AF600594

The Prophet's Ascension

The Prophet's Ascension

Cross-Cultural Encounters with the Islamic *Miʿrāj* Tales

Edited by
Christiane Gruber and Frederick Colby

Indiana University Press
Bloomington and Indianapolis

The inclusion of colored illustrations in this volume was made possible by a generous grant from the Ilex Foundation.

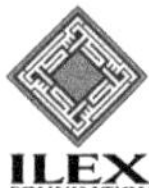

This book is a publication of

Indiana University Press
601 North Morton Street
Bloomington, IN 47404-3797 USA

www.iupress.indiana.edu

Telephone orders 800-842-6796
Fax orders 812-855-7931
Orders by e-mail iuporder@indiana.edu

∞ *The paper used in this publication meets the minimum requirements of the American National Standard for Information Sciences—Permanence of Paper for Printed Library Materials, ANSI Z39.48-1992.*

MANUFACTURED IN THE UNITED STATES OF AMERICA

Library of Congress Cataloging-in-Publication Data

The Prophet's ascension : cross-cultural encounters with the Islamic mi'raj tales / edited by Christiane Gruber and Frederick Colby.
p. cm.
Includes bibliographical references and index.
ISBN 978-0-253-35361-0 (cloth : alk. paper) 1. Muhammad, Prophet, d. 632—Isra' and Mi'raj. 2. Legends, Islamic—History and criticism. I. Gruber, Christiane J., date– II. Colby, Frederick Stephen, date–
BP166.57.P76 2009
297.6'33—dc22
2009021910

1 2 3 4 5 15 14 13 12 11 10

Contents

Foreword

Powerful spiritual experiences, be they plunging into the abysses of consciousness or journeying through the mysteries of being, are almost invariably described by those who have savored them as inexpressible and ineffable. In their myriad of forms and manifestations in various cultural traditions, accounts of "celestial ascensions" appear to have formed one of the preeminent ways to communicate a kind of occurrence that otherwise cannot be easily described. There are two reasons for this: first, because the contents of such narratives can mirror the most intense form of initiatory experience; and second, because these narratives' intricate structure—in various incarnations and through numerous symbols—can provide the most suitable narrative model to convey the complexity of this sort of experience.

Since time immemorial, many spiritual traditions have emphasized the metaphysical and organic link between the internal world of the human being and the external world of the universe. As the old Hermetic proverb goes, "That which is below is like that which is above." A celestial ascension can be considered a double helix dive into the depths of the soul. In a cosmos governed by harmonious conjunctions, an ascent through the celestial stages finds its match in a descent into the occult levels of the self. As Aristotle notes in his *De Anima* (I:3): "One of them, the Demiurge divided into seven circles so that the movements of the soul conform to the movements of the heavens." A celestial ascension, contemplation, and even ecstasis—or rather "enstasis," as Mircea Eliade fittingly describes it—correlates to a vision of the world that seeks to grasp the totality of being. The skies and the celestial worlds form the macrocosmos; the earth, which has its center at the temple or the royal palace, constitutes the mesocosmos; and finally the mysteries of the soul represent the microcosmos that is the human being.

The number seven, which Aristotle mentions, finds its roots in Sumerian astronomy. The construct of the seven spheres at the core of ancient cosmologies appears first in the Mesopotamian and Hellenistic worlds, and develops later in Gnostic and Manichaean traditions. In such cosmologies, this seven-part ordering of the sky is reflected on earth, which is divided into seven climes. It is also echoed in the "mirror of the world" that is the king's palace, most famously attested by the antique city of Ecbatana, capital of the Median ruler Deioces (Diyāokū): this city was said to have been fortified by seven ramparts of seven different colors (Herodotus, *History,* I, 98).

Below the earth, the dark kingdoms of death comprise the seven rings of the Sumerian hell, thereby forming a reverse image of the sky. Ancient philosophers were convinced that this spinning world, ordered according to the septuple rule, also contained the mysteries of the soul, much like a coded cipher.

As the last great successor to the intellectual and spiritual traditions of late Antiquity, Islam inherited these cosmo-psychological elements. And yet this is often overlooked. Although we fully acknowledge that Islam forms an extension of the two great antecedent monotheistic traditions, we must recall here that Judaism and Christianity, in the multiple forms in which they reached the Muslims, had already passed through turning points of thought at the hands of the Byzantine monk of Syria known as Dionysius the Areopagite, the deeply Hellenized Jewish philosopher Philo of Alexandria, and the Prophet Mani, keeping in mind that the last of these left very deep and long-lasting traces upon subsequent religious traditions spread over a vast region. Well before the widespread effort to translate older works into Arabic during the so-called Golden Age of Islam, both the presence of older religions in Arabia and subsequent Muslim conquests put Islam into contact with Greece, Rome, Egypt, Mesopotamia, and Iran. As a consequence, older traditions subtly infused Islam with wise teachings harking back to Zoroaster and Mani, as well as to the philosophers Alexander of Aphrodisias, Plotinus, Porphyry of Tyre, and Iamblichus of Chalcis.

Based on a few highly enigmatic qur'anic cues, the celestial ascension that Islamic tradition very quickly accredited to the Prophet Muḥammad (as well as to the imāms in Shiʿi circles) is one of the most stunning attestations to this heritage that adapted itself so well to this new religion. Indeed, the Prophet's night journey and his visits through the seven levels of the heavens and the seven layers of hell reiterate some of the most important elements of ancient spiritual systems. The tale also reflects later developments of ascension tales, such as the Zoroastrian *Book of Ardāvīrāf,* Jewish *Hekhalot* literature, the Gnostic *Merkava* traditions, or even the "Hymn of the Pearl" in the apocryphal *Gospel of Thomas.*

The crucible par excellence where, through a dazzling alchemy, a congruent synthesis of these multiple traditions took place and tremendous efforts to assimilate them were expended was undoubtedly the domain of Islamic mysticism. We need only to look to a few masterpieces such as Niẓāmī's *Haft Paykar* (Seven Beauties), ʿAṭṭār's *Manṭiq al-Ṭayr* (Conference of the Birds), or even the correspondence of the seven-part structure of the universe with the seven stations of the soul in Sufism and the seven prophets of the heart as described by the Sufi philosopher ʿAlā' al-Dawla Simnānī. A verse composed by Sanā'ī of Ghazna describes this mystery, articulated earlier by Aristotle: "In the kingdom of the soul there are heavens / that regulate the sky of [this] world." (*Āsmānhāst dar vilāyat-i jān / kārfarmā-yi āsmān-i jahān*). Thus the theme of the ascension is vitally important for spiritual life: knowledge of the self and that of the cosmos unlock each other, and both go through an intense, internal experience that cannot be expressed except through symbols, paradoxes, or poetry.

What a tremendous joy for me that two outstanding scholars, Christiane Gruber and Frederick Colby, have decided to celebrate the tenth anniversary of a volume of collected articles dedicated to the theme of the ascension that I organized and edited in 1996. It is a great honor for me to see research in this field moving forward thanks to sixteen original and very rich studies on a theme that I consider essential to a better understanding of the diverse thought, doctrine, and spirituality of Muslims. By providing a wealth of novel information and by opening new and exciting venues for research, the distinguished scholars who have contributed to this volume are pushing research forward in the best and most beautiful manner, namely with rigor and erudition. I am honored and touched, and I extend to them my wholehearted thanks.

Mohammad Ali Amir-Moezzi
École Pratique des Hautes Études (Sorbonne)
Paris, France

Acknowledgments

This volume grew out of a pair of scholarly panels organized at the annual meetings of the American Academy of Religion (AAR) and the Middle East Studies Association (MESA) in November 2006, commemorating the tenth anniversary of Mohammad Ali Amir-Moezzi's collection of essays entitled *Le voyage initiatique en terre d'Islam: ascensions célestes et itinéraires spirituels* (1996). We wish to thank both MESA and the Islamic Mysticism Group at AAR for providing us with public forums in which we were able to present our preliminary research, as well as Mohammad Ali Amir-Moezzi for his enthusiastic support of our research.

We extend our appreciation to the authors who contributed to this volume for their excellent work and for many effervescent conversations over the course of two years. We have learned much in the process and are convinced that more research on the subject of the Prophet's ascension is needed. This volume, we hope, will provide a small but textured and polyphonous contribution to what promise to be ongoing, lively discussions.

We also wish to thank the staff at Indiana University Press, who graciously took on this project and worked with us through the various steps towards publication. A warmhearted thanks goes to Robert Sloan, Editorial Director, for his unwavering support of this project; to Miki Bird, Managing Editor, for supervising the volume's editing; to Candace McNulty for her tireless copyediting work; and to Anne Clemmer and Bernadette Zoss for their help in laying out the color plates.

Last but certainly not least, we are most grateful to the ILEX Foundation for having provided us with a grant to support the inclusion of thirty-two color plates. Their generous support of this project—as well as of many others that engage in the humanistic study of Mediterranean and Near Eastern civilizations—comes with our deep appreciation.

Christiane Gruber and Frederick Colby

The Prophet's Ascension

Introduction

CHRISTIANE GRUBER AND FREDERICK COLBY

From the very earliest period of Islamic history until today, the story of how the Prophet Muḥammad was taken by night on a celestial journey has sparked both the interests and the imaginations of many Muslims (Plate 1). In the versions that have come to be widely accepted, the story often involves Muḥammad being guided by the angel Gabriel to mount a fantastic steed named Burāq, to ride it at incredible speed from Mecca to Jerusalem (the portion of the journey that comes to be identified as the "night journey" or *isrā'*), and to lead in prayer the prophets such as Abraham, Moses, and Jesus, whom Muslims consider as Muḥammad's spiritual forerunners. Many accounts of the story continue by describing how Gabriel leads Muḥammad from Jerusalem on an otherworldly ascension up through the seven heavens (the portion of the journey that comes to be identified as the "ascension" or *miʿrāj*), witnessing fantastic sites and encountering awe-inspiring figures along the way. In a number of versions, Muḥammad is given a tour of the pleasures of paradise and the tortures of hellfire. The story of the Prophet's ascension usually depicts how, at the climax of his journey, Muḥammad enjoys some form of interaction with God, receiving the charge for the Muslim community to perform ritual prayers five times per day. At the conclusion of this amazing journey, the angel Gabriel returns Muḥammad to Mecca, and he comes to realize that his remarkable experience took place in the span of a single night. He informs his community about his experience, causing some to doubt its veracity and to turn away from him, while causing others to accept it and to rejoice in this confirmation of his prophetic mission and exalted status. Accounts of this journey—which one can refer to in its entirety as Muḥammad's *miʿrāj*—have been transmitted, developed, and transformed in fascinating ways in the diverse contexts in which the story was told and retold over the course of many centuries.

This collected volume of essays analyzes the theme of the Prophet Muḥammad's *miʿrāj* in a variety of cultural, literary, and artistic contexts from the ninth century until the present day. The essays break fresh ground by discussing new materials and by providing alternative methodological approaches to the study of one of the most popular of Muslim tales. Collectively, they seek to provide a broad cross-cultural perspective on this subject, not only in its foundational discourses in Arabic, Persian, and Turkic spheres, but also through its adaptations by various communities from Europe to South Asia.

The chapters are organized around three principle themes: the *miʿrāj* as a formative and missionary text, its adaptations in diverse esoteric and literary contexts, and its use in performance and ritual. In constructing these themes, we have deliberately sought to go beyond the conventional geographical and linguistic categories that have informed previous scholarship on the ascension. Likewise, visual materials serve as a unifying thread that is woven throughout the volume, rather than a marginal element relegated to a separate field of inquiry. As a result, this study places in conversation topics, texts, and images that otherwise might seem unconnected to one another in the hopes of challenging and transcending traditional disciplinary boundaries.

The tales of the *miʿrāj* fulfilled a variety of functions and responded to disparate concerns over the course of Muslim history. In many instances, they served as narratives designed to buttress claims of legitimacy or to promote the worldview of a particular group of Muslims. They also played a significant role in internal dialogues on the construction of normative communal behavior and ritual practices. Replete with admonitory and proselytizing themes, they functioned as tools to assert the superiority of Islam vis-à-vis competing religious traditions as well.

The first group of chapters in this collection addresses many of these issues by examining the use of *miʿrāj* narratives in community building, as well as the deployment of the narrative in the service of both inter-communal struggles and wide-ranging missionary efforts. These chapters pay particular attention to how textual reworkings may shed light on contemporary religious and cultural circumstances, as well as how ascension tales could include gendered messages, serve as a battlefield for otherworldly knowledge (and thus worldly legitimacy), and function as a powerful mechanism in regulating communal behavior.

Roberto Tottoli's chapter examines how the "tour of hell" scenes received increasing prominence in *miʿrāj* narratives as they developed over the formative period of Islamic history, demonstrating how they served the moral and polemical purposes of the leaders of the growing Arab Muslim community. His diachronic examination of how ascension tales were expanded through various eschatological details, with a particular attention to women's sins and their consequent punishments, reveals how such texts attempt to define the moral parameters of communal mores.

Christiane Gruber's study of an early Ilkhanid *Miʿrājnāma* proves that the rise of illustrated ascension works around the turn of the fourteenth century served to promote a Sunni Muslim worldview while offering pedagogical resources to newly converted communities on the proper ways to pray to and petition God. Through a detailed text and image analysis, her study argues that illustrated manuscripts of the *miʿrāj* could serve as a means to promote a specific worldview in Persian lands during the medieval period.

The chapter by Maria Subtelny argues that the famous Timurid *Miʿrājnāma* written in Chaghatay Turkish in Uighur script ca. 1436 CE is best understood as a missionary text that preserves an older Persian-language narrative that was created with the goal of converting Persian-speaking Jewish communities in Iran and Central Asia. Through the methods of positive argumentation rather than confrontation, the original text that the Timurid Book of Ascension preserves thus uses the theme of Muḥammad's prophetic mission to create what is essentially a manual of conversion.

Max Scherberger's study presents an analysis and English translation of a versified eastern Turkish *Miʿrājnāma* ascribed to the twelfth-century Central Asian mystic Ḥakīm Ata. Through an analysis of later manuscripts, he argues that the text should be understood as original. As a result, it provides further evidence of Sufi efforts to spread the Islamic faith in Central Asia during the twelfth and thirteenth centuries. The text's dual didactic-missionary function reveals how the ascension tale could be used to strengthen the faith of its Muslim audience, and how it simultaneously could be applied toward conversion efforts among non-Muslim communities in Turkish-speaking Central Asia.

In her analysis of illustrated texts of Beatus's *Commentary on the Apocalypse,* Heather Coffey argues that select Christian authors in medieval Spain came to parody and subvert *miʿrāj* texts in order to claim legitimacy for the Christian faith at a time of Christian-Muslim tension in the Iberian Peninsula. Her study shows how both texts and images of Beatus's *Commentary* dealing with otherworldly themes, themselves possibly prompted by the spread of *miʿrāj* texts in translation in Spain, functioned as arenas of religious confrontation. Much as in Islamic traditions, in this case the eschaton is deployed as a "weapon" for Christian (re)conversion and indoctrination.

Although the chapters in this first section consider widely divergent historical moments, they each demonstrate how *miʿrāj* texts were at the center of efforts at constructing group identity and regulating social interactions and behavior in contradistinction to one or more opposing groups. Time and time again in the chapters, not only in this section but throughout this volume, one comes to see that the story of Muḥammad's ascension, with its frequent emphasis on the honoring of Muḥammad and his exalted status among all created beings, provides a powerful template that could be adopted and adapted to serve a particular group's missionizing efforts among its co-religionists or toward adherents of different religious communities. A tool of religious and cultural suasion par excellence, the ascension tale thus fulfills a significant role within the domain of inter- and intra-communal polemics.

Many of the studies in the second group of chapters in this volume share a similar concern with group formation and/or missionary efforts, but they have been set apart here in order to emphasize the esoteric and literary dimensions of *miʿrāj* texts. The composition of ascension accounts in the middle and later periods of Islamic history developed into a high art, and until very recently the literary aspects of these remarkable poetic and prose adaptations of the *miʿrāj* have not received the attention that they deserve. Several chapters in the second group begin to address this significant lacuna. Furthermore, as Mohammad Ali Amir-Moezzi mentions in his preface to this volume, a number of Muslim mystics refined and developed discussions of Muḥammad's *miʿrāj*, using it to illustrate key mystical concepts. Several chapters in this section examine adaptations of the *miʿrāj* by particular Sufis, while several others pay attention to the mystical or esoteric appropriations of the *miʿrāj* by non-Sufi Shiʿi thinkers.

Frederick Colby's study describes how details included in the scenes of Muḥammad's encounter with God can be shown to illustrate how early Sunnis and Imami Shiʿis wrestled over the control of *miʿrāj* narrative in order to promote their own particular religious agendas. By focusing in particular on the intimate colloquy scenes between God and the Prophet, his chapter attempts to show how supercessionist discourses can be detected within early ascension tales. Without a doubt, such details underscore the theme's centrality for sectarian claims to legitimacy and authority.

Elizabeth Alexandrin's chapter demonstrates how the pivotal Ismaʿili thinker Qāḍī al-Nuʿmān draws on key passages of the Qur'an regarding the prophethood of Abraham and the ascent of Muḥammad in order to construct a paradigm that charts the progress of Ismaʿili spiritual aspirants as they are initiated into increasingly deeper levels of mystical knowledge and practice. By using esoteric language and initiatory motifs, Qāḍī al-Nuʿmān's text helps to build a complex system of exoteric knowledge that can only be gained through a careful training in the Ismaʿili "Calling" (*daʿwah*).

In his study of the medieval philosophical use of the *miʿrāj* in the works of Avicenna and Abraham ibn Ezra, Aaron Hughes contends that the general theme of the heavenly ascent provides a conceptual language of legitimation. For Avicenna, a proper understanding of Muḥammad's ascent provides an authoritative model for his philosophical enterprise. For ibn Ezra, similarly, recontextualizing elements of the *miʿrāj* in his own work provides a mechanism to assert the primacy of Jewish texts with regard to the idea of a heavenly ascent, vision, or initiation.

Selim Kuru's chapter is one of the first studies to investigate the versification of the *miʿrāj* in the early Anatolian Turkish literary tradition of the fourteenth and fifteenth centuries. He traces a development from early "religio-didactic" verse narratives that focus on the theme of piety and prayer to "lyric romance" verse narratives that focus on the theme of love and unification with God. These formative texts in Turkish cultural spheres reveal a general move from expository writing to allegorical thought, in which the Prophet acts as the embodiment of divine communion.

The chapter by Gottfried Hagen investigates the use of the *miʿrāj* within a masterpiece of Ottoman Turkish prose, Veysī's *Dürretü t-tāc*, in order to reflect on how the work's author draws upon and adapts *sīra* accounts of Muḥammad's journey within an Ottoman literary context. He demonstrates how Veysī's text both highlights the physical reality of the otherworlds that Muḥammad visits and emphasizes the promise of salvation for Muslims that the Prophet secures through his intercession for humankind.

Moving forward, Ayesha Irani describes how the Bengali author Saiyad Sultan adapts the *miʿrāj* narrative to local concepts and symbols. By using a vernacular idiom and by drawing upon yogic motifs in particular, this Sufi teacher depicts the Prophet as the quintessential ascetic. By localizing his narrative through an "indigenous" language and motifs, Saiyad Sultan produces a fascinating text in which his prophetic protagonist echoes and legitimizes his own mission to promote Islam among both non-Muslims and nominal Muslims in the region.

The final essay in this second group of chapters, written by Ali Boozari, shows how illustrated lithographed books depicting Muḥammad's *miʿrāj* produced in Iran during the Qajar period essentially served as graphic novels, promoting education in Imami Shiʿism among children and young adults. These illustrated texts blend various Persian tales (*dāstāns*) with narratives of the Prophet's ascension in a larger bid to inculcate a juvenile audience into various fields of knowledge at a time when both texts and images were mobilized in popular practices to promote and strengthen Shiʿi Islam in Persian lands.

The *miʿrāj* narrative proved malleable enough in diverse instances to be adapted to a wide variety of contexts. The chapters in this section illustrate how there existed some ascension narratives displaying links to Persian tales and others containing references to Indian deities. There were those that developed mystical and esoteric concepts on the one hand and Greek philosophical ideas on the other. Still others argued fine points on the nature of reality while waxing poetic on the supple contours of lyric romances. Together such examples demonstrate how this story was and remains eminently suitable to serve varied purposes in innumerable cultural, religious, and political contexts. Through such creative syntheses over many centuries, the theme of the Prophet's ascension has continued to provide a nodal point for the expression of piety and spirituality in both elite and popular spheres in the Muslim (and non-Muslim) world.

The third group of chapters also examines the narrative's great potential for adaptability, examining it through a lens that is relatively new in the study of Islamic ascension narratives, namely the performative and ritual dimensions of the *miʿrāj*. The chapters in this section provide new theoretical approaches and methodological tools to examine the dramatic aspects of Muslim ascent tales in both the pre-modern and modern periods. They also provide a window into the world of the *miʿrāj* as a living tradition, illustrating how different communities "perform" the text of the otherworldly journey, and how such performances generate meaning.

For instance, Özgen Felek's chapter takes an innovative perspective on the ascension narrative in Muʿin al-Miskīn's *Maʿārij al-nubuwwa*, arguing that the late Timurid author of the work constructs his narrative in such a vivid and dramatic fashion that it resembles a type of theater performance. Given the particularly dramatic quality of the text, Felek shows how theories of narratology and dramatology can help to shed new light on the construction and function of this *miʿrāj* account. Her cross-disciplinary exploration of the ascension tale highlights its essentially "visual" character as developed through the author's vivid rhetorical techniques.

Phokion Kotzageorgis's chapter provides a window onto a hitherto little-known area, namely the adaptation of the *miʿrāj* tale during the eighteenth century in the Greek-speaking region of Epirus. Not only does the text show peculiar features reflecting the majority Christian environment in which it was produced and its likely audience (Christian converts to Islam), but it also contains aspects suggesting that the text was recited orally as part of a ritual or public performance during the festival days at the end of the month of Ramaḍān. Written in Greek and disclosing elements emanating from local religious traditions, this rare text on the ascension appears to have served as a catechism for a minority Muslim community living on the westernmost borders of the Ottoman empire.

The final two chapters in the volume both deal with a dynamic ritual enactment of the *miʿrāj* account central to Turkish Alevis known as the *ayīn-i cemʿ* (ritual of assembly). In the first of the two essays dedicated to this fascinating performance, Amelia Gallagher delves into the history and legend surrounding the literary corpus ascribed to Shāh Ismāʿīl Ṣafevī (often known by his pen-name, Ḫaṭā'ī), a corpus whose works—both authentic and pseudonymous—are foundational to the Alevi understanding of the mystical meaning of the Prophet's *miʿrāj*, and to the way this mystical meaning becomes enacted through the Alevi *ayīn-i cemʿ* ritual.

Vernon Schubel brings the discussion of the ritual enactment of this central Alevi ceremony up to the present day, describing how Turkish Alevis in recent years continue to transmit and transform their *miʿrāj* tradition in music, drama, and narrative. Schubel draws on theories from anthropology and religious studies not only to demonstrate how the performance fulfills a community function that can be analyzed and appreciated by outsiders to the tradition, but also to explain the reason that the evocation of the *miʿrāj* plays such a profoundly crucial role and enjoys such a prominent place of reverence among members of the Alevi community.

From its beginnings to its later manifestations, the tale of the Prophet's *miʿrāj* has undergone countless creative syntheses depending on the religious and cultural needs of the day. Much as written texts could serve as tools in missionary efforts or as purveyors of spiritual expression, so too could ascension images carry or embed specific messages. Such images could promote certain cosmological views (Plate 2) or expose systems of faith, not only during previous centuries but also in the modern period (Plates 3 and 32) and stretching from the Indian subcontinent (Plates 29 and 30) to mainland Europe (Plate 31). The visual iterations of the Prophet's ascension produced between ca. 1300 to the present day disclose motifs that bear undeniable cultural and religious implications, which can be examined and decoded through careful scrutiny. The thirty-two color plates included in this volume, which relate to the chapters and admittedly provide only a small selection of a much larger corpus of extant *miʿrāj* illustrations, therefore aim to bring text and image studies together in order to stimulate further research into the ascension tale's rich and varied literary and artistic heritage.

By expanding previous scholarship and investigating new scholarly venues, *The Prophet's Ascension: Cross-Cultural Encounters with the Islamic Miʿrāj Tales* endeavors to encourage further interdisciplinary research, perspectives, and discussion into this pivotal theme. We hope these essays will appeal to both specialists and the general public, from students and scholars of Islamic history, religion, comparative literature, and art, to a broader readership interested in tales of otherworldly journeys as transmitted and performed in diverse cultural contexts.

Note to the Reader

The transliteration of Arabic words follows the Library of Congress system as described in the *International Journal of Middle East Studies*. Persian words generally follow the Arabic transliteration system, but their slight variations in pronunciation are taken into consideration. Transliteration of most Ottoman and Chaghatay Turkish words are given according to modern Turkish standards. The transliteration of Bengali largely follows the Library of Congress system, with a few modifications that seek to harmonize it with the Library of Congress system for Sanskrit. Titles of Islamic Bengali texts and the names of Bengali Muslims are romanized according to the conventions for Bengali.

Names of individuals are followed by the years of their death (d.), regnal years (r.), or, for authors, the years during which their literary activities flourished (fl.) if their dates of death are unknown. Dates follow the Gregorian A.D. (*anno Domini*) and the Islamic A.H. (*anno Hegirae*) calendars. The A.D. calendar is solar, while the A.H. calendar is lunar, so sometimes an A.H. date spans two A.D. years. In such a case, the span of two A.D. years is provided. Many scholars choose to refer to A.D. years with the abbreviation C.E. (Common Era) in an attempt to express greater neutrality with respect to the Christological implications of the A.D. ("Year of Our Lord") calendar system.

Following the convention of most Muslim scholars, who have come to use the terms *isrā'* (night journey) and *miʿrāj* (ascension) relatively interchangeably, we will make frequent use of the terms *miʿrāj* and ascension in this volume as easy and convenient ways to refer to Muḥammad's entire journey, rather than simply a defined portion of it. In the cases where authors use these terms in a more specific or more general sense, they will indicate that usage in their chapters.

PART 1

☾

The Formation of Miʿrāj *Narratives as Missionary Texts*

1

Tours of Hell and Punishments of Sinners in *Miʿrāj* Narratives: Use and Meaning of Eschatology in Muḥammad's Ascension

ROBERTO TOTTOLI

The various and rich literature on the night journey and the heavenly ascent of the Prophet Muḥammad comprises many narratives ranging from the first brief descriptions in early exegetical and hadith literature to later more lengthy works. This literature not only displays differing theological and literary attitudes but also is characterized by what is most typical in the elaboration of the works of a peculiar genre or *corpus* of works on the same topic, i.e., that of excluding or including various motifs depending on authorial choice. Many *miʿrāj* narratives include descriptions of paradise and hell, which Muḥammad visited during the night of his ascension. A theme of particular interest in these eschatological sections includes the description of the categories of sinners and evil-doers, along with their respective punishments.[1]

Eschatological themes as found in *miʿrāj* narratives have attracted little scholarly attention. Only recently has Frederick Colby touched upon some passages that raise the question of the description of the tortures of the evil-doers in the tour of hell scenes in *miʿrāj* literature, and Brooke Olson Vuckovic has devoted some pages to the description of sinners whom the Prophet saw punished during his *miʿrāj*.[2] In this study, I wish to explore why some versions of the Prophet's night journey and ascension came to include mention of specific classes of sinners and particular categories of sins, while others did not. Further, following Vuckovic, I also will endeavor to uncover the moral concern behind the inclusion or exclusion of particular sins and sinners, and thus the polemical peculiarities of a selection of ascension stories taken from medieval Arabic literature.

By juxtaposing data present in the tours of hell in *miʿrāj* literature with information found in Muslim traditions, an interplay between narratives on the ascent to heaven and other Muslim literature on this topic can be seen in action.[3] Indeed, the Prophet's tour of hell as described in two controversial hadiths on the *miʿrāj* was the main and only reference in early literature. Only in later popular literature was this motif expanded with a peculiar emphasis on the description of sinful women and their punishments, a theme which was first borrowed from Shiʿi traditions but subsequently became a relevant theme in Sunni popular *miʿrāj* narratives. This emphasis on the sins and punishments of women is attested neither in eschatological literature as a whole nor in other narratives including tours of hell. This new concern certainly points to the audience of listeners and readers of these narratives on the *miʿrāj,* which were read and recited during popular meetings and festivals that emerged during and after the tenth century. The mention of women reflects the relevance of regulating women's behavior as well as female participation in these celebrations.

Sins and Sinners in Early *Miʿrāj* Narratives

Early long hadith reports on the night journey and the heavenly ascent of the Prophet Muḥammad,[4] such as those transmitted by Anas b. Mālik, do not include descriptions of the tortures of sinners in hell, nor do they even mention Muḥammad's tour of hell.[5] Among other early sources, Muqātil's (d. 767) *tafsīr,* for instance, does not mention categories of sinners, nor does Ibn Saʿd (d. 845) in his *Kitāb al-Ṭabaqāt al-kubrā* (The Book of the Major Classes), although he does make an oblique reference to such issues by stating that Muḥammad specifically requested that God show him paradise and hell.[6] These early reports containing no mention of eschatological details are the most frequently cited in later literary works dealing with the Prophet's *miʿrāj.* Some narratives, however, include reports drawn from other sources, which describe Muḥammad's vision of sinners and their punishments. Among the various versions attested in early major works ranging from hadith literature to qur'anic *tafsīr*s commenting upon Q 17:1, two reports that mention sinners and their tortures in hell stand out: one can be traced back to Abū Hurayra, and the other to Abū Saʿīd al-Khudrī. These reports are particularly relevant because they attest to the early circulation of *miʿrāj* narratives that describe the Prophet's vision of hell. However, these two reports were considered by later literature to be of minor importance and, as we shall see, of doubtful authenticity.

The first of these reports is attributed to Abū Hurayra. It is found both in the *Dalā'il al-Nubuwwa* (Proofs of Prophecy) of al-Bayhaqī (d. 1066) and the *tafsīr* of al-Ṭabarī (d. 923). Muḥammad is shown sinners and their punishments during his night journey from Mecca to Jerusalem, at which time he witnesses the punishments of the following classes of sinners: those who do not follow prescribed prayer; those who do not give alms; those who commit adultery; those who sit in the way and block it; those who engage in usury; those who cannot liquidate money they had on deposit in a trust; preachers who incite sedition in the community (*khuṭabā' al-fitna*) and do not practice what they preach; those who eat the flesh of other people, that is, who are guilty of slander and gossip; and the man who gives his word and then reneges on it.[7]

In the second report transmitted by Abū Saʿīd al-Khudrī, sinners and their punishments are presented to the Prophet upon his arrival in the first heaven. Here, Muḥammad observes those who commit adultery; those who commit usury; those who consume the goods of orphans; women who commit adultery and subsequently kill their infants; and those who slander others. This tradition is mentioned in some early qur'anic commentaries, including those of ʿAbd al-Razzāq (d. 827) and Yaḥyā b. Sallām (d. 216).[8] It is also mentioned frequently in later literature, with some variants.[9]

In these two accounts, the physical location of hell remains contested. According to Abū Hurayra's report, Muḥammad's tour of hell occurred during his night journey, thus raising the question of the present existence of hell somewhere on earth, a theme of major controversial theological debate by Muʿtazilites and their opponents. According to Abū Saʿīd al-Khudrī, on the other hand, the Prophet's witnessing of sinners took place in the first heaven after his meeting with Adam, thus localizing hell within the lowest of the heavenly realms.

Furthermore, both of these traditions were deemed untrustworthy. Al-Bayhaqī, for example, provides an overview of the principal reports on Muḥammad's night journey and ascension—most of which do not include any eschatological contents—and then introduces these two reports by stating that they have weak *isnād*s (chains of transmission) and it is for this reason that they were not included in the most important hadith collections. It would be tempting to hypothesize that the description of hell and its denizens comprised the element that prompted doubts on the reports' authenticity. This is, in fact, the stance of al-Suyūṭī (d. 1505): he concludes that Abū Hurayra's report interpolates elements from a long hadith of a dream by Muḥammad quoted by al-Bukhārī and going back to Samura, and, consequently, that the Abū Hurayra report most probably represents a questionable compilation of various hadiths.[10] It is thus clear that it was not only a problem with the reports' chains of transmission but also one which concerned textual context (*matn*) as well. Though al-Suyūṭī offers an exegetical explanation with the aim of dismissing these versions, his particular discussion of eschatological motifs suggests the way that such particulars came to enter into extended reports on the *miʿrāj*.[11]

Leaving aside hadith literature and the question of the acceptance or rejection of these two reports going back to Abū Hurayra and Abū Saʿīd al-Khudrī, we find some other significant *miʿrāj* narratives that include tours of hell with descriptions of sinners and their torments. One of the most important of these appears in Ibn Hishām's (d. 833) *Sīra* (Biography) of the Prophet. In his chapter dealing with Muḥammad's night journey and ascent to heaven, he includes a report transmitted on the authority of Abū Saʿīd al-Khudrī that states that once the Prophet arrived in the lowest heaven, he encountered the following sinners: those who devour the wealth of orphans (Plate 4); those who commit usury; those who forsake the women whom God has permitted and go after those whom he has forbidden; and women who give birth to adulterous children and then secretly force the babies upon their husbands as if they belonged to them.[12] It is not necessary to discuss in detail these four classes of sinners described by Ibn Hishām because they are quite similar to the ones found in the hadith attributed to Abū Saʿīd al-Khudrī, itself the most probable source.[13]

The Shiʿi author al-Qummī (fl. 919) also offers a long report from Jaʿfar al-Ṣādiq, whose only description of evil-doers and their punishments in hell is close to that of Abū Saʿīd al-Khudrī. They are located in the first heaven and form six categories of sins. These categories are similar to those in al-Khudrī's report, excluding the adulterers, those who sleep instead of praying, and women who bequeath the wealth of their husbands to children who are not their own (Plate 5).[14] Although Ibn Hishām and al-Qummī provide only two select reports, they are nevertheless important since they further attest to the early diffusion of Abū Saʿīd al-Khudrī's report.

Tours of Hell and Sinners in later *Miʿrāj* Narratives

Muslim literature on the story of the night journey and heavenly ascent of the Prophet Muḥammad is rich, and it goes well beyond early hadith collections. Indeed, medieval Muslim literary activity displayed a strong capacity for the reworking of motifs included in such narratives. Creative syntheses and innovations resulted, first of all, in the writing of numerous new texts on the topic. As it is impossible to review subsequent texts in a comprehensive manner, only a selection of works will be examined here in relation to the Prophet's tour of hell. These date from the eleventh century to the middle of the eighteenth century.

One of the most significant elaborations and alterations of motifs contained in the tours of hell appears in the various *miʿrāj* narratives attributed to Abū al-Ḥasan al-Bakrī (fl. ninth century). Many of these texts display substantial differences, the result of a number of textual reworkings throughout various periods and of distinct textual traditions all attributed to one single author.[15] The tours of hell in these various al-Bakrī ascension narratives also reveal diverging contents. Likewise, some contain rather brief descriptions of sinners and their punishments, while others include longer descriptions, thereby displaying a steady and growing interest in the genre.[16] One version, for instance, places the tour of hell in the fifth heaven, where Muḥammad is shown seven levels or doors that represent the future destinations of the damned. The first level is reserved for Muslims who commit major sins (*kabāʾir*), after which only seven further categories of sinners are given.[17] These include the common sins related to stealing orphans' goods, dishonesty, wine consumption, adultery, killing, abandoning prayer, usury, and, much more unusual, disobeying one's parents. This version, however, does not delineate any specific categories of sinners that include women.

Quite different is the picture painted by another manuscript attributed to al-Bakrī. This particular narrative includes a list of sinners entirely different from the first one discussed above, and adds a description of a whole series of punishments specifically reserved for women. After the text mentions the well-known categories related to sins—such as eating what is forbidden, adultery, and usury, among many—it lists various women suffering a number of tortures.[18] Although it is not easy to answer why this long report about women was inserted, it is possible to determine its source. It is in fact very close to a report found in one of the works by the Imāmī Shiʿi Ibn Bābawayh (d. 992), in which Fāṭima and ʿAlī are described as finding the Prophet Muḥammad weeping. In the report, Muḥammad tells them that during his night journey he saw women of his community being punished, and at Fāṭima's request he gives them a description of the sins and their consequent punishments. We find here eleven categories similar in wording to those mentioned above and largely connected to marital relations or women's social behavior. These categories include women who did not cover their head to conceal it from men other than their husband; who irritated their husbands; who abstained from marital relations; who went out without their husbands' permission; who beautified themselves for other people; who did not clean themselves from impurity; who bore children from adultery and imposed them upon their husbands; who did not cover themselves from men; who acted as matchmakers; who slandered and lied; and who sang and mourned. It is clear that the aim of this particular report consists in delineating the parameters of women's moral behavior toward men, further strengthened by Muḥammad's final statement in this report: "Woe unto a woman who makes her husband angry and blessed be the woman with whom her husband is satisfied."[19]

The insertion of this description of women's sins reveals a clear shift in the tours of hell included in *miʿrāj* narratives. The sinners and punishments discussed thus far were not so different from the general assessments in the hadiths by Abū Hurayra and Abū Saʿīd al-Khudrī. However, it cannot be excluded that reports of this kind could also have been in circulation before the redaction of the various versions of ascension texts attributed to al-Bakrī, especially since Ibn Bābawayh wrote his works in the tenth century.

The mention of lists of women characterizes other works that provide long descriptions of hell, along with evil-doers and their respective tortures. The best known example in this genre is the apocryphal work on the *miʿrāj* ascribed to Ibn ʿAbbās. The origin and definition of this popular version of the ascension story—attested in various manuscript recensions and diffused in the modern and contemporary Muslim world through a frequently printed version that became a sort of standardized *Qiṣṣat al-isrāʾ wa-l-miʿrāj*—has been discussed in detail by Frederick Colby.[20] As regards the topic at hand, the printed version attributed to Ibn ʿAbbās is particularly relevant since it mentions a list of twenty-four sinners and their punishments. After Muḥammad arrives in the fifth heaven and sees Mālik, the keeper of hellfire, he is shown hell and the punishments of wayward women.

These include: women who make themselves up for men other than their husbands; those who mock their husbands; those who say "divorce me" to their husbands without reason; those who do not cover their hair in front of strangers; those who nurse the sons of other people without their husbands' permission; those who do not perform ablutions and are dirty; those who have sons from men other than their husbands; those who henpeck their husbands; those who bring together couples for illicit liaisons; those who arouse enmity between their husbands and their neighbors; those who stir up hatred among people; those who ingest substances in order to kill their babies; those who sing professionally for others; those who mourn at funerals for pay; and those who dye their hair and alter the image of [their bodies as created by] God.[21]

Rather than forming a standard text, the *miʿrāj* narratives attributed to Ibn ʿAbbās should be considered a corpus of variant texts that share a number of peculiarities. Thus, later reworkings of narratives traceable to Ibn ʿAbbās further elaborate this list of women's sins, which share many elements in common with those ascribed to al-Bakrī. Other *miʿrāj* narratives attributed to Ibn ʿAbbās include similar categories of sinners and punishments, either reduced or enlarged in number. For instance, the text edited by Nazeer al-ʿAẓma lists seventeen classes of evildoers and their punishments.[22] We recognize in this list the same categories listed previously, although in some cases with a different wording.[23]

A number of other authors follow in these steps and elaborate upon the various lists given in Ibn ʿAbbās' texts. For example, Zayn al-Dīn, in his work dedicated to Muḥammad's ascension, places the tour of hell in the fifth heaven and lists more than twenty classes of evildoers and their respective tortures, following closely the lists present in Ibn ʿAbbās' texts.[24] Only a few divergences from the pattern of the whole occur, such as the mention of commercial sins (including making deficient measures) or gender-specific offenses (including women who strike their hands against their cheeks to show despair for the dead).[25]

A large section on sinners also is included in another ascension narrative preserved in the Kahle Library at the University of Turin.[26] This work lists thirty categories of evildoers and their tortures but presents them at the end of the ascent, after the seventh and last heaven. The major peculiarity of this list is that only a few punishments are reserved for women. Moreover, it includes classes of evil-doers that are rarely mentioned, such as those who disobey their parents and poets who are condemned to different forms of punishments. The location of the tour of hell in the seventh sky, along with that of paradise (Plate 6), is further attested in some other well-known ascension works such as the *Liber Scale Machometi* (Book of Muḥammad's Ladder)[27] and especially the Chaghatay Turkish illustrated *Book of Ascension*.[28] In the latter manuscript, fourteen categories of sinners and their punishments are listed after the description of the cursed Tree of Hell (*al-Zaqqūm*), categories in general similar to those mentioned above and in which only four are devoted specifically to women.[29] These four categories include: women who did not cover their hair in public and committed immoral acts, who are punished by hanging by the hair; women who did not pray and remained in a state of impurity, who are punished by being chained by the hands and feet and by being assaulted by scorpions and snakes; women who insulted their husbands and went out without their permission, who are punished by hanging by the tongue; and women who had children by men other than their own and introduced the children into their household, who are punished by hanging by the breasts.

Later *miʿrāj* works reveal various attitudes toward the tours of hell, sinners, and their punishments. Some authors may be defined as hadith-oriented and consequently deal with questions related to the *miʿrāj* as originating in various reports and sayings traced back to the Prophet in traditional literature. Rather than adding new data, these works are nevertheless relevant because they discuss categories of sinners and their sins, and disclose a variety of authorial opinions. Al-Ujhūrī (d. 1655), for instance, is most interested in harmonizing the peculiarities of the two early reports going back to Abū Hurayra and Abū Saʿīd al-Khudrī, and so he emphasizes that the Prophet saw some of the sinners during his night journey and others during his heavenly ascension.[30] He quotes the report of Abū Hurayra from the *tafsīr* of al-Ṭabarī,[31] and then he adds that Muḥammad saw five classes of sinners during his ascent to heaven in the first heaven.[32] What he comments upon first is that the punishments of usurers and adulterers are given differently in the two descriptions.[33] Some other works avoid this issue by not mentioning any particulars of the tour of hellfire. This is particularly the case with Ibn Diḥya (d. 1236) and with the prolific Muḥammad Shāmī (d. 1535), the latter of whom devoted more than one work to Muḥammad's *miʿrāj*.[34]

Yet others take a kind of middle position. Such is the case of Najm al-Dīn al-Ghayṭī (d. 1576), who authored one of the major works on the *miʿrāj*, itself an official-popular synthesis of various ascension works.[35] In his text, he mentions sinners three times. First, he mentions the various categories of sinners seen by Muḥammad during the night journey according to the hadith attributed to Abū Hurayra; second, he briefly hints at the categories of sinners in the first heaven mentioned in the hadith attributed to Abū Saʿīd al-Khudrī; and third, he points to Muḥammad's experiences beyond the seventh heaven, where Muḥammad is shown the portion of hell in which one finds the punishment of slanderers.[36] The end result thus forms a compromise: Ghayṭī includes the tour of hell motif as found in the two early hadith reports, but he also relies on other reports by including the final vision of hell at the conclusion of the Prophet's ascension.

Differing approaches and degrees of attention paid to the categories of sinners can lead to different results. This is quite clear from the text of al-Iznīqī (d. 1429), which includes one of the longest tours of hell in ascension literature. It lists thirty categories of sinners and their punishments by mixing information from previous works along with more innovative motifs.[37] The final part of Iznīqī's description of the Prophet's tour of hell is dedicated to listing the nine classes of sinful women, which are similar to those mentioned above in connection to al-Bakrī.[38]

It thus appears that later *mi*ʿ*rāj* literature developed the tour of hell motif and introduced new particulars about the sinners witnessed by Muḥammad. The major innovation is first attested in Sunni works by al-Bakrī or in works attributed to him, in which numerous female sinners first appear. This expansion of the narrative allowed for a major shift in the meaning of the Prophet's tour of hell and in its moral intention. The morality of women and their sins in marital relations emerge here as major themes related to these scenes. All subsequent authors had thus to deal with this varying list of female sinners, either by including and discussing it or by entirely excluding it from their works.

Sinners Destined to Hell in Muslim Literature

Having reviewed the various sins and sinners mentioned in a selection of early and later *mi*ʿ*rāj* works, it is now necessary to examine the Muslim tradition on hellfire as a whole. This brief survey will permit us to better identify the originality of this literature, the interplay between official reports and more popular and extended versions of hellfire scenes, and furthermore the novelty of the list of women's punishments. First of all, it is important to recall that the issue of Muslim sinners and their destiny in hell is a problematic question in Muslim tradition. Although Ashʿarī theology has finally come to the solution that those who commit major sins are destined to temporary punishments, Muslim traditions and theological speculation as a whole never felt at ease in specifying which sins condemned Muslims to this temporary punishment. This hesitancy explains why Muslim hadith-oriented literature neither includes lists of sinners nor describes Muslim sinners in hell like those in the ascension texts discussed so far.

Only in rare cases does the Qur'an connect a category of sinners with their respective punishments, stating for example that, "those who devour the property of orphans unjustly, devour fire in their bellies and shall assuredly roast in a blaze" (Q 4:10).[39] Major hadith collections and Muslim tradition as a whole did include some relevant reports on the topic, but long lists of sinners and punishments are quite rare. Hadith literature instead displays in this regard a wide use of formulae on these eschatological traditions, such as describing the conditions of some sinners on the Day of Judgment. Such works state that those committing a specific sin will not enter paradise, or they describe which sinners are subjected to the most exacting punishment. Thus, although hadith literature is rich in the description and identification of particular sins, most of these reports lack the eschatological element of interest to us, that is, the connection of sins to their specific punishments in the Hereafter.

The report most similar to the list of sinners mentioned in some *mi*ʿ*rāj* reports is a long hadith going back to Samura b. Jundab. In this report, Muḥammad describes one of his dreams, in which he is shown four types of punishments for the following sinners: a liar, a man not acting according to the Qur'an and sleeping at night, those who commit adultery, and a usurer.[40] Other reports in the major hadith collections mention sinners and their punishments in a manner directly connected to the *miʿrāj*, but as discussed above, these hadiths are short and describe the torture of only one category of sinners.[41] Shiʿi literature does not provide much more information on this topic. The most relevant report is the one already mentioned from Ibn Bābawayh. Likewise, other Shiʿi sources, such as the encyclopedic *Biḥār al-anwār* (Seas of Lights) by al-Majlisī (d. 1699), present a picture similar to that in Sunni sources.[42]

This same approach is also well explicated by the Sunni body of eschatological literature. A comprehensive discussion is beyond the scope of this brief study, but offering a few considerations will be enough to serve the present purpose. The most famous work on eschatology is the *al-Tadhkira fī aḥwāl al-mawt wa-umūr al-Ākhira* (Memorial on the Conditions of Death and the Concerns of Afterlife) of al-Qurṭubī (d. 671/1272), which resembles an encyclopedia of traditions dealing with eschatological themes. The work mentions sinners and the punishments they suffer, but this only occurs in a short chapter collating some brief traditions. The chapter describes the punishment of those who make images, and of the *ʿālim* (man of knowledge) whose *ʿilm* (knowledge) is not useful. It then presents two longer reports that include short lists of categories of sinners with their specific torments. In the first of these two longer reports, one of which is transmitted from Ibn al-Mubārak, there are three classes of sinners: haughty people, usurpers of the rights of people, and slanderers. In the second long report, the text mentions four categories of offenders: those who did not settle their debts, those who did not wash away their urine, those who took pleasure from spreading calumny and obscenity, and those who slandered others.[43] Other works on eschatological themes do not alter this basic picture.[44]

The situation is completely different if we leave normative traditional literature of the *ʿulamāʾ* circles—defined with different names such as elite or traditional hadith-oriented literature—and turn instead to other works of medieval Muslim literature, such as popular works or those belonging to non-*ʿulamāʾ* circles.[45] One story of interest is that of Jesus and the skull (*Hadith/Qiṣṣat al-jumjuma*), which includes a tour of hell by a man who describes this tour to Jesus and who is then brought back to life by him.[46] In the many versions of this story, we find mention of various classes of sinners and their specific punishments in hell. Versions of this narrative state that the first layer of hell is reserved for the evil-doers among Muḥammad's community. Further sinners who are also without a doubt from the Muslim community are in the seventh heaven, and they include rebels and liars (*mujrimūn* and *mukadhdhibūn*).

Among the various versions of the "Jesus and the Skull" story, some of them explore in more detail sinners and their relation to the layers of hell in which they reside. Furthermore, some indicate more specific categories, although not mentioning a correlated kind of punishment. In such a case, sinners include hypocrites; usurpers of orphans' money; those who commit *zinā* (adultery); usurers; those who drink and eat forbidden food; unbelievers and idolaters; Satan (Iblīs) and his followers; those who slander honest women; those who do not believe in doomsday; the *ʿulamā'* who do not apply the precepts of religious law; women who kill their children and betray their husbands; women who neglect prayer; worshippers of the sun; tyrants and their helpers; those who forbid *zakāt;* adulteresses and adulterers; apostates; Pharaohs; and Shiʿites/Rafiḍites mentioned as those who offended Abū Bakr, ʿUmar and ʿUthmān (Plate 7).[47]

A few elements are of primary importance for our purposes. First of all, the variant reports of the "Jesus and the Skull" narrative reveal that every version of the narrative contains original particulars. This holds true for the various lists of sinners as well. However, the element deserving closer attention here is that the sinners mentioned are typologically different from those found in *miʿrāj* narratives, with the exception of a few "classical" categories of sinners, such as those who commit usury and those who devour orphans' goods. Unlike the categories in most *miʿrāj* accounts, the classes of sinners found in the "Jesus and the Skull" tradition are more related to theological issues and to major questions involving the community of believers, especially in relation to other communities of faith. Minor and private faults in marital relations, as well as other sins connected to the morality of men and women, do not form a major concern of the authors of stories in this genre, nor by extension to their audience of readers and listeners.

This same tendency is confirmed by other traditions containing visions of sinners and their punishments. In fact, along with normative and hadith-oriented literature, other eschatological texts that preserve a wide range of categories of various sins of Muslim sinners destined to hell did circulate quite widely. One of these is the apocryphal *Kitāb al-ʿajā'ib wa-l-gharā'ib* (The Book of Marvelous and Strange Things) attributed to ʿAbd Allāh b. Salām (d. 43/663). This report contains, among other things, a long tour of hell narrated through a dialogue between Ibn Salām and the third caliph ʿUthmān. In the long description of the fire of *Jahannam,* many categories of sinners are included, and, most interestingly, these categories are largely distinct from those previously discussed.[48] The narrative includes a long passage describing people who complain because they were punished for presumably minor faults, after which various types of sinners are mentioned. The most relevant among these are those who heighten their position before kings and rulers; those who give away their riches without charity to the poor; teachers who go first to the children of the rich and only afterward to the children of the poor; imāms who are reluctant in leading people in prayer; those who wear kings' attire and desire to be in their place; those among kings, rulers, emirs, and their assistants who take people's goods and rule without right; and the calumniators of kings, emirs, and their assistants.

These categories attest to what is the main concern of the work, namely to offer advice regarding the relationship between men of power and the wider populace. It thus appears that the various texts—or more precisely the various corpuses of texts—each contain differing types of traditions on the subject of the sinners and their punishments in hell. These details in turn echo the distinct concerns and aims of their authors and at the same time the differing circulation and audience that these narrative traditions had.

Final Considerations

A series of questions remains to be answered, foremost among them the question of when the tours of hell with visions of sinners and their punishments became included in *miʿrāj* narratives. We have described above the path of the motif in reports on Muḥammad's night journey and his heavenly ascension, and have shown how most probably such reports were inserted in traditions circulating during the second Hijrī century. The hadith of Abū Hurayra and that of Abū Saʿīd al-Khudrī attest to this, and the criticism surrounding both reports further supports the thesis that they represented a sort of middle ground between the popular and the official recountings of the Prophet's *miʿrāj*.[49] Such evidence and other indirect references connected to our topic suggest that long reports including tours of hell connected to popular literature or to differing layers than those originating in hadith-oriented literature were in circulation during the first centuries of Islam. Their aim, as previously suggested by Vuckovic, was to define the moral borders of a community of believers and to indicate clearly which sins would lead Muslims to suffer temporary punishment and torture in hell.

The later appearance of long narratives that include comprehensive lists of sinners no doubt reflects the tendency of this material to grow, sometimes exponentially. Such texts also attest to the growing influence of the concept of Muḥammad's intercession and thus his ability to lead a certain number of Muslim sinners out of hell.[50] Alongside the Prophet's intercessory power (*shafāʿa*), one should not underestimate the later interest in many questions related to eschatological beliefs, most importantly the destiny of Muslim sinners. The attention paid to this particular issue is in clear contrast with the reluctance of hadith-oriented scholars and authors to touch upon this material or to use it when discussing hellfire and the punishments awaiting sinners.

Another question is not only when and why lists of sinners in *miʿrāj* narratives grew longer, but also why later versions included different types of sinners, especially long lists of women sinners mostly attested in the cycles attributed to al-Bakrī and Ibn ʿAbbās. Regarding this issue, we can only offer some suggestions that may point toward possible answers. Although a peculiar emphasis on the morality of women and on the nature of their sins is well attested in early literature,[51] such extended lists of sins represent a major development in the genre. It is relevant to note again that the first attestation of this new development, to my knowledge, can be traced to the tenth-century *ʿUyūn akhbār al-Riḍā* of Ibn Bābawayh, and a version of this report appears to have found its way into some versions of Bakrī's work on the *miʿrāj*. This situation offers a confirmation of the interplay between

Shiʿi and Sunni traditions, a possibility most recently discussed by Colby in his study included in the present volume.[52] This Shiʿi report may well have been at the foundation of long descriptions of female sins found in later Sunni reports.

As regards the general interest in sins involving women, suggestions by Himmelfarb in her work on Jewish and Christian tours of hell provide some possible parallels. Himmelfarb theorizes that the emphasis given to sexual sins and sins of speech may be connected to the invisibility of women, and thus to their being impervious to legislation.[53] The intent of such tours of hell is thus moral in nature, and it emphasizes behaviors not easily detected. This is also evidenced in the Muslim tours of hell emerging in this literature, in which along with "canonical" sins we find what Bencheikh calls the "wretchedness of daily life."[54] Himmelfarb's hypothesis can offer an apt answer to the peculiarities of the list of sinners given in the various later texts, where along with more classical categories of sinners connected to usury and the theft of orphans' goods, a consistent emphasis is given to the sexual sins and to the morality of women.

One should not lose sight of the fact that this emphasis upon the punishment of women's sins, however, applies primarily to categories of sinners and sins included in *miʿrāj* narratives. We have shown how this concern with women and for the kinds of sin described above are specific to *miʿrāj* narratives, since in comparison to similar narratives including tours of hell with other different concerns, it appears clear that *miʿrāj* narratives were interested in more popular definitions of morality. Ascension narratives, for instance, show scarce attention to the relations between rulers or generic men of power and their constituencies. One possible reason for this different type of emphasis may be connected to the participation of women in festivals and celebrations of the "night of ascension" (*laylat al-miʿrāj*), at which time ascension texts were read out loud or recited. There was a significant involvement of women in various celebrations of the life of Muḥammad after the tenth–eleventh centuries. Indeed, as has been underlined recently by Marion Katz, the high degree of concern with female characters in the literature about the *mawlid* (birth, or celebrations of the birth) of the Prophet Muḥammad reflects the high degree of female participation in such events.[55]

In the case of *miʿrāj* texts, the particular concern over the sinful behavior of women fits well with the chronology of narratives of this theme. Further, this concern displays a strong moral suasion against and a censuring of the sinful behaviors of the very women who likely were participating in the recitation and reading of ascension texts. At the same time, the new focus on the sins of women shows the authors' new moral attitude as influenced by their intended audience of men and women, and as informed by their differing attitudes revealed by the range from canonical hadith-oriented literature to the growing diffusion of popular motifs. These differing attitudes attest to the richness of Muslim literature after the so-called classical period. This literary output consisted of a corpus of texts that did not rely exclusively on the discussion of material in early hadith collections, but also introduced and reworked novel motifs, thus contributing and responding to the development of moral interests and needs.

Notes

1. Colby, "Constructing an Islamic Ascension Narrative" (Ph.D. diss., Duke University, 2002), ch. 1, 17–70. I wish to thank Frederick Colby for sharing his dissertation and unpublished works with me and for discussing questions related to this study.

2. Vuckovic, *Heavenly Journeys, Earthly Concerns* (New York and London: Routledge, 2005), 112–121.

3. As stated by Bencheikh, *Le Voyage nocturne de Mahomet* (Paris: Imprimerie Nationale, 1988), 219, the sins are more interesting than the kinds of tortures because they reveal concerns over social behavior.

4. The specification of long narratives on the night journey and the ascent is important since short inclusions of one category of sinners seen by Muḥammad are also attested in canonical collections. But what makes these statements different is that they are not lists but instead only mention one class of evil-doers. Notwithstanding this, such attestations are quite relevant, since they point to the circulation at that time of various reports on the topic, which generated differing evaluations in the authors of these hadith collections. In a short report, the Prophet states that during his ascent to heaven he saw people with wide bellies from which snakes were seen coming out: these were the usurers (see Ibn Abī Shayba, *Muṣannaf* [Beirut: Dār al-kutub al-ʿilmiyya, 1995] vol. 7, 335 no. 36574; Ibn Māja, *Sunan* [Cairo: Muṣṭafā al-Bābī al-Ḥalabī, n.d.], vol. 2, 763 no. 2273; Aḥmad b. Ḥanbal, *Musnad* [Beirut: Dār al-Fikr, 1991], vol. 3, 269–270 no. 8648, 289 no. 8765). A saying traced back to Anas b. Mālik mentions those who preach (*khuṭabā'*) what they do not follow or those forbidding evil and prescribing good but not acting according to this precept (Aḥmad ibn Ḥanbal, *Musnad*, nos. 12232, 12879; Abū Yaʿlā, *Musnad* [Beirut: Dār al-Ma'mūn li-l-turāth, 1992], vol. 7, 72, 180 nos. 3996, 4160, etc. This tradition is quoted in many sources; see also the longer version in Yaḥyā b. Sallām, *Tafsīr* (Beirut: Dār al-kutub al-ʿilmiyya, 2004), vol. 1, 111). We also find here sinners and punishments that some other versions include in the larger reports, such as slanderers (Abū Dāwūd, *Sunan* (Cairo: Dār al-hadith, n.d.), vol. 4, 269, no. 4878; Aḥmad ibn Ḥanbal, *Musnad*, nos. 2324, 13364; al-Suyūṭī, *al-Durr al-manthūr* (Beirut: Dār al-Fikr, 1983), vol. 5, p. 212).

5. Some other versions simply mention that Muḥammad saw paradise and hell without any further description. See, for instance, al-Tirmidhī or later authors such as Ibn Kathīr or Ibn Diḥya, in Colby, "Constructing an Islamic Ascension Narrative," 130, 367, 266–267. It is interesting to note that the eschatological matters are almost completely absent in the Shiʿi versions of the *mi'rāj*. On this see topic, see Amir-Moezzi, *La religion discrète* (Paris: Librairie Philosophique J. Vrin, 2006), 145.

6. As regards Muqātil, *Tafsīr* (Cairo: al-Hay'a al-miṣriyya, 1979–1989), vol. 2, 519, although he does not list any category of sinners, he indeed mentions two specific Meccans tortured for their worship of Allāt and al-ʿUzzā (as discussed also by Colby, "Constructing an Islamic Ascension Narrative," 92); cf. Ibn Saʿd, *al-Ṭabaqāt al-kubrā* (Beirut: Dār al-Ṣādir, n.d.), vol. 1, 213.

7. al-Bayhaqī, *Dalā'il al-nubuwwa* (Beirut: Dār al-kutub al-ʿilmiyya, 1985), vol. 2, 397f.; the other sources include some variants, for example al-Ṭabarī, *Jāmiʿ al-bayān* (Cairo: Muṣṭafā al-Bābī al-Ḥalabī, 1968), vol. 15, 7, gives seven out of these categories; see also al-Thaʿlabī, *al-Kashf wa-l-bayān* (Beirut: Dār al-kutub al-ʿilmiyya, 2002), vol. 6, 57; and al-Suyūṭī, *al-Durr al-manthūr*, vol. 5, 199–200 (quoting various sources such as al-Bazzār, Abū Yaʿlā, al-Ṭabarī, al-Marwazī, Ibn Abī Ḥātim, Ibn ʿAdī, Ibn Mardawayh and al-Bayhaqī). On this hadith, see Colby, "Constructing an Islamic Ascension Narrative," 196–203.

8. ʿAbd al-Razzāq, *Tafsīr* (Riyadh: Maktabat al-Rushd, 1989), vol. 1, 367–368; Yaḥyā b.

Sallām, *Tafsīr,* vol. 1, 107–108; Hūd b. Muḥakkam, *Tafsīr* (Beirut: Dār al-Gharb al-Islāmī, 1990), vol. 2, 402–403. On this hadith see Colby, "Constructing an Islamic Ascension Narrative," 191–196.

9. Al-Ṭabarī, *Jāmiᶜ al-bayān,* vol. 15, 13; al-Bayhaqī, *Dalāʾil al-nubuwwa,* vol. 2, 389f.; and al-Suyūṭī, *al-Durr al-manthūr,* vol. 5, 196. Instead of the women committing adultery and killing their babies, these versions mention those who leave the permitted and take the forbidden.

10. al-Suyūṭī, *al-Āya al-kubrā fī sharḥ qiṣṣat al-isrāʾ,* in Ibn Ḥajar al-ᶜAsqalānī and al-Suyūṭī, *al-Isrāʾ wa-l-miᶜrāj* (Cairo: Dār al-ḥadith, 1989), 38. There are various versions of this hadith of Muḥammad's dream, discussed subsequently. The relevance of this dream tradition to the *miᶜrāj* narratives was already noted by M. Asín Palacios in his seminal work *La escatología musulmana en la Divina Comedia* (Madrid: Real Academia Española, 1919), 8–14.

11. The insertion of independent narremes is also attested or probable in other cases. On the matter, see Bencheikh, *Le Voyage nocturne de Mahomet,* 283; and Colby, "Constructing an Islamic Ascension Narrative," 135–139.

12. Ibn Hishām, *al-Sīra al-nabawiyya* (Beirut: Dār al-Fikr, 1992), 272.

13. According to Colby, "Constructing an Islamic Ascension Narrative," this vision of hellfire probably represents an interpolation into the middle of Abū Saᶜīd al-Khudrī's report.

14. Al-Qummī, *Tafsīr* (Beirut: Dār al-surūr, 1991), vol. 2, 6–7, translated in Colby, "Constructing an Islamic Ascension Narrative," 206–210; and in particular 211 on the relation of Qummī's version to that of Abū Saᶜīd al-Khudrī regarding the classes of evildoers.

15. On Abū al-Ḥasan al-Bakrī and all the problems connected to his works and his lifetime, see Shoshan, *Popular Culture in Medieval Cairo* (Cambridge: Cambridge University Press, 1993), ch. 2; on his identity and his work on Muḥammad's *miᶜrāj,* see Colby, "Constructing an Islamic Ascension Narrative," 272–298.

16. On this point, see Colby, "Constructing an Islamic Ascension Narrative," 303.

17. Bibliothèque nationale de France, Paris, ms. arabe 1931, folios 78r–79r.

18. Süleymaniye Kütüphanesi, Istanbul, Ayasofya 867, folios 172v–173r; see Colby, "Constructing an Islamic Ascension Narrative," 291. This version of al-Bakrī's narrative is translated by Colby, "Constructing an Islamic Ascension Narrative," 442–462.

19. Ibn Bābawayh, *ᶜUyūn akhbār al-Riḍā* (Beirut: Muʾassasat al-aᶜlamī li-l-maṭbūᶜāt, 2005), vol. 2, 13–14, no. 24; and al-Majlisī, *Biḥār al-anwār* (Beirut: Muʾassasat al-wafāʾ, 1983), vol. 18, 351.

20. See his dissertation "Constructing an Islamic Ascension Narrative"; and also his book based on a portion of his dissertation, *Narrating Muḥammad's Night Journey* (Albany, N.Y.: SUNY Press, 2008).

21. See *al-Isrāʾ wa-l-miᶜrāj li-l-imām Ibn ᶜAbbās* (Cairo: Maktabat al-Qāhira, n.d.), 18–22; *Hādhā miᶜrāj al-nabī (ṣ) taʾlīf al-Imām Ibn ᶜAbbās* (Damascus: Maktabat Muḥammad al-Ḥalabī, 1948), 15–19, and the many other printed editions of this work. For an English translation see el-ᶜAẓma, *al-Miᶜrāj wa-l-razm al-ṣūfī* (Beirut: Dār al-Bāḥith, 1982), Engl. Sec., 30–32; and for a Spanish translation, see F. Cisneros, *El Libro del viaje nocturno y la ascensión del Profeta* (México: El Colegio de México, 1998), 89–94.

22. el-ᶜAẓma, *al-Miᶜrāj wa-l-razm al-ṣūfī,* 143–145.

23. One manuscript preserved in the Kahle Library of the Department of Oriental Studies of the University of Turin, titled *Miᶜrāj Ibn ᶜAbbās,* is almost identical to the one edited by el-ᶜAẓma, thus attesting to the diffusion of a version of the narrative of Ibn ᶜAbbās that includes seventeen categories of sinners. See Turin Kahle ms. no. 180, folios 45r-50v. On this manuscript see Tottoli, "Two *Kitāb al-miᶜrāj* in the manuscripts collection of the Paul Kahle Library of the University of Turin," *Loquentes linguis: Studi linguistici e orientali in onore di Fabrizio A. Pennacchietti,* edited by Pier Giorgio Borbone et al. (Wiesbaden: Harrassowitz Verlag, 2006), 708–709.

24. See Zayn al-Dīn, *al-Najm al-wahhāj fī al-masrā wa-l-miᶜrāj,* Dār al-kutub, Cairo, ms. 829 Majāmīᶜ, folios 12r-13v. On this work, see Colby, "Constructing an Islamic Ascension Narrative," 337–344, and especially 339, where he defines Zayn al-Dīn's text as a "redacted synthesis of diverse early recensions of pseudo-Ibn ᶜAbbās Ascension narratives."

25. Zayn al-Dīn, *al-Najm al-wahhāj fī al-masrā wa-l-miᶜrāj,* folios 12b and 13b.

26. Turin Kahle ms. no. 179, folios 162r-179r. See Tottoli, "Two *Kitāb al-miʿrāj* in the manuscripts collection of the Paul Kahle Library," 705–708. The name of the author of this work is given at the beginning; it is a certain Abū ʿAbd Allāh Muḥammad b. Aḥmad al-Mālikī.

27. Toward the end of the work, the author describes which sinners Muḥammad saw and their specific punishments: those who commit mischief, those who commit adultery and work as prostitutes, and finally rich members of the community who, though giving charity, were too haughty. See Cerulli, *Il "Libro della scala"* (Vatican: Biblioteca apostolica vaticana, 1949), 192–194 (ch. 72), 210–212 (ch. 79).

28. See Scherberger, *Das Miʿrājnāme: Die Himmel- und Höllenfahrt des Propheten Muḥammad in der osttürkischen Überlieferung* (Würzburg: Ergon Verlag, 2003), 109–113, listing fourteen categories and their punishments. See also el-ʿAẓma, *al-Miʿrāj wa-l-ramz al-ṣūfī*, 22–23; and Colby, "Constructing an Islamic Ascension Narrative," 317–321. For English and French translations of the Timurid Book of Ascension, see Wheeler Thackston, "The Paris Miʿrājnāma," *Journal of Turkish Studies* 18 (1994), 263–299; Christiane Gruber, *The Timurid Book of Ascension (Miʿrajnama): A Study of Text and Image in a Pan-Asian Context* (Valencia: Patrimonio Ediciones, 2008), Appendix I; and Abel Pavet de Courteille, *Mirâdj-Nâmeh, Récit de l'Ascension de Mahomet au Ciel Composé A.H. 840/1436–1437* (Amsterdam: Philo Press, 1985).

29. Only one category of sinners in this "Book of Ascension" is particularly relevant to the current discussion, and it is that of those men who hypocritically treat their leaders (*emirs*) with deference. This detail clearly reflects a general praise of the morality of people toward their rulers, which also occurs in later presentations of tours of hell in other literary forms.

30. Nūr al-Dīn al-Ujhūrī, *al-Nūr al-wahhāj fī al-kalām ʿalā al-isrāʾ wa-l-miʿrāj* (Beirut: Dār al-kutub al-ʿilmiyya, 2003), 174f.

31. Ibid., 174–175, 199.

32. Ibid., 199–201.

33. Ibid., 199.

34. Ibn Diḥya, *al-Ibtihāj fī aḥādīth al-miʿrāj* (Cairo: Maktabat al-Khānjī, 1996); and, e.g., M. Shāmī, *Khulāṣat al-faḍl al-fāʾiq fī miʿrāj khayr al-khalāʾiq* (Cairo: Dār Ibn Ḥazm, 2003). On these works and their approaches, see Colby, "Constructing an Islamic Ascension Narrative," 300, 352–363, 372–375.

35. On al-Ghayṭī, see Colby, "Constructing an Islamic Ascension Narrative," 375–398. The narrative portion of his major work, *al-Miʿrāj al-kabīr*, is translated in A. Jeffery, *A Reader on Islam* (The Hague: Mouton & Co., 1962), 621–639.

36. al-Ghayṭī, *Qiṣṣat al-miʿrāj* (Muṣṭafā al-Bābī al-alabī, 1949) 10–11, 16, 22. On this point see Colby, "Constructing an Islamic Ascension Narrative," 381, 385.

37. Such as the punishment of rich people; see Mūsā Iznīqī, *Kitāb al-miʿrāj*, Marmara Üniversitesi, Ilahiyat Oğüt ms. 1229, folios 22r-24r. On this work, see Colby, "Constructing an Islamic Ascension Narrative," 309–317.

38. Iznīqī, *Kitāb al-miʿrāj*, folio 23v.

39. On orphans, see also Q 17:34. On the topic, see Smith and Haddad, *The Islamic Understanding of Death and Resurrection* (Oxford and New York: Oxford University Press, 1981), 86. Other passages of interest include Q 4:145, where it is stated that the hypocrites "will be in the lowest reach (*dark*) of the Fire"; and further, the passage stating "surely those who cast it upon women in wedlock that are heedless but believing (*al-muḥṣanāt al-ghāfilāt*) shall be accursed in the present world and the world to come; and there awaits them a mighty chastisment" (Q 24:23).

40. Al-Bukhārī, *Ṣaḥīḥ* (Beirut: Dār al-kutub al-ʿilmiyya), no. 7047. This hadith is mentioned by Aḥmad ibn Ḥanbal, and there are also other versions with variants on all of these categories. See al-Muttaqī al-Hindī, *Kanz al-ʿummāl fī sunan al-aqwāl wa-l-afʿāl* (Beirut: Muʾassasat al-Risāla, 1989), vol. 16, 659f. nos. 39793–39801 (see in particular no. 39801). Along with the other four categories, this version also adds people acting as Lot's people. The mention of punishment in hell is used in another hadith, in which it is said that women who display golden necklaces and earrings will wear similar jewelry on the Day of Resurrection, but instead made of fire. See al-Nasāʾī, *al-Sunan al-kubrā* (Beirut: Dār al-kutub al-ʿilmiyya, 1992),

vol. 5, 434 no. 9439; and see similar statements, prompting the use of silver instead of gold also for women, in Abū Dāwūd, *Sunan,* vol. 4, 90–91 nos. 4236, 4238.

41. See above, n. 5.

42. Admittedly, there are some reports that no doubt attest to the circulation of traditions and even long narrations on the topic, but the theme of sinners and their punishments in hell does not appear to be a major one for Shiʿis, or at least not one with which authors wanted to deal comprehensively. See for example, al-Majlisī, *Biḥār al-anwār,* vol. 8, 311 (from *al-Khiṣāl* by Ibn Bābawayh), stating that in hell there is a mill grinding five categories of people, *ʿulamāʾ*, bad rulers, etc.; or see vol. 8, 309 from the same source, stating that various specific kinds of bad *ʿulamāʾ* are in the seven stages of hell. In other places, it discusses the fate of sinners on the Day of Judgment, where it also cites specific punishments; see al-Majlisī, *Biḥār al-anwār,* vol. 7, 213–216); or see the long tradition ascribed to Abū Hurayra and Ibn ʿAbbās in the *Thawāb al-aʿmāl* by Ibn Bābawayh (Qumm: Manshūrāt al-Sharīf al-Riḍāʾ, 1984), pp. 280–295, which lists various punishments connected to sins and various rewards connected to good acts.

43. al-Qurṭubī, *al-Tadhkira fī aḥwāl al-mawt wa-umūr al-ākhira* (Medina: Maktabat dār al-minhāj, 2005), vol. 2, 887–890. Hadiths are quoted after these reports; see for instance the report from Anas b. Mālik on hypocritical preachers, *al-Tadhkira,* vol. 2, 891.

44. Such works include the *Durra al-fākhira* attributed to al-Ghazālī, *al-Baʿth wa-l-nushūr* by al-Bayhaqī, the *Budūr al-sāfira fī umūr al-ākhira* by al-Suyūṭī, or the *Daqāʾiq al-akhbār fī dhikr al-janna wa-l-nār* by al-Qāḍī. For example, when dealing with the seven doors of hell, al-Suyūṭī does not mention the categories of damned destined to inhabit them. It is only said that the first one is for the sinners of the Muslim community (al-Suyūṭī, *al-Budūr al-sāfira fī umūr al-ākhira* [Cairo: Maktabat al-Qurʾān, 1990], 310–312). Only a few other passages mention scanty particulars of interest in connection with the long chapters dealing with punishments of disbelievers and sinners: e.g. ibid., 354f., which lists punishments for those prescribing right and forbidding evil but acting differently, those whose knowledge was not useful to themselves, women wearing golden necklaces and earrings, those having "two tongues" (the duplicitous), those who drink from vessels of gold and silver, those who commit suicide, and those who drink wine.

45. For stratifications and interplay between various levels of the elite to popular spectrum, I make reference to Sadan, "Hārūn al-Rashīd and the Brewer," *Studies in Canonical and Popular Arabic Literature* (Toronto: York Press, 1998), 1–22, and in particular 6.

46. For a comprehensive study of this story in Arabic literature and a study of the approximately thirty manuscript versions, see Tottoli, "The Story of Jesus and the Skull in Arabic Literature: the Emergence and Growth of a Religious Tradition," *Jerusalem Studies in Arabic and Islam* 28 (2003): 225–259.

47. On all these reports, see the various manuscript versions of the narrative quoted in Tottoli, "The Story of Jesus and the Skull."

48. Ps.-ʿAbd Allāh ibn Salām, *Kitāb al-ʿajāʾib wa-l-gharāʾib wa-mā khalaqa Allāh Taʿālā min al-makhlūqāt,* Gotha ms. A 745, folios 9r–15v.

49. On this point, see Colby, "Constructing an Islamic Ascension Narrative," 302.

50. Colby, "Constructing an Islamic Ascension Narrative," 268, 296, 303–304, 328, 391; and also Smith and Haddad, *The Islamic Understanding of Death and Resurrection,* 81–82, 93. The new approach may also reflect the tendency of popular culture to revolve around themes of suffering and misery, as maintained elsewhere by Colby, "Constructing an Islamic Ascension Narrative," 406–407.

51. For example, see Smith and Haddad, "Women in the Afterlife," *Journal of the American Academy of Religion* 43 (1975): 39–50.

52. Also see his "Constructing an Islamic Ascension Narrative," 298.

53. Himmelfarb, *Tours of Hell: An Apocalyptic Form in Jewish and Christian Literature.* (Philadelphia: University of Pennsylvania Press, 1983), 73.

54. Bencheikh, *Le Voyage nocturne de Mahomet,* 219: "Les misères du quotidien."

55. Katz, *The Birth of the Prophet Muḥammad: Devotional Piety in Sunni Islam* (London and New York: Routledge, 2007), 48–49.

2

The Ilkhanid *Miʿrājnāma* as an Illustrated Sunni Prayer Manual

CHRISTIANE GRUBER

Over the years, scholarship concerned with Islamic painting has grappled with the enduring problem of how religious feeling manifests itself in pictorial form within an artistic tradition generally described as lacking in developed cycles of religious imagery. A number of scholars have contended that some Ottoman illustrated manuscripts depicting events from the life of the Prophet Muḥammad, such as the *Siyer-i Nebî* (Biography of the Prophet) commissioned by the Ottoman Sultan Murād III in 1595–1596[1] and other sixteenth-century illustrated hagiographic works such as al-Nīshāpūrī's *Qiṣaṣ al-Anbiyā'* (Stories of the Prophets), are not "true works of religious art, although they may, and often do, have a spiritual element."[2] Other scholars, however, have attempted to explore how religious sentiment may mediate an image, adopting it as a means of pious expression and thus engendering a genre of artistic production one might call "religious painting."[3] Although still in its early stages and faced with a number of challenges, the study of Islamic painting can nonetheless serve to explore the function of images and their relationship to devotional practices within the religious life of pre-modern Islamic cultures.

Illustrated manuscripts from the period of Ilkhanid rule in Iran (1256–1353) in particular served as powerful vehicles for the promotion of specific forms of religiosity and the official view on a shared cultural history at a time when neither was safe from the fluctuations of interpretation. For example, Öljeïtu (r. 1304–1316)—the most religiously erratic ruler, who was a baptized Nestorian Christian (under the name Nicholas) and who converted first to Sunni and later Shiʿi Islam—attempted to impose Shiʿi doctrine on a majority Sunni Iran.[4] He did so not just by executive order, but by patronizing architectural projects and the arts of the book. His mausoleum at the new capital of Sulṭānīya, it has been argued, originally was intended to house the relics of ʿAlī and Ḥusayn and thus promote Shiʿi pilgrimage in Iran,[5] while his illustrated copy of al-Bīrūnī's *al-Āthār al-Bāqīya* (Chronology of Nations) included two illustrations of scenes that were particularly promoted by and dear to the Shiʿi cause.[6]

Through these artistic endeavors, themselves marked by overt gestures of ostentatious piety,[7] he carefully endorsed a particular branch of Islam, an endorsement that was as unconcealed as it was short-lived.

Much as Öljeïtu remains best known among all Ilkhanid sultans for merging religious polemics with the pictorial arts, the last Ilkhanid ruler Abū Saʿīd (r. 1317–1335) promoted himself as the champion who restituted Sunni Islam to Iran after his predecessor's religious equivocations. The first Ilkhanid ruler to bear a purely Islamic name and no other, he changed the coins and the Friday sermon (*khuṭba*) back to the Sunni tradition upon his accession to the throne.[8] A number of extant works believed to have been produced during his rule, such as the Great Mongol *Shāhnāma* (Book of Kings) of the 1320s or 1330s, appear to comment upon contemporary events and to assert, through carefully selected ideological programs, rightful lordship over Persian lands.[9] These manuscripts certainly constituted didactic works of art that were intended to promote the Ilkhanid rulers' commitment to a shared political and cultural heritage in lands where they were still deemed foreign intruders.[10]

Abū Saʿīd's promotion of Sunni Islam in and through the visual arts has been less apparent, and thus less studied, than Öljeïtu's carefully orchestrated espousal of Shiʿism. It seems plausible to assume, however, that Abū Saʿīd would have wanted to provide a set of counter-narratives and counter-images to his forerunner's Shiʿi projects, thereby creating a competing pictorial mission to forward Sunni Islam. Just as Abū Saʿīd's copy of the *Shāhnāma* must have highlighted particular episodes pictorially for political purposes, one can assume that the illustrated *Miʿrājnāma* (Book of Ascension) of ca. 1317–1335 could have fulfilled religious aims as well.

Abū Saʿīd is known to have commissioned a *Miʿrājnāma,* and there is strong evidence to suggest that nine fragmentary Ilkhanid paintings represent images that may have originated from that particular illustrated manuscript.[11] These paintings, attributed to the Ilkhanid master painter (*ustād*) Aḥmad Mūsā and whose now missing text was written by the famed calligrapher ʿAbdallāh Ṣayrafī, are included in the Bahrām Mīrzā Album held in the Topkapı Palace Library in Istanbul.[12] Both their date and their function have remained subject to speculation, as the paintings were cropped from their original setting and therefore have lost their attending text due to remounting.[13] Even the identification and the sequence of the paintings have not yet been resolved, since no other extant ascension text—such as the thirteenth-century European "Book of Muḥammad's Ladder" or other autonomous *Miʿrājnāmas* written in Arabic and Chaghatay Turkish—closely match the paintings' contents.[14] Certainly these texts help identify episodes depicted in the fragmentary paintings, but none provides a close enough parallel to propose a tentative reconstruction of the painting series or, more importantly, formulate a hypothesis about the function of the original illustrated manuscript.

As a result of these uncertainties, the remnants of the illustrated "Book of the Prophet's Ascension" attributed to Abū Saʿīd's patronage have not found their proper place in discussions of Ilkhanid painting and *miʿrāj* narratives more generally. However, an anonymous and unillustrated Persian-language *Miʿrājnāma* dated 685/1286 (henceforth "SK text") can fill this lacuna.[15] This particular Ilkhanid Book of Ascension helps to identify the paintings and to reconstruct their sequence, as well as to determine the symbolic function of *miʿrāj* tales during the Ilkhanid period. By collating evidence from the SK text with an iconographic analysis of the fragmentary paintings intended to accompany Abū Saʿīd's royal *Miʿrājnāma,* it is possible to propose that narratives of the Prophet's ascension—illustrated or unillustrated, written or oral—could serve as powerful propaedeutic tools for the implementation of a particular branch of Islam during the Ilkhanid period.

This study aims to demonstrate that Ilkhanid paintings of the Prophet's *miʿrāj* could function as visual facilitators for the promotion of Sunni Islam in Persian lands, for the learning of Arabic-language *tasbīḥ*s,[16] and for the instruction of bodily movements used in oral petitionary prayers (*duʿā*s). The basis for such evidence can be traced through a formal analysis of the paintings' iconography. Moreover, a comparison between the paintings and their coeval SK text makes it clear that the paintings once belonged to an artistic genus that one could call an "illustrated prayer manual." This kind of pictured guidebook mediated oral behavior and religious practice primarily through the dual mechanism of a text and its attending images, in a manner not unlike Christian prayer manuals that may well have been in circulation in Ilkhanid Iran.

The Ilkhanid *Miʿrājnāma* Text

The SK Book of Ascension provides salient evidence for the Ilkhanid paintings, even though it bears neither the name of its author nor a discrete title on the first folio (Figure 2.1). Rather than immediately launching into the ascension narrative with Gabriel's arrival in Mecca, the text includes an introductory paragraph highlighting the problem of the location and date of the *miʿrāj.* This preliminary discussion is similar to those found in exegetical and philosophical works.[17] According to the text, the Prophet's first *miʿrāj* occurred between Mecca and *Bayt al-Maqdis,* while the second *miʿrāj* made Muḥammad ascend from *Bayt al-Maqdis* through the heavens to the realm of the Lord.[18] The introductory paragraph concludes that every person who denies the Prophet's ascension is an unbeliever (*kāfir*)[19] because he thereby denies God's divine revelation of the "Verse of the Night Journey" (*sūrat al-isrāʾ*) as included in the Qurʾan.[20] The text then includes a partially rubricated citation of *āyat al-isrāʾ,* the qurʾanic verse responsible for the later narrative elaborations of the Prophet's ascension.[21] The tone is set quickly at the opening of the work: the story of the Prophet's *miʿrāj* is a matter of faith, and any Muslim who rejects it is guilty of apostasy.

This rather dogmatic prolegomenon finds a strong echo in many of the details inserted throughout the text, which, albeit narrative and miraculous in character,

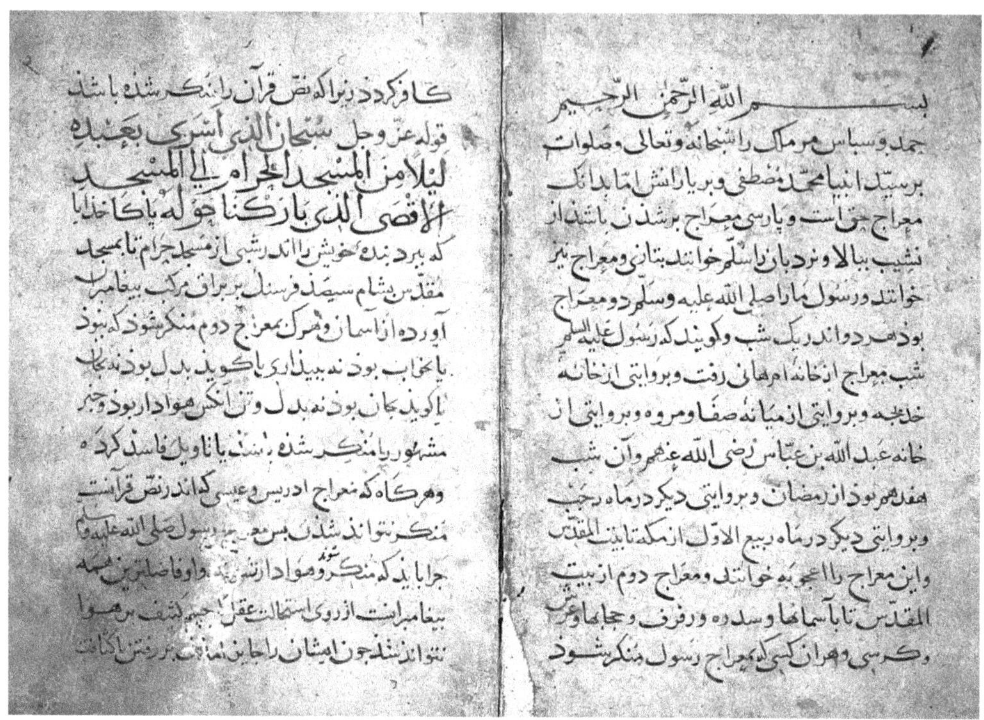

FIGURE 2.1. Incipit of the anonymous *Miʿrājnāma*, probably Iran, dated 685/1286. Istanbul, Süleymaniye Library, Ayasofya 3441, folios 1v–2r.

provides a template for the laying out of Muslim conviction and prayer. Many of the verbal exchanges that occur between Muḥammad, the prophets, and a variety of angels take the form of the uttered, personal invocations (*duʿā*) addressed in Arabic directly to God.[22] Although these invocations include excerpts from the Qur'an or proclaim the *takbīr* ("Allah is Great") and the *tahlīl* ("There is no God but God"), they largely consist of variations on the *tasbīḥ*.

The *tasbīḥ* formula begins with the introductory exclamation *subḥān* ("Glory to . . ."), followed by a variety of phrases or epithets describing God.[23] It is favored in the *Miʿrājnāma* manuscript, most probably since the term *subḥān* initiates *āyat al-isrāʾ* ("*subḥān al-ladhī asrā bi-ʿabdihi . . .*"). *Tasbīḥ* prayers glorify God as "Royal," "Eternal," "Living," "Powerful," and so forth. Even dialogues between the *Miʿrājnāma*'s protagonists appear in the guise of a verbal prayer toward the Lord, and each repetition of a *tasbīḥ* orison reverberates throughout the text much like the harmonic intonation of a repeated personal *duʿā*. Along with various qur'anic verses, these petitionary prayers in the SK ascension text create a cantillated exaltation of the Divine.

The repeated *tasbīḥ* phrases endow the text with a character unlike that of any other surviving *miʿrāj* narrative. It transforms an otherwise entertaining, biographical story into a teaching tool or, more precisely, into a "prayer manual" or guide to the proper performance of *duʿā* and *tasbīḥ* prayers intended for a non-Arabic speaking audience. Indeed, some of the prayers in the manuscript can be performed in direct emulation of the Prophet. Upon his arrival at the highest heaven, for example, Muḥammad encounters an angel circumambulating *al-bayt al-maᶜmūr* (the Frequented House) while praising the Lord with a *duᶜā*. Upon hearing the prayer, the Prophet states that he decided to memorize it and perform two prayer cycles (*rakᶜat*).[24] The Prophet's action implies that the reader should follow suit.

Much as the *Miᶜrājnāma* text includes rather prescriptive details with regards to prayer formulas, it also emerges as a cautionary tale. Throughout the text, it is stated that men who do not follow God's ordinances are bound for hell and its tortures. As Gabriel takes Muḥammad through the seven valleys of hell, both witness the punishments of the hypocrites, polytheists, Sabians (*Ṣābiyān*), unbelievers, and many other errant or rebellious men.[25] The emphasis on this particular narrative cluster—which represents the longest episode described in the manuscript—underscores the admonitory nature of the composition.[26] Not unlike earlier and later *Miᶜrājnāma* compositions, the focus of the Prophet's ascension tends to revolve around, and draw inspiration from, the detailed description of Inferno's punishments.[27]

At its conclusion, the SK text essentially takes on the form of a conversion narrative, and thus belongs to a larger storytelling genre intended to impart moral lessons. In the narrative, when the Prophet recounts his ascension to the Quraysh, Abū Jahl complains to Abū Bakr that Muḥammad has gone mad, to which Abū Bakr responds that the Prophet is not a liar. He adds that whatever Muḥammad says must be true.[28] At that precise moment, the caravans arrive in Mecca as the Prophet had predicted, and the conclusion to the narrative is given: he who believes in the *miᶜrāj* solidifies his faith (*īmān*), and his faith is that of Abū Bakr. The believers thus attain true conviction (*yaqīn*), and this knowledge (*ᶜilm al-yaqīn*) constitutes one of the principal moral lessons to be learned from the story of the Prophet's ascension.[29]

The most important section in the manuscript's conclusion includes the following exaltation: "Praise be to God who made us part of *ahl-i sunnat wa jamāᶜat* by means of the ascension."[30] The term *ahl-i sunnat wa jamāᶜat* refers undoubtedly to traditional Sunni Islam as practiced by the community at large.[31] It differentiates itself from the *ahl al-shīᶜa* (Shiᶜis) or *ahl al-bidaᶜ* (literally, "innovators," or those who interject new and arbitrary rules into Muslim practice). The stress on Sunni "orthodoxy" at the close of the SK text confirms that it is the product of a Sunni author feeling the pressures of non-Islamic religions such as Buddhism or the recrudescent and "innovative" forms of Islam such as Shiᶜism. The author certainly responded to the problematic theological climate at the time, as the year 1286 marked the period between the rule of Aḥmad (1281–1284), the first Ilkhan to convert to Islam, and the succession of Arghūn (1284–1291), a zealous Buddhist. As individual religious beliefs and official doctrines continued to vie for implementation, the *Miᶜrājnāma* takes a clear stance in favor of the *ahl-i sunnat,* one that Abū Saᶜīd would see fit to adopt in his own (anti-Shiᶜi, post-Öljeïtu) projects.

The SK text's character thus consists of four basic elements. First and foremost, it is a prayer manual used to teach non-native Arabic speakers parts of the Qur'an and a variety of oral prayers. Secondly, it appears as an elaborate forewarning of what lies ahead for those who stray from the right path. Thirdly, it promotes the acceptance of Muḥammad's prophetic miracles and conversion to the Islamic faith through the lessons learned upon the Quraysh's doubting. Lastly, it advances Sunni Islam over all other forms of religion and Islamic "heterodox" movements. In other words, this Ilkhanid *Miʿrājnāma* text is a Persian Sunni prayer book with a strong penchant toward the monitorial as provided through the narrative of the Prophet's ascension.

Text-Image Analysis

Although the *Miʿrājnāma* text dates from 685/1286, or approximately three to five decades earlier than the Ilkhanid ascension paintings' proposed date of ca. 1317–1335, a textual continuity probably existed in ascension narratives that circulated from the 1280s to the 1330s. Just as its date and provenance make it the most suitable chronological and linguistic match for the Ilkhanid paintings, the SK text's narrative content and religious tenor harmonize well with the paintings' themes and character.[32] Although not an Ur-narrative per se, the SK text provides the most fruitful narrative to date for the identification and sequential reconstruction of the Ilkhanid *miʿrāj* depictions. Just as importantly, the SK text also suggests that the paintings accompanying an ascension text during the Ilkhanid period may have been used as visual facilitators for the instruction of pious behavior and the promotion of Sunni Islam.

Based on the contents of the SK text, I propose the following sequence of paintings, along with a proper identification for each one of the depicted scenes:

1) folio 62r: The Prophet Muḥammad encounters prophets in Jerusalem and undergoes the "testing of the cups" (Figure 2.2)
2) folio 121r: Muḥammad flies on Gabriel's shoulders over the *Qāżīya* Ocean
3) folio 61r (upper): Muḥammad and Gabriel arrive at the gate of the first heaven, made of emerald
4) folio 61v: The Prophet Muḥammad encounters the celestial rooster in the first heaven and a group of angels raising their hands in prayer (Figure 2.3 and Plate 8)
5) folio 31v: The Prophet Muḥammad arrives in the seventh heaven, made of light, and encounters the gate-keeper angel Nūryābīl, accompanied by a host of angels (Figure 2.4)
6) folio 42r: Muḥammad rides on Gabriel's shoulders through the seventh heaven, made of light
7) folio 42v: Muḥammad and Gabriel fly over the "Swollen Ocean"
8) folios 61r (lower) and 121r (lower): Paradise, the *ḥūrīs* (black-eyed inhabitants of heaven), and the Lote Tree of the Limit (*sidrat al-muntahā*)

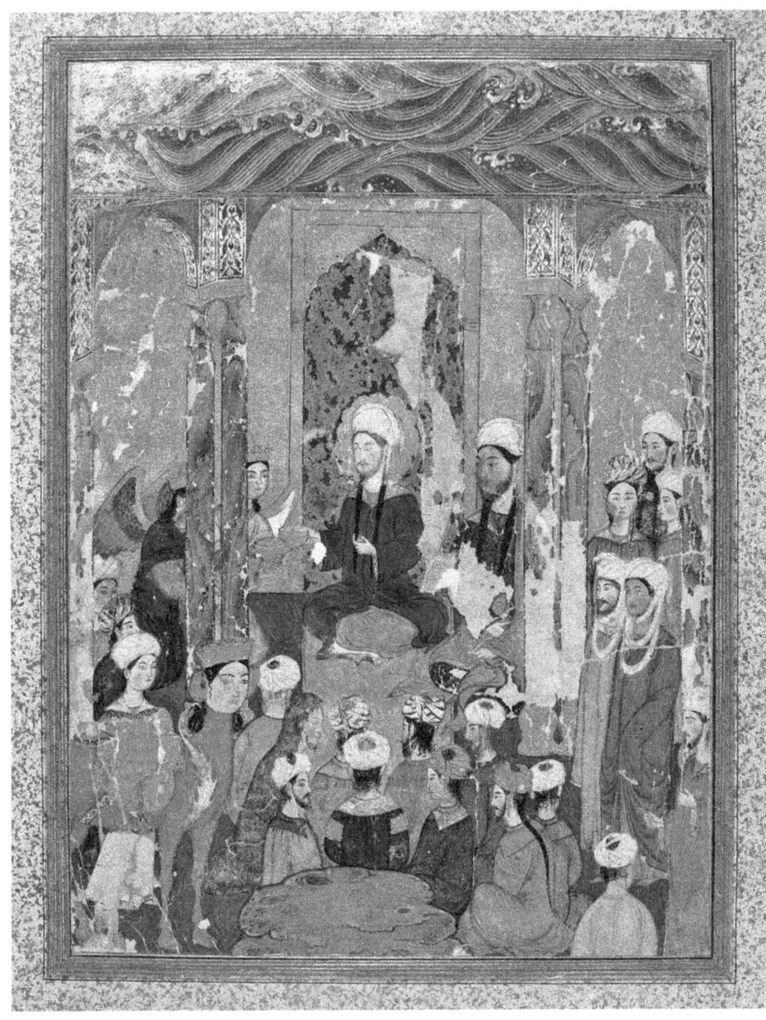

FIGURE 2.2. The Prophet Muḥammad encounters prophets in Jerusalem and undergoes the "testing of the cups," anonymous, *Miʿrājnāma*, probably Tabriz, ca. 1317–1335. Istanbul, Topkapı Palace Library, H. 2154, folio 62r.

9) folio 107r: The Prophet Muḥammad has a miraculous vision of Jerusalem upon his return to Mecca and correctly describes it to Abū Bakr, Abū Jahl, and members of the Quraysh tribe (Figure 2.5 and Plate 9)

For the sake of succinctness, only four paintings (1, 4, 5, and 9) bearing overtly doctrinal or ritual implications are discussed in this study.[33]

The first depiction in the fragmentary illustrated Ilkhanid *Miʿrājnāma* represents Muḥammad's arrival in Jerusalem, his encounter with prophets, and the testing of the cups immediately prior to his ascension through the heavens (Figure 2.2).[34] The SK text describes in detail this amalgamated narrative episode, which serves to ascertain and to strengthen Muḥammad's supreme prophetic status.[35]

The text specifies that upon his arrival at the mosque in Jerusalem, the Prophet sees the angel Gabriel attach his winged, human-headed steed Burāq to one of the mosque's columns, a textual detail that matches closely the depiction of Burāq in close proximity to a green column in the painting's lower left corner. The SK text, furthermore, describes Burāq as having large ears as green as emeralds and a body as red as coral, two very specific details to which this painting has remained loyal.[36]

The text then describes Muḥammad as stating that Gabriel placed him in front of the rock (that is, Mount Moriah) next to the Prophet Adam, who joyfully salutes him.[37] In the painting, Muḥammad can be identified as the figure with a golden aureole around his head sitting cross-legged in the center of the painting's background, while Adam (Ādam) must be the individual with an oversize head on the Prophet's left. The rock also is included in the center of the painting's foreground. One by one, the other prophets, many of whom are described in the SK text, welcome Muḥammad in their midst: first Noah (Nūḥ), then Abraham (Ibrāhīm) and Moses (Mūsā), and finally David (Dā'ūd), Solomon (Sulaymān), Jacob (Ayyūb), and Jonas (Yūnus).[38] More than twenty precursor prophets are represented as standing and sitting in a circular fashion, a compositional device that hints that the event transpires in a centrally planned building such as the Dome of the Rock in Jerusalem.

The composition provides a pictorial exposition of the blessings conferred upon Muḥammad on the night of his ascension, itemized one by one in the SK text. The Prophet states here that God has granted him the following blessing: He created him the first and the last; He made the Qur'an the most blessed book; He made his community the best of all communities; He ensured that his religious laws are the easiest to follow; He granted him the most rewards from his religious laws; He made his *qibla* (direction of prayer) the best *qibla* of all; He invested him with prophethood; and He made him the first to appear on the Day of Resurrection as an intercessor for his community.[39] The enumeration of God's favors serves to emphasize Muḥammad's pre-eminence within a long genealogy of prophets and Islam's supremacy within an unbroken continuum of monotheistic religions. This textual panegyric is echoed in the painting's compositional arrangement, in which a centrally located Muḥammad is depicted in heroic proportions.

The same holds true for the Prophet's success at the testing of the cups, which takes place immediately after the inventory of the gifts conferred upon him. The SK text states that Muḥammad is offered four golden vessels filled with water, milk, grape wine, and honey.[40] He selects the cup of milk and drinks it, at which time Gabriel states that his community will be saved from drowning in error.[41] This episode also appears in the painting: two angels to the Prophet's right offer him four golden cups filled with liquid. He gently reaches with his right hand for the gold vessel containing milk, and thus engages in an observable action that serves as an exclusive selection of his prophecy and his community's engagement on the right path.

The testing of the cups constitutes a frequently occurring narrative cluster, or narreme, in *miʿrāj* narratives over the centuries. From very early on, texts describe an offering of two, three, or four cups to the Prophet, and his correct selection of the vessel filled with milk offers the concrete proof of his decision to follow the right path (*al-fiṭra* or *al-ṣirāṭ al-mustaqīm*) and to ascertain his flawless character before entering into God's celestial abode.[42] Both an initiatory and legitimizing event, the narreme of the testing of the cups provides further confirmation of Muḥammad's divinely granted prophethood.

While this first painting in the Ilkhanid *Miʿrājnāma* serves to affirm the Prophet's superior status, subsequent paintings establish a set pattern of pious invocations and gestures. This is most clear in the two paintings representing Muḥammad's encounter with the celestial rooster in the first heaven (Figure 2.3 and Plate 8) and the angel Nūryābīl in the seventh heaven (Figure 2.4). The SK text describes conversations between Muḥammad and the various angels he encounters in the skies as consisting largely of uttered and exchanged *duʿās*. In a similar manner, the paintings "tell the story" by depicting the different gestures that accompany such *duʿā*-dialogues. Altogether, the SK text and the *Miʿrājnāma* paintings thus form a pedagogical picture book that illustrates the correct way to perform this devotional activity that forms one significant aspect of Islamic religious observances (*ʿibādāt*).

Upon his arrival in the first heaven made of emerald, Muḥammad sees an angel in the shape of a standing rooster (Figure 2.3 and Plate 8).[43] The SK text describes the rooster's body as consisting of white snow, and its prayer reaches all confines of the earth. It cries out twenty-four thousand prayers day and night, one thousand prayers for each hour in the day.[44] Muḥammad hears its *tasbīḥ* prayer, "Praise be to God, the Great, the Exalted, there is no God but God, the Living, the Eternal."[45] In response, the earthly roosters exclaim in unison with a warning to humans, "Remember God, O negligent ones."[46] The text cautions the reader to repeat the prayer and not to neglect the continuous remembrance of God. In effect, the narrative episode of Muḥammad's encounter with the celestial rooster serves as a prompting of the daily prayers and the teaching of yet another *tasbīḥ* formula to the text's reader-viewer.

As the rooster calls out to prayer, the anticipated human response is epitomized by angels on the left side of the painting, who raise their hands in petitionary prayer with palms and faces raised upward. The practice of raising the two hands (*rafʿ al-yadayn*) is common in Islamic prayer traditions, and several manuals contain discussions about its particular role in ritual prayer or *ṣalat*. For instance, the famous hadith transmitter al-Bukhārī (d. 870) composed a tract titled *Kitāb Rafʿ al-Yadayn fī'l-Ṣalāh* (The Book on Raising the Two Hands in Prayer),[47] which describes this gestural practice by collecting and presenting a wide array of sayings on the topic.

In his treatise, al-Bukhārī considers several components central to the raising of the hands. First and foremost, he states that the *rafʿ al-yadayn* is an essential part of religious observances because it is performed at the very opening (*iftitāḥ*) or welcoming (*istiqbāl*) of ritual prayer with the initiatory proclamation of the *takbīr* (the exclamation that God is Great), when going into bowing down (*al-rukūʿ*), and upon standing up again (*al-qiyām*).[48] The Prophet's practice of raising his hands at these three fixed points in prayer reveals how his own practice of raising the hands became a critical reference in the Muslim community's subsequent canonization of communal

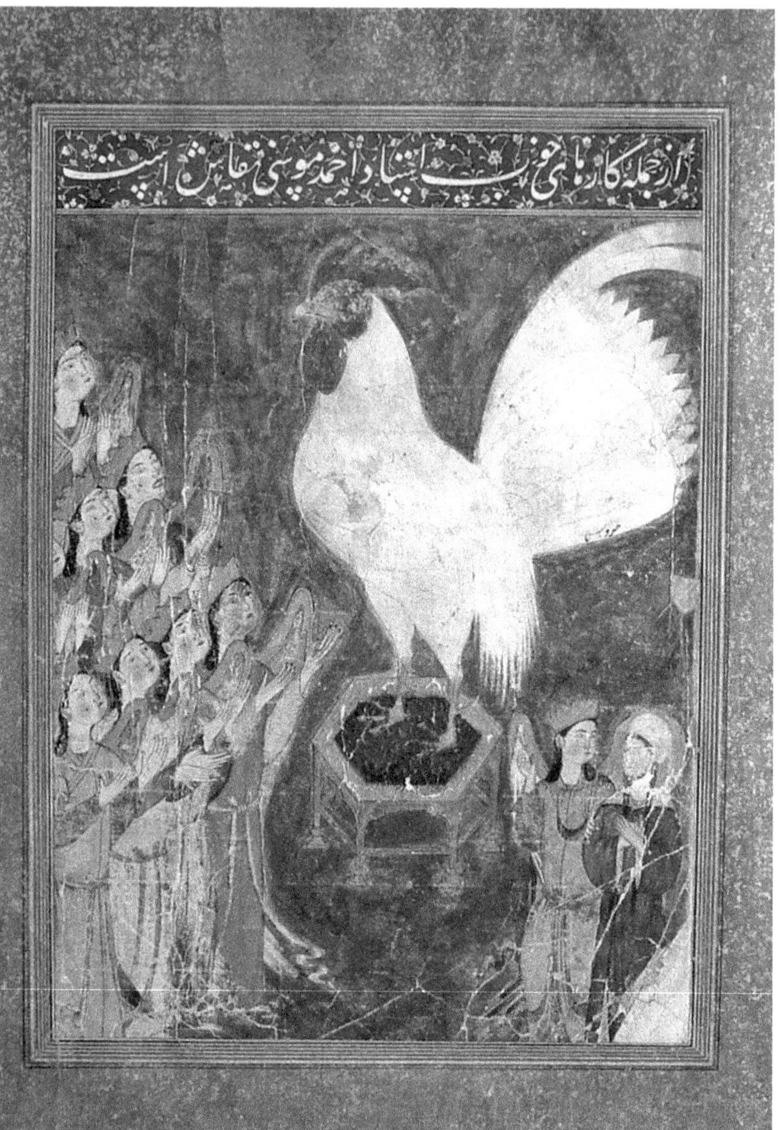

FIGURE 2.3. The Prophet Muḥammad encounters the celestial rooster in the first heaven and a group of angels raising their hands in prayer, anonymous, *Miʿrājnāma*, probably Tabriz, ca. 1317–1335. Istanbul, Topkapı Palace Library, H. 2154, folio 61v. See color plate 8.

prayer and its attending bodily movements. In this painting, we thus see at least one significant component of prayer practices—namely the *rafʿ al-yadayn*—deployed in visual form.

As al-Bukhārī emphasizes, the practice of raising the hands is accepted as canon by the *ahl al-sunna,* that is, Sunni Muslims.[49] Those who deny the practice await punishment because they oppose the prophetic tradition of the *rafʿ al-yadayn.*[50] The stress on the Prophet's *sunna* by the emulation of his and his companions' prayer practices appears entirely appropriate in an illustrated manuscript that stresses the acceptance of the *miʿrāj* as an essential component of pious behavior as propounded in Sunni Islam.

Al-Bukhārī's discussion of the *rafʿ al-yadayn* bears a number of symbolic correspondences with the ascension painting depicting the heavenly rooster and the choir of angels raising their hands in prayer. In particular, the theme of flight links al-Bukhārī's discussion of the raising of the two hands with the painting. In his treatise, he records the saying transmitted by Mūsā b. Ismāʿīl: "When the Prophet's companions were praying, their hands in front of their ears were like fans or vanes (*marāwiḥ*)."[51] The painting of the rooster with the choir of angels raising their hands preserves this notion of flight: the angels' wings and outstretched arms rise upward through the spiritual "lift" of devotional practice.

The Prophet and the angel Gabriel, on the other hand, do not stand in the posture of *rafʿ al-yadayn,* suggesting that other prayer positions are permissible in Islamic prayer traditions (and showing that the Prophet learned the "raising of the two hands" from the angels).[52] As Gabriel points to the scene of the heavenly rooster and the angels in adoration, he touches Muḥammad gently on his right upper arm. By his bodily movement, he suggests that the Prophet (and, by extension, the viewer) witness the depicted event and learn from it. As an intermediary figure, the archangel invites the Prophet and his community to observe firsthand a sacred cosmological event.

For his part, Muḥammad stands with his right hand gently folded above his left hand at chest level in the position of *qabḍ* (grasping or clutching). The depicting of the *qabḍ* position shows a preference, once again, for common communal practice (*ʿamal*) rather than prescriptive forms in the sound hadith collections, which tend to prefer *sadl al-yadayn* (the two hands at one's sides). This depiction reveals that physical imitation may provide a firm affirmation of the prophetic tradition.[53] The representation of both the *qabḍ* and *rafʿ al-yadayn* positions in this painting therefore lays emphasis on common practice, creating together a prescriptive visualization of various hand movements used in communal prayer. Much as the companions followed the Prophet's example, the image's viewer is invited to mimic the *sunna* of the Prophet, in particular the use of a range of hand movements in ritual prayer.

After ascending through six more heavens, the Prophet arrives in the seventh heaven, where he encounters the guardian angel Nūryābīl and a host of other angels (Figure 2.4). The SK text describes the seventh heaven as made of light, a substance that is matched in the painting by the inclusion of a gold background.[54] Nūryābīl informs Muḥammad that everyone from his community who utters the following *tasbīḥ* prayer will earn God's reward in paradise: "Praise be to the Creator of light, praise be to the most High, praise be to the Exalted and Blessed One, praise be to the Knower of the unseen, for He does not make anyone acquainted with His secret." Angels in Nūryābīl's entourage rejoice in the Prophet's presence and also utter praises for him and his community.[55] The interchange between the angels of the seventh heaven and Muḥammad thus consists of prayers that the community of believers must recite in order to seek forgiveness from God in the afterworld.

The painting shows the action unfolding, as the Prophet and Gabriel approach a large angel (Nūryābīl), set apart by his impressively sized, colorful wings and a

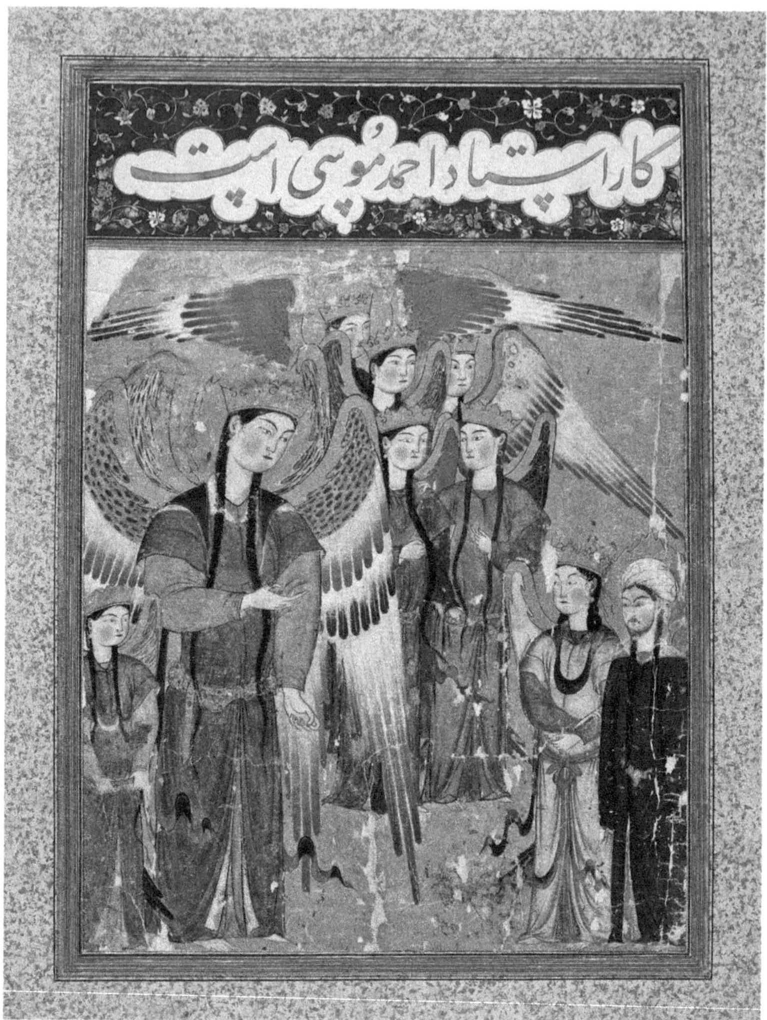

FIGURE 2.4. The Prophet Muḥammad arrives in the seventh heaven, made of light, and encounters the gate-keeper angel Nūryābīl, accompanied by a host of angels, anonymous, *Miʿrājnāma*, probably Tabriz, ca. 1317–1335. Istanbul, Topkapı Palace Library, H. 2154, folio 31v.

flaming gold nimbus around his head. Nūryābīl welcomes Muḥammad by extending his right hand toward him, while other crowned angels stand around him. All angels wear long black hair plaits, golden crowns, and jeweled belts typical of Mongol attire; interestingly, the belts are mentioned as jewel-studded waistbands in the SK text, much as they are depicted in this composition.[56] The angel Gabriel stands next to the Prophet with his right hand over his left forearm at navel height in the position known as *qabḍ,* while the Prophet stands with both arms at his sides, his hands hidden beneath the long blue sleeves of his robe, in the position called *sadl al-yadayn* (the two hands at one's sides).[57]

The inclusion of the *qabḍ* and *sadl* positions in the painting reveals the artist's pictorial attempt to find a middle ground between the customary Medinan practice (*ʿamal*) of crossing the hands at the chest and subsequent hadith prescriptions of placing the hands at one's side. The inclusion of both positions forces the viewer to observe the totality of the *sunna* of the Prophet, based upon the consensus between group practice and a codified system of rules and regulations. This compromise is of prime importance to the SK text, as it proclaims in several instances to represent an authoritative account of the Prophet's ascension. Although the text is prescriptive in a fashion similar to the hadiths in its manner of teaching certain prayers, it is closer in spirit to other works that prefer to define the *sunna* of Muḥammad as both hadith and *ᶜamal.*[58] The *Miᶜrājnāma* painting, therefore, represents the performing or enactment (i.e., the *ᶜamal* component) of an accompanying text, whose character is not entirely removed from that of regulatory manuals.

Where the teaching of group practice is concerned, this kind of painting thus appears to help fill a didactic role. It can visually teach bodily positions to accompany prayers, forcing the viewer to learn through oral as well as physical emulation. Furthermore, it also makes a clear case for the learning of laudatory prayers which Muḥammad and the angels address to one another and to God, along with the hand positions with which Muḥammad and his followers perform such prayers. The Prophet's interactions with Nūryābīl and with the angels of the seventh heaven form a powerful visual vehicle for the viewer-reader's indoctrination into various aspects of Islamic prayer.

Toward the end of the text and in the last extant painting, the emphasis moves away from the topic of prayer to the promotion of proper Sunni belief. After passing through all seven heavens, encountering God, and witnessing the delights of heaven and the torments of hell, Muḥammad returns to Jerusalem, straddles Burāq again, and rides back to Mecca. The SK text records that, once back in Mecca, the Prophet's public declaration that he embarked on a heavenly ascension during the previous night was derided by the Quraysh tribesmen and, most of all, Muḥammad's life-long enemy Abū Jahl. The latter states that traveling from Mecca to Jerusalem and back in one night is impossible and that Muḥammad has gone mad or is simply a liar. Only Abū Bakr, who sits next to Abū Jahl, argues to the contrary and maintains that if Muḥammad states that he did so, then he speaks verily.[59]

Abū Jahl insists that the Prophet provide proof to him and to the Quraysh of his visit to Jerusalem by describing what he saw. At that moment, God orders Gabriel to gather *bayt al-maqdis,* all of its cities, neighborhoods, rivers, and gardens to show to Muḥammad.[60] The Prophet so astonishes his entourage with his accurate descriptions of the city that his detractors become believers on the spot. As the SK text concludes succinctly, all those who believe in the ascension are of Abū Bakr's faith, while all those who doubt it belong to the fraternity of Abū Jahl. As a result, God must be praised because "He made us part of the community of [Muḥammad's] example and consensus (*mārā az ahl-i sunnat wa jamāᶜat kard*)."[61] In other words, the text suggests that only the Sunnis are the true followers of Abū Bakr, and all others who reject Abū Bakr—such as certain Shiᶜis, who reject and/or curse the first three rightly guided caliphs in prayer practices—fall into the camp of Abū Jahl, enemies of the Prophet.[62] The episode of the doubting Quraysh, here as in many other ascension texts, serves as the primary vehicle for confirming the Prophet's miracles, prompting conversions to Islam and reinforcing Sunni principles.

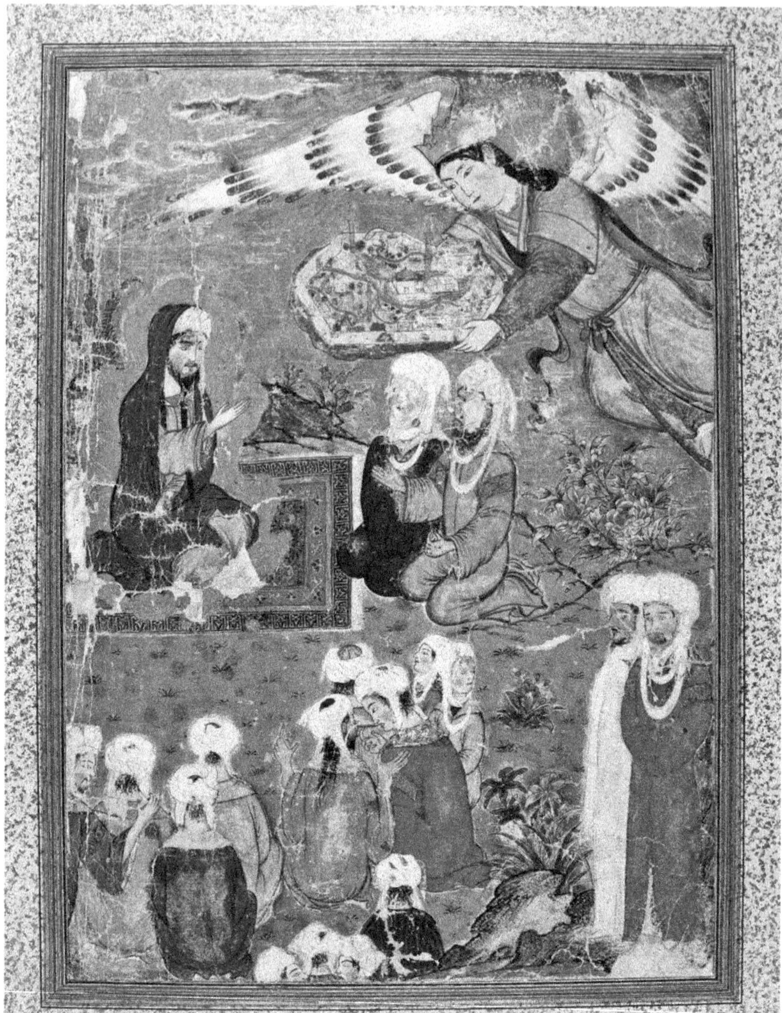

Figure 2.5. The Prophet Muḥammad has a miraculous vision of Jerusalem upon his return to Mecca and correctly describes it to Abū Bakr, Abū Jahl, and members of the Quraysh tribe, anonymous, *Miʿrājnāma*, probably Tabriz, ca. 1317–1335. Istanbul, Topkapı Palace Library, H. 2154, folio 107r. See color plate 9.

The last painting in the *Miʿrājnāma* series represents this particular episode (Figure 2.5 and Plate 9). The Prophet Muḥammad, wearing his black *burda* over his robe, sits on his prayer rug while God grants him a vision of Jerusalem through the angel Gabriel.[63] At least one other ascension narrative describes his donning of the *burda* and the use of a prayer rug at this ultimate moment of divine disclosure.[64] Both his *burda* and his prayer rug thus represent the twin symbols of utmost solemnity.[65]

The three-dimensional model presented by Gabriel contains a variety of mosques, minarets, rivers, neighborhoods, houses, etc., and therefore must represent Jerusalem and its dependencies as noted in the anonymous SK text. It bears little or no resemblance to the actual city, and, as a consequence, has resulted in misinterpretations of the scene depicted.[66] A documentalist approach to identifying the model based on precise topographical representations and geographical knowledge at the time has shed very little light on the scene. Not a mimetic rendering of the city or *bilād al-shām* (the province of Syria), it rather reflects the creative imagination of the artist Aḥmad Mūsā or another contemporary painter, who probably relied on verbal descriptions and Ilkhanid building types for the architectural details depicted in the model. For example, the centrally planned, gold-domed structure portrayed in the center of the model—probably intended as a representation of the Dome of the Rock—may have drawn inspiration from Ghāzān's tomb in Ghāzāniyya, a suburb of the capital city of Tabrīz,[67] or Sulṭān Öljeïtu's tomb in his later capital of Sulṭāniyya (1305–1317).[68] Other no longer extant buildings in Tabrīz, such as those in the ruined complex of Rashīd's quarter (*rabᶜ-i Rashīdī*), could have provided inspiration as well.

The figures who interact with the Prophet are identifiable thanks to the SK text. Opposite Muḥammad sit Abū Bakr and Abū Jahl. Abū Bakr has a white beard and rosy cheeks and wears a blue cloak, while Abū Jahl has a darkened gray face with touches of red. His face, just like the facial skin of the two standing men in the lower right corner of the painting, turns to an almost diabolic red, an outward sign of his soul ignited by the sin of disbelief.[69] He gesticulates toward the Prophet as if in a heated discussion. The other groups of men, seated in three groups in the foreground of the painting, engage in astonished deliberation with their mouths gaped open and hands in agitated motion. They are teetering between belief and disbelief.

The Prophet's ascension represents a stumbling block to unbelievers, but an encouragement to men of faith: it tests both sides to choose whether to accept the prophetic mission or to reject it in its entirety. Ultimately, Muḥammad's correct description of Jerusalem to the Quraysh tribesmen provides proof of his prophecy, and his miraculous ascension wins converts to his cause. Along with the episode of the testing of the cups, his vision of Jerusalem constitutes the primary "proof" narreme[70] present in the story of the *miᶜrāj* that validates, once and for all, his prophetic standing. The story's conclusion with the vision of Jerusalem as evidence of the Prophet's ascension provides a powerful argument for accepting his honorable status and the inevitable necessity to accept Islam. In a similar manner, the painting offers proof of Muḥammad's utmost status through the pictorial mode.

Historical Significance

The SK text of 685/1286 and the *Miᶜrājnāma* paintings attributed to the patronage of the last Ilkhanid sultan Abū Saᶜīd (r. 1317–1335) span several decades of religious and political turmoil under Mongol domination in Persian lands. The major themes that emerge both in the ascension text and in the paintings permeated the theological climate of the time. These included efforts to establish a particular Islamic religious doxa and praxis under Mongol rule.

Arab and Persian authors considered the initial Mongol invasions of Persia as the end of the world unfolding in real time and space. In popular imagination,

Chinghīz Khān and his descendants were viewed as the Riders of the Apocalypse, wrathful beyond measure and ready to ruthlessly slaughter Muslims who stood in their way.[71] The subsequent wavering between Buddhism and various branches of Islam by the Mongol rulers revealed a fluctuating relationship between their old customs and a naturalization to the culture and religion of their subject lands. Religious battles punctuated Ilkhanid rule in Iran, first under the Buddhist Abāqā (d. 1282) and his Muslim brother Aḥmad (d. 1284), and later his zealously Buddhist son Arghūn (d. 1291).[72]

The SK text of 685/1286 emerges in the context of these Buddhist-Islamic struggles for supremacy in the eastern Islamic world. Its open endorsement of Sunni Islam finds a particular echo in the contemporary fight for political and religious sovereignty. As the text argues, the only way to achieve true salvation consists in belonging to the *ahl-i sunnat,* that is, the community of people who follow the religious precedents (*āthār*) set by the Prophet Muḥammad.[73] Ultimate authority and legitimacy are defined here solely through Sunni terms.

Abū Saʿīd's pro-Sunni position and his attempts to draw others to Sunni Islam forms one of the most substantial efforts at persuading the elite and the masses to embrace (or to re-embrace) a well-established communal doctrine. Despite the firm roots of Sunni Islam in Iran, Abū Saʿīd faced some lingering opposition from members of the Mongol elite, who were not keen to abandon their religious traditions linked to Buddhist religious practices, ethnic definitions, and an adherence to the great Mongol *Yāsā* (code of laws) of Chinghīz Khān. The substitution of Islam, Arab-Persian culture, and *sharīʿa* (Islamic law) for these other traditions was cause for great discomfort, if not rebellion. For instance, Sulṭān Aḥmad's earlier conversion to Islam (1282–1284) offended the amirs, who saw in his action an abandonment of Mongol tradition and a siding with their mortal enemies, the Mamluks.[74] During Abū Saʿīd's reign, a number of members of the elite again insisted on a return to their ancestral traditions and the restoration of the *Yāsā* of Chinghīz Khān as well.[75] Theirs was a longing for "traditional" Mongol rule and a last bid at solidifying their waning authority.

While Abū Saʿīd was in no a hurry to alienate his base, he decided to make a push for the permanent establishment of Islam in Persia, and his call to Sunni Islam was persuasive and practical. Perhaps the illustrated *Miʿrājnāma* produced under his patronage constituted a subtle means to invite his immediate Mongol entourage to embrace Sunni Islam as a theological doctrine transcending political differences. Indeed, it might have provided a creative and compelling medium to bridge the gap between himself and his rebelling amirs, chief among whom Amīr Chupān.[76] Turning his attention to the all-inclusive concept of the *ahl-i sunnat wa jamāʿat* (people of the way and consensus), the last Ilkhanid ruler may have found in the pictured promotion of Sunni Islam a more compelling force than raw political might.

Painting as Praxis

One can only conjecture whether the illustrated *Miʿrājnāma* was produced as a polemical, pro-Sunni missionary tool guided to members of Abū Saʿīd's immediate entourage, themselves second and third generation Mongols who had acculturated to Persian lands. Indeed, the Persian language used in the SK text suggests that a local language served as an appropriate exegetic and narrative tool to explain the story of the ascension and to offer an intelligible context for the many Arabic-language prayers interspersed throughout. In this case, it seems possible to hypothesize that the illustrated *Miʿrājnāma* prayer manual was read and recited aloud in a "native" Persian idiom, buttressed by its large-scale "show-and-tell" images.

Although ethnographic evidence and *miʿrāj* oral stories do not survive from the Ilkhanid period, more contemporary studies on ascension narratives can prove a helpful, though admittedly speculative, means to understand the social and religious context of the Ilkhanid illustrated *Miʿrājnāma*. For example, some ascension texts written during the eighteenth and nineteenth century were intended as "chat books" for a variety of festive reading events, especially the celebrations of the Prophet's ascension on the night of the 27 Rajab.[77] A group of men would gather around a reciter, whose duty consisted in reading the text and encouraging his listeners to follow him in uttering prayer formulas aloud. This kind of "literacy event," or special occasion for storytelling prompted by a written text, facilitated the oral delivery of praise formulas within the very specific framework of celebrating the Prophet's *miʿrāj*. Didactic and engaging, oral stories of the ascension seem to have had the religious goal of inducing attitudes of praise among their audiences.

A parallel can be made for the Ilkhanid rulers as well, since there is evidence to suggest that *miʿrāj* celebrations were observed and lavishly sponsored. For example, the powerful vizier Rashīd al-Dīn (d. 1318) was particularly fond of the Prophet's ascension. He composed a theological tract on the subject titled "*fī bayān al-miʿrāj*" (An Explanation of the Ascension),[78] and his endowment deed (*waqf*) provided ample annual funding for *miʿrāj* celebrations.[79] One cannot help but wonder whether such illustrated manuscripts produced in the *rabʿ-i Rashīdī* in Tabrīz might have been used as visual prompts during the formal observances of this formidable event, in a manner similar to eighteenth-century "festive readings" accompanying the celebration of *laylat al-miʿrāj* on 27 Rajab.

Ghiyāth al-Dīn, Rashīd al-Dīn's son and the vizier to Sultan Abū Saʿīd, must have inherited this tradition of depicting and celebrating the Prophet's ascension. He was a pious Muslim[80] and it is to him that the ruler must have turned when he decided to commission an illustrated manuscript of the "Book of the Prophet's Ascension." With its overt Sunni message and its explicit endorsement of oral *tasbīḥ* formulas, it is not impossible that Abū Saʿīd intended his royal manuscript to function as a pictured chat book to be used during an elite, festive gathering celebrating the Prophet and his miracles.

Based on an iconographic and textual study, the illustrated *Miʿrājnāma* of Abū Saʿīd provides evidence for the existence of a picture book that illustrates a credal canon through a symbiotic relationship between a text and its corresponding images. This pictorial system of faith is bound by a narrative theme and enlivened by a cycle of oral *duʿās* and their associated hand gestures. In this sense, the *Miʿrājnāma*'s character parallels some of the illustrated manuscripts of late medieval Europe, most notably manuscripts of the Dominican prayer manual known as *De Modo Orandi* (On the Manner of Prayer). Composed ca. 1250 and used by Dominicans like Fra Angelico (1395–1455), a number of *De Modo Orandi* manuscripts include images of devout friars depicted in various positions of prayer while contemplating events in the life of Jesus Christ.[81] The paintings were used for instruction through the double procedures of *verbo et exemplo,* that is, a text and its corresponding visual examples.[82] In these Christian illustrated texts, the devout's inner state is shown as summoned by bodily gestures: ecstasy is expressed as a standing position and imploring divine power as arms outstretched and hands upraised.

Providing moralizing messages, stressing orthodoxy, and exposing a system of personal worship through pictures, illustrated prayer manuals like the *De Modo Orandi* offered mnemonic devices to study and perform devotions, a pattern that finds an intriguing echo in Abū Saʿīd's illustrated *Miʿrājnāma.* The doxologies, or ritual praises of the Lord, and hymns in Christian texts certainly recall the repeated *tasbīḥ* prayers and *duʿās* present in the SK text, which allow readers to become participants in ritual action and meditation of the divine.[83] Bodily positions as represented in Christian texts also appear rather analogous to the pious hand gestures in the *Miʿrājnāma,* such as those of *qabḍ, sadl,* and *rafʿ al-yadayn.* For these reasons, one cannot help but wonder whether the Ilkhanid ruler might have been inspired by illustrated Christian devotional works, which missionaries may have carried with them on their way to Persian lands in order to convert the "heathen" Mongols to Christianity.[84]

Not so entirely removed from its contemporary western counterparts in terms of its symbolic character and practical applications, the Ilkhanid *Miʿrājnāma* appears to have operated as a didactic tool for the implementation of a perceived communal tradition (Sunni orthodoxy) and its established ceremonial practices (Sunni orthopraxy). It necessitated a dialectic response on the part of the reader-viewers, and its paintings supplied a series of *tableaux vivants* for the expression of the Islamic faith and the activation of its concomitant observances. Without a doubt, Abū Saʿīd's illustrated *Miʿrājnāma* thus provides new and compelling evidence for the existence of religious painting in Islamic traditions at a time when a similar trend was well underway in the Christian devotional art of western Europe.

Notes

This chapter received the Margaret B. Sevcenko Award for Best Article on Islamic Art by a Young Scholar, College Art Association, 2006. I wish to thank the members of the Sevcenko committee for their comments and suggestions, as well as Frederick Colby for his meticulous—and always generous—feedback. All remaining shortcomings and mistakes are my own to bear.

1. Tanındı, *Siyer-i Nebî;* Garrett Fisher, "A Reconstruction of the Pictorial Cycle of the *Siyar-i Nabî* of Murād III"; and idem, "The Pictorial Cycle of the *Siyer-i Nebi:* a Late Sixteenth Century Manuscript of the Life of Muḥammad."

2. Milstein et al., *Stories of the Prophets*; James, *The Master Scribes*, 11.

3. İpşiroğlu and Eyüboğlu, *Fatih Alumuna Bir Bakış*, 120. Earlier in their study, the authors claim that Muslim prayer does not call for the intervention of images (117), a statement that goes contrary to their final conclusion. On religious painting, see Rogers, "The Genesis of Safawid Religious Painting." Religious painting and religious imagery have been the focus of more recent studies on Islamic painting. For example, Oleg Grabar describes the Timurid *Miʿrājnāma* (Bibliothèque nationale de France [BnF] Supplément Turc [Sup Turc] 190) as a pictorial awakening of religious sensibility and thus a classic monument to the theme of "religion" in Islamic painting (Grabar, *Mostly Miniatures*, 91). In a similar manner, Eleanor Sims identifies religious painting as a separate genus of representation in her study of Persian painting titled *Peerless Images*, 60–68.

4. Pfeiffer, "Conversion Versions."

5. Blair, "The Mongol Capital of Sulṭāniyya"; and Godard, "The Mausoleum of Öljeïtu at Sultaniya."

6. The manuscript provides the earliest set of depictions of the Prophet Muḥammad, including the Day of Cursing (*mubāhala*), at which time he names Fāṭima and ʿAlī his closest friends, as well as his investiture of ʿAlī at Ghadīr Khumm during his farewell pilgrimage (Hillenbrand, "Images of Muḥammad in al-Biruni's *Chronology of Ancient Nations*," 133–135 and pls. 13–14).

7. Hillenbrand, "The Arts of the Book in Ilkhanid Iran," 136.

8. Pfeiffer, "Conversion Versions," 47; and Sheila Blair, "The Coinage of the Later Ilkhanids." Abū Saʿīd's coins include the names of the first four rightly guided caliphs (*al-rashīdūn*), although at least two extant coins bear the names of the imams (see Howorth, *History of the Mongols from the 9th to the 19th Century*, part III, 628).

9. Grabar and Blair, *Epic Images and Contemporary History*, 27.

10. Blair, "The Development of the Illustrated Book in Iran," 270–271.

11. For a detailed discussion of their attribution to Abū Saʿīd's patronage, see Gruber, *The Ilkhanid Book of Ascension*, Introduction.

12. Thackston, *Album Prefaces and Other Documents on the History of Calligraphers and Painters*, 12; Topkapı Sarayı Kütüphanesi (TSK) H. 2154, folios 31v, 42r–v, 61r–v, 62r, 107r, and 121r. The paintings have been published in a number of works on the history of Persian painting, *inter alia* Tanındı and Çağman, *The Topkapı Saray Museum*, 65–70 and pls. 45–47; and Ettinghausen, "Persian Ascension Miniatures of the Fourteenth Century." Two other ascension-related paintings also are held in the Baysunghur album (TSK H. 2152, folios 64r, 68v, and 69r). They represent a man riding a giant phoenix (*sīmurgh*) and a young prince carried in the arms of an angel. They appear to depict secular themes or epic tales (*dāstān*) such as the exploits of Amīr Hamza, the Prophet's uncle, and are otherwise unconnected to the set of ascension paintings in TSK H. 2154 (see Ettinghausen, "Persian Ascension Miniatures of the Fourteenth Century," 378–383 and Figs. 10–12).

13. A number of scholars have proposed a later date of ca. 1360–1370 and have argued on stylistic grounds that the manuscript might be attributable to the patronage of the Jalayirid sultan ʿUways (Tanındı and Çağman, *The Topkapı Saray Museum*, 67–70; and Grube, *Persian Painting in the Fourteenth Century*, 193). The present author maintains the attribution of the *Miʿrājnāma* to Abū Saʿīd's reign based on Dūst Muḥammad's presumably well-informed pref-

ace. Stylistic arguments pushing the manuscript to a later date have not been convincing, as artistic schools were still in the process of formation and were subject to artistic fluctuation. Unfortunately, no portion of the original ascension narrative has survived on the paintings' folios. Text included in the paintings consists of minute "labels" identifying the figures of Muḥammad, Gabriel, and the heavenly rooster (*khurūs*), as well as Dūst Muḥammad's illuminated panels, added in the sixteenth century, attributing the compositions to the master painter (*ustād*) Aḥmad Mūsā.

14. The *Liber Scale Machometi* (The Book of Muḥammad's Ladder) was first written in Castilian at the request of King Alphonso X (r. 1252–1284). The text later was translated into Latin and old French ca. 1300 (see *Liber Scale Machometi*). Antecedent Arabic-language "Books of Ascension" were composed by Ibn ʿAbbās (d. 69/688) and al-Qushayrī (d. 465/1073). For Ibn ʿAbbās' work, see his "al-Isrāʾ wa'l-Miʿrāj"; Colby, "Constructing an Islamic Ascension Narrative"; and idem, *Narrating Muḥammad's Night Journey.* For al-Qushayrī's work, see his *Kitāb al-Miʿrāj;* and al-Samarrai, *The Theme of Ascension in Mystical Writings,* 245–265. A number of Chaghatay *Miʿrājnāmas* have survived. These include a versified text attributed to the twelfth-century mystic Ḥakīm Sulaymān Ata (see Max Scherberger's chapter in this volume) and the Timurid illustrated *Miʿrājnāma* manuscript of ca. 1436–1437 (see Gruber, *The Timurid Book of Ascension*).

15. Süleymaniye Kütüphanesi (SK), Ayasofya 3441. The manuscript contains seventy-six thick beige rag folios with fifteen lines of text written in crisp *naskh* script per page. The colophon on folio 75r specifies that the book was completed on 1 (*ghurrat*) Ṣafar 685/ 29 March 1286. This Persian text is available, along with an English translation, in Gruber, *The Ilkhanid Book of Ascension.*

16. That is, invocations to God using the "*Subḥān*/Praise to God" prayer formula.

17. SK Ayasofya 3441, folio 1v, lines 8–10. The text records various traditions (*riwāyāt*) stating that the *miʿrāj* from Mecca to Jerusalem (*bayt al-maqdis)* began either from the house of Umm Hāniʾ, the house of Khadīja, Ṣafā and Marwa (in between which Hajar ran seven times looking for water for her thirsty son; the two hillocks now marking the course of pilgrims to Mecca), or finally the house of ʿAbdallāh b. ʿAbbās. The text also includes the debate over the date of the event, making note of 17 Ramaḍān, as well as the months of Rajab and Rabīʿ I.

18. Ibid., folio 1v, lines 12–15. The term *isrāʾ* (the night journey from Mecca to Jerusalem) is replaced with the term *miʿrāj.* Thus, the text states that the Prophet experienced two *miʿrāj*s in one night, a proposition not at odds with other narratives (both Sunni and Shiʿi) that argue that he experienced multiple ascensions. However, since the Ilkhanid author views the *isrāʾ* and *miʿrāj* as two continuous events, here it is simply a question of terminology, i.e., the word "*miʿrāj*" signifying both journey and ascension. On folio 2r, line 6, the author specifies that *bayt al-maqdis* refers to the city of Jerusalem, as it is specified as being "*bi-shām*" (in the historical province of *bilād al-shām,* i.e., the Levant) or *bi-Filisṭīn* (in Palestine).

19. Ibid., bottom line of folio 1v and top line of folio 2r.

20. Qur'an 17:1. The act of denying the ascension also would constitute a refusal to accept *sūrat al-ḥamd* (Qur'an 1, *al-fātiḥa*) and the end of the "Chapter of the Cow" (*sūrat al-baqara*), that is, Qur'an 2:286. According to the *Miʿrājnāma* text, God granted Muḥammad these verses and, in fact, the entirety of the Qur'an at the same time as he offered him the five daily prayers and other benefits reserved for the Muslim community (ibid., folios 53r–v).

21. Verses from *sūrat al-najm* (53: 1–18) also describe the Prophet's ascension.

22. The practice of personal invocation or request (*duʿā*) differs from the ritual and liturgical prayer of *ṣalāh.*

23. The *tasbīḥ* resembles the *taḥmīd* ("thanks be to God") and *taʿālā* ("God is Great") expressions, all three essentially meaning, "praise be to God."

24. SK Ayasofya 3441, folios 42r–v. The *rakʿa* (Persian *rakʿat*) is the basic unit of communal prayer. It consists in uttering a series of prayers, genuflecting the body from an initial upright position, and then performing two prostrations.

25. The seven valleys of hell in the manuscript reflect the seven names of hell in the Qur'an.

These include: *hāwiya* (abyss), *jaḥīm* (blaze), *sa*ʿ*īr* (fierce fire), *jahannam* (hell), *laẓā* (flame), *saqar* (scorch), and *ḥuṭama* (crush). For a discussion of these names, see O'Shaughnessy, "The Seven Names for Hell in the Qur'an." It is not clear here whether the term *Ṣābiyān* refers specifically to the Manicheans practicing in Iran around the end of the thirteenth century or to polytheistic religions more generally (De Blois, "Ṣābi'," *Encyclopaedia of Islam*, new ed. [E.I.[2]], vol. 8, 672–675). SK Ayasofya 3441, folios 31v–34v. The visit to the valleys of hell occurs in the fifth heaven, after the Prophet meets Aaron (Harūn).

26. It is unfortunate that no related Ilkhanid paintings have survived, given the text's detailed elaborations of hell.

27. The description of hell in some narratives attributed to Ibn ʿAbbās is also highly detailed and occurs in the fifth heaven (Ibn ʿAbbās, *al-Isrā' wa'l-Mi*ʿ*rāj*, 18–21) while Muḥammad's witnessing of hell and its tortures occurs immediately prior to his descent to earth in the *Liber Scale Machometi* (295–323). The Timurid *Mi*ʿ*rājnāma* contains an elaborate series of paintings representing hell and its tortures as well (Séguy, *The Miraculous Journey of Mahomet*, pls. 44–57). For a further discussion of "hell tours" in ascension narratives, see Roberto Tottoli's contribution to this volume.

28. SK Ayasofya 3441, folio 59v, lines 6–8. Here, Abū Bakr is also given the epithet *al-Ṣiddīq* (the Righteous, Confirmer, or Veracious).

29. Ibid., folio 60v, lines 7–10. Al-Qushayrī elaborates on the term *yaqīn* (conviction) and links it to a visual experience (*ru'yat al-yaqīn*). See al-Qushayrī, *Kitāb al-Mi*ʿ*rāj*, 111. ʿ*Ilm al-yaqīn*—Qur'an 102:5. This term appears in tandem with ʿ*ayn al-yaqīn*, or "certainty of sight" (102:7), when men observe hell on the Day of Judgment. See also SK Ayasofya 3441, folio 41v, line 13. The other *ḥikmas* include the forgiveness of men's errors prior to the Day of Judgment, the Prophet Muḥammad reaching the highest station (*maqām*) of all prophets, and his vision of Malik al-Mawt (the Angel of Death).

30. SK Ayasofya 3441, folio 60v, lines 11–12.

31. Gardet and Berque, "Djamāʿa," E.I.[2], vol. 2, 411–413.

32. Although the SK text is not an exact match to the paintings, its overlapping details outweigh its disjunctures. For example, the painting of the rooster angel (Figure 2.3 and Plate 8) includes angels raising their hands in prayer; these angels are not described in the SK text. They may have been described in the later illustrated Book of Ascension or added by the painter to strengthen and illustrate the importance of physical movements in petitionary prayers.

33. These and the manuscript's other paintings are analyzed in detail in the introduction to Gruber, *The Ilkhanid Book of Ascension*.

34. Several antecedent episodes that play an important role in the *Mi*ʿ*rājnāma* text may have been depicted but do not survive: these could have included the arrival of Gabriel in Mecca with Burāq, as well as Gabriel's splitting open of the Prophet's breast and the removal of several black blood clots to be washed in a gold vessel (SK Ayasofya 3441, folios 7r–9v).

35. Ibid., folios 16r–19r.

36. Ibid., folios 10r–11r.

37. Ibid., folio 16r, lines 6–8.

38. Ibid., folio 17v, line 14. In the *Liber Scale Machometi* (1991), 104–109, the prophets are described as standing along the inside wall of the Temple (*templum/masjid*) as they wait for the Prophet Muḥammad to arrive and pray with them.

39. SK Ayasofya 3441, folio 18r, lines 1–10.

40. Ibid., folios 18v–19r.

41. Ibid., folio 18v, line 9.

42. Early texts such as Ibn Isḥāq's (d. 151/768) *Sīrat al-Nabī* (Biography of the Prophet) include variant reports, in which angels offer two cups filled with milk and wine or three cups filled with milk, wine, and water (Ibn Isḥāq, *The Life of Muhammad*, 181–182). Sayings of the Prophet also record either two or three cups (see al-Bukhārī, *Ṣaḥīḥ*, book 55, nos. 607 and 647; book 58, no. 227; and book 69, nos. 482 and 514; and Muslim, *Ṣaḥīḥ*, book 75, no. 309). In the Ilkhanid text, two or three cups expand to four (milk, wine, water, and honey).

43. SK Ayasofya 3441, folio 20v, lines 11–12. Many ascension texts include the celestial rooster in the first heaven and describe it as an ornithomorphic angel of cosmic proportions, whose head reaches God's throne and whose feet grasp the earth. Its movements, however, are not described in any detail.

44. Ibid., folio 21r, lines 5–6.

45. Ibid., folio 21r, lines 1–2.

46. Ibid., folio 21r, line 4.

47. al-Bukhārī, *Kitāb Rafᶜ al-Yadayn fī'l-Ṣalāh.*

48. Ibid., 5, 46, 61, 74, and 112–117.

49. Throughout his treatise, al-Bukhārī also states that the practice is accepted by the *ahl al-ᶜilm* (theologians) and the *ahl al-naẓar* (jurists). Although he does not explicitly state so, it is clear that al-Bukhārī heralds this Sunni practice in contraposition to Shiᶜi "innovations."

50. al-Bukhārī, *Kitāb Rafᶜ al-Yadayn fī'l-Ṣalāh,* 59 and 95.

51. Ibid., 75.

52. A number of Islamic sources describe the Prophet learning how to pray from the angels. For instance, we are told the he learned the call to prayer from the angel Gabriel and that he witnessed the angels in various positions of ritual prayer during the night of his ascension. For a discussion of this motif, see Colby, "Constructing an Islamic Ascension Narrative," 357–358, and footnotes 143 and 147.

53. Dutton, "*ᶜAmal v. Ḥadīth* in Islamic Law," 36–37.

54. SK Ayasofya 3441, folio 38r. This is the only painting in the series representing the Prophet's encounter with angels on a plain gold background, hence its identification as the seventh heaven made of light. The upper left corner of the painting's gold background is damaged, creating a white triangle immediately below the attribution panel at the top.

55. SK Ayasofya 3441, folio 38v.

56. Ibid., folio 43r.

57. Dutton, "*ᶜAmal v. Ḥadīth* in Islamic Law."

58. Ibid., 35.

59. SK Ayasofya 3441, folios 58v–59v.

60. Ibid., folio 60r, lines 6–8. In this case, *bayt al-maqdis* stands for Jerusalem and its immediate surroundings.

61. Ibid., folio 60v, lines 9–12.

62. For a general discussion of Shiᶜi ritual cursing, see in particular Calmard, "Les rituels shiites et le pouvoir."

63. The Prophet is well known to have owned a *burda,* a long piece of woolen cloth usually of brown or grayish color that is wrapped around the body during the day and serves as a blanket at night (Dozy, *Dictionnaire détaillé des noms des vêtements chez les arabes,* 59).

64. The earliest Chaghatay Turkish *Miᶜrājnāma* composed during the 6th/12th century and attributed to Ḥakīm Sulaymān Ata describes the Prophet pulling out a rug to pray to God (*Resul secade saldı Tenri'ga namaz kıldı*) so that he could describe Jerusalem accurately to his opponents (Akar, *Türk Edebiyantında Manzum Mi'râc-Nâmeler,* 97).

65. In the illustrated manuscript of al-Bīrūnī's *al-Athār al-Bāqīya* (Chronology of Nations) dated 707/1307–1308, the Prophet also wears the *burda* in the painting depicting his investiture of ᶜAlī at Ghadīr Khumm (See Hillenbrand, "Images of Muḥammad in al-Biruni's *Chronology of Ancient Nations,*" pl. 13). This suggests that, at an iconographic level, the *burda* denotes a moment of religious revelation.

66. Grube (*Persian Painting in the Fourteenth Century,* 33–34, fn 113) states that the scene depicts an encounter between the Prophet and the people of Medina, while scholars such as Ettinghausen ("Persian Ascension Miniatures of the Fourteenth Century," 376), followed by İpşiroğlu (*Painting and Culture of the Mongols,* 62), suggest that the painting represents an apocalyptic vision of the Prophet predicting the conquest of Constantinople by a great Muslim ruler. However, it seems that both scholars are basing their findings on the misinterpretation of a prophetic saying on the conquest of Rome. Tanındı and Çağman (in their *The Topkapı Saray*

Museum, 69, fig. 47) also reject the identification of the model as Jerusalem, as the city had no walls at the time and too many rivers are depicted in the model.

67. Ghāzān's no longer extant tomb was built 1297–1305 and later was destroyed by Shāh ʿAbbās I (Wilber, *Architecture of Islamic Iran,* 24–26).

68. See Blair, "The Mongol Capital of Sulṭāniyya"; and Godard, "The Mausoleum of Öljeïtu at Sultaniya."

69. These two standing men are not identified in the SK text. However, judging from their ruddy skin tone and their lack of interaction with the seated men, it is possible to hypothesize that they are Quraysh tribesmen who did not ultimately accept the veracity of the Prophet's ascension.

70. Colby, "Constructing an Islamic Ascension Narrative," 100.

71. Spuler, *History of the Mongols Based on Eastern and Western Accounts of the Thirteenth and Fourteenth Centuries,* 118.

72. Aḥmad's name before his conversion to Islam was Tegüder, and he ruled from 1282 to 1284. His conversion was a social and political matter. He implemented Islamic law (*sharīʿa*) in Ilkhanid lands and used it as a means to establish peace with the Mamluks. He also transformed several pagan shrines and monasteries into mosques (Amitai, "The Conversion of Tegüder Ilkhan to Islam").

73. Gardet and Berque, "Djamāʿa," E.I.[2], vol. 2, 411–413.

74. Amitai, "The Conversion of Tegüder Ilkhan to Islam," 35–37.

75. Calmard, "Le chiisme imamite sous les Ilkhans," 271.

76. Melville, *The Fall of Amir Chupan and the Decline of the Ilkhanate;* and idem, "Abū Saʿīd and the Revolt of the Amirs in 1319."

77. Millie, "The Narrative Potential of Mi'râj."

78. His treatise is included in his compendium of theological writings titled *al-Majmūʿa al-Rashīdiyya* (Rashīd's Miscellany) held in the BnF (Arabe 2324, folios 129r–131v). See Gruber, "The Prophet Muḥammad's Ascension (*Miʿrāj*) in Islamic Art and Literature, 1300–1600," 86 and Appendix I/2 (which includes a complete copy of the text).

79. Soucek, "The Life of the Prophet," 204; and Jahn, "The Still Missing Works of Rashid al-Din."

80. Howorth, *History of the Mongols from the 9th to the 19th Century,* 618.

81. Hood, "Saint Dominic's Manners of Praying"; and Tugwell, "The Nine Ways of Prayer of St. Dominic."

82. Hood, "Saint Dominic's Manners of Praying," 197.

83. Lewis, *Reading Images,* 259.

84. Between 1250 and 1350, many Franciscan friars and missionaries traveled to Iran to proselytize. They brought with them religious objects, Gospel books, and possibly illustrated devotional manuscripts (see Blair, "The Religious Art of the Ilkhanids," 112).

3

The Jews at the Edge of the World in a Timurid-era *Miʿrājnāma*: The Islamic Ascension Narrative as Missionary Text

MARIA E. SUBTELNY

The illustrated manuscript of the Islamic ascension narrative, or *Miʿrājnāma,* copied in Timurid Iran or Central Asia during the first half of the fifteenth century and today in the collection of the Bibliothèque nationale de France (Supplément turc 190), has always been something of a puzzle.[1] In the eighteenth century, French Orientalists could not even decipher the script in which it was written, and, since Abel Pavet de Courteille's ground-breaking edition and translation of the text in the late nineteenth century, subsequent scholarly studies have raised more questions than there are ready answers for.

The main issue has been the precise nature of the manuscript's relationship to its Timurid context. By whom was it commissioned? When and why was it translated into Middle Turkic? Why was Uighur script used in transcribing the Turkic text? Who was the intended audience? This study will attempt to answer these questions, first by tracing the complex process by which the particular version of the ascension narrative represented by the Timurid *Miʿrājnāma* was transmitted, and second by examining certain key elements of the narrative that may shed light on the function of the Islamic ascension narrative in medieval Islamic societies in general, and in Iran and Central Asia in particular. Since I am not an art historian, I will not comment on the iconography of the manuscript, which consists of sixty paintings that illustrate the progress of the narrative in an almost literal manner, replicating specific details mentioned in the text.[2] My observations and conclusions, however, may influence the way art historians approach the iconographic analysis of the manuscript in the future.

My argument is based on what I perceive to be an exceedingly important but largely overlooked historical function of the Islamic ascension narrative, namely, its use as a missionary text in proselytizing about Islam among various religious communities in the early medieval Islamic world. The apocalyptic features of the account lent themselves to the presentation of Islamic beliefs, especially regarding eschatology, in a narrative structure that would not have been unfamiliar to adherents of Judaism, Christianity, and Zoroastrianism. The fact that there was no canonical version of the narrative meant that the account could be creatively adapted to appeal to the religious sensibilities of a particular faith community. To anticipate my conclusions regarding the Middle Turkic text of the Timurid *Miʿrājnāma*, it is my contention that it preserves a much earlier Persian version of the Islamic ascension narrative that was originally directed toward Persian-speaking Jews living in Iran or Central Asia, with a view to converting them to Islam. As for the manuscript itself, which was transcribed in Uighur characters and sumptuously illustrated, I believe it was intended only for elite or court use, serving as a tangible token of the new pro-Islamic policies espoused by the early Timurids, albeit not to the exclusion of their own, often contradictory, Turko-Mongolian customs and traditions. This is perhaps a radical thesis, but the intractability of the problems connected with the provenance and function of the Timurid *Miʿrājnāma* manuscript called for nothing short of cutting the proverbial Gordian knot.

The *Miʿrājnāma* in Middle Turkic Translation

The manuscript of the *Miʿrājnāma* that constitutes the object of our inquiry is not mentioned in any of the literary or historical sources of the Timurid period, and the little that is known about it can only be gleaned from the internal evidence the manuscript itself provides. The illustrated text constitutes the first item in a bound volume that also contains an abridged translation of the hagiographical work *Tadhkirat al-awliyā'* (Memorial of Saints) by Farīd al-Dīn ʿAṭṭār (d. 1220).[3] According to the colophon at the end of the latter work, the manuscript was copied in Herat by a scribe named Harī-Malik Bakhshi on 10 Jumādā II 840 (i.e., 20 December 1436), which, according to him, corresponded to the Year of the Horse in the Turko-Mongolian animal calendar.[4] The manuscript contains no dedication and no mention of the patron who may have commissioned it.

Both works in the volume are Middle Turkic translations from Persian, and both are written in Uighur script. As indicated in its introduction, the *Miʿrājnāma* was translated into "the language of the Turks" (*türk tiligä*) from a work titled *Nahj al-farādīs* (Pathway to Paradise).[5] Although there is no explicit statement to this effect in the text, the language in which the *Nahj al-farādīs* was written must have been Persian.[6] Support for this contention is found in the *Miʿrājnāma* itself, which refers to a prophetic Tradition (hadith), supposedly cited from the *Maṣābīḥ al-sunna* (The Lanterns of Tradition) of al-Baghawī (d. 1122), as having been "written in Persian" (*fārsī bitildi*).[7] In other words, the prophetic Tradition, which was originally in Arabic, had been translated in the *Nahj al-farādīs* into Persian and, in turn, into Turkish. This reflects the usual process of transmission of Arabic works of a religious nature into Turko-Islamic culture through the intermediacy of Persian translations, since Persian literary influence predominated in the eastern Islamic world.[8] Further circumstantial evidence that the *Miʿrājnāma* was translated from the Persian is provided by the fact that the *Tadhkirat al-awliyā'*, with which it was bound together in the same manuscript, was also translated "into the Turkish language from Persian" (*fārsīdin türkchä tilgä*), as clearly stated in its introduction.[9]

The Timurid *Miʿrājnāma* is thus not an original Middle Turkic work but a translation.[10] Attempts by some scholars to ascribe the Turkic text to the Chaghatay poet Mīr Ḥaydar are not supported either by internal evidence or by the primary sources of the Timurid period.[11] Moreover, since the Islamic ascension narrative belongs to the literary genre of apocalypse, the "author" of the narrative is in fact its narrator—the Prophet Muḥammad—whose own account is related in the form of extended prophetic Traditions transmitted through the required chains of authority. Just as the Hebrew Apocalypse of Enoch, to which the Islamic ascension narrative has a great affinity, was ascribed pseudepigraphically to the famous second-century Palestinian sage Rabbi Ishmael, who is also its hero and narrator, many versions of what might properly speaking be called the Apocalypse of Muḥammad were attributed to such well-known early Islamic authorities and traditionists as Ibn ʿAbbās, Anas b. Mālik, Abū Hurayra, and Mālik b. Ṣaʿṣaʿa, among others, who transmitted the words of the Prophet without altering the first person narrative structure that is one of the defining features of the Near Eastern apocalyptic genre.[12]

It is not known when the Middle Turkic translation of the *Miʿrājnāma* was completed. It is possible that the translation was done roughly at the same time the copy of the manuscript was made. In view of the wording of the introduction ("We have translated [the *Miʿrājnāma*] from the book titled *Nahj al-farādīs* into the language of the Turks"), the translator may have been the scribe, Harī-Malik Bakhshi, but this is by no means certain.[13] A linguistic analysis of the text indicates that the Middle Turkic idiom into which it was translated is closer to Khwarazmian Turkish than to Chaghatay, thus reflecting an earlier stage in the development of the Eastern Turkic literary language.[14] This would support an argument for the text having been translated well before it was copied in ca. 840/1436. On the other hand, a simpler, less Persianized Turkic idiom than Chaghatay, a sophisticated hybrid literary language cultivated mainly within the framework of Timurid court culture, would have been more appropriate for conveying a popular religious narrative like the *Miʿrājnāma*.

As for the Persian work titled *Nahj al-farādīs,* from which the *Miʿrājnāma* was translated, some scholars have identified it with an anonymous Middle Turkic (Khwarazmian) work, also titled *Nahj al-farādīs,* a manuscript copy of which was produced in 761/1360 at the Golden Horde capital, Saray.[15] However, thorough comparisons of the two works by János Eckmann, who edited the Khwarazmian manuscript, and Max Scherberger, the latest editor and translator of the *Miʿrājnāma,* have shown that the two texts are not identical.[16] The Khwarazmian Turkic *Nahj al-farādīs* belongs to the "forty hadith" genre and includes, besides the *miʿrāj* account, the biography of the Prophet (of which the *miʿrāj* represents but a single episode), the biographies of the Prophet's companions, Orthodox caliphs, and members of the family of ʿAlī, as well as an exposition of the main features of Islamic religious practice and ethical conduct.[17] There are also significant differences between the two accounts of the *miʿrāj* itself, particularly with regard to the description of the heavenly spheres and the prophets associated with them, and some of the mythic motifs, such as the cosmic cock, do not occur in the Khwarazmian version, nor does the account of Muḥammad's visit to the Jews at Mount Qāf, which will be discussed in due course.[18]

The citation of the same prophetic Tradition at the very beginning of the *miʿrāj* narrative in both texts, which is described as being taken from the *Maṣābīḥ al-sunna* of al-Baghawī but which is actually a less common version of the Tradition recorded in the Qur'an commentary of al-Ṭabarī (d. 923), would seem to suggest that, since both texts repeat the same erroneous attribution, the Timurid *Miʿrājnāma* was directly dependent on the Khwarazmian Turkic *Nahj al-farādīs.*[19] This is not the case, however. Since, in Eckmann's view, the Khwarazmian Turkic *Nahj al-farādīs* was probably also translated from a Persian original, and given the fact that the Turkic idiom of the Khwarazmian *Nahj al-farādīs* is different from that of the Timurid *Miʿrājnāma,* it appears that the two Middle Turkic translations were made from different Persian texts bearing the same name, at different times and in different locales.[20] We may posit, then, that the beguiling title of the *Nahj al-farādīs,* which held out the promise of Paradise to those who heeded its message, served as a generic designation for conversion manuals or practical handbooks that were used by popular preachers and Muslim missionaries in medieval Iran and Persianate Central Asia as a guide in the exposition of fundamental Islamic beliefs and practices.[21] Based chiefly on prophetic Traditions, qur'anic citations, and a common fund of Islamic religious knowledge, works of this type were necessarily anonymous and of similar, although not identical, content.

On the basis of the foregoing discussion, it may be hypothesized that the Timurid *Miʿrājnāma* served to preserve an earlier Persian version of the Islamic ascension narrative that is now lost. Like a fly in amber, the Persian "original" survived intact thanks to its translation into Middle Turkic, which was itself preserved in the copy that has come down to us from the early Timurid period. The strength of this hypothesis depends, of course, on the faithfulness of the Turkic translation of the Persian. An indication that the translation adhered strictly to the Persian original is the citation, mentioned earlier, of a prophetic Tradition that had evidently been translated in the *Nahj al-farādīs* into Persian. The statement indicating this was then rendered verbatim into Middle Turkic, despite the fact that it was not necessary to do so since the Tradition was being translated into Middle Turkic anyway. It seems that religious texts in particular, which belonged to a supranational Islamic culture and hence did not require cultural transfer, were less susceptible to alteration in the course of translation from Persian to Turkic languages. Additionally, it may be ventured that, in general, medieval Turkic (including Ottoman Turkish) translators followed the Persian originals they were translating quite closely, perhaps even slavishly, unless they had literary pretensions themselves or the text was stylistically less straightforward than the narrative under discussion.[22]

In this respect, the function of the *Miʿrājnāma* may be compared to that of the so-called Book of Muḥammad's Ladder, a Castilian translation of which, completed at the court of Alfonso X the Wise (r. 1252–1284), served to preserve a lost original Arabic version of the Islamic ascension narrative from medieval Spain. Although the Castilian translation was also lost, it was preserved, in turn, in thirteenth-century Latin and Old French translations titled *Liber Scale Machometi* and *Le livre de l'eschiele de Mahomet,* respectively.[23] The Book of Muḥammad's Ladder is thus not a polemical text, as many European medievalists have maintained.[24] Rather, in its original Arabic form, it played the same role, albeit in a different historical context, as did the original Persian version of the ascension narrative from which the Timurid *Miʿrājnāma* was translated. Whereas the Persian version preserved in the Timurid *Miʿrājnāma* was used as a missionary text among Persian-speaking Jews in Iran or Central Asia, the Arabic version preserved in the Book of Muḥammad's Ladder appears to have been addressed to Arabic-speaking Christians in Muslim Spain.[25]

The Timurid Context

The historical context in which the *Miʿrājnāma* manuscript was produced corresponds to the reign of the Timurid ruler Shāhrukh (r. 1409–1447) in Herat. Located in the large eastern Iranian province of Khorasan, Herat became the new capital of the Timurid realm thanks to Shāhrukh who moved it there from Samarqand. As a ruler in the first generation after his nomadic warlord father, Temür, who had exhibited profound attachment to the Chinggisid *yasa*, or customary law, Shāhrukh tried to establish his credentials as a Muslim monarch. He adopted the title *pādshāh-i Islām* and reportedly abrogated Turko-Mongolian customary law in favor of the *Sharīʿa.*[26] Portraying himself as the "renewer" (*mujaddid*) of Islam, who according to a well-known prophetic Tradition was destined to appear at the start of every Islamic century, Shāhrukh conducted a vigorous policy of Islamization that included his establishment of a *madrasa* in Herat to promote Hanafite doctrinal uniformity, as well as the direction of missionary activity in the Ismāʿīlī enclave of Quhistan, among the nomads of the Qipchaq steppe, and in India.[27] In his correspondence with the Ming emperor, Shāhrukh boasted about his implementation of Islamic policies throughout the Timurid realm and expressed the hope that the emperor would do the same in his own kingdom.[28]

At the same time, however, Shāhrukh did not entirely abandon Turko-Mongolian customs and traditions, which were referred to by the Timurids as the *törä.* As the Timurid elaboration of the Chinggisid *yasa,* the *törä* represented a kind of unwritten constitution by means of which the Timurid rulers and their military elites maintained their "Chaghatay" identity as distinct from the sedentary Iranian Muslim population over which they ruled. Among its characteristic features were the Chinggisid ranking of military offices, the maintenance of the *yarghu* courts of investigation, and the centrality of the imperial guard corps (*keshik*) in the organization of the patrimonial household.[29] The Timurids retained the use of the Turko-Mongolian twelve-animal calendar and Turko-Mongolian titles for military-administrative and household appointments, such as *tovachi* (troop inspector), *yarghuchi* (chief judge), *qushchi* (falconer), and *bökävül* (taster), and despite being highly acculturated and adopting the Persian system of bureaucratic administration, they did not abandon the use of the Turkic language even in the chancery, where they maintained a parallel system of Turkic scribes proficient in the use of Uighur script alongside the Tajik (i.e., Iranian) secretaries who employed Persian, the chief language of Timurid bureaucratic and diplomatic correspondence. As attested in the Timuro-Chinggisid genealogical history *Muᶜizz al-ansāb*, commissioned by Shāhrukh in 830/1426–1427, the names of many Turkic scribes (*bitikchiyān* or *nawīsandagān-i türk*) in the various Timurid administrations contain the title *bakhshi*, which denoted a literate individual of great learning, who was often of Uighur descent.[30] It will be recalled that the scribe who copied the *Miᶜrājnāma* manuscript, Harī-Malik Bakhshi, also bore this title. Unfortunately, his name does not appear in the list of the Turkic scribes of Shāhrukh's administration in the *Muᶜizz al-ansāb*.[31]

Like the Ilkhanid Mongols, whom they often regarded as models, the Timurids cultivated the symbolic use of the Uighur script as a distinctive marker of their dynastic culture.[32] Ibn ᶜArabshāh (d. 1450), the author of a polemical but insightful history of Temür, noted the widespread use of Uighur script in the early Timurid administration and the high demand for scribes expert in it:

> In this script they write their orders and edicts, official correspondence, historical chronicles, poems . . . and everything concerning administrative matters (*al-umūr al-dīwāniyya*) and Chinggisid customary law (*al-tūrāt al-jankīzkhāniyya*). Whoever is proficient in this script does not perish among them, for it is among them the key to a livelihood.[33]

A number of manuscripts of important Middle Turkic works or Middle Turkic translations from Persian were transcribed in Uighur script during the early Timurid period.[34] The most telling expression of Timurid interest in classical Turkic political culture was the Karakhanid mirror for princes, *Qutadgu bilig* (The Wisdom that Brings Royal Glory), composed in 1069 or 1070 by Yūsuf Khāṣṣ Ḥājib, which was copied in Herat in 843/1439.[35] As for the *Miᶜrājnāma* manuscript under discussion, its significance lies in the fact that it contained what were, arguably, the two most popular religious texts of the time—the Islamic ascension narrative, or apocalypse of Muḥammad, and the *Tadhkirat al-awliyā'*, or biographies of Muslim saints and mystics, by ᶜAṭṭār.[36] The transcription in Uighur script of Middle Turkic translations of these two seminal religious works may be regarded as symbolizing the symbiosis of the two cultural systems in which the Timurids functioned simultaneously—the Turko-Mongolian and the Perso-Islamic.[37] Although there is no direct proof that the manuscript was commissioned by Shāhrukh himself, the fact that it remained in the Timurid royal library before being brought to Istanbul, along with so many other precious Timurid manuscripts (including the Paris manuscript of the *Muᶜizz al-ansāb*), probably by the last Timurid ruler of Herat, Badīᶜ al-Zamān Mīrzā, who was taken to the Ottoman court by Sultan Selim I after the Battle of Chaldiran in 1514, provides strong circumstantial evidence for its having emanated from Shāhrukh's court atelier.[38]

The Ascension Narrative as Missionary Text

The narrative account of the Prophet Muḥammad's heavenly ascension is not a mythological tale or a pious legend intended simply for popular entertainment. It embodies a theologumenon that was considered a touchstone of faith in Islam.[39] The authoritative biography, or *sīra*, of the Prophet, which is based on Muḥammad's own words as reported by his closest Companions and relatives, including his wife ᶜĀ'isha, states the matter in the following way:

> The matter of the place of the nocturnal journey (*masrā*) and what is recounted about it is a trial and a test (*balā' wa tamḥīṣ*) and a matter of God's power and authority wherein is a lesson for those endowed with [intuitive] understanding (*ᶜibrat li-ūlī al-albāb*),[40] and a guidance, and a mercy, and a confirmation for those who believe.[41]

In other words, those who believed in Muḥammad's heavenly ascension were regarded as having accepted his prophetic mission and place in religious history as the "seal of the prophets," whereas those who did not were considered to have rejected Islam itself.[42] The model of the former was Abū Bakr (d. 634), Muḥammad's faithful Companion and son-in-law and later first caliph of Islam, and the representatives of the latter were first and foremost members of Muḥammad's own tribe of Quraysh, in particular Abū Jahl, who became the symbol of the obstinate unbeliever.[43] Thus the primary function of the ascension narrative was to demonstrate Muḥammad's confirmation by his Jewish and Christian predecessors as the last prophet in an unbroken chain of prophetic history as well as to underscore the favored eschatological status of the Muslim community.

But there is another function of the narrative to which virtually no attention has been paid by modern scholarship, namely, its use as a missionary text among the various religious communities—Zoroastrian, Christian, and Jewish—with which Muslims came into contact during the course of their political expansion from the mid-seventh to the mid-eighth centuries. This dramatic account, related in the first person by the Prophet himself, was a highly effective vehicle for capturing the imagination of prospective converts. The text of the ascension narrative itself contains a number of indications that support this contention. The first is a narreme, or narrative fragment, that occurs at the very beginning of most versions of the account, that subtly yet unmistakably sets its proselytizing tone. In it Muḥammad is described as hearing two, three, or even four voices calling to him as he is traveling from Mecca toward the Temple in Jerusalem (Plate 10). He does not pay any attention to the voices at the time, and the angel Gabriel later interprets their meaning for him, explaining that they represented the various religions, and had Muḥammad responded to any one of them, his community would have become Jewish, Zoroastrian, Christian, or even polytheist, as the case may be.[44]

Unlike qur'anic scripture, the Islamic ascension narrative never assumed a canonical form and, as already indicated, it was recounted in many versions that differed from each other in subtle yet significant ways. This served the purposes of missionaries perfectly, as the narrative could be manipulated to respond to the exigencies of a particular time and place, and to appeal to the particular religious community targeted for conversion. Contributing to the fluid and even ephemeral nature of the narrative was its oral and performative dimension, as has been demonstrated in the case of the contemporary Malay context and in Özgen Felek's study in this volume.[45] In this way, many elements drawn from the belief systems of the various religious communities were appropriated and, once integrated into the narrative, remained standard features in later versions even as their original meaning became obscured. Therefore, those who would seek a "complete" or definitive version of the ascension narrative are, in my view, pursuing a futile and faulty line of investigation. By the same token, to interpret the absence of certain details in a given version as a lacuna in the manuscript, and to fill that lacuna with details from another version, is to distort the original intent of a particular version of the narrative.[46]

While it is possible, thanks to the heuristic model assembled by Richard Bulliet, to reconstruct the rate and degree of conversion in various regions of the Islamic world, we know next to nothing about the strategies employed by Muslim missionaries in specific medieval Middle Eastern societies.[47] Acknowledging the truism that forced conversion played an insignificant role in the spread of Islam to such outlying regions as Central Asia, Devin DeWeese has formulated the most sophisticated approach available to date for understanding the meaning of conversion to a particular Islamicizing society, namely, that of the nomadic Turks of the Qipchaq steppe, by analyzing legendary and hagiographical conversion narratives that integrated indigenous Inner Asian religious themes into Islamic paradigms.[48] The use of such narrative "mechanisms" to explain communal conversion from a socio-historical perspective can also shed light on the means by which conversion took place. The narrative account of the *miʿrāj,* which could be adapted to appeal to different religious groups through the inclusion of culturally specific narremes and religious motifs, was just such a "mechanism" that could be used by Muslim missionaries, popular preachers, and Sufis, many probably recent converts themselves, in "calling" non-Muslim communities to Islam.[49]

Judging from the way in which the ascension narrative was manipulated to appeal to different religious groups, we may posit that the strategy employed by Muslim missionaries was one of positive argument, rather than of polemical confrontation or refutation, that stressed shared truths and reinforced the religious beliefs of the target audience, which were integrated into an Islamic framework. This strategy is remarkably similar to that propounded by the Catalan theologian Ramón Llull (d. 1315), who, in his many works on the subject of the conversion of Muslims and Jews to Christianity, expressed the view that rather than arguing "against the faith," it was necessary to argue "through the faith" by starting a dialogue from basic principles common to both religions and employing techniques characteristic of the other religion.[50] Jamsheed Choksy, who has surveyed the patterns of conversion and resistance among Zoroastrians in Iran in the ninth and tenth centuries, opines that intellectual persuasion had the most lasting effect in the case of voluntary acceptance of Islam. He also suggests that popular preachers and Sufi missionaries operating on the oral level played an important role in presenting Islam as compatible in many respects with Zoroastrian beliefs and rituals, thereby convincing Zoroastrians that they would not be abandoning their religious traditions if they accepted Islam.[51] In the final analysis, the Muslim attitude to conversion appears to have reflected the qur'anic dictum, "There is no compulsion in religion" (*lā ikrāha fī'l-dīni*) (Q 2:256), the *locus classicus* for discussions of the Islamic view on interfaith relations and religious tolerance, which actually denies the feasibility of coercion in matters of religion and leaves the decision to convert up to the volitional subject.[52]

In his edition and translation of the text, Wheeler Thackston suggested that the Timurid *Miʿrājnāma* may have been used as part of a missionary initiative to convert the "heathen Mongolized Turks" of Moghulistan, that is, the Turko-Mongolian nomads of Inner Asia.[53] In view of the fact that a "re-Islamization" of the steppe regions of Central and Inner Asia was undertaken during the early Timurid period, this may not be out of the question.[54] But the suggestion could apply to the Turkic text of the narrative and not to the manuscript itself, which was a luxury item intended for elite use. As mentioned earlier, the manuscript was more an ideological expression of the Timurids' hybrid culture than a practical manual for proselytizing among the nomads of the steppe regions. Moreover, it appears that the ascension narrative was not as central to the process of the Islamization of Central and Inner Asia as were legendary conversion narratives and popular hagiographical accounts that, although they did not ignore the theme of the *miʿrāj,* focused primarily on the role of charismatic Sufi shaykhs and prominent converts as Islamizers of particular historical communities.[55]

As I will attempt to demonstrate in this study, in view of the specifically Jewish allusions that occur in the text, the intended audience of the Persian original from which the Timurid *Miʿrājnāma* was translated must have been a Jewish one. Jews in the medieval eastern Islamic world were, as a rule, Persian-speaking, and aside from such well-known Iranian centers as Isfahan, Shiraz, and Hamadan, they also lived in Balkh and Herat, the main cities of Khorasan, as well as in Transoxiana, Azerbaijan, and Khwarazm, the cities of Bukhara, Shirvan, and Urgench (Khiva) being the most noteworthy in this respect.[56] My contention is that the version of the ascension narrative that is preserved in the Timurid *Miʿrājnāma* was a missionary text intended for use in proselytizing among Jews living in the Persian cultural sphere. The fact that the text is in Middle Turkic should not mislead us, because, as already established, the translation only served to preserve a Persian original that dated from an earlier period. Just how much earlier must remain a matter of conjecture.

The citation of a prophetic Tradition from al-Ṭabarī's *Jāmiʿ al-bayān*, which as mentioned earlier was ascribed instead to al-Baghawī's *Maṣābīḥ al-sunna*, might, however, provide a clue with regard to dating, for it may be interpreted to mean that the original Persian account was circulating as early as the end of the ninth and beginning of the tenth centuries. The reference to the *Maṣābīḥ al-sunna*, regarded as a more popular (and perhaps theologically less daunting) source of prophetic Traditions than al-Ṭabarī's long-winded exegetical work, would simply have been added in later redactions.[57] Such a conjecture would fit the historical conversion curve proposed for Iran by Richard Bulliet, according to whom the bulk of conversions occurred in the ninth and early tenth centuries, the process being by and large completed by the mid- to late thirteenth century.[58]

With this background in mind, let us examine the narreme alluded to earlier about the Jews who live at the edge of the world on Mount Qāf with a view to determining why it should have resonated with a Jewish audience.

The Narreme about the Jews at the Edge of the World

At the very end of the Timurid *Miʿrājnāma*, after reaching the throne of God in the highest heavenly sphere and being given tours of Paradise and Hell, the Prophet Muḥammad is transported to the edge of the world by the angel Gabriel in order to pay a visit to the Jews who live in the mythical cities of Jābalqā and Jābalsā on Mount Qāf.[59] These cities, which are situated, respectively, on the eastern and western sides of the mountain, are described as being of monumental proportions, with a thousand gates each, the distance between each gate being a *farsang*, or league. The houses in which the Jews live are described as all being of the same height and located far from their places of worship, whereas their cemeteries are situated close by.[60] When Muḥammad inquires about the identity of these people, Gabriel informs him that they are "from among the people of Moses" (*Mūsā ummatläridin*).

After being introduced to them, Muḥammad asks the Jews a series of questions. In response to the question why their houses are all the same height, they reply, "Because among us there is neither envy nor pride."[61] In response to the question why their places of worship are far from their homes while their cemeteries are close by, the Jews answer that it is so that by exerting themselves to reach their places of worship, their reward will be greater, and so that they will always be mindful of death.[62] After assuring Muḥammad that they perform their prayers, fast, honor their parents, and so on, the Jews ask him for some words of "advice" (*naṣīḥat*).[63] Muḥammad complies by exhorting them to "Fear God, do not be prideful, and obey the commandments!" The Jews accept Muḥammad's words, thereby expressing their belief in him as a prophet. That they also accept the religion of Islam is indicated by Muḥammad's final commentary, with which this version of the ascension narrative ends:

> They all accepted [me] (*qabūl qıldılar*) . . . They all expressed their belief (*īmān*) [in Islam].[64] May God, who is exalted, grant them all success in [the performance of] good deeds (*yakhshılıq*) and in obedience (*ṭāʿat*) [to the faith and practice of Islam].[65] May He deliver them from the torments of hell and grant them the reward of Paradise. Amen, O Lord of the Worlds![66]

The narreme under discussion is not unique to the version of the ascension narrative preserved in the Timurid *Miʿrājnāma*. Variants of it are also attested in versions of the narrative ascribed pseudepigraphically to such early Islamic authorities as Ibn ʿAbbās (d. 686), a renowned Qur'an exegete and transmitter of prophetic Traditions.[67] In a Persian version that survives in a manuscript dating possibly from the Ilkhanid period, Muḥammad is described as visiting the "righteous people" (*qawm-i ṣāliḥ*) who live in the cities of Jābalqā and Jābalsā.[68] The inhabitants of the latter are identified as those Jewish proto-Muslims mentioned in Qur'an 7:159 who were believed to constitute a separate community from the general community of Jews.[69] According to the narrative, after Muḥammad instructs them in the fundamentals of the Islamic faith, they all convert to Islam.

In a more elaborate version of the narreme preserved in an early fifteenth-century Arabic translation of the ascension narrative compiled by Mūsā b. Ḥājjī Ḥusayn al-Izniqī, Muḥammad encounters a separate community of Jews who live between the earth and the first heavenly sphere, that is, at the edge of the world.[70] They are described as living on an island in a river of sand where no one can reach them and where they lead a pure and ascetic lifestyle.[71] Their houses are described in the same detail as in the Timurid *Miʿrājnāma,* namely, as all being the same height, with no doors, and located far from the people's places of worship but close to their cemeteries. The Jews tell Muḥammad that they pray and fast, perform their religious duties, do not fornicate, and do not take interest on loans; moreover, they say they have no need of kings or judges because they are all just. Muḥammad recognizes them as the community of the Jews mentioned in the Qur'an, and the Jews recognize Muḥammad as the prophet promised by Moses.[72] When the Jews ask Muḥammad to teach them about Islam's commandments, he responds by saying,

"Fear God, do not be proud or arrogant; do not place trust in your possessions or actions; live life amid hope and with fear," which represents a close variant of the "advice" he gives them in the narreme preserved in the Timurid *Miʿrājnāma*.[73]

Linked exegetically to the scriptural verse, "Among the people of Moses (*min qawm Mūsā*) there is a [separate] community (*umma*) who guide with truth and exercise justice thereby" (Qur'an 7:159), the motif of the righteous Jews who live at the edge of the world is attested in medieval Qur'an commentaries, Islamic legends of the prophets (*qiṣaṣ al-anbiyā'*), and historical, cosmological, and cosmographical works, most of which appear to have been of Persian provenance.[74] Citing Jewish sources, the Persian cosmographer Yāqūt (d. 1229), for example, identifies the inhabitants of the city of Jābars, which he locates in the far east, with the descendants of Moses (*awlād Mūsā*), who were deposited there by God during the wars of Saul (Ṭālūt) or of Nebuchadnezzar (Bukht-Naṣṣar).[75] They live by themselves in this unattainable place, keeping the true faith that their co-religionists had allegedly corrupted, and even going so far as killing those Jews who try to join them there. Yāqūt calls them "the remnant of the Muslims" (*baqāyā al-muslimīn*), by which he means those Jewish proto-Muslims mentioned in Qur'an 7:159 who presumably separated themselves from the Rabbanites and, having recognized the prophesy of Muḥammad's coming in the Torah, remained faithful to their belief in him.[76]

According to the account of the Creation in the universal history of the late ninth–early tenth-century Persian Qur'an commentator, al-Ṭabarī, the cities of Jābalq and Jābars were created by God in the east and west, respectively.[77] Al-Ṭabarī does not explicitly mention that they were located on Mount Qāf, but he does describe them as having the same monumental proportions as in the narreme preserved in the Timurid *Miʿrājnāma*, that is, as having ten thousand gates each, with a distance of a *farsang* between each gate. Al-Ṭabarī identifies their inhabitants as belonging to the "remnant" of the ancient people of ʿĀd and Thamūd, who are mentioned in the Qur'an as believers in the pre-Islamic prophets.[78] The most significant aspect of al-Ṭabarī's account is that it incorporates what may be the earliest textual reference to the narreme about Muḥammad's visit to the mythic cities of Jābalqā and Jābalsā during the course of his heavenly ascension. Although he does not identify the inhabitants of the cities as Jews, al-Ṭabarī's description of the Prophet's assessment of the "remnant" of these people allows us to identify them with the separate community of Jewish proto-Muslims alluded to in the above-mentioned scriptural verse:

> Gabriel then took me to the inhabitants of the two cities. I called on them to follow the religion of God [i.e., Islam] and to worship Him. They agreed and repented [i.e., converted]. They are our brothers in the [true] religion. Those of them who do good are together with those of you [i.e., Muslims] who do good, and those among them who do evil are together with those of you who do evil.[79]

The narreme about the righteous Jews who anticipate the coming of the Prophet Muḥammad and accept Islam when he visits them in their isolated dwelling place at the edge of the world must have been introduced into the Persianate cultural milieu during the historical process of conversion in Iran, which, according to Bulliet's conversion curve, began in the mid-eighth century and peaked during the ninth and early tenth centuries.[80] Due to the conservative nature of the transmission of textual sources in medieval Islam, once the narreme was included in a particular version of the ascension narrative and fixed in writing, it remained a standard feature even as its original significance could no longer be discerned. This was particularly true of Zoroastrian elements incorporated into the ascension narrative, such as the motif of the rooster angel, symbol of the deity Sraosha, which would immediately have been recognized by a Zoroastrian audience in, say, the eighth or ninth century, but which by the fifteenth century had lost its relevance and become trivialized.[81] The narreme of the Jews who live at the edge of the world thus relates to an earlier historical reality that no longer obtained in fifteenth-century Iran when the Timurid *Miʿrājnāma* was copied. It is in fact a kind of fossilized relic embedded in a version of the ascension narrative that was, in turn, preserved in a translation. But by examining its mythic and symbolical associations, it is possible to reconstruct the significance it may have had for a Jewish audience living in the Persianate sphere, and it is to this task that we now turn.

Alexander, Bulūqiyā, and Muḥammad

The ancient Iranian mythological motif of the cosmic mountain at the edge of the world was incorporated early on into medieval Islamic cosmology. Known as Mount Qāf, it was described as an inaccessible place, situated at the point where the earth meets the first heavenly sphere of the moon.[82] Believed to have been fashioned by God out of green emerald, Mount Qāf was the abode of such fabulous creatures as the jinn and the mythical bird Sīmurgh, and since it contained the "tree of all seeds" and the spring of eternal life, it was reckoned to be the source of all plant and animal life on earth.[83] Mount Qāf and its mythical cities were perhaps most closely associated in the Perso-Islamic literary tradition with the epic of Alexander, whose wanderings to the ends of the earth in search of the spring of eternal life and his meeting there with an angel caused him to be identified with the Dhū'l-Qarnayn mentioned in the Qur'an.[84]

Often conflated with the Alexander romance was the legend of Bulūqiyā, a Jewish figure whose apocalyptic journey takes him across the seven seas to the ends of the earth; there he visits the cosmic mountain and encounters angelic beings who provide him with a glimpse of the world beyond.[85] In the Islamic tradition, the legend of Bulūqiyā was refocused to illustrate the theological doctrine of *taḥrīf,* which held that the original text of the Torah, corrupted at the hands of the Rabbanites, contained the prophesy of the coming of Muḥammad.[86]

According to the version of the tale in the legends of the prophets compiled by al-Thaʿlabī (d. 1036), Bulūqiyā gained foreknowledge of Muḥammad's coming from a book left behind by his father, who had recognized the prophesy in the Torah but had concealed it from his son.[87] Overcome by a desire to find Muḥammad, Bulūqiyā sets out on a quest for him. After crossing the seven seas, he reaches Mount Qāf at the edge of the world where he meets an angel with the Hebrew theophoric name Khazqīyā'īl, who is the custodian of the mountain.[88] Bulūqiyā wishes to know what lies beyond Mount Qāf, a region where, according to Islamic legend, there are created beings that only God knows about. He sees a locked gate, which the angel Gabriel opens for him, beyond which he sees many marvels and fabulous creatures. He asks the angels about the Prophet Muḥammad, but since Muḥammad has not yet made his appearance in history, they respond that they have not seen him and ask Bulūqiyā to convey their greetings to him should he meet up with him himself.

The Jewish associations of the tale of Bulūqiyā are further affirmed in a version preserved in a thirteenth-century Persian miscellany of a cosmological, talismanic, and cabalistic nature, in which Bulūqiyā's full name is given as Bulūqiyā b. Yamlīkhā b. Isrā'īl, which suggests he was the son of Moses, since Yamlikhyah was considered to be Moses's name before he received his prophetic calling.[89] At Mount Qāf, the angel Bulūqiyā meets is named Maḥarā'īl, who is described as one the Children of Israel (*az Banī Isrā'īl*) who are the custodians of the spring of eternal life located there. As in the case of Khazqīyā'īl, the theophoric name Maḥarā'īl derives from Jewish angelology, Mahariel being the angel of Paradise associated with the first heavenly gate.[90]

In short, the tale of the Jewish hero Bulūqiyā, with its many features in common with the epic of Alexander, would have been sufficiently well known to a Jewish audience for them to interpret Muḥammad's journey to the mythic cities of Mount Qāf at the edge of the world in terms of the epic quests of both Alexander and Bulūqiyā, and to see themselves in the righteous, albeit socially marginal, Children of Israel who have been waiting for the prophet of Islam promised to them in their own Scripture.

In keeping with the strategy of positive argument, the portrait presented of the Jews in the narreme under discussion is necessarily a flattering one, and the responses they give to the questions posed by Muḥammad cast them in a positive light. Muḥammad's line of questioning ultimately has its origins in the philosophical questions posed by Alexander in India to the Brahmans, or gymnosophists (i.e., the naked philosophers), in order to test their philosophical knowledge.[91] Aside from such well-known medieval sources as al-Qazwīnī's cosmographical work mentioned above, the account would also have been familiar to Jews from medieval Hebrew translations of the classical Alexander romance.[92] In the Islamicized versions of the account, Alexander's role is assumed by the Prophet Muḥammad, while the gymnosophists become the Jews who live at the edge of the world and who are ascetic, God-fearing, strictly vegetarian, never quarrel among themselves, and so on.[93]

It will be recalled that, in response to Muḥammad's question why their houses are all the same height, the Jews explain that this is because they do not possess envy (*ḥasad*) or pride (*takabbur*). These were the character traits most often ascribed to Jews by popular opinion in medieval Islam, but that are refuted in their positive portrayal.[94] The Jews' response echoes that given by the naked philosophers to Alexander's questioning of them in medieval Hebrew translations of the Alexander romance.[95] Likewise, the motif of the cemeteries that are located close to the Jews' houses is borrowed from the Alexander romance and attested in its Hebrew translations, and the Jews' response to the question regarding the reasons for this is the same or similar.[96]

Most telling, from the point of view of conversion strategy, is the advice (*naṣīḥat*) Muḥammad gives the Jews in the narreme under discussion. The term *naṣīḥat* had a religio-ethical connotation in medieval Islam, denoting the good counsel a Muslim was morally obliged to give a co-religionist with regard to Islamic beliefs and practices.[97] Hence, by providing them with such advice, Muḥammad is addressing the Jews as quasi-Muslims. What has not been noticed before in the translations and scholarly discussions of the narreme is that Muḥammad's words represent an interpolation of the well-known verse with which the Book of Ecclesiastes ends: "Fear God, and keep His commandments, for this is the whole duty of man" (Eccles. 12:13).[98] With its characteristic Jewish themes of fear of God and obedience to the commandments, or *mitsvot* (rendered by means of the Persian word *farmān*), Muḥammad's "advice" could not but have resonated with a Jewish audience.[99] In fact, it serves in the narrative as the catalyst for their conversion to Islam.

Prophets and Heavenly Spheres

Aside from the narreme about the Jews at the edge of the world, there are a number of other indications in the Timurid *Miʿrājnāma* that support my contention that the version of the Islamic ascension narrative it preserves was addressed specifically to Jews. The most compelling is the absence of Jesus in the pantheon of prophets Muḥammad meets on his journey through the heavenly spheres. In most versions of the ascension narrative, Jesus is associated with the second heaven, which he customarily occupies with John the Baptist, known in Islamic tradition as John, the son of Zachariah (Yaḥyā b. Zakariyyā).[100] In the Timurid *Miʿrājnāma,* instead of meeting Jesus and John the Baptist in the second heavenly sphere, Muḥammad meets John (Yaḥyā) *and* his father Zachariah (Zakariyyā), with the result that, although two prophets are still named, the reference to Jesus has been eliminated.[101] Jesus is mentioned only in connection with Muḥammad's brief preliminary stop at the Aqṣā mosque in Jerusalem, where he is described as being led in prayer, along with Abraham and Moses, by the Prophet of Islam (Plate 11).[102] Meanwhile, the description of the fourth heaven, which is the sphere of the sun, with which Jesus was popularly associated in medieval Persian culture, makes no mention of any prophet as occupying it and meeting with Muḥammad.[103]

On the other hand, Old Testament Hebrew prophets figure very prominently in the version of the ascension narrative preserved in the Timurid *Miʿrājnāma*. Not only are Moses and Abraham accorded the distinction of inhabiting the highest heavenly spheres, the sixth and seventh, respectively,[104] but there are more references to Old Testament prophets in the Timurid *Miʿrājnāma* than in any other version of the narrative. Besides Abraham and Moses, also mentioned are Jacob, Joseph, David, Solomon, Ishmael, Isaac, Aaron, Lot, Noah, and Enoch, all of whom meet Muḥammad as the long-awaited prophet, thereby conferring their legitimacy on his prophetic mission.[105]

It would appear that the kinds of prophets that figure in a given version of the ascension narrative, and the particular heavenly sphere with which they are associated, are not without significance, since certain prophets would have appealed to certain religious communities, while others would not have been suitable for inclusion or emphasis. The placement of prophets in the heavenly spheres in the various versions of the Islamic ascension narrative deserves to be investigated further, as the differences in their arrangement must have served a purpose.[106] If the Timurid *Miʿrājnāma* does not include Jesus among the prophets Muḥammad meets on his heavenly journey, it may be because this would not have been palatable for the Jewish audience targeted for conversion. By the same token, the placement of Adam in the highest heaven (usually reserved for Abraham) in the version of the ascension narrative preserved in the Latin and Old French translations of the Book of Muḥammad's Ladder, which I believe was directed at a Christian audience, may have been meant to symbolize the role of Jesus as the "new Adam."[107]

Other themes and motifs in the narrative preserved in the Timurid *Miʿrājnāma* that would have resonated with a Jewish audience include the angel encountered by Muḥammad in the first heaven, that is described as being half snow or ice and half fire, a motif that also occurs in a late Midrashic account of the Ascension of Moses.[108] The reference to Muḥammad's sandals would have been another theme to which Jews would have been sensitive. As Muḥammad approaches the throne of God in the highest heavenly sphere, he makes the gesture of removing his sandals out of respect for the sanctity of his surroundings, but he is prevented from doing so by God who states, "Let the blessing of your sandals (*naʿlayn*) reach Our throne."[109] The episode, which alludes to Moses's being commanded by God to take off his sandals when he approached the burning bush on Mount Sinai, provides yet another instance of Muḥammad's proximity to God and his superiority over the greatest prophet of the Jews.[110] Indeed, in many versions of the ascension narrative, including the one preserved in the Timurid *Miʿrājnāma*, Moses is described as weeping on account of the fact that God has preferred Muḥammad over himself and promised Muḥammad that the Muslim community will be the first to enter Paradise.[111]

Like the narreme about the Jews who live at the edge of the world, these motifs already occur in versions of the Islamic ascension narrative that date back several hundred years.[112] They too are not unique to the Timurid *Miʿrājnāma;* rather, they attest to the early provenance of the versions of the narrative in which they are preserved. This is not to say that they would not have had meaning for a Muslim audience. On the contrary, despite the fact that the original significance of many of the motifs became obscured over time, the inherent ambiguity and esoteric content of the apocalyptic genre, with its journeys to otherworldly regions and encounters with angels and other otherworldly beings, called for a suspension of the rational in the interests of spiritual transformation through the uniquely personal experience of the Prophet of Islam.

Far from being an original literary creation, the Timurid *Miʿrājnāma,* which attracted the attention of modern scholarship largely by reason of its stunning illustrations, served to preserve in Middle Turkic translation a lost Persian version probably dating back to the period of conversions in Iran that began in the mid-eighth century and peaked during the ninth and early tenth centuries. As I have attempted to argue, this Persian version (or an earlier version of it), with its distinctively Jewish motifs and allusions, must have been used for proselytizing among Persian-speaking Jews in Iran or Persianate Central Asia. Employing a sophisticated strategy of positive argument, Muslim missionaries, popular preachers, and professional storytellers used the Islamic ascension narrative as a vehicle for addressing different religious groups by manipulating it in ways that stressed common beliefs and shared truths. The apocalyptic nature of the ascension narrative, with its emphasis on personal experience, visionary imagination, and prophetic revelation, would have appealed to members of religious communities who were already familiar with the genre in their own traditions and who believed that by accepting Islam they would be preserving their own beliefs and practices in an "updated" Islamic framework.

As for the Timurid-era manuscript itself, I have suggested that its production under elite or royal patronage served a dual and contradictory purpose. On the one hand, the Turkic-language text, transcribed in the revered Uighur script, represented for the Timurids a cultural artifact that expressed their adherence to the *törä,* or Turko-Mongolian custom, which had been championed by their eponymous founder, Temür, and which they were committed to uphold as a marker of their "Chaghatay" identity. On the other hand, since it consisted of what were arguably the two most popular religious texts in the medieval eastern Islamic world, the lavishly illustrated manuscript provided tangible evidence of the Timurids' newly professed commitment to Islam. A paradox, perhaps, but one that captures nicely the dual cultural loyalties of the Timurids, whose checkered transition from a nomadic empire organized according to Chinggisid principles to a centralized Persianate polity governed by Islamic law is reflected in the complex historical, cultural, and artistic legacy they left behind for us to ponder.

Notes

1. For the history of the French acquisition of the manuscript in the seventeenth century, see Abel Pavet de Courteille, ed. and trans., *Mirâdj-nâmeh: Récit de l'ascension de Mahomet au ciel composé A.H. 840 (1436/1437). Texte turk-oriental, publié pour la première fois d'après le manuscrit ouïgour de la Bibliothèque Nationale et traduit en français* (Paris, 1882; repr. ed., Amsterdam: Philo, 1975), i–xiv; Francis Richard, *Splendeurs persanes: Manuscrits du XIIe au XVIIe siècle* (Paris: Bibliothèque nationale de France, 1997), 77; and Christiane Gruber, *The Timurid Book of Ascension (Miʿrajnama): A Study of Text and Image in a Pan-Asian Context* (Valencia: Patrimonio Ediciones, 2008), app. 4, 391–401.

2. For a reproduction of the illustrations, see Marie-Rose Séguy, *The Miraculous Journey of Mahomet: "Mirâj Nâmeh," Bibliothèque Nationale, Paris (Manuscrit Supplément Turc 190)*, trans. Richard Pevear (New York: George Braziller, 1977). For a recent discussion of the iconography, see Gruber, *Timurid Book of Ascension*, chaps. 3–4.

3. The title of the work is provided in its introduction—see W. M. Thackston, "The Paris *Miʿrājnāma*," in "Annemarie Schimmel Festschrift: Essays Presented to Annemarie Schimmel on the Occasion of Her Retirement from Harvard University by Her Colleagues, Students and Friends," ed. Maria Eva Subtelny, special issue, *Journal of Turkish Studies* 18 (1994): 265; and Max Scherberger, ed. and trans., *Das Miʿrāğnāme: Die Himmel- und Höllenfahrt des Propheten Muḥammad in der osttürkischen Überlieferung*, Arbeitsmaterialien zum Orient 14 (Würzburg: Ergon, 2003), 48, Tafel 1 (fol. 1v), line 9.

4. For a description of the manuscript, see Pavet de Courteille, *Mirâdj-nâmeh*, xv–xvii; E. Blochet, *Catalogue des manuscrits turcs*, 2 vols. (Paris: Bibliothèque nationale de France, 1932–1933), 1:254–255; Richard, *Splendeurs persanes*, 77; Thackston, "Paris *Miʿrājnāma*," 263; and Scherberger, *Das Miʿrāğnāme*, 38–40. Despite the fact that the scribe's name is clearly written Harī-Malik Bakhshi in the colophon, many scholars have incorrectly shortened it to Malik Bakhshi, while others misread it as Abū Malik Bakhshi—see Pavet de Courteille, *Mirâdj-nâmeh*, xv; Emil Esin, "The Bakhshi in the 14th to 16th Centuries: The Masters of the Pre-Muslim Tradition of the Arts of the Book in Central Asia," in *The Arts of the Book in Central Asia, 14th–16th Centuries*, ed. Basil Gray (London: Serindia; Paris: UNESCO, 1979), 288 (citing O. Sertkaya); and Gruber, *Timurid Book of Ascension*, 274–275. It is unclear why Max Scherberger, the most recent editor and translator of the Timurid *Miʿrājnāma*, should refer to him as Muḥammad Malik Bakhshi, since most of the sources he cites for this do not even give his name in this form—see Scherberger, *Das Miʿrāğnāme*, 38. The information in Séguy's *Miraculous Journey of Mahomet* is to be avoided altogether (see also n. 6 below); the same applies to Metin Akar's *Türk edebiyatında manzum Mi'râc-nâmeler* (Ankara: Kültür ve Turizm Bakanlığı, 1987), a popular publication that incorrectly states that the Timurid manuscript was copied in Merv (p. 99).

The Timurid *Miʿrājnāma* also exists in an Arabic-script copy completed in Cairo in 917/1511 by a certain Nūr al-Dīn ʿAlī b. Kichkinä Sayyid ʿAlī al-Ṭāliqānī (MS, Istanbul, Süleymaniye Library, Fatih 2848). It, too, contains a translation of ʿAṭṭār's *Tadhkirat al-awliyāʾ*. However, the text is not identical with that of the Timurid *Miʿrājnāma*, and the Middle Turkic idiom in which it is written is closer to classical Chaghatay. For a description of the manuscript, see Hellmut Ritter, "Philologika XIV. Farīduddīn ʿAṭṭār. II," *Oriens* 11 (1958): 70; János Eckmann, "Die kiptschakische Literatur," in *Philologiae Turcicae Fundamenta*, vol. 2, ed. Louis Bazin et al. (Wiesbaden: Franz Steiner, 1964), 292; and Scherberger, *Das Miʿrāğnāme*, 36–38.

5. Thackston, "Paris *Miʿrājnāma*," 265 (fol. 1b); and Scherberger, *Das Miʿrāğnāme*, 48, Tafel 1 (fol. 1v), lines 9–10. In transliterating Turkic words, I have not indicated long vowels and I have maintained only a degree of vowel harmony. Persian and Arabic words in Middle Turkic have been transliterated according to the *International Journal of Middle East Studies* system for transliterating Arabic followed in this volume.

6. See E. Blochet, "Études sur l'histoire religieuse de l'Iran, II: L'ascension au ciel du prophète Mohammed," *Revue de l'histoire des religions* 40 (1899): 2 n. 1 ("Comme tous les livres ouïgours, il est traduit du persan"); and Blochet, *Catalogue*, vol. 1:254 ("vraisemblable-

ment écrit en persan"). Séguy's statement that the *Miʿrājnāma* was translated directly from an Arabic original is patently incorrect—see Séguy, *Miraculous Journey of Mahomet,* 8.

7. Thackston, "Paris *Miʿrājnāma,*" 277 (fol. 44b); and Scherberger, *Das Miʿrāǧnāme,* 68, Tafel 38 (fol. 44r), line 4. János Eckmann had already drawn attention to this reference—see János Eckmann, ed., *Nehcü'l-feradis,* 3 vols. (Ankara: Türk Tarih Kurumu Basımevi, 1956–1998), vol. 1:x–xi.

8. For Persian literary influence on the emerging Eastern Turkic literatures, and the translation and/or adaptation into Turkic languages of such classics of Persian literature as Niẓāmī's *Khusraw wa Shīrīn* and Saʿdī's *Gulistān,* see Eckmann, "Die kiptschakische Literatur," 280, 298; and János Eckmann, "Die tschaghataische Literatur," in *Philologiae Turcicae Fundamenta,* vol. 2, ed. Louis Bazin et al. (Wiesbaden: Franz Steiner, 1964), 311, 318ff.

9. Pavet de Courteille, *Mirâdj-nâmeh,* xvii–xviii.

10. In the opinion of Blochet, the Timurid *Miʿrājnāma* "n'a d'ailleurs aucune valeur originale" and would never have been published (by Pavet de Courteille) if it had not been written in Uighur characters—see Blochet, "Études sur l'histoire religieuse," 2 n. 1.

11. The source of this misinformation, which has been repeated by many art historians, appears to have been Marie-Rose Séguy—see Séguy, *Miraculous Journey of Mahomet,* 7–8. For others, see Scherberger, *Das Miʿrāǧnāme,* 32 n. 134.

12. For a comprehensive definition of the genre of apocalyptic or revelatory literature, see John J. Collins, "Towards the Morphology of the Genre," in "Apocalypse: The Morphology of a Genre," ed. John J. Collins, special issue, *Semeia* 14 (1979): 5–9; and the chapter by Roberto Tottoli in this volume. For the Hebrew Book of Enoch, see P. Alexander, trans., "3 (Hebrew Apocalypse of) Enoch (Fifth–Sixth Century A. D.): A New Translation and Introduction," in *The Old Testament Pseudepigrapha,* Vol. 1, *Apocalyptic Literature and Testaments,* ed. James H. Charlesworth (New York: Doubleday, 1983), 255ff. The study of the affinities between Jewish and Islamic apocalyptic literature, which has scarcely been undertaken, would yield many important insights into the structure and characteristic features of the Islamic ascension narrative, and it would also bring it into the wider conversation about the Near Eastern apocalypse, from which it is usually excluded.

13. The introduction to the translation of the *Tadhkirat al-awliyā'* contains similar wording: "We have rendered this book into the Turkish language from Persian." See n. 9 above. A linguistic and stylistic comparison of the two translations, which to my knowledge has never been attempted, might possibly reveal whether they were translated by the same person.

14. See Scherberger, *Das Miʿrāǧnāme,* 122, 131.

15. See Eckmann, *Nehcü'l-feradis,* vol. 1:x–xi. The work is sometimes attributed to a certain Maḥmūd b. ʿAlī al-Sarā'ī al-Kerderī, although the evidence for this is rather flimsy—see Eckmann, "Die kiptschakische Literatur," 287, 290.

16. See Eckmann, *Nehcü'l-feradis,* vol. 1:xi–xii; and Eckmann, "Die kiptschakische Literatur," 291. According to Max Scherberger, "No definitive statement regarding the role of the [*Nahj al-farādīs*] in the formation of the [*Miʿrājnāma*] can be made"—see Scherberger, *Das Miʿrāǧnāme,* 36.

17. For a discussion of the contents of the work, see Eckmann, "Die kiptschakische Literatur," 287–288. For the *miʿrāj* account, see Eckmann, *Nehcü'l-ferādīs,* vol. 2:38–50 (ch. 1, sections 7–8).

18. For purposes of comparison, the prophets who occupy the heavenly spheres in the Timurid *Miʿrājnāma* are: first heaven—Adam; second heaven—John the Baptist and his father Zachariah; third heaven—Jacob, Joseph, David, and Solomon; fourth heaven—no prophet mentioned; fifth heaven—Ishmael, Isaac, Aaron, and Lot; sixth heaven—Moses, Noah, and Enoch; seventh heaven—Abraham. In the Khwarazmian Turkic *Nahj al-farādīs:* first heaven—Adam; second heaven—Jesus and John the Baptist; third heaven—Joseph; fourth heaven—Enoch; fifth heaven—Aaron; sixth heaven—Moses; seventh heaven—Abraham. See Eckmann, *Nehcü'l-ferādīs,* vol. 2:39–41. For these and other differences, see Scherberger, *Das Miʿrāǧnāme,* 35–36.

19. See Muḥammad b. Jarīr al-Ṭabarī, *Jāmiʿ al-bayān ʿan ta'wīl āy al-Qur'ān,* 30 vols. in 12 (Cairo: Muṣṭafā al-Bābī al-Ḥalabī, 1388/1968), vol. 15:15; and Thackston, "Paris *Miʿrājnāma,*"

266 n. 16. For the form of the Tradition in al-Baghawī, which reflects the more common versions found in the canonical compilations of hadiths, see Abū Muḥammad al-Ḥusayn b. Masʿūd al-Baghawī, *Maṣābīḥ al-sunna,* ed. Yūsuf ʿAbd al-Raḥmān al-Marʿashlī, Muḥammad Salīm Ibrāhīm Samāra, and Jamāl Ḥamdī al-Dhahabī, 4 vols (Beirut: Dār al-Maʿrifa, 1407/1987), vol. 4:76; and Rifʿat Fawzī ʿAbd al-Muṭṭalib, *Aḥādīth al-isrāʾ wa al-miʿrāj: Dirāsa tawthīqiyya* (Cairo: Maktabat al-Khānjī, 1400/1980), 18, 22, 25.

20. See Eckmann, *Nehcü'l-feradis,* vol. 1:x–xi; and Eckmann, "Die kiptschakische Literatur," 287, 291. I am thus in agreement with Max Scherberger's conclusion that "the widespread notion that the [Timurid *Miʿrājnāma*] was translated from a Persian version of the [Khwarazmian *Nahj al-farādīs*] must be revised." See Scherberger, *Das Miʿrāğnāme,* 130.

21. For other manuscripts with this title (all apparently dating from the fourteenth century), see Eckmann, "Die kiptschakische Literatur," 290; and János Eckmann, "Nehcü'l-Feradis'in bilinmiyen bir yazması," in János Eckmann, *Harezm, Kipçak ve Çağatay Türkçesi üzerine araştırmalar,* ed. Osman Fikri Sertkaya (Ankara: Türk Dil Kurumu, 1996), 49–51.

22. See Gottfried Hagen, "Translations and Translators in a Multilingual Society: A Case Study of Persian-Ottoman Translations, Late Fifteenth to Early Seventeenth Century," *Eurasian Studies* 2, no. 1 (2003): 130–133.

23. See Gisèle Besson and Michèle Brossard-Dandré, eds. and trans., *Le livre de l'échelle de Mahomet (Liber Scale Machometi): Édition nouvelle* (Paris: Le Livre de Poche, 1991); and Reginald Hyatte, trans., *The Prophet of Islam in Old French: "The Romance of Muhammad" (1258) and "The Book of Muhammad's Ladder" (1264)* (Leiden: Brill, 1997).

24. See, for example, John V. Tolan, *Saracens: Islam in the Medieval European Imagination* (New York: Columbia University Press, 2002), 193.

25. See my forthcoming article, "'Holy, Holy, Holy': The Book of Muhammad's Ladder as Missionary Text among Christians of Muslim Spain."

26. See Maria E. Subtelny, *Timurids in Transition: Turko-Persian Politics and Acculturation in Medieval Iran* (Leiden: Brill, 2007), 25.

27. Maria Eva Subtelny and Anas B. Khalidov, "The Curriculum of Islamic Higher Learning in Timurid Iran in the Light of the Sunni Revival under Shāh-Rukh," *Journal of the American Oriental Society* 115, no. 2 (1995): 211–214, 218; and Maria Eva Subtelny, "The Sunni Revival under Shāh-Rukh and Its Promoters: A Study of the Connection between Ideology and Higher Learning in Timurid Iran," in *Proceedings of the 27th Meeting of Haneda Memorial Hall: Symposium on Central Asia and Iran, August 30, 1993* (Kyoto: Haneda Memorial Hall, Institute of Inner Asian Studies, Kyoto University, 1994), 15–17.

28. For the correspondence, which was in Persian and Arabic and concerned chiefly with the creation of favorable conditions for trade between the two realms, see Ralph Kauz, *Politik und Handel zwischen Ming und Timuriden: China, Iran und Zentralasien im Spätmittelalter* (Wiesbaden: Reichert, 2005), 101–106.

29. For a discussion of the Timurid *törä* and its relationship to the Chinggisid *yasa* on the one hand and to Islamic law on the other, see Subtelny, *Timurids in Transition,* 15–18, 24–28.

30. See Subtelny, *Timurids in Transition,* 68–69. The Turkic term *bakhshi* derives from the ancient Chinese title *bakşi* (modern Chinese *bóşì*). The older opinion that it derives from Sanskrit *bhikṣu,* meaning a Buddhist monk or mendicant, has now been discarded in favor of the Chinese etymology. See Gerhard Doerfer, *Türkische und mongolische Elemente im Neupersischen: Unter besonderer Berücksichtigung älterer neupersischer Geschichtsquellen, vor allem der Mongolen- und Timuridenzeit,* 4 vols. (Wiesbaden: Franz Steiner, 1963–1975), vol. 2:271–277, s.v. *baḫšī.* The famous Chaghatay poet Mīr ʿAlīshīr Uighur, known by the pen-name Nawāʾī, was descended from a family of Uighur *bakhshis*—see Maria Eva Subtelny, "ʿAlī Shīr Nawāʾī: *Bakhshī* and *Beg,*" in "Eucharisterion: Essays Presented to Omeljan Pritsak on His Sixtieth Birthday by His Colleagues and Students," ed. Ihor Ševčenko and Frank E. Sysyn, special issue, *Harvard Ukrainian Studies* 3–4 (1979–1980), 2:799. For an updated reference, see Mirza Haydar Dughlat, *Tarikh-i Rashidi: A History of the Khans of Moghulistan,* ed. and trans. W. M. Thackston, 2 vols. (Cambridge, Mass.: Department of Near Eastern Languages and Civiliza-

tions, Harvard University, 1996), vol. 2:126. It might be noted in passing that the use of the Uighur script by scribes whose names contained the title *bakhshi* had nothing to do with Buddhist influence in the Timurid realm, as some have suggested. Although the Uighur scribes in various Mongol realms may have been Buddhists, they could also have been Nestorian Christians or Muslims. As for the Turkic scribes in the Timurid administrations, they were undoubtedly Muslim.

31. The suggestion that Harī-Malik Bakhshi is to be identified with Amīr Harī-Malik, the son of Mūsāka Nukuz, one of Ulug Beg's leading commanders, is unsupported by the available sources—see Thackston, "Paris *Miʿrājnāma*," 263; and Richard, *Splendeurs persanes*, 77. As indicated by his title, Amīr Harī-Malik was a military commander whose name never appears with the scribal title *bakhshi*. There is also no evident basis for identifying Harī-Malik Bakhshi with the Muḥammad Bakhshi who served as Timurid envoy to the Ming emperor, as their names are clearly different. Christiane Gruber's attempted identification of "Malik Bakhshi" not only with the aforementioned Amīr Harī-Malik (whom she in turn identifies with the anonymous scribe of a *soyurghal* document issued by Shāhrukh), but also with the envoy Muḥammad Bakhshi, is based on a number of unproven assumptions—see Gruber, *Timurid Book of Ascension*, 274–275. For the *soyurghal* document she cites, which is dated 825/1422, see J. Deny, "Un *soyurgal* du Timouride Šāhruḫ en écriture ouigoure," *Journal asiatique* 245, no. 3 (1957): 255. Unfortunately, Max Scherberger has confused the matter further by calling him Muḥammad Malik Bakhshi—see Scherberger, *Das Miʿrāğnāme*, 38; and n. 4 above.

32. See Subtelny, *Timurids in Transition*, 40.

33. Ibn ʿArabshāh, *ʿAjā'ib al-maqdūr fī nawā'ib Taymūr*, ed. Aḥmad Fā'iz al-Ḥimṣī (Beirut: Mu'assasat al-Risāla, 1407/1986), 479.

34. For a list, see Tourkhan Gandjeï, "Note on the Colophon of the *Laṭāfat-nāma* in Uighur Characters from the Kabul Museum," *Annali dell'Istituto Universitario Orientale di Napoli*, n.s., 14 (1964): 162.

35. See [Yūsuf Khāṣṣ Ḥājib], *Kutadgu bilig*, vol. 1, *Viyana nüshası*, facsimile ed. (Istanbul: Alâeddin Kıral, 1942), 14–15. For the ideological significance of the work, see Yūsuf Khāṣṣ Ḥājib, *Wisdom of Royal Glory (Kutadgu Bilig): A Turko-Islamic Mirror for Princes*, trans. Robert Dankoff (Chicago: University of Chicago Press, 1983), 1–10; and Thomas W. Lentz and Glenn D. Lowry, *Timur and the Princely Vision: Persian Art and Culture in the Fifteenth Century* (Los Angeles: Los Angeles County Museum of Art; Washington, D.C.: Arthur M. Sackler Gallery, Smithsonian Institution, and Smithsonian Institution Press, 1989), 230.

36. For the latter work, see Farīd al-Dīn Nīshāpūrī ʿAṭṭār, *Tadhkirat al-awliyā'*, ed. Muḥammad Istiʿlāmī (repr. ed., Tehran: Kitābkhāna-i Millī-i Īrān, 1382/2003–2004); and A. J. Arberry, trans., *Muslim Saints and Mystics: Episodes from the Tadhkirat al-Auliya' ("Memorial of the Saints") by Farid al-Din Attar* (London: Routledge and Kegan Paul, 1966; repr. ed., 1979).

37. I concur on this point with Thomas Lentz and Glenn Lowry, who state that "No manuscript more tellingly reveals the Timurid's [read: Timurids'] ideological duality"—see Lentz and Lowry, *Timur and the Princely Vision*, 97.

38. On this point, see Ghiyāth al-Dīn b. Humām al-Dīn al-Ḥusaynī Khwāndamīr, *Tārīkh-i Ḥabīb al-siyar fī akhbār afrād-i bashar*, ed. Jalāl al-Dīn Humā'ī, 4 vols. (Tehran: Khayyām, 1333/1954–1955; repr. ed., 1362/1984), vol. 4:394; Ivan Stchoukine, "Les images de Sultân Hosayn dans un manuscrit de son *Dîvân* de 897/1492," *Syria* 53 (1976): 146; and *Muʿizz al-ansāb (Proslavliaiushchee genealogii)*, facsimile ed. and trans. Sh. Kh. Vokhidov (Alma Ata: Daik, 2006), 9–10.

39. See Josef van Ess, "Le *miʿrāğ* et la vision de Dieu dans les premières spéculations théologiques en Islam," in *Le voyage initiatique en terre d'Islam: Ascensions célestes et itinéraires spirituels*, ed. Mohammad Ali Amir-Moezzi (Louvain: Peeters, 1996), 55–56; and Josef van Ess, *Theologie und Gesellschaft im 2. und 3. Jahrhundert Hidschra: Eine Geschichte des religiösen Denkens im frühen Islam*, 6 vols. (Berlin: Walter de Gruyter, 1991–1997), vol. 4:387–388. The Qur'an contains several allusions to Muḥammad's critics calling for a miraculous sign, such as a heavenly ascension or a book, to prove the truth of his prophesy. Qur'an 17:90–93 states: "They say, 'We shall not believe in you until you . . . mount [a ladder] to the sky (*tarqā fī al-*

samā'). And we will not even believe in your mounting (*li-ruqiyyika*) until you send down to us a book (*kitāban*) that we may read.'" The divine response to calls for such prophetic miracles is that all miracles come from God, and if God wanted to, He could make believers of the skeptics without the aid of any signs. Thus Qur'an 6:35 states: "If their spurning is hard on you, yet even if you were able to seek . . . a ladder (*sullaman*) to the sky and bring them a sign, [what would it mean]? If God wills, He could bring them all to true guidance. So do not be among those who are swayed by ignorance." The Prophet's ascension was and continues to be celebrated in most Islamic cultures, usually on the eve of the twenty-seventh of the lunar month of Rajab. For the term theologumenon, which refers to a theological point that does not necessarily represent a dogmatic teaching, but that is nevertheless "the outcome and expression of an endeavour to understand the faith by establishing connections between binding doctrines of faith," see Richard N. Soulen and R. Kendall Soulen, *Handbook of Biblical Criticism*, 3rd rev. ed. (Louisville, Ky.: Westminster John Knox Press, 2001), 196.

40. An allusion to Qur'an 12:111.

41. [ʿAbd al-Mālik] Ibn Hishām, *al-Sīra al-nabawiyya*, ed. Muṣṭafā al-Saqqā, Ibrāhīm al-Abyārī, and ʿAbd al-Ḥafīẓ Shalabī, 4 vols. (repr. ed., Beirut: Dār Iḥyā' al-Turāth al-ʿArabī, n.d.), 2:37; and Alfred Guillaume, trans., *The Life of Muhammad: A Translation of Isḥāq's* Sīrat Rasūl Allāh (London: Oxford University Press, 1955), 181.

42. For an explicit statement to this effect in a version of the ascension narrative, see al-Rabghūzī, *The Stories of the Prophets: Qiṣaṣ al-Anbiyā'. An Eastern Turkish Version*, ed. H. E. Boeschoten, M. Vandamme, and S. Tezcan, trans. H. E. Boeschoten, J. O'Kane, and M. Vandamme, 2 vols. (Leiden: E. J. Brill, 1995), vol. 2:617–621. The orthodox view is that the Prophet's ascension was in body and not just in spirit.

43. Abū Bakr apparently received the epithet al-Ṣiddīq (The one who testifies to the truth) on account of his belief in the Prophet's ascension—see Guillaume, *Life of Muhammad*, 183.

44. For example, *Kitāb-i Miʿrājnāma*, MS, Istanbul, Süleymaniye Library, Ayasofya 3441, fols. 11v–12r (where the voices are those of Jews, Zoroastrians, Christians, and polytheists); and Mûsâ b. Hacı Hüseyin el-İznikî, *Miʿrac*, trans. Hikmet Özdemir (Istanbul: Gonca, 1986), 40 (where the voices are those of Jews, Christians, and "the world"). See also Frederick Colby, "Constructing an Islamic Ascension Narrative: The Interplay of Official and Popular Culture in Pseudo-Ibn ʿAbbās" (Ph.D. diss., Duke University, 2002), 444; and Brooke Olson Vuckovic, *Heavenly Journeys, Earthly Concerns* (New York: Routledge, 2005), 29. It does not occur, however, in the Timurid *Miʿrājnāma*.

45. See Julian Millie, "The Narrative Potential of Mi'râj: Two Contexts for Its Interpretation," in *Epic Adventures: Heroic Narrative in the Oral Performance Traditions of Four Continents*, ed. Jan Jansen and Henk M. J. Maier (Münster: LIT, 2004), 128–139. For the role of popular preachers and storytellers called *quṣṣāṣ* in the transmission of the ascension narrative, see Richard Hartmann, "Die Himmelsreise Muhammeds und ihre Bedeutung in der Religion des Islam," in "Über die Vorstellungen von der Himmelsreise der Seele," special issue, *Vorträge der Bibliothek Warburg* 8 (1928–1929): 46–49. See also *The Encyclopaedia of Islam*, new ed., s.v. "Ḳāṣṣ."

46. This was the method employed by Pavet de Courteille, who believed that the absence of the description of the fourth heaven in the Timurid *Miʿrājnāma* was a lacuna in the Timurid-era manuscript, which he filled in with the description of the fourth heaven from the Turkish translation of the Persian *Maʿārij al-nubuwwa fī madārij al-futuwwa* by the Timurid traditionist Muʿīn al-Dīn Muḥammad Amīn al-Farāhī, known as Miskīn (d. 907/1501–1502), as well as from a sixteenth-century Ottoman Turkish version of the *miʿrāj* account. See Pavet de Courteille, *Mirâdj-nâmeh*, xxi–xxii, 42–43, 51–53. For a discussion of Miskīn's text, see Özgen Felek's chapter in this volume. Not only was this a distortion of the original intent of the version in the Timurid *Miʿrājnāma*, but it made no sense, since in the first instance, the fourth heaven was occupied by Moses, who in the Timurid *Miʿrājnāma* was already represented in the sixth heaven, while in the second instance, the fourth heaven was occupied by David and Solomon, who in the Timurid *Miʿrājnāma* were already associated with the third heaven! The French Islamicist Jamel Eddine Bencheikh went even further, producing a composite text of the ascension narrative in French, in

which he conflated a number of Arabic versions dating from various periods and including the Latin Book of Muḥammad's Ladder. See Jamel Eddine Bencheikh, comp. and trans., *Le voyage nocturne de Mahomet* (Paris: Imprimerie Nationale, 1988), 233–234, 238.

47. See Richard W. Bulliet, *Conversion to Islam in the Medieval Period: An Essay in Quantitative History* (Cambridge, Mass.: Harvard University Press, 1979). For a discussion of approaches to the history of conversion in Islam, see R. Stephen Humphreys, *Islamic History: A Framework for Inquiry,* rev. ed. (Princeton, N.J.: Princeton University Press, 1991), 273–283; and Devin DeWeese, *Islamization and Native Religion in the Golden Horde: Baba Tükles and Conversion to Islam in Historical and Epic Tradition* (University Park: Pennsylvania State University Press, 1994), 17–27.

48. DeWeese, *Islamization and Native Religion,* 25.

49. The technical term for missionary activity in Islam is *daʿwa,* meaning "call" or "invitation."

50. For Llull's views on conversion, which were at variance with contemporary Christian missionary strategies, see Tolan, *Saracens,* 260; and Harvey J. Hames, *The Art of Conversion: Christianity and Kabbalah in the Thirteenth Century* (Leiden: Brill, 2000), 2. It is not out of the question that Llull was influenced by Islamic techniques of conversion, as he had studied Arabic and was very familiar with Islam.

51. See Jamsheed K. Choksy, *Conflict and Cooperation: Zoroastrian Subalterns and Muslim Elites in Medieval Iranian Society* (New York: Columbia University Press, 1977), 76–93.

52. For a discussion of the qur'anic verse and its interpretations, see Yohanan Friedmann, *Tolerance and Coercion in Islam: Interfaith Relations in the Muslim Tradition* (Cambridge: Cambridge University Press, 2003), 94–106. It is interesting to note that the Latin translation of the Book of Muḥammad's Ladder from Spain ends, appropriately enough, with a reference to this qur'anic verse: "Bene credentes non coactione ulla sed uoluntate propria credere bene debent" (Those who would believe should do so of their own accord and not because of any coercion)—see Besson and Brossard-Dandré, *Le livre de l'échelle,* 338.

53. See Thackston, "Paris *Miʿrājnāma,*" 264.

54. On this point see DeWeese, *Islamization and Native Religion,* 20.

55. See D. DeWeese, "Sayyid ʿAlī Hamadānī and Kubrawī Hagiographical Traditions," in *The Legacy of Mediaeval Persian Sufism,* ed. Leonard Lewisohn (London: Khaniqahi Nimatullahi Publications, 1992), 149–150; Devin DeWeese, "Yasavian Legends on the Islamization of Turkistan," in *Aspects of Altaic Civilization, III: Proceedings of the Thirtieth Meeting of the Permanent International Altaistic Conference, Indiana University, Bloomington, Indiana, June 19–25, 1987,* ed. Denis Sinor (Bloomington, Ind.: Research Institute for Inner Asian Studies, Indiana University, 1990), 1–3; and DeWeese, *Islamization and Native Religion,* 25 (this is in fact the thesis of the book). The *miʿrāj* is mentioned, for example, in the legendary tale of Satuq Bughra Khan, the first Karakhanid ruler to convert to Islam, whose soul Muḥammad encounters among the prophets he meets during his ascension, and who the angel Gabriel explains will one day spread Islam in Turkestan—see Julian Baldick, *Imaginary Muslims: The Uwaysi Sufis of Central Asia* (New York: New York University Press, 1993), 77. The account of the *miʿrāj* was also included in the biography of the Prophet in the Middle Turkic translation of prophetic legends by al-Rabghūzī (d. 1310)—see al-Rabghūzī, *Stories of the Prophets,* vol. 1:475–498 (Turkic text), vol. 2:593–623 (trans.).

56. See Walter J. Fischel, "Isfahān: The Story of a Jewish Community in Persia," in *The Joshua Starr Memorial Volume: Studies in History and Philology* (New York: Conference on Jewish Relations, 1953), 111ff.; Walter J. Fischel, "The Jews of Central Asia (Khorasan) in Medieval Hebrew and Islamic Literature," *Historia Judaica* 7, no. 1 (1945): 35–43; Moshe Gil, *Jews in Islamic Countries in the Middle Ages,* trans. David Strassler (Leiden: Brill, 2004), 522–532; and Michael Shterenshis, *Tamerlane and the Jews* (London: RoutledgeCurzon, 2002), 57–63. The compilation of Hebrew-Persian dictionaries intended for Jews studying the Torah and other sacred texts attests to the fact that Persian was the mother tongue of Jews even in such regions as Khwarazm and Azerbaijan in the fourteenth and fifteenth centuries. See Wilhelm Bacher,

Ein hebräisch-persisches Wörterbuch aus dem vierzehnten Jahrhundert (Strassburg: Karl Trübner, 1900), 10; and Wilhelm Bacher, "Ein hebräisch-persisches Wörterbuch aus dem 15. Jahrhundert," *Zeitschrift für die alttestamentliche Wissenschaft* 16 (1896): 241.

57. For the popularity of the *Maṣābīḥ al-sunna* in the curriculum of Islamic religious studies in early fifteenth-century Iran and Central Asia, see Subtelny and Khalidov, "Curriculum of Islamic Higher Learning," 228–229, nos. 1.39, 2.3.

58. Bulliet, *Conversion to Islam*, 44–52; and Richard W. Bulliet, "Conversion to Islam and the Emergence of a Muslim Society in Iran," in *Conversion to Islam*, ed. Nehemia Levtzion (New York: Holmes and Meier, 1979), 35, 47.

59. For the narreme, see Pavet de Courteille, *Mirâdj-nâmeh*, 41–43 (fols. 67v–68r) (Turkic text in Arabic script), 27–28 (French trans.); Thackston, "Paris *Miʿrājnāma*," 284–285; and Scherberger, *Das Miʿrāğnāme*, 79–80, Tafel 58A–58B (transliterated Turkic text), 114–115 (German trans.), 152–153 (facsimile ed.). Although I have consulted all three translations, I am relying on my own rendering, which in some instances differs from that of the above-mentioned scholars.

60. The reference to the size or height of the Jews' houses is unclear. Thackston interpreted the Turkic word *täng* to mean "strange," "wonderful," and he translated the phrase to mean that the Jews' houses had strange shapes, which does not make sense in view of the Jews' response—see Thackston, "Paris *Miʿrājnāma*," 284. Pavet de Courteille's interpretion that all the houses "had exactly the same dimensions" would appear to be closer to the mark—see Pavet de Courteille, *Mirâdj-nâmeh*, 27; and Scherberger, *Das Miʿrāğnāme*, 115, Tafel 58A, lines 15–16. My translation of the phrase to mean that all the houses were of the same height is corroborated by other sources, which provide the Jews' own explanation that they did not build their houses higher than their neighbors' so as not to deprive them of sunlight or prevent the nightly breeze from reaching everyone. See, for example, el-İznikî, *Miʿrac*, 151; Brannon M. Wheeler, "The Prophet Muḥammad Dhu al-Qarnayn: His Journey to the Cities at the Ends of the Earth," in "The Acts of Alexander the Great: The Unique Monument of Medieval Toreutics Found in the Village Muzhi of Yamal-Nenetz Autonomic District. Proceedings of the Colloquium Held by the Saint-Petersburg Society for Byzantine and Slavic Studies, September 10–12th, 1998" (Russian title page: "Deianiia tsaria Aleksandra"), ed. C. C. Akentiev and B. I. Marshak, special issue, *Byzantinorossica/Vizantinorossika* 2 (2003): 207, 209 (based on al-Qazwīnī); and al-Rabghūzī, *Stories of the Prophets*, vol. 2:616.

61. It is noteworthy that these two negative character traits are treated in some detail in the fourth chapter (sections 4 and 8) of the Khwarazmian Turkish *Nahj al-farādīs* (dated 1360), which is devoted to those things that prevent a person from entering Paradise—see Eckmann, *Nehcü'l-ferādīs*, vol. 2:257ff., vol. 2:286ff.

62. The explanation that walking the distance to their places of worship is a meritorious act is reminiscent of the variations on the cycle of prophetic Traditions that recommend walking to the mosque from a distant place of habitation as one of the expiatory actions (*kaffārāt*). See Daniel Gimaret, "Au coeur du *Miʿrāğ*, un hadith interpolé," in *Le voyage initiatique en terre d'Islam: Ascensions célestes et itinéraires spirituels*, ed. Mohammad Ali Amir-Moezzi (Louvain: Peeters, 1996), 77–78.

63. The Jews' assurances that they fulfill these obligations would seem to be in response to Qur'an 2:83, which was addressed to the Children of Israel (Banū Isrā'īl) regarding their failure to fulfill their covenantal obligations, except for a small number among them (*illā qalīlan minkum*). It is noteworthy that the obligation to honor one's mother and father is also treated in a separate chapter (ch. 3, sec. 6) of the Khwarazmian Turkic *Nahj al-farādīs*—see Eckmann, *Nehcü'l-ferādīs*, vol. 2:195ff.; and Eckmann, "Die kiptschakische Literatur," 288–290.

64. In qur'anic usage, *īmān* is the customary term for faith or belief in Islam—see Hanna E. Kassis, *A Concordance of the Qur'an* (Berkeley and Los Angeles: University of California Press, 1983), 159.

65. The Arabic root *ṭwʿ* occurs frequently in the Qur'an to denote willing or voluntary obedience to God, the Prophet, and Islamic prescriptions, such as payment of the alms tax. See Kassis, *Concordance of the Qur'an*, 1240–1242. Pavet de Courteille translated the term *ṭāʿat* as "la pratique du culte," which I believe conveys the notion well.

66. Pavet de Courteille, *Mirâdj-nâmeh,* 43 (Turkic text), 28 (French trans.); Thackston, "Paris *Miʿrājnāma,*" 284–285; and Scherberger, *Das Miʿrāğnāme,* 80, Tafel 58B, lines 13–17.

67. For the role of Ibn ʿAbbās in the transmission of the narrative, see Colby, "Constructing an Islamic Ascension Narrative," 80–87; and Frederick Colby, *Narrating Muḥammad's Night Journey: Tracing the Development of the Ibn ʿAbbās Ascension Discourse* (Albany: State University of New York Press, 2008).

68. *Kitāb-i Miʿrājnāma,* Ayasofya 3441, fols. 57v–58r. Christiane Gruber has interpreted the date in the colophon, which is not entirely legible, as 685/1286, but it could also be read 805/1402. See Christiane Gruber, *The Ilkhanid Book of Ascension: A Persian-Sunni Devotional Tale* (London: I. B. Tauris, 2009). The transmitter of the narrative was a certain Khwāja Imām Muḥammad b. Muḥammad b. ʿAbd al-Malik al-Balkhī—see Colby, "Constructing an Islamic Ascension Narrative," 306–309. I am grateful to Frederick Colby for providing me with a photocopy of the manuscript and to Christiane Gruber for sharing her study and translation of the Persian text.

In this version, which is not as extended as the version in the Timurid *Miʿrājnāma,* the Jews are not the only ones who are called "righteous," since Muḥammad visits them only after having visited another "righteous people," who inhabit the city of Jābalqā in the east, and who might be identified as Christians, seeing as the narrative makes frequent reference to Christians and the Gospel. These people never lie, eat unlawful food, or even get sick, since illness is interpreted as a punishment for sin. Muḥammad invites them to accept Islam and they too become members of his community.

69. For the qur'anic reference, see below.

70. See el-İznikî, *Miʿrac,* 148–156. For this version, see Colby, "Constructing an Islamic Ascension Narrative," 309–317. Most of the manuscripts of this translation are of fairly recent vintage, the oldest dating from 1095/1684. I have used the modern Turkish translation.

71. The motif of the river of sand occurs in the classical epic of Alexander, for which see Richard Stoneman, trans., *The Greek Alexander Romance* (London: Penguin Books, 1991), 175; and the discussion below.

72. The allusion was believed to be to Deut. 18:15 (addressed to Moses), "The Lord thy God will raise up unto thee a Prophet from the midst of thee, of thy brethren, like unto me; unto him ye shall hearken."

73. In this version of the narreme, after their meeting with Muḥammad, the Jews tell him that they have two wishes—that God should remove the distance between them and Mecca so that they could perform the pilgrimage, and that they might be able to do so without meeting anyone. Their wish is granted, and they perform the *ḥajj* in secret.

74. For Qur'an commentaries, see al-Thaʿlabī, *al-Kashf wa al-bayān, al-maʿrūfbi Tafsīr al-Thaʿlabī,* ed. Abū Muḥammad b. ʿĀshūr, 10 vols. (Beirut: Dār Iḥyā' al-Turāth al-ʿArabī, 1422/2002), vol. 4:293–294. For references in legends of the prophets, see the Middle Turkic compilation by al-Rabghūzī (d. 1310), which was based on the eleventh-century Persian work by Nīshāpūrī—al-Rabghūzī, *Stories of the Prophets,* vol. 1:492–493 (Turkic text), vol. 2:615–617 (trans.). For cosmographical works, see Zakariyyā b. Muḥammad b. Maḥmūd al-Qazwīnī, *Āthār al-bilād wa akhbār al-ʿibād* (Beirut: Dār Ṣādir, 1380/1960), 27–28, s.v. Jābarsā; and Wheeler, "The Prophet Muḥammad Dhu al-Qarnayn," 207–208 (for a translation of the passage).

75. For this variant spelling of Jābarsā or Jābalsā, see n. 77 below.

76. Shihāb al-Dīn Abū ʿAbdullāh Yāqūt b. ʿAbdullāh al-Ḥamawī al-Rūmī al-Baghdādī, *Muʿjam al-buldān,* 7 vols. (Beirut: Dār Ṣādir, 1955–1957; repr. ed., 1995), 2:90–91, s.v. Jābars; and Brannon M. Wheeler, *Moses in the Quran and Islamic Exegesis* (London: RoutledgeCurzon, 2002), 93ff. (for a partial translation and discussion of the passage).

77. Muḥammad b. Jarīr al-Ṭabarī, *The History of al-Ṭabarī (Ta'rīkh al-rusul wa'l-mulūk),* vol. 1, *General Introduction* and *From the Creation to the Flood,* trans. Franz Rosenthal (Albany: State University of New York Press, 1989), 237–238. Jābalq and Jābars are variant spellings of Jābalqā and Jābarsā or Jābalsā. al-Ṭabarī provides pseudo-Syriac equivalents for Jābalq (Marqīsīyā) and Jābars (Barjīsīyā). As Franz Rosenthal notes (237 n. 457), however, there is no

etymological explanation for these names in Syriac, aside from the final -ā, which imitates the definite article in Aramaic. It is noteworthy that, in medieval Islamic literature, whenever the ancient nature of a work or writing was to be emphasized, it was usually described as having been written in Aramaic/Syriac. Interestingly enough, al-Thaʿlabī also provides a Hebrew equivalent for Jābars (Jāyir Sāniyūt), for which see al-Thaʿlabī, *ʿArāʾis al-majālis fī qiṣaṣ al-anbiyāʾ or "Lives of the Prophets" as Recounted by Abū Isḥāq Aḥmad ibn Muḥammad ibn Ibrāhīm al-Thaʿlabī,* trans. William M. Brinner (Leiden: Brill, 2002), 34.

78. For the ʿĀd and Thamūd, see Wheeler, *Moses in the Quran,* 102ff.

79. al-Ṭabarī, *History of al-Ṭabarī,* 238. See also al-Ṭabarī, *Jāmiʿ al-bayān* 8:87 (where he states that they are separated from the rest of humanity by a river of sand (or honey) and that they are *ḥunafāʾ muslimūn,* Muslim monotheists); and compare al-Thaʿlabī, *al-Kashf wa al-bayān,* vol. 4:293–294.

80. See n. 58 above.

81. See my article, "Zoroastrian Elements in the Islamic Ascension Narrative: The Case of the Cosmic Cocks," in *Proceeding of the 6th European Conference in Iranian Studies,* in press.

82. From Old Persian/Avestan *kaofa,* meaning "mountain" (New Persian, *kūh*). See Christian Bartholomae, *Altiranisches Wörterbuch* (1904; repr. ed., Berlin: Walter de Gruyter, 1979), 431.

83. See Muḥammad Jaʿfar Yāḥaqqī, *Farhang-i asāṭīr wa dāstānwārahā dar adabiyāt-i fārsī* (Tehran: Farhang Muʿāṣir, 1386/2007), 643–646; al-Thaʿlabī, *ʿArāʾis al-majālis,* 9; and Anton M. Heinen, *Islamic Cosmology: A Study of as-Suyūṭī's al-Hayʾa as-sanīya fī l-hayʾa as-sunnīya* (Beirut: Franz Steiner, Wiesbaden, 1982), 171.

84. Qurʾan 18:83–98. See al-Thaʿlabī, *ʿArāʾis al-majālis,* 605–621; Wheeler, "Prophet Muḥammad Dhu al-Qarnayn," 181ff.; and Wheeler, *Moses in the Quran,* 26ff.

85. Bulūqiyā is often described as an ancient Israelite or as a Jewish king of Egypt, and sometimes identified with the son of the king Josiah or with the prophet Jeremiah, who lived during the reign of the king Josiah, known for instituting a religious reform based on the discovery of the lost books of the law by the high priest Ḥilqiyahu. See A. Abel, "L'apocalpse de Balūqīya," in *Eschatologie et cosmologie,* ed. Armand Abel et al. (Brussels: Éditions de l'Institut de Sociologie, Université Libre de Bruxelles, 1969), 191; Stephanie Dalley, "The Tale of Bulūqiyā and the *Alexander Romance* in Jewish and Sufi Mystical Circles," in *Tracing the Threads: Studies in the Vitality of Jewish Pseudepigrapha,* ed. John C. Reeves (Atlanta, Ga.: Scholars Press, 1994), 243–247; Josef Horovitz, "Bulūqjā," *Zeitschrift der Deutschen Morgenländischen Gesellschaft* 55 (1901): 522; and Steven M. Wasserstrom, "Jewish Pseudepigrapha and *Qiṣas al-Anbiyāʾ,*" in *Judaism and Islam: Boundaries, Communication and Interaction. Essays in Honor of William M. Brinner,* ed. Benjamin H. Hary, John L. Hayes, and Fred Astren (Leiden: Brill, 2000), 246–247. The current scholarly consensus is that the tale of Bulūqiyā represents a further adaptation of the ancient Mesopotamian epic of Gilgamesh—see Dalley, "Tale of Bulūqiyā," 261; and Stephanie Dalley, "Gilgamesh in the Arabian Nights," *Journal of the Royal Asiatic Society,* ser. 3, vol. 1, no. 1 (1991): 7–8.

86. See Dalley, "Tale of Bulūqiyā," 248. For the doctrine of *taḥrīf,* see Camilla Adang, *Muslim Writers on Judaism and the Hebrew Bible: From Ibn Rabban to Ibn Hazm* (Leiden: E. J. Brill, 1996), 223.

87. See al-Thaʿlabī, *ʿArāʾis al-majālis,* 593–604. For al-Thaʿlabī's Jewish sources and their significance, see Wasserstrom, "Jewish Pseudepigrapha," 244–245. According to Wasserstrom, the Apocalypse of Abraham may have served as a source for the version in al-Thaʿlabī—see Wasserstrom, "Jewish Pseudepigrapha," 240–247.

88. Probably Hebrew Hizqiel, who in Jewish angelology is the angel who serves as the chief aide to Gabriel—see Gustav Davidson, *A Dictionary of Angels, Including the Fallen Angels* (New York: Free Press, 1967), 141. According to another Islamic legend, Khazqīyāʾīl was a proto-monotheist who concealed his beliefs from Pharoah until Moses's triumph over Pharoah's sorcerers. He is the true believer alluded to in Qurʾan 40:28—see al-Thaʿlabī, *ʿArāʾis al-majālis,* 311.

89. *Daqāʾiq al-ḥaqāʾiq,* MS, Bibliothèque nationale de France, persan 174, fols. 105r–107v.

The tale occurs in the chapter on the marvels of Mount Qāf. For a description of the manuscript, see Francis Richard, *Catalogue des manuscrits persans,* vol. 1, *Ancien fonds* (Paris: Bibliothèque nationale de France, 1989), 191–195. For Yamlikhyah (meaning "God rules"), the name of Moses when he was still with his tribe, see R. Payne Smith, *Thesaurus Syriacus,* 2 vols. (1879–1901; repr. ed., Hildesheim: Georg Olms, 1981), vol. 1:1606. My thanks to my colleague Amir Harrak for his assistance with the Syriac.

90. See Davidson, *Dictionary of Angels,* 180.

91. For the episode in the Pseudo-Callisthenes version, dating from ca. 300 CE, see Stoneman, *Greek Alexander Romance,* 131–133. The episode is also found in the anonymous Arabic and Persian "Advices of Alexander." See Charles-Henri de Fouchécour, *Moralia: Les notions morales dans la littérature persane du 3e/9e au 7e/13e siècle* (Paris: Éditions Recherche sur les Civilisations, 1986), 32; and Minoo S. Southgate, trans., *Iskandarnamah: A Persian Medieval Alexander-Romance* (New York: Columbia University Press, 1978), 180–181.

92. These date from the eleventh to the fourteenth centuries—see Wout Jac. van Bekkum, ed. and trans., *A Hebrew Alexander Romance According to MS London, Jews' College, no. 145* (Louvain: Peeters and Departement Oriëntalistiek, 1992), 137–139; Wout Jac. van Bekkum, ed. and trans., *A Hebrew Alexander Romance According to MS Héb. 671.5 Paris, Bibliothèque Nationale* (Groningen: Styx, 1994), 99; and Jean-Pierre Rothschild, "Alexandre hébreu, ou Micromégas," *Mélanges de l'École Française de Rome* 112, no. 1 (2000): 27–42. Alexander is also mentioned in the Talmudic and Midrashic literature, as well as in such works as the *Sefer Yosippon* (comp. 953). See van Bekkum, *Hebrew Alexander Romance According to MS London,* 2–13, 16–17; and Giuliano Tamani, "La tradizione ebraica del *Romanzo di Alessandro,*" in *La diffusione dell'eredità classica nell'età tardoantica e medievale: Forme e modi di trasmissione,* ed. Alfredo Valvo (Alessandria: Edizioni dell'Orso, 1997), 222–227.

93. See, for example, Wheeler, "The Prophet Muḥammad Dhu al-Qarnayn," 207.

94. One is reminded of the negative depiction of Jews in the well-known tale in the *Mathnawī* of Jalāl al-Dīn Rūmī about the evil Jewish king who persecuted Christians and his devious vizier who, motivated by envy, or *ḥasad,* feigned conversion to Christianity in order to subvert the Christians' beliefs. See Jalāl al-Dīn Rūmī, *Kitāb-i Mathnawī-i maʿnawī.,* ed. and trans. Reynold A. Nicholson, 6 bks. in 8 vols. (London: Luzac, 1925–1940; repr. ed., vols. 1–6, 1985), bk. 1, lines 429–439.

95. See van Bekkum, *Hebrew Alexander Romance According to MS London,* 151: "Envy and rivalry have been turned away from us, and not one of us rises up against another, nor does any one of us desire or covet anything, because his property is enough for him."

96. See Stoneman, *Greek Alexander Romance,* 131–133; Charles Genequand, "Alexandre et les sages de l'Inde," *Arabic and Middle Eastern Literatures* 4, no. 2 (2001): 142; and van Bekkum, *Hebrew Alexander Romance According to MS London,* 139 (where the sages reply that their bodies are their graves).

97. For the concept of *naṣīḥa* in Islam, see van Ess, *Theologie und Gesellschaft,* vol. 1:194.

98. The use of scriptural interpolations is also attested in versions of the ascension narrative that were aimed at a Christian audience. The Book of Muḥammad's Ladder, which preserves an original Arabic text in Latin and Old French translations dating from thirteenth-century Spain, contains slightly paraphrased citations from the New Testament Book of Revelation (4:6–8), or Apocalypse of St. John. See Besson and Brossard-Dandré, *Le livre de l'échelle,* 158, 160; and my article, "'Holy, Holy, Holy.'"

99. This fundamental idea was summed up succinctly by the nineteenth-century Hasidic Rabbi Moshe of Kobryn (d. 1858) who stated:

> At the close of Ecclesiastes (i.e., Eccles. 12:13) we read, 'The end of the matter, all having been heard: fear God!' Now whatever matter you come to the end of, you will always hear this one maxim, 'Fear God!' and this is one is the whole. There is not a single thing in all the world that does not show you a way to fear God and to serve him. All is commandment.

See Martin Buber, *Tales of the Hasidim*, trans. Olga Marx, 2 books in 1 (New York: Schocken Books, 1947; repr. ed., 1991), vol. 2:161. From the Islamic viewpoint, in the Abrahamic family of religions, the dominant aspect of Judaism is believed to be fear of God (*makhāfa*), of Christianity it is love of God (*maḥabba*), and of Islam it is knowledge of God (*maʿrifa*)—see Seyyed Hossein Nasr, *Islamic Art and Spirituality* (Albany: State University of New York Press, 1987), 134, 145 n. 3.

100. Contrary to the Semitically-inspired *miʿrāj* narrative, in medieval Persian popular culture Jesus is always identified with the fourth heaven, the sphere of the sun. This is vividly illustrated in the Persian *Kitāb-i Miʿrājnāma,* Ayasofya 3441: whereas in the narrative itself, Jesus and John the Baptist are associated with the third heaven (fol. 23v), in the author's commentary Jesus's station is described as being in the fourth heaven (fol. 67v).

101. Thackston, "Paris *Miʿrājnāma,*" 269.

102. Thackston, "Paris *Miʿrājnāma,*" 267 (fol. 5b).

103. Scholars have assumed that this represents a lacuna in the manuscript—see Pavet de Courteille, *Mirâdj-nâmeh,* xxi; and Thackston, "Paris *Miʿrājnāma,*" 270 n. 22.

104. Thackston, "Paris *Miʿrājnāma,*" 271–272. Moses and Abraham are associated, interchangeably, with the sixth and seventh heavens in other versions of the narrative—see Vuckovic, *Heavenly Journeys,* 62, 57.

105. Thus also Frederick Colby—see Colby, "Constructing an Islamic Ascension Narrative," 321.

106. For example, in the Persian *Miʿrājnāma* that possibly dates from the Ilkhanid period, Jesus is mentioned not in the second heaven, with which he is usually associated, but in the third together with John the Baptist. The second heaven is occupied by Joseph, which perhaps reflects the Syrian Christian view that he prefigured Jesus—see *Kitāb-i Miʿrājnāma,* Ayasofya 3441, fols. 22v–23v; and A. S. Rodrigues Pereira, "Two Syriac Verse Homilies on Joseph," *Ex Oriente Lux* 31 (1989–1990): 95ff. I owe this particular insight to Amir Harrak.

107. See Besson and Brossard-Dandré, *Le livre de l'échelle,* 148–149.

108. See Louis Ginzberg, comp., *Legends of the Jews,* trans. Henrietta Szold and Paul Radin, 2nd ed., 2 vols. (Philadelphia: The Jewish Publication Society, 2003), vol. 1:504 (citing *Gedullat Moshe*). It is not out of the question that the Midrashic account may itself have been influenced by the Islamic ascension narrative.

109. Thackston, "Paris *Miʿrājnāma,*" 277 (fol. 44a); and Scherberger, *Das Miʿrāğnāme,* 68, Tafel 37 (fol. 42v), lines 4–5 and Tafel 38 (fol. 44r), line 1. For the Islamic legend of Muḥammad's "noble sandals" that were believed to have touched the Throne of God, see Annemarie Schimmel, *And Muhammad Is His Messenger: The Veneration of the Prophet in Islamic Piety* (Chapel Hill: University of North Carolina Press, 1985), 40.

110. Ex. 3:5, "Come no closer! Remove the sandals from your feet, for the place on which you are standing is holy ground"; and Qur'an 20:12, "Verily, I am your Lord, so remove your sandals, for you are in the sacred valley of Ṭuwā."

111. See Thackston, "Paris *Miʿrājnāma,*" 271 (26a); and Scherberger, *Das Miʿrāğnāme,* 59, Tafel 23 (fol. 26r), lines 1–5.

112. See, for example, the accounts recorded in the Qur'an commentaries of al-Thaʿlabī and Abū al-Futūḥ Rāzī, dating, respectively, from the early eleventh and early twelfth centuries—al-Thaʿlabī, *al-Kashf wa al-bayān* 6:54–68; and Abū al-Futūḥ Rāzī, *Rawḍ al-jinān wa rawḥ al-janān fī tafsīr al-Qur'ān,* ed. Muḥammad Jaʿfar Yāḥaqqī and Muḥammad Mahdī Nāṣiḥ, 20 vols. (Repr. ed., Mashhad: Intishārāt-i Āstān-i Quds-i Riḍavī, 1378/1999), vol. 12:129–159. For a translation of the latter account, see Angelo M. Piemontese, "Le voyage de Mahomet au Paradis et en Enfer: Une version persane du *miʿrâj,*" in *Apocalypses et voyages dans l'au-delà,* ed. Claude Kappler et al. (Paris: Les Éditions du Cerf, 1987), 301–317.

4

The Chaghatay *Miʿrājnāma* Attributed to Ḥakīm Süleymān Ata: A Missionary Text from the Twelfth or Thirteenth Century Preserved in Modern Manuscripts

MAX SCHERBERGER

The *Miʿrājnāmatu-ʿl-Ḥaẓrat ṣallā-ʿl-lāhu ʿalayhi* (The Book of Ascension of His Majesty, May God Bless Him, henceforth *MNḤ*) attributed to Ḥakīm Süleymān Ata (d. 1186/7?), along with the Timurid *Miʿrājnāma* of ca. 1436–1437,[1] is one of the few compositions describing Muḥammad's ascension to heaven in eastern middle Turkish. Instead of being written in prose, as several other ascension narratives are, it is instead composed in distiches following the *qaṣīda* meter, thus offering a rare example of *miʿrāj*-poetry in eastern Turkish.[2] This work has attracted scholarly interest in the past, but still has not been analyzed in detail. It never has been translated into another language. The present study aims to fill this lacuna by providing a full English translation of the text. Moreover, it also aims to address another insufficiently investigated issue, that of the authorship of the *MNḤ*. The work itself pretends to be composed by a certain "Süleymān."[3] All published studies dealing with the *MNḤ* have identified or accepted this particular "Süleymān" as Ḥakīm Süleymān Ata (twelfth or thirteenth century),[4] a famous Turkish Sufi saint from Bāqirghān in Khwārazm (modern-day Uzbekistan) who is said to have been a disciple of Aḥmad Yasawī (d. 1166/7?).[5] If this attribution is correct, the work translated herein would be the most ancient extant ascension narrative in a Turkic language.[6]

The present chapter argues in favor of this theory, accepting the attribution of the text to Ḥakīm Süleymān Ata, despite two important objections that can be raised against it. First, there is no surviving manuscript from such an early time. The oldest complete recension of the text does not date prior to the seventeenth century.[7] Second, the idiom of the *MNḤ* is Chaghatay, the most recent form of eastern middle Turkish that was used from the fifteenth to the nineteenth century. Ḥakīm Ata would have expressed his verses in Qara-Khanid, the earliest form of eastern middle Turkish (eleventh-thirteenth centuries).[8] Relying on this data and following these two objections, one could postulate that the *MNḤ* is not the work of Ḥakīm Ata but of a much later author (sixteenth/seventeenth century) who decided for unknown reasons to attribute his writings to Ḥakīm Ata.[9] If one decides in favor of this theory, one has to answer three difficult questions: Who might such an author be, for what kind of audience in this later period might this mysterious author have composed the *MNḤ*, and what might have been his intention in attributing the text to Ḥakīm Ata? If one examines the contents of the story, one cannot find a satisfactory answer to any of these questions, and thus this chapter will argue that the best solution to the question of authorship, given our current state of knowledge, is to accept the conventional attribution of the text to Ḥakīm Ata himself.

As will be shown subsequently, the *MNḤ* can be identified as a missionary-didactic text. It encourages people to accept Islam and preaches love for the Prophet. The Islamization of Central Asia was completed by the fifteenth century at the latest.[10] It is therefore pointless to look for an author of missionary literature and a corresponding audience in the region after that period. Ḥakīm Ata's lifetime (whether it took place in the twelfth or thirteenth century)[11] and his personal religious background instead are much more compatible with the missionary motifs present in the text. Mystic dervishes like Ḥakīm Ata played an important role in the spread of Islam, whether in Central Asia or in other regions that became part of the Muslim world. The converts-to-be whom the *MNḤ* appears to address may have comprised members of different social and religious communities, since certain parts of the text reflect an adaptation of Muslim elements to nomadic tastes and Buddhist concepts.

The present chapter contends that the *MNḤ* preserves an early Turkish ascension narrative, or at least several motifs of such a narrative, that was composed by the Yasawī dervish Ḥakīm Ata for use in his missionary activities. A possible explanation for why there are no early manuscripts of narratives like the *MNḤ* is that they were intended for an audience that was largely illiterate, and therefore the early versions of the text would only have been recited orally.[12] The surviving manuscripts of the *MNḤ* must be the work of later disciples, supporters or venerators of the Yasawī tradition who were trying to preserve the spiritual inheritance of their ancestors. Since the literary language of their time was Chaghatay, they understandably used this idiom in order to record the narrative in written form. Except for this adaptation of the text to the new idiom, they largely preserved the original spirit and style of a twelfth/thirteenth–century missionary text.

English Translation of the *MNḤ*

Not having access to any of the extant manuscripts of the text, the present translation is based on a collation of two slightly different versions of the *MNḤ* published by Eraslan. The first is included in the *Dīwān-i Ḥikmat*.[13] This manuscript was in the possession of Caferoğlu and henceforth will be referred to as "the *Caferoğlu* manuscript." The second copy forms part of the *Bāqirghān Kitābı*.[14] This particular text was published in 1884 for the second time in Kazan, and henceforth will be referred to as "the *Kazan* edition." A translation of both versions is not necessary, since they do not differ substantially from one another. The *Caferoğlu* manuscript contains a total of 122 verses, 19 of which are not included in the *Kazan* edition. On the other hand, the *Kazan* edition contains 11 verses not found in the *Caferoğlu* manuscript, and is thus 8 verses shorter than the latter. Therefore, the slightly longer *Caferoğlu* manuscript has been selected as the base text for the present English translation. The supplementary verses in the *Caferoğlu* manuscript are mentioned in the footnotes. There are a few exceptions where preference is given to the *Kazan* edition; the reasons for this preference are explained in the footnotes. Moreover, the eleven verses of the *Kazan* edition that complement the *Caferoğlu* manuscript also appear in the present English translation. They are cited after the corresponding verses of the *Caferoğlu* manuscript, having the same numbers but distinguished with the letters "a" and "b." Their original verse numbers in the *Kazan* version and the pages on which they occur in Eraslan's edition are given in the footnotes. All verses have thus been included here so as to achieve as complete an edition of the *MNḤ* as possible. I have taken some creative liberties in translating several of the verses into English, in order to convey a sense of the text's many details and its rich layers of meaning.

The Book of Ascension of His Majesty, May God Bless Him

1 See how the only existing God granted [us] a favor,
He sent down Muṣṭafā and made of us a community of believers.
2 He sent to us the Prophet as a gift for the community,
thus He gave the Prophet to a rebellious community like ours.
3 The community of the Prophet will be fortunate on the Day of Resurrection
and will wander about freely, released from hell.
3a Anybody who did not follow him and did not accept his religion
will be burned and will remain in hell forever.
3b He [God] created him from His Own light and named him "Beloved,"
and he [the Prophet] crossed the veils and came within two bows' length from Him.[15]
4 The Prophet entered the mosque and carried out his evening prayer,
when suddenly Abū Jahl came in through the door.
5 With Abū Jahl there were eighty people,
they suddenly saw the Prophet and looked at him respectfully.
6 The Cursed [Abū Jahl] said: "Aḥmad the Magician,
you are the greatest sorcerer in the world.
7 You have distorted our religion and corrupted mankind,
you have brought [to us] your extremely false sorcery!"
8 The Prophet heard this and it hurt him very much,
so he went to the house of Umm Hāni' and entered it.
9 The Prophet spread out a carpet and prayed to God,
and he thanked God and cried before the Lord.
10 Then he made the three hundred and thirteen prophets his advocates,

he entrusted his secret to God and found [in Him] a firm support.
10a The Prophet relied [on God], and his body was soothed,
his soul came into a turmoil and his heart was awakened.[16]
11 See what God did: He invited the Prophet,
who came to have a vision of the Divine Truth.
12 Gabriel was called by God, Who said: "Go on!
I commanded you [Gabriel] to send my regards.
13 You were commanded to go and tell the *ḥūrī*s and palaces
to gather, this is the time of the Vision."
14 Gabriel arrived immediately, delivered God's greetings,
entered paradise, took Burāq and left [with this steed].
15 Heaven's gate was opened, he took Burāq, and they exited.
He [Gabriel] said: "I told Riżwān that he [the Prophet] is supposed to ride Burāq."[17]
16 Burāq remained at the door, Gabriel entered the house,
took Muḥammad, and they exited.
17 The Prophet said: "This matter is strange and difficult to understand.
You are coming to me very soon, [Gabriel], so is this the Day of Resurrection?"[18]
18 He answered: "Until the Day of Resurrection there will be good fortune and happiness.
The Friend [God] tells a secret to a friend—this is the night of [your] ascension!"[19]
19 The Prophet went out and saw Burāq,
he looked at [this creature made from] God's power and was highly amazed.
20 Its face was created from light, its eyes from gems,
that is how only the Living Creator has created it.
21 Its head was of ruby, its ears of agate,
its body of white gems, its teeth of pearls,
22 Its back of pure emerald, its bones of ruby,
its flesh of saffron and amber,
23 Its coat of white musk, its tails of gems,
and its feet of gems, silver, and gold.
24 It was bigger than a horse and smaller than a camel,
and with each step it traversed a seventy thousand years' way.
25 Its saddle was of red ruby and its stirrups of emerald.
Burāq saw the Prophet and greeted him effusively;
26 The Prophet responded to the greeting and went in front of Burāq.
Burāq looked at the Prophet, dropped its bridle, and fled.
27 Burāq fled from the Prophet, and Gabriel said: "Hey, hey,
do not be recalcitrant and disobedient!
28 The disobedient ones are in a difficult position: They will not have a vision of the Divine Truth,
the Almighty will torture them, and their place will be in hell."

29 Burāq heard these words, lowered its head to the ground,
shed tears, and uttered: "I have one wish.
30 A hundred thousand *burāqs*[20] are at your command, they long for [your] majesty,
they amble in paradise, and all of them are inferior [to me].
31 O Aḥmad, let us come to an agreement:
You will ride me on the Day of Resurrection!"
31a The Prophet agreed and said: "Enjoy that privilege, come!"
He [the Prophet] took a hair from his head and said: "You can really believe it!"[21]
32 Muḥammad, the pride of the world, concluded an agreement with Burāq.
Gabriel witnessed it and seized its bridle.
32a Gabriel grabbed hold of its bridle, Michael stepped on its stirrup,
Isrāfīl gave him a hand, and the Prophet mounted [Burāq].[22]
33 Gabriel was standing by its halter, Michael to its right,
Isrāfīl to its left.
34 It was Monday night: The Prophet mounted Burāq,
and embarked from Mecca.[23]
35 There was a voice coming from the right: The Prophet heard it immediately,
did not respond, and continued on his way.
36 There was a voice coming from the left: He did not respond,
did not even look, and went on his way.
37 The Prophet said: "O Gabriel, this occurrence is strange,
what were these voices coming from the right and from the left?"
38 Gabriel said: "How well you acted, Aḥmad, rejoice!
If you had responded to them, your community would have been destroyed.[24]
39 The voice coming from the right was the accursed Jews;
you paid no heed to them, and your community has found peace.
40 The voice coming from the left was the world that wanted to deceive you;
it is good that you did not pay attention to her, thus she remained poor."[25]
41 The Prophet heard these words and his difficulties were solved.
He closed his eyes and when he opened them he saw the "Furthest Place of Worship."
42 The Prophet was thirsty and wanted to drink some sherbet:
He looked [around], stopped, and saw four vessels.
43 In one there was wine, in one there was honey,
in one there was white milk, and in one there was honey with sugar.
44 The Prophet refused the wine as well as the honey,
but he took the two other vessels and drank them without delay.
45 Then four garments [were offered] to the Prophet: a yellow one, a black one, a green one, and a white one.
He left behind the yellow and the black ones, and selected the green and white ones.[26]

46 Gabriel said: "My friend, you left the yellow and the black ones,
you have proven that you are a prophet, well done!"
47 The Prophet heard these words and his difficulties were solved.
He witnessed the secrets and went to the "Furthest Place of Worship."[27]
48 [There] the Prophet entered the mosque and saw other prophets:
They all were standing, and they greeted him.
49 The Prophet responded to their greeting and talked to all of them.
In their midst, the Prophet was the moon and the others were the stars.
50 [There were] three hundred thirteen apostles, four hundred forty-four messengers,
and lastly the saints came to join them and were all in attendance, too.
51 Moses said: "O Adam, how fortunate you are at this time!
You are God's best friend, be our prayer leader."
52 Adam looked at Moses and said: "How could this be appropriate?"
He grasped Muṣṭafā and said: "He has to be our prayer leader!"
53 The Prophet was chosen as the prayer leader with the other prophets standing in a line [behind him].
He gave thanks to God and he offered his greetings.
54 He went back to the *miḥrāb*[28] and looked at the other prophets.
He prayed silently to God, and all responded: "Amen!"
55 He finished praying, rose, and approached the Rock.[29]
He ascended from the Rock, and the other prophets remained [behind].
56 A ladder of light was erected in front of the Prophet:
He climbed it and reached the gate of heaven.[30]
57 The gate of heaven was opened, and he saw angels.
They came in throngs and observed Muṣṭafā.[31]
58 He flew to the first heaven and saw angels;
[in it] he thanked God and implored Him.
59 He passed through it and reached the second heaven;
[there] he saw a rooster and asked Gabriel [about it].
60 Gabriel said: "That is the rooster who oversees time:
When it crows, the other roosters [on earth] crow as well."
61 He flew to the third heaven and saw angels,
whose bodies were half of fire and half of snow.[32]
62 He ascended to the fourth sky and saw the prophet Jesus,
who looked at him, stopped, and greeted him.
63 The Prophet responded to his greeting and entered the Frequented House.
[In it] he offered thanks and greetings to God.
64 He ascended to the fifth heaven, where he saw the prophet Moses.
They [Muḥammad and Moses] were talking at this opportunity.
64a Moses said: "O Aḥmad, for the sake of your community ask
[that God] reduce [the number of daily] prayers!"[33]
65 He ascended to the sixth heaven and saw angels:
There were no heads on their bodies.[34] He exclaimed: "God is the most Exalted!"

66 He ascended to the seventh heaven and saw angels,
some of whom he did not know and with whom he spent some time.
67 Some of them were standing, some were kneeling,
some touched the ground with their foreheads. He uttered: "God is the most Exalted!"
68 The Prophet looked above and saw the exalted throne:
It was seven thousand times the size of the world, and so he was greatly astonished.
69 He approached the throne and witnessed the attributes of the Divine.
A thousand drops were falling into Muṣṭafā's mouth:
70 They were sweeter than honey and colder than snow.
His three hundred sixty arteries were shining bright.
71 The [drops] fell into the Prophet's throat. His heart was shining bright like daylight,
and he was overwhelmed by the knowledge of wisdom.[35]
72 From God came the call: "Step onto the throne!"
At this instant, God's Beloved said: "Let me take off my shoes."
73 However, God ordered: "Do not remove your shoes,
approach with your shoes on, and with the dust on them!"
73a [So] the Prophet did not take off his shoes, and he stepped onto the throne.
From God came the request: "Walk quickly!"[36]
74 He went past the throne and arrived at the Lote Tree of the Limit.
He reached this place and said: "O my followers!"
75 They reached the exalted place, his majesty Gabriel turned back,
cried, and apologized many times.
76 He said: "The horizon is my boundary, there is no place for me beyond it.
O Prophet, please understand and believe me!"[37]
77 *Rafraf* arrived, and the Prophet mounted it.
He traversed countless veils and came within a two bows' distance from Him.[38]
78 See what God did: He invited the Prophet
and greeted Muṣṭafā.
79 The Prophet went into ecstasy and when he heard God's greeting,
he lost consciousness and remained lying there for some time.[39]
80 The Prophet came to and quickly responded to the greeting:
He opened his hands and prayed.
81 From God came the call: "What did you bring?
When a friend visits a Friend, he does not come empty-handed!"
82 [The Prophet responded:] "Grant me my wish, and after that I will make a request!
I brought something that You do not have.
83 I brought four things that do not exist in Your treasury:
crime, indigence, poverty, and sin."

84 He [the Prophet] said: "To my right there is my wish, to my left there is my desire,
please forgive the sins of my followers!"
84a He [God] said: "Ask, O Prophet, this is the time of asking,
whatever request you make will be granted!"
84b The Prophet said: "I want to ask, for the sake of my followers,
the forgiveness of the sins of the rebellious community!"[40]
85 He said: "Chief of prophets, leader of saints,
light of the two worlds, come, be welcome!
86 I have created all the oceans as honey and sugar:
Wherever you go, they shall go there, too.
87 I have created all trees as roses and corals:
Wherever you like, they shall bear fruit.
88 O my friend Muḥammad, whatever you say [about your] community,
I have forgiven the sins of your followers!"
88a I [God] said to you: "If you didn't exist, I wouldn't have created the spheres!"
He [God] said: "Light of the two worlds, you are my Beloved![41]
89 You are my Beloved, Muḥammad, I have forgiven your community!"
The Prophet rejoiced a great deal.[42]
90 He [God] said: "I have created this world and the other world for you,
and you will be satisfied on the Day of Resurrection."
91 He put on the garment of mercy and put the crown of forgiveness [on his head].
Whenever the Prophet requested [a favor], he always was satisfied.
92 The Prophet came back from his Majesty, turned around,
and saw the seven hells spurting fire.
93 In each hell he saw angels,
who were holding clubs of fire.
94 Their faces were black, their eyes blue-brown,
and their bodies were half of fire and half of snow.
94a They seized a group (of people), took clubs[43] of fire,
cut off their lips, and tortured them incessantly.[44]
95 They seized a group (of people), pushed them into the fire,
and pulled out their tongues through their backs.[45]
96 They seized a group [of women] and hung them by their breasts.
[There was another] group [of people] with chains around their necks.
97 He saw two persons in the abyss,
he recognized [that they were his] father and mother. He was truly shocked.
98 Their shoes were of fire and their garments were of tar.
The Prophet saw them and was confounded.
99 They said: "O son, look at us and mourn [us];
weep [for us] and make them show mercy [upon us].[46]
100 Do not leave us in here, [rather] petition your God [for mercy]!
Do not leave us without hope, and do not leave [us behind], O son!"

101 The Prophet heard these words and was discouraged.
From God came the call: "Renounce them!"
102 The call of the Almighty came: "O my Beloved,
two friends never fit into one heart!"
103 He said: "O my friend Muḥammad, do one of [these] two tasks!
Say either: 'your father and mother' or 'your community'!"[47]
104 The Prophet said: "O Merciful One, my father and mother are [only] two lives,
[but] my followers are thousands. Accept [my following decision]!"[48]
105 He said: "I abandon my father and mother,
I request, for the sake of my followers, [Your] forgiveness of them!"
106 The Prophet passed hell and looked to the right:
He saw the eight paradises and was much amazed.
107 They went toward paradise, and the *ḥūrī*s came out to meet them.
They strewed pearls and gems onto Muṣṭafā's head.
108 He passed over the threshold and saw paradise:
[In it], he saw four channels and was quite astonished.
109 One of them was of water, one of white milk,
one of honey, and one of honey with sugar.
110 How many rivers did they see! They looked [at them]
and enjoyed them. They were overwhelmed [by their beauty] and went into ecstasy.[49]
111 They saw a paradise created of camphor,
its environs of emerald. They observed it and were amazed.[50]
112 Its thrones were of camphor and its domes of amber.
He look at it and was perplexed.
113 In each paradise there were marvelous domes;
in each dome, there were seventy thousand *ḥūrī*s.
114 For the sake of the believers, the *burāq*s were grazing on basil,
drinking the water of Kawthar, and walking about.[51]
115 The Prophet observed all of this and returned to his house.
He reached the city of Mecca and entered it.
116 The Prophet came and apologized to Burāq:
He asked Burāq for permission [to withdraw], and went into his home.
117 The Prophet's bed was still warm,
the chains were still shaking as in the moment when the Prophet had left.[52]
118 Dawn arrived and the Prophet went to the mosque.
He told [his] secret to his friend, and they all said yes
119 They all said yes *(belī dêdi)* and were obedient.
The faces of the hypocrites blackened with disbelief.
120 ʿAbdallāh b. al-ʿAbbās[53] asked the Prophet:
"Did you have a vision of the Divine Truth?" The Prophet said: "Yes!"
121 Listen to [the tale of] the Prophet's ascension, polish your belief,
and polish your exterior and interior. Purity comes from the brightness.

122 The servant Süleymān spoke a word and spread the [story of] the Prophet's ascension,
he talked about Aḥmad's ascension, implanting it into the memory of [God's] friends.

Missionary Aspects of the *MNḤ*

The *MNḤ* contains many aspects of a missionary text. Before beginning this analysis, it has to be stated clearly that the story of Muḥammad's ascension in general is a suitable motif for promoting conversion to Islam. All classical Islamic ascension narratives, whether Arabic, Turkic, or Persian, contain several elements that can be shown to be missionary in character. The following details common to many Islamic ascension narratives can be included in this category: the superiority of the Prophet Muḥammad to all former prophets; the message that a life according to Islam leads to salvation and the delights of paradise; the threat that rejecting the Prophet and his religion will lead to eternal damnation and infernal punishment; the presentation of examples of belief (Abū Bakr and/or Ibn ʿAbbās and the other companions of the Prophet in Mecca increasing their faith in Islam by accepting the veracity of the ascension) and unbelief (Abū Jahl insulting the Prophet by calling him a sorcerer, or the hypocrites in Mecca denying the veracity of the ascension); Muḥammad being a model for the true believer (evident when he fulfils his prayers, resists the temptations of the Jews and the world, refuses a cup of wine and a cup of honey, selects the "good colors" green and white from the "bad colors" yellow and black or red, and so on); the exaltation of the Prophet to God; and his visions of reward and retaliation in the hereafter, making him the guarantor of the Divine and Ultimate Truth, etc. These are clear enticements to embrace Islam: Who would not want to follow the most exalted of the prophets, who would risk to go to hell instead of being granted the delights of paradise, who would not trust in the person who knows the secrets of the hereafter and can guarantee every individual salvation, and who would want to be on the side of his enemies, who are obviously embarked on the wrong path?

At this point the question has to be asked whether all *miʿrāj* literature can be identified as missionary literature. What about Arabic ascension narratives like those attributed to Ibn ʿAbbās (tenth/eleventh century), al-Qushayrī's (d. 1073) *Kitāb al-Miʿrāj*, or al-Bakrī's (thirteenth century) *Kitāb Qiṣṣat al-Miʿrāj*, which circulated in the Arab world when the latter had been Islamized for centuries? If one gives the term *mission* a broader sense than "converting non-Muslims to Islam," as for example "subjecting people considered to be defective Muslims to a lesson in Islam," "strengthening the individual's beliefs," "teaching religious-moral knowledge," then every ascension narrative can be interpreted as a missionary text.[54] Was the story used in one case (e.g., the Arab world) to exhort certain Muslim people to a stricter observation of religious law, while in others (e.g., Central Asia) it was used to convert non-Muslims to Islam? It is also possible that the story could serve both purposes, especially in Central Asia in the twelfth or thirteenth century, when some individuals in the region were still converting and others had already embraced Islam. Either way, one can surmise that Ḥakīm Ata composed his ascension text in order to strengthen the faith of Central Asian Muslims, and to attempt to convert non-Muslims in the region to Islam.

The Yasawī order of dervishes was often considered to have played a key role in converting the Turks of Central Asia to Islam. Köprülü even speaks of a "national Turkic mission" of the *Yasawiyya.* According to him, Aḥmad Yasawī preached a "simple" form of Islam to his audience consisting of "unsophisticated" Turkish nomads. This definitely is a simplification and exaggeration of the phenomenon, and has correctly been criticised by DeWeese.[55] But the dervishes undoubtedly made a substantial contribution to the Islamization of several formerly non-Muslim regions, such as Central Asia, parts of the Indian subcontinent, Indonesia, and Africa, especially between the eleventh and the fourteenth centuries. Moreover, their influence on popular piety is obvious.[56] The reasons for the success and popularity of mystic missionaries are easily identifiable. The Sufis' understanding of Islam centered on love and trust in the Prophet and God, and was not affected by the theoretical, theological, and juridical speculations of classical Muslim scholarship. Such a warm and emotional form of religiosity was impressive and attractive for many people. In contrast to scholars, Sufis used local idioms rather than Arabic to express their thoughts, Arabic being largely unintelligible to the natives of the eastern regions of Islam's expanding borders.[57] The eastern middle Turkish description of the Prophet given in the *MNḤ* is a typical example of this religious attitude. The *Kazan* version of the text especially reflects the main elements of love and veneration of the Prophet characteristic of Sufism and folk Islam. In this regard, three main motifs can be cited.

First, the text says that Muḥammad has been created from God's light and is the "light of the two worlds."[58] These references allude to the idea of the Prophet's eternal light (the so-called *nūr Muḥammad*), a light already existing before anything else that in turn created everything in this world and the other world.[59] This doctrine was first fully formulated by the Iraqi Sufi Sahl al-Tustarī (d. 896) and is further developed by Ḥusayn b. Manṣūr al-Ḥallāj (d. 922) and others.

Second, the text maintains that God loves the Prophet so much that He created the whole universe and everything that is inside it only for him or, in other words, Muḥammad is the reason and purpose of creation: "I have created all the oceans as honey and sugar, wherever you go, they shall go there, too [. . .] I have created all trees as roses and corals, wherever you like, they shall bear fruit [. . .] I have created this world and the other world for you."[60] This idea reaches it climax when the text cites a famous hadith qudsī ("Holy Saying") especially popular in mystic circles: "If you didn't exist, I wouldn't have created the spheres!"[61]

Third, the Prophet's main concern is to help his community on the imminent and terrifying Day of Resurrection and Divine Judgement.[62] Thanks to him, all members of his community may hope for God's mercy: "Ask, O Prophet, this is the time of asking, whatever request you make will be granted. [. . .] O my friend Muḥammad, whatever you say [about your] community, I have forgiven the sins of your followers. [. . .] You are my Beloved Muḥammad, I have forgiven your community!" This idea of Muḥammad's intercession is a theme that receives special emphasis and attention in popular Islam, and appears to be one motif that comes to enjoy a certain prominence in medieval Turkish ascension texts.

Given this background, what Kara has stated about Ḥakīm Ata and the *MNḤ* succinctly sums up the situation: "Ḥakīm Ata, with his didactic poems, is one of the first architects of the new religious-moral understanding of the Turks who became familiar with the religion of Islam [. . .] With his vernacular poetry he has [. . .] inculcated the love of God and the Prophet in them. His ascension narrative [. . .] is one of the first Turkish examples of this phenomenon."[63] In other words, dervishes like Ḥakīm Ata had become the Islamizers of the Turks, and they used the story of Muḥammad's ascension and other popular mystical tales in order to spread their doctrine. Ḥakīm Ata's ascension narrative blazed a trail that many subsequent Turkish ascension narratives were quick to follow.

Despite the connection between Ḥakīm Ata's version of the story and subsequent ascension narratives, there is one special detail present in the *MNḤ* that is not to be found in other ascension narratives: the Prophet's encounter with his parents in hell. His parents implore him to invoke God to release them from hellfire, but God tells him that he must choose either to save his parents or to save his community. The Prophet becomes saddened by this situation, but has no choice but to decide in favor of his community.[64] This episode is not only missing in other versions of *miʿrāj*, but also, to my knowledge, never appears in that specific form in any other Islamic source. Before one can consider the significance of this singular motif, it is important to review briefly here what Muslim sources do say about the eschatological fate of Muḥammad's parents.

Muḥammad's parents ʿAbdallāh b. ʿAbd al-Muṭṭalib and Āmina died before the prophetic career of their son, and therefore could not have been or have become Muslim. The question of whether they therefore must be considered infidels and thus in hell has preoccupied Muslim scholars for some time. If one categorizes Muḥammad's parents along with other non-Muslim "pagans," then the Qur'an (9:113) addresses the issue of whether such pagans can have any hope of God's forgiveness: "It is not fitting for the Prophet and those who believe that they should invoke (God) for forgiveness for pagans, even though they be of kin, after it has become clear to them that they are companions of the fire." If one applies this verse to the case of Muḥammad's parents, clearly they are beyond hope.

The canonical compendia of Traditions, however, agree that the above verse does not refer to Muḥammad's parents, but rather to his uncle Abū Ṭālib.[65] Only al-Nasā'ī's (d. 915) *Kitāb al-sunan al-kubrā* (Book of the Great Traditions) contains a hadith pointing to the unbelief of Muḥammad's mother. It is mentioned in the chapter about the visit to tombs of idolaters, and it goes as follows: Abū Hurayra said, "The Prophet visited the tomb of his mother and cried and made the others around him cry, and he said, 'I wanted to ask my Lord for allowance to invoke Him for forgiveness for her, but He did not grant it to me, so I asked for allowance to visit her tomb, and He granted it to me. So [believers], visit the tombs so that you may be aware of death!'"[66] This hadith offers a rare exception to the norm, for Muslim tradition and scholarship usually tried to make Muḥammad's parents appear as true believers and quasi-Muslims.

This mainstream Muslim position on the faithfulness of Muḥammad's parents is illustrated by Jalāl al-Dīn al-Suyūṭī's (d. 1505) *Masālik al-ḥunafā' fī wāliday al-Muṣṭafā* (The Orthodox Actions of Muṣṭafā's Parents), a treatise in which he examines the question of whether Muḥammad's parents are in hell or in paradise.[67] Suyūṭī gives three reasons to explain why ʿAbdallāh and Āmina cannot be in hellfire. First, they lived in a period when the former revelations of the "True Faith" had been long since forgotten, and the new revelation had not yet taken place. The people of that period (*ahl al-fatra*) have not yet been condemned, but will instead get a new chance to embrace the "True Faith" on the Day of Resurrection. Second, Suyūṭī maintains that Muḥammad's parents did not belong to the idolaters, but to a class following the monotheism of Abraham (*dīn al-ḥanīf*) already before Muḥammad's revelation,[68] and thus have to be judged as Muslims. Third, he states that they were temporarily awakened from the dead, during which time they accepted Islam, and then were subsequently restored to the state of death. Suyūṭī cites many verses from the Qur'an, all kinds of hadiths, and the positions of such famous Muslim authorities as al-Ṭabarī (d. 923), al-Ṭabarānī (d. 971), al-Ḥākim (d. 1014), al-Bayhaqī (d. 1066), Fakhr al-dīn al-Rāzī (d. ca. 1209), al-Dhahabī (d. 1352/3), Ibn Kathīr (d. 1373), etc., in order to prove the correctness of the theory that Muḥammad's parents cannot possibly be in hell.[69]

Despite this broad consensus among a number of Muslims that Muḥammad's parents can be found in paradise rather than hell, Ḥakīm Ata's narrative takes the opposite position, depicting Muḥammad's parents in hell and beyond the ability of the Prophet's intercession. Since this detail cannot be found in Muslim sources other than the *MNḤ*—neither in the Qur'an, tradition, other ascension narratives, nor in exegetical and theological literature—one can consider it an element that belongs to the very special context of Ḥakīm Ata's text. This context is, as Gruber already has correctly noted, the spread of Islam by Yasawī dervishes like Ḥakīm Ata in Central Asia, where remnants of pre-Islamic beliefs had resisted the process of Islamization. Gruber states: "This particular anecdote provides a pattern for members of Ḥakīm Ata's audience, whom he encourages to embrace Islam despite their parents' adherence to another faith (Buddhism, for example)."[70] She points to further examples of oral narratives with a missionary background like tales of "supernaturally conceived convert infants who refuse their infidel mother's milk," and explains that such motifs served to undermine "paternal and/or maternal authority" when such authority was portrayed as a threat to the children's conversion.[71] Gruber's interpretation is convincing, and numerous examples from this text and others provide further support for it. For instance, the following formulation also confirms that the *MNḤ* alludes to people having a conflict with their parents because of their different faiths: when Muḥammad's parents implore the Prophet for help, they say "petition *your* God," as if they worshipped a different one than he did.[72] The motif of Muḥammad's encounter with his parents in hell, therefore, makes the most sense when interpreted as a narrative addressed to an audience in the midst of intergenerational upheaval, composed in a missionary context in which this text could be deployed in order to help convince those who were considering conversion to Islam of the pressing need to abandon the other religious tradition(s) of their families.

There are two final examples of the missionary-didactic and instructive character of the *MNḤ*. First, the text repeatedly describes the procedure of the Muslim ritual prayer (*ṣalāt*) with its direction (*qibla* as symbolized by the *miḥrāb*) and different positions (*qiyām, rukūᶜ, sujūd*): "The Prophet was chosen as the prayer leader with the other prophets standing in a line (behind him). [. . .] He went back to the *miḥrāb* [. . .]. He [the Prophet] prayed silently to God, and all [prophets] responded: 'Amen!'"[73] When the Prophet ascends to the seventh heaven he sees praying angels: "Some of them were standing, some were kneeling, some touched the ground with their foreheads."[74] These parts of the *MNḤ* seem to be intended to instruct new Muslims in the norms of Muslim worship. In other ascension narratives with a missionary aim, for example the Ilkhanid *Miᶜrājnāma* text of ca. 1317–1335, the instructive effect of the text could be intensified by means of paintings portraying various prayer positions.[75] The second example of the didactic nature of the *MNḤ* can be seen in its use of the second person imperative (in both the singular and plural) to draw the audience in to consider the importance of what they were hearing: "*see* (*körüng*) how the only existing God looked, [. . .] *see* (*körgil*) what God performed, [. . .] *listen* (*êşit*) to [the tale of] the Prophet's ascension and *polish* (*yarut*) your belief, *polish* your exterior and interior." This type of rhetorical device appears throughout the text, and makes one final appearance in the last verse of the narrative: "The servant Süleymān spoke a word and *spread* the [story of] the Prophet's ascension, he talked about Aḥmad's ascension, *implanting it into the memory* of [God's] friends."[76] These examples illustrate how Ḥakīm Ata's narrative has the immediacy of an oral narrative addressed to an audience of listeners, told with the didactic purpose of drawing moral lessons from the story, with the goal of either converting the audience to Islam or strengthening their Islamic faith.

Despite the text's modern idiom and the late date of extant manuscripts, there is a wealth of evidence to justify attributing the *MNḤ* to Ḥakīm Ata, and identifying it as a missionary-didactic work used in the context of the *Yasawiyya*'s contribution to the Islamization of Central Asia in the twelfth or thirteenth centuries. However, what was the possible religious affiliation of the people Ḥakīm Ata aimed to reach with his religious propaganda?

In her examination of the Timurid *Miʿrājnāma* in the present volume, Subtelny, dealing with the question of the strategies used by Muslim missionaries, plausibly explains that the latter tended rather to adapt Islamic elements to the religious ideas and tastes of their target group than to confront them in a hostile and polemical way. As for the *MNḤ*, one might see the reflection of such a tendency in two of its features, namely the presentation of Burāq as the leader of a group of a hundred thousand heavenly steeds grazing in paradise like earthly horses in the steppe—doubtlessly a familiar scenario for a nomadic audience—and the depiction of infernal retaliation following the karmic principle of a physical-symbolic analogy between sin and punishment (e.g., liars or calumniators are tortured by their tongues, women who have committed adultery or nursed bastards are tortured by their breasts, etc.)[77]—commonly found in Turkic Buddhist eschatological literature.[78] Given this background, it seems that Ḥakīm Ata was concerned with Islamizing both a tribal Shamanist and sedentary Buddhist populace.

By presenting an English translation of the *MNḤ*, analyzing the missionary character of Islamic ascension literature in general and of the *MNḤ* in particular, and referring to the fact that Islamization procedures, carried out by dervishes in peripheral and superficially Islamized regions of the Muslim world such as Central Asia, were in their heyday during the lifetime of Ḥakīm Ata, we hope to have proven that the latter is the probable author of the verses preserved in the *MNḤ*. We also hope that our closer examination of the *MNḤ* has shown that the Turkic poetry contained in the classical works attributed to the Yasawī tradition—the *Dīwān-i Ḥikmat* and the *Bāqirghān Kitābı*, for example—despite being repeatedly edited and commented upon for over a century, still offers important and insufficiently exploited sources for the religious history of the Turks, a subject awaiting closer scholarly analysis in the future.

Notes

1. For more information on this *Miʿrājnāma* written in Khwārazmian Turkish and preserved in the Bibliothèque nationale de France, Paris, Supplément Turc 190, see Gruber, *The Timurid Book of Ascension*; idem, "The Prophet Muḥammad's Ascension," 180–239; and Scherberger, *Das Miʿrāǧnāme.*

2. There is another eastern Turkish poem titled *Ḥikāyet-i Miʿrāj* (The Story of the Ascension, henceforth *ḤM*) which is attributed to Aḥmad Yasawī. For more information about this text, see note 6.

3. See the last verse of the *MNḤ*: "The servant Süleymān spoke a word and spread the [story of] the Prophet's ascension, he talked about Aḥmad's ascension and implanted it into the memory of friends" (Eraslan, "Hakîm Ata ve Mi'râc-Nâmesi," 256, verse 122).

4. These studies are, in chronological order, the following: 1) Alpay, "Ḥakīm Ata," an *En-*

cyclopaedia of Islam, new ed., article just mentioning the *MNḤ* among other works attributed to Ḥakīm Ata. 2) Eraslan, "Hakîm Ata ve Mi'râc-Nâmesi," an edition of two slightly different manuscripts of the text. It consists of a Turkish introduction containing biographical data of Ḥakīm Ata (244–247), the transcription in Latin characters of the Chaghatay manuscripts written in Arab characters (247–256, 256–264), critical annotations to the text's metrical and linguistic features (265–272) and a list of Chaghatay words incomprehensible to the modern western Turkish reader, alongside their Turkish equivalents (273–302). The present translation and analysis of the *MNḤ* are based on this edition. 3) Akar, *Manzum Mi'râc-Nâmeler,* a vast presentation of ascension poems from Turkish Muslim literature also including the *MNḤ* (96–99). Akar describes the text's meter and rhyme, summarizes its contents, and cites some of its verses. He defines the idiom of the *MNḤ* as "12th-Century Central Asian Turkish" and sees the work as the most ancient Turkish ascension poem (ibid., 99). 4) Kara, "Hakîm Ata," a T.D.V. *İslâm Ansiklopedisi* article briefly mentioning the *MNḤ* and emphasizing its didactic character. 5) Gruber, "The Prophet Muḥammad's Ascension"; Gruber is the first western scholar dealing with the *MNḤ*. In her 2005 dissertation on the motif of the *miʿrāj* in Islamic art and literature, she presents the *MNḤ* as "the earliest extant Chaghatay-language *Miʿrājnāma,*" examines some of its contents, and identifies it as a missionary text.

5. This information is given by ʿAlī Shīr Nawā'ī (d. 1501) in his biography *Nasā'im al-Maḥabba min Shamā'im al-Futuwwa* (The Breezes of Love from the Fragrances of Generosity). See Eraslan, *Nesâyimü'l-Mahabbe,* 384.

6. As already mentioned in note 2, the *ḤM* pretends to be the work of Aḥmad Yasawī. If this is correct, and if we consider that Ḥakīm Ata was Aḥmad's younger disciple, the *ḤM* must be at least a decade older than the *MNḤ*. The *ḤM* is not, however, an ascension narrative in the true sense with the necessary classical elements (night journey from Mecca to Jerusalem, ascension from Jerusalem to heaven, visits to the seven heavens and meetings with former prophets, visions of paradise and hell, etc.). It is rather a eulogy of the Prophet containing allusions to the ascension. It is preserved in a manuscript of the *Dīwān-i Ḥikmat.* For a transcription and Turkish translation of this text, see Eraslan, *Ahmed-i Yesevî,* 256–266.

7. The *MNḤ* is included in the *Dīwān-i Ḥikmat* (Compendium of Wisdom, henceforth *DḤ*), a compilation of mystic-didactic poems ascribed to Aḥmad Yasawī and other authors. The earliest manuscripts of the *DḤ* are from the seventeenth century (İz, "Aḥmad Yasawī," 299). It also is preserved in the *Bāqirghān Kitābı* (*Book of Bāqirghān*, henceforth *BK*), a collection of mystic-didactic poems attributed to Ḥakīm Ata and other authors. This collection was in circulation since the later eighteenth century and was printed in 1857 for the first time in Kazan (DeWeese, "Ḥakim Atā," 574). In addition to the *DḤ* and the *BK*, there must be a further manuscript, copied around 1560 and preserved in Moscow, containing several verses that are found in later versions of the *MNḤ* (DeWeese, personal communication to the author, 26 September 2006). I wish to thank Devin DeWeese for providing me with this information.

8. The Chaghatay character of the *MNḤ* becomes evident by an analysis of its phonetic features. A few examples may illustrate this. Instead of *ä, d,* and *b,* as would be the archaic spelling, our text writes *i, y,* and *v,* as in the following examples: *kiltürdüm* ("I have brought"), not *kältürdüm; ayaḳ* ("foot") and not *adaḳ;* and *yavlaḳ* ("bad, badly"), not *yablaḳ* (see Eraslan, "Hakîm Ata ve Mi'râc-Nâmesi," 253, verse 82b; 249, verse 23b; and 263, verse 100a). The text's Chaghatay character also is recognizable by some of its grammatical features, such as its use of the following Perfect II forms as used in Chaghatay and not in Qara-Khanid: *yörüpdürler* ("they have walked"), *turupdur* ("it has been"), *saḳlap turupdur* ("he has counted") (see ibid., 249, verse 30b; 255, verse 117a; and 251, verse 60a). There are many other examples that could be cited here. For the development of eastern middle Turkish, see Eckmann, "Charakteristik"; ibid., "Das Chwarezmtürkische"; ibid., "Das Tschaghataische"; and Mansuroğlu, "Das Karakhanidische."

9. The theory that the *MNḤ* is a fake from an earlier period, based on the late date of extant manuscripts and the wholly Chaghatay character of its idiom, is not to be found in the secondary sources, but it still exists. For instance, DeWeese believes that the text, as "the entire body of Turkic verses ascribed to sheikhs of the Yasawī tradition, [. . .] is most likely the prod-

uct of dervishes of the Yasawī order during the 15th and 16th centuries" (DeWeese, personal communication to the author, 26 September 2006). I wish to thank Devin DeWeese for sharing this perspective with me. As for DeWeese's refusal of Aḥmad Yasawī's authorship for the poems in the *DḤ*—equally because of the late date of their manuscripts, their Chaghatay idiom, etc.—see his foreword in Köprülü, *Early Mystics,* xx–xxi.

10. Laut, "Vielfalt," 31; Scharlipp, *Die alttürkische Literatur,* 13.

11. Unfortunately it is not entirely clear when Aḥmad Yasawī and Ḥakīm Ata lived. Most scholars (Barthold, "Ḥakīm Atā," 239; İz, "Aḥmad Yasawī," 299; Gruber, "The Prophet Muḥammad's Ascension," 49) agree that Aḥmad Yasawī died in 1166/7, whereas DeWeese argues that he probably lived in the early thirteenth century (DeWeese, *"Mashā'ikh-i Turk,"* 183; and idem, foreword to Köprülü, *Early Mystics,* xvii). As for Ḥakīm Ata, the majority of secondary sources (Akar, *Manzum Miʿrâc-Nâmeler,* 98; Alpay, "Ḥakīm Ata," 76; Arat, "Hakîm Ata," 101; Eraslan, "Ahmed-i Yesevî," 161; Gruber, "The Prophet Muṇammad's Ascension," 49; and Kara, "Hakîm Ata," 183) state either that he died in 1186/7 or else that he lived in the twelfth century (without giving a precise date). But if the attribution of Aḥmad Yasawī to the thirteenth century is correct and if Ḥakīm Ata was Aḥmad's disciple, the former has to be placed accordingly later. DeWeese writes that 1186/7 as the date of Ḥakīm Ata's death was first mentioned in Ghulām Sarwar Lāhurī's nineteenth-century Muslim-Indian Sufi biography *Khazīnat al-aṣfiyā'* (Treasure of the Pure), and the date "seems not to have been based on any reliable information" (DeWeese, "Ḥakim Atā," 573). As in the case of Aḥmad Yasawī, DeWeese attributes Ḥakīm Ata to the early thirteenth century (ibid.). For the present chapter, the dispute about the date of Ḥakīm Ata's death is not crucial, since missionary efforts in Central Asia make sense in both the twelfth and the thirteenth centuries.

12. The *MNḤ* itself gives some evidence that it was recited orally and did not circulate in written form. In its penultimate verse, the text says "*listen* to [the tale of] the Prophet's ascension," and not "*read* [the tale of] the Prophet's ascension" (Eraslan, "Hakîm Ata ve Miʿrâc-Nâmesi," 256, verse 121a).

13. See note 7.

14. See note 7.

15. Verses 3a and 3b are included in *Kazan,* not in *Caferoğlu* (Eraslan, "Hakîm Ata ve Miʿrâc-Nâmesi," 256, verses 4 and 5).

16. This verse is included in Kazan only (ibid., 257, verse 13).

17. This verse is included in *Caferoğlu* only (ibid., 248, verse 15).

18. This verse is included in *Caferoğlu* only (ibid., 248, verse 17).

19. This verse is included in *Caferoğlu* only (ibid., 249, verse 18).

20. That is, heavenly steeds in general, rather than Burāq proper.

21. This verse is included in *Kazan* only (ibid., 258, verse 32).

22. This verse is included in *Kazan* only (ibid., 258, verse 34).

23. This verse is included in *Caferoğlu* only (ibid., 250, verse 34).

24. This verse is included in *Caferoğlu* only (ibid., 250, verse 38).

25. In *Kazan,* the voices are reversed: the voice coming from the right is the world and the voice coming from the left is the Jews (ibid., 259, verses 36 and 37).

26. In *Kazan,* the colors are yellow, green, red, and white, and the Prophet left behind the yellow and the red ones, and selected the green and white ones (ibid., 259, verse 41).

27. This verse is included in *Caferoğlu* only (ibid., 251, verse 47).

28. *Miḥrāb*: Niche in the wall of the mosque indicating the *qibla*, i. e., the direction of the Kaʿba in Mecca that Muslims are obliged to face while fulfilling the ritual prayer.

29. Ibid., 251, verse 55. Eraslan transcribes the term as *ṣaḥrā* ("desert" or "steppe"). However, it should be read as *Ṣakhra* ("Rock"), because the Prophet's heavenly ascension began from the rocky outcrop (that is, Mount Moriah) in Jerusalem.

30. This verse is included in *Caferoğlu* only (ibid., 251, verse 56).

31. This verse is included in *Caferoğlu* only (ibid., 251, verse 57).

32. This verse is included in *Caferoğlu* only (ibid., 251, verse 61).

33. This verse is included in *Kazan* only (ibid., 260, verse 62).

34. This is a very rare depiction of angels. It is difficult to trace the origins of this motif. In Buddhist Turkish eschatological literature (*Maitrisimit*), people in hell who were executioners while alive are described as having no heads; they have to suffer the same punishment in hell that they meted out in life (Laut, *Uigurische Sünden,* 147). It is possible that this trope survived in Islamic Turkish eschatology in this same form, but with a modified content. For more information about the *Maitrisimit,* see note 78.

35. This verse is included in *Caferoğlu* only (Eraslan, "Hakîm Ata ve Mi'râc-Nâmesi," 252, verse 71).

36. This verse is included in *Kazan* only (ibid., 261, verse 71).

37. The corresponding verse in *Kazan* mentions that Gabriel's wings would burn if he passed this limit (ibid., 261, verse 74).

38. In *Kazan,* the Divine Presence is described as the "no-place" (*lā mekān*), that is, a location beyond temporal and spatial limits (ibid., 261, verse 75).

39. This verse is included in *Caferoğlu* only (ibid., 253, verse 79).

40. Verses 84a and 84b are included in *Kazan* only (ibid., 262, verses 81 and 82).

41. This verse is included in *Kazan* only (ibid., 262, verse 88).

42. This verse is included in *Caferoğlu* only (ibid., 253, verse 89).

43. Literally, "sandalwood" (ibid., 263, verse 94).

44. This verse is included in Kazan only (ibid., 263, verse 94).

45. The corresponding verse of *Kazan* specifies that the angels use hooks to pull out the sinners' tongues (ibid., 263, verse 95).

46. This verse is included in *Caferoğlu* only (ibid., 254, verse 99).

47. This verse is included in *Caferoğlu* only (ibid., 254, verse 103).

48. This verse is included in *Caferoğlu* only (ibid., 254, verse 104).

49. This verse is included in *Caferoğlu* only (ibid., 255, verse 110).

50. This verse is included in *Caferoğlu* only (ibid., 255, verse 111).

51. This means that the heavenly steeds eat the best food and drink the best water so that they are in a brilliant state and can serve the inhabitants of paradise in the best possible way.

52. This metaphor expresses that the Prophet was removed from earthly time during the ascension and dipped into divine time, so it was possible for him to experience years, decades, and even centuries in a split second (Schimmel, *Muhammad ist sein Prophet,* 141–142).

53. ʿAbdallāh b. al-ʿAbbās (d. 686 or 688), often referred to in brief as Ibn ʿAbbās, was Muḥammad's cousin and one of the most famous transmitters of the Prophet's Sayings. A number of ascension tales are attributed to him; see Colby, "Constructing an Islamic Ascension Narrative"; and idem, *Narrating Muḥammad's Night Journey.*

54. For a discussion of the use of *miʿrāj* narratives as missionary literature, see Gruber, "The Prophet Muḥammad's Ascension," 108–179, 180–239.

55. DeWeese in Köprülü, *Early Mystics,* xx.

56. For the importance of Aḥmad Yasawī and his order for the Islamization of Central Asia, see Bodrogligeti, "Yasavī Ideology," 42; Caferoğlu, "La littérature Turque," 272; Eraslan, "Ahmed-i Yesevî," 160–161; İz, "Aḥmad Yasawī," 299; and Zarcone, "Ṭarīḳa," 250. For Sufi missionaries in the Subcontinent, the following examples can be cited: Muʿīn al-dīn Chishtī (d. 1236), the founder of the Chishtiyya order in India; Laʿl Shahbāz Qalandar (d. 1262 or later) in Sindh; Shāh Jalāl Mujarrad (d. 1346), a native of Yemen (according to another tradition, he was from Konya), in Bangladesh; Sayyid ʿAlī Hamadānī (d. 1385), an Iranian, in Kashmir (see Frembgen, *Derwische,* 21, 32; Harder, "Bangladesch," 366; and Schimmel, *Mystische Dimensionen,* 341, also pointing to the missionary activity of Sufi preachers in Indonesia and Africa, 365–366). Further evidence for the missionary activity of Sufi orders in Africa is given by Müller, "Islamisierung," 454.

57. Schimmel, *Mystische Dimensionen,* 341.

58. Eraslan, "Hakîm Ata ve Mi'râc-Nâmesi," 256, verse 5a and 262, verse 88b.

59. On the concept of the *nūr Muḥammad,* see Rubin, "Pre-existence and Light: Aspects of the Concept of Nūr Muḥammad," 62–119; and idem, "Nūr Muḥammadī," 125.

60. Eraslan, "Hakîm Ata ve Miʿrâc-Nâmesi," 253, verse 90 and 262, verses 85–86 and verse 89.

61. In Arabic, it appears as follows: *Law lāka law lāka, mā khalaqtu 'l-aflāka* (ibid., 262, verse 88a). A hadith qudsī is an expression believed to be uttered by God rather than the Prophet. Many of them are mystic traditions not dating prior to the tenth or eleventh century. This specific tradition is included in al-Ḥākim (d. 1014), *al-Mustadrak* (The Correction), 615, but in a different wording, and in al-ʿAjlūnī (d. 1749), *Kashf al-Khafāʾ* (Revelation of the Hidden), 232, with the same wording as in the *MNḤ*. For further information on "Holy Sayings," and on the subject of hadith qudsī in general, see Demirci, "Hakîkat-i Muhammediyye," 180; Graham, *Divine Word;* Robson, "Ḥadith Ḳudsī"; Schimmel, *Mystische Dimensionen,* 305; idem, "The Prophet in Popular Muslim Piety," 377; idem, *Muhammad ist sein Prophet,* 114, 117, 220 and 231; and Süleyman Uludağ, "İslâm kültüründe Hz. Muhammed," *İslâm Ansiklopedisi* 30 (2005): 449.

62. Eraslan, "Hakîm Ata ve Mi'râc-Nâmesi," 247, verse 3, 253, verses 83–84 and verse 88a, and 254–255, verses 104–105.

63. Kara, "Hakîm Ata," 184.

64. Eraslan, "Hakîm Ata ve Miʿrâc-Nâmesi," 254, verses 97–255, verse 105.

65. Muhsin Khan, *Ṣaḥīḥ al-Bukhārī,* 6:158; Muslim, *Ṣaḥīḥ,* 1:54; al-Nasāʾī, *Kitāb al-sunan,* 2:465–466.

66. al-Nasāʾī, *Kitāb al-sunan,* 2:465.

67. Suyūṭī has written five more treatises on the subject: 1) *al-Taʿẓīm wa-'l-minna fī anna abaway al-nabī fī 'l-janna* (The Grace and Blessing that the Parents of the Prophet are in Paradise) or *al-Fawāʾid al-kāmina fī īmān al-sayyida Āmina* (The Hidden Proofs of Āmina's True Belief), 2) *al-Maqāma al-sundusiyya fī khabar wāliday khayr al-bariyya* (The Silk Tune of the Best Parents of Creation), 3) *al-Daraj al-munīfa fī 'l-ābāʾ al-sharīfa* (The Exalted Path to the Honorable Fathers), 4) *Nashr al-ʿalamayn al-munīfayn fī iḥyāʾ al-abawayn al-sharīfayn* (The Revelation of Two Exalted Signs for the Reanimation of the Honorable Parents), 5) *Subul al-najāḥ* (The Ear of Success). On these works, see Brockelmann, *Geschichte,* 2:185.

68. For a discussion of this phenomenon, see Montgomery Watt, "Ḥanīf."

69. Suyūṭī, *Masālik al-ḥunafāʾ,* 15–39, 39–85, and 85–92. All his other works, as can already be recognized by their titles, are also defending the innocence of Muḥammad's parents.

70. Gruber, "The Prophet Muḥammad's Ascension," 51.

71. Ibid., 51, note 120.

72. Eraslan, "Hakîm Ata ve Miʿrâc-Nâmesi," 254, verse 100a.

73. Ibid., 251, verse 53–54.

74. Ibid., 252, verse 66–67.

75. For the Ilkhānid *Miʿrājnāma,* see Gruber's chapter in this volume; idem, *The Ilkhanid Book of Ascension;* and idem, "The Prophet Muḥammad's Ascension," 108–179.

76. Eraslan, "Hakîm Ata ve Miʿrâc-Nâmesi," 247, verse 1a, 248, verse 11a, 253, verse 78a and 256, verses 121–122.

77. The *MNḤ* describes such forms of punishment without telling us the sin the punished have committed (ibid., 254, verses 95–96; 263, verses 94–95). It is obvious, however, that the people being tortured by their tongues (ibid., 254, verse 95) must have been liars or calumniators or women having insulted their husbands, and that the women hung up by their breasts (ibid., verse 96) must have been women having nursed children who have been born as a result of their mothers' adulterous relationships. This can be evidenced by consulting the contents of several other ascension narratives like those attributed to Ibn ʿAbbās and the Timurid *Miʿrājnāma* (Ibn ʿAbbās, *al-Isrāʾ wa-'l-Miʿrāj,* 12–16; and Scherberger, *Miʿrāğnāme,* 109–114.)

78. Compare, for example, the depiction of hell as given in the *Maitrisimit,* a text of Turkic Buddhist eschatology preserved in manuscripts from the eighth or eleventh century (see also note 34). For further information about this work, see Scherberger, *Miʿrāğnāme,* 126–128, with further references.

5

Contesting the Eschaton in Medieval Iberia: The Polemical Intersection of Beatus of Liébana's Commentary on the Apocalypse and the Prophet's *Miʿrājnāma*

HEATHER M. COFFEY

The peculiar power of eschatological literature rests not only with its enigmatic, otherworldly imagery but also in its soteriological content, which expounds a particular philosophy of redemption. This characteristic marks the genre as a prime resource for the reinforcement of communal solidarity during periods of religious fluctuation and strife. With the infiltration of Islam into the Iberian Peninsula through the Umayyad conquest in 711 and the establishment of the Caliphate of Córdoba (929–1031), acculturation and conversion to Islam threatened the integrity of the Hispanic Christian church. This investigation will show how the veridical claim of eschatological material was marshaled as a polemic device in Christian-Muslim disputations. Christians engaged publicly with Islam in both literary and visual forums, not only through widely disseminated polemical tracts but also through the proliferation of pictorial imagery in lavishly illustrated manuscripts.

This latter enterprise was dominated by the production of various copies of the *Commentarius in Apocalipsin* (Commentary on the Apocalypse) written by the Asturian monk Beatus of Liébana (c. 730–800).[1] Illustrated copies of Beatus's text proliferated in monastic scriptoria throughout the frontier zone between al-Andalus and the northern Hispanic Christian kingdoms from the tenth to the thirteenth centuries. Referring to select images drawn from two manuscripts representative of the Beatus tradition, the Girona Beatus[2] (completed ca. 975) and the Las Huelgas Beatus[3] (completed in 1220), this investigation will show how these manuscripts' imagery reflected the position espoused by their Christian patrons regarding the Muslim presence: the culture of resistance to inculcation that prompted northward migration in the case of the former, or the crusading efforts of the *Reconquísta* to liberate the Iberian peninsula from Muslim rule in the case of the latter. In so doing, it will expose how the historical vector of the ideological deployment of eschatological material created a direct intersection with the Islamic *Miʿrājnāma* genre, the central repository of eschatological imagery within Islam, at key moments in its own evolutionary trajectory.

The Illustrated Beatus Tradition

Beatus's commentary was an exegetical product that relied upon the selection and careful arrangement of passages penned by earlier patristic writers rather than his inspired authorship in the modern sense. The commentary is introduced by a series of prefatory entries and a *Summa dicendorum*,[4] while the core of the commentary is structured according to interchanging *storia* and *explanatio:* each of the sixty-eight *storiae* contains a portion of verses from the Book of Revelation followed by an *explanatio* comprising a woven sequence of preexisting interpretations.[5] Although the commentary has repeatedly been characterized as a response against the Adoptionist theology upheld by Archbishop Elipandus of Toledo,[6] and on that basis dated to ca. 785, recent scholarship has positioned the commentary as an earlier project of ca. 776, well before the inception of the Adoptionist controversy.[7]

No illustrated copies of Beatus's commentary survive from the eighth century. Evidence of a painted tradition makes its first appearance in a single ninth-century fragment preserved in Silos, which bears a small image inserted into the lower left corner of one of the folio's two columns of text.[8] The surviving corpus suggests that it is only from the tenth century onward that one witnesses the production and dissemination of lavishly illustrated manuscripts. This pictorial revision is associated with the so-called Branch II manuscripts,[9] initiated by the sudden production of numerous volumes in the mid- to late tenth century, such as the mid-century Morgan Beatus,[10] the mid-century Vitrina Beatus, the Tábara Beatus of 970, the Valladolid Beatus of 970, and the Girona Beatus of 975. Indeed, John Williams has convincingly argued that the archetype of all Branch II manuscripts, which inaugurated this expanded pictorial form when compared to that operative in the Silos fragment, was produced between approximately 940 and 950.[11] All of these manuscripts share a format characterized by the insertion of an illustration pertaining to each *storia* prior to the beginning of the *explanatio.* Their illustrations include half and full page images as well as numerous remarkable double-page compositions. This tenth-century efflorescence is also marked by the appearance of supplemental addenda or "extra-Apocalyptic imagery" of a Christological nature, including frontispieces of the Evangelists, genealogical tables that chart a "schema of the Incarnation," oftentimes a Crucifixion scene, and an illustrated version of Jerome's *Commentarius in Danielem* (Commentary on the Book of Daniel), considered the Old Testament counterpart to the Apocalypse of John.[12]

Together, the entire corpus of illustrated Beatus manuscripts comprises a singular tradition of medieval painting consisting of twenty-seven extant full or partial copies comprising over one thousand five hundred illustrations.[13] Such overt visual splendor is proof of investment in their production, yet the specific function of these manuscripts is somewhat elusive. All are the product of monastic scriptoria and evidently intended for monastic use, save the so-called Facundus Beatus produced in 1047 for Fernando I of Castile, who ruled León-Castile from 1038–

1065.[14] The original purpose of Beatus's commentary and its eventual application (which need not be the same) is addressed obliquely within the introductory preface. Here Beatus dedicates his text to Etherius, bishop of Osma, "for the edification of the brothers' study,"[15] although much of the preface—including the above phrase—is directly appropriated from earlier writings by Isidore of Seville, which somewhat complicates its reflection of our author's motives.[16]

Scholars have traditionally explained the prevalence of the commentary by the fact that the special liturgical role of the Book of Revelation was affirmed in 633 at the Fourth Council of Toledo as a canonical book to be read in the church from Easter to Pentecost.[17] Yet this prescription of Apocalyptic *lectiones* during the Easter season extended beyond the Iberian peninsula, appearing in both the Gallician liturgy and the earliest *Ordines Romani.*[18] Furthermore, it has become clear that the function of these illustrated manuscripts must be evaluated according to a trajectory of liturgical change, because their history overlaps with the transition from the Mozarabic to the Roman liturgy sanctioned at the Council of Burgos in 1080.[19] Rose Walker has demonstrated that a sample of surviving Mozarabic liturgical manuscripts lack readings for the monastic office, suggesting that Beatus's text could not have fulfilled this function.[20] This insight lends credence to the position, popularized in earlier studies, that the commentary was employed as a contemplative monastic tool oriented around personal study.[21] Close interaction with these manuscripts, either individually or in small groups, would have functioned as an ideal didactical venue wherein the tribulation characterizing much of contemporary Christian-Muslim encounters, that is, interpretations of current and recent Iberian history, could be articulated through an eschatological lens.

The Rise of Polemical Eschatology

The production of a pictorially expanded version of Beatus's commentary during the mid-tenth century attests to the peculiar resonance of its eschatological material at a specifically identifiable moment within the manuscripts' conventual history. Although it may be something of a natural impulse to suspect millenarist expectations as a possible motivation, it must be remembered that "the *era hispanica,* the chronology then practiced in Spain, reached 1000 already in the year 962 of the common *annus domini* chronology still used today," and therefore only two of the surviving copies of the commentary actually predate the turn of the millennium.[22] A much more convincing explanation for the motive to produce these manuscripts revolves around the polemical contexts of the era in which the works were created.

All of the extant tenth-century manuscripts were manufactured in monastic scriptoria scattered beyond the Duero River, then the northern lip of al-Andalus, concurrent with the immigration of Mozarabic monks to the Kingdom of León.

From the mid-ninth century onward, King Alfonso III (r. 866–910) encouraged the mass migration of Christians northward in order to repopulate the marshes between the Asturias and Andalusia.[23] A multitude of surviving foundation inscriptions and charters document that this process was most prominent between 910 and 940.[24] Salient examples of migration include the monastery of San Cosme de Abellar, which was founded in 905 by the Córdoban Bishop Cixila, and the monastery of Sahagún, restored by monks from the Córdoban monastery of San Cristóbal under the leadership of Abbot Adefonso. Córdobans also founded the monastery of San Cebrián de Mazote in 915 and San Martin de Castañeda in 916.[25] The construction of these and other monasteries attempted to bolster the strength of Christianity near the shifting, embattled frontier.

Exodus from al-Andalus constituted an act of protest and a radical solution to the strain of subordinate status. The term "Mozarabic" derives from the Arabic word *mustaʿrab,* meaning "arabized," but also "one who claims to be Arab without being so."[26] It thus refers to those Christians subjugated to Islamic rule living within al-Andalus who, as *dhimmīs*, were allowed to practice their religion and to maintain a measure of internal communal authority provided they paid the *jizya* tax. The majority of these Christians were members of communities of pre-Islamic origin that were loosely clustered into nodes reflecting the bishoprics of the Hispanic church.[27] By no means, however, did their protected status erect an impermeable boundary between the conquerors and the conquered. Although the social and legal relations regulated by the *dhimma* were intended to maintain a clear division between the Arab Muslim authorities and their subject population, this division was undermined by a gradual yet persistent process of acculturation, accelerated by the twin phenomenon of ethno-religious intermarriage and conversion.[28] Such acculturation is theoretically bidirectional,[29] but Andalusian Christians garnered significant financial and social advantages upon the full or partial adoption of Arabic language and culture. In contrast, there was little to no incentive for the Muslim elite to show a similar interest in Latin language and literature. While the majority of the Christian population was likely indifferent to this situation, for those Christians closely engaged with and fully immersed in traditional Latin Christian culture, particularly monks, nuns, and clerics, this constituted a palpable erosion of cultural identity.[30]

This simmering anxiety eventually resulted in an outburst of anti-Muslim activism by radical Christians. Throughout the 850s a number of Christians engaged in public denunciations of Muḥammad and his teachings and were executed for blasphemy. Provocation for these acts may have been found in two relatively spontaneous events. The first was the execution of a priest from the basilica of St. Acisclus named Perfectus on 18 April 850, who was accused of insulting the Prophet Muḥammad.[31] The second was the assault and arrest of a merchant named John in May 851, who was accused of swearing by the Prophet although he was a Christian.[32] It was not long after these initial incriminations that a monk named Isaac walked from the monastery of Tabanos to Córdoba and publicly railed against the

Prophet in front of the emir's palace and in the presence of a Muslim judge *(qāḍī);* predictably, he was decapitated for this blasphemy on 3 June 851.[33] Isaac's death initiated a persistent practice of intentional executions such that by the close of the decade almost fifty individuals had engaged in near identical confrontations.[34] Twenty-one of these individuals were monks or nuns who engaged in strict ascetic practices.[35] A significant subgroup came from volatile ethno-religiously mixed families; members of this subgroup were executed as apostate Muslims who refused to recant their Christian beliefs.[36] Offering a clear index of their acculturation, the wider Christian community refused to champion these deaths as anything other than meaningless agitations orchestrated by zealots. This indifference was fought not with the sword but with the pen, through the circulation of polemical texts underscoring the heroism of these acts.

Previous treatises had been penned by learned Latin ecclesiastics in response to the encroachment of Islam. The earliest of these is the *Disputatio Felicis cum sarraceno* (The Disputation of Felix with a Saracen), likely penned by Bishop Felix of Urgell and mentioned by title in a letter from the scholar Alcuin to Charlemagne (r. 768–814); unfortunately, nothing at all remains of the work beyond this brief allusion.[37] A second anti-Islamic *disputatio* was composed by the Córdoban Abbot Speraindeo in the 820s or 830s in response to the execution of the brothers Adulphus and John, of which only a minute portion survives, having been incorporated into a later text.[38] Significant for our purposes is the fact that, fueled throughout the 850s by the controversy sustained by the continual deaths before the *qāḍī,* such literary activity gained new urgency and was imprinted with decidedly eschatological imagery.

The figureheads of this literary campaign were Eulogius and Paulus Alvarus. Eulogius initially composed *passiones* in the summer following Isaac's death and the numerous individuals who so quickly followed his example.[39] As one of many supposedly dissident clerics incarcerated by the Muslim authorities in 851 accused of inciting unrest, Eulogius wrote the *Documentum martyriale* (Martyrology) intended to encourage two young women, Maria and Flora, similarly imprisoned but also facing execution, to maintain their resolve and face death.[40] During his incarceration Eulogius also dedicated himself to the completion of the *Memoriale sanctorum* (Memorial of the Saints), a "combination apology and martyrology" widely circulated after his release.[41] In his final literary endeavor, the polemical *Liber apologeticus martyrum* (Apologia of the Martyrs), composed ca. 857–859, the priest Eulogius attempted to garner support for these deaths by accentuating the Christological component that distinguished the two religions.[42] While the wider Mozarabic community was willing to find between Christianity and Islam general parity (rooted in their shared monotheism), Eulogius presented Muḥammad as a heresiarch, a modern incarnation of Arius, who acknowledged the exemplary nature of Christ but was "bestowed with none of the power of the deity."[43] In his treatises Eulogius further scorns Muḥammad as both a pseudo-prophet and *praecursor antichristi,* although Eulogius does not attend to this latter invective at any length.[44] Eulogius also buttressed these denigrations by emphasizing the falsity of the Islamic afterlife, quoting the only surviving passage from the earlier *disputatio* written by Abbot Speraindeo. This passage dismissed the Islamic conception of heaven as "more of a lunapar than a paradise,"[45] and accused the Prophet of perverting the Christian model of the afterlife "until it resembled a brothel,"[46] therein undermining Islam as a credible theological system.

Written around 854, at the height of the controversy, the first half of Paulus Alvarus's *Indiculus luminosus* (Luminous Catalogue) progresses much like Eulogius's texts.[47] The second half, however, begins with the explication of passages drawn from chapters seven and eleven of Daniel, which had been identified in Jerome's commentary as referring to Antichrist,[48] and devotes an elaborate exegesis to the exposure of Muḥammad as such. From a theological perspective, Muḥammad could not be considered the ultimate Antichrist, immediate harbinger of the end of the world, because such a figure is prophesized as living during the last days. Muḥammad was clearly a historical figure who was agreed to have died an earthly death over two centuries prior.[49] This did not dissuade Alvarus from also constructing his literary image of him as a precursor to, or instrument of, Antichrist, one of the many manifestations that would precede and accelerate the arrival of the end of the world.[50]

In his defamation of Muḥammad, Alvarus pursued descriptions of the Islamic afterlife with a biting enthusiasm unequalled even in the rhetorical flourishes attending similar content in Eulogius's tracts. Alvarus was particularly inspired by one opportune line from Daniel (11:37–38)—"And he shall follow the lust of women"—through which he exposes Muḥammad as a sexually deviant polygamist.[51] To offer but one colorful assertion inspired by this phrase, the *Indiculus luminosis* claims that Muḥammad "enjoys the wives of other men like a pimp, concealing the scabbiness of his filth behind an angelic command, promising as a gift for those who believe in him harlots for the taking, scattered about in the paradise of his god."[52] In this vitriolic attack Alvarus displays some concrete knowledge of the Qur'an; his description of the "harlots for the taking" must be inspired by the celestial houris promised to the faithful in various chapters (*sūras*) in the Qur'an.

These polemical authors did not gravitate randomly toward paradisiacal content in their literary efforts. Discourse over the nature of the afterlife was a strategic move with a logical explanation. Knowledge of the heavenly realm presupposes the disclosure of transcendent reality through a precise moment of revelation, an experience neither Eulogius nor Alvarus could grant Muḥammad. To accept the image of the celestial spheres recorded in the Qur'an, ḥadīths, and other Islamic writings would not only verify his elect status in the eyes of God—confirming his prophethood—it would also invalidate the redemptive value of Christian belief, based upon its perceived monopoly on veridical knowledge of the divine. For these polemical authors, the existence of competing narratives on the nature of heaven was a ludicrous impossibility. There was nothing heinous for Eulogius and Alvarus in mocking the Muslim image of heaven: as a heretic, Antichrist and false prophet, Muḥammad's teachings were themselves fanciful constructions or paradisiacal imaginings, contingent upon the parasitical inversion of Christological content. Given this belief in the inherent corruption of Islam as a theological entity, once removed from Christian truth, Eulogius's and Alvarus's denigrations of the Prophet were merely parody in the second degree.

Furthermore, disputations on the nature of the afterlife were inherently topical. In the minds of the Córdoban martyrs, the price of acculturation was forfeiture of its splendors. This is particularly true for those secretly engaging in Christian worship, who, as a result of these covert practices, may have been sacrificing their salvation. Certainly the radical Christian position espoused that "only an open profession of faith would save them from hell," and this is one of the central motivations Eulogius describes in his defense of the martyrs' actions.[53] Yet in their combination of paradisiacal and eschatological content, neither of our polemical authors espouses the literal arrival of the eschaton. In defaming Muḥammad as a precursor of the Antichrist, they seek to understand the popularity of his teachings within the realm of Christian history; rather than anticipating the end of the world, Eulogius and Alvarus anticipate the end of Muslim rule[54] and the restoration of a prosperous church in Iberian lands and beyond.

The construction of such denunciations of Muḥammad required a solid grasp of the details of both his life and the tenets of Islam *a priori* in order to be persuasive. It has been noted that an essential tool in Eulogius's arsenal was the exploitation of a brief, spurious biography of the Prophet that relayed the year of his birth as 666, the number of the Beast of the Apocalypse (Rev. 13:18),[55] which he had discovered in the monastic library of Leyre near Pamplona in Navarre ca. 850.[56] It is reasonable to assume that both authors derived some knowledge of the Islamic afterlife from the Qur'an itself, but Alvarus seems also to have known of the defamatory *vita*, which he summarizes in a letter to Joannes of Seville.[57]

Yet it is startling to realize that this spurious biography of Muḥammad is *itself* a subversion of the very bio-historical texts essential to the formation of a narrative of the Prophet's ascension, the central repository of Islamic eschatological imagery. Over the course of its history, the developmental trajectory of the "Book of the Prophet Muḥammad's Ascension" moved from the circulation and performance of oral accounts of the Prophet's *miʿrāj* in the earliest decades of Islam toward its emergence by the tenth century as an established, amplified ascension narrative.[58] The propagation of successive biographies of the Prophet was one of several literary genres, in addition to the transmission of hadiths, and the development of exegetical works, histories, and mystical poetry, pivotal to this process of narrative expansion. Yet biography played a distinguished role: indeed, the earliest explication of a complete ascension related by Muḥammad appears in Ibn Isḥāq's (d. 768) *Sīrat al-Nabī* (Biography of the Prophet). In Ibn Isḥāq's text the qur'anic allusion to Muḥammad journeying to "the farthest mosque" is definitively connected to the sacred sanctuary in Jerusalem (Aelia, that is, al-Quds) and Muḥammad not only travels up into the heavens—meeting various earlier prophets and angels along the way—but also briefly witnesses the gruesome punishments of the denizens of hell.[59] This and other biographies of the Prophet would certainly have been available in Muslim Spain and particularly among the Córdoban literary elite, and may or may not have been known to Eulogius and Paulus Alvarus.

Eulogius's and Paulus Alvarus's own works would most certainly have been available in the Kingdom of León. After his death, Eulogius himself became an object of veneration, prompting Alfonso III (r. 866–910) to negotiate the transfer of his relics, and possibly some of his books,[60] from Emir Muḥammad I (r. 852–886), thereby providing a channel through which these texts, and a copy of the original *vita* from Leyre, could have entered (or reentered, as the case may be) northern terrain. We can also presume that copies of these texts would have been brought directly by the exodus of monks seeking refuge from the cultural and religious tensions marking al-Andalus, if indeed they were not already in circulation among northern Christian communities.[61]

This is the historical and religious context in which Beatus of Liébana's Commentary on the Apocalypse gained popularity: on the heels of an established textual practice of exploiting defamatory eschatological material with the implicit aim of crafting a conversion narrative to inculcate Islamicized Christians, with its own peculiar parallel to the nascent tradition of narrating and visualizing the Prophet's ascension.[62] The tenth-century proliferation of illustrated Commentaries within scriptoria along the frontier could therefore be recognized as an adaptive extension of this practice in its championing of Christian eschatology, buttressed by the newly inserted Christological context and the *Commentarius in Danielem* by Jerome mined by Paulus Alvarus. In this contentious environment, the seemingly atopical nature of much of John's Revelation and Beatus's commentary adopts a declarative function, affirming, or more accurately reaffirming, Christian cosmology in a visceral, visual statement of Christian orthodoxy over and against the competing assertions of that which these polemicists considered Muslim heresy.

Visual Resonances in the Girona Beatus

The affirmative function of the illustrated editions of Beatus's text oftentimes relies upon semi-veiled pictorial commentaries upon Islamic-Christian tensions. This is most prominently displayed in the so-called Girona Beatus, named for the cathedral in which it was preserved. It is not an original product of Catalonia but rather seems to have arrived there prior to 6 October 1078.[63] Although the colophon does not provide the specific name of the scriptorium responsible for its manufacture, it attributes its illustration to the artistic talents of the monk Emeterius and the nun Ende.[64] Critical information is also provided by an inscription following the conclusion of the text on folio 284r, which informs the reader that the scribe was one "presbyter Senior," and a second inscription on folio 285v provides the name of the patron, Dominicus.[65] Thus the manuscript is generally considered to be a product of the monastery of San Salvador de Tábara, in part because the names of Senior and Emeterius both appear in the colophon of the Tábara Beatus.[66] The colophon of the Girona manuscript also reveals that martial conflict informed the production of the commentary, recording how the codex was "successfully completed on Friday, 6 July. In those days Ferdenando Flaginiz was at Villas, the Toledan town, fighting the Moors. The year was 975."[67] Carlos García-Tejedor notes that this surname appears in ninth-century Asturian documents; indeed the name "Ferdenando Flaginiz" has been identified as one Count Fernán Láinez (959–995), the governor of the Duero region of León, who has also been recorded in archival documents by the name of Fernando ben Falain.[68] It has also been suggested that this particular military expedition refers to the campaign initiated in Navarre in March, 975 by García Fernández, Count of Castile from 970–995.[69] Word of the Christian defeat did not reach Córdoba until 15 July of that year, suggesting that artists and scribes laboring in Leónese scriptoria may still have been hoping for news of victory when the codex was completed.[70]

An underlying current of conquest is captured in the notorious image of a mounted warrior spearing a serpent which graces the bottom third of folio 134v. It is neither a regular component of the commentary illustrations nor is it adequately explained by the content of the *storia* that precedes it or the *explanatio* that follows. As such, it has been the locus of varying interpretations, both as "an ideal portrait of a warrior of the Reconquest," who remains a venerable Christian figure despite his oriental costume,[71] but also inversely, as a representation of Islam against an erect serpent who withstands his onslaught in a Christian posture of defiance.[72] Such disagreement is the casualty of the highly symbolic nature of the commentary's visual imagery, which often contains an element of elusiveness despite the most sensitive and detailed explications.

Nonetheless, a thematic sequence of four full-page illustrations in the Girona Beatus could have provided eschatological vindication of the radical Christian resistance to acculturation under Islamic rule that prompted monastic migration northward. The first is the full-page illustration of Rev. 10:1–11:2, *John Receives the Book and Measures the Temple*, which encompasses folio 161v (Figure 5.1 and Plate 12). These biblical passages describe how a mighty angel descends to John from heaven, so immense that he stands with one foot on the sea and the other on land. John then hears a heavenly voice, who orders him to take the scroll held open in the angel's hand. The angel then commands John to "take it [the scroll] and eat; it will be bitter to your stomach, but sweet as honey in your mouth" (Rev. 10:9).[73] That John then consumes the text proves that he announces a message that originates from an external, divine source and that it is not his own fabrication.[74] Given a reed for a measuring rod, John is then commanded to go and "measure the temple of God and the altar

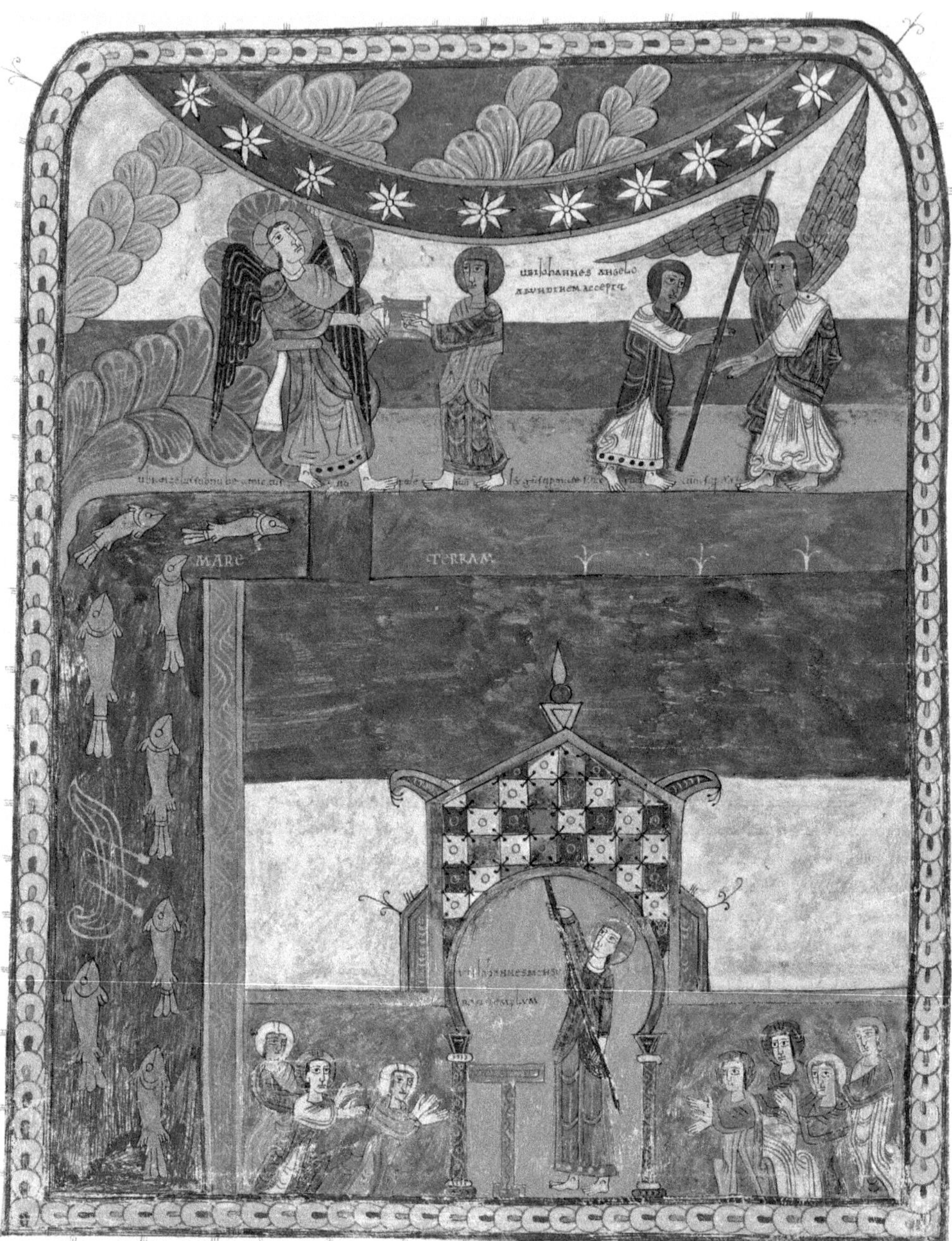

FIGURE 5.1. John receives the book and measures the temple, folio 161v. Girona Beatus, 6 July 975. Museu de la Catedral de Girona, Num. Inv. 7(11). See color plate 12.

and those who worship there, but do not measure the court outside the temple, leave that out, for it is given over to the Gentiles" (Rev. 11:2–3).[75]

These events are depicted in the upper register of the image, where, under the star-filled canopy of heaven, John is represented on two occasions. To the left within the upper register, he is shown receiving a book from the angel (whose one foot is planted on "Mare," the other on "Terram"), and again to the right, grasping the reed proffered by the angel. This John puts to good use in the lower register where he appears for a third time. He is shown standing by an altar actively measuring the curve of a splendid horseshoe arch articulated by polychrome tiles. Several haloed figures flank this structure in gestures of worship. Within the confines of the biblical text, these may represent souls ready to enter God's 'temple,' the coming New Jerusalem erected upon the arrival of the eschaton. Typologically, John functions as a New Testament Ezekiel: the first Temple having been destroyed by Nebuchadnezzar upon his conquest of Jerusalem ca. 578 BC, Ezekiel is given a vision of the new Temple that will restore the worship of God within the holy city (Ezek. 40–43). The inclusion of exterior polychromy is a significant detail in that it evokes the colored patterning that permeates the illustration *The Burning of Babylon* illustration later in the manuscript (folio 215v). There, the city of Babylon is symbolized through the schematic rending of an architectural façade, the entire surface of which is encrusted with geometric shapes and colored patterns, precious vases, and bowls. Referring to these same pictorial strategies within *The Burning of Babylon* illustration in the Morgan Beatus,[76] Jerrilynn Dodds has convincingly demonstrated how the artist pursued an "unorthodox variety of nonrepresentational motifs" to represent the city of Babylon as a Spanish Islamic palace.[77] The fact that the upper façade of the temple John measures displays similarly opulent geometric patterning (albeit on a smaller scale) suggests a covert allusion to Islamic architecture and thus to Islam, which, like the court "given over to the Gentiles," encroaches upon God's altar throughout much of southern Iberia.

Allusion to Christian-Muslim interaction is even more likely when we consider John's task at hand. The measurement of an architectural space—particularly for its preservation and/or restoration—would be an especially charged theme considering the destruction of countless churches within the territory of the caliphate throughout the previous century. The loss of these churches, combined with the prohibition against the construction of new structures, was emphasized repeatedly within the writings of Eulogius and Alvarus.[78] If the suppression of Christian architecture was a method of circumscribing and subduing a religious minority within al-Andalus, then the inception of architectural projects throughout the frontier zone following monastic migration was a significant reassertion of Christian authority. The extensive appearance of architectural imagery in the iconographic cycle of the Girona Beatus could well have functioned as a repository of communal memory of this process.

The next full-page image to confront the reader, *The Two Witnesses* on folio 164r, illustrates the motif found in Rev. 11:3–6 (Figure 5.2). Here the witnesses stand in an elaborate horseshoe arch that is both scaffold and frame for the attributes described in Rev. 11:4: "These are the two olive trees and the two lamp stands which stand before the Lord of the earth."[79] Although the witnesses are not named in the *storia*, these figures are clearly labeled in the image as "ELIAS" and "ENOC." However, that the two figures are represented wearing monastic habits and carry-

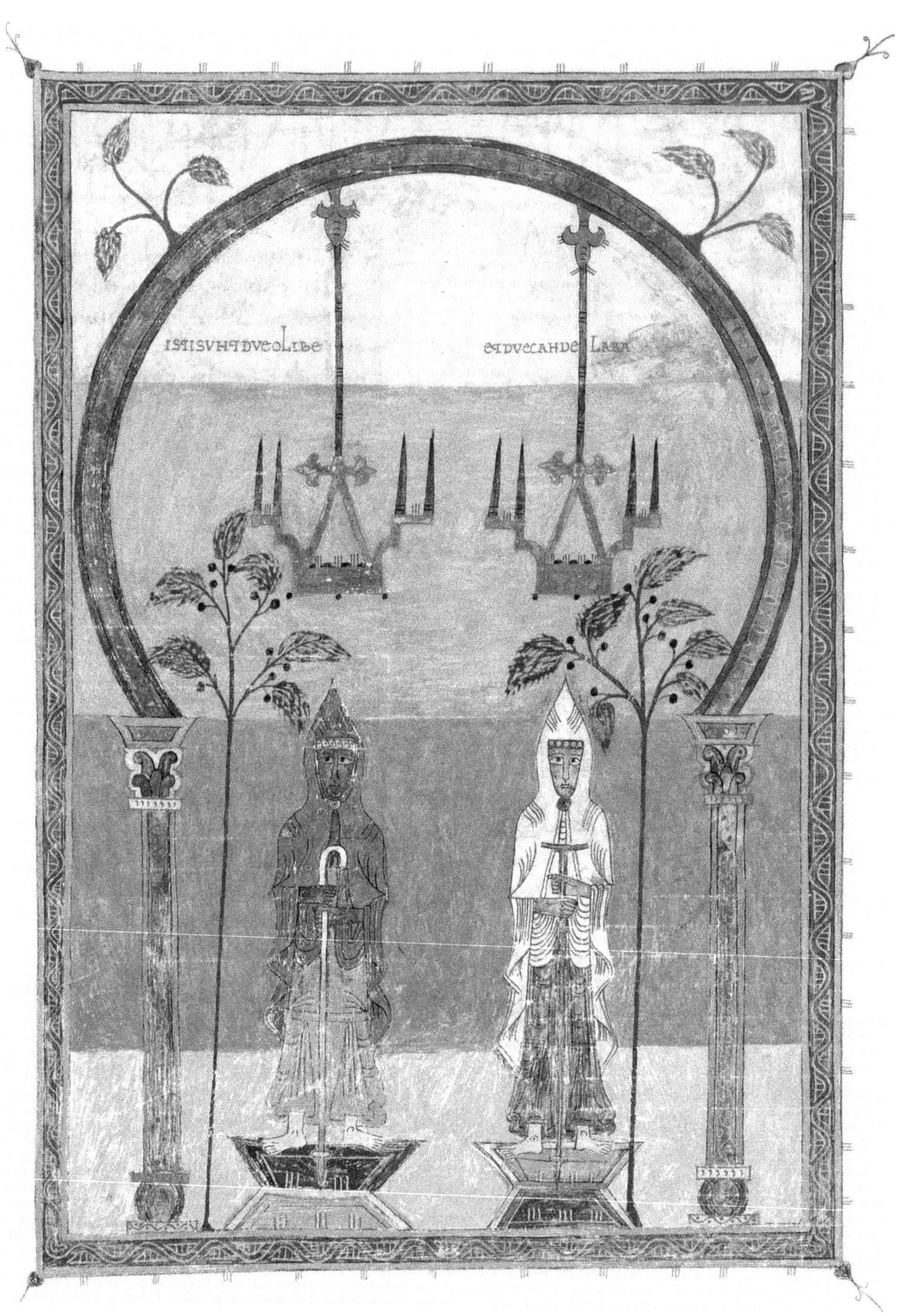

FIGURE 5.2. The Two Witnesses, folio 164r. Girona Beatus, 6 July 975. Museu de la Catedral de Girona, Num. Inv. 7(11).

ing the attributes of the abbot's staff accords with Isidore of Seville's identification of Elijah and Enoch as Old Testament prototypes of the monk.[80] These two figures are intended to function as vivid exemplars for their conventual viewer, as literally communicated through the manner of their representation, namely their actual elevation onto geometric podiums, upon which they stand in a hieratic pose, directly facing the reader/viewer for his contemplation.

The fate of these two figures is revealed in the next full-page illustration, *The Two Witnesses Killed by the Antichrist*, on folio 166r (Figure 5.3). The biblical text describes Elijah and Enoch facing the consequences of publicly declaring their faith, after which (Rev. 11:7–8): ". . . [it] will conquer them and kill them, and their dead bodies will lie in the street of the great city that is prophetically called Sodom and Egypt, where also their Lord was crucified."[81] In the Beatus text this episode is expanded over two *storiae,* and both ensuing *explanationes* clarify that "it" indicates the beast/Antichrist. Malevolence is detectable in the uppermost register of the image, where an angry mob attacks an architectural structure representative of Jerusalem. Within this structure are painted five haloed figures that stand momentarily protected from this onslaught by its thick walls. These walls, however, are beginning to crumble as bricks shatter and split under repeated blows. In the lower register of the image the two witnesses are decapitated for their unswerving resolve by a coterie of armed protagonists.[82]

Significantly, this is the sole moment in the corpus of iconographic themes common to all Beatus manuscripts where an element of an image has been inspired by its exegetical *explanatio* rather than adhering to the content of the biblical verses constituting its *storia,* which in this instance says nothing of a city itself under siege.[83] The *explanatio* is more particular, citing Luke 21:24, which states how "the city of Jerusalem will be trodden down by the Gentiles, until the times of the nation be fulfilled."[84]

In light of this fact, Peter Klein has asserted that *The Killing of the Two Witnesses* constitutes an authentic reflection of Christian-Muslim conflict within the Beatus tradition.[85] Klein found support for this theory in the text of the *Chronica Muzarabica* (Mozarabic Chronicle) of ca. 754, which contains a comparison of the fall of Jerusalem with the conquest of Spain, perhaps reflecting a widespread association between the two.[86] If indeed viewers were conditioned to make this association, then the scene, combined with the killing of the two witnesses below, would have functioned as a symbolically analogous reference to the executions in Córdoba. John Williams cautioned this interpretation, noting the *Chronica Muzarabica*'s discussion of the fall of Jerusalem with respect to the capture of Troy, the destruction of Babylon, and the fall of Rome—that is, within an overall discussion of the transience of power.[87] Williams also noted that this architectural motif, labeled "*Antichristus civitatem Iherusalem subvertit*" (the Antichrist overthrows the city of Jerusalem) is present in both Branch I and Branch II manuscripts, suggesting its presence in a Beatus archetype that predates the Córdoban martyrdoms; he thus interprets the scene primarily as an expression of the *explanatio.*[88]

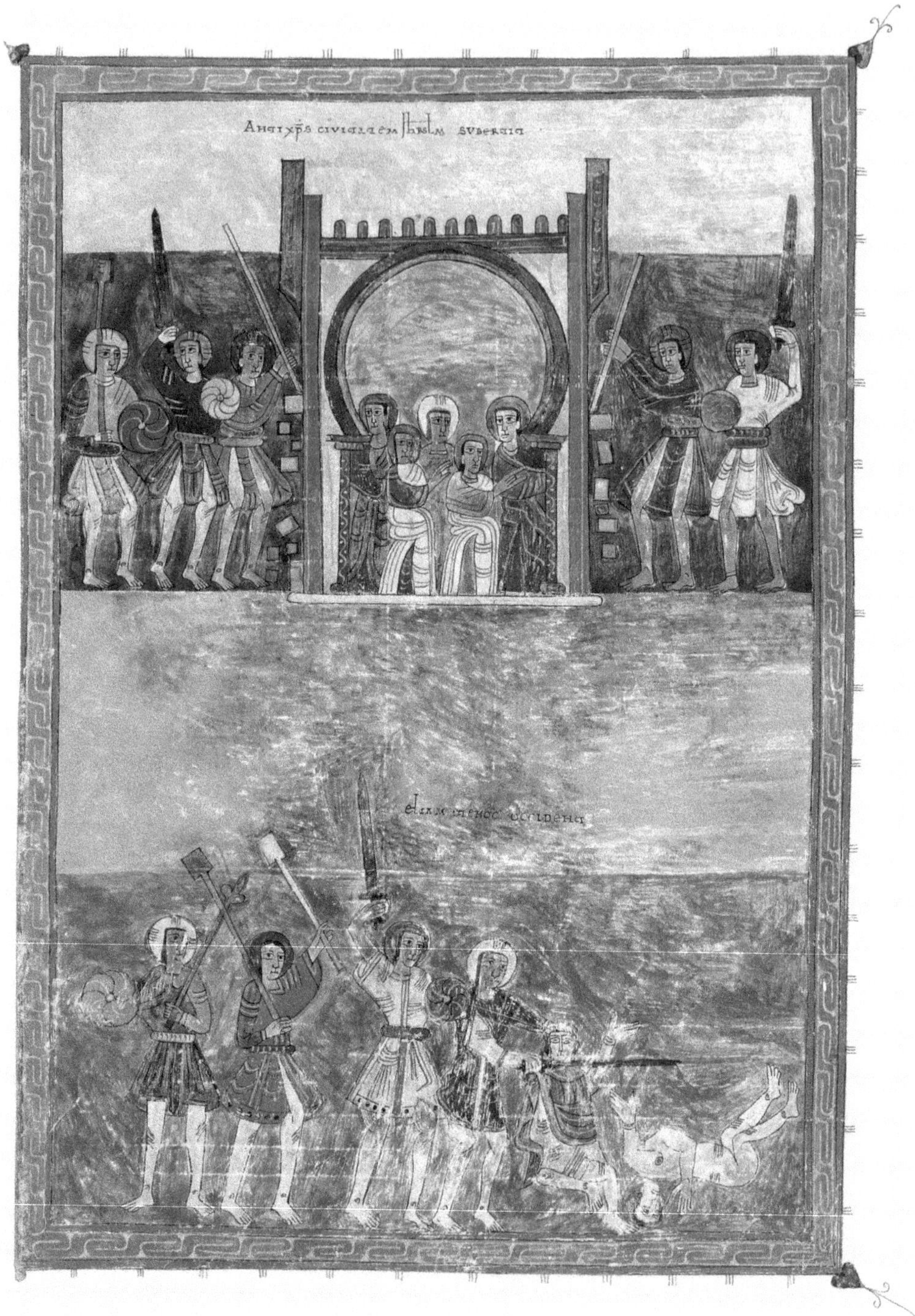

FIGURE 5.3. The Two Witnesses killed by the Antichrist, folio 166r. Girona Beatus, 6 July 975. Museu de la Catedral de Girona, Num. Inv. 7(11).

Yet, the vivid and at times bizarre symbolism of John's eschatological narrative inherently resists concrete, infallible interpretation. It is precisely because of this intrinsic multivalent capacity that we should be fairly confident that its readers expected to navigate multiple interpretations for any one visual or textual element. It is widely accepted that *The Feast of Belshazzar*, on folio 202v in the Morgan Beatus, directly equates the Umayyad rulers with the irreverent Babylonian King. The king and his court are shown gathered at a table beneath a horseshoe arch composed of the variegating red and white voussoirs characteristic of the Great Mosque of Córdoba.[89] That the artist Maius could be confident this insult would be recognized by his audience requires that they be primed to explore layered meanings within the text and its images, even ones not immediately apparent to our modern eyes.

As a result, we cannot discount that the image of the slaying of the two witnesses on folio 166r in the Girona Beatus did not evoke the Córdoban martyrs, and similarly that the subsequent image of the siege of Jerusalem did not trigger sorrow over the past destruction of Córdoban churches. Paulus Alvarus also considered Elijah to be a critical monastic exemplar, citing Elijah's sacrifice in the *Indiculus luminosis* as "the biblical paradigm" for the steadfast commitment to Christianity demonstrated by the Córdoban martyrs.[90] Incidentally, while the witnesses in the image are beheaded, it is intriguing that neither the *storia* nor the *explanatio* mention decapitation per se, but instead use the verb *occidere,* which encompasses a great variety of deaths. The likelihood of topical political reverberation within this and the preceding full-scale images increases given their sequential presentation. The reader's study of the illustration *John Receives the Book and Measures the Temple*, followed by the striking image *The Two Witnesses* (save the interpolated *storia* and *explanatio*) would provide momentum to these sorts of allusions.

Of course, this need not be the exclusive allusion beyond the literal biblical narrative achieved by the image on folio 166r. The figures constrained behind the walls of Jerusalem directly parallel the enclosure of the monastic audience studying the manuscript's text and images. That these figures undergo attack would have had immediate resonance for the tenth-century Leónese monk, given the constant pressure of numerous military excursions into Christian territories throughout the reign of al-Ḥakam II (r. 961–976)[91] and the militaristic tenor of the manuscript's own colophon.

The thematic sequence of these illustrations (fs. 161v, 164r, 166r) culminates with a fourth full-page illustration on folio 167v, *The Two Witnesses' Ascension to Heaven* (Figure 5.4). Elijah and Enoch are shown ascending on a cloud toward God enthroned in heaven, while crowds of their enemies watch in terror and are punished by a sudden calamitous earthquake. The soteriological nature of the image could be directed toward a range of hopes and expectations: toward a commendation of the radical resolve of the Córdoban martyrs; toward the end of Muslim rule and the renewed primacy of the church throughout the Iberian peninsula; and naturally the ultimate reward of the reader and those comprising the religious

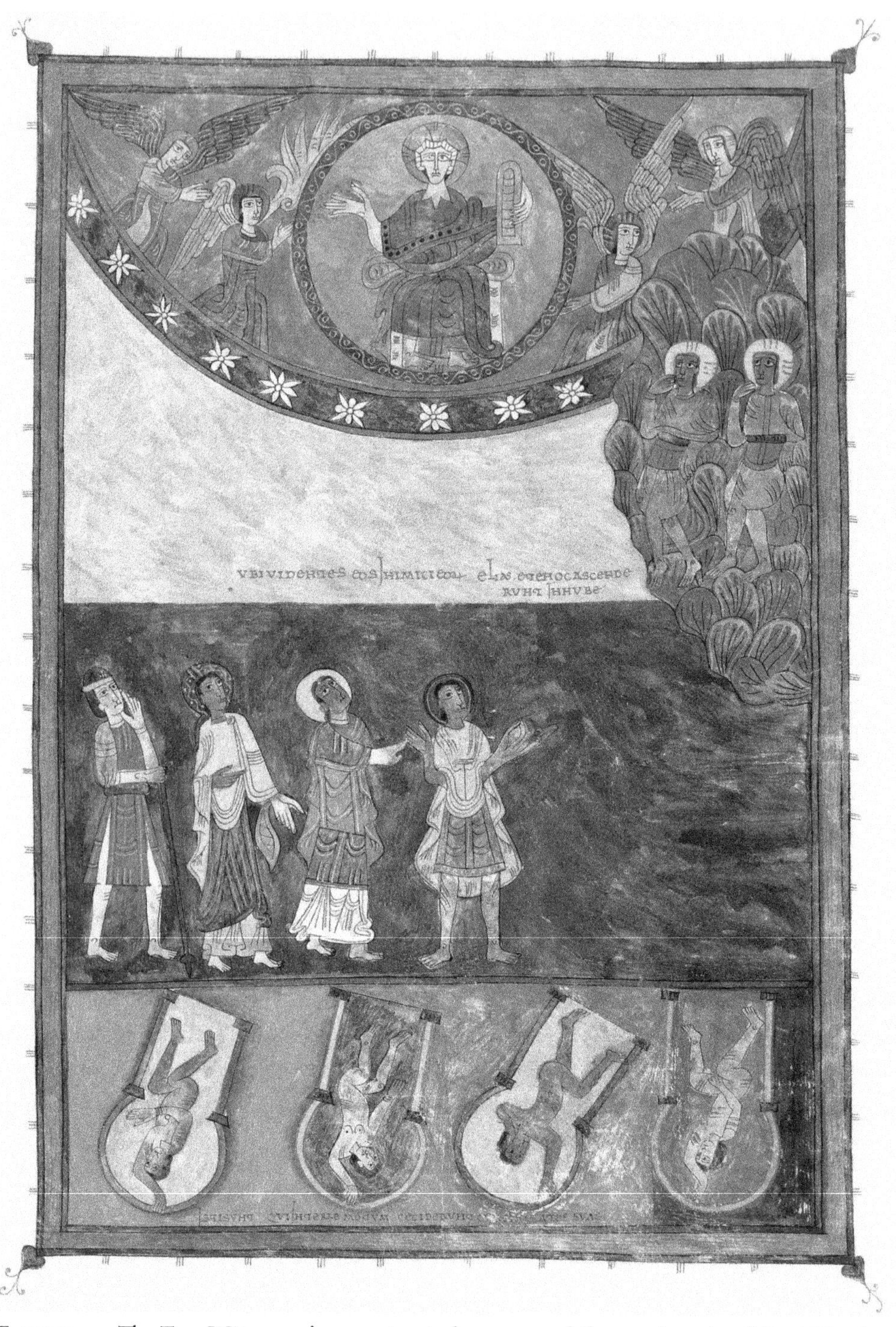

FIGURE 5.4. The Two Witnesses' ascension to heaven, and the earthquake, folio 167v, 6 July 975. Museu de la Catedral de Girona, Num. Inv. 7(11)

community of San Salvador de Tábara, who trust that their unwavering devotion to God has made them worthy of paradise. The fact that these two witnesses touch their lips "in a ritual gesture of silence that denotes a traditional monastic virtue"[92] underscores the manuscript's role as a spiritual aid for its audience.[93]

Symbolic Intersections in Apocalyptic Imagery

Given these veiled allusions to Islamic-Christian relations, it is striking to consider the various commonalities between Beatus's *Commentary on the Apocalypse* and the tradition of illustrated *Miʿrājnāmas*. The core text of the commentary, John's Book of Revelation, and the *Miʿrājnāma* are both apocalyptic narratives that seek to reveal the transcendent character of heavenly geography. By definition, Beatus's commentary is the product of exegetical practice, but so too is the *Miʿrājnāma*. In Beatus's text this is confined to the *explanatio* following each *storia;* it is also overtly cumulative, in that Beatus's interpretive efforts relied upon the summation of the exegetical products of earlier authors. The *Miʿrājnāma* narrative is in its entirety a product of sustained and expanded exegesis based upon a few abstract references in the Qur'an. These include Qur'an 17:1, which describes the Prophet Muḥammad's night journey (*isrā'*) from the sacred mosque in Mecca to the "farthest sanctuary" (*al-masjid al-aqṣā*), which has been variously interpreted to mean a number of locations, particularly Jerusalem or the Temple Mount (*al-ḥarām al-sharīf*).[94] Qur'an 53:4–18 further describes a somewhat ambiguous process of divine revelation, where Muḥammad "reached the highest pinnacle" and "He [God] revealed to His servant what He revealed."[95] Curiously, nowhere in either of these verses, nor any other verses in the Qur'an, is the word *miʿrāj* (ascension) used. The term per se is indicative of the development of a wider, autonomous corpus of narratives on the Prophet's ascension from the tenth to the thirteenth centuries. Furthermore, interaction with the painted images within illustrated manuscripts of either of these revelatory narratives can itself be described as a sort of visual exegetical practice, as the reader/viewer engages with the various layers of meaning intertwined in each illustration, both for its role relative to a portion of text, but also as a gloss on the contemporary events that may have inspired the illustration of that particular episode in the narrative.

Both narratives additionally partake of common narremes constructed from a shared repository of widely diffused symbols in their account of the celestial realms. Scholars have argued that this confluence of symbolic imagery is in no way accidental, but rather reflects multidirectional influences and interactions between distinct traditions of ascension narratives. Michael Sells conceptualized this phenomenon as a "language world," which he defines as "a set of words, themes, myths, [or] symbols which holds a certain consistency and which serves as a locus of meaning."[96] Not only do these narratives therefore display an innate, intersecting matrix of imagery, but many of these symbols are deployed in a manner well suited to the espousal of their particular belief system in an atmosphere of religious flux or strife. This is hardly surprising given the social context of tribulation which the biblical Apocalypse of John was authored to address, and its exhortation to its readers to remain steadfast in their religious commitment and to anticipate deliverance from persecution and repression.[97]

For the purpose of a broad comparison between Christian and Muslim eschatological traditions, let us now consider some of the symbolic intersections detectable between the Book of Revelation that is the focus of Beatus's commentary and the anonymous Chaghatay text accompanying the illustrated Timurid *Miʿrājnāma* of ca. 840/1436–37.[98] Because the development of a mature *Miʿrājnāma* narrative was characterized by continuous exegetical elaboration by countless reciters and authors, the Chaghatay text encapsulates a much fuller tradition of oral and written ascension narratives within Islam, and therefore can be used as a template to excavate narremes present in earlier accounts of the Prophet's ascension that antedate Beatus's text.[99]

One of the common themes between the two narratives is the symbol of the cup or bowl, the contents of which function as an index of wickedness or righteousness. Within the Book of Revelation, references to the pagan Roman Empire are indirect; Rome is called the new Babylon because it is the second empire to raze the Hebraic temple in Jerusalem.[100] In Rev. 17:4–6 John receives a vision of Babylon, personified by a woman, seated astride a scarlet beast, lasciviously holding aloft a great golden goblet full of abominations and "drunk with the blood of the saints and the blood of the martyrs of Jesus."[101] The first proclamation of her defeat (Rev. 14:8) reads: "Fallen, fallen, is Babylon the great! She has made all nations drink of the wine of the wrath of her fornication."[102] Divine retribution is again clothed as intoxicating wine in Rev. 16–19: "God remembered great Babylon, and gave her the wine-cup of the fury of his wrath."[103] These latter images partake of an Old Testament metaphor of the cup of wine as the wrath of God.[104] Other imagery within the revelatory narrative involving cups and bowls is rooted in the ritualistic vessels of the cult of the Hebraic temple. This is particularly present in the cycle of the Seven Bowls comprising Rev. 15:5–16:21.[105] Throughout these verses seven angels dispense seven plagues from golden bowls, wreaking havoc by pouring their devastating contents upon the earth. When the first angel emptied his bowl onto the earth, "a foul and painful sore came on those who bore the mark of the beast."(Rev. 16:2).[106] The second angel pours his bowl into the sea, and "it became like the blood of a corpse," (Rev. 16:3)[107] and so on, in a sorrowful litany of destruction and deprivation.

Within the *Miʿrājnāma* narrative the symbol of the cup or bowl manifests in the singular event of a test administered to the Prophet. When Muḥammad reaches the Lote Tree of the Limit (*sidrat al-muntahā*) in the heavens, he is greeted by angels who offer him three vessels. One vessel contains milk, one wine, and the other honey. Muḥammad selects the milk and is commended by the angels, for in this choice the Prophet demonstrates his *fitra,* that is, his innate and rightly guided disposition.[108] This narrative vignette appears already in Ibn Isḥāq's *Sīrat al-Nabī,* but the event takes place in Jerusalem; he also records various versions of the story in which different numbers of cups are offered. Yet the merit of Muḥammad's choice remains the same, illustrating that he is "rightly guided toward nature (*al-fitra*) and his nation is guided rightly, as wine is prohibited to them."[109]

Although the motif is used inversely in these texts—with a negative inflection in the biblical apocalypse and in a more positive, initiatory sense in the *Miʿrājnāma*—ingestion and imbibition appear in both to allegorically represent moral virtue. This is literally enacted in the *Miʿrājnāma,* as it is the selection of the proper cup that proves Muḥammad's elect status, ensuring that he may enter the heavenly realm.[110] Within a religiously contentious environment, literary and pictorial illustration of the dispensation of final judgment and the selectivity of redemption clearly summons the reader to be prudent in his/her affiliations.

Another parallel theme is the use of the motif of clothing to signify rightful membership among the elect. The Book of Revelation is replete with references to white garments worn by the righteous.[111] The use of this symbolism is likely influenced by both baptismal practice and the priestly clothing of ancient Israel.[112] A prominent expression of this clothing motif occurs in Rev. 4:4 and 7:9. The throne of God and the Lamb are encircled by a heavenly court composed of twenty-four elders seated on thrones, dressed in white garments and wearing golden crowns,[113] along with a great multitude of standing souls holding palm branches and wearing white robes.[114] That the elect are all enrobed in white, unblemished garments indicates their spiritual purity, reminding the reader of the exclusiveness of salvation.

Explicit differentiation between the elect and the damned occurs during Muḥammad's celestial journey. The Timurid *Miʿrājnāma* relates that when Muḥammad ascends to the seventh heaven he meets Abraham (Ibrāhīm) seated before an emerald pavilion into which seventy thousand angels enter every day. The Prophet is instructed by Gabriel to lead his community in prayer. Before he commences this task Muḥammad suddenly sees a "group of people, half of whom had white robes and half of whom had striped robes."[115] While the white-robed souls raise their hands in prayer, those wearing impure robes are denied entry into the heavenly mosque. This visual threat of judgment and exclusion from a heavenly precinct reinforces communal identity by demonstrating the importance of dutiful worship and the consequences of impious behavior.[116]

Thirdly, both narratives describe the throne of God indirectly, through the description of rich materials as the focus of acts of devotion intended to inspire emulation. That these incitements to worship occur in conjunction with the description of the heavenly throne within both texts sanctions these devotional practices as reliable vehicles through which to reach and to anticipate access to the divine. By "authorizing" particular ritual activities, these texts naturally affirm their own belief system, exhorting the readers to have confidence in their salvation.

In John's revelatory narrative, the heavenly theophany is first described in Rev.

4:3–5: "and he who sat there appeared like jasper and carnelian, and round the throne was a rainbow that looked like an emerald. [. . .] From the throne issued flashes of lightning, and voices and peals of thunder." God is not described directly; the divine is instead articulated through an account of the events around the heavenly throne and its attributes. The throne is surrounded by four living creatures, each with six wings and covered in eyes,[117] who unceasingly intone the trisagion, "Holy, holy, holy, the Lord God the Almighty, Who was and is and was to come" (Rev. 4:8), the first of a sequence of five related hymns that praise the creator.[118] The fact that the words of the angels' song are included in the text invites their recitation by the reader.[119] Also, John specifically notes that he was in a state of prophetic illumination "on the Lord's day" (Rev. 1:10), a declaration suggesting that this recitation may initially have been a weekly event within the nascent Christian community, as part of an earthly liturgy believed to enact a heavenly prototype.[120] The twenty-four elders and multitude of souls also complete acts of adoration: the former place their crowns before the throne while the latter prostrate themselves in a posture of adoration.[121]

In contrast, the Timurid *Miʿrājnāma* narrative recounts that upon reaching the "place of proximity" (*maqām al-qurba*) in the seventh heaven, Muḥammad was rewarded with a vision of God. Whether this vision involved the bodily eye, the heart, or a spiritual vision "of faith" is a matter of debate; the text does not provide further detail.[122] However, the text does reveal that God's throne is made of ruby, and "is so immense that if the seven layers of the earth and sky were placed next to it, they would not be visible."[123] The throne is unceasingly circumambulated by numerous angels, evoking the ritual motion performed around the Kaʿba in Mecca. The throne is also surrounded by seven hundred thousand tents, each seventy times the size of the earthly realm. Five hundred thousand angels worship God within each tent, "some standing, some sitting, and some in prostration."[124] Given the fact that all versions of the *Miʿrājnāma* developed through a continual process of exegesis, the mention within these texts of the angels' multiple positions of prayer likely originated among antecedent instructions of ritual behavior. This seemingly innocuous narrative detail also provides an opportunity for the inclusion of didactical representations of ritual actions. Indeed, one of the illustrations that accompanies the Timurid *Miʿrājnāma* depicts Muḥammad at the throne (*ʿarsh*) of God.[125] Perhaps in accordance with mainstream Muslim theology, which maintained that God was beyond both human comprehension and representation, the artist avoided a literal interpretation of the scene. Muḥammad is portrayed in a position of prostration (*sajda*) amid whorls of light enhanced by the direct application of burnished gold to the folio. In this way, the artist captures the rapture of the soul in the presence of God and entices the reader/viewer to directly imitate Muḥammad's devotional action through the implicit promise that he/she can experience a similarly ecstatic colloquy with God through prayer and its concomitant physical position of prostration.

The Las Huelgas Beatus and the Alfonsine Translations

While the earliest surviving illustrated copies of Beatus's commentary date to the tenth century, the latest copies of this pictorial tradition are products of the thirteenth century. Singular among these later editions is the Las Huelgas Beatus. With dimensions measuring 540 by 340 mm, the Las Huelgas Beatus is the largest extant illustrated copy of Beatus's exegetical text.[126] The manuscript derives its name from the Cistercian convent of Sta. María la Real de las Huelgas, near Burgos, where it was discovered in the eighteenth century.[127] It is one of four Beatus manuscripts produced in Castile in this period.[128] Although a lengthy colophon felicitously records the year of its production as 1220,[129] it is less forthcoming about the identity of its scribe(s) and its place of origin, telling us only that it was a gift from an unnamed "lady, most generous to God," also referred to as "servant N." This "lady" is widely agreed to have been Berenguela, daughter of Alfonso VIII (r. 1158–1214) and his wife Leonor Plantagenet, and the mother of Ferdinand III of Castile (r. 1217–1252).[130] It was Alfonso VIII who ruled during the decisive battle of Las Navas de Tolosa on 16 July 1212, at which time the tapestry covering the opening to the tent of the Almohad Caliph al-Nāṣir (r. 1199–1213) was seized and dispatched to the monastery of Las Huelgas, where it was displayed as a trophy of war.[131] The military consortium under the command of Ferdinand III and Jaume I of Aragòn defeated the Almohad state. It was Ferdinand who reconstructed the great mosque at Córdoba as a cathedral and who sent captured Muslims to Santiago with its cathedral bells, seized over two centuries prior by al-Manṣūr (r. 981–1002). This relationship to Alfonso and Ferdinand reveals the spirit of *Reconquísta* that permeated the age of the manuscript's production.[132]

The convent of Las Huelgas was founded in 1187 under the patronage of Berenguela's father and mother, and served as the royal funerary pantheon by 1199.[133] Shortly after its foundation, the convent was favored as a *specialis filia* (a "special daughter") of Cîteaux, a status that granted it jurisdiction over a network of convents in Castile, and in territories belonging to Navarre and León.[134] Despite its royal affiliations, it is uncertain whether a scriptorium existed within the monastic community; all of the illuminated manuscripts associated with Las Huelgas seem to have been externally produced, either at the monastery of San Pedro de Cardeña or imported from England.[135] The artists responsible for the illustration of the manuscript could well have traveled to the monastery for all or part of its production.[136] However, a stylistic analysis of its pictorial cycles provides compelling evidence that the manuscript was completed offsite, within the cultural ambit of Toledo.[137]

Perhaps the image most emblematic of John's revelatory narrative is the depiction of *Heavenly Jerusalem* on folio 140v, "the new earth" that is the culmination of his panoramic, eschatological vision (Rev. 21:1–27).[138] The illustration represents the divine city diagrammatically, constructed from multiple perspectives that converge on a central space (Figure 5.5). This architectural representation is character-

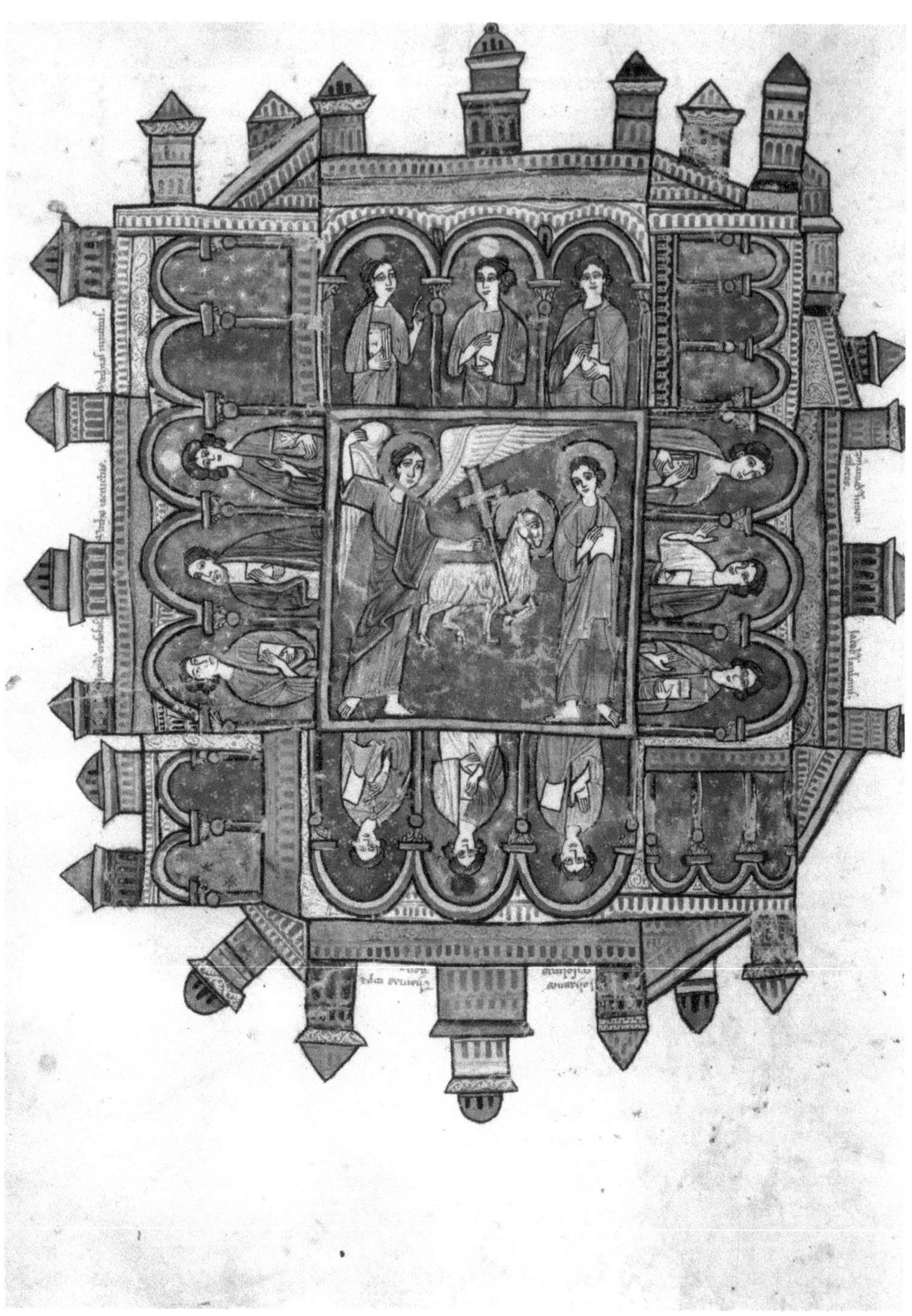

FIGURE 5.5. Heavenly Jerusalem, folio 140v. Las Huelgas Beatus, 1220. New York, Pierpont Morgan Library, M. 429.

ized by restrained architectonic detailing such as bare curved arcades and lintels lacking figural sculpture, both common strategies within Cistercian architecture. It has been posited by Rose Walker that this may symbolize the specific cloister of Las Huelgas, Las Claustrillas, built in the 1180s and intended as the final resting place for the founders and their deceased children.[139] This is naturally supported by the biblical text, which explicitly describes the shape of the city as a square, with high walls and many gates (Rev. 21:12–21).[140] Members of the monastic community are inspired to envision themselves within the *Civitas Dei*, motivated by the figures of the twelve apostles[141] who are each depicted within the heavenly arcades, evocative of the cloister walk of Las Claustrillas.

Within the Las Huelgas Beatus, *The Two Witnesses* is not granted the luxurious treatment dispensed by the painters Emeterius and Ende, who devoted an entire folio to its depiction in the Girona Beatus. In the Las Huelgas Beatus the image has been reduced to the lower third of a folio, suppressed below two substantial columns of text (Figure 5.6). The polylobed arch that framed the earlier image has been removed from the illustration. The two figures, still dressed in contemporary monastic garb and identified by small painted inscriptions as "HELIAS ET HENOCH" (Elias and Enoch), instead stand erect against a schematic, geometric background of segments of painted red, blue, and blush. These fields of color are overlaid with stars, evoking a heavenly, cosmic realm. Here again, the two monks are each buttressed by an olive tree and a candlestick, to which they are likened in the biblical text (Rev. 11:4), although the abbots' staffs they hold within the Girona manuscript have been replaced with codices. These they present to the reader/viewer and, through this self-referential detail, reinforce interaction with the large-scale manuscript of which they are a part. Enoch (the figure to the right) raises his right hand in a gesture of oration, clearly offering the profession of faith for which he and Elijah are killed (Rev. 11:7). That this is a more understated image, lacking the grandeur accorded the theme within the Girona Beatus captures the decreased importance of this particular moment in the revelatory narrative, which in the earlier manuscript functioned as an ideological blazon. Significantly, the comparative reduction of the scale and spirit of this illustration within the Las Huelgas Beatus cannot be explained by the codex's ultimate pictorial model within the Beatus corpus, the Tábara Beatus. Because the only surviving images of the Tábara edition comprise three illustrations of the Book of Revelation and two reflective of Jerome's *Commentarius in Danielem,* the nature of its iconography is adduced from the Girona manuscript, which is ascribed to the same scriptorium.[142] The diminution of the illustration is best explained as symptomatic of the shift of cultural priorities inherent to the passage of almost three centuries: that is, the cult of the Córdoban martyrs is not the vehicle of self-definition that it was previously in the Girona manuscript.

Yet the evincing of overtly Islamic features within the general aesthetic of the Las Huelgas Beatus does not mean that the manuscript is ideologically devoid of references to Islam and to contemporary Christian-Muslim interaction. Just as reverbera-

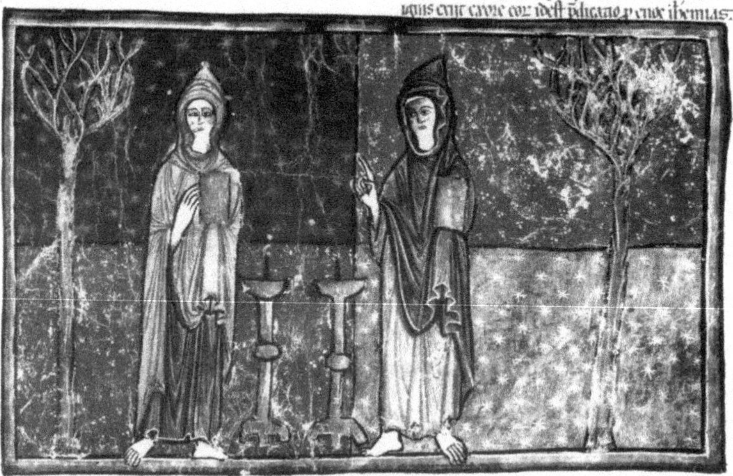

FIGURE 5.6. The Two Witnesses, folio 97r. Las Huelgas Beatus, 1220. New York, Pierpont Morgan Library, M. 429.

tions of contemporary political events permeate the Girona Beatus, select folios within the Las Huelgas Beatus provided its readers/viewers with opportunities to affirm the *Reconquísta* of southern Iberia and military action against Muslim territories further abroad. Perhaps the most vivid example of this is the double-page illustration of *The Siege of Jerusalem and the Lamentation of Jeremiah*, comprising folios 149v–150r (Figure 5.7 and Plate 13). The image accompanies Jerome's commentary on Daniel, characteristically appended to Beatus's text. On its surface the illustration depicts the troops of King Nebuchadnezzar attacking the holy city as described in the Book of Daniel (1:1): "In the third year of the reign of King Jehoiakim of Judah, King Nebuchadnezzar of Babylon came to Jerusalem and besieged it." The illustration, however, conflates two separate occurrences from ancient history. On the one hand the image contends with the struggle between Nebuchadnezzar and Jehoiakim, yet on the other it also refers to a previous siege of Jerusalem by Nebuchadnezzar during the reign of Zedekiah, king of Judah.[143] The lowest register of imagery on folio 149v is inspired by 2 Kings 25:7: "They slaughtered the sons of Zedekiah[144] before his eyes, then put out the eyes of Zedekiah; they bound him in fetters and took him to Babylon." Nebuchadnezzar appears enthroned along the bottom edge of the left folio, somewhat lost among the colorful rows of cavalry and infantry that advance toward the city gate. To the left of the enthroned king appears the bound king of Judah, his head roughly twisted to enable a view of his sons' decapitations to the far right; at the same time Zedekiah suffers the loss of his sight. These tragedies that befall Zedekiah are absent from the Book of Daniel, although they are present in various books of the Old Testament referred to in Jerome's commentary.[145] These events are also recounted at length in the Book of Jeremiah (Jer. 39:1–7); indeed, it is Jeremiah, displaying a traditional gesture of grief, who sits sorrowfully on a rock to the far right on folio 150r.

That the city of Jerusalem is contained within a half-page illustration on the right hand folio gives prominence to its conquest rather than to the decorous features of its architecture. The military action is made more remarkable through the modernization of the soldiers' costume and weaponry, transforming ancient events into contemporary wars. These pictorial strategies make it very difficult to believe that the readers of the Las Huelgas Beatus would not have immediately equated the devastating campaigns of the Chaldean king with the recent siege and capture of Jerusalem in 1187 by the Ayyubid Sultan Ṣalāḥ al-Dīn (r. 1174–1193). Although the diplomatic efforts of Frederick II ensured that Jerusalem was once again under Christian control by 1229, at least one viewer found the image of the loss of Jerusalem sufficiently antagonistic to assault the image by vehemently scratching out the face of Nebuchadnezzar.[146]

This capacity for anti-Muslim sentiment is also present in the image gracing folio 94r, *The Death-Dealing Cavalry*, pertaining to Rev. 14–19 (Figure 5.8). This image represents the sixth of seven plagues, each heralded by a trumpet, which prepares the way for the restoration of the kingdom of God on earth. After the sixth angel sounds his trumpet, God instructs the creature to "Release the four angels who are bound at

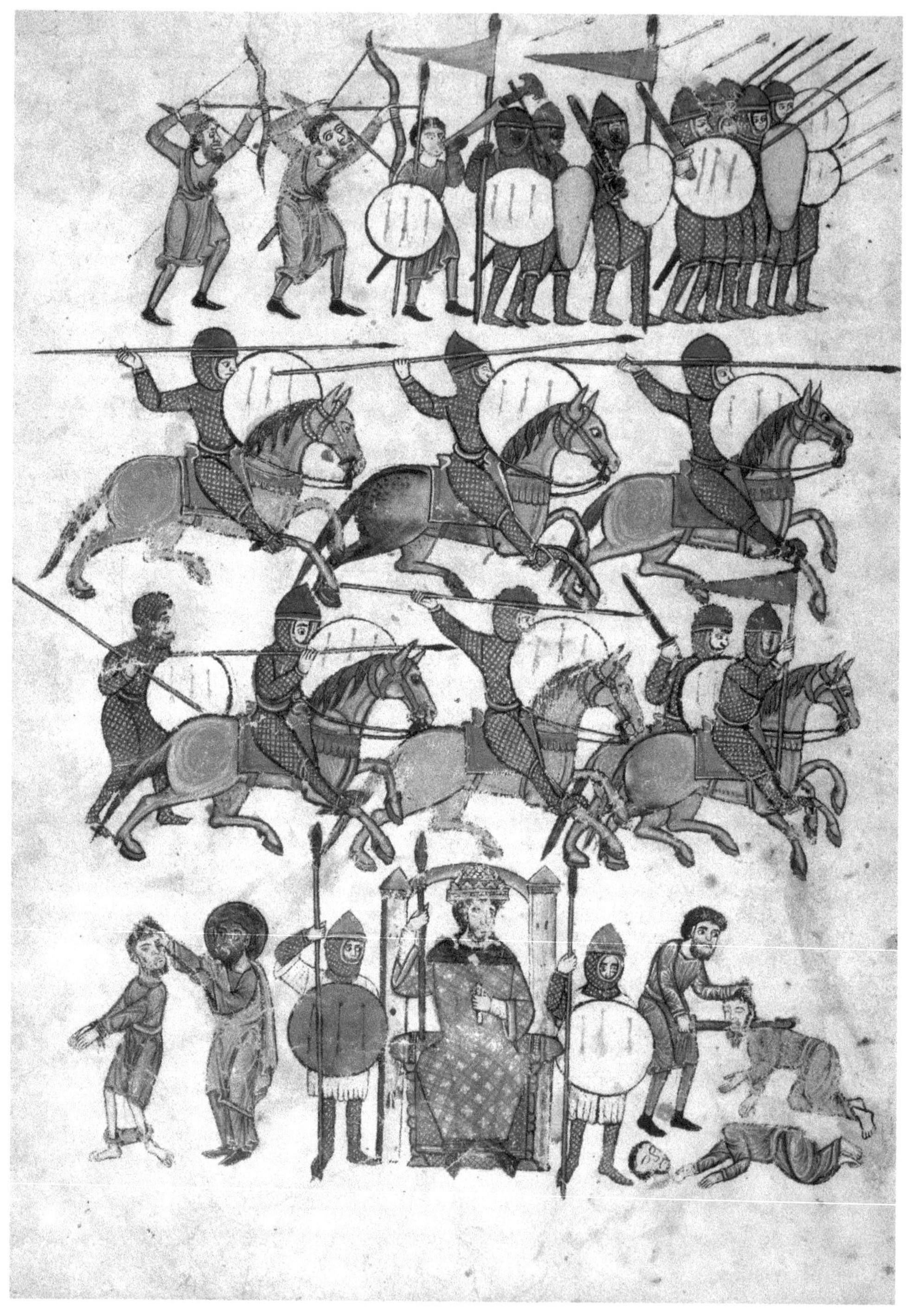

FIGURE 5.7. The Siege of Jerusalem and the Lamentation of Jeremiah, folios 149v–150r. Las Huelgas Beatus, 1220. New York, Pierpont Morgan Library, M. 429. See color plate 13.

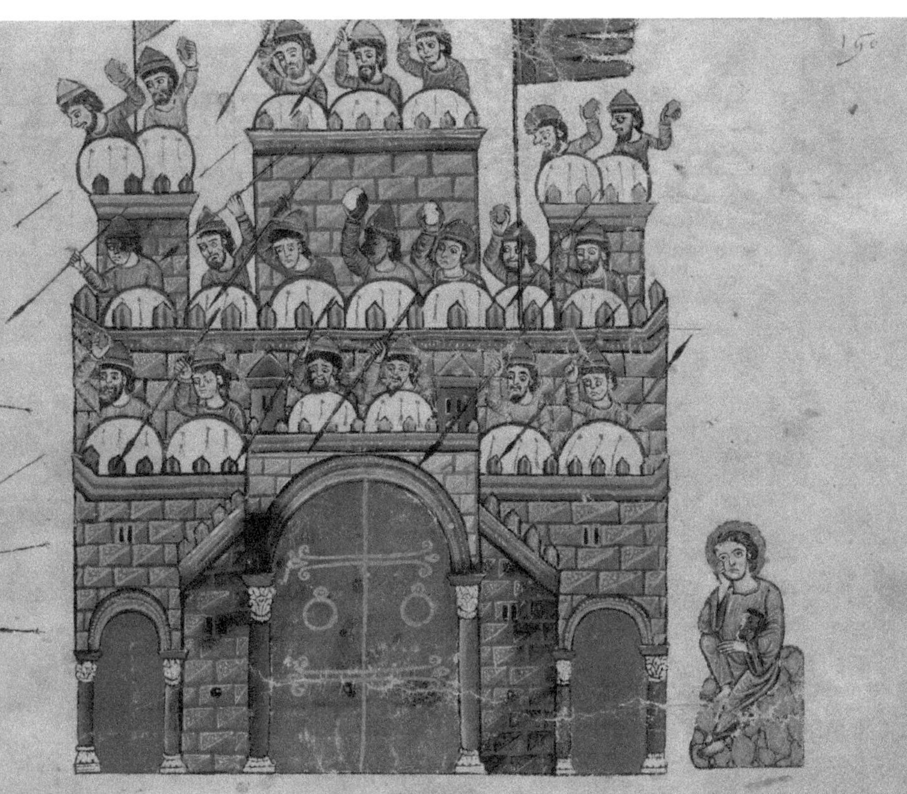

Anno tertio regni ioachim regis iuda:
uenit nabuchodonosor rex babi
lonis in ihelm: et obsedit eam io
achim filius iosie. cuius tertio
decimo anno prophetare orsus est iheremias.
Sub quo etiam holda mulier prophetauit.
Ipse est qui alio nomine appellatur ioachim:
et regnauit super tribum iudam et ihe
rusalem annis undecim. Cui successit
in regnum filius eius ioachim. Cognomi
to iechonias qui tertio mense regni sui die
decimo captus a ducibus nabuchodonosor:
ductusque est in babilonem. et in loco eius co
in regnum filius eius ioachim. Cognomi
to iechonias qui tertio mense regni sui die
decimo captus a ducibus nabuchodonosor:
ductusque est in babilonem. et in loco eius co
in regnum filius eius ioachim. Cognomi
to iechonias qui tertio mense regni sui die
decimo captus a ducibus nabuchodonosor:
ductusque est in babilonem. et in loco eius co
in regnum filius eius ioachim. Cognomi

atque subuersa est. Nemo igitur putet
eundem in danielis principio esse ioa
chim: qui in ezechielis exordio ioachin
scribitur. Iste enim extremam sillabam
chim habet. ille chin. et ob hanc causam
in euangelio secundum matheum una uidetur
esse generatio. quia secunda chim desinet fili
um iosie. et tertia incipit a ioachim filio
ioachim. Quod ignorans porphirius: ca
lumpniam instruit ecclesie. suam osten
dens imperitiam: dum euangeliste ma
thei arguere nititur falsitatem quoque tradi
tus scribitur ioachim monstrat. non ad
lumpniam instruit ecclesie. suam osten
dens imperitiam: dum euangeliste ma
thei arguere nititur falsitatem quoque tradi
tus scribitur ioachim monstrat. non ad
lumpniam instruit ecclesie. suam osten
dens imperitiam: dum euangeliste ma
thei arguere nititur falsitatem quoque tradi
tus scribitur ioachim monstrat. non ad
lumpniam instruit ecclesie. suam osten

the river Euphrates!"[147] The biblical text describes how these four angels "who had been held ready for the hour . . . wore breastplates the color of fire and of sapphire and of sulphur; and the heads of the horses were like lions' heads, and fire and smoke and sulphur issued from their mouths."[148] Their horses kill by means of their breath, and by the bite of their tails, which terminate in venomous serpents' heads.[149] Within the Las Huelgas Beatus, the four riders are depicted in profile against a chromatic background similar to that which appears in its *Two Witnesses*. Each horseman resides in his own star-filled colored segment and charges forward as his reptilian tail attacks a helpless victim, shown either splayed lifelessly across the divide of two chromatic fields or curled up in one of the image's upper corners. The biblical narrative further reveals that the advance of these beasts, and the two hundred million troops of cavalry at their command, kills a third of humanity (Rev. 9:16–18). This destruction is symbolized in the lowest register of the image where the artist has painted seven pale figures representative of the souls of the dead. Against the eschatological panorama of John's visions, these fiery creatures are agents of divine vengeance against those who pursue infidel practices under the guise of Christianity. Despite this widespread calamity, those who survive these creatures persist in their worship of demons and idols, in murder, theft, fornication and other transgressions.

Yet the fact that these agents of destruction dispense calamity through military action primes them for the superimposition of more contemporary, earthbound military engagements. Their surging forth from the river Euphrates reflects a pervasive fear of invasion along the eastern border of the Roman Empire by the Parthians within the original context in which John wrote his revelatory text.[150] Within a thirteenth-century context, this invocation of the Euphrates was no less charged, alluding to the heart of Nebuchadezzar's Babylonian Empire but also to Baghdad, the seat of the Abbasid Caliphate and thus a symbol of Muslim rule. In this way the image of *The Death-Dealing Cavalry*, like the elaborate double-folio illustration *The Siege of Jerusalem and the Lamentation of Jeremiah*, could argue for military action against Islam through carefully crafted imagery.

In light of these sociopolitical reverberations within the manuscript's eschatological matrix, it is noteworthy that the Las Huelgas Beatus was produced just prior to the inception of the rule of Alfonso X (1252–1284). It is under Alfonsine patronage that the propagandistic use of Muslim eschatological content decisively infiltrates the contemporary literary realm. As a strategic move in the crafting of his imperial ideology, Alfonso commissioned the translation of numerous Arabic materials into Castilian, particularly astronomical and other scientific treatises.[151] This endeavor included the translation of a version of the Prophet's *miᶜrāj* in which Muḥammad ascends to heaven not on the back of the winged steed Burāq but by climbing a ladder. This calculated translation of an ascension narrative by Alfonso's Jewish physician, Abraham of Toledo,[152] likely drew from a variety of Arabic sources in order to produce a Castilian composite text.[153] Although the Castilian version no longer survives, it was subsequently translated by royal commission

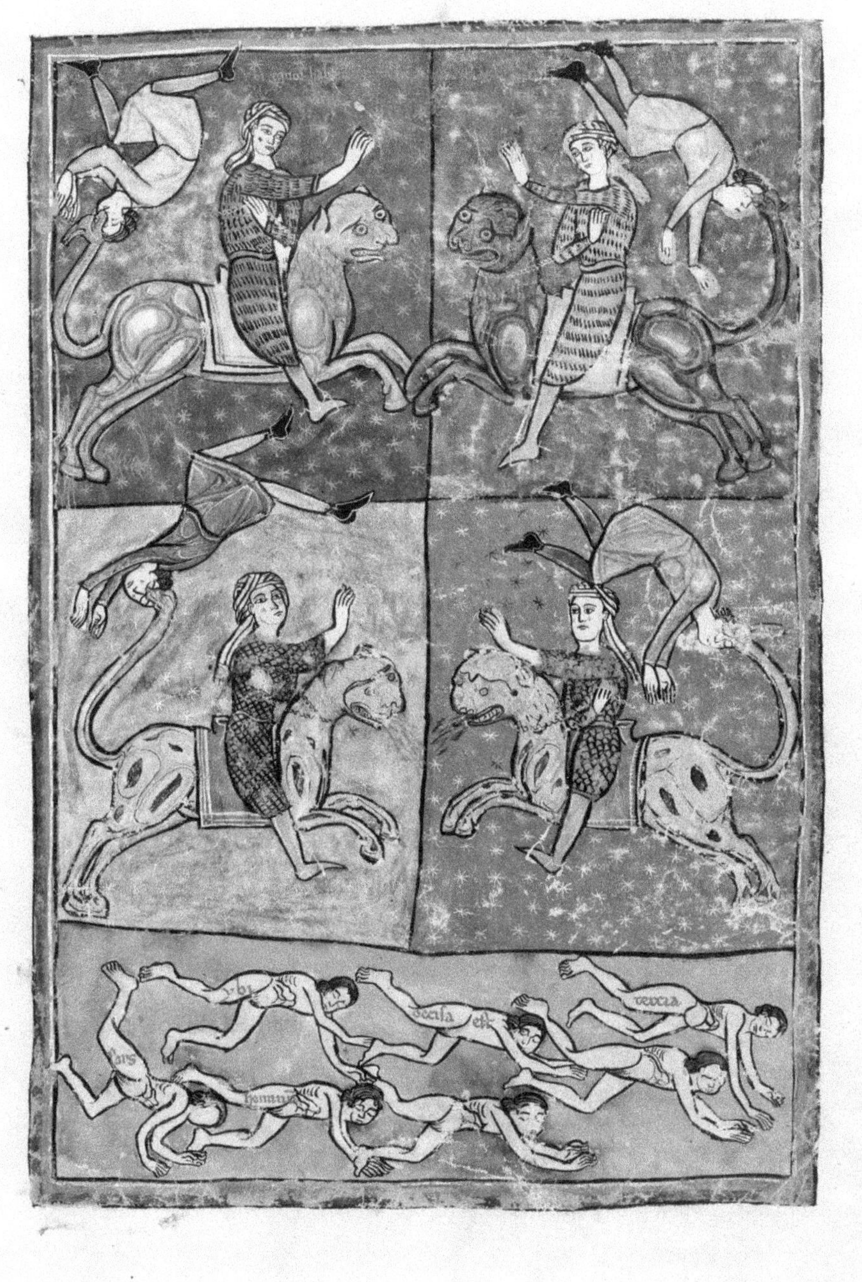

FIGURE 5.8. The Death-Dealing Cavalry, folio 94r. Las Huelgas Beatus, 1220. New York, Pierpont Morgan Library, M. 429.

into Latin circa 1264 by Bonaventura da Siena.[154] This Latin version of the narrative, the *Liber Scale Machometi* (The Book of Muḥammad's Ladder) served as the base for yet another translation of the ascension narrative into Old French in or shortly after 1264, titled *Le livre de l'eschiele de Mahomet.* Although the preface and colophon of the French text claim also to have been completed by Bonaventura, it has been suggested that it was more likely the work of an anonymous Provençal in the service of the king.[155]

The motivation for the serial translation of a Muslim ascension narrative into Castilian, Latin, and French is fairly clear. By the mid-thirteenth century, Muslim Spain had been constrained to a small portion of the Iberian Peninsula comprising the eastern Algarve and the kingdoms of Granada and Murcia.[156] As a result, the kingdom of Castile-Léon housed a substantial Muslim population. Multiple translations of a Muslim religious text, at least one of which was royally commissioned, attests both to a widespread interest in Islam, and that various documents in Arabic and Latin, if not also Old French and Castilian, were already in circulation at this time. The successive translations of *The Book of Muḥammad's Ladder* ensured it was equally accessible to both clergy and laity and therefore could serve as an efficient conduit for the dissemination of information about Islam with the specific aim of discrediting its theological validity. The preface to the Old French version makes this explicit. It describes the goal of the book's translation being that

> people may learn about Muḥammad's life and knowledge so that after they are acquainted with the errors and unbelievable things that he recounts in this book, the legitimate Christian religion and truth which is in [Christ] will thus be more fitting and pleasing to embrace and keep for all those who are good Christians.[157]

It was thus hoped that contemplation of *The Book of Muḥammad's Ladder* would fortify the Christian community against the potentially divisive effects of mutual coexistence. The suitability of the *miʿrāj* narrative for this purpose derives partially from its authoritative tenor: it is narrated by the Prophet himself, and in its final chapter both Abū Bakr and Ibn ʿAbbās swear to have faithfully recorded the words of the Prophet.[158] Christian theologians eager to attract attention to *The Book of Muḥammad's Ladder* even claimed that it was "Muḥammad's 'second book,'" and that he was in fact the true author of both it and the Qur'an.[159] Yet it was its eschatological character that made the text an indispensable tool for proselytizing against Islam, particularly given the assertion of Muḥammad's supposed authorship. This claim, like the lurid descriptions of paradise publicized by Eulogius and Paulus Alvarus in ninth-century Córdoba, was levied to deny its divine revelation. This rendered the text and the belief system it encapsulated open to trenchant criticism. Curiously, however, potential readers were not provided with any supplemental commentary (save the short paragraph of the preface) to guide their reaction to the text, which in many instances glorifies Muḥammad.[160] This omission reveals a certain confidence in the self-evidence of Islam's deficiencies and that Christian readers would automatically find elements of it theologically preposterous (for example, Jesus appears in the lowest heaven and is nowhere to be found during the Last Judgment).[161]

This marshalling of Islamic eschatological material through the Alfonsine translations effected the naturalization of the *miʿrāj* narrative within thirteenth-century Castile-Léon. With this realization the beginning and end points of the present investigation converge. *The Book of Muḥammad's Ladder* was intentionally assembled and translated under Alfonsine patronage in the thirteenth century so that it could be ideologically deployed by a Christian audience against the supposedly deleterious effects of Christian-Muslim contact. This literary enterprise mirrors the ninth-century circulation of texts propagated by Córdoban polemicists among a Christian community experiencing strife precisely *because* of Christian-Muslim contact.

This mobilization bisects the *Miʿrājnāma* genre at two discrete points in its historical development. The first is through the exploitation of prophetic biography, one of the genres pivotal to the formation of an independent, fully elaborated ascension narrative. The second is through the redaction and dissemination of one of these mature versions. That these textual enterprises were accompanied by the efflorescence of an illustrated tradition of Beatus of Liébana's Commentary on the Apocalypse not only makes it possible to track a change in Christian attitudes toward Muslims across time, but indicates that this battle over the eschaton was not confined solely to the literary realm. Within the medieval world, the explanation and affirmation of the natural and supernatural order occurred through the exegesis of authoritative texts, which in turn required revision and illustration to be of optimal effectiveness in a period of tense interreligious relations in the Iberian Peninsula.

Notes

I am sincerely grateful to Christiane Gruber for encouraging my pursuit of this subject. I would also like to express my heartfelt appreciation to both Christiane and Frederick Colby for their generous commentary and counsel over the course of the development of this chapter.

1. The author has tried to restrict sources to those in English to allow the generalist reader to access the material.
2. Girona, Catedral de Girona, Num. Inv. 7(11), 6 July 975, 284 folios, 40 × 26 cm.
3. New York, Pierpont Morgan Library MS. M. 429, 1220, 184 folios, 53 × 34 cm.
4. These include a brief preface written by Beatus, in which he dedicates his text to "holy father Etherius," Bishop of Osma, a Prologue attributed to Jerome, and part of a letter written by Jerome which introduced his edition of the *Commentary of Victorinus on the Apocalypse*. These were followed by selections from the works of Isidore of Seville that addressed St. John, and then what Enrique Flórez termed the *Summa dicendorum* (literally "a summary of what is said"), that is, a reiteration of the main themes of Beatus's commentary. See John Williams, *The*

Illustrated Beatus: A Corpus of Illustrations of the Commentary on the Apocalypse (London: Harvey Miller, 1994), vol. 1: 20; and Enrique Flórez, *Sancti Beati, Presbyteri Hispani Liebanensis, in Apocalypsin, ac Plurimas Ultriusque Foederis Paginas Commentaria, ex Veteribus, Nonnullisque Desideratis Patribus, Mille Retro Annis Collecta, Nunc Primum Editia* (Madrid, 1770).

5. Beatus's sources include Jerome, Augustine, Gregory the Great, Ambrose, Fulgentius, Irenaeus, Tyconius, Apringius, Isidore of Seville, Gregory of Elvira, and Baquiarius. See John Williams, "Purpose and Imagery in the Apocalypse Commentary of Beatus of Liébana," in *The Apocalypse in the Middle Ages,* ed. Richard K. Emmerson and Bernard McGinn (Ithaca, NY: Cornell University Press, 1992), 218.

6. For a list of relevant literature, see Williams, "Purpose and Imagery," 1992, note 13.

7. Wilhelm Neuss proposed a date of 785 in his "Probleme der christlichen Kunst in maurischen Spanien des 10. Jahrhunderts," in *Neue Beträge zur Kunstgeschichte des 1. Jahrtausends: Frühmittelalterliche Kunst,* vol. 1, 2nd ed., ed. A. Alföndi (Baden-Baden: Verlag für Kunst und Wissenschaft, 1954), 249–284. In this position Neuss rejected the opinions of Leopold Delisle and Henry Sanders, both of whom considered a date of 776 to have witnessed the first of successive editions; Neuss envisioned a complete archetype rather than a progressive evolution. Peter Klein affirmed the date of 776 in his *Der ältere Beatus-Kodex Vitr. 14-1 der Biblioteca Nacional zu Madrid: Studien zur Beatus-Illustration und der Spanischen Buchmalerei des 10. Jahrhunderts* (Hildesheim: Olms, 1976). John Williams also favors the year 776 and reminds us that "Beatus *did* compose an anti-Adoptionist tract: the *Ad Elipandum,* which attacked Elipandus and his theology directly and explicitly." See Williams, "Purpose and Imagery," 1992, 220–221 and notes 15 and 16.

8. Silos, Biblioteca del Monasterio de Santo Domingo, Fragment 4.

9. For an overview of the stemma proposed by Williams in relation to those proposed by Neuss and Klein, see Williams, *The Illustrated Beatus,* vol. 1, 21–26 and 50ff.

10. John Williams proposed a date of 940–945 (Williams, *The Illustrated Beatus,* vol. 2, 27) while Peter Klein prefers the slightly later date of 950–960. See Peter Klein, "Eschatological Expectations and the Revised Beatus," in *Church, State, Vellum and Stone: Essays on Medieval Spain in Honor of John Williams,* ed. Therese Martin and Julie A. Harris (Leiden: Brill, 2005), 150.

11. Wilhelm Neuss theorized that the first illustrated commentary was composed c. 785 and that it equaled the lavishness of the fully illuminated Beatus manuscripts that survive today. In contrast to this supposition of a visually sophisticated archetype, Peter Klein asserted that Beatus's written text evolved through repeated editions, which coincided with the development of the commentary's imagery. Klein further situated the production of all of Branch II manuscripts between 800 and 950, and very likely between 925 and 950. Following Klein's position, Williams has argued convincingly that the archetype of the Branch II manuscripts—and thus its pictorial expansion—was produced approximately 940–950. See Wilhelm Neuss, *Die Apokalypse des hl. Johannes in der altspanischen und altchristlichen Bibel-Illustration* (Spanische Forschungen der Görresgesellschaft, Reihe II, 2 and 3), Münster in Westfalen, 1931, 2 vols., 5; "Probleme der christlichen Kunst," 254; Klein, *Der ältere Beatus-Kodex,* 176, 216 and 299; "La tradición pictória de los Beatos," in *Actas del Simposio para el estudio de los códices del "Comentario al Apocalipsis" de Beato de Liébana,* vol. 2 (Madrid: Joyas Bibliográficas, 1980), 97–98; "Beatus v. Liébana," *Lexikon des Mittelalters,* I (Munich: Artemis Verlag, 1980), col. 1747. See Williams, *The Illustrated Beatus,* vol. 1, 50 and 76.

12. Williams, *The Illustrated Beatus,* vol. 1, 55–56 and 58. Citing an entry in Juan Gil, *Corpus scriptorum muzarabicorum* (Madrid: Instituto Antonio de Nebrija, 1973), 126–133, Williams notes that ". . . there is evidence to indicate that at least by the middle of the ninth century the Daniel commentary was coupled with that on the Apocalypse. A text titled *Indiculum de adventum Enoc et Elie adque Antichrist: libris duobus id est Danielis et Apocalipsin Ioannis a beato Iheronimo expositum,* a work dating from the middle of the ninth century apparently based on Jerome's *Commentarium in Danielem* and Beatus's *Commentarius in Apocalipsin,* is witness to their early combination." Whether this commentary was illustrated is unknown. See Williams, *The Illustrated Beatus,* vol. 1, 26 and n. 32.

13. This estimation of the scale of the visual corpus is found in Williams, *The Illustrated Beatus,* vol. 1, 8, with the addition of the fragment of San Pedro de León discussed in vol. 5, 50. I would like to thank David Raizman for confirming the number of extant illustrated Beatus manuscripts and fragments. Regarding the component illustrations in those Beatus Manuscripts representative of the tradition's mature form, I cannot improve upon the summation provided by John Williams, which is worth quoting in full here: "In the final stage of its evolution, Beatus's commentary on the Apocalypse was illustrated by as many as one hundred and eight canonical images. Sixty-eight of these were inspired by and immediately followed the *storiae* into which the Apocalypse text had been divided. Seven were based on the text of the commentary: the map of the world, the Apostles, the Four Beasts and the Statue, the Woman on the Beast, the Ark of Noah, the palm, and the fox and the cock. To these were added the eight prefatory miniatures of the evangelists and their Gospels, fourteen pages presenting the genealogy of Christ, and the eleven illustrations that accompany Jerome's commentary to Daniel. This total could then be augmented in the most luxurious copies by the labyrinth of an ex-libris, the authors, the cross, the Alpha and Omega, and the allegorical combat of bird and serpent." See Williams, "Purpose and Imagery," 226.

14. Williams, "Purpose and Imagery," 225.

15. Henry Sanders, ed., *Beati in Apocalipsin libri duodecim* (Rome: American Academy, 1930), 1–2.

16. Beatus drew specifically from the prefaces to Isidore's *Contra Iudaeos, De ortu et obitu partum,* and *De oficiis.* Williams, "Purpose and Imagery," 219.

17. Canon XVII states: ". . . si quis eum [sc. Apocalypsum librum] deinceps aut non receperit aut a Pascha usque ad Pentecosten missarum tempore in ecclesia non praedicaverit, excommunicationis sententiam habebit." José Vives, ed., *Concilios visigóticos e hispano-romanos* (Barcelona and Madrid: Consejo Superiod de Investigaciones Científicas, Instituto Enrique Flórez, 1963), 198. Quoted in Otto Werkmeister's "The First Romanesque Beatus Manuscripts and the Liturgy of Death," in *Actas del Simposio para el Estudio de los Codices del 'Comentario al Apocalipsis' de Beato de Liébana* (Madrid: Joyas Bibliográficas, 1980), vol. 1, 172, n. 33, and further explicated in n. 34.

18. Williams, *The Illustrated Beatus,* vol. 1, 169, note 10. Evidently some other factor must account for the widespread proliferation of Apocalyptic text and imagery through the manufacture of numerous copies of Beatus's commentary.

19. For further information on this transition, see Bernard F. Reilly, *The Kingdom of León-Castilla under King Alfonso VI, 1065–1109* (Princeton: Princeton University Press, 1988); *Santiago, Saint-Denis and Saint Peter. The Reception of the Roman Liturgy in León-Castile in 1080,* ed. Bernard F. Reilly (New York: Fordham University Press, 1985), especially J. F. O'Callaghan, "The Integration of Christian Spain into Europe: the Role of Alfonso VI of León-Castile," 101–120.

20. Rose Walker, *Views of Transition: Liturgy and Illumination in Medieval Spain* (London: British Library Press, 1998), 88. Walker succinctly summarizes the presence and absence of readings in the two liturgies on p. 85: "The most striking change of all in terms of content in these liturgical manuscripts was the introduction of readings in the Roman books. As there are no readings in the Mozarabic manuscripts for any of the offices, the contrast is an absolute one between their presence in the Roman manuscripts as opposed to their absence in the Mozarabic manuscripts. It may indeed be that the *lectio,* as the new element in matins, was the distinguishing feature *par excellence* of the new liturgy."

21. Werkmeister, "The First Romanesque Beatus," 167–170. Significantly, Rose Walker also discovered excerpts from Beatus's text in a late eleventh century breviary containing the Roman liturgy from the Abbey of Silos, which were used as *lectiones* for the first and second nocturns from the first to the fourth Sunday after the Easter octave (see Walker, *Views of Transition,* 88). Therefore, one may conclude that over the long durée the illustrated tradition of Beatus's commentary navigated both a semi-public and para-liturgical status.

22. Klein, "Eschatological Expectations," 149.

23. Williams, *The Illustrated Beatus,* vol. 1, 132.

24. Roger Collins, *Early Medieval Spain: Unity in Diversity, 400–1000* (New York: St. Martin's

Press, 1983), 218. The most famous of these is the foundation inscription of the monastery of San Miguel de Escalada, settled in 912 and the recipient of the celebrated Morgan Beatus. The inscription begins "This place, of old dedicated in honor of the archangel Michael and built with a little building, after falling into pieces, lay long in ruin until Abbot Alfonso, coming with his brethren from Córdoba his fatherland, built up the ruined house. . . ." See Jerrilynn Dodds, *Architecture and Ideology in Early Medieval Spain* (University Park: Pennsylvania State University Press, 1989), 50.

25. José Fernández Arenas, *Mozarabic Architecture* (Greenwich, CT: New York Graphic Society, 1972), 254. See also Margarita López Gómez, "The Mozarabs: Worthy Bearers of Islamic Culture," in *The Legacy of Muslim Spain*, ed. Salma Khadra Jayyusi (Leiden and New York: E. J. Brill, 1992), 171.

26. Mikel de Epalza, "Mozarabs: An Emblematic Christian Minority in Islamic Al-Andalus," in *The Legacy of Muslim Spain*, ed. Salma Khadra Jayyusi (Leiden and New York: E. J. Brill, 1992), 149. De Epalza notes that the term has also been linked by some Arabists to the word *mustaʿrib*, meaning "tribes not originally descended from Arabs." See I. Lichtendsdâdter, "Mustaʿrib(a)," *Shorter Encyclopaedia of Islam* (Leiden and London: E. J. Brill, 1961), 418. Cited by de Epalza in footnote 3, page 163.

27. De Epalza, "Mozarabs: An Emblematic Christian Minority," 150.

28. Jessica Coope, *The Martyrs of Córdoba: Community and Family Conflict in an Age of Mass Conversion* (Lincoln: University of Nebraska Press, 1995), 1–3 and 11–14.

29. Coope, *The Martyrs of Córdoba*, 3. Coope writes elegantly on this point: "The word "acculturation" implies a process of mutual change, but in practice in any given situation the extent of cultural borrowing is rarely equally balanced. I believe that the 850s in Córdoba were so turbulent at least partly because whatever balance had existed between Christians and Muslims was fairly suddenly upset in favor of Arab Muslim culture. . . . This is not to say that cultural borrowing moved in only one direction in ninth-century Córdoba, but what happened there begins to look less like mutual acculturation and more like assimilation—that is, a one-way cultural shift pulling Christians into Arab Muslim culture."

30. Coope, *The Martyrs of Córdoba*, 9.

31. Coope, *The Martyrs of Córdoba*, xv and 17–18. See also Kenneth Baxter Wolf, *Christian Martyrs in Muslim Spain* (Cambridge: Cambridge University Press, 1988), 24.

32. Coope, *The Martyrs of Córdoba*, 18–19.

33. Kenneth Baxter Wolf, "The Earliest Spanish-Christian Views of Islam," *Church History* 55/3 (Sept. 1986), 289.

34. Ibid.

35. Coope, *The Martyrs of Córdoba*, 21.

36. Ibid., 23.

37. Wolf, "The Earliest Spanish-Christian Views of Islam," 288; Williams, *The Illustrated Beatus*, vol. 1, 130.

38. Wolf, "The Earliest Spanish-Christian Views of Islam," 288; idem, *Christian Martyrs in Muslim Spain*, 63.

39. Wolf, *Christian Martyrs in Muslim Spain*, 62.

40. Wolf, *Christian Martyrs in Muslim Spain*, 66–68; Coope, *The Martyrs of Córdoba*, 25.

41. Wolf, *Christian Martyrs in Muslim Spain*, 56–57.

42. Wolf, "Earliest Spanish-Christian Views of Islam," 291.

43. *Liber apologeticus martyrum* 19, *Corpus scriptorum muzarabicorum*, ed. Juan Gil, vol. 2, 487. Quoted by Wolf, "Earliest Spanish-Christian Views of Islam," 291.

44. Wolf, *Christian Martyrs in Muslim Spain*, 91. When considering Eulogius's project, it is fascinating to ponder Wolf's observation that the Muslim authorities "apparently did not regard Latin treatises which contained disparaging remarks about Islam or its founder as violations of the proscriptions against blasphemy, because the audience of such works was so restricted." See his *Christian Martyrs in Muslim Spain*, 73.

45. *Memoriale sanctorum* 1.7, *Corpus scriptorum muzarabicorum*, vol. 2, 375–376. Cited in Wolf, "Earliest Spanish-Christian Views of Islam," 288, note 29.

46. Ibid. See Wolf, "Earliest Spanish-Christian Views of Islam," 292; and the paragraph in full in idem, *Christian Martyrs in Muslim Spain*, 52: "In the next life," they say, "all the fortunate shall be born into paradise. There God will give us beautiful women, more comely than usual, and ready to serve our pleasure." Response: By no means will they obtain the state of blessedness in paradise if both sexes partake freely in the flow of desire. This is not paradise but a brothel, a most obscene place. The Lord, responding to the Pharisees who had asked whose wife the woman would be upon resurrection who had married seven brothers so that, according to the Mosaic law, she might raise up the seed of the next of kin, said: "You err, not knowing the scripture, nor the power of God. The children of this world marry and are given in marriage. But they who shall be as angels of God in heaven shall neither marry nor be given in marriage upon resurrection." Wolf notes that because Speraindeo was a teacher of Eulogius, this passage, written by the Abbot, in all likelihood comes from a lesson or "textbook" suited to clergymen soon to practice in a pluralistic environment.

47. Kenneth Baxter Wolf, "Muhammad as Antichrist in Ninth-Century Córdoba," in *Christians, Muslims, and Jews in Medieval and Early Modern Spain*, ed. Mark D. Meyerson and Edward D. English (South Bend, IN.: Notre Dame Press, 1999), 6.

48. Wolf, "Muhammad as Antichrist," 7.

49. Suzanne Conklin Akbari, "The Rhetoric of Antichrist in Western Lives of Muhammad," *Islam and Christian-Muslim Relations* 8, no. 3 (1997): 299.

50. Wolf, "Muhammad as Antichrist," 15.

51. Ibid., 9–10.

52. *Indiculus luminosus*, 23, *Corpus scriptorium muzarabicorum*, vol. 1, 314–315. Quoted by Wolf, "Muhammad as Antichrist," 11. Wolf's clever article contains further examples of this colorful rhetoric.

53. Coope, *The Martyrs of Córdoba*, 70.

54. John V. Tolan, *Saracens: Islam in the Medieval European Imagination* (New York: Columbia University Press, 2002), 91.

55. Williams, *The Illustrated Beatus*, vol. 1, 131.

56. *Liber apologeticus martyrum* 16, *Corpus scriptorium muzarabicorum*, vol. 2, 483–486. Quoted in Wolf, "Earliest Spanish-Christian Views of Islam," 288, n. 30. That Eulogius returned from the north with a *vita* of Muḥammad is also noted by Williams, *The Illustrated Beatus*, vol. 1, 131; and Collins, *Early Medieval Spain*, 212. A copy of the *vita* was preserved in the eleventh-century Codex of Roda (Biblioteca de la Academia de Historia 3, folios 187r–188r), rediscovered in 1927. For a full transcription and English translation of the *vita*, see Kenneth Baxter Wolf, "The Earliest Latin Lives of Muhammad," in *Conversion and Continuity: Indigenous Christian Communities in Islamic Lands, Eighth to Eighteenth Centuries*, ed. Michael Gervers and Ramzi Jibran Bikhazi (Toronto: Pontifical Institute of Mediaeval Studies, 1990), 89–101, esp. 96–99.

57. *Epistulae* 6.9, *Corpus scriptorium muzarabicorum*, vol. 1, 200–201. Wolf, "Earliest Spanish-Christian Views of Islam," 288, n. 30.

58. Christiane Gruber, "The Prophet Muhammad's Ascension (*Miʿrāj*) in Islamic Art and Literature, ca. 1300–1600" (Ph.D. diss., University of Pennsylvania, 2005), 40.

59. ʿAbd al-Malik Ibn Hisham, *The Life of Muhammad: A Translation of Ishaq's Sirat rasul Allāh*, intro. and notes by Alfred Guillaume (London: Oxford University Press, 1955), 181–187.

60. Collins, *Early Medieval Spain*, 218.

61. Carlos Miranda García-Tejedor lists Alvarus's *Indiculus luminosis* as a prominent literary work that would have been very popular among these northern religious communities. See Carlos Miranda García-Tejedor, "Stylistic Analysis of the Gerona Beatus," in *Codex of Gerona: Commentarius in Apocalypsin*, vol. 2 [Commentary volume accompanying facsimile edition] ed. Mónica Miró (Barcelona: M. Moleiro, 2004), 263.

62. To access further literature that discusses images and texts of the *miʿrāj*, please see the above-mentioned dissertation by Christiane Gruber (note 58) and also her chapter in this vol-

ume. Also see Frederick Colby, "Constructing an Islamic-Ascension Narrative: The Interplay of Official and Popular Culture in Pseudo-Ibn ʿAbbās." Ph.D. diss., Duke University, 2002; and Brook Olson Vuckovic, *Heavenly Journeys, Earthly Concerns: The Legacy of the Miʿraj in the Formation of Islam* (New York: Routledge, 2005).

63. This date is based on the loan of an *Exposito Apocalipsin* given to the Cathedral of Girona recorded in Madrid, RAH [Real Academia de la Historia], Doc. Sala, 9, 2309, pp. 27–30. See John Williams, *The Illustrated Beatus,* vol. 2, 51.

64. Ibid. The colophon states "*ENDE PINTRINX ET D(E)I AIUTRIX FR(A)T(E)R EMETERIUS ET PR(E)S(BITE)R*" (Ende painter and servant of God. Emeterius monk and presbyter). Ibid.

65. The inscriptions read "*SENIOR PRESBITER SCRIPSIT*" (presbyter Senior wrote it) and "*D(OMI)NICUS ABBA FIERI PRECEPIT*" (Abbot Dominicus had the book made).

66. Ibid. For an introduction to the Tábara Beatus (Madrid, Archivo Histórico Nacional, Cod. 1097B, 27July 970, 168 folios, 36 × 25.5 cm), see Williams, *The Illustrated Beatus,* vol. 2, 43–49.

67. The colophon states "*INVENI PORTUM VOLUMINE VIA F IIA N(O)N(A)S IULIAS. IN IS DIEBUS ERAT FREDENANDO FLAGINIZ A VILLAS TOLETA CIVITAS AD DEVELLANDO MAURITANIE. DISCURRENTA ERA MILLESIMA XIII.*" Williams observes that this was not a Friday but a Tuesday (ibid).

68. Carlos Miranda García-Tejedor, "Stylistic Analysis of the Gerona Beatus," 274.

69. See Gonzalo Menéndez Pidal, "Mozárabes y asturianos en la cultura de la Alta Edad Media en relación especial con la historia de los conocimientos geográficos," *Boletín de la Real Academia de la Historia* 134 (1954), 206–207. Cited in Carlos Miranda García-Tejedor, "Stylistic Analysis of the Gerona Beatus," 274.

70. García-Tejedor, "Stylistic Analysis of the Gerona Beatus," 275.

71. Williams, *The Illustrated Beatus,* vol. 2, 60–61. Williams first makes this identification in *Early Spanish Manuscript Illumination,* 99. It is reaffirmed in his "Purpose and Imagery," 232.

72. See Otto Werkmeister, "The Islamic Rider in the Beatus of Girona," *Gesta* 36/2 (1997), 101–108.

73. Sanders, ed., *Beati in Apocalipsin,* 437.

74. Adela Yarbro Collins, *The Apocalypse* [New Testament Message: A Biblical-Theological Commentary, Volume 2] (Collegeville, Minn.: A Michael Glazier Book published by the Liturgical Press, 1979), 64.

75. Sanders, ed., *Beati in Apocalipsin,* 437.

76. New York, Pierpont Morgan Library, M. 644, 300 folios, 38.7 × 28.5 cm. For an introduction to the Morgan Beatus, see Williams, *The Illustrated Beatus,* vol. 2, 21–33.

77. Jerrilynn Dodds, "Islam, Christianity, and the Problem of Christian Art," in *The Art of Medieval Spain, 500–1200 A.D.* (New York: Abrams, 1993), 30.

78. Eulogius mentions this four times in his *Memorale sanctorum.* The entirety of Book III ("On the Destruction of Basilicas") addresses this issue, where he discusses the architecture destroyed within the reign of Muḥammad I, particularly his destruction of the monastery of Tábanos. In his *Indiculus luminosis,* Paulus Alvarus wrote "that the Christians' churches were destroyed daily, and their sacred buildings pulled to the ground." (quoted in Dodds, *Architecture and Ideology,* 64).

79. Sanders, ed., *Beati in Apocalipsin,* 444.

80. Otto Werkmeister, "Art of the Frontier: Mozarabic Monasticism," in *The Art of Medieval Spain* (New York: Abrams, 1993), 128.

81. Rev. 11:9–10 continues: "For three and a half days members of the peoples and tribes and languages and nations will gaze at their dead bodies and refuse to let them be placed in a tomb; and the inhabitants of the earth will gloat over them and celebrate and exchange presents, because these two prophets had been a torment to the inhabitants of the earth." See Sanders, ed., *Beati in Apocalipsin,* "Storia Eliae, Sive Legis et Evangeli," 445 and "Storia de Eodem Testamento," 448–449. The subject of *vincet* and *occidet,* though supplied in the *explanationes,* remains ambiguous in the *storiae* as Beatus omits the portion of Rev. 11:7 that names the Beast

as the slayer of the two witnesses, and appends the phrase "vidi inquit bestiam ascendentem de abysso" to the end of chapter eleven (11:19) in a later *storia*. See Sanders, ed., *Beati in Apocalipsin*, 456–457; Roger Gryson, ed., *Apocalypsis Johannis. Vetus Latina. Die Reste der altlateinischen Bibel. Nach Petrus Sabatier neu gesammelt und herausgegeben von der Erzabtei Beuron unter der Leitung* 26/2 (Freiburg: Herder, 2000), 85–89 and 431–432. I would like to express my appreciation to Andrew Hicks for his discussion of the *Vetus Latina* and for his skillful translation of select portions of Beatus's commentary.

82. The labels on the page read "*Antichristus civitatem Iherusalem subvertit / eliam et enoc occident.*"

83. Williams, *The Illustrated Beatus*, vol. 1, 32.

84. Sanders, ed., *Beati in Apocalipsin*, 449; cited in Williams, *The Illustrated Beatus*, vol. 1, 32.

85. Klein, *Der ältere Beatus-Kodex*, 103–105.

86. The *Chronica Muzarabica* appears in J. Gil, *Corpus scriptorium muzarabicorum*, vol. 1, 14–54.

87. Williams, *The Illustrated Beatus*, vol. 1, 134.

88. Ibid.

89. Dodds, "Islam, Christianity, and the Problem of Christian Art," 29–30. This pictorial conceit appears in other Branch II manuscripts, including the Girona Beatus.

90. Paulus Alvarus, *Indiculus luminosus*, 6, quoted in Werkmeister, "Art of the Frontier: Mozarabic Monasticism," 131.

91. García-Tejedor, "Stylistic Analysis of the Gerona Beatus," 275.

92. Werkmeister, "Art of the Frontier: Mozarabic Monasticism," 128.

93. Gestures intended for pious emulation are also used in illustrated *Miʿrājnāmas* (see the chapter by Christiane Gruber in this volume).

94. Qur'an 17:1 reads: "Glory (*subḥān*) to Him who made His servant travel (*asrā*) by night from the sacred mosque (*al-masjid al-ḥarām*) to the farthest place of worship (*al-masjid al-aqṣā*), whose precincts We have blessed, in order that We may show him some of Our signs. Indeed, He hears and sees (all things)." All qur'anic translations are taken from Ahmed Ali, *al-Qur'ān*, 5th edition (Princeton: Princeton University Press, 1994). For a comprehensive discussion of the interpretive issues surrounding the term *al-masjid al-aqṣā*, see Heribert Busse, "Jerusalem in the Story of Muḥammad's Night Journey and Ascension," *Jerusalem Studies in Arabic and Islam* 14 (1991), 1–40.

95. Qur'an 53:4–18 reads: "So he acquired poise and balance, and reached the highest pinnacle. Then he drew near and drew closer until a space of two arcs (*qāb qawsayn*) or even less remained, when He revealed to His servant what He revealed. His heart did not falsify what he perceived. Will you dispute with him what he saw? He saw Him indeed another time by the Lote Tree of the Limit (*sidrat al-muntahā*) beyond which no one can pass, close to which is the Garden of Tranquility, when the Lote Tree of the Limit was covered over with what it was covered over; neither did sight falter nor exceed the bounds. Indeed he saw some of the greatest signs of the Lord."

96. Michael Sells, "3 Enoch (*Sefer Hekhalot*) and the Miʿrāj of Abū Yazīd al-Bisṭāmī" (paper presented before the American Academy of Religion, 1989, 9). Quoted in Colby, "Constructing an Islamic-Ascension Narrative," 33–34.

97. The majority of scholars concur that portions of the Book of Revelation were written during the 60s AD, following the persecution of Christians that marked the reign of Nero (r. 13 October 54–9 June 68 AD). Other aspects of the text, however, suggest that it was not completed until the reign of Domitian (r. 14 September 81–18 September 96). Bart D. Ehrman, *The New Testament: A Historical Introduction to the Early Christian Writings*, 3rd ed. (New York and Oxford: Oxford University Press, 2004), 470.

98. Translated into French by Abel Pavet de Courteille, *Mirâdj-Nâmeh, Récit de l'ascension de Mahomet au ciel composé A. H. 840/1436–37* (Amsterdam: Philo Press, 1975); into German by Max Scherberger, *Das Miʿrajname: die Himmel und Höllenfahrt des Propheten Muhammad in der osttürkischen überlieferung, Arbeitsmaterialien zum Orient* 14 (Würzburg: Ergon, 2003); and into

English by Wheeler Thackston, "The Paris *Mi^crajnama*," *Journal of Turkish Studies*, vol. 18 (1994), 263–299; Christiane Gruber, *The Timurid Book of Ascension (Miʿrajnama): A Study of Text and Image in a Pan-Asian Context* (Valencia: Patrimonio Ediciones, 2008), Appendix I.

99. For a further discussion of this development in the early period, see Colby, "Constructing an Islamic-Ascension Narrative," esp. chapter 2.

100. Yarbro Collins, *The Apocalyspe*, 102.

101. Sanders, ed., *Beati in Apocalipsin*, 557.

102. Ibid., 514. The second proclamation of Babylon's defeat occurs in Rev. 18:2.

103. Ibid., 551.

104. For example, Ps. 75:8 and Is. 51:17, 22. See Yarbro Collins, *The Apocalypse*, 110.

105. Yarbro Collins, *The Apocalypse*, 110.

106. Sanders, ed., *Beati in Apocalipsin*, 531.

107. Ibid., 536.

108. Thackston, "The Paris *Miʿrajnama*," 273.

109. Ibn Hisham, *The Life of Muhammad*, 182. Quoted by Gruber, "The Prophet Muhammad's Ascension," 29.

110. On the choice of the cups in ascension narratives and images, see Gruber, "The Prophet Muhammad's Ascension," 81–99.

111. See Rev. 3. 4–5, 6.11, 7.9, 19.14, and 22.14.

112. Charles A. Gieschen, "Baptismal Praxis in the Book of Revelation," in *Paradise Now: Essays on Early Jewish and Christian Mysticism*, ed. April D. DeConick (SBL Symposium Series 11, Atlanta: Society of Biblical Literature, 2006), 346. By the third century, baptismal initiates to Christianity were stripped of their clothing, washed, and clothed in a white robe. Gieschen notes that "later baptismal praxis in the church is not rooted primarily in the visions of Revelation, but is a continuation of extant baptismal praxis that is reflected in the Israelite priesthood," 347.

113. Sanders, ed., *Beati in Apocalipsin*, 266.

114. Ibid., 364.

115. Thackston, "The Paris *Miʿrajnama*," 272.

116. Gruber, "The Prophet Muhammad's Ascension," 233.

117. Sanders, ed., *Beati in Apocalipsin*, 276.

118. Gottfried Schimanowski, "Connecting Heaven and Earth: The Function of Hymns in Revelation 4–5," in *Heavenly Realms and Earthly Realities in Late Antique Religions*, eds. Ra'anan Boustan and Annette Yoshiko Reed (Cambridge: Cambridge University Press, 2004), 67 and 71. This hymnal sequence includes Rev. 4:8; 4:11, 5:9–10, 5:12, and 5:13.

119. Schimanowski, "Connecting Heaven and Earth," 83.

120. Ibid., 71.

121. Sanders, ed., *Beati in Apocalipsin*, 276 and 364.

122. For a full discussion of these debates see A. J. Arberry, "The Divine Colloquy in Islam," *The Bulletin of the John Rylands Library* (1956–1957), 18–44. The Timurid Book of Ascension text argues for an inward vision. Muḥammad relates that upon reaching "the station of proximity [he] prostrated [himself], and with [his] heart's eye saw God" (Thackston, "The Paris *Miʿrajnama*," 272).

123. Ibid., 272.

124. Ibid., 276.

125. Paris, Bibliothèque nationale de France, Supplément Turc 190, folio 44r. The image may also be accessed in Marie-Rose Séguy, *The Miraculous Journey of Mahomet: Mirâj nâmeh: Bibliotèque nationale (Manuscrit supplément Turc 190)*, trans. Richard Pevear (New York: G. Braziller, 1977), Pl. 38.

126. Raizman, "The Later Beatus, (M. 429) in the Morgan Library: Description, Function, Style, and Provenance," in *Estudio del Manuscrito del Beato de las Huelgas M. 429*, vol. 2, 209; idem, "Prayer, Patronage, and Piety at Las Huelgas: New Observations on the Later Morgan Beatus (M. 429)," in *Church, State, Vellum and Stone: Essays on Medieval Spain in Honor of*

John Williams, ed. Therese Martin and Julie A. Harris (Leiden: Brill, 2005), 253; and Williams, *The Illustrated Beatus,* vol. 5, 40.

127. Williams, *The Illustrated Beatus,* vol. 5, 38.

128. The other copies include the Cardeña Beatus, of c. 1180, divided mostly among Madrid's Museo Arqueológico Nacional, MS 2, 165ff and the Metropolitan Museum of Art in New York, (formerly Paris, Coll. Vasselot,) 15ff; the Rylands Beatus of c. 1175 in Manchester, John Rylands University Library, MS. Lat. 8, 248ff; and the Arroyo Beatus dating to the first half of the thirteenth century in Paris, Bibliothèque nationale de France, nouv. acq. lat. 2290, 167ff.

129. This is the second of two colophons in the manuscript. The first colophon appears on folio 182v and was transcribed directly from the tenth-century Tábara Beatus (Madrid, Archivo Histórico Nacional, Cod. 1097B, which served as the model for the Las Huelgas Beatus). The second colophon, contemporary to the context of the manuscript's production, is found on folio 184v. For an introduction to the Tábara Beatus, see Williams, *The Illustrated Beatus,* vol. 2, 43–49.

130. Williams, *The Illustrated Beatus,* vol. 5, 38. Although Williams considers Berenguela the "likely candidate," he notes that in November of 1219 Berenguela's son, Ferdinand III, "took the sword of a Crusader from the altar of Las Huelgas" and shortly married Beatrice of Swabia. Because this marriage was commemorated with gifts to the convent, Queen Beatrice is another potential patron for the manuscript's production. As Williams explains, because of "the precedent of his namesake Fernando I of León and Queen Sancha, who jointly commissioned the Facundus Beatus in 1047, one can imagine a commission in 1219 designed to honour the new Queen." See Williams, *The Illustrated Beatus,* vol. 5, 39. For further information on the Facundus Beatus, see Williams, *The Illustrated Beatus,* vol. 3, 34–38. David Raizman also favors an attribution to Berenguela. See Raizman, "Prayer, Patronage, and Piety," 238.

131. Joseph F. O'Callaghan, *Reconquest and Crusade in Medieval Spain* (Philadelphia: University of Pennsylvania Press, 2003), 72 and fig. 2.

132. Melveena McKendrick, *A Concise History of Spain* (London: Cassell, 1972), 69. For a discussion of the removal of the bells by al-Manṣūr, see Jerrilynn Dodds, "The Great Mosque of Córdoba," in *Al-Andalus: the Art of Islamic Spain,* ed. idem (New York: Abrams, 1992), 24.

133. James D'Emilio, "The Royal Convent of Las Huelgas: Dynastic Politics, Religious Reform and Artistic Change in Medieval Castile," in *Studies in Cistercian Art and Architecture,* ed. Meredith Parsons Lillich, vol. 6 (Kalamazoo, MI.: Cistercian Publications, 2005), 194 and 211.

134. Raizman, "Prayer, Patronage, and Piety," 245.

135. David Raizman, "The Later Beatus (M. 429) in the Morgan Library: Description, Function, Style, and Provenance," in *Estudio del Manuscrito del Beato de las Huelgas M. 429* vol. 2 [Commentary volume accompanying facsimile edition titled *Beato del Monasterio de Santa Maria la Real de Huelgas de Burgos*], William M. Voelkle et al. (Valencia: Scriptorium, 2004), 217; and Williams, *The Illustrated Beatus,* vol. 5, 40.

136. Raizman, "The Later Beatus," 232–233; and idem, "Prayer, Patronage and Piety," 256.

137. The 184 folios that compose the Las Huelgas Beatus present subtle stylistic variances indicating the contribution of three distinct artists. The first of these artists completed the prefatory images gracing folios 1v through 13v. A second artist is associated with the illustrations on folios 100r, 100v, 101v–102r, 106r, 112r, 115r, 116v, and 146v, and all of the painted imagery that accompanies Jerome's *Commentarius in Danielem.* The craftsmanship of both of these artists has been identified in separate surviving versions of the treatise *De virginitate sanctae Mariae,* authored in the seventh century by St. Ildefonsus, archbishop of Toledo (d. 667). For a discussion of the intricacies of these manuscripts (Madrid, Biblioteca Nacional de España, Cod. 21546 and Cod. 10087) and their probable Toledan provenances, see Raizman, "The Later Beatus," 226–228 and 230; also addressed in idem, "A Rediscovered Illuminated Manuscript of St. Ildefonsus's *De Virginitate Beatae Mariae* in the Biblioteca Nacional in Madrid," *Gesta* 26/1 (1987), 37–46. The second artist is also recognized as the "Master of Toledo" who completed frescoes in the Toledan church of Santa Cruz (El Cristo de la Luz). See Raizman, "The Later Beatus," 230, also mentioned in idem, "The Church of Santa Cruz and the Beginnings of Mudejar Architecture in Toledo," *Gesta* 38/2

(1999), 136; and Williams, *The Illustrated Beatus,* vol. 5, 40. The third artist, comparatively "uneven" and "haphazard" in execution, was responsible for the remaining sixty-four Beatus illustrations. Raizman has observed that the hand of this latter artist closely resembles illuminated initials present in another extant copy of *De virginitate sanctae Mariae.* This third version of the Ildefonsine treatise survives in the Cathedral of Burgos (Sig. 15), raising the possibility that production of the Las Huelgas Beatus occurred closer to or within Las Huelgas itself. See Raizman, "The Later Beatus," 231–232; and Williams, *The Illustrated Beatus,* vol. 5, 40. On the other hand, palaeographic analysis of Arabic glosses preserved in the Tábara Beatus, of which Las Huelgas is a copy, are fairly consistent with Toledan script of the twelfth century, providing further support for a Toledan provenance. See Raizman, "The Later Beatus," 216; and Williams, *The Illustrated Beatus,* vol. 1, 144 and fig. 85. Finally, the invoice provided to the Pierpont Morgan Library upon its 1910 purchase of the Beatus manuscript records that it was acquired from the Cistercian convent of San Clemente in Toledo, itself under the jurisdiction of the Las Huelgas monastery further north. The manuscript was purportedly given to San Clemente by Alfonso VI, but this Alfonsine association is erroneous, because the death of Alfonso VI in 1109 clearly predates the manuscript. Certainly the manuscript was at the monastery of Las Huelgas by the eighteenth century, where it was examined by Enrique Flórez (1702–1773). Raizman, "Prayer, Patronage and Piety," 256, note 67; Williams, *The Illustrated Beatus,* vol. 5, 40; and Flórez, *Sancti Beati,* XXXVIII.

138. Sanders, ed., *Beati in Apocalipsin,* 616–618.

139. Rose Walker, "Looking into the Cloister: The Case of Las Huelgas," paper presented at the XXXVII International Congress on Medieval Studies, Kalamazoo, Michigan, May 2002. Cited in Raizman, "Prayer, Patronage, and Piety," 250.

140. Sanders, ed., *Beati in Apocalipsin,* 617–618.

141. These figures are surmounted by small painted circles representative of the lustrous jewels from which the foundations of the celestial city are constructed. This pictorial strategy, present in some other Beatus manuscripts, originates in the literal conflation of two biblical verses. Rev. 21:14 describes how "the wall of the city has twelve foundations, and over them are the twelve names of the apostles of the Lamb." Shortly thereafter, Rev. 21:19 describes how the foundations are adorned with precious stones: "the first was jasper, the second sapphire, the third chalcedony, the fourth emerald, the fifth sardonyx, the sixth sard, the seventh chrysolite, the eighth beryl, the ninth topaz, the tenth chrysoprase, the eleventh jacinth, the twelfth amethyst." See Sanders, ed., *Beati in Apocalipsin,* 617–618. Inscriptions pertaining to eight of the figures depicted on folio 140v are composite labels, identifying the name of the apostle but also the name of the stone depicted above them, e.g., "johannes crisolitus" (John chrysolite), "Thomas topation" (Thomas topaz) and so on. The presence of these labels is also noted in Klein, "Illumination of the *Las Huelgas Beatus* Codex," in *Estudio del Manuscrito del Beato de las Huelgas M. 429* [Commentary volume accompanying the facsimile edition titled *Beato del Monasterio de Santa Maria la Real de Huelgas de Burgos*], ed. William M. Voelkle et. al. (Valencia: Scriptorium, 2004), 155.

142. Williams, *The Illustrated Beatus,* vol. 2, 44.

143. Klein, "Illumination of the Las Huelgas Beatus Codex," 159.

144. Alternatively spelled Sedecias.

145. Ibid., 159.

146. Ibid., 160.

147. Sanders, ed., *Beati in Apocalipsin,* 430.

148. Ibid., 430 and 432.

149. The labels on the folio read "Ubi Occisa Est Tercia Pars Hominum / Ubi Equos Capita Sicut Leonum Et Ignis Exit Ex Ore Eorum."

150. Collins, *The Apocalypse,* 62.

151. See Joseph O'Callaghan, *The Learned King: the Reign of Alfonso X of Castile* (Philadelphia: University of Pennsylvania Press, 1993), 141–144.

152. Reginald Hyatte, trans., *The Prophet of Islam in Old French: The Romance of Muhammad (1258) and the Book of Muhammad's Ladder of 1264* (Brill: Leiden, 1997), 21.

153. I. Heullant-Donat and M.-A. Polo de Beaulieu, "Histoire d'une Traduction," in *Le Livre de l'Échelle de Mahomet (Liber Scale Machometi),* trans. Gisèle Besson and Michèle Brossard-Dandré (Paris: Librairie Générale Française, 1991), 26.

154. Hyatte, *The Prophet of Islam in Old French,* 21. The text of the *Liber Scale* may be accessed through various publications. In addition to the English translation offered by Hyatte, the Latin version may be found in *Le Livre de l'Échelle de Mahomet (Liber Scale Machometi),* trans. Gisèle Besson and Michèle Brossard-Dandré (Paris: Librairie Générale Française, 1991) and also *Liber Scale Machometi: die Lateinische Fassung des Kitab al-Mi'radj,* ed. Edeltraud Werner (Düsseldorf: Droste, 1986); to compare the Latin, Castilian, and Old French translations, see José Muñoz Sendino, ed. *La Escala de Mahoma: Traducción del Árabe al Castellano, Latín y Francés, Ordenada par Alfonso X el Sabio* (Madrid: Ministerio de Asuntos Esteriores, Dirección General de Relaciones Culturales, 1949).

155. Peter Wunderli, *Études sur "Le livre de l'eschiele Mahomet." Prolégomènes à une nouvelle édition de la version française d'une traduction alphonsine* (Winterthur: P. G. Keller, 1965), 20–24.

156. O'Callaghan, *The Learned King,* 165.

157. Hyatte, *The Prophet of Islam in Old French,* 23 and 97.

158. Ibid., 22. Ch. 85 begins on page 198 in Hyatte's text. The claim for authenticity reads: "We, Habubekar [Abū Bakr] and Abnez [Ibn ʿAbbās] attest with true heart and pure conscience that all the matters which Muḥammad related above are completely true, so that all those who will hear them told ought surely to place their trust in them."

159. Ana Echevarría, "Eschatology or Biography? Alfonso X, Muhammad's Ladder and a Jewish Go-Between," in *Under the Influence: Questioning the Comparative in Medieval Castile,* eds. Cynthia Robinson and Leyla Rouhi (Leiden: Brill, 2005), 135.

160. Hyatte, *The Prophet of Islam in Old French,* 29.

161. Ibid.

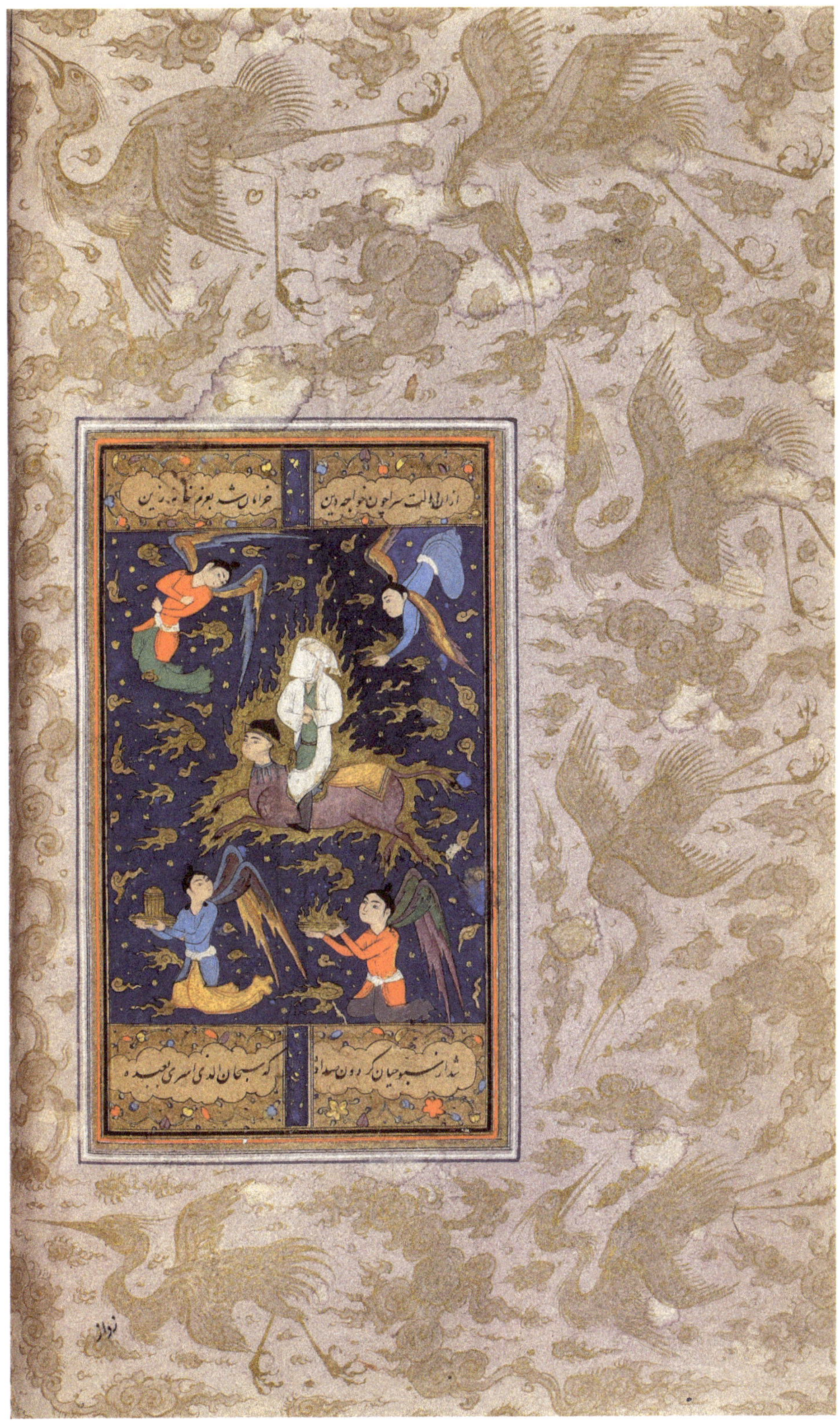

PLATE 1. The Prophet's ascension, Jāmī, *Yūsuf va Zulaykhā* (Joseph and Potiphar's Wife), Shiraz, 975/1567–1568. Istanbul, Topkapı Palace Library, H. 812, folio 10v.

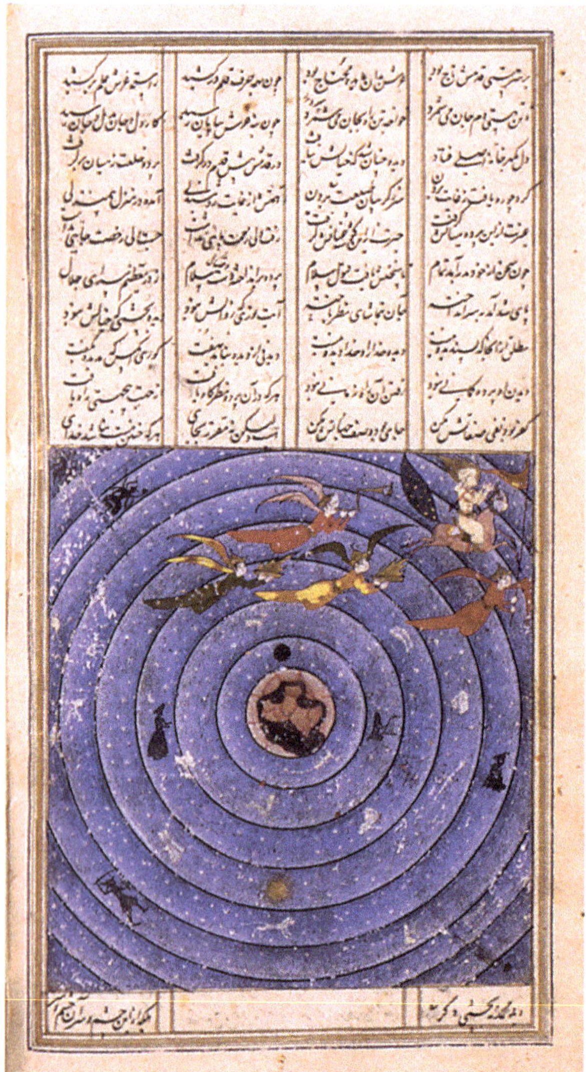

PLATE 2. The Prophet ascends through the celestial spheres, constellations, and signs of the zodiac, Niẓāmī, *Khamsa* (Quintet), Isfahan, 1076-7/1665-1667. London, British Library, Add. 6613, folio 3v.

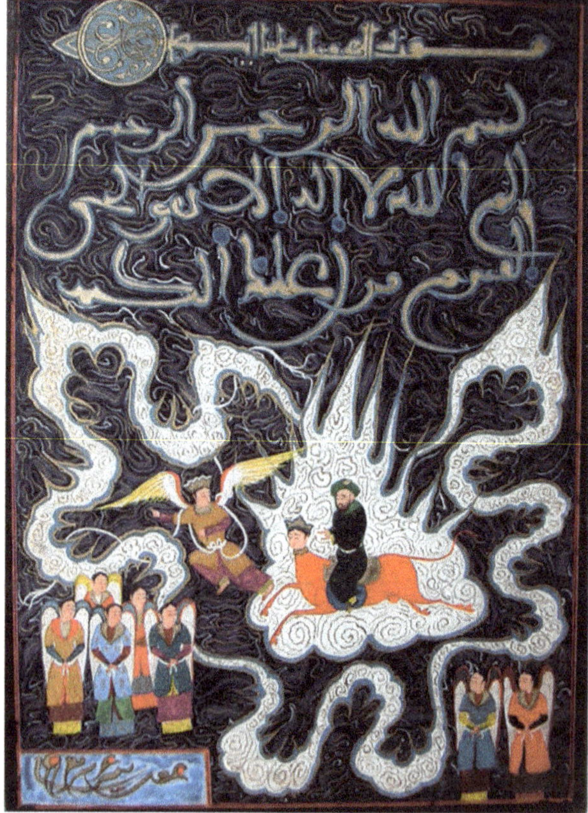

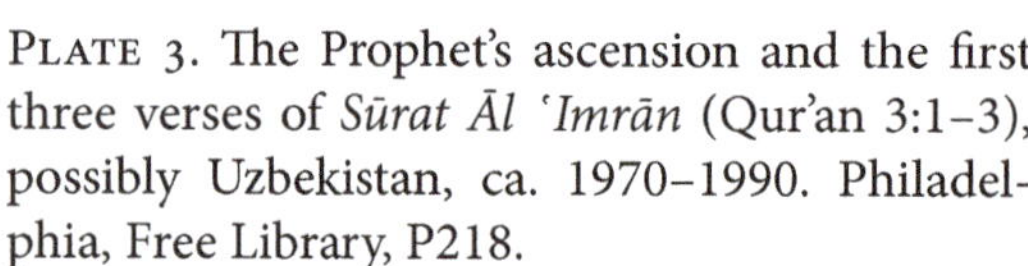

PLATE 3. The Prophet's ascension and the first three verses of *Sūrat Āl ʿImrān* (Qur'an 3:1–3), possibly Uzbekistan, ca. 1970–1990. Philadelphia, Free Library, P218.

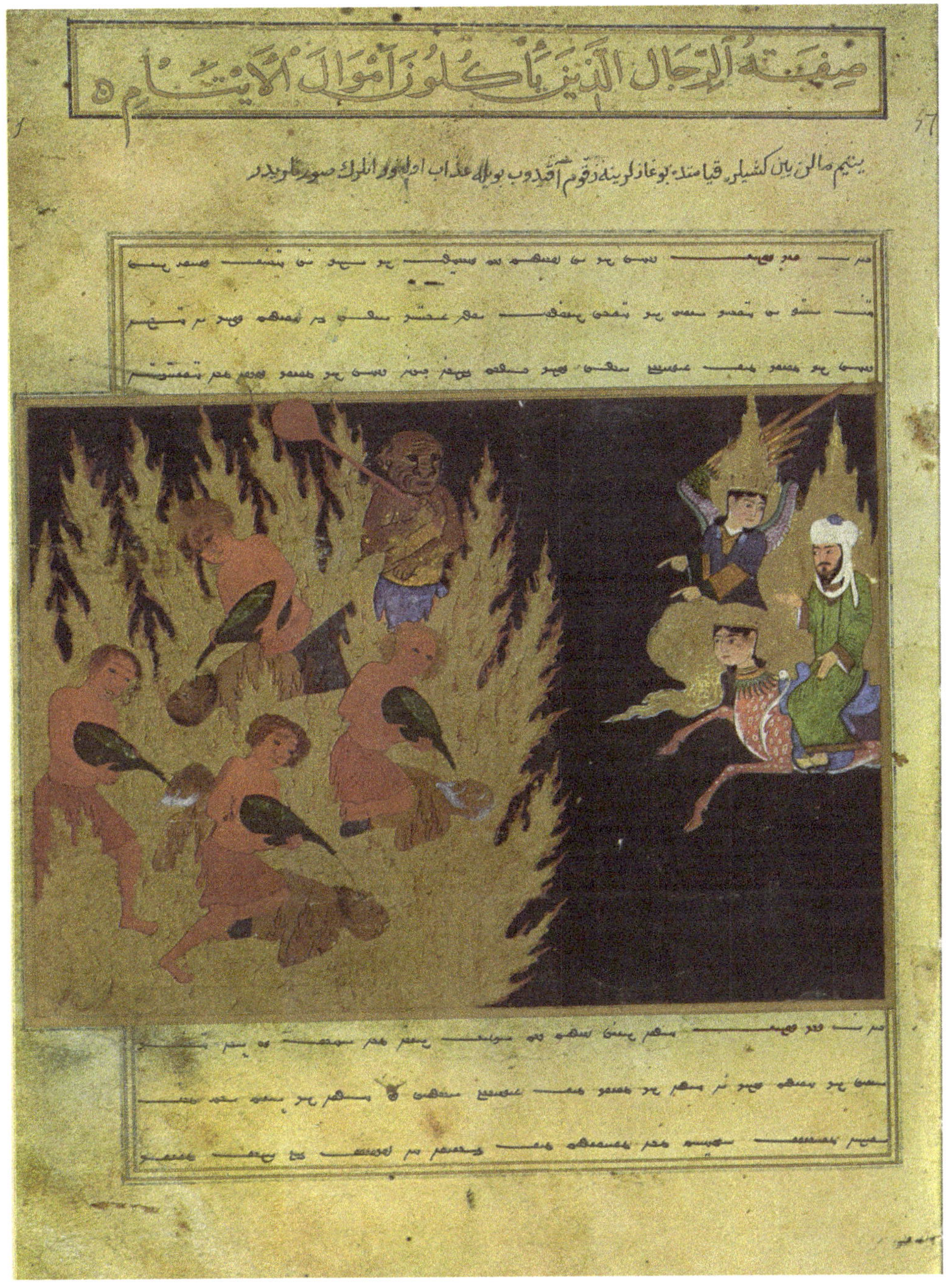

Plate 4. The Prophet witnesses the torture of those who steal the wealth of orphans, anonymous, *Miʿrājnāma,* Herat, ca. 840/1436–1437. Paris, Bibliothèque nationale de France, Suppl. Turc 190, folio 61r.

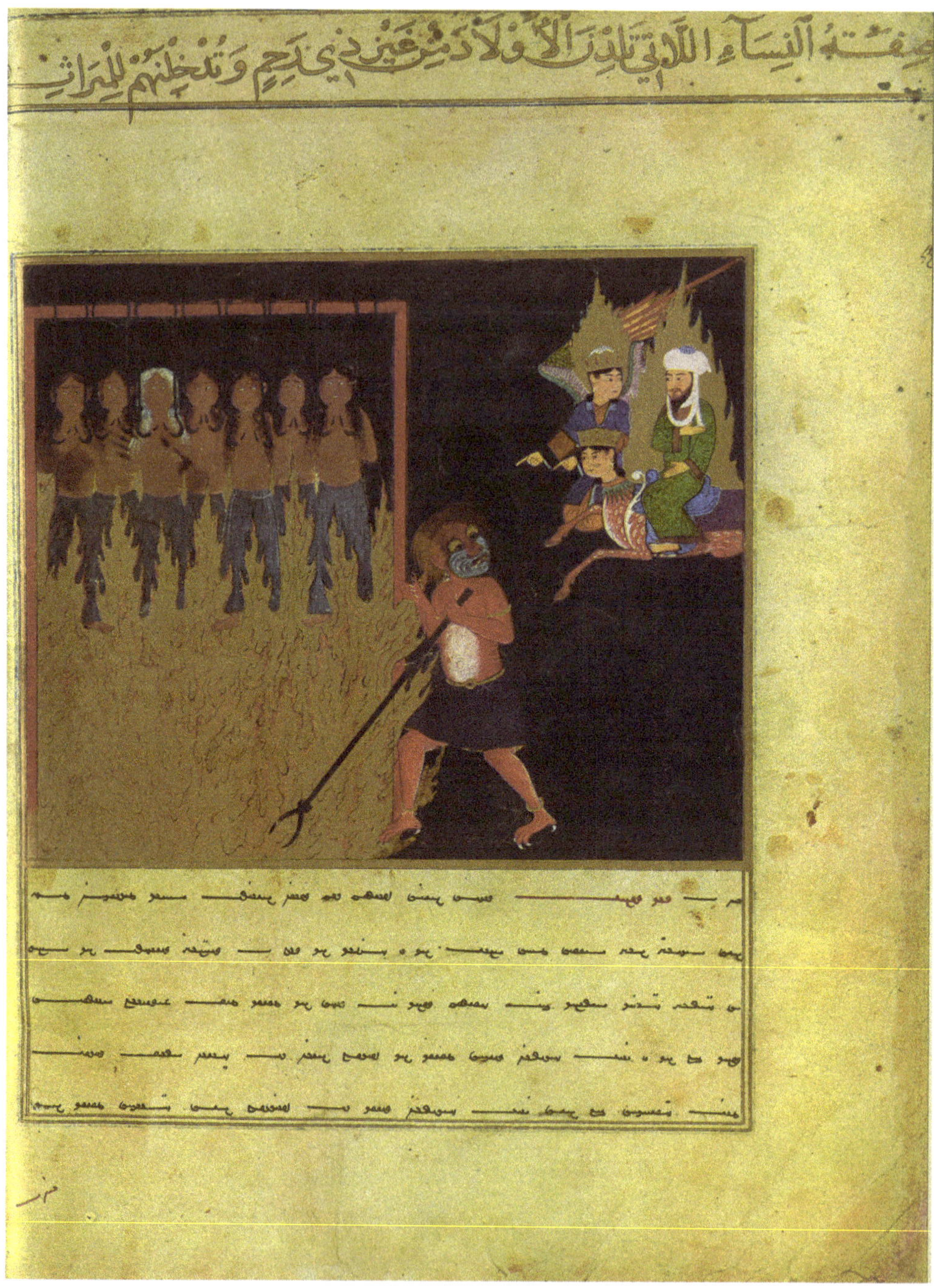

Plate 5. The Prophet observes the torture of women who engage in adulterous relations and whose illegitimate offspring receive the inheritance of their legal children, anonymous, *Miʿrājnāma,* Herat, ca. 840/1436–1437. Paris, Bibliothèque nationale de France, Suppl. Turc 190, folio 61v.

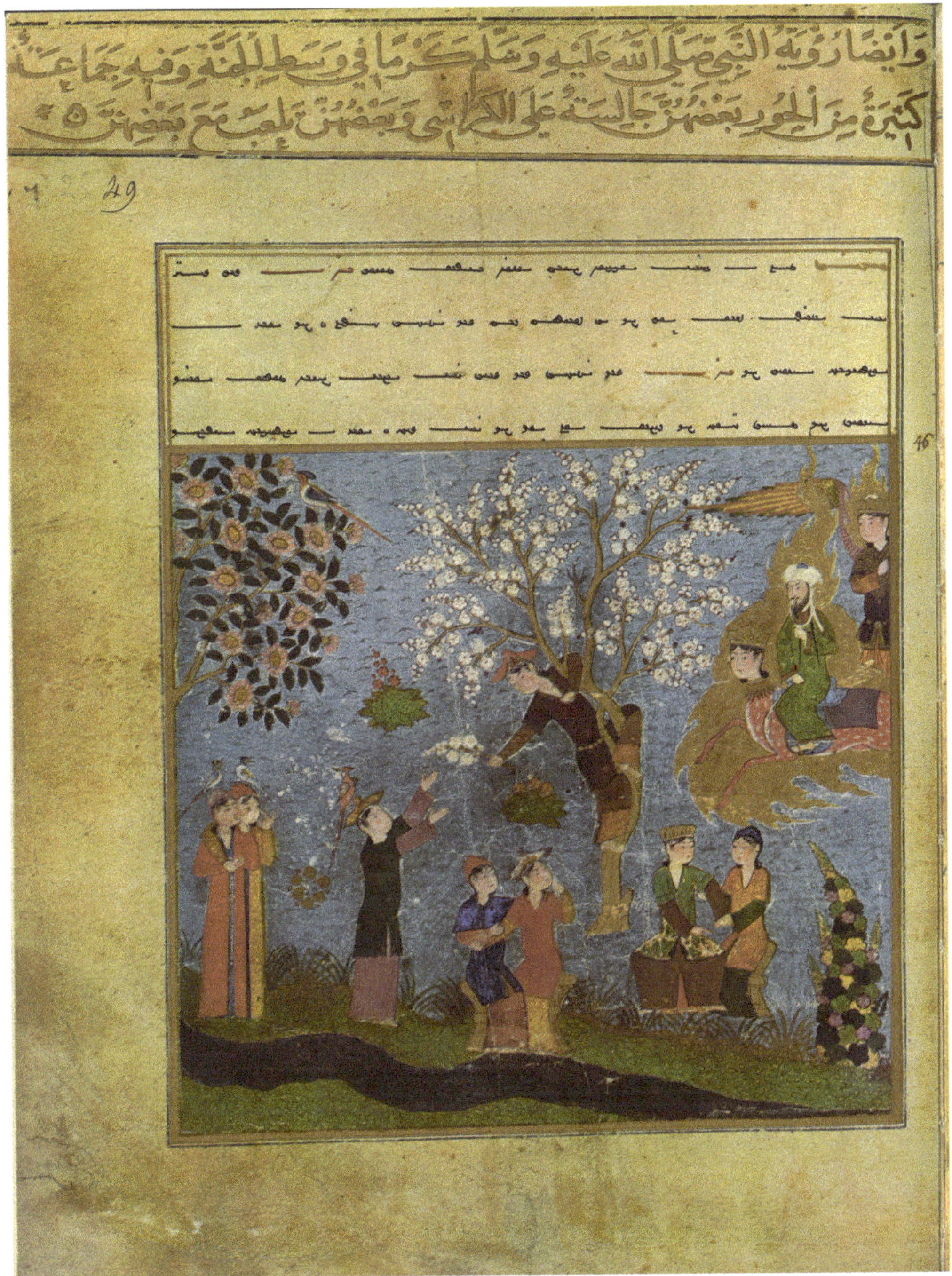

PLATE 6. The Prophet visits heaven and observes the amusement of the *ḥūrīs*, anonymous, *Miʿrājnāma*, Herat, ca. 840/1436–1437. Paris, Bibliothèque nationale de France, Suppl. Turc 190, folio 49r.

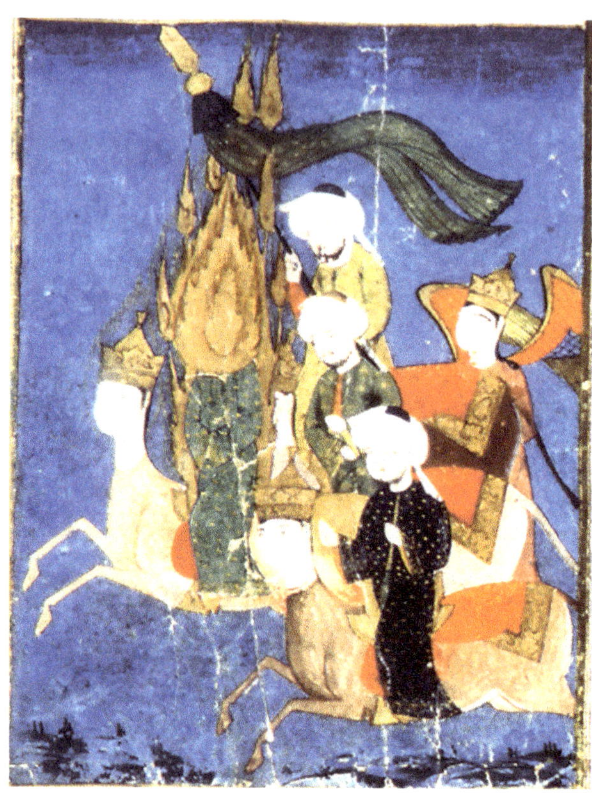

PLATE 7. The Prophet, with his head as a flaming bundle, ascends with the first three rightly guided caliphs, anonymous, *Aḥwāl al-Qiyāma* (The Conditions of Resurrection), Istanbul, ca. 1600–1630. Staatsbibliothek zu Berlin, Ms. Or. Oct. 1596, folio 49r.

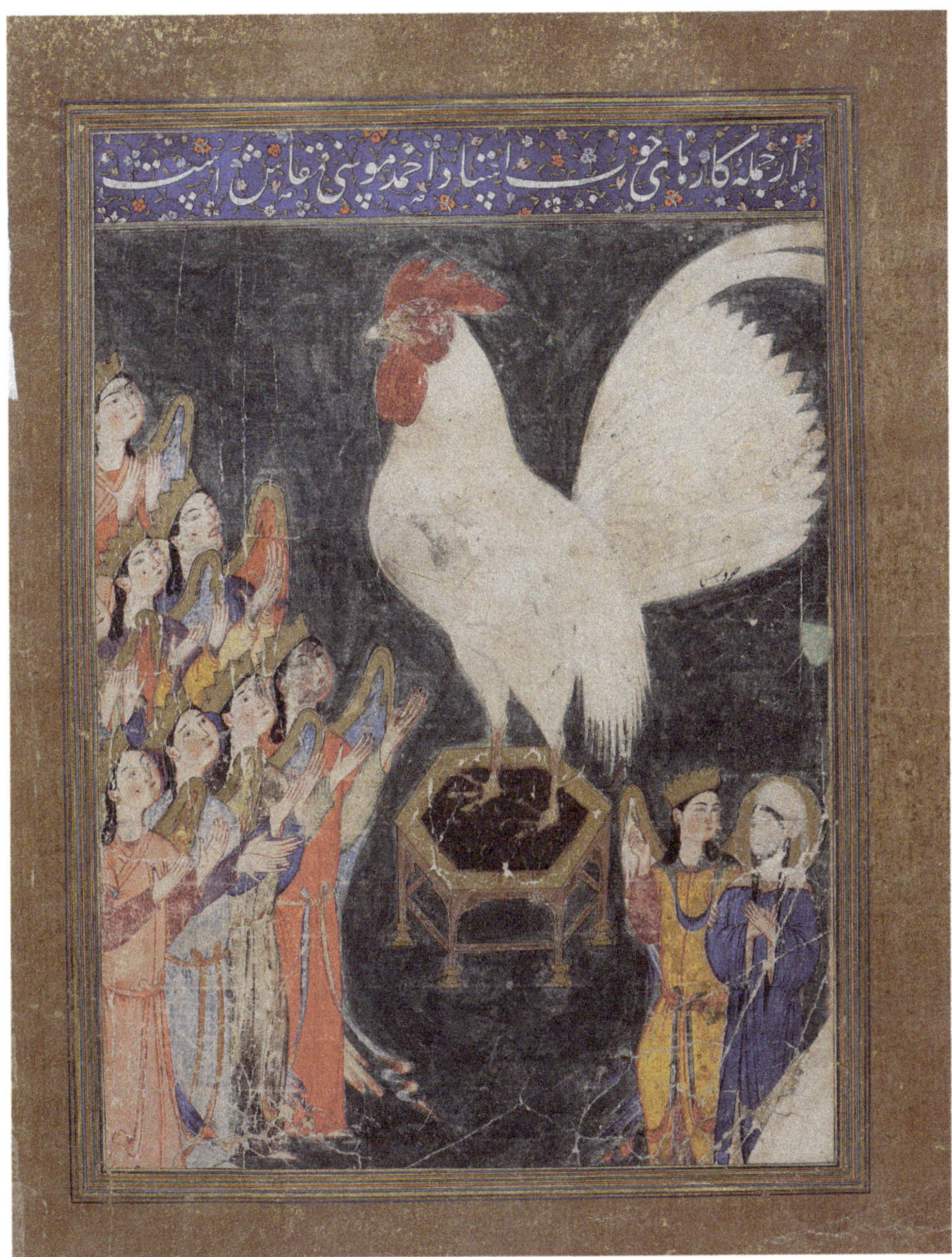

PLATE 8. The Prophet encounters the celestial rooster in the first heaven and a group of angels raising their hands in prayer, anonymous, *Miʿrājnāma,* possibly Tabriz, ca. 1317–1335. Istanbul, Topkapı Palace Library, H. 2154, folio 61v.

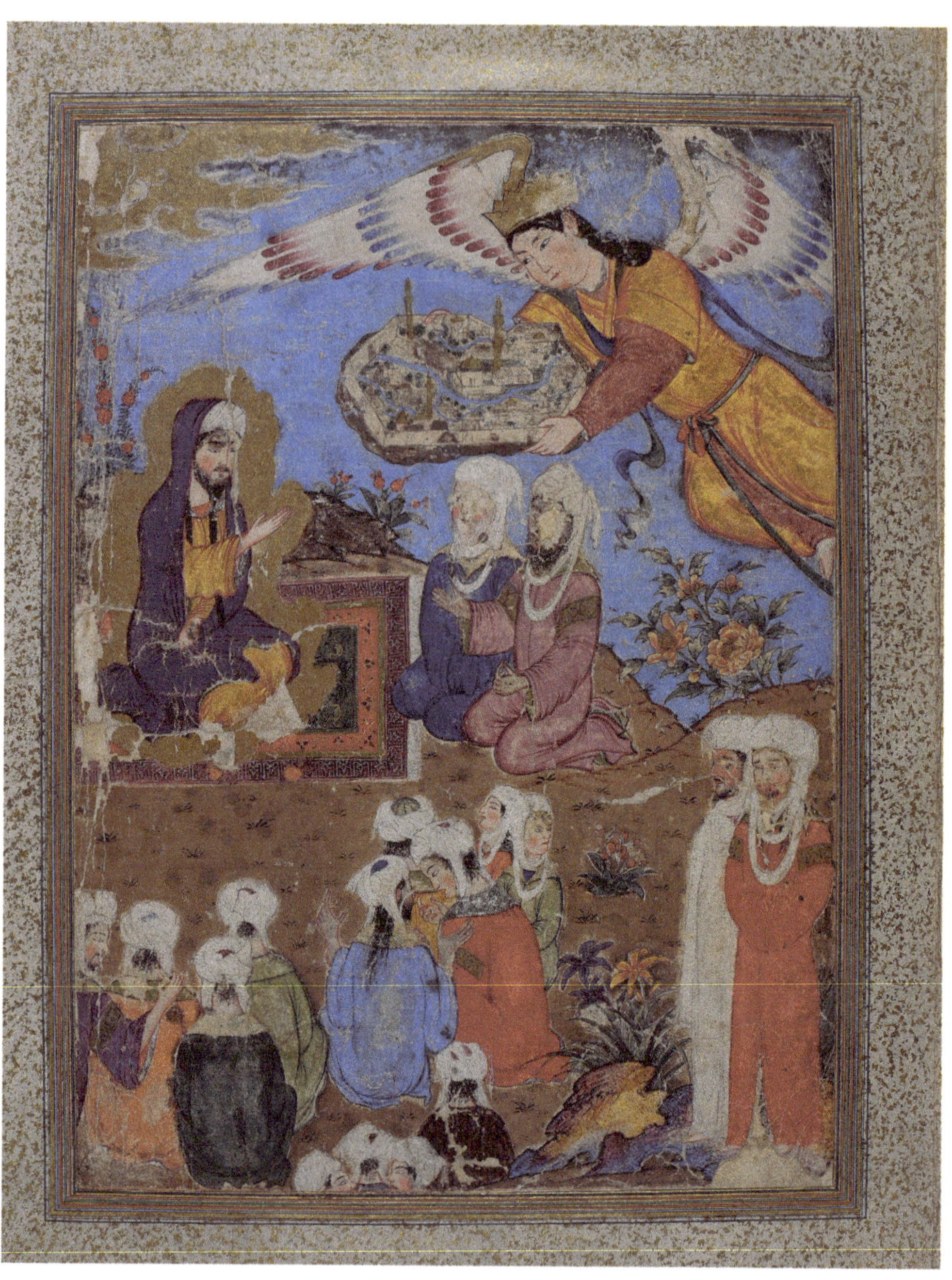

PLATE 9. The Prophet has a miraculous vision of Jerusalem upon his return to Mecca and correctly describes it to Abū Bakr, Abū Jahl, and members of the Quraysh tribe, anonymous, *Miʿrājnāma*, probably Tabriz, ca. 1317–1335. Istanbul, Topkapı Palace Library, H. 2154, folio 107r.

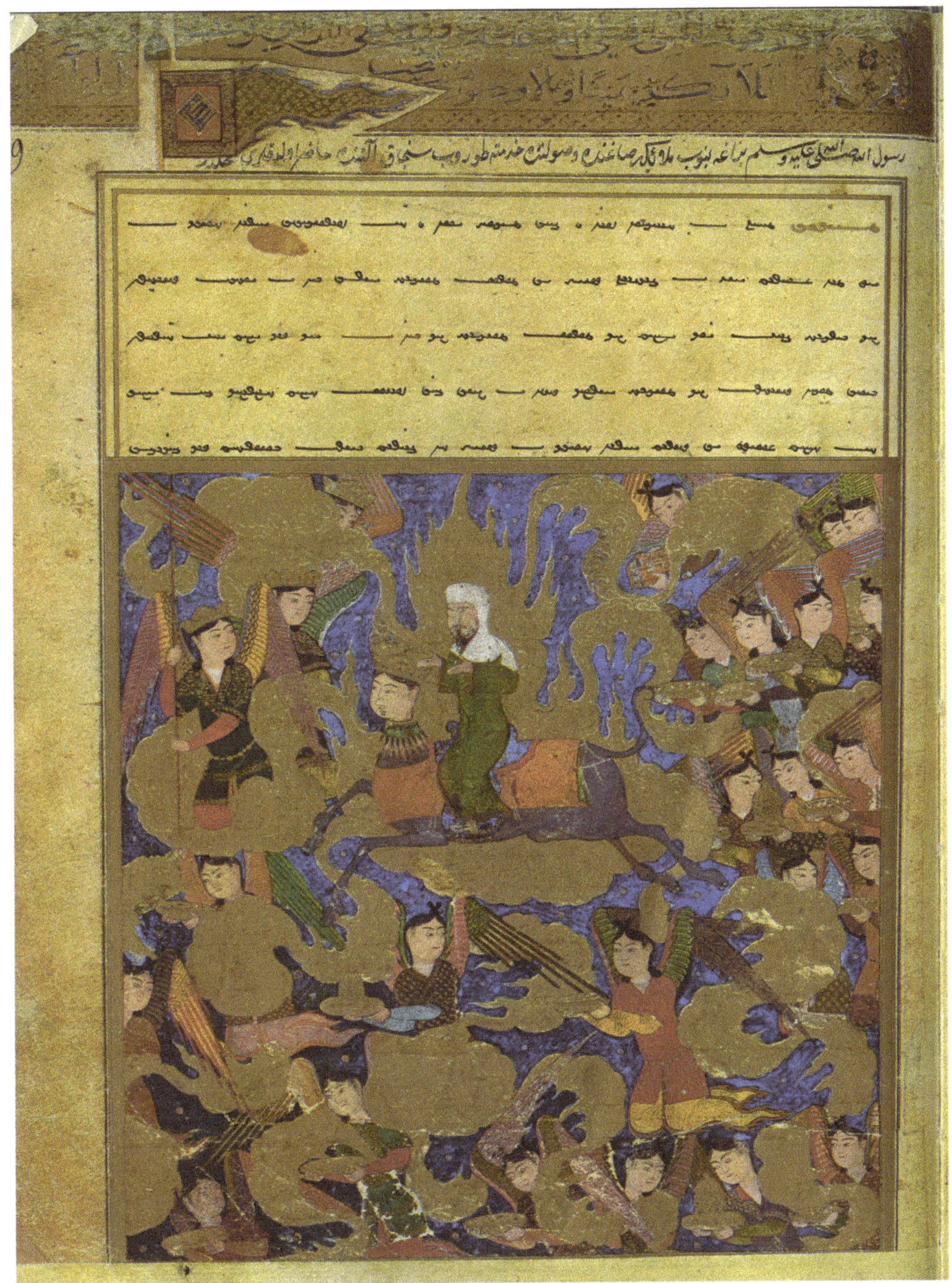

PLATE 10. The Prophet, accompanied by angels, rides Burāq from Mecca to Jerusalem, anonymous, *Miʿrājnāma,* Herat, ca. 840/1436–1437. Paris, Bibliothèque nationale de France, Suppl. Turc 190, folio 5r.

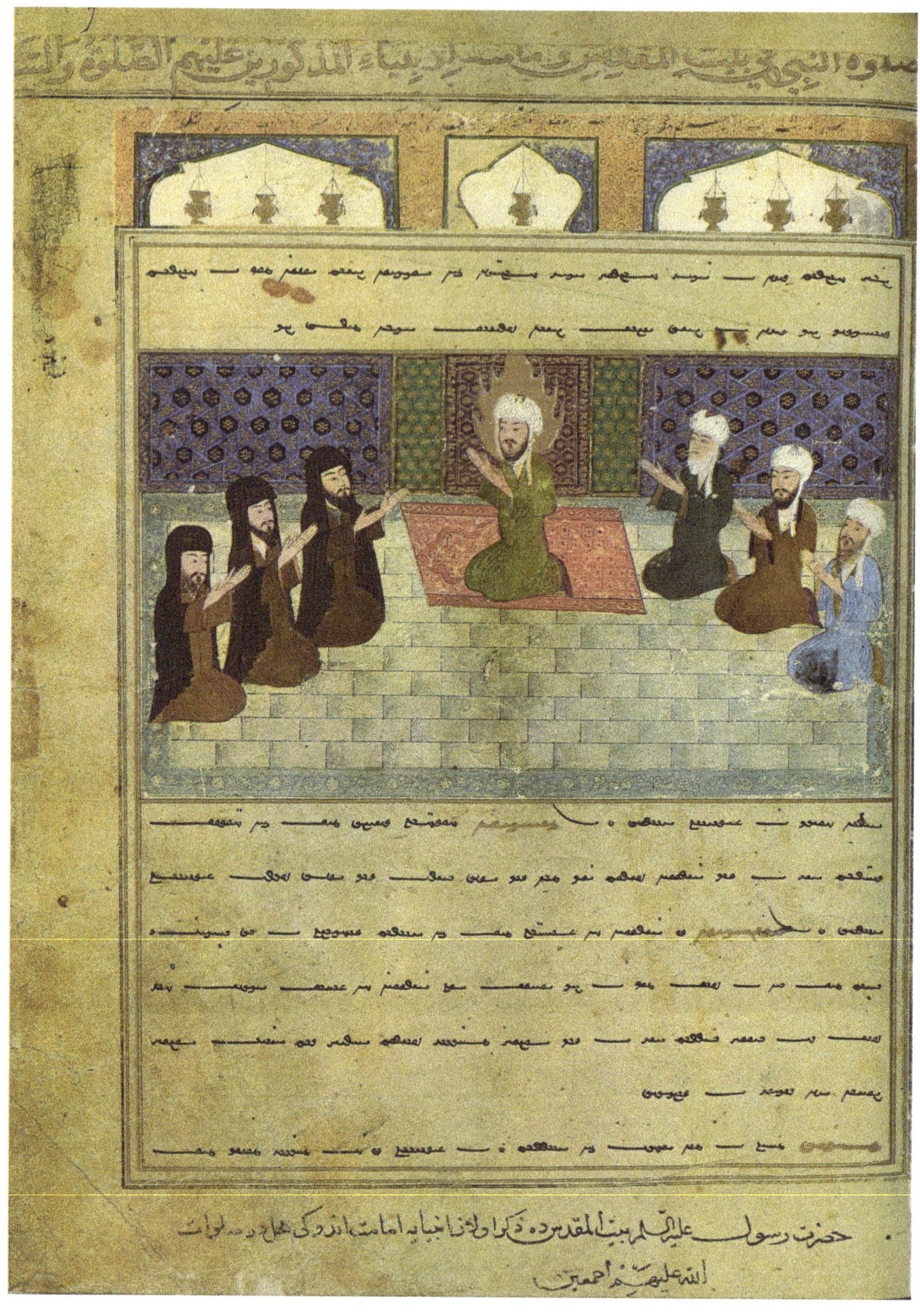

Plate 11. The Prophet Muḥammad leads other prophets in prayer in Jerusalem, anonymous, *Miʿrājnāma,* Herat, ca. 840/1436–1437. Paris, Bibliothèque nationale de France, Suppl. Turc 190, folio 7r.

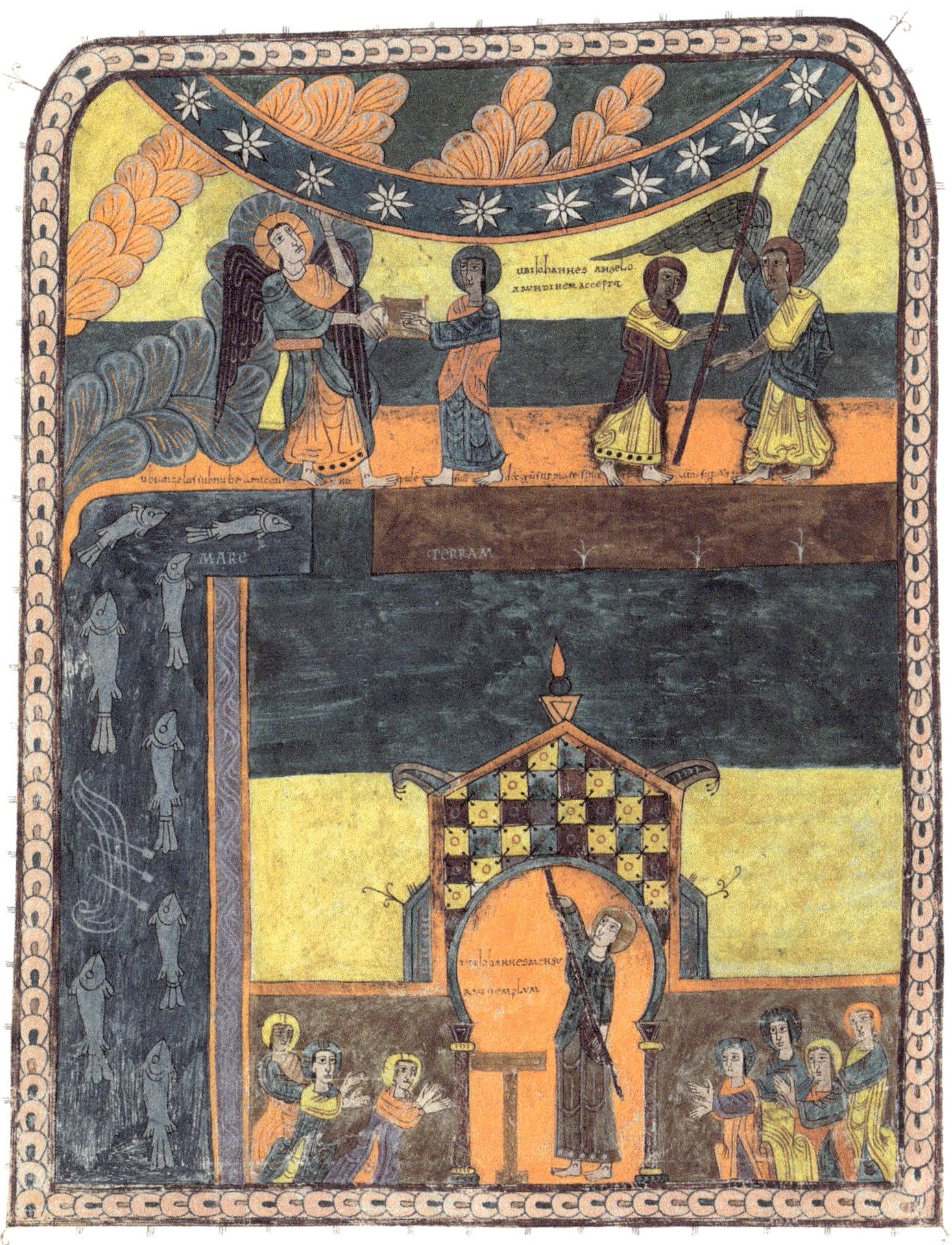

PLATE 12. John receives the book and measures the temple, Girona Beatus, 6 July 975. Museu de la Catedral de Girona, Num. Inv. 7(11), folio 161v.

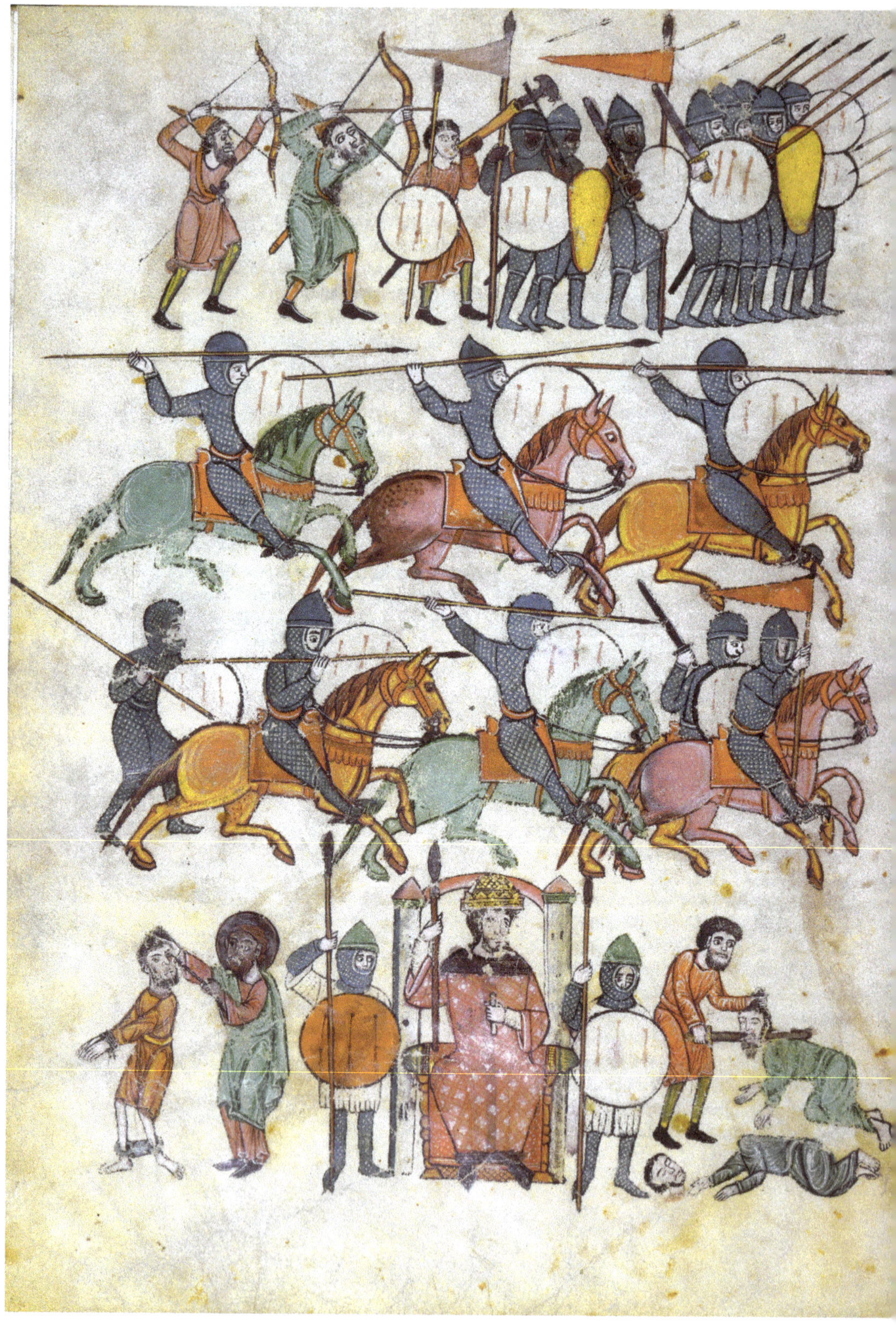

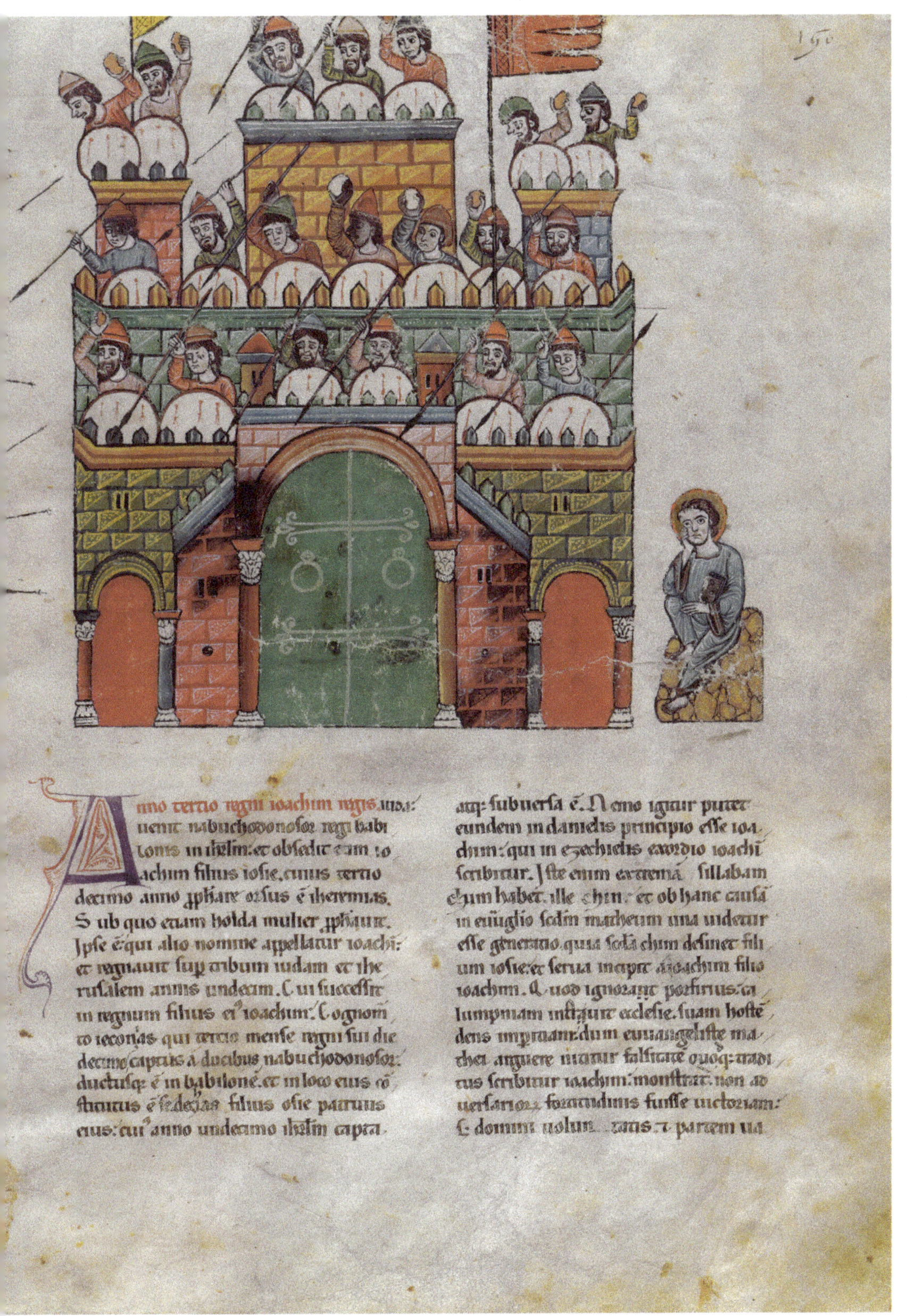

PLATE 13. The Siege of Jerusalem and the Lamentation of Jeremiah, Las Huelgas Beatus, 1220. New York, Pierpont Morgan Library, M. 644, folios 149v–150r.

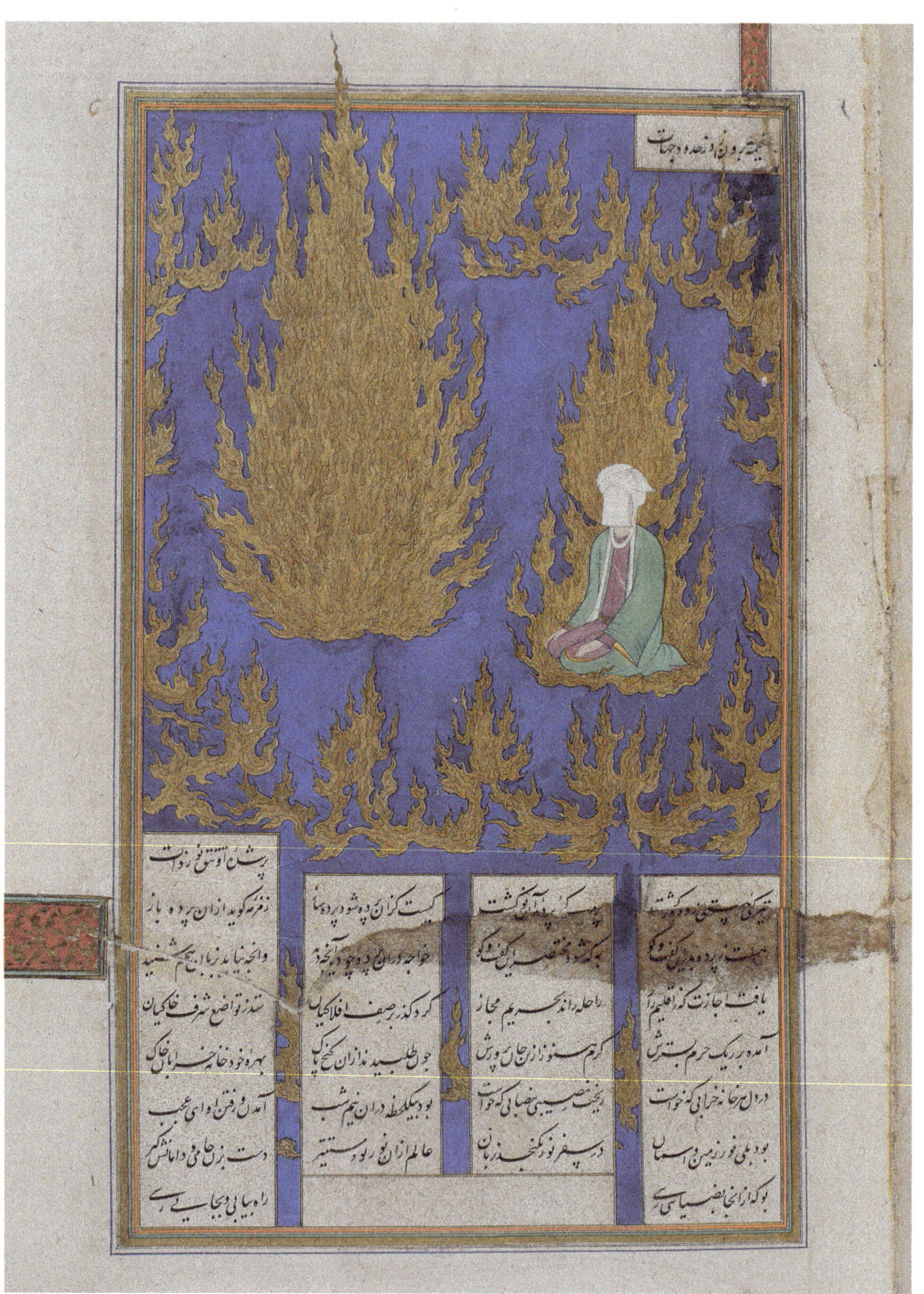

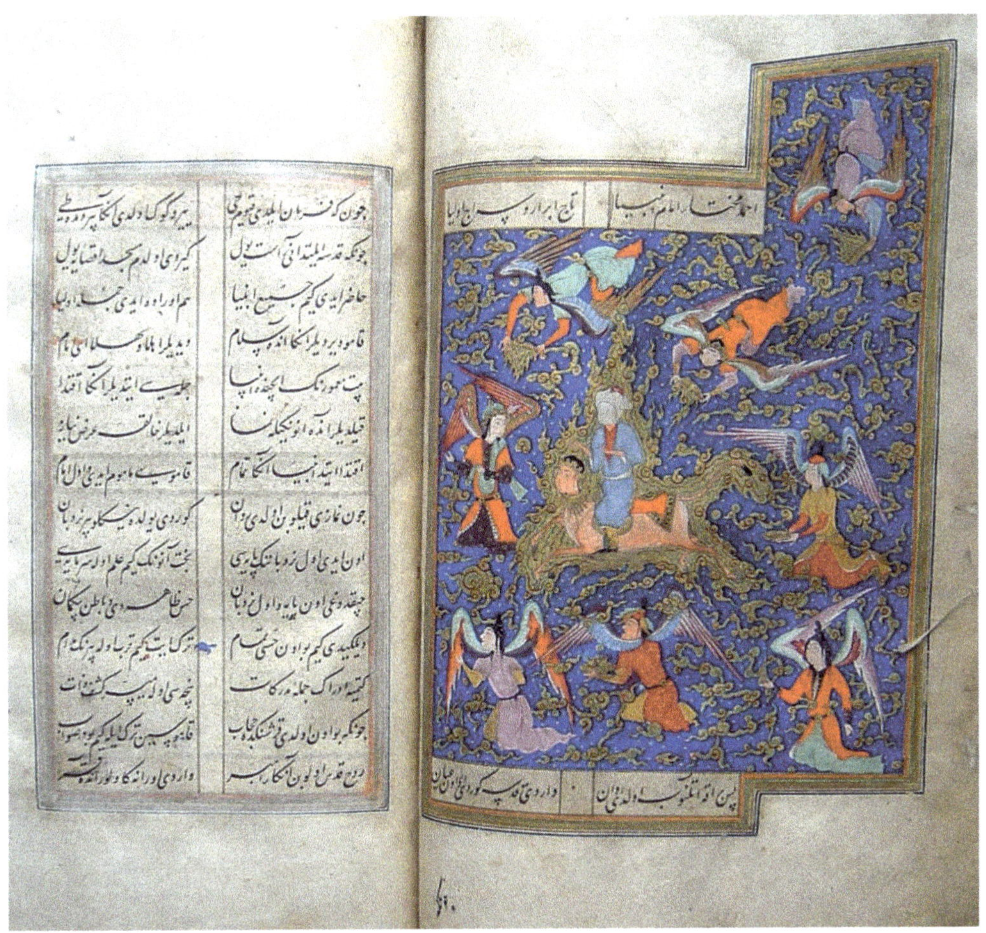

PLATE 15. The Prophet ascends on Burāq, Aḥmedī, *İskendernāme* (Book of Alexander), Shiraz, 966/1559. Istanbul, Topkapı Palace Library, R. 812, folios 235v–236r.

PLATE 14. *(opposite)* The Prophet speaks with God, represented as a large gold flame, Jāmī, *Yūsuf va Zulaykhā* (Joseph and Potiphar's Wife), Iran, 978/1570–1571, Istanbul, Topkapı Palace Library, H. 1483, folio 42r.

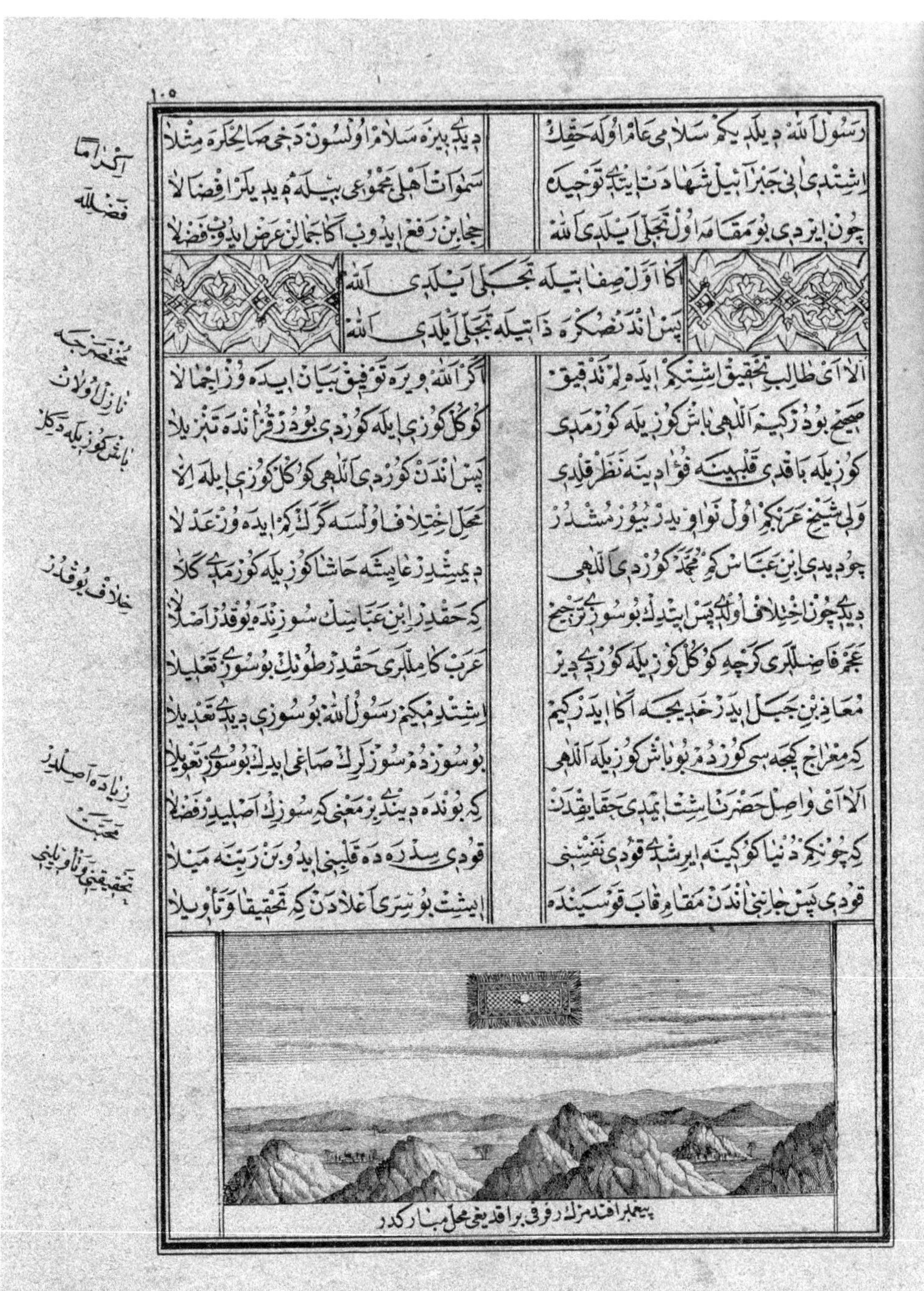

PLATE 16. The Prophet, as a small white ball, ascends on *rafraf* past the seventh heaven to the realm of God, Yazıcıoğlu, *Muḥammediyye,* Istanbul, 1880s. Collection of Tobias Heinzelmann.

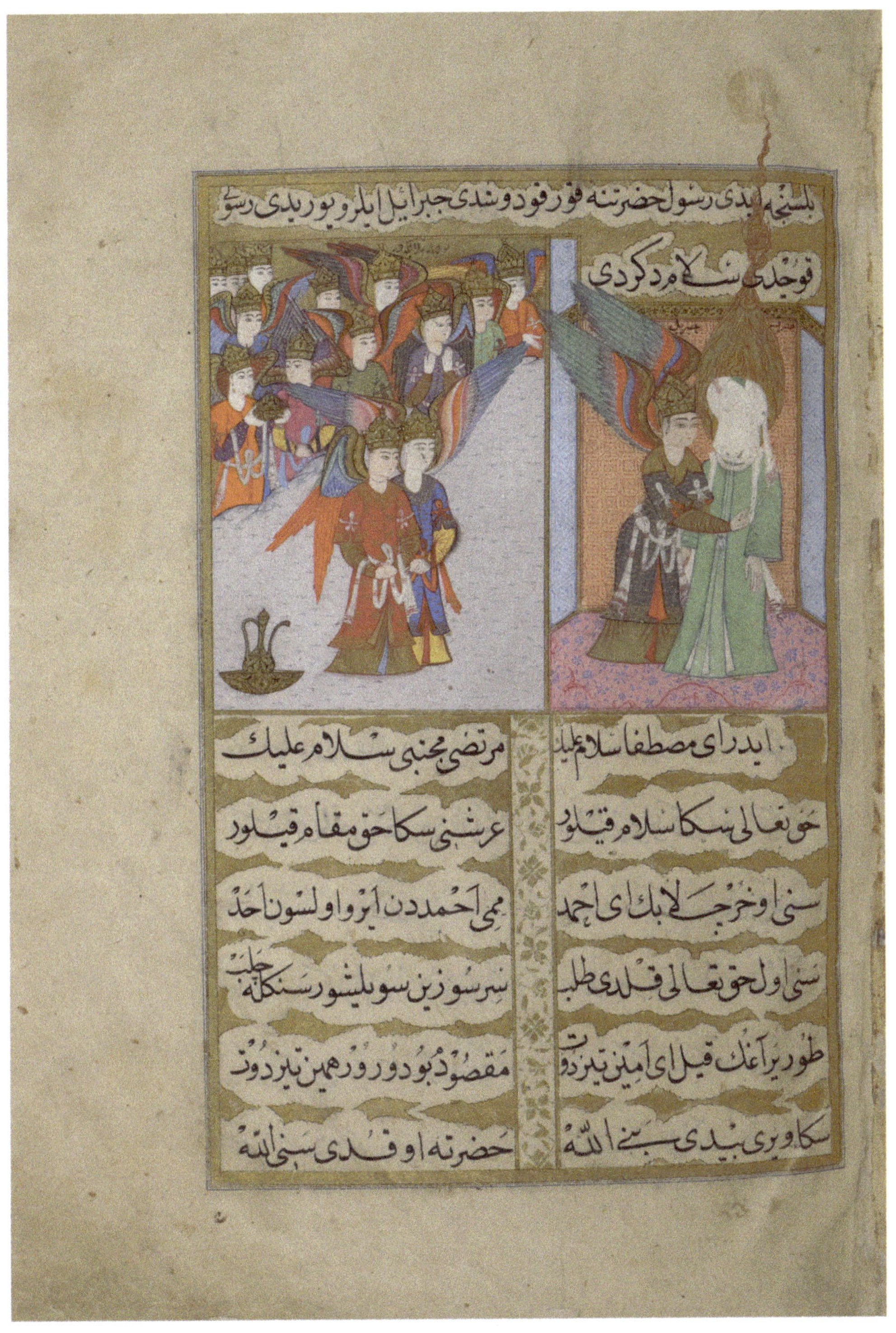

PLATE 17. Gabriel announces the ascension to the Prophet, Ḍarīr, *Siyer-i Nebī* (The Biography of the Prophet), Istanbul, 1595–1596. New York Public Library, Spencer Collection, Turk ms. 157, folio 3r.

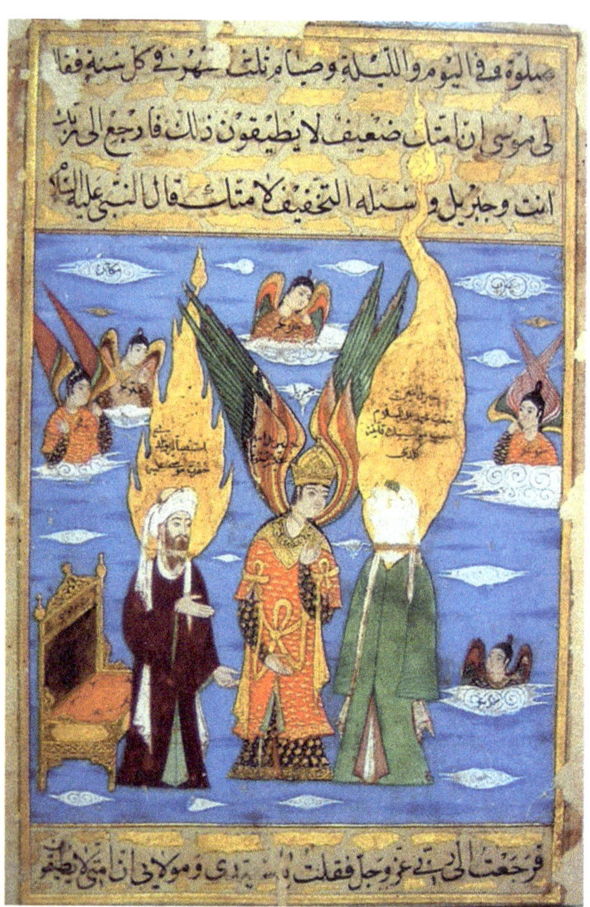

Plate 18. The Prophet meets Moses in the heavens and they discuss the reduction of daily prayers, Ḍarīr, *Siyer-i Nebī* (The Biography of the Prophet), Istanbul, 1595–1596. Berlin, Islamic Art Museum, I.26/78.

Plate 19. *(opposite)* The Prophet ascends on Burāq, Qāḍī ʿIyād al-Yaḥṣubī, *al-Shifā bi-Taʿrīf Ḥuqūq al-Muṣṭafā* (Healing by the Recognition of the Rights of the Chosen One), possibly north Africa, 1172/1759. New York Public Library, Spencer Collection, Turk ms. 24, folio 120r.

ففقال خذ العفو وقال فاعف عنهم واصفح وقال له جبريل
وقد سأله عن قوله خذ العفو قال ان تعفو عمن ظلمك
وقال في التورية والانجيل في الحديث المشهور في صفته
ليس بفظ ولا غليظ ولكن يعفوا ويصفح ومن اسمائه عفو

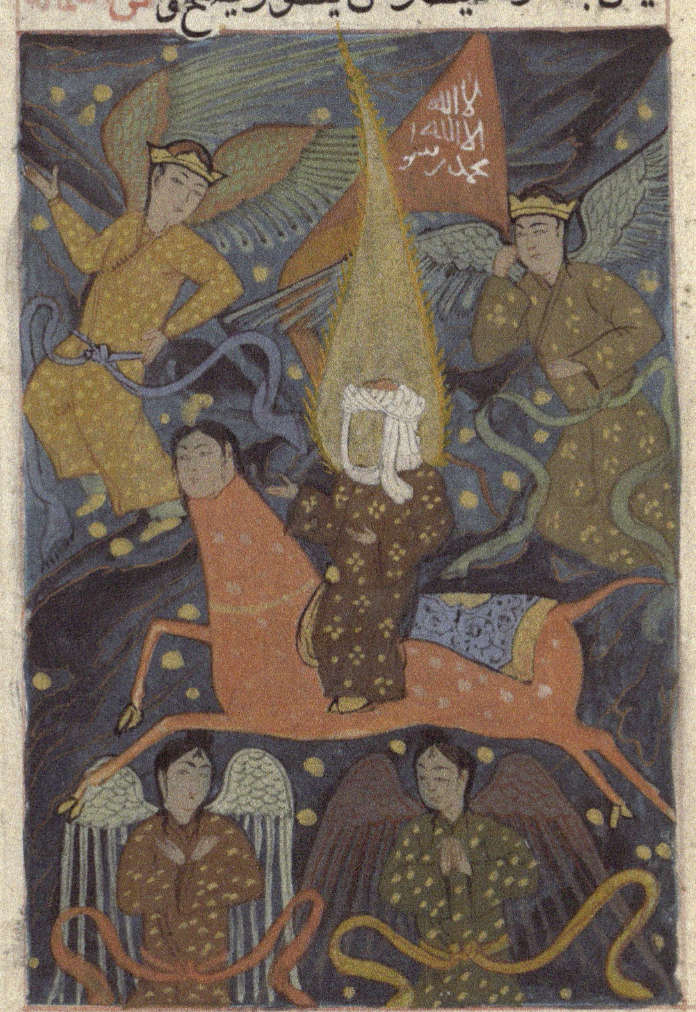

Plate 20. The Prophet ascends on Burāq, ʿAṭṭār, *Mihr u Mushtarī*, Shiraz or Tabriz, 860/1456. Keir Collection (on permanent loan to the Islamic Art Museum, Berlin), III.104–126, folio 2v.

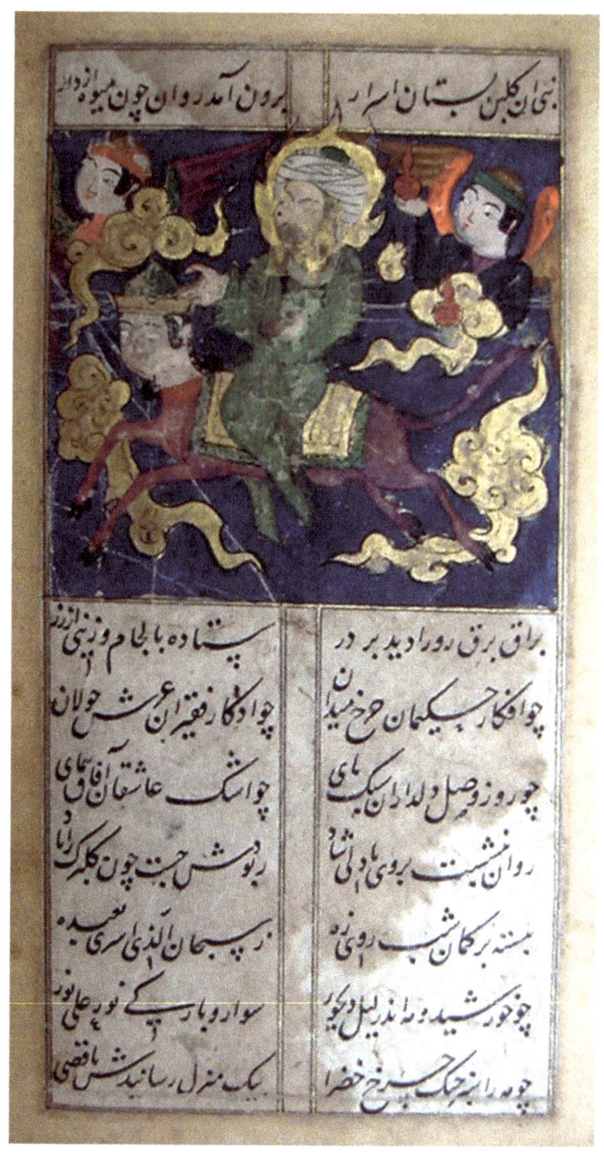

Plate 21. *(opposite)* The Prophet ascends on Burāq, Ibn Ḥusām, *Khavarānnāma* (The Book of Eastern Exploits), Tabriz, ca. 1480–1500. Gulistan Palace, Tehran.

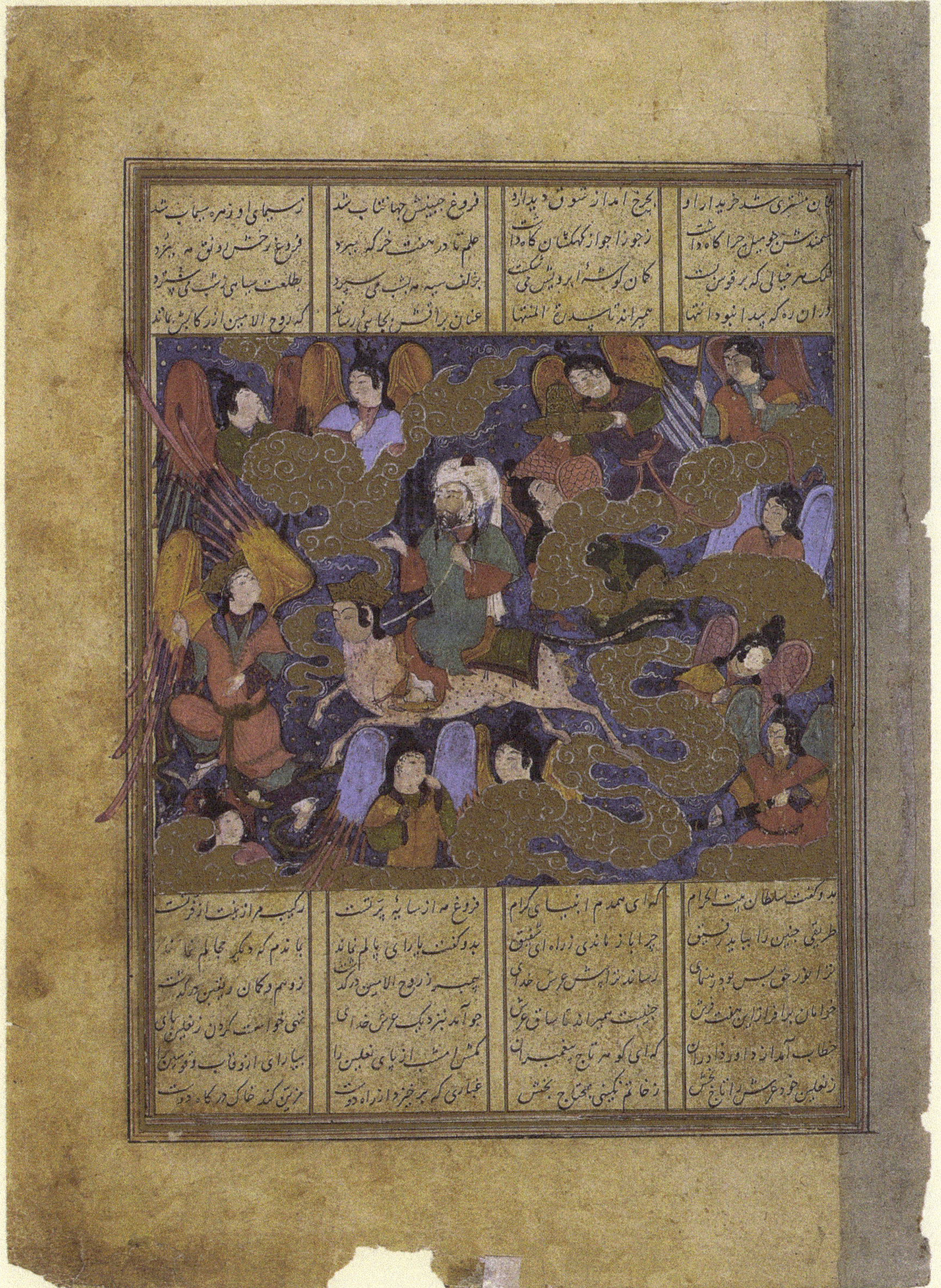

PLATE 22. The Prophet is offered gold and silver staircases to ascend to the heavens, anonymous, Shiʿi *Miʿrājnāma*, Iran, ca. 1850–1880. New Haven, Beinecke Rare Book and Manuscript Library, Yale University, Persian mss. 8, folio 17r.

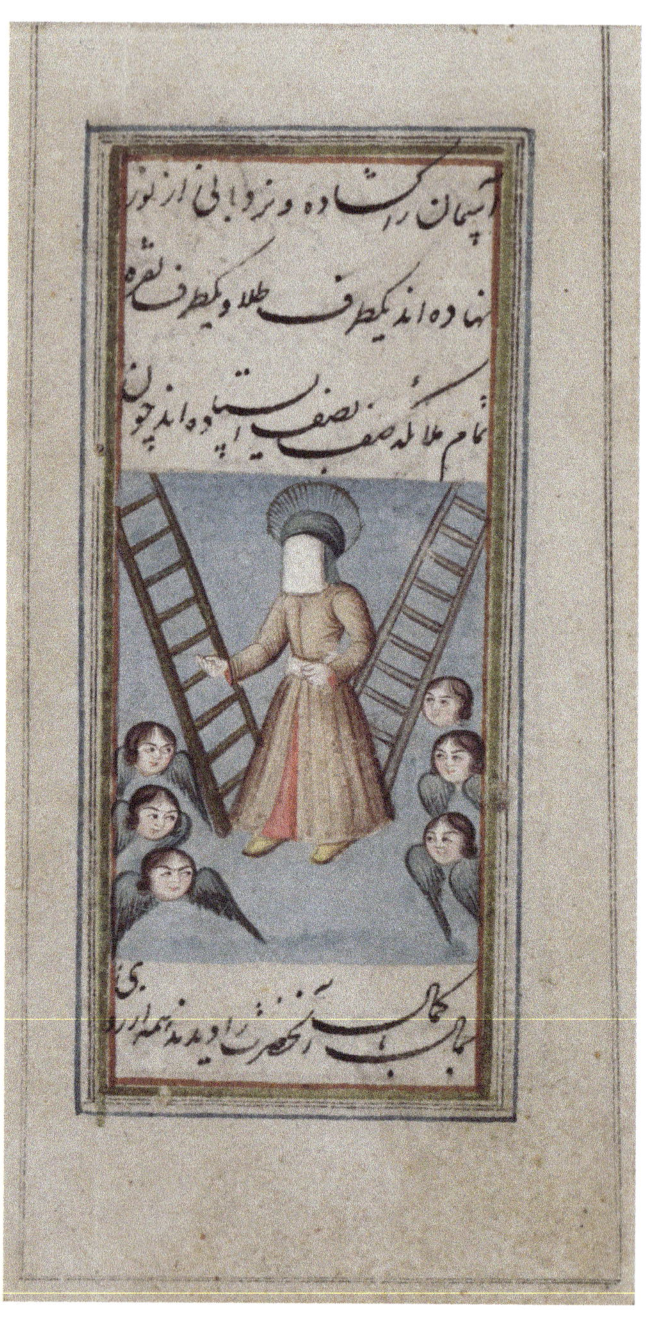

PLATE 23. *(opposite)* The Prophet ascends above Mecca and the Kaʿba, Niẓāmī, *Makhzan al-Asrār* (Treasury of Secrets), Herat, 1494–1495. London, British Library, Or. 6810, folio 5v.

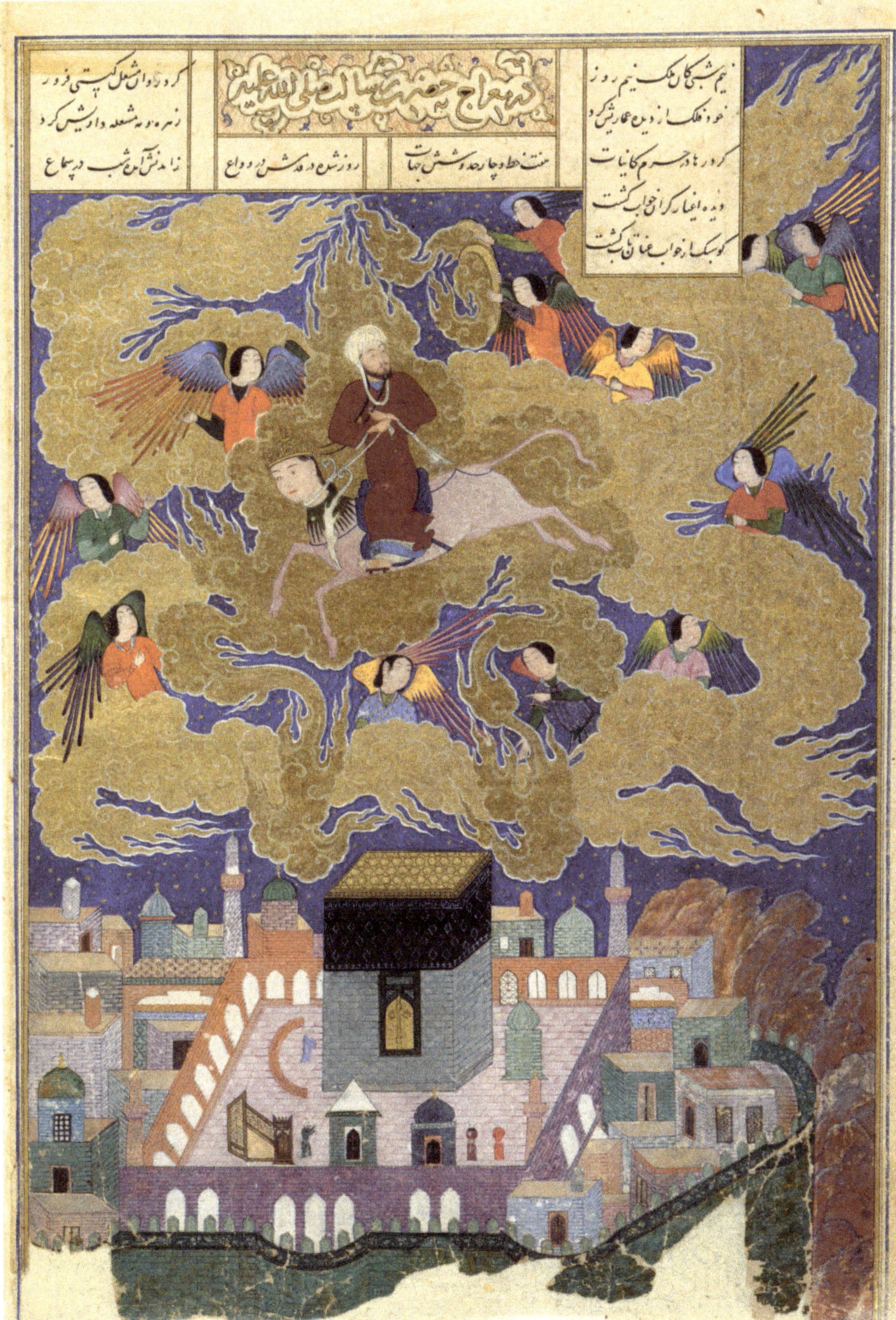

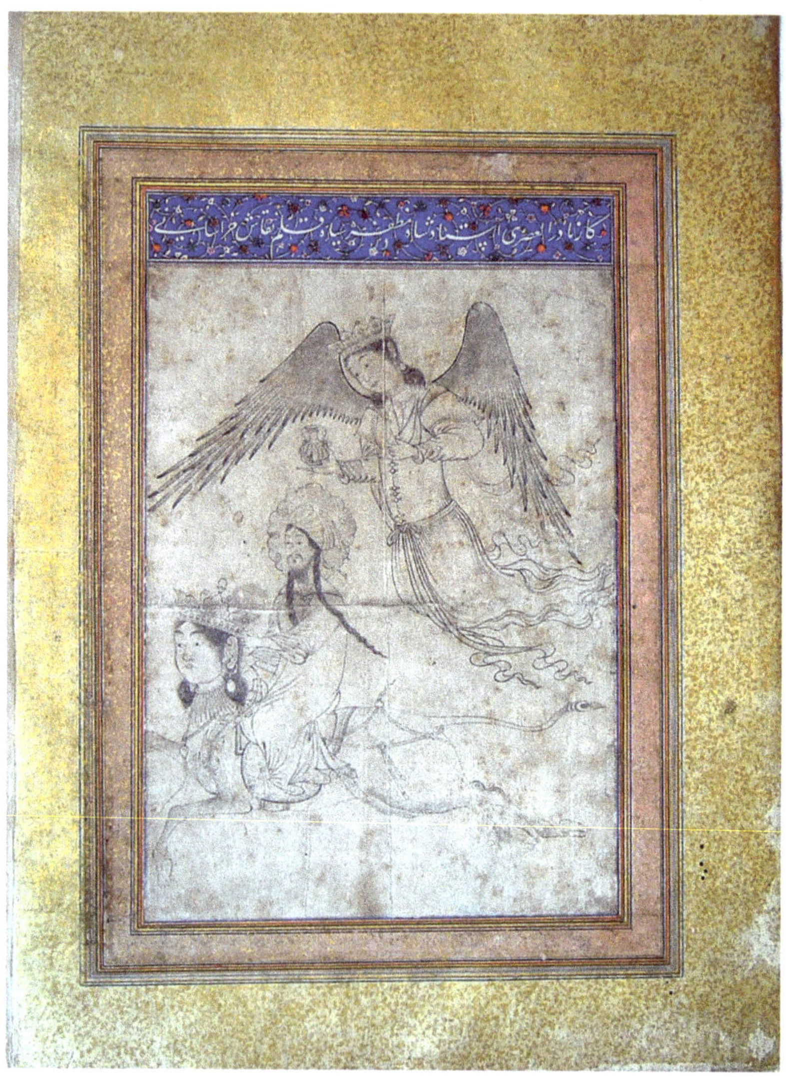

PLATE 24. Shāh Muẓaffar (attr.), ink sketch of the Prophet ascending on Burāq, Herat, ca. 1475–1500. Istanbul, Topkapı Palace Library, H. 2154, folio 40v.

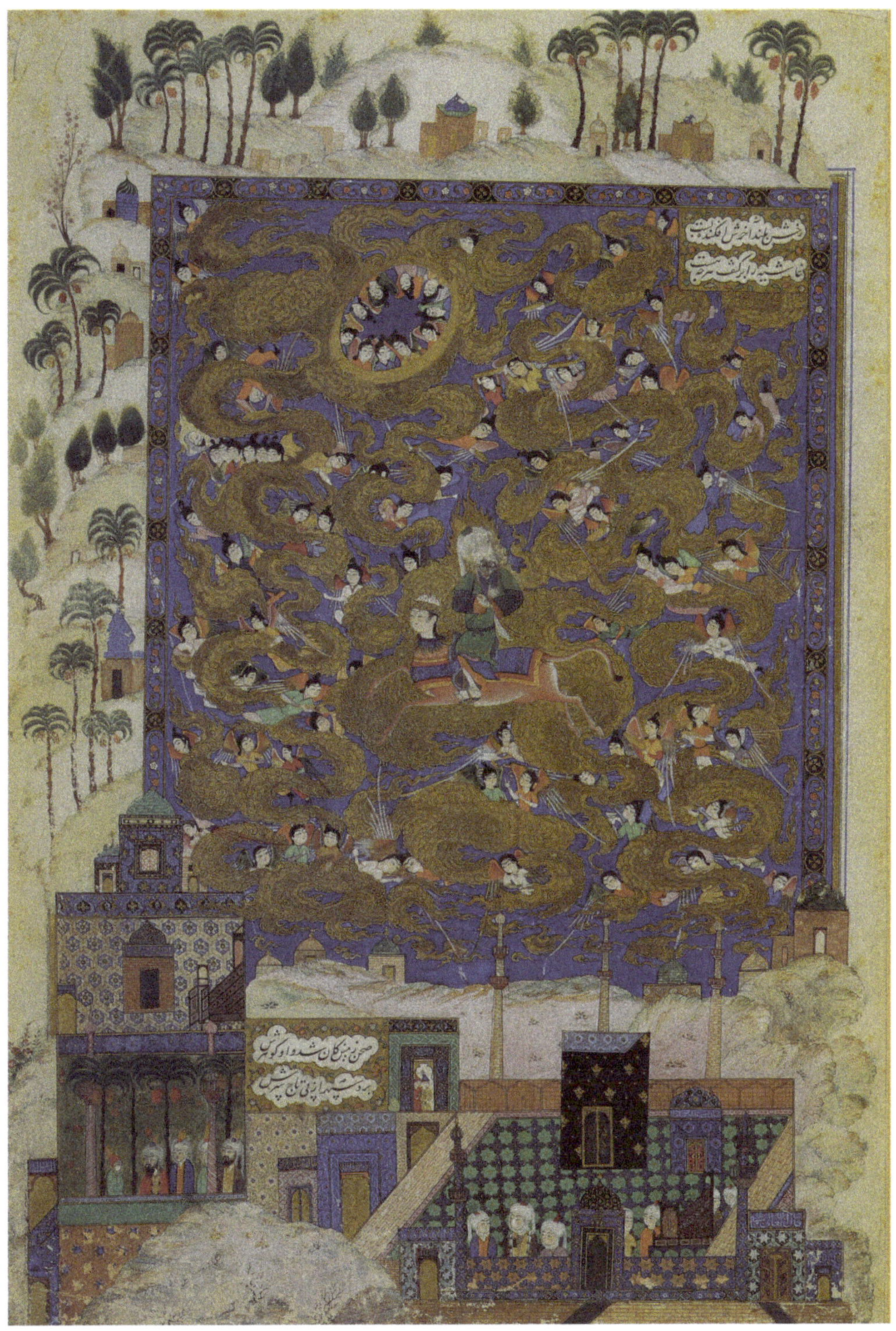

PLATE 25. The Prophet ascends over Mecca and the Kaʿba, Niẓāmī, *Khamsa* (Quintet), Tabriz, completed in 910/1505. Keir Collection (on permanent loan to the Islamic Art Museum, Berlin), III.207.

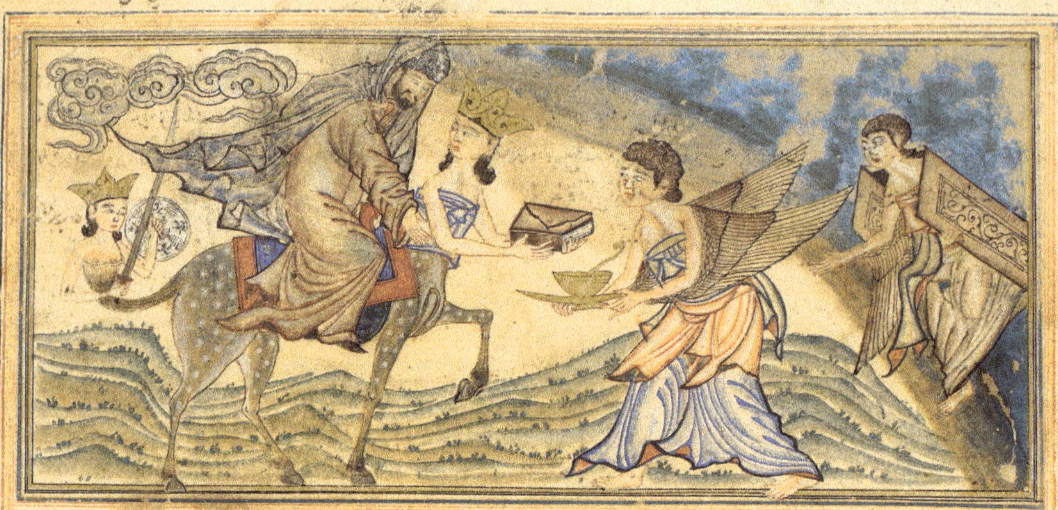

لو اخترت الخمر لارتدت من امتك من بعدك واضلوا كثيرا ولو اخترت الماء كانوا على خطر عظيم من الغرق فحيث اخترت اللبن سوف
تجد امتك الهداية والصراط المستقيم فلما سرت ساعة قال لى جبرئيل انزل يا رسول الله وصل ههنا ركعتين فنزلت وصليت قال هذه طيبة
يعنى به المدينة التى يكون هجرتك اليها فركبت وسرت زمانا ثم قال لى انزل يا محمد وصل ركعتين فنزلت وصليت فقال هذا طور سينا الذى
كلم الله تعالى عليه موسى بن عمران عليه السلم فركبت ثم سرت هنية فقال لى انزل يا محمد وصل ههنا ركعتين فنزلت وصليت فقال هذا مولد عيسى
عليه السلم ثم ركبت وسرت الى بيت المقدس فلما انتهيت الى باب المسجد الاقصى نزلت عن البراق فاخذ جبرئيل البراق وشده فى حلقة الباب
فى المكان الذى شد فيه الانبياء قبلى فدخلت المسجد فاذا انا بالانبياء وقد اجتمعوا هناك فلما راونى سلموا على فسالت اخى جبرئيل من هولاء
فقال اخوتك الانبياء الذين سبقوك فاصطفوا للصلاة فقال جبرئيل عليه السلم تقدم وصل بهم فتقدمت وسلمت عليهم وصليت بهم ركعتين
ثم انطلقت الى الصخرة وهذه الصخرة هى التى تعرج الملائكة عندها والانبياء الى المعراج والسماء من عندها فعرج بى ايضا من هناك الى السماء
فلما انتهيت الى السماء الاولى استفتح جبرئيل عليه السلم فقالت الملائكة من هذا قال انا جبرئيل وفى صحبتى محمد عليه السلم قد اختص برسالة الاسلام
فقالوا مرحبا به وفتحوا الباب فرايت رجلا تام الخلقة جالسا وعلى يمينه باب مفتوح يفوح من داخله رائحة طيبة وعلى يساره ايضا باب يخرج منه رائحة
كريهة وهذا الجالس اذا نظر الى اليمين تبسم وكلما نظر الى جانب اليسار بكى فسالت اخى جبرئيل عليه السلم ما هذان البابان ومن هذا الرجل قال
هذا ابوك آدم عليه السلم والباب الذى عن يمينه باب الجنة والباب الذى عن يساره باب جهنم فاذا نظر الى اولاده الذين يتنعمون فى الجنة تبسم واذا نظر
الى اولاده وهم يشقون فى النار بكى فسلمت عليه فرحب بى ثم عرج بى الى السماء الثانية ففتح لى الباب كما فتح فى الاولى وفرحت الملائكة بمقدمى
واستبشروا فرايت شابين جالسين فسالت اخى جبرئيل عليه السلم عنهما فقال هذا عيسى روح الله والاخر يحيى بن زكريا عليهما السلم وهما ابنا خالة ثم
عرج بى من هناك الى السماء الثالثة ففتح لى الباب على الطريقة المذكورة فرايت رجلا جميلا فى غاية الحسن والجمال فسالت جبرئيل عليه السلم من هذا
قال اخوك يوسف الصديق عليه السلم ثم عرج بى ايضا الى السماء الرابعة فرايت هناك رجلا فسالت جبرئيل عليه السلم عنه فقال هذا اخوك ادريس
النبى عليه السلم ثم عرج بى الى السماء الخامسة فرايت رجلا جالسا يتكلم وحوله خلق كثير فسالت اخى جبرئيل من هذا الرجل قال هذا هرون
عليه السلم وهولاء الجماعة المحدقين به يسمعون كلامه بنو اسرائيل ثم عرج بى الى السماء السادسة فرايت رجلا جالسا فلما جاوزته بكى قلت من هذا يا
جبرئيل فقال هذا موسى عليه السلم كليم الله قلت ولماذا بكى قال لانه يقول ان بنى اسرائيل ادعوا انى اكرم عند الله من آدم وهذا احد اولاد آدم
عليه السلم قد جاوزنى فبقيت متاخرا عنه ثم عرج بى الى السماء السابعة فرحبت بى الملائكة وفتحوا الباب فرايت رجلا كهلا جالسا فوق كرسى
على باب الجنة وحوله جماعة لا تحصى عددهم لهم وجوه بيض كالقراطيس وقوم آخر وجوههم متغيرة وهناك نهر ماء فاذا نزل اليه المتغير لونه واغتسل
منه صفى لونه وصار فى البياض كوجه هولاء البيض الوجوه فسالت اخى جبرئيل من هولاء البيض الوجوه ومن هولاء المتغيرة وجوههم ومن هذا الرجل
الجالس على الكرسى فقال اما الرجل الجالس فهو ابوك ابرهيم عليه السلم وهولاء البيض الوجوه هم جماعة لم يذنبوا قط وهولاء الاخر قوم قد عملوا اعمالا صالحة

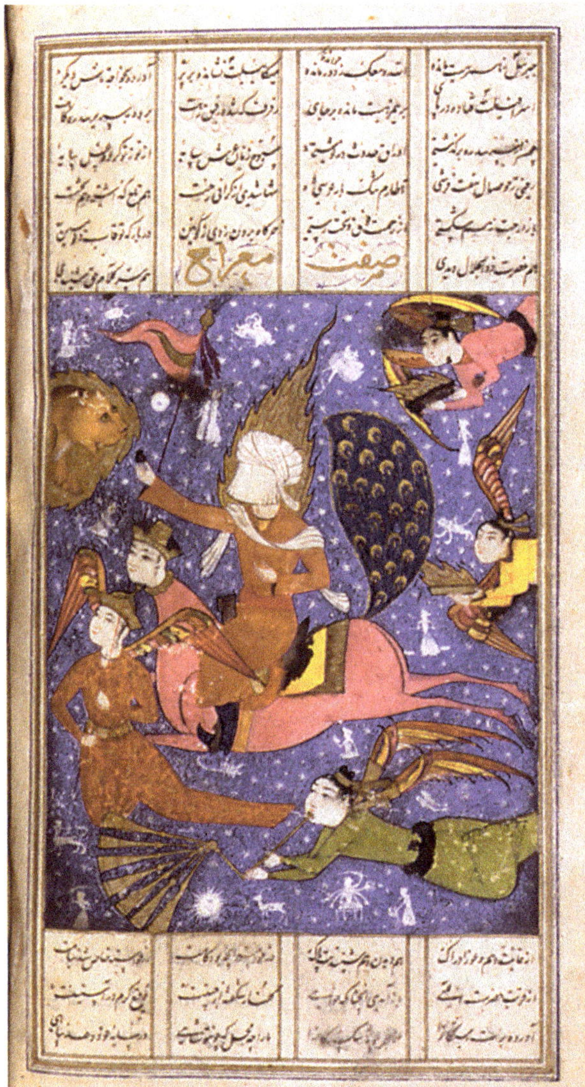

PLATE 27. Accompanied by the angel Isrāfīl, the Prophet ascends towards ʿAlī as an angelic lion while flying past the constellations, Niẓāmī, *Khamsa* (Quintet), Isfahan, 1076–1077/1665–1667. London, British Library, Add. 6613, folio 92v.

PLATE 26. *(opposite)* The Prophet arrives at the gate of the first heaven and must select the cup of milk, Rāshīd al-Dīn, *Jāmiʿ al-Tawārīkh* (Compendium of Chronicles), Tabriz, 706/1306–1307. Edinburgh University Library, Or. Ms. 20, folio 55r.

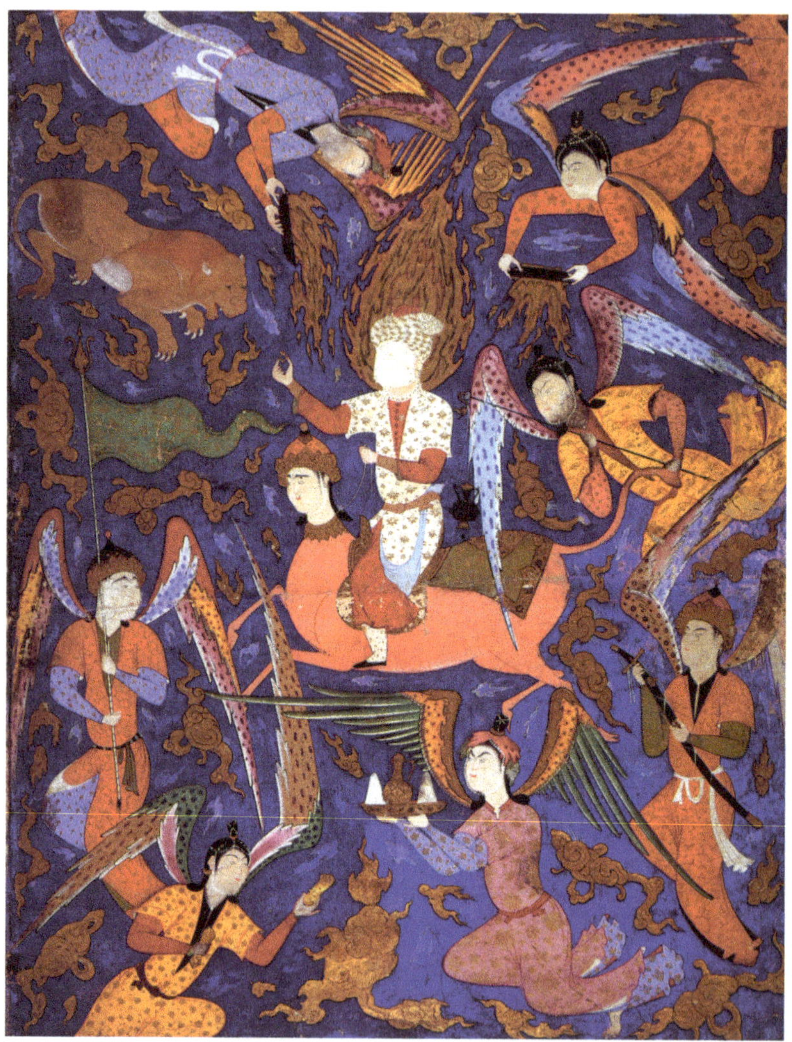

PLATE 28. The Prophet encounters ʿAlī as an angelic lion during his ascension, Jaʿfar al-Ṣādiq (attr.), *Fālnāma* (Book of Divination), Tabriz or Qazvin, ca. 1550. Washington, D.C., Smithsonian Institution, Arthur M. Sackler Gallery, S1986.0253.

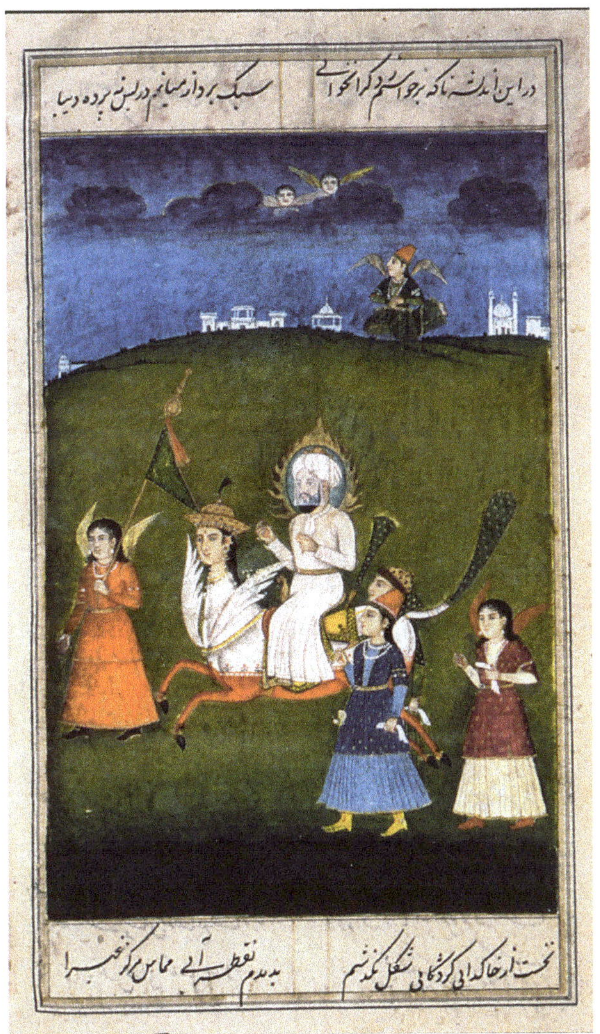

Plate 29. The Prophet rides Burāq, accompanied by the angel Gabriel and peris, Qamar al-Dīn, *Dīvān* (Compendium of Poems), Provincial Mughal (Oudh), ca. 1782. London, British Library, Or. 6633, folio 4v.

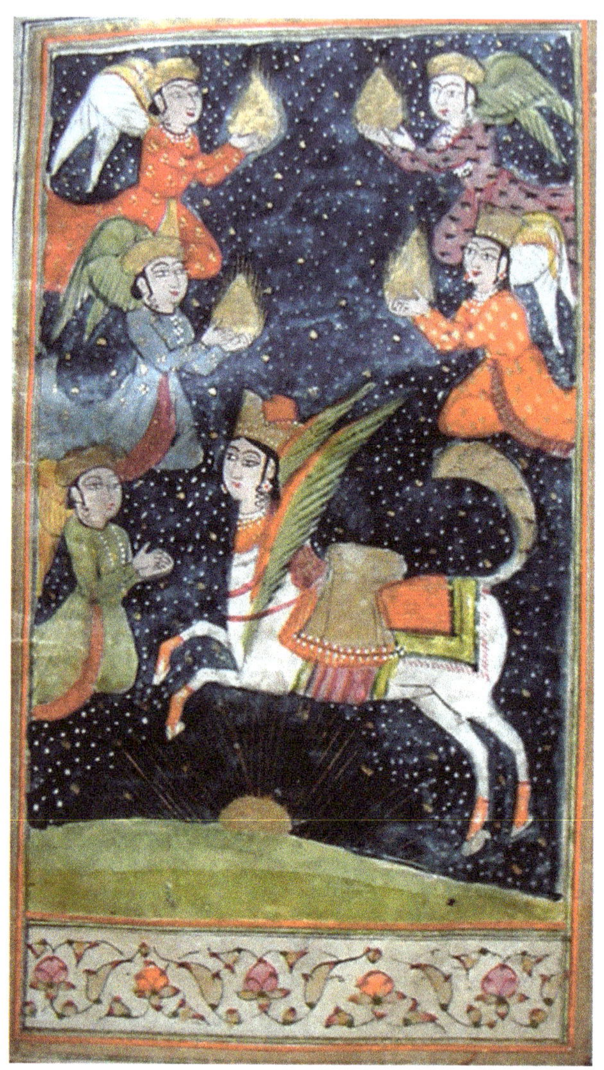

PLATE 30. The Prophet (not depicted) ascends on Burāq, accompanied by angels, Firdawsī, *Shāhnāma* (Book of Kings), Kashmir, 18th century. London, British Library, Add. 7763, folio 21r.

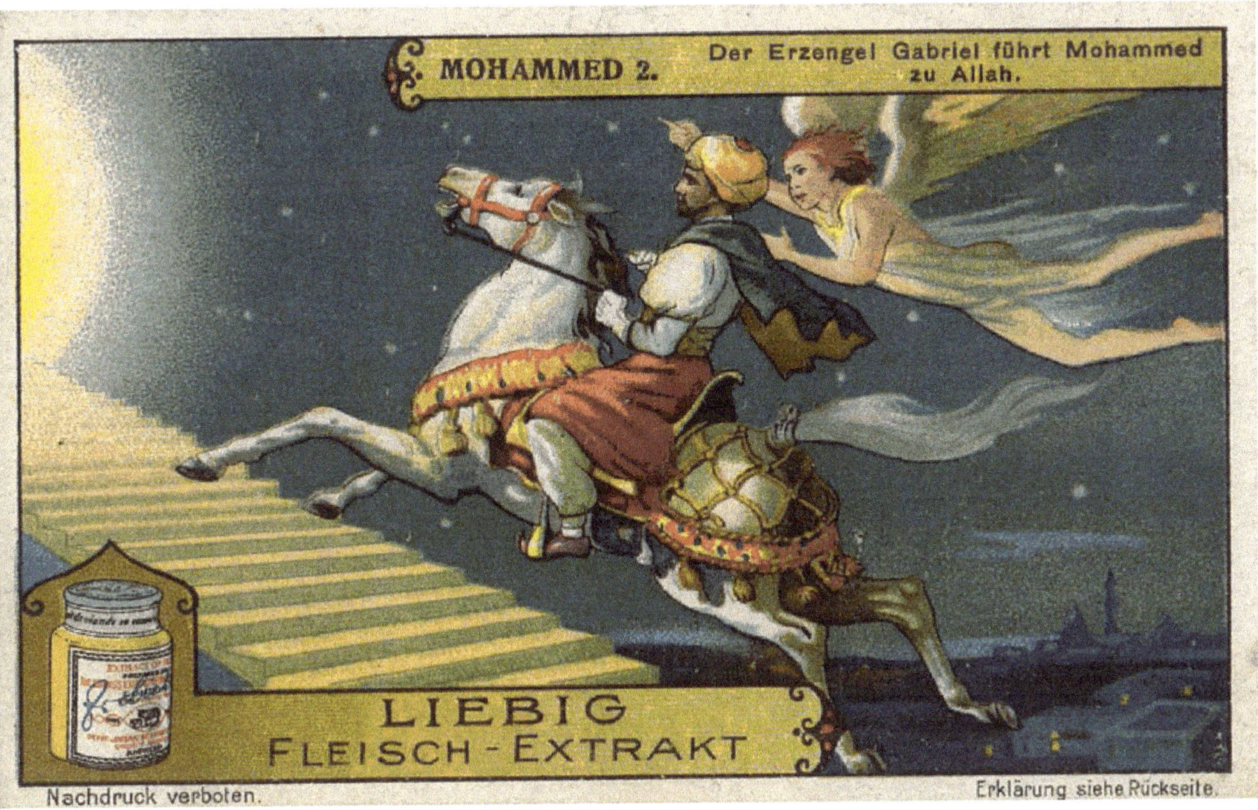

Plate 31. German broth label representing Gabriel leading the Prophet toward God on the night of his ascension, Giessen, Germany, 1928.

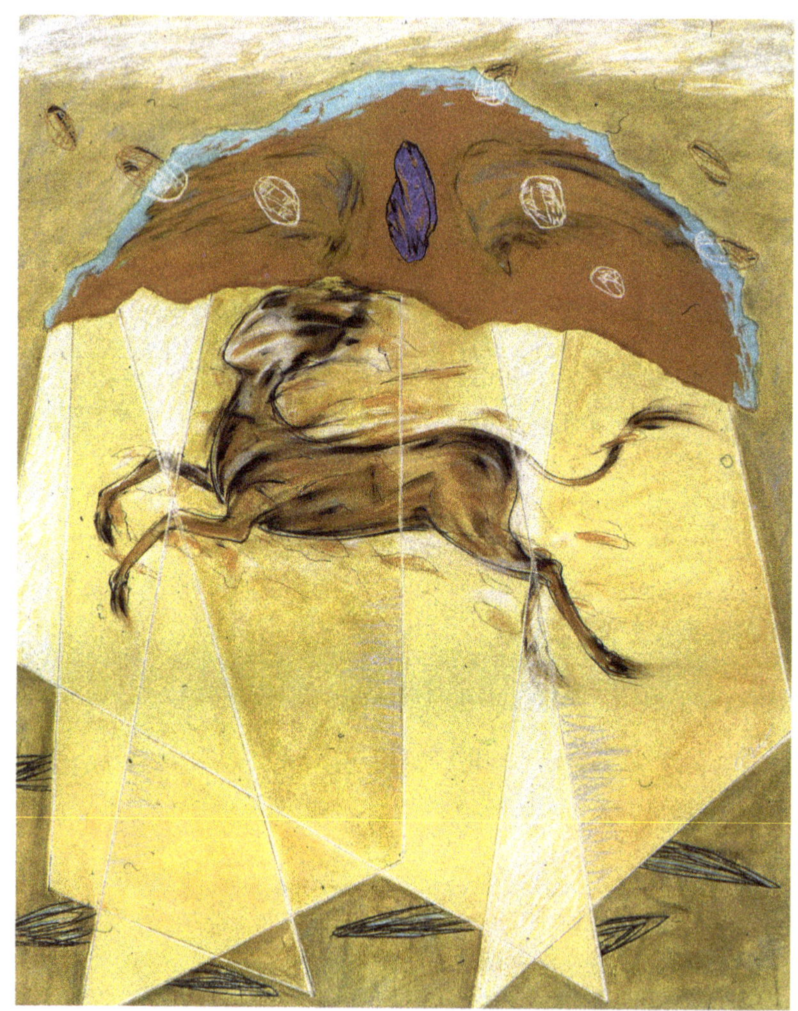

PLATE 32. Behnam Kamrani, *Burāq*, Tehran, 1982. Courtesy of the artist.

PART 2

☾

The Adaptation of Miʿrāj *Narratives in Esoteric and Literary Contexts*

6

The Early Imami Shiʿi Narratives and Contestation over Intimate Colloquy Scenes in Muḥammad's *Miʿrāj*

FREDERICK COLBY

The composite story of Muḥammad's night journey and ascension describes how Muḥammad was taken by night from Mecca to Jerusalem, how he prayed with prophets such as Abraham, Moses, and Jesus there, how he was then taken upon a tour of the seven heavens, meeting angels and prophets at each level, and finally how he enjoyed some kind of revelatory exchange with the divinity at the climax of the ascent before he was brought back to Mecca that same night.[1] The Qur'an contains only the briefest and vaguest of references to Muḥammad's night journey and ascension, while the extra-qur'anic stories that circulated in the first centuries of Islamic history primarily in the form of oral reports enriched the telling of these tales. The contemporary scholarly approach to this oral material typically has been to turn from the Qur'an immediately to the Sunni collections of sound (*ṣaḥīḥ*) hadith reports, imagining that these reports preserve the earliest versions of the story as told among the majority of Muslims.[2] And yet, these sound Sunni reports on the night journey and ascension did not arise in a vacuum, and they should not be treated as comprehensive accounts of how the first generations of Muslims understood and discussed Muḥammad's journey. Just as Carl Ernst argues that observers of contemporary Muslim movements repeatedly and mistakenly take puritanical interpretations of Islam as representative of the only "true" or "orthodox" Islam of a majority of Muslims today,[3] so I would argue that contemporary historians of the early period repeatedly and mistakenly take the sound Sunni hadith reports as representative of the "true" or "orthodox" mainstream position embraced by the majority of the community in the formative period of Islamic history. While the Sunni sound collections (the so-called "six books," and especially those known by the title *Ṣaḥīḥ* or *Sound*) certainly came to enjoy an authoritative position among many later Sunni Muslims, the situation in the first centuries of Islamic history was more fluid and complex, as a study of the early night journey and ascension narratives makes clear.

The historical record shows that in this early period, proto-Shiʿis made use of the ascension narrative as a context through which to assert the God-given right of ʿAlī and his descendants, the imams, to the leadership of the Muslim community after Muḥammad.[4] Concentrating on the proto-Shiʿi approach to the ascension discourse helps one to see how the narratives of proto-Sunnis appear to have been in conversation with this early partisan use of the *miʿrāj* narrative. By focusing upon the scenes of Muḥammad's encounter with God during the ascension (Plate 14), this study will suggest that the proto-Shiʿi depictions of these scenes as a site for the assertion of ʿAlī's leadership was countered by two different approaches on the part of distinct groups of proto-Sunni scholars: on the one hand, groups appropriated and adapted these scenes, and, on the other, groups rejected and silenced them. Although it is not possible at this time to prove whether the early Shiʿi or Sunni ascension narratives arose first, because written evidence for both flourishes only in the ninth century, I argue that viewing the Sunni narratives as reactions to early Shiʿi narratives helps to explain some of the major ways in which later Sunni scholars came to develop discourses on Muḥammad's journey. The sectarian contest over the ascension discourse as it played out at the beginning of the tenth century demonstrates the need to study the dialectical relationship between Shiʿi and Sunni ascension narratives. Through such an approach, one might gain a more accurate understanding of the sectarian contexts within which this ascension discourse first developed and then flourished among Muslims.

Even the earliest of Muslim historical accounts of Muḥammad's night journey and ascension bear witness to the fact that this narrative provoked differences of opinion among the Muslims of the formative period. For example, Ibn Isḥāq's night journey account, with its references to scholarly debates over the nature of Muḥammad's experience, proves that the narrative was the site of scholarly controversy even in the eighth century.[5] With the unrealized political ambitions of the ʿAlid loyalists during the early period of the ʿAbbāsid caliphate, it is reasonable to conjecture that some of these partisans might have turned to otherworldly narratives in order to provide arguments in favor of their ʿAlid cause. Such pro-ʿAlid arguments would have become especially useful for them prior to and during the "Shiʿi century" (beginning in the first half of the tenth century), when ʿAlid forces gained political control in the central lands of Islamdom, ruling over a majority population of non-Shiʿis.[6] As I will argue in what follows, those who rejected the claims of these ʿAlid loyalists about the exalted status of ʿAlī might naturally have responded to this partisan use of the ascension narrative by offering their own partisan versions of these same narratives, versions that supported their Sunni worldviews and the legitimacy of Sunni leaders. Rather than considering such theological and political struggles over the control of the ascension discourse as an anomaly, given the potential religious and political stakes involved, one might instead expect to find such conflicts over the narrative in general and the scenes of Muḥammad's encounter with God in particular in early scholarly works.

Although this study concentrates upon conflicts over the ascension narrative among different groups of Muslims in the formative period of Islamic history, it is important to recognize that such conflicts were not limited to debates among Muslims alone, as demonstrated by Aaron Hughes's study of Jewish-Muslim conflicts over the ascension discourse in al-Andalus.[7] Michael Sells introduces the useful concept of the "language world" in an essay comparing a Jewish and a Sufi Muslim ascent text, explaining how diverse groups often draw upon and adapt a common set of symbols.[8] According to Sells's theory, competition over the proper use and interpretation of these common symbols often leads to conflict both within and among religious groups:

> The notion of a language world does not involve the assumption that those who share it share a common ideology or theology. In fact, it is more often the opposite that is true. One group will reappropriate the territory of a given language world when it feels threatened by what another group is doing with that symbolic system. . . . The language world of the ascent through the levels to the divine throne was not the locus of unified ideology within Islamic literature. Rather, it was the polemical scene of debate, controversy, and conflict.[9]

The present chapter provides an example of this debate, controversy, and conflict by illustrating several ways that proto-Shiʿis and proto-Sunnis struggled over the general representation and specific content of the encounter between Muḥammad and God on the night of the ascension. Beginning in the ninth century it becomes a political issue whether or not to mention figures like ʿAlī or Abū Bakr in one's account of the intimate colloquy scenes, and even whether or not to include these scenes in one's account in the first place. I contend that the way each subsequent storyteller or author deals with these issues in narrating the story of Muḥammad's *miʿrāj* tells us something about that person's particular sectarian preferences, as an analysis of select early references will suggest.

Proto-Shiʿi Accounts and Their Intimate Colloquy Scenes

For the purposes of the present argument, it is important to begin with a brief survey of proto-Shiʿi accounts of Muḥammad's ascension, given that they tend to be less familiar to most contemporary readers than the proto-Sunni accounts. As Josef van Ess and others have noted, the proto-Shiʿis seem to have taken an early interest in the Prophet's otherworldly journey, and apparently they were the first to have composed entire works dedicated to the subject of Muḥammad's ascension.[10] Mohammad Ali Amir-Moezzi has studied the ascension reports of what he terms the "esoteric non-rational" proto-Shiʿis, illustrating the centrality of the imams in many of these reports.[11] Though the present chapter takes a wider frame of analysis and asks different questions of this material, Amir-Moezzi's dedicated spadework uncovering ascension references in the proto-Shiʿi sources provides the foundation for my own research in this area. His groundbreaking research demonstrates how formative Shiʿi thinkers often included in their discussions of Muḥammad's ascension (and the related ascensions attributed to the imams) the idea that at the most exalted stage of Muḥammad's journey, God informs Muḥammad of ʿAlī's high station and the rightful role of ʿAlī and his spiritual inheritors to succeed Muḥammad to the leadership of the Muslim community.[12] While it will not be possible here to explore these esoteric proto-Shiʿi intimate colloquy scenes in depth, a survey of key ascension anecdotes in a few central works will serve to demonstrate this common proto-Shiʿi trope.[13]

In the earliest extant of these proto-Shiʿi works that discusses Muḥammad's ascension, Ṣaffār Qummī (d. 902–903) draws upon a qur'anic reference in the chapter of the Star to the phrase "*He revealed to his servant what he revealed*" (Q 53:10), seeing in it an allusion to the intimate colloquy scene in which God teaches Muḥammad about ʿAlī's extraordinary status:

> [Jaʿfar Ṣādiq] reported that the Messenger of God said, "My Lord caused me to travel by night. *He revealed to* me—*from behind a veil—what he revealed,* and *he spoke* to me (Q 53:10, 42:51). Among what he said to me was the following: 'Muḥammad, ʿAlī is the first, and ʿAlī is the last, [ʿAlī is the manifest and ʿAlī is the hidden], and *he is of all things most knowing*' (Q 57:3). I said, 'My Lord, is that not you? Is that not you?' He replied, 'Muḥammad, *I am God, there is no God but me* (Q 20:14), *the King, the Holy, the Peaceful, the Faithful, the Protector, the Powerful, the Omnipotent, the Proud. Glorified be God above what they associate* (Q 59:23). Indeed I am God, there is no God but me: *the Creator, the Fashioner, the Shaper, to him are the beautiful names with which those in the heavens and the earths glorify him. He is the Powerful, the Wise* (Q 59:24). O Muḥammad, I am God, there is no God but me. I am *the First,* for there is nothing before me; I am *the Last,* for there is nothing after me. I am *the Manifest,* for there is nothing above me; I am *the Hidden,* for there is nothing below me. I am God, there is no God but me, *of all things Most Knowing.* [But] O Muḥammad, ʿAlī is *the first:* the first of the imams who accepted my covenant. O Muḥammad, ʿAlī is *the last:* the last of the imams whose soul I will seize. . . . O Muḥammad, ʿAlī is *the manifest:* I will make manifest to him all that I have entrusted to you. You need not conceal anything from him. O Muḥammad, ʿAlī is *the hidden:* I will hide in him the secret that I kept secret with you. No secret between us will be kept from ʿAlī. About all that I created, and of the permissible and the forbidden, ʿAlī is *most knowing.*'"[14]

Amir-Moezzi interprets this passage as an expression of a "cosmic ʿAlī," a figure that deliberately conflates ʿAlī with the divinity.[15] Read on another level, however, it does not claim a divine status for ʿAlī but rather employs an esoteric commentary on select qur'anic verses in order to describe ʿAlī's most exalted status among created beings. In either case, this revelation to Muḥammad, depicted as taking place during the latter's intimate colloquy with God at the climax of his ascension, offers a powerful example of how some proto-Shiʿis made use of this symbolically charged setting in order to promote partisan ideas regarding the high status of ʿAlī.

The daring conception of an exalted, or even quasi-divine, figure of ʿAlī in Ṣaffār Qummī's text becomes only slightly tempered in the work of his contemporary, Furāt b. Furāt Kūfī (d. ca. 912). Just as Ṣaffār Qummī's report found hidden references to ʿAlī in qur'anic passages that on the surface had nothing to do with ʿAlī, so Furāt Kūfī sees a reference to a dialogue between Muḥammad and God on the night of the ascension in a passage that on the surface has nothing to do with the *miʿrāj*. He presents this interpretation in his commentary on the final verses (or "seals") of the Cow chapter in the Qur'an:

> 285) *The Messenger believes what was sent down to him from his Lord. The believers all believe in God, his angels, his books, and his messengers. We do not differentiate between any of his messengers. They say, "We hear and obey." Forgive us, Lord. To you is the arrival.*
>
> 286) *God does not burden a soul beyond what it can bear. It has what it has earned, and upon it is what it earned. Lord, do not blame us when we forget or err. Lord, do not make us bear a heavy weight like the one you made those before us to bear. Lord, do not make us carry what we are not able. Forgive us and pardon us and have mercy on us. You are our Master, so give us victory over the unbelievers.*[16]

Furāt Kūfī understands these two "seals of the Cow chapter" collectively as recording an account of the way that Muḥammad responds to a question God poses to him on the night of the ascension. Instead of analyzing separate phrases in these verses, Furāt Kūfī cites a report that begins with a reference to this trope, but turns quickly from it to a broader discussion of God's revelation of ʿAlī's exalted status:

> Muḥammad [Bāqir] reported that the Messenger of God said, "When I was caused to journey by night to the heaven[s], the Almighty said to me, 'Does *the Messenger believe what was sent down to him from his Lord?*' I replied, '*And the believers* [*all believe*]. . . .' (Q 2:285) He said, 'You speak the truth, Muḥammad, peace be upon you. Whom have you left in your place for your community after you?' I said, 'The best of [the community] for its people.' He said, 'ʿAlī b. Abī Ṭālib?' I said, 'Yes, Lord.'
>
> He replied, 'Muḥammad, I caused some to rise up upon the earth, and I chose you from among them. I split off for you a name from among my names. I am never mentioned anywhere without you being mentioned with me. I am "*Maḥmūd*" ("the praised one") and you are "*Muḥammad*" ("highly praised"). Then I caused a second one to rise, and I chose ʿAlī. I split off for him a name from among my names. I am "*al-Aʿlā*" ("the Most High") and he is "*ʿAlī*" ("high").
>
> 'Muḥammad, I created you, ʿAlī, Fāṭima, Ḥasan and Ḥusayn as figures of light out of my light. I showed your authority to the heavens and their residents as well as to the earths and their residents. Those who accept your authority become close companions in my eyes, and those who struggle against it become unbelievers. Muḥammad, were a servant to serve me until he becomes cut apart or like a worn out waterskin, and then he struggles against your authority, I will not forgive him until he acknowledges your authority.'
>
> 'O Muḥammad, would you like to see them?' I said, 'Indeed, Lord!' He said, 'Turn to the right side of the throne.' I turned to the right side of the throne, and there I found myself with the reflections of ʿAlī, Fāṭima, Ḥasan, Ḥusayn, and all of the imams until the Mahdī, in a pool of light. They began to perform ritual prayer, the Mahdī in their midst as if he were a shining star. He said to me,

> ʿMuḥammad, these are the proofs, and this is the avenger of your stock. [I swear] by my power and grandeur, he is a necessary proof to my friends, [and he is] one who takes vengeance upon my enemies.'"[17]

In this anecdote, God confirms ʿAlī as the best choice for Muḥammad's successor, explains that both ʿAlī and Muḥammad bear names that derive from divine names, and shows that the luminous essence of ʿAlī and other figures in his household reside near the foot of the divine throne, the messianic figure of the Mahdī prominent among them. Once again, this passage demonstrates how a proto-Shiʿi scholar draws upon the scene of Muḥammad's dialogue with God during the Prophet's ascension in order to convey explicitly partisan ideas about God's favor toward ʿAlī, his family, and his spiritual successors.

Ṣaffār Qummī and Furāt Kūfī's contemporary, the famous early Shiʿi exegete ʿAlī Qummī (d. ca. 919), includes a number of ascension-related anecdotes in reference to the night journey verse (Q 17:1), one of which consists of a long and detailed report ascribed to Imam Jaʿfar Ṣādiq. This narrative by Jaʿfar Ṣādiq as recorded by ʿAlī Qummī lacks overt ʿAlī-partisan references, leading Amir-Moezzi to characterize it as little more than an appropriation of the proto-Sunni ascension report ascribed to Abū Saʿīd Khudrī.[18] Despite this characterization of ʿAlī Qummī's commentary on the night journey verse, just as Ṣaffār Qummī and Furāt Kūfī find references to the intimate colloquy scene elsewhere in the Qur'an, so also ʿAlī Qummī preserves a more partisan approach to the intimate colloquy elsewhere in his commentary, specifically in his discussion of a qur'anic reference to a debate among the heavenly host (Q 38:67–71):

> 67) *Say: It is a great prophecy*
> 68) *One which you oppose*
> 69) *I did not have knowledge of the heavenly host when they were debating*
> 70) *It was only revealed to me that I am a clear warner*
> 71) *When your Lord said to the angels, "I am creating a human being out of clay"*

ʿAlī Qummī does not interpret this "heavenly host debate" passage as a reference to the objections of the angels to God's creation of human beings, but rather reads the passage as a reference to yet another topic of conversation in the intimate colloquy between Muḥammad and God on the night of the ascension. For example, what follows is the detailed report that ʿAlī Qummī transmits regarding this heavenly host debate passage, beginning with a debate over the proper understanding of the night journey verse:[19]

> [ʿAlī Qummī] said that . . . Ismāʿīl Juʿfī reported, "I was sitting near the sacred mosque and Abū Jaʿfar [Muḥammad Bāqir] was present. He raised his head and gazed once at the sky, and once at the Kaʿba. Then he said, "*Glorified be the one who caused his servant to journey by night from the sacred mosque to the furthest*

mosque. . . ." (Q 17:1). He recited it three times, then he turned to me and said, "What do the people of Iraq say about this verse, Iraqī?" I said, "They say, he *caused* him *to journey by night from the sacred mosque to the furthest mosque,* that is, the house of the sanctuary [in Jerusalem]." He said, "It is not as they say. Rather, he caused him to journey by night from this to that." And he pointed with his hand to the sky. "Anything besides those is free [from playing any role in his journey]."

He said, "When [Muḥammad] ended up at the Lote Tree of the Boundary, Gabriel turned back. The Messenger of God said, 'Gabriel, in this spot you desert me?' He said, 'Advance forward. By God, you have reached [a place] where no created being before you has reached.'[20]

I saw the light of my Lord, and immediately between him and me there was a glorification. I asked, "What glorification should you perform as your sacrifice?" He gestured with his head to the ground and with his hands to the sky, and said, "The sublimity of my Lord, the sublimity of my Lord!," three times.

[God] said, "O Muḥammad." I replied, "Here I am." He said, "What do the heavenly host debate?" I said, "Glorified are you, I have no knowledge except what you teach me." He put his hand, that is, the "hand of power" (*qudra*) between my nipples, and I felt their coldness between my shoulderblades. I knew everything that he asked me about, what had passed and what remained. He said, "Muḥammad, what do the heavenly host debate?" I said, "Lord, [about] the degrees, the penitential acts, and the goodnesses."

He said, "Muḥammad, when your property has passed and you have stopped eating, who will be your trustee?" I said, "Lord, I have tested your creation and have not seen among them any more obedient to me than ʿAlī." He said, "Same with me, Muḥammad." I said, "Lord, I have tested your creation and did not see anyone more intensely in love with me than ʿAlī." He said, "It is the same with me, Muḥammad. Rejoice, for he is the archer of guidance, the leader of my saints, and a victory to those who obey me."[21]

After dealing with several issues, including the proper understanding of the destination indicated in the night journey verse, the reason Gabriel made Muḥammad proceed unaccompanied beyond the Lote Tree, the proper way to glorify God during one's approach, etc., this passage describes how the divinity teaches Muḥammad the meaning of the heavenly host debate. The lesson is conveyed through the touch of God's hand, here understood in a metaphorical sense. ʿAlī Qummī's report describes how God approves of Muḥammad's choice of ʿAlī as his successor, and God showers ʿAlī with praise. Once again, this passage illustrates how a proto-Shiʿi scholar near the turn of the tenth century preserves a report on Muḥammad's night journey and ascension that presents the intimate colloquy scene as the stage upon which God voices his support for ʿAlī in a sectarian fashion. In each of the instances cited above, proto-Shiʿi scholars interpret qur'anic references as allusions to a conversation between Muḥammad and God on the night of the ascension, intimate colloquies through which Muḥammad receives confirmation of God's favor toward ʿAlī, and of God's support for a particularly partisan view in which ʿAlī and his descendants receive the divine mandate to lead the Muslim community after Muḥammad's death.

Proto-Sunni Accounts and their Intimate Colloquy Scenes

If one accepts that the proto-Shiʿis were some of the first to compose and circulate works dedicated to night journey and ascension narratives,[22] then in the midst of these partisan versions of the intimate colloquy that highlighted ʿAlī's special status, some proto-Sunni scholars in the tenth century would have been faced with the dilemma of how best to respond. I would maintain that one avenue of Sunni response was to reclaim the intimate colloquy scene in their own accounts, divesting it of ʿAlid-partisan language. Sells's language world theory anticipates such a process: "One group will re-appropriate the territory of a given language world when it feels threatened by what another group is doing with that symbolic system."[23] While examples of such a response may well have circulated in hadith reports prior to the turn of the tenth century,[24] Ibn Jarīr Ṭabarī (d. 923) preserves at least two references in his Qur'an commentary on the night journey verse (Q 17:1) that prove that the full-fledged appropriation of this intimate colloquy scene had certainly begun by this period.

First, Ṭabarī records a long version of the ascension narrative ascribed to Abū Hurayra in which God's showering of praise upon ʿAlī in the intimate colloquy scene becomes transformed into God's showering of praise upon Muḥammad himself.[25] The relevant passage begins when Muḥammad cites references to blessings received by previous prophets, and he asks God if he himself will receive similar divine favors. While Muslims may certainly have had a number of reasons for developing what I call this "favor of the prophets" trope and its exaltation of Muḥammad, not least among these its usefulness in their debates with non-Muslims, its appearance as a major trope of the intimate colloquy scenes at the beginning of the tenth century, precisely when versions of proto-Shiʿi ascension narratives exalting ʿAlī were circulating, suggests that it may have functioned partially as a rejoinder to the Shiʿi ascension tales. That is, God's expression of particular titles and favors that God bestows upon ʿAlī as conveyed in the proto-Shiʿi texts may well have their parallel in God's expression of particular titles and favors that God bestows upon Muḥammad in the proto-Sunni texts. Ṭabarī's Abū Hurayra anecdote, then, could be said to preserve an early example of this competitive approach.

A second allusion in Ṭabarī's Qur'an commentary that offers evidence of a proto-Sunni rejoinder to Shiʿi use of the intimate colloquy scene appears in a brief reference to Ibn ʿAbbās's position on Muḥammad's vision of God during his heavenly ascension:

> . . . Ibn ʿAbbās reported that the Messenger of God said, "I saw my Lord in the best form. [God] said to me, 'Muḥammad, do you know what the heavenly host debate?' I said, 'No, Lord.' So he placed his hand between my shoulder blades and I felt the coldness between my nipples. I knew what was in the heaven[s] and what was in the earth. I said, 'Lord, [they discuss] the degrees (*al-darajāt*) and the pen-

itential acts (*al-kaffarāt*), going on foot to the congregational prayers (*al-jumuʿāt*) and waiting for prayer after prayer (*al-ṣalāt*).' I said, 'Lord, you *took Abraham as an intimate friend* (Q 4:125) and you *spoke to Moses directly* (4:164), and you did this and that.' He said, '*Did I not open your breast? Did I not remove your burden from you?* (Q 94:1–2). Did I not do this and that with you?' [Muḥammad] said, 'Then he informed me of things that he did not permit me to tell you about.' He said, 'That is [God's] saying in his book that he does tell you: *Then he drew closer and descended, and was a distance of two bows or closer. He revealed to his servant what he revealed. The heart did not lie in what it saw* (Q 53:8–11). He made the light of my vision in my heart, and I gazed upon him with my heart.'"[26]

This passage in Ṭabarī's commentary highlights the intimate colloquy scene of a longer Ibn ʿAbbās ascension narrative, citing from that narrative in passing in order to make a larger point about Muḥammad's vision of God. The citation refers briefly to both the heavenly host debate and the favor of the prophets tropes in its account of the intimate colloquy. These tropes were described above with reference to the proto-Shiʿi versions, but in the Ibn ʿAbbās narrative they are presented without any Shiʿi-partisan language.[27] Not long after Ṭabarī's death, a traditionist from Nishapur named Ibn Ḥibbān (d. 965) records a full version of the Ibn ʿAbbās ascension narrative, one that continues to develop and expand the details of such types of references in the centuries that followed.[28]

Versions of the Ibn ʿAbbās ascension narrative repeatedly transform symbols that appear in these early Shiʿi narratives and appropriate them into its Sunni-valenced discourse. For example, in its intimate colloquy scene, the fully elaborated Ibn ʿAbbās narrative comes to include the heavenly host debate, the seals of the Cow chapter, and the favor of the prophets themes as prominent tropes. The favor of the prophets trope in the Ibn ʿAbbās narrative often segues into a discussion of the special gifts that God has chosen to bestow upon Muḥammad (with no mention of ʿAlī or his family). Ṭabarī's reference to the Ibn ʿAbbās ascension narrative does not contain all these nuances, but the anecdote cited above offers clear proof that Ṭabarī was aware of this type of narrative that was circulating in Ibn ʿAbbās's name. In Ṭabarī's time, if not before, such Ibn ʿAbbās narratives formed part of a growing body of oral literature that began increasingly to take a Sunni partisan approach to what appear to have been originally Shiʿi ascension themes.

In later Sunni versions of the Ibn ʿAbbās discourse, the appropriations of Shiʿi tropes become even more explicit. For instance, in one version an angel in the form of ʿAlī described in the proto-Shiʿi ascension reports is replaced in later Sunni Ibn ʿAbbās ascension reports with an angel in the form of Abū Bakr.[29] Abū Bakr, of course, is the companion of the Prophet whom the majority of Muslims accepted as the leader of the Muslim community upon Muḥammad's death, but who was cursed as a usurper by the early partisans of ʿAlī. Inserting Abū Bakr in the place of ʿAlī in this otherworldly narrative, then, becomes a symbolic way to inject an assertion of Sunni allegiance into an originally Shiʿi-valenced account.

In another instance of this same type of appropriation, the idea of God speaking to Muḥammad in the voice of ʿAlī gets transformed into God speaking to Muḥammad in the voice of Abū Bakr.[30] Elsewhere accounts that occasionally depict a prominent Shiʿi figure such as ʿAlī or the Mahdī as wielding a sword near the base of God's throne become adapted in the Ibn ʿAbbās narratives into a trope in which a "sword of vengeance" hangs from the side of God's throne, used to explain the divine purpose behind the strife that befalls the Muslim community.[31] Such examples could be multiplied, but the preceding references provide adequate support for the idea that debates between Shiʿi and Sunni partisans become inserted into and narrated through the story of the Prophet's ascension in general, and the account of his intimate colloquy with God on the night of the ascension in particular.

That such types of appropriations were not merely unidirectional (from Shiʿi to Sunni narratives) becomes clear upon turning to consider the lengthy and less sectarian proto-Shiʿi narrative ascribed to Jaʿfar Ṣādiq in ʿAlī Qummī's commentary on the night journey verse (Q 17:1). The intimate colloquy scene in the Jaʿfar narrative, which makes no mention of ʿAlī or the imams, mirrors the reports of the seals of the Cow chapter and favor of the prophets tropes that form standard elements (along with the heavenly host debate) of nearly every subsequent Sunni ascension narrative that is ascribed to Ibn ʿAbbās:

> I ended at the Lote Tree of the Boundary, one leaf of which would shade an entire community. I was [a distance] from it as God says [in the verse], "*a distance of two bows or closer*" (Q 53:9), when [God] called out to me, "*The Messenger believes what was sent down to him from his Lord* (Q 2:285), which [is something] I have written in the chapter of the Cow."
>
> I said, "My Lord, you gave your prophets favors, so give me [some as well]." God said, "I have given you [favors], among which are two phrases from under my throne: 'There is no might nor power save with God, and there is no refuge from you except to you.'"[32]

While this account by Jaʿfar Ṣādiq offers an abbreviated form of these tropes, it is clear from this section and elsewhere in the narrative that it draws liberally from the Sunni-valenced Ibn ʿAbbās ascension narrative.[33] Furthermore, as mentioned above, the long "Jaʿfar hadith" combines the primitive Ibn ʿAbbās ascension narrative with another major ascension account embraced by early Sunnis, namely the extended report attributed to Abu Saʿīd Khudrī that is cited by Ibn Hishām, Ṭabarī, Qushayrī, and others. From the evidence advanced thus far, a case can be made that the proto-Shiʿi depictions of the intimate colloquy scene played a pivotal role in determining the direction in which one strand of the Sunni ascension narratives would develop, namely the appropriation and reinterpretation of early Shiʿi tropes. As evidenced by the above Jaʿfar narrative, such Sunni developments may also have affected the development of formative Shiʿi accounts.

Accounts that Silence the Intimate Colloquy Scenes

Diverging from the aforementioned anecdotes that show partisan debates over the control of the ascension narrative in general and the divine colloquy scenes in particular, a different response among early traditionists was to marginalize all such constructions by downplaying any notion that Muḥammad enjoyed a substantive exchange with God on the night of the ascension apart from his negotiations over the number of daily ritual prayers that Muslims were commanded to observe.

In view of the above descriptions of the intimate colloquy scenes that were circulating among both proto-Sunnis and Shiʿis between the ninth and tenth centuries, the absence of such scenes in the relatively unadorned ascension narratives recorded in the two most important collections of Sunni hadith reports, those of Muḥammad Bukhārī (d. 870) and Muslim b. Hajjāj Qushayrī (d. 875), can be seen in a new light.[34] Those sound Sunni reports that tell the narrative in its entirety, rather than isolated anecdotes or narremes, nearly without exception trace their origin to the accounts of a single individual: Anas b. Mālik.[35] Furthermore, these sound reports transmitted by Anas b. Mālik all come to a narrative climax with the imposition of the five daily ritual prayers, making absolutely no mention of an intimate colloquy scene between Muḥammad and God. By limiting the interaction between Muḥammad and God to such a brief exchange over the number of daily ritual prayers, these "official" accounts leave no room for any partisan debate over the content of God's other message(s) to the Muslim community that might have been expressed to Muḥammad in person on the night of the ascension.

It is certainly possible that the intimate colloquy scenes reflect a development in the ascension narratives that appeared later, only after these official hadith collections were assembled. Viewing the evidence from this perspective would lead to the conclusion that the lack of substantial colloquy scenes in the ascension narratives appearing in the sound Sunni collections helps us to date the appearance of these scenes to the end of the ninth century. It is also possible, however, that their absence reflects a deliberate choice on the part of "official" scholars to exclude these intimate colloquy scenes from those reports selected for inclusion in the Sunni Sound collections. That is, the fact that they do not appear in the sound reports may be the result of a strategy on the part of a group of Sunni scholars who sought to inoculate the ascension narratives against the types of creative partisan rhetoric that competing groups might seek to inject into the body of the ascension text. The fact that Bukhārī and Muslim's extended ascension reports only include those narratives transmitted by Anas b. Mālik, not reports by others—for instance, those whom Ibn Hishām cites in his recension of Ibn Isḥāq's work, such as ʿĀ'isha, Muʿāwiyya, Qatāda, Umm Hāni', Abū Saʿīd Khudrī, et al.[36]—further suggests that the simplicity of the Sunni sound reports may have more to do with an ideological decision to promote a stripped-down ascension narrative than with concerns over preserving the most widely attested and most authentic hadith reports.

The sound Sunni collections may have maintained a deliberate silence about the intimate colloquy as a strategy to counter and/or to render moot the partisan use of these scenes in which God endorses the leadership of ʿAlī and the imams. This effort at silencing the intimate colloquy scenes can be traced not only in Sunni hadith collections but also in the widely accepted collections of Shiʿi hadith reports. I would suggest that this silence in the official sources did not satisfy subsequent generations of Muslims, as references in the work of the famous Nishapuri Sufi Abū ʿAbd al-Raḥmān Sulamī (d. 1021),[37] his student Abū al-Qāsim Qushayrī (d. 1072),[38] and many others attest.[39] The popularity of *miʿrāj* narratives that included the intimate colloquy scenes grew over time, either because of the political usefulness of these scenes for sectarian posturing, or because of the religious usefulness of these scenes for providing extra-qur'anic divine legitimacy to key concepts such as intercession. As a result, the appropriation of and contestation over the intimate colloquy scenes comes to form a central part of the ascension discourse in the middle periods of Islamic history, despite their absence from the official collections of ascension hadith reports, and the widespread perception among Sunni scholars that these official collections record the most reliable versions of the story of Muḥammad's journey.

The widespread circulation of the Ibn ʿAbbās ascension narratives in the middle periods of Islamic history demonstrates that the effort at marginalizing the more elaborate versions of the story, ones that often included a detailed account of the intimate colloquy between Muḥammad and God, was not generally successful in the pre-modern era. The evidence presented above suggests that esoteric proto-Shiʿi anecdotes about the revelation of ʿAlī's status during the intimate colloquy between Muḥammad and God on the night of the ascension, reports for which we have written evidence beginning in the ninth century, seem to have affected the emerging Sunni ascension discourse. There was undoubtedly a political dimension to the development and spread of the intimate colloquy scenes, and the political contexts in the years immediately before, during, and after the "Shiʿi century" might well have precipitated this process. Some early Shiʿi and Sunni scholars clearly used the intimate colloquy scenes of the *miʿrāj* narrative as a sectarian battleground. Meanwhile, some other scholars apparently attempted to reduce the threatening potential of these scenes by limiting the discourse, promoting as authentic only those ascension narratives originating with a single individual (Anas b. Mālik), and only those reports that remained silent about Muḥammad's intimate colloquy with God. In the contemporary era this latter approach has gained significant ground among Muslims, but in the middle periods of Islamic history it faced serious competition from the rising popularity of more detailed and full *miʿrāj* narratives, a number of which were circulated in the name of Ibn ʿAbbās, narratives that preserved evidence of the partisan contexts in which they originally were articulated.

This study has made the case that understanding the partisan use of the early *miʿrāj* accounts is crucial to a proper understanding of the formative development of the Islamic ascension discourse. The Sunni appropriations of originally Shiʿi tropes transform praise for ʿAlī into praise for the Prophet himself. References to qur'anic passages that on their surface have little to do with Muḥammad's ascension, such as the seals of the Cow chapter and the reference to the heavenly host debate, which were associated with the intimate colloquy by esoteric proto-Shiʿi authors, become adopted as standard tropes in Sunni depictions of the conversation between Muḥammad and God on the night of the ascension. While the struggle between Shiʿis and Sunnis over the content and meaning of Muḥammad's night journey was to continue in the centuries that follow, by the end of the ninth and beginning of the tenth centuries the emergence of this sectarian struggle influenced how Muslims came to narrate the story of Muḥammad's ascension, and thereby to forward and legitimize their own sectarian belief systems in the process.

Notes

This chapter was delivered as a paper at the Annual Meeting of the American Academy of Religion in Philadelphia in November 2006. Special thanks are due to Christiane Gruber for her constructive remarks both at that panel and subsequently. Errors herein are, however, my own.

1. On the basic outlines of the night journey and ascension narratives, and their development in the formative period of Islamic history, see my *Narrating Muḥammad's Night Journey: Tracing the Development of the Ibn ʿAbbas Ascension Discourse* (Albany: State University of New York Press, 2008); Brooke Olson Vuckovic's *Heavenly Journeys and Earthly Concerns: The Legacy of the Miʿrāj in the Formation of Islam* (New York and London: Routledge, 2005); Christiane Gruber's "The Prophet Muḥammad's Ascension (*Miʿrāj*) in Islamic Art and Literature, 1300–1600" (Ph.D. diss., University of Pennsylvania, 2005) and idem, *The Ilkhanid Book of Ascension: A Persian-Sunni Devotional Tale* (London: I. B. Tauris, 2009). See also the relevant encyclopedia articles, such as those by Gerhard Böwering, s.v. "Miʿrāj," *Encyclopedia of Religion;* Jamel Eddine Bencheikh, s.v. "Miʿrādj," *Encyclopaedia of Islam*; Frederick Colby and Michael Sells, "Miʿrāj," *Encyclopedia of Islam and the Muslim World.*

2. Such a pattern, long followed by Sunni Muslim scholars since the formative period, was established as the typical approach in western scholarship from the end of the nineteenth and beginning of the twentieth centuries in studies by European scholars.

3. Carl Ernst, *Following Muḥammad* (Chapel Hill: University of North Carolina Press, 2003), 46, 140.

4. On this early period of proto-Shiʿi history, see Mohammad Ali Amir-Moezzi, *La religion discrète* (Paris: Librairie Philosophique J. Vrin, 2006), especially the essay included therein titled "L'Imām dans le ciel: ascension et initiation," which was first published as "L'Imām dans le ciel: ascension et initiation (aspects de l'Imāmologie Duodécimaine)," in idem (ed.), *Le Voyage initiatique en terre d'Islam: Ascensions célestes et itinéraires spirituels* (Louvain-Paris: Peeters, 1996). Subsequent references to this essay will give the page number(s) for the 2006 edition, followed by the page number(s) for the 1996 edition in parentheses.

5. Debates in Ibn Isḥāq's narrative range from simple questions such as the number of cups that Muḥammad was offered in the "cup test" to more complex and abstract questions such as whether Muḥammad's journey took place in body, in spirit, or in some other manner. Ibn Isḥāq's version is most easily accessed in the recension of the *Biography of the Messenger of God* by Ibn Hishām, *Sīrat Rasūl Allāh,* ed. Ferdinand Wüstenfeld, vol. 1/I (Göttingen, 1856). Readers of Eng-

lish may wish to consult the translation by A. Guillaume, *The Life of Muḥammad* (Oxford: Oxford University Press, 1955), 181–187. Although I refer here to the position of "Ibn Isḥāq" as represented by the version of his account given by Ibn Hishām, I do so after having compared the Ibn Hishām recension with that of another student of Ibn Isḥāq by the name of Ibn Bukayr. I discuss the issue of interpolating Ibn Isḥāq's portrayal of the night journey and ascension accounts from the two different extant versions in my *Narrating Muḥammad's Night Journey,* 51–57.

6. For a discussion of the phrase "Shiᶜi century" in connection with the rise of the Buyids and the Fatimids in the central lands of Islamdom in the tenth and eleventh centuries, see Marshall Hodgson, *The Venture of Islam,* vol. 2 (Chicago: University of Chicago Press, 1974), 36–39.

7. See Aaron Hughes, "*Miᶜrāj* and the language of Legitimation in the Medieval Islamic and Jewish Philosophical Traditions: A Case Study of Avicenna and Abraham ibn Ezra," chapter 8 in the present volume.

8. Michael Sells, "3 Enoch (Sefer Hekhalot) and the Miᶜrāj of Abū Yazīd al-Bisṭāmī," paper read before the American Academy of Religion in Anaheim, California, November 1989. This paper was kindly provided by Michael Sells to the author.

9. Sells, "3 Enoch," 10.

10. The earliest independent work dedicated to the Prophet's ascension appears to be that of the Shiᶜi compiler Hishām b. Sālim Jawālīqī (fl. eighth century). See the notice on this figure by Josef van Ess, *Theologie und Gesellschaft im 2. und 3. Jahrhundert Hidschra* (Berlin: de Gruyter, 1991–1997), vol. 1, 345; ibid., vol. 5, 69; this work is cited and briefly discussed in Mohammad Ali Amir-Moezzi's "L'Imām dans le ciel," 136 (100).

11. In addition to his pivotal study cited above, Amir-Moezzi develops the more general concept of the "esoteric non-rational" strand of proto-Shiᶜism in his work *The Divine Guide in Early Shiᶜism: The Sources of Esotericism in Islam,* translated by David Streight (Albany: State University of New York Press, 1994).

12. See Amir-Moezzi, "L'Imām dans le ciel," 136–144 (100–110).

13. Ibid.; also see my *Narrating Muḥammad's Night Journey,* ch. 4.

14. Muḥammad b. Ḥasan Ṣaffar Qummī (d. ca. 902), *Baṣā'ir al-darajāt fī faḍā'il Āl Muḥammad,* ed. Mīrzā Muḥsin Kuchabāghī Tabrīzī (Qum: Maktabat Āyat Allāh al-ᶜUẓmā Marᶜashī Najafī, 1982), 515 (sec. 10, ch. 18, no. 36); the passage is translated into French in Amir-Moezzi, "L'Imām dans le ciel," 139–140 (104). All English translations in the present chapter are my own, made from the original language, unless otherwise stated. Here and elsewhere in this chapter, words or phrases directly quoted from the Qur'an are given in italics.

15. Amir-Moezzi, "L'Imām dans le ciel," 139 (104).

16. Q 2:285–286.

17. Furāt b. Furāt Kūfī (d. ca. 912), *Tafsīr Furāt al-Kūfī,* ed. M. al-Kāẓim (Tehran: Mu'assasat al-Ṭabᶜ wa'l Nashr, 1990), 74–75, commentary to Q 2:285–286. There are references to this passage, and other related passages among the early Shiᶜis, in Amir-Moezzi, "L'Imām dans le ciel," 139 n. 18 (103 n. 18).

18. Amir-Moezzi, "L'Imām dans le ciel," 136 n. 6 (100 n. 6), where he claims that this Jaᶜfar narrative "constitutes a parallel version to that of the Sunni Abū Saᶜīd Khudrī." While the Jaᶜfar narrative certainly draws upon the Khudrī version, it also draws substantially upon the Ibn ᶜAbbās ascension discourse, as I discuss in *Narrating Muḥammad's Night Journey,* 101–104.

19. Although the consensus of the Muslim community would come to form around the idea that the destination of Muḥammad's night journey to the furthest place of prostration (*al-masjid al-aqṣā*) represented an allusion to Jerusalem, in the formative period some Muslims apparently understood the verse differently. Instead of reading the allusion as representing a terrestrial journey to Jerusalem, some of these Muslims interpreted it as a celestial journey to the heavens directly from Mecca. An example of this latter position can be seen in the following anecdote from ᶜAlī Qummī's commentary. For a discussion of the nuances of this early debate, see Heribert Busse, "Jerusalem in the Story of Muḥammad's Night Journey and Ascension," *Jerusalem Studies in Arabic and Islam* 14 (1991): 1–40. Busse follows the lead of earlier Orientalists who argued that this fashion of interpreting Q 17:1 as a reference to a heavenly

journey preceded that of the Jerusalem interpretation. However, the fact that Ibn Hishām's recension of Ibn Isḥāq's very early discussion of the night journey already equates *al-masjid al-aqṣā* with Jerusalem proves that both interpretations originated in the formative period. I would contend that it is no longer possible, if it ever were, to determine which interpretation should be considered the original one.

20. This passage alludes to the trope that would become more developed in the Ibn ʿAbbās ascension discourse and later Sufi texts, namely that Muḥammad was forced to leave Gabriel behind during the highest stages of the night journey. In some of these versions, Gabriel explains that he would burn up were he to continue the shortest distance beyond his "known station" near the Lote Tree in the seventh heaven. See *Narrating Muḥammad's Night Journey,* chapters 8 and 9.

21. ʿAlī b. Ibrahīm al-Qummī (d. ca. 919), *Kitāb tafsīr ʿAlī b. Ibrāhīm* (Tabriz lithograph, 1895), 572–573, commentary to Q 38:67–71.

22. As cited above, this theory has been articulated with reference to the work of Jawālīqī (eighth century) by Josef van Ess, *Theologie und Gesellschaft im 2. und 3. Jahrhundert Hidschra,* vol. 1, 345; ibid., vol. 5, 69.

23. Sells, "3 Enoch," 10.

24. For example, the "heavenly host debate" trope appears in the proto-Sunni collection of sound hadith reports compiled by Tirmidhī (d. 892); see my *Narrating Muḥammad's Night Journey,* 90–92.

25. Muḥammad b. Jarīr Ṭabarī (d. 923), *Tafsīr al-Ṭabarī* (Beirut: Dār al-Kutub al-ʿIlmiyya, 1992), vol. 8, 7–12, commentary to Q 17:1. The Abū Hurayra report has been translated by Reuven Firestone in John Renard, ed., *Windows on the House of Islam* (Berkeley: University of California Press, 1998), 336–345. It has been discussed by Étienne Renaud, "Le Récit du miʿrāj: une version arabe de l'ascension du Prophète, dans le Tafsīr de Tabarī," in *Apocalypses et voyages dans l'au-delà,* ed. Claude Kappler (Paris: CERF, 1987), 267–290; see also my *Narrating Muḥammad's Night Journey,* 96–101.

26. Ṭabarī, *Tafsīr,* vol. 11, 510, commentary to Q 53:11; this passage is both quoted and discussed in my *Narrating Muḥammad's Night Journey,* 44–45.

27. On the formative development of the Ibn ʿAbbās ascension narrative, see my dissertation, "Constructing an Islamic Ascension Narrative: The Interplay of Official and Popular Culture in Pseudo-Ibn ʿAbbās" (Duke University Ph.D. diss, 2002); see also my *Narrating Muḥammad's Night Journey, passim,* but especially chapters 2, 8, and 9.

28. A hadith report recorded by Ibn Ḥibbān Bustī (d. 965), preserved by Jalāl al-Dīn al-Suyūṭī (d. 1505) in his *Lālī al-maṣnūʿa fī aḥādīth al-mawḍūʿa,* ed. Abū ʿAbd al-Raḥmān Ṣalāḥ b. Muḥammad b. ʿUwayḍa (Beirut: Dār al-Kutub al-ʿIlmiyya, 1996), 62–75. I have discovered two other recensions of the same early ḥadīth, recorded by Abū al-Qāsim Qushayrī (d. 1072) and ʿAbd al-Raḥmān Wāsiṭī (d. 1343). I examine these recensions in my *Narrating Muḥammad's Night Journey,* ch. 2, and I include a full translation of this hadith in appendix A of the same work.

29. In addition to the luminous form of ʿAlī and his family presented in the passage quoted above from Furāt Kūfī's *Tafsīr,* in another anecdote the same exegete records how God explains that he created an angel in ʿAlī's image (*fī ṣūratihi*) because of the other angels' longing for ʿAlī. The anecdote is discussed in my *Narrating Muḥammad's Night Journey,* 75–76; a French translation and further references appear in Amir-Moezzi, "L'Imām dans le ciel," 140–141 (105). As for an angel in the form of Abū Bakr, one version of the hadith in which God creates an angel "in his image" (*fī ṣūratihi*) is recorded by Muḥammad b. Yūsuf Shāmī Ṣāliḥī (d. 1535) in the final chapter of his massive work titled *"al-Āyāt al-ʿaẓīma al-bāhira fī miʿrāj sayyid ahl al-dunyā wa ʿl-ākhira,"* MS Murad Molla 332, Bayezit Kütüphanesi, Istanbul, fol. 82v. See my "Constructing an Islamic Ascension Narrative," 361.

30. References to God speaking to Muḥammad in the voice of ʿAlī can be found in Amir-Moezzi, "L'Imām dans le ciel," 140 (104); God speaking to Muḥammad in the voice of Abū Bakr appears in the modern printed version of the Ibn ʿAbbās ascension narrative, which appears to have been a later recension. Nevertheless, the latter trope certainly circulated prior to the time of Shāmī,

who records it among his collection of fabricated ascension reports; see *al-Āyāt al-ʿaẓīma,* fols. 82r–82v, a passage I translate in my "Constructing an Islamic Ascension Narrative," 359–361.

31. In Furāt Kūfī, *Tafsīr Furāt al-Kūfī,* vol. 2, 372–374 (commentary on Q 39:74), an anecdote describes an inscription on a tree at the gate of Paradise: "There is no god but God, Muḥammad is the Messenger of God, ʿAlī b. Abī Ṭālib is God's solid grip . . . the sword of his vengeance upon the idolators." The hanging sword trope, in which Muḥammad spies the "sword of vengeance" (*sayf al-nuqma*) that hangs from the throne, serves as a common feature of many Ibn ʿAbbās ascension narratives since the recension of Abū al-Ḥasan al-Bakrī (fl. thirteenth century at the latest). See my *Narrating Muḥammad's Night Journey,* chapter 8.

32. ʿAlī Qummī, *Tafsīr Qummī* (1895 lithograph), 374–375, commentary on Q 17:1. The entire Jaʿfar narrative spans 368–376 in the 1895 lithograph edition. The narrative was reproduced wholesale in Majlisī, *Biḥār al-anwār* (Tehran and Qum: Ḥaydarī, 1956–1972), vol. 18, 319–331; this later version of Majlisī was translated into English by James Merrick in *The Life and Religion of Muḥammad* (Boston: Phillips, Sampson & Co, 1850), vol. 2, 192–199.

33. A discussion of this Jaʿfar ascension hadith report appears in my *Narrating Muḥammad's Night Journey,* 105–108.

34. Abū ʿAbd Allāh Muḥammad b. Ismaʿīl Bukhārī (d. 870), *Ṣaḥīḥ Bukhārī,* ed. Muḥammad Nizār Tamīm and Haytham Nizār Tamīm (Beirut: Sharikhat Dār al-Arqām b. Abī Arqām, n.d.); Muslim b. Ḥajjāj al-Qushayrī al-Naysabūrī (d. 875), *Ṣaḥīḥ Muslim,* (Beirut: Dār al-Kutub al-ʿIlmiyya, 1998).

35. See my *Narrating Muḥammad's Night Journey,* 81–82.

36. Ibn Hishām, *Sīrat Rasūl Allāh,* 263; Guillaume, *The Life of Muḥammad,* 181; and Colby, *Narrating Muḥammad's Night Journey,* 51–57.

37. Sulamī, *The Subtleties of the Ascension,* trans. Frederick Colby (Loisville, KY: Fons Vitae, 2006).

38. al-Qushayrī, *Kitāb al-Miʿrāj,* ed. ʿAlī Ḥasan ʿAbd al-Qādir (Cairo: Dār al-Kutub al-Ḥadītha, 1964).

39. Subsequent Sunni authors of Arabic books dedicated to working out the issues arising from the accounts of Muḥammad's ascension are too numerous to mention; see the extensive, if incomplete, bibliography of works in the introduction to Suyūṭī, *al-Āya al-kubrā,* ed. Muḥyī al-Dīn Mistū (Beirut: Dār Ibn Kathīr, 1987; Medina: Dār al-Turāth, 1987).

7

Prophetic Ascent and Initiatory Ascent in Qāḍī al-Nuʿmān's *Asās al-Taʾwīl*

ELIZABETH R. ALEXANDRIN

The image of the Prophet Muḥammad as an exemplar and model of individual practice is especially compelling in the mystical traditions of Islam. Two esteemed scholars of the mystical traditions of Islam, Schimmel and Sells, have examined the Prophet Muḥammad's ascent (*miʿrāj*) as a paradigm for the narration of individual mystical experience.[1] Less scholarly attention, however, has been directed to Ismāʿīlī Shiʿism as one of the mystical traditions of Islam. In this study, we shall see how the medieval Fatimid Ismāʿīlī tradition interpreted the qur'anic passages concerned with prophetic ascent in order to construct a set of parallel symbolic discourses for narrating mystical and prophetic experiences. Key to understanding the ascension motif in the Ismāʿīlī tradition is that the ascent may take on the meaning of the individual's gradual apprehension of the continuum of exoteric and esoteric knowledge in tandem with the revealed religions and the interpretation of their scriptures. The necessary training (*tarbiyyah*) in the Ismāʿīlī missionary organization itself, the "Calling" (*daʿwah*), leads to the individual's acquisition of exoteric and esoteric knowledge through religious instruction and mystical or initiatory experience. While occasionally providing glimpses into the rich and varied expanse of the Fatimid Ismāʿīlī tradition, this study will draw upon on select passages from Qāḍī al-Nuʿmān's *Asās al-Taʾwīl* (The Foundation of Allegorical Interpretation) in order to explore the themes of prophetic and initiatory ascent. As shall be seen in what follows, the parameters of the individual practitioner's potential for spiritual perfection *qua* mystical ascent are defined on the basis of a reading of the qur'anic verses on the prophethood of Abraham (Ibrāhīm) and the Prophet Muḥammad's Night Journey (*isrāʾ*) and ascension (*miʿrāj*).

Definitions

Just as there are many different academic approaches for studying diversity in the Islamic tradition, there are many scholarly definitions of what constitutes Islamic mysticism. At times the terms mysticism and esotericism are conflated, as are such expressions as "mystical knowledge" and "esoteric knowledge." Morris has argued that most definitions of Islamic mysticism have relied exclusively on establishing a set of distinct modes of piety that allude to the interiorization of religious knowledge or individual mystical experience. These definitions, by and large, refer to Western academic perceptions of the historical development of Sufism. Morris's position is that Sufi texts, as a result, have thus frequently been studied in isolation, without much regard for a larger understanding of the spirituality entailed in the Qur'an and Islam's religious tenets. Reconsidering the scope of Islamic mysticism, as Morris has suggested, would provide a means for approaching Shiʿism, and by extension Ismāʿīlism, as mystical traditions of Islam.[2]

Before beginning our discussion of prophetic and initiatory ascent in Qāḍī al-Nuʿmān's *Asās al-Ta'wīl,* it is important first to present in general terms some of the central concepts of Ismāʿīlī thought. Therefore, what follows is a brief presentation of how the medieval Ismāʿīlī tradition has approached and interpreted key Islamic practices and religious tenets in the light of the qur'anic text and the layers of meaning incorporated in it as revealed scripture, that is, how it has been interpreted both "literally" and "metaphorically."

Ismāʿīlism features two dimensions of prophetic thought. Both dimensions of prophetic thought place particular emphasis on the redemptive strategies available to the individual practitioner through the emulation of the prophetic exemplar of Muḥammad and the Ismāʿīlī *imāms* who will take his place after his death. In the Ismāʿīlī tradition, the horizontal dimension of history leads to salvation. Sacred history is recapitulated in the Shiʿi concept of *imāmah,* where the *imāms* represent the sole historical, authoritative continuation of prophecy and where they, after the death of the Prophet Muḥammad, take on his role as "divine guides" on earth.[3] Due to the fact that in the Ismāʿīlī tradition the *imāms* transmit to the community of believers the esoteric interpretation of the Qur'an (*ta'wīl*), they are also granted the love and obedience that is foremost due to the Prophet Muḥammad. The qur'anic verse "Say: if you love God, follow me and God will love you" (Q 3:29) best exemplifies the love and obedience reserved for the *imāms* in the Ismāʿīlī tradition.

Another aspect of the horizontal dimension of history and perhaps even more indicative of some central beliefs in the Ismāʿīlī tradition is the concept of the cycles of prophetic history. In the Ismāʿīlī tradition, the cycles of prophecy commenced with Adam as the first human being and will draw to a close at an undisclosed point in the future with the advent of a seventh figure, the messianic "Rising One" (*al-Qā'im*).[4] Of particular importance to understanding Ismāʿīlī soteriology is to grasp how the two dimensions of prophetic thought are embodied and represented by the hierarchies of the missionary organization of the Ismāʿīlīs, the Calling (*daʿwah*), and the ranks of religion (*ḥudūd al-dīn*). For example, Ismāʿīlī authors of the medieval period discuss how gradual perfection takes place on the macrocosmic and microcosmic levels. This perfection transpires through the individual's acquisition of the esoteric knowledge that the Calling and the ranks of religion provide. In this sense, the Calling provides both the exoteric and esoteric aspects of religion, that is, exoteric revelation and esoteric interpretation. In terms of the horizontal dimension of history, it is the perfecting guidance of the ranks of religion that brings the cycles of prophetic history to a close and ushers in the appearance of the *Qā'im* and the Resurrection (*qiyāmah*) at the end of time.

As for the vertical dimension of prophetic thought, an ascent (*miʿrāj*) is implied in conjunction with allegorical interpretation (*ta'wīl*), and a descent with the divine assistance (*ta'yīd*) associated with the revelatory experience. In fact, two qur'anic themes, the designation of prophethood and the reception of prophetic revelation, are implied in the arcs of ascent and descent. Parallel to employing qur'anic themes and examples, medieval Ismāʿīlī authors often introduced Neoplatonic concepts into their discussions of prophetic and initiatory ascent. For example, just as the Universal Soul may incline toward the natural world, turn downward, and become entrapped in the material domain and the sensate (an arc descending downward), so may the Universal Soul yearn for the Universal Intellect's perfection and ascend upward in order to apprehend pure intelligibles (an arc ascending upward).[5] In terms of the individual practitioner's gradual perfection, the dynamic of descent and ascent occurs on the microcosmic level. The very same dynamic is most clearly seen in the examples of the divine assistance and the esoteric interpretation of the Qur'an that the perfected human being may receive directly from Intellect itself, without any sort of intermediaries.

This chapter is concerned with this second, vertical dimension of Ismāʿīlī prophetic thought, and in particular with the themes of initiatory ascent and prophetic ascent as discussed in the medieval Ismāʿīlī tradition. This study introduces how in the Fatimid Ismāʿīlī tradition, individual initiatory ascent is modeled in part on the ascent of the Prophet Muḥammad. Qāḍī al-Nuʿmān's (d. 974) Fatimid Ismāʿīlī work, *Asās al-Ta'wīl,* forms an early example of the medieval Islamic employment of the Prophet Muḥammad's ascent as a model for individual mystical, or more specifically, initiatory experience. Yet *Asās al-Ta'wīl* reflects the methods of tenth-century Fatimid Ismāʿīlī qur'anic interpretation, which promotes the centrality of the "stories of the prophets" (*qiṣaṣ al-anbiyā'*) to medieval Ismāʿīlī thought. As this study will present, the symbolic significance of the Prophet Muḥammad's ascension is intimately intertwined with the qur'anic story of Abraham's prophethood. Muḥammad's ascension maintains its central importance as a core Islamic belief even as the story of Abraham comes to denote the role of the *imāms* throughout the cycles of prophecy. Therefore, the Fatimid Ismāʿīlī tradition of the allegorical interpretation of the qur'anic passages concerning prophetic ascent receives attention in what follows in order to show how Qāḍī al-Nuʿmān's theory of the cycles of prophecy lends its hand to the elaboration of two parallel ascent narratives in which the Prophet Muḥammad and Abraham figure most prominently.

Qur'anic Exemplars of Obedience and Perfection: The Ascents of Abraham and Muḥammad

As we turn our attention to the medieval Ismāʿīlī tradition, it is important to note that the Fatimid Ismāʿīlī author Qāḍī al-Nuʿmān introduces a certain premise concerning the ranks of religion in his *Asās al-Ta'wīl.* Most notably, Qāḍī al-Nuʿmān introduces the pivotal importance of the practice of obedience (*ṭāʿah*) to the *imām* as exemplified by the prophet Abraham. He correlates the practice of obedience to the function of divine guidance and authority (*walāyah*) in order to hyper-articulate the centrality of the Ismāʿīlī Calling throughout sacred history. For Qāḍī al-Nuʿmān, as for later Fatimid Ismāʿīlī authors, the Calling in each of the prophetic cycles comes to signify the corporeal, physical component of the ranks of religion. The Calling of each epoch, like the ranks of religion, thereby provides the necessary training (*tarbiyyah*) not least for individual practitioners but for the prophets as well.[6]

In many respects, Qāḍī al-Nuʿmān's works on the central tenets of the Islamic tradition came to form the "core curriculum" of the Fatimid Ismāʿīlī missionary organization and its associated instructional lectures (*majālis*) in Cairo during the tenth and eleventh centuries.[7] For this reason, we would like to use the work of a later Fatimid Ismāʿīlī author, al-Mu'ayyad fī al-Dīn al-Shīrāzī (d. ca. 1078), in order to introduce the themes of initiatory and prophetic ascent in the medieval Ismāʿīlī tradition.[8] In fact, there are two particular passages on the "absolute human being" (*al-insān al-muṭlaq*)[9] in al-Mu'ayyad's main doctrinal work that address the significance of the parallel ascent narratives of Muḥammad and Abraham in the Fatimid Ismāʿīlī tradition. These passages clarify specifically how prophethood and prophetic ascent are linked to the gradual perfection of the human being that takes place initially with the training that the Calling provides in each prophetic cycle. As is the case in *Asās al-Ta'wīl,* the two prophetic ascents of Abraham and Muḥammad run along parallel lines: each ascent narrative commences with initiation into the ranks of religion and culminates in the recognition of God's unity (*tawḥīd*) and the attainment of proximity to God.

Al-Mu'ayyad also couches individual ascent in the metaphoric language of human birth, growth, and development. The individual human being, in his/her process of ascent and perfection, emulates both the Universal Soul and the Universal Intellect.[10] Spiritual development and perfection occur parallel to human physical growth and maturation, where the individual is "nurtured" and assisted by both the physical and spiritual realms, that is, the "Heavens and Earth" (Q 50:38) of the ranks of religion.[11] This is the meaning behind al-Mu'ayyad's metaphor when he states that only the individual who has been properly nurtured through the Calling's upbringing while in this world will enter into the vast and unlimited space of the World of Intellect and Soul, which is "what no eye has seen, and no ear heard, nor has entered the heart of man."[12] Al-Mu'ayyad's account also presents one of the more subtle narratives on the proximity to God that the absolute human being may potentially attain through spiritual ascent.[13] An important question, nonetheless, emerges: do al-Mu'ayyad's comments suggest that even prophets must receive the initial training provided by the Calling before receiving prophetic revelation?

In another set of lectures on the "stories of the prophets" from the *Majālis al-Mu'ayyadiyyah* (The Lectures), al-Mu'ayyad aims to answer this question. He addresses the implications of the paradigm of prophetic ascent for the individual practitioner in terms of the prophet Abraham's initiatory ascent and his reception of prophetic revelation.[14] Al-Mu'ayyad's discussions of prophetic ascent are not limited to the interpretation of the qur'anic narratives on the Prophet Muḥammad's ascent or Night Journey (Q 17:1). As we shall see in what follows, Qāḍī al-Nuʿmān similarly does not restrict his discussion of prophetic ascent to Muḥammad's ascension alone. On the one hand, al-Mu'ayyad's treatment of the qur'anic narrative on the prophet Abraham's ascent through the corporeal and celestial ranks of religion offers a parallel commentary on the concept of the human being from the perspective of the soul's ascent and acquisition of divine assistance. On the other hand, with regard to the issue of prophetic inheritance, al-Mu'ayyad sets the record straight that Abraham is a human being, like any other individual. Al-Mu'ayyad does this through the example of Abraham's initial training in the elite circle of the Calling before he could receive prophetic revelation and the designation of prophethood symbolized by his acceptance of the covenant (*mīthāq*).[15]

As in al-Mu'ayyad's work, Qāḍī al-Nuʿmān's *Asās al-Ta'wīl* addresses the theme of initiatory ascent through the corporeal and celestial ranks of religion. In allegorical reference to the qur'anic material, the individual soul's ascent serves as one of the main focal points of Qāḍī al-Nuʿmān's work, because the reception of divine assistance necessarily implies having transcended the limits of the corporeal ranks of the Calling's hierarchy, thereby proceeding from the sensible (*maḥsūs*) to the intelligible (*maʿqūl*) through the means of allegorical interpretation. The reception of divine assistance and the initiatory ascent itself are doubly nuanced as a *miʿrāj*, in the sense that they are modeled on the prophet Muḥammad's *isrā'* or Night Journey (Q 17:1). The Prophet Muḥammad's *miʿrāj* thus represents the spiritual progress and noetic journey of the individual.[16] Stressing the importance of the cycles of prophetic history in conjunction with presenting the pivotal function of the spiritual hierarchy in terms of the training of each prophet, the issue of prophetic revelation is broached in terms of the different modalities of scripture as well as the apprehension of the "vision of God." For example, the scriptures of the Torah, the Gospels, and the Qur'an, bestowed upon the prophets Moses (Mūsā), Jesus (ʿĪsā), and Muḥammad respectively, allude to their distinctive and exclusive prophetic experiences. That is to say, each of these scriptures alludes to the prophetic ascent unique to each of these prophets.[17]

In Qāḍī al-Nuʿmān's presentation of Abraham's ascent and reception of prophetic revelation, the transmission of divine assistance (*ta'yīd*) from God's word (*ka-*

limah) occurs through the ranks of religion, from the upper (*ʿulwiyyah*) or celestial realm, downward to the lower (*sufliyyah*) or terrestrial (*arḍiyyah*) ranks.[18] This too comprises an arc of descent. From within the realm of Ismāʿīlī sacred history, the prophet Abraham's training, initiatory ascent, and designation of prophetic mission defines the potential range of visionary experience for the individual human being as capable of transcending the senses' perceptions. It calls attention to the fact that the ascent under discussion is a spiritual ascent of the soul. Abraham's training and ascent demarcate the ranks embodied in the hierarchy of the Calling and the ranks of religion that exist in each of the prophetic cycles. Additionally, the cycle of Abraham's prophetic mission marks the epoch in which religious practices, such as prayer, pilgrimage, and monotheistic worship, were first established.[19]

Prophetic Ascent in Qāḍī al-Nuʿmān's *Asās al-Ta'wīl*

In order to better understand Qāḍī al-Nuʿmān's theory of prophetic ascent, and the Prophet Muḥammad's ascension in particular, we must turn to his commentary on the story of Abraham (*qiṣṣat Ibrāhīm*) in the *Asās al-Ta'wīl,* which constitutes one chapter of the work. First, however, a few words on the text of the *Asās al-Ta'wīl* are necessary. In sum, the *Asās al-Ta'wīl* reflects some of the central doctrinal interests and exegetical concerns of the tenth-century Fatimid missionary organization in Cairo. The work's main focus is the "stories of the prophets." Qāḍī al-Nuʿmān devotes a chapter to the life of each prophet with the Ismāʿīlī doctrine of the "cycles of prophecy" clearly in mind. The reason for this focus is that the history of prophecy commences with Adam and concludes with the appearance of the *Qā'im.* Not only the prophets but the Ismāʿīlī *daʿwah* plays a significant role in the course of prophecy's dramatic history, foremost by providing the *ta'wīl* of revealed scriptures. The *Asās al-Ta'wīl*'s exegetical approach can be defined in simple terms as moving, verse by verse, phrase by phrase, and word by word, from the literal meaning of the qur'anic text to other deeper readings. Much attention is paid to drawing out through *ta'wīl* the range of meanings connected to each set of qur'anic verses on the pre-Islamic prophets and the Prophet Muḥammad. Through *ta'wīl,* key qur'anic passages and phrases are likewise drawn back to the meaning and significance of Ismāʿīlī doctrines.

In the *Asās al-Ta'wīl,* Qāḍī al-Nuʿmān's commentary on the story of Abraham serves a distinct purpose in terms of laying the foundation for the parallel symbolic discourses previously mentioned. In order to define the initiatory experience of the prophetic ascent, Qāḍī al-Nuʿmān employs the examples of the prophets Enoch, Jesus, and Muḥammad to indicate how God "raised" (*rafʿ*) individual human beings. He thus marks the prophetic ascent as foremost involving the soul's spiritual ascent. The ascension narrative of the Prophet Muḥammad first receives attention in the course of Qāḍī al-Nuʿmān's commentary on the story of Abraham.

For Qāḍī al-Nuʿmān, the *isrā'* epitomizes the Prophet Muḥammad's ascent. He begins his commentary on prophetic ascent by quoting Qur'an 17:1, and then goes on to explain that Muḥammad's Night Journey, in which he saw the angels, the prophets, and the messengers, alludes to his ascent in the heaven.[20] Also in the course of this initial presentation of Muḥammad's prophetic ascent, Qāḍī al-Nuʿmān cites an example of existing reports on Muḥammad's Night Journey. In this part of his commentary on the story of Abraham, the author's brief comments are directed to the widespread discussion concerning the prophetic ascent of Muḥammad in terms of whether it constituted a physical or a solely spiritual ascent.[21] With implications for an Ismāʿīlī theory of initiatory ascent, Qāḍī al-Nuʿman advances the argument that the prophetic ascent is one in which the souls of the prophets are purified and perfected through their contact with the upper souls (*al-arwāḥ al-ʿulwiyyah*).[22] He asserts that, just as God has previously selected individual prophets and "raised" them spiritually, the Prophet Muḥammad's ascent is likewise an ascent of the soul. Implicit in Qāḍī al-Nuʿmān's initial commentary on the Night Journey in the story of Abraham is that individual practitioners may potentially experience spiritual ascent through their training in the *daʿwah*.

The Prophet Muḥammad's Night Journey also defines the parameters of the reception of prophetic revelation. Situated in the context of Ismāʿīlī symbolic cosmology, the focal point of mystical apprehension in the initiatory ascent is, in fact, the hierarchy of the ranks of religion and the Calling in God's creation. The order and the arrangement of the spiritual hierarchy, as it specifically culminates in Muḥammad's prophetic mission, is most clearly seen in one particular passage from *Asās al-Ta'wīl*. Qāḍī al-Nuʿmān explains that the true and faithful followers of Muḥammad established his command during his lifetime and continued to uphold and maintain it after his death. Together, his followers form the "rope of God" (*ḥabl Allāh*), establishing the links of a chain that continuously connect individual practitioners, on the lower end of the continuum, to the *imāms*, the *asās* (that is, the direct legatee to the speaking-prophet of the cycle, the *nāṭiq*), and then to the Prophet Muḥammad himself.[23] Qāḍī al-Nuʿmān's aim here is to clarify his arguments concerning the superiority of the Prophet Muḥammad while supporting the necessity of obedience to the lower ranks of religion in terms of individual practice.[24]

But what precisely is the role of the ranks of religion in the process of ascent? As Gilliot has indicated, the *Imāmī* treatise that al-Māturīdī draws upon in his qur'anic commentary bears striking similarities with what is found in the Persian School's treatment of Q 6:75–79, where the ranks of religion from Ismāʿīlī cosmology assist in the prophet Abraham's ascent and in his reception of prophethood.[25] This qur'anic passage is correlated to Abraham's vision of "the dominion of the Heavens and the Earth" (Q 6:75). Gilliot's observations hold much relevance to the medieval Ismāʿīlī commentaries on the story of Abraham, especially with regard to the question of whether or not the prophets are exempt from error if they, like Abraham, were not originally monotheists and worshipped other gods before the designation of their respective prophetic missions.[26] There exists another dimension to the debate on the gradual reception of prophetic revelation in tandem with the ontological perfection of the individual human being. The medieval Ismāʿīlī commentaries on the story of Abraham also focus on the question of Abraham's rejection of the cult of astral bodies as a feature of his development, maturation, and perfection as a human being.[27]

In the Fatimid Ismāʿīlī context, the figure of Abraham comes to signify an alternative modality of receiving prophetic revelation, inasmuch as the defining features of his prophetic mission are specific to his epoch. Abraham is characterized by the qualities of being the friend of God (*khalīl Allāh*) and the faithful one (*wafā'*) in comparison to the other prophets.[28] According to Qāḍī al-Nuʿmān, Abraham's exclusivity as a prophet rests on the fact that "God the Most High mentioned disclosing to Abraham the kingdom of the heavens and the earth, because God, may He be praised, does not reveal this except to the one approved of from His creation."[29] Implied in this passage is that God selects the most praiseworthy individuals, foremost the prophets and the "friends of God," to witness the glory of His creation. Yet in other passages of his commentary on the story of Abraham, Qāḍī al-Nuʿmān notes the gradual progression of Abraham through the Calling and that God "promised to him to establish him as an *imām*."[30] Ascending upward through the ranks of religion, from the rank of proof (*ḥujjah*), "God raised him to the rank (*darajah*) of *imām*-hood (*al-asāsiyyah*) and honored him with prophethood and messengership."[31] He stresses that even the prophets are not exempt from the necessary training the *daʿwah* provides in each cycle of prophetic history.

Qāḍī al-Nuʿmān is well known in the Ismāʿīlī tradition for his commentaries on the central ritual practices and religious tenets of Islam, and in particular for the following two works: *Kitāb Daʿā'im al-Islām* (The Book of the Pillars of Islam) and *Ta'wīl Daʿā'im al-Islām* (The Allegorical Interpretation of the Pillars of Islam). The *Asās al-Ta'wīl* is therefore informed in part by the author's other "legalistic" works. In the *Asās al-Ta'wīl,* his discussion of the qur'anic verses on Abraham aims to introduce Abraham as a qur'anic exemplar from within the realm of sacred history. Abraham maintains a certain special status as a prophet because he established for the future religious community (*ummah*) of Islam the fundamental religious tenets of prayer and pilgrimage to the Kaʿba (*al-bayt al-ḥarām*).[32] Abraham's foundation of the Kaʿba in Mecca forms a substantial focal point in Qāḍī al-Nuʿmān's commentary on the story of Abraham. In *Asās al-Ta'wīl,* there are levels of reverberation within the narrative concerning how Abraham constructed the Kaʿba. At the outset of his commentary, the author does not posit an exclusively Ismāʿīlī interpretation of prophetic history. Further into his commentary, however, he puts forth his allegorical interpretation of Q 2:127 with reference to the cycles of prophecy.[33] The foundations (*qawāʿid*) of the Kaʿba (*al-bayt*) represent the four speaking-prophets (*nuṭaqā'*—the prophets who bring scriptures): Moses and Jesus from the lineage of Isaac (Isḥāq), and Muḥammad and the *Qā'im,* from the lineage of Ishmael (Ismāʿīl).[34]

In addition, while the architectural structure of the Kaʿba takes on the significance of a strand of prophetic history narrated by the Qur'an, it symbolizes the ranks of the Ismāʿīlī missionary organization in both ideal and abstract terms. Implied in the passage that follows in Qāḍī al-Nuʿmān's commentary on the story of Abraham is the ranking of the members in the hierarchy of the Calling: the *imām,* the *ḥujjah,* the speaking-prophet (*nāṭiq*), and the legatee of the prophet (*asās*). Abraham serves as a qur'anic exemplar of the practice of obedience to the *imām,* and by extension, the Ismāʿīlī *daʿwah.* Qāḍī al-Nuʿmān clarifies that in relation to the meaning of obedience and the two prayers alluded to in the qur'anic verse, Abraham turned toward the speaking-prophet of his time, but only first through the speaking-prophet's legatee, emulating the gradual initiation into the hierarchy of the Calling itself.[35] In this manner, first through the means of obedience to the legatee, Abraham was then able to rely on the speaking-prophet of his epoch and to turn toward him in the practice of obedience.[36] Attaining to these particular ranks in the Calling indicates Abraham's training and gradual perfection, all of which precede his designation as a prophet himself. The very same paradigm, modeled on Abraham's gradual reception of prophethood, is central to the Fatimid Ismāʿīlī treatment of prophetic ascent in general, and the Prophet Muḥammad's Night Journey in particular.

In *Asās al-Ta'wīl,* the esoteric interpretation of the Prophet Muḥammad's Night Journey from the "Blessed Mosque" (*al-masjid al-ḥarām*) to the "Furthest Mosque" (*al-masjid al-aqṣā*)—or, as Qāḍī al-Nuʿmān elucidates, from the Kaʿba in Mecca to the Holy Mosque in Jerusalem—is correlated to the ranks of the Calling and the degrees embodied in the ranks of religion.[37] According to Qāḍī al-Nuʿmān's allegorical interpretation, the Prophet's ascent to heaven is tantamount to the disclosure of the dominion of both the lower and the celestial degrees, in the same manner that the knowledge of the degrees was revealed and disclosed to the prophet Abraham. At this point in the allegorical interpretation of the Night Journey, Qāḍī al-Nuʿmān then returns to the commentary he initially put forth in the section on the story of Abraham, specifically on the qur'anic verse "Abraham saw the dominion of the Heavens and the Earth" (Q 6:75). Reflecting the emphasis of his commentary on prophetic ascent in fundamental ways, the author's correlation between the prophetic ascent of Abraham and the Night Journey of the Prophet Muḥammad indicates the common ground of the initiatory experience, in terms of observing the ranks of religion in the process of ascent.[38]

Qāḍī al-Nuʿmān nevertheless distinguishes between the prophetic experiences of Abraham and Muḥammad. The main point of differentiation lies in the fact that, as he explains, when the Prophet Muḥammad reached the proximity to God of "two bow-lengths" (*qāb qawsayn*) (Q 53:9), he was still only capable of perceiving the upper celestial ranks, but "He saw them purely, clearly, with the eye of his heart."[39] Hence, the ranks the Prophet Muḥammad observed in his Night Journey are the "signs" mentioned in Q 17:1. Qāḍī al-Nuʿmān treats the sign from Q 17:1 as equivalent to "the dominion of the Heavens and the Earth" from Q 6:75 that Abraham perceived: the celestial degrees or uppermost ranks of religion.[40] Muḥammad's vision of the ranks during the Night Journey, however, is distinguished from Abraham's initiatory ascent, based on Qāḍī al-Nuʿmān's interpretation of the end of the Night Journey verse: "in order that We might show him some of Our signs: for He is the All-Hearing and All-Seeing" (Q 17:1).[41] The correlation of the ranks of the Calling to the Night Journey provides a visionary topography to Muḥammad's prophetic ascent. In conjunction with Qur'an 48:1, "Verily we have granted you a manifest victory," Qāḍī al-Nuʿmān states:

> Then God made him ascend to the world of His dominion (*ʿālam malakūtihi*) and disclosed to him the degrees of His Heavens, and He informed him of the knowledge of His unseen (*ghayb*).[42] By this, He distinguished him over all of His prophets. He drew him near to His presence from the uppermost celestial ranks, and that is the saying of God the Most High, "Glory to the one who took His servant for a journey by night from the sacred mosque to the farthest mosque whose precincts We did bless, in order that We might show him some of Our signs: for He is the All-Hearing and the All-Seeing" (Q 17:1).[43]

The distinctiveness of the Prophet Muḥammad's ascent assures his superiority over the other prophets. Qāḍī al-Nuʿmān's commentary also provides further insight into his theory of the prophetic cycles, where Muḥammad is the final and most perfect of the prophets and ʿAlī's role as *imām* lends additional weight to the importance of the Ismāʿīlī Calling in the last cycle of prophetic history. As noted by Qāḍī al-Nuʿmān: "Muḥammad (prayers and peace be upon him) is the most excellent of the Houses (*al-buyūt*) and his Gate (*Bāb*), ʿAlī, is the most preferred of the Gates."[44] He further explains, "ʿAlī (prayers and peace be upon him) is the most preferred (*afḍal*) Gate of the ranks of God, who are the speaking-prophets, and the wisdom of God is preserved, concealed in His Houses, and the most preferred of his Houses is Muḥammad."[45] Qāḍī al-Nuʿmān's statements on the relationship between the speaking-prophets and their legatees (the *imāms*) speaks to the necessary relationship between the transmission of the exoteric revelation of scripture and its exoteric interpretation to the community of believers. In structural terms, the upper (spiritual) ranks and the lower (corporeal) ranks of religion are the vehicles that transmit the exoteric and esoteric forms of knowledge to individuals. Abraham's initiatory ascent, or his gradual recognition of God's unity, demarcates the lower and upper stages of the ranks of religion. Abraham's obedience to the ranks of religion represents the practice of *ṭāʿah* that individual practitioners owe to the *imām* of the time.

In the example of the story of Abraham, the upper (*ʿulwiyyah*) and lower (*sufliyyah*) ranks parallel each other, but they function with respect to the ascent of the souls of the prophets (that is, the arc of ascent) and the transmission of divine assistance from the celestial realm to the earthly realm (the arc of descent).[46] As noted previously, in the earthly realm, the corporeal intermediaries, such as the ranks, are of unequivocal importance for the spiritual development of the individual practitioner.[47] The ascent through the Calling and the ranks of religion does not attenuate the necessity of the corporeal intermediaries, but rather the corporeal intermediaries form an intrinsic part of the prophet Abraham's vision itself. As Qāḍī al-Nuʿmān explains:

> Likewise Abraham (may God's prayers be upon Him) said when he saw the first of the upper (celestial), divine (*malakūtiyyah*), heavenly ranks of religion (*ḥudūd*), "He said: This is my Lord" (Q 6:78). He likewise said it for the second and the third, for when he saw it, he attained to what was above him and he abandoned the independent utmost limit (*al-mutanahī al-mustaqill*), and he held fast to the highest one until it came to an end. Then he abandoned it, as it was described by God the most Exalted and Glorious in His book, that he turned himself toward the Creator of Creation (*bāri al-bari'ah*), and the Endower (*Fāṭir*) of "the Heavens and the Earth" (Q 6: 79), [for] every limit (*ḥadd*) and delimited thing (*maḥdūd*) is beneath him, and he is the one who is elevated (*al-mutaʿalli*) above the limits (*ḥudūd*) and the ones delimited (*maḥdūdāt*) according to his capacity. This is just as "the dominion of the heavens" (Q 6:75), which God the Exalted and Glorious mentioned that Abraham saw, are the upper limits (*al-ḥudūd al-ʿulwiyyah*) that transfer the *ta'yīd* from them to the lower limits (*al-ḥudūd al-sufliyyah*).[48]

Why are the examples of prophetic ascent through the ranks of religion drawn from *Asās al-Ta'wīl* significant? The visionary aspect of prophetic ascent lays the groundwork for a symbolic and technical lexicon of Ismāʿīlī terms, based on qur'anic verses, in such a manner that the qur'anic narratives are drawn back into the realm of the individual practitioner's obedience, the religious duty of *walāyah* entailed in the practice of *ṭāʿah*. In *Asās al-Ta'wīl,* individual human beings are set apart into groups on the basis of the distinctions of individual soul. Individual human beings possess two types of soul with the potential for mystical and initiatory ascent. The two types of soul the individual possesses echo the ranks of religion in terms of the upper and lower demarcations of God's creation into the realm of the heavens and their dominion, the earth.

> God the Most Exalted and Glorious reveals to him the pure, superior souls (*al-arwāḥ al-zakiyyah al-fāḍilah*) who devoted themselves to Him, and commended His obedience (*ṭāʿah*), and He chose them to praise Him. He selected them, distinguished them, and was pleased with them. Then He discloses to them the dominion of the heavens (*malakūt al-samāwāt*), so they unite with the upper, heavenly souls (*bi al-arwāḥ al-ʿulwiyyah al-samawiyyah*) without the bodies (*al-ajsād*) that seek refuge in the earthy density (*al-kathīfah al-arḍiyyah*).[49]

With this passage, Qāḍī al-Nuʿmān discusses how the individual, as was mentioned in the beginning of this chapter, may yearn for Universal Intellect's perfection. He or she may cast aside the material domain and turn upward, emulating the qur'anic exemplars of obedience and perfection, Abraham and Muḥammad, the models for the spiritual ascent of the perfect human being.

Reflecting the richness of the Fatimid Ismāʿīlī tradition, Qāḍī al-Nuʿmān's *Asās al-Ta'wīl* presents a theory of individual mystical or initiatory experience based on two qur'anic exemplars, Abraham and Muḥammad. In ascent, the hierarchies of the *daʿwah* and the ranks of religion come to function as external symbolic referents in order to articulate the profoundly initiatory aspect of the very knowledge the human being may attain through God's selection.[50]

This chapter has explained how Qāḍī al-Nuʿmān's commentaries on the Prophet Muḥammad's Night Journey and the story of Abraham outline a doctrinal position where individual practitioners may potentially experience spiritual ascent through their training in the *daʿwah*. Arguably, more research is required in terms of situating medieval Fatimid Ismāʿīlī texts within the scope of the medieval mystical traditions of Islam.

Notes

1. Annemarie Schimmel, *And Muhammad is His Messenger* (Chapel Hill: University of North Carolina Press, 1985), 1–66; Michael Sells, *Early Islamic Mysticism* (New York: Paulist Press, 1996), 47.

2. J. W. Morris, "Situating Islamic 'Mysticism': Between Written Traditions and Popular Spirituality," in *Mystics of the Book*, ed. Richard Herrera (New York/Berlin: P. Lang, 1993), 293–334.

3. Shin Nomoto, "Early Ismāʿīlī Thought on Prophecy according to the *Kitāb al-Iṣlāḥ* by Abū Ḥātim al-Rāzī (d. ca. 322/ 934–5)," Ph.D. diss., McGill University, 2000, 2–3.

4. Mohammad Ali Amir-Moezzi, *Le Guide divin dans le shi'isme originel* (Paris: Verdier, 1992); trans. David Streight, *The Divine Guide in Early Shiʿism* (Albany: State University of New York Press, 1994), 19; and Nomoto, "Early Ismāʿīlī Thought on Prophecy," 2–3.

5. One of the most remarkable Neoplatonist authors in the medieval Ismāʿīlī tradition is Abū Yaʿqūb al-Sijistānī (d. ca. 982 CE). Two of his works, *Kashf al-Maḥjūb* (The Unveiling of the Hidden) and *Kitāb al-Yanābīʿ* (The Wellsprings of Wisdom), present several theories on the relationship between Universal Intellect and Universal Soul on the macrocosmic and microcosmic levels of God's creation. See Sijistānī, *Kashf al-Maḥjūb*, ed. Henri Corbin (Tehran and Paris: Département d'Iranologie de l'Institut francoiranien, 1949); intro. and trans. Hermann Landolt, in *An Anthology of Philosophy in Persia*, ed. Seyyed Hossein Nasr and Mehdi Aminrazavi (Oxford: Oxford University Press, 2001); and *Kitāb al-Yanābīʿ*, in *Trilogie ismaélienne*, ed. Henri Corbin (Tehran and Paris: Département d'Iranologie de l'Institut francoiranien, 1961); trans. Paul Walker, *Wellsprings of Wisdom* (Salt Lake City: University of Utah Press, 1994).

6. For the use of the term *tarbiyyah* in the *Majālis al-Mu'ayyadiyyah*, see vol. I and III, ed. Muṣṭafā Ghālib, Majlis 57, 67; and vol. III (Ghālib edition), 200. In vol. III, four lectures are specifically devoted to Abraham's upbringing (*tarbiyyah*) in the cave (see vol. III, Majlis 367–370, 191–203). The correlation between the gradual training of the prophet Moses and the initiatory ascent of the individual practitioner is notable in *Asās al-Ta'wīl*. See Qāḍī al-Nuʿmān, *Asās al-Ta'wīl*, ed. ʿĀrif Ṭāmir (Beirut: Dār al-Thaqāfa, 1966), 190. God guides His friends (*awliyā'*) on the Straight Path (*al-ṣirāt al-mustaqīm*): "Then He entrusted them with souls, and He brought them forth from the wombs as children, not knowing anything, but then He taught them with the assistance of His servants, and in that manner, conveys them in knowledge (*ʿilm*), grade (*darajah*) after grade."

7. On Qāḍī al-Nuʿmān and the Fatimid *majlis*, see Heinz Halm, *The Empire of the Mahdi*

(Leiden: E. J. Brill, 1996); and idem, "The Ismāʿīlī Oath of Allegiance (*ʿahd*) and the Sessions of Wisdom (*majālis al-ḥikma*) in Fāṭimid Times," in *Medieval Ismāʿīlī History and Thought,* ed. Farhad Daftary (Cambridge: Cambridge University Press, 1996), 91–116.

8. On al-Mu'ayyad's life and career, see Verena Klemm, *Die Mission des fāṭimidischen Agenten al-Mu'ayyad fī d-Dīn in Sīrāz* (Frankfurt: P. Lang, 1989). On al-Mu'ayyad's doctrinal thought and his collection of lectures, see Elizabeth Alexandrin, "The 'Sphere of *Walāyah.*' Ismāʿīlī *Ta'wīl* in Practice according to al-Mu'ayyad (d. ca. 1078 CE)," Ph.D. diss., McGill University, 2006.

9. As originally discussed by Landolt in his seminal article on *walāyah,* and elaborated upon in detail in my Ph.D. dissertation, al-Mu'ayyad introduces into the Fatimid Ismāʿīlī technical lexicon an original term for the "absolute human being" (*al-insān al-muṭlaq*), tantamount to the "perfect human being" (*al-insān al-kāmil*) frequently discussed in medieval Sufi and Shiʿi literature. According to al-Mu'ayyad, the absolute human being is the representative of the true Adamic form (the Gnostic anthropos, as it were) in each prophetic cycle (*dawr*) and each time-period (*ʿaṣr/zamān*). In the final cycle of prophetic history, the Prophet Muḥammad (during his life-time) and the *imāms* (after his death) are all the absolute human being. See Hermann Landolt, "Walāyah," in *Encyclopaedia of Religion,* ed. Mircea Eliade (New York: Macmillan, 1987), 316–323; Alexandrin, *The "Sphere of Walāyah,"* ch. 4.

10. al-Mu'ayyad, *Majālis,* vol. I, Majlis 8, 36–37, ln. 11–21 and ln. 1–17. Also see Habib Feki, *Les Idées religieuses et philosophiques de l'ismaelisme fatimide* (Algiers: Université de Tunis, 1978), 173–174.

11. *Majālis,* vol. I, Majlis 8, 36–37, ln. 11–21 and ln. 1–17; Feki, *Les Idées religieuses,* 173–174.

12. This is similar to what is alluded to in Qur'an 32:17, but it is in fact a hadith *qudsī* on the authority of Abū Ḥurayrah. Al-Mu'ayyad also refers to this hadith in vol. I, Majlis 59, 290, ln. 8–9.

13. *Majālis,* vol. II (Ḥamīd al-Dīn edition), *Majālis al-Mu'ayyadiyyah,* vol. I & II, ed. Ḥātim Ḥamīd al-Dīn (Oxford and Bombay: Z. H. Nooruddin/Leaders Press Private Limited, 1395–1407/1975–1986), Majlis 41, 244, ln. 89–94. This is also tantamount to becoming separated from the placenta (*al-mashīmah*), after being born, of "this world" (*dār al-dunyā*). See vol. I, Majlis 75, 366–367, ln. 3–20 and ln. 10; vol. II, Majlis 3, 20–21, ln. 81–85; and vol. III, Majlis 19, 57–58, ln. 16–23 and ln. 1–6.

14. Some other material on Abraham may be found in volumes I, II, and V of the *Majālis al-Mu'ayyadiyyah.* See in this connection vol. I, Majlis 15, 21, 51, 56, 67, 74; and vol. II, 6, 94.

15. In *Asās al-Ta'wīl,* the *mīthāq* of Abraham, 123–124 (longer passage, in relation to *ḥadd* and *ta'yīd* as well as Ishmael and Isaac), 126. Qāḍī al-Nuʿmān uses the term *mīthāq* in his commentary on the story of Moses and the story of Muḥammad (see *Asās al-Ta'wīl,* 205, 343). In the context of classical Sufism, Sahl al-Tustarī, al-Ḥallāj, and Junayd employed the term *mīthāq* in conjunction with individual mystical ascent (see Gerhard Böwering, *The Mystical Vision of Existence in Classical Islam* [Berlin and New York: de Gruyter, 1980], 152–157; and Louis Massignon, "Le 'Jour du covenant' (*Yawm al-Mīthāq*)," *Oriens* 16 [1962]: 86–92). In the early Jewish mystical tradition, the theme of "adjuration" also appears in relation to prophetic ascent and the "vision of God," in which the prophet Moses serves as a "prototype" of the "Merkavah mystic," with a notable initiatory and theurgic aspect (see Peter Schäfer, *The Hidden and Manifest God,* trans. Alan Pomerance [Albany: State University of New York Press, 1992], 143–161).

16. Gerhard Böwering, "From the Word of God to the Vision of God," in *Le Voyage initiatique en terre d'Islam,* ed. Mohammad Ali Amir-Moezzi (Louvain and Paris: Peeters, 1996), 208–209. Böwering has noted that in both the mystical and classical commentaries, Muḥammad's *isrā'* is combined with his *miʿrāj.* In *Asās al-Ta'wīl* (337–339), the *isrā'* of the Prophet Muḥammad is included in the story of Muḥammad (*qiṣṣat Muḥammad*). Qāḍī al-Nuʿmān, however, first comments on the *isrā'* in the introductory section of the story of Abraham (see ibid., 108–109; and Feki, *Les Idées religieuses,* 232, n. 49).

17. *Asās al-Ta'wīl,* 321–326: on how the *Qā'im* will make manifest the *bāṭin* of the religious

law (*sharīʿah*) and its *ta'wīl*. Cf. ibid., 332, which contains examples of Moses, Jesus, and Muḥammad receiving (respectively) the Torah, Gospels, and Qur'an.

18. *Asās al-Ta'wīl,* 109–113, 338–339. Also see ibid., 192, where Qāḍī al-Nuʿmān puts forth another example of the transmission of *ta'yīd* from the upper to the lower *ḥudūd* but in the context of the story of Moses (*qiṣṣat* Mūsā). *Asās al-Ta'wīl,* 112 in particular discusses the ascent of Abraham. The text on 112–113 is foremost concerned with the *Ta'wīl* of Qur'an 6:76, "When the night covered him over," offering an interpretation of the term *al-layl* (the night) in correlation with the rising and setting of the sun and moon of the following verses, Qur'an 6:77–78. In *Asās al-Ta'wīl,* 113, as in the *Majālis al-Mu'ayyadiyyah,* vol. III, Majlis 72, 207, both authors situate Abraham's upbringing in the cave as part of the story of Abraham. For the story of Muḥammad, see in particular *Asās al-Ta'wīl,* 338–339.

19. *Asās al-Ta'wīl,* 107–129.

20. Ibid., 108. A more detailed interpretation of the *isrā'* appears in the section on the story of Muḥammad (ibid., 337–338). On 338 in particular, Qāḍī al-Nuʿmān presents his *ta'wīl* of Muḥammad's ascent in the heaven.

21. *Asās al-Ta'wīl,* 108–109.

22. Ibid., 108–109. In this passage, Qāḍī al-Nuʿmān explains that in the context of Muḥammad's ascent, the soul has two aspects, one that is "heavy" (*thaqīl*) and one that is not. According to Qāḍī al-Nuʿmān, though Muḥammad's Night Journey has been commonly misconstrued as a physical ascent, it is a spiritual ascent. In fact, according to Qāḍī al-Nuʿmān, the "heavy" component of the prophetic soul is what ascends and becomes purified in the process of ascent. Feki states that "Qāḍī Nuʿmān gives to *waḥy* the meaning of an intimate conversation (*mushāfaha*) of the lower souls with the superior souls" (Feki, *Les Idées religieuses,* 230). In this particular passage from the *Asās al-Ta'wīl,* Qāḍī al-Nuʿman uses the terms lower souls (*al-arwāḥ al-sufliyyah*) and upper souls (*al-arwāḥ al-ʿulwiyyah*). On this point, see in particular, Yves Marquet, "L'Ascension spirituelle chez quelques auteurs ismailiens," in Amir-Moezzi, ed., *Le Voyage initiatique,* 117–126.

23. *Asās al-Ta'wīl,* 344–345.

24. Ibid., 345. See, in conjunction with this passage, p. 343.

25. Claude Gilliot, "Abraham eût-il un regard peccamineux?," in *Autour du regard: Mélanges Gimaret,* ed. Eric Chaumont with the collaboration of Denis Aigle, Mohammad Ali Amir-Moezzi, and Pierre Lory (Louvain: Peeters, 2003), 40–46.

26. Ibid., 45–46; Hermann Landolt, "Ghazālī and '*Religionswissenschaft*': Some Notes on the *Mishkāt al-Anwār* for Professor Charles J. Adams," *Asiatische Studien (Etudes asiatiques)* 45/1(1991), 35–39; Nomoto, "Early Ismāʿīlī Thought on Prophecy," 229; Dominique Sourdel, *L'Imāmisme vu par le cheikh al-Mufīd* (Paris: Guethner, 1974), 16–17. Sourdel addresses the theory of the impeccability (*ʿiṣmah*) of the *imām* as a "divine distinction" (*tafaḍḍul min Allāh*), as well as the parameters of the *imām*'s knowledge, including his knowledge of the unseen and unknowable (*ghayb*). See also Ḥamīd al-Dīn al-Kirmānī, *Kitāb al-Riyāḍ,* ed. ʿĀrif Ṭāmir (Beirut: Dār al-Thaqāfa, 1960), 168–172. Prior to his presentation of the story of Moses, Kirmānī notes the distinctions between the *ḥudūd,* the *ʿulwiyyah,* and the *sufliyyah,* (from Abū Yaʿqūb al-Sijistānī's no longer extant *Nuṣrah*). Of decidedly more interest with regard to the story of Abraham and his perception of the ranks of religion in the form of the star, the moon, and the sun, Kirmānī (ibid., 168) cites Sijistānī's comparison of the *sābiq* (the "preceder," or Universal Intellect) and the *tālī* (the "follower," or Universal Soul) to the *nāṭiq* and *asās,* and the *nāṭiq* and the *asās* to the sun (*al-shams*) and the moon (*al-qamar*) in the three realms of the world of origination (*ʿālam al-ibdāʿ*), the world of the body, or the physical domain (*ʿālam al-jism*), and the world of religion (*ʿālam al-dīn*). A matter addressed in further detail in ch. 4 of my Ph.D. dissertation, al-Mu'ayyad discusses the roles of the sun (*al-shams:* the prophet), the moon (*al-qamar:* the legatee), and the stars (*al-nujūm:* the *imāms*), which constitute the world of religion (*ʿālam al-dīn*). See *Majālis,* vol. I (Ḥamīd al-Dīn edition), Majlis 19–20, 81–84; on the physical composition (*tarkīb*) of the sun, the moon, and the stars, see vol. I (Ghālib edition), Majlis 50; Majlis 63, 311: how in this world (*dār al-dunyā*), the prophets, the *awṣiyā'* and the *imāms* are in the station (*manzilah*) of the sun, the moon, and the stars. On the sun and moon in relation to *walāyah,* see ibid., 24. Also see vol. II, Majlis 208.

27. Abraham's association of other deities to the one God, or polytheism (*shirk*), is addressed in particular in four lectures from the *Majālis al-Mu'ayyadiyyah.* See vol. III, Majlis 367–340.

28. *Asās al-Ta'wīl,* 107; and Henri Corbin, *Face de Dieu, face de l'homme* (Paris: Flammarion, 1983), 117. There are six periods of prophetic cycles. The "legislating" prophets, or those who bring scriptures and religious laws, are as follows: Adam, Noah, Abraham, Moses, Jesus, and Muḥammad. For additional information on Qāḍī al-Nuʿmān's theory of the prophetic cycles, see Henri Corbin, "L'Histoire secrète des prophètes, d'après le Kitab Asas al-Ta'wil de Qazi No'man," in *Itinéraire d'un enseignement,* ed. Christian Jambet (Tehran and Paris: Bibliothèque iranienne, 1993), 80–81.

29. *Asās al-Ta'wīl,* 108.

30. Ibid., 127.

31. Ibid., 126.

32. Ibid., 114–115. On the building of the Kaʿba in Mecca as a place of pilgrimage, see 115 in particular.

33. Qur'an 2:127: "And remember Abraham and Ismāʿīl raised the foundations of the House."

34. *Asās al-Ta'wīl,* 116.

35. Ibid., 118.

36. Ibid., 116–117. Also see 117 in particular, where the *sujūd* and *rakaʿ* are equated to the *ḥudūd* and the *daʿwah.*

37. Ibid., 337–338; and Marquet, "L'Ascension spirituelle chez quelques auteurs ismailiens," 120–122.

38. *Asās al-Ta'wīl,* 337. According to Qāḍī al-Nuʿmān, the *ta'wīl* of the night (*al-layl*) of Muḥammad's Night Journey (Q 17:1) signifies "the veil and concealment in the *bāṭin,* meaning that the Glorious and Exalted made him ascend and progress in the knowledge of the 'hidden' (*ʿilm al-bāṭin*)."

39. *Asās al-Ta'wīl,* 339: "*bi ʿayn qalbihi al-ṣafiyyah al-baṣīrah.*" On the expression "the eye of the heart," see Amir-Moezzi, *The Divine Guide in Early Shiʿism,* 48–50.

40. *Asās al-Ta'wīl,* 338.

41. Ibid., 336–337.

42. A reference to Qur'an 27:65, "Say: none in the heavens or on earth, except God, knows what is hidden."

43. *Asās al-Ta'wīl,* 337; and Sells, *Early Islamic Mysticism,* 47. There are, needless to say, other medieval Ismāʿīlī interpretations of Muḥammad's Night Journey and ascension. See, in conjunction with this passage, Marquet, "L'Ascension spirituelle chez quelques auteurs ismailiens," 121. Marquet suggests that the "furthest mosque" is an esoteric reference to the sixth *imām* or the *mutimm.* By way of comparison, see Nomoto, "Early Ismāʿīlī Thought on Prophecy," 223 (citing Rāzī, *Iṣlāḥ,* f. 58v., ll. 5–13/ f. 57r., l. 16-v., l. 8/120).

44. *Asās al-Ta'wīl,* 365.

45. Ibid., 366.

46. In the story of Moses from the *Asās al-Ta'wīl,* 192, Qāḍī al-Nuʿmān explains that of the three portions (*aqsām*) of *ta'yīd* that flow from the upper to the lower *ḥudūd,* the most preferred portion is the portion of the prophets.

47. See *Asās al-Ta'wīl,* 109, for the example of Abraham and the transmission of *ta'yīd* by the means of the *ḥudūd.*

48. Ibid., 109.

49. Ibid., 108.

50. An example of this dynamic at work may be seen in the *Asās al-Ta'wīl,*198. Qāḍī al-Nuʿmān states: "This is from the hidden symbols (*al-rumūz al-khafiyyah*) whose meaning is not to be found except with the 'friends of God.'" Also, see *Asās al-Ta'wīl,* 348–349 (in the story of Muḥammad), on *tanzīl* and *ta'wīl.* The apparent Calling (*al-daʿ wah al-ẓāhirah*) is paired with the hidden Calling (*daʿwah al-bāṭinah*) for the purpose of explanation and facilitation (*taysīr*). Another reference to the hidden Calling appears in a passage concerning ranks of religion (ibid., 327).

8

*Mi*ᶜ*rāj* and the Language of Legitimation in the Medieval Islamic and Jewish Philosophical Traditions: A Case Study of Avicenna and Abraham ibn Ezra

AARON W. HUGHES

This study explores the translation of the *mi*ᶜ*rāj* into the intellectual categories associated with the medieval Islamic and Jewish philosophical traditions. It argues that the *mi*ᶜ*rāj* provided a conceptual language to legitimate foreign ideas that were potentially dangerous and thus subversive to religious orthodoxy.[1] To demonstrate this, I examine several texts, one written in Persian, one in Arabic, and the other in Hebrew. The first two, *Mi*ᶜ*rājnāma* and *Ḥayy ibn Yaqẓān* (written by Avicenna, 980–1037), show how Islamic philosophers employed the *mi*ᶜ*rāj* to contextualize some of the generic features associated with philosophical ascent. The latter, *Ḥay ben Meqitz*, composed by Abraham ibn Ezra (1092–1167), also deals with such contextualization, but in addition enables us to examine how minorities could appropriate the *mi*ᶜ*rāj* to legitimate their own cultural and intellectual projects.

If Avicenna's text reveals how Muslim philosophers used the *mi*ᶜ*rāj* to ground the truth claims of ancient philosophy within the religious sources of Islam, ibn Ezra's shows to just what extent this trope could be deployed and manipulated among Islamicate subcultures.[2] Yet in dealing with ibn Ezra's text, a problem immediately presents itself: although his Hebrew composition employs elaborate accounts of ascent, initiation, and vision, nowhere does he employ the term "*mi*ᶜ*rāj*." This raises the theoretical question of the extent to which it is proper or even useful to perceive echoes of the *mi*ᶜ*rāj*, the raison d'être of Muḥammadan prophecy, in works of non-Islamic literatures. This issue, I maintain, can only be resolved by a comparative use of this trope in a manner that is sensitive to the limits of the conceptual analogy. I use the term *mi*ᶜ*rāj* here in reference to *Ḥay ben Meqitz* because I believe that the concepts of ascent, vision, and initiation have their own indigenous history in Judaism. My aim is not to distort our understanding of this historical tradition by indiscreetly applying concepts borrowed from one set of literature, nor to examine the thorny question of which tradition influenced the other, but rather to examine these concepts carefully and locally in order to explore some of the literary techniques and historical permutations that developed in the Islamicate world, a world in which Jews participated and to which they made important contributions.

So although ibn Ezra nowhere explicitly employs the term *miʿrāj*,[3] we do know that he composed *Ḥay ben Meqitz* with the primary intention of competing with Avicenna's Arabic *Ḥayy ibn Yaqẓān*.[4] Since Islamicate Jews spoke and wrote in Arabic, it is important to understand that what ibn Ezra effectively offered his audience was the exact same allegorical account of ascent and vision as Avicenna, but one that was now firmly embedded within the familiar language and categories of the Bible and other Jewish texts from late antiquity.[5] I contend that when ibn Ezra decided to rewrite *Ḥayy ibn Yaqẓān* for a Jewish audience, he had no choice but to engage, either directly or indirectly, certain themes associated with the *miʿrāj* and that, in so doing, he adapted them to show how they were intrinsic to the defining texts of Judaism.

Within this context it is important to be clear that my definition of *miʿrāj* is perhaps broader than that employed by other contributors to this volume. Like others, I define this technical term as dealing with ascent, in particular that of Muḥammad; but I perhaps differ in that I primarily regard this term as a trans-cultural and trans-religious symbol, whose manipulation is a convenient way to legitimate a particular ideology (e.g., philosophy) or group (e.g., Jews). Framed positively, this enables me to use the trope of the *miʿrāj* comparatively, showing how it could be used in non-Islamic cultures. Yet, the flipside is that it is necessary to avoid hasty generalizations, *viz.*, invoking the *miʿrāj* as a convenient omnibus category for numerous types of stories dealing with ascent. In what follows I shall make the case that both *Ḥayy ibn Yaqẓān* and *Ḥay ben Meqitz* are not simply allegorical stories of ascent, but can be classified as philosophical treatments of the *miʿrāj*. In arguing for this, however, I do not want to imply that any Islamicate story involving themes of ascent, initiation, and vision need necessarily be labeled as such.

The major methodological difficulty that confronts me here is that, with the exception of the *Miʿrājnāma*, neither Avicenna's nor ibn Ezra's texts make explicit mention of Muḥammad's ascent, the latter text perhaps for obvious reasons. On one level, it is evident that Avicenna clearly models his *Ḥayy ibn Yaqẓān* on his *Miʿrājnāma*, itself a commentary on a less conventional *miʿrāj* narrative tradition, by employing the trope of ascent, travel with a representative from the celestial world, using the same (Aristotelian) cosmology and symbolism, and explicating the concept of initiation leading to higher and higher degrees of understanding. In addition to these features, I contend that it is equally important to be aware of the form or genre of *Ḥayy ibn Yaqẓān*. The *miʿrāj* presented Avicenna with a convenient, preexisting mythic narrative with which both to ground and to explore the concepts associated with philosophical ascent. What links these two narratives philosophically for Avicenna is the notion of prophecy. For it is the prophetic act, as he makes clear in his *Miʿrājnāma*, that the *miʿrāj* ultimately recounts and unfolds. The crucial difference between the two texts of Avicenna that I shall deal with here— namely, that one explicitly mentions Muḥammad's ascent and that one does not—can be explained in part by the philosophical system with which Avicenna works: prophecy is not a one time phenomenon localized in Muḥammad, but something that every person can theoretically aspire to by means of intellectual perfection.

The case with ibn Ezra is much more difficult to fit into this schema. I persist, however, because I think the repercussions are significant enough when it comes to understanding how Islamic ideas and ideals filtered into non-Islamic cultures. By rewriting *Ḥayy ibn Yaqẓān,* ibn Ezra clearly deals with the same themes and symbols of not only *Ḥayy* but also *miʿrāj* narratives more generally. On one level this may simply be coincidental: in providing a Hebrew and Jewish version of *Ḥayy ibn Yaqẓān,* he had no choice but to tap, perhaps unintentionally, into such themes. However, I wish to take this a step further and suggest that he also tried to demonstrate to his Jewish audience that the themes that circulated around the *miʿrāj* are also Jewish. This is not to say that he wants to claim that the *miʿrāj* is of Jewish origin, but that these themes are ultimately grounded within the biblical narrative.

Avicenna and the Philosophical Reworking of the *Miʿrāj*

In this section my goal is not so much to examine the philosophic content of Avicenna's work as to show how his two texts that deal significantly with the theme of the *miʿrāj* attempt to translate it into the philosophical ideas associated with Neoplatonism.[6] Within this context, it is important not to lose sight of the fact that Neoplatonism provided a generic framework of ascent, virtue ethics, initiation, and vision of the First Cause that coincided neatly, at least on the surface, with certain religious aspects of the Islamic tradition. I say on the surface because although both stressed notions of ascent and vision, they differed dramatically when it came to the prerequisites, and thus the *telos,* for their respective journeys. In this regard, the Islamic tradition put pride of place on the religious perfection of the believer, whereas the classical Neoplatonic tradition emphasized the intellectual perfection of the philosophical initiate. It was precisely this tension that Avicenna attempted to assuage when he grafted the discourse of scientific knowledge and intellectual perfection onto the familiar terms and categories of the *miʿrāj.* The result, as we shall see, is that the speculative tradition associated with the latter became an important way to domesticate non-Islamic philosophical ideas.

Avicenna's most explicit elucidation of the *miʿrāj* may be found in his Persian-language *Miʿrājnāma* (The Book of Ascension).[7] In this work we encounter an interpretation of Muḥammad's ascent using the psychological and epistemological framework of medieval Neoplatonism. We see this in the very structure of the treatise, which is divided into two sections. The first section provides an account of Avicenna's taxonomy of the soul, focusing on its various powers, function, and modalities; the second part is a commentary on Muḥammad's *miʿrāj* in light of the categories imported from the previous section.[8]

In the beginning of the second part of the work, for example, Avicenna informs his audience that there exist two categories of ascent:

> Ascensions are of two types, either corporeal, by means of the power [*quvvat*] of [corporeal] upward motion, or spiritual, by means of the power of cogitation [*quvvat-i fikrī*] toward intelligibles. Since the conditions of the ascension [*miʿrāj*] of our prophet, upon whom be peace, are not in the sensible world, it is known that he did not go in the body, because the body cannot traverse a long distance in one moment. Hence, it was not a corporeal ascension, because the goal was not sensual. Rather, the ascension was spiritual because the goal was intellectual.[9]

Avicenna argues that Muḥammad's ascension was purely an internal and intellectual journey. Since the essence of being human is the intellect (which is permanent), not the body (which is impermanent), true ascent is contingent upon the former, which by definition is incorporeal.[10] Since the body and its various powers are non-essential, or accidental, Muḥammad's ascension must occur through the faculty that distinguishes him, as indeed it does all humans, from all other types of animals—the intellect:

> Then [Muḥammad] said: *Suddenly Gabriel descended in his own form with such beauty, splendor, and majesty that the house was alit.* Here [Muḥammad] means: the faculty of the Holy Spirit [i.e., the Active Intellect] in the form of the Divine Command united with me. It had so great an effect that all the faculties of the rational soul became renewed and alit.[11]

According to the psychological system employed by Avicenna and other medieval Neoplatonists,[12] the Active Intellect, here referred to by the more religiously sanctioned term Holy Spirit, is the last of the celestial intellects. Its main responsibility is the emanation of forms abstracted from matter into the human rational faculty that is able to receive them. Not every human intellect, however, is able to receive these forms, but only those intellects that have understood primary general truths (e.g., the whole is greater than its parts) and the secondary ones derived from them. These truths emerge, not from prayer or ritual activity, but from intellection.[13]

The archangel Gabriel, according to Avicenna's reading of the *miʿrāj,* refers not to an actual angel or a celestial guide, but to the technical philosophical term Active Intellect. In grafting the impersonal Active Intellect onto the well-known persona of Gabriel, Avicenna allegorizes the traditional Islamic account, thereby signaling to his audience, which is well read in philosophy, that when the normative or orthodox tradition says one thing it often actually means something quite different. This, of course, would be the main criticism leveled at Avicenna and other Islamic philosophers by critics of the philosophical program, such as Abū Ḥāmid al-Ghazālī (d. 1111 CE).[14] Yet, rather than claim, as Ghazālī would, that Avicenna is here being disingenuous, we should, as I have already mentioned, better understand his allegoresis as the attempt to harness the foreign into the familiar, thereby legitimating the former using the categories of the latter.[15] In employing familiar characters (e.g., Muḥammad, Gabriel), familiar narratives (e.g., the *miʿrāj*), and terms (e.g., Holy Spirit), Avicenna seeks to make explicit what he takes to be latent in the text. Muḥammad now becomes a metaphor for the perfected human intellect; the Holy Spirit is none other than the Active Intellect, that divine intellect responsible for bringing human intellects from passivity into activity; finally, the *miʿrāj*, as will become even clearer in *Ḥayy ibn Yaqẓān*, becomes an allegorical tale recounting the very process of intellection.[16]

Near the middle of the traditional *miʿrāj* account, as the various prophets meet and welcome Muḥammad, Avicenna writes:

> Their greeting him is his comprehension of all the rational faculties, because Absolute Truth [*ḥaqq*], may He be praised and exalted, when He created human beings, divided their nature [*nahād*] into two domains: an external one and an internal one . . . Just as someone who wishes to go on a roof first needs a ladder and then ascends rung by rung until reaching the roof, rational faculties are like ladder rungs. Someone who ascends rung by rung will reach his or her goal.[17]

When the traditional narrative refers to the prophets, according to Avicenna, it does not mean literal prophets whom Muḥammad would have encountered physically; rather, since he has already established that Muḥammad's journey was one of interiority, these "prophets" are personifications for his own internal (e.g., common sense, rational faculty) and external (e.g., touch, sight) senses. When they greet him, Avicenna implies, this signals a philosophical understanding on the part of Muḥammad that is tantamount to an awareness of the proper functioning of each one of these senses as they relate to the rational faculty. For it is only with such knowledge in place that his subsequent journey through the various celestial spheres can proceed.

At the conclusion of the narrative, as Muḥammad approaches the divine presence, Avicenna comments that

> [Muḥammad] attained pleasure the like of which he had never experienced. He understood that the Necessary Existent was deserving of all praise, but he knew he could not praise it with language. This type of praise is only connected with particulars and universals, but it is not appropriate for the Necessary Existent, which is neither a universal nor a particular.[18]

Once again, Avicenna here argues that what Muḥammad saw was not corporeal, but intellectual. However, he also implies that this vision is also supra-intellectual, an understanding that ultimately transcends the categories both of the particular and of the universal. This is in keeping with his more discursive philosophical works, in which he describes the Necessary Existent—that whose existence all other things are contingent upon—as superseding all noetic categories.[19] The result is that the *telos* of

Muḥammad's *miʿrāj,* as in keeping with the tenor of his commentary, involves the rational faculty: a vision of the divine presence *qua* the Necessary Existent. The truth of Muḥammad's prophecy, the legacy of his ascension, is ultimately philosophical.[20]

In the final analysis, Avicenna interprets Muḥammad's *miʿrāj* as a grand allegorical journey documenting his internal ascension toward intellectual perfection. In his hands, the *miʿrāj* becomes a narrative account documenting, non-discursively, philosophical ideas and terminologies within the familiar terms provided by traditional Islamic teachings. This enables Avicenna to legitimate in as smooth a way as possible non-Muslim teachings. If Muḥammad can reach intellectual perfection, then there is nothing stopping other Muslims from engaging in the same type of activity. The study of philosophy, Avicenna wishes to imply, is not only a very Islamic activity, but also obligatory on the pious believer.[21] In taking this approach, however, it is clear that what Avicenna does here is manipulate the base narrative of the *miʿrāj* to suit his own philosophical program.

Avicenna further legitimates the philosophical ideals of intellectual perfection through the notion of ascent in general and the *miʿrāj* tradition in particular in his allegorical *Ḥayy ibn Yaqẓān.* Here, however, he is less concerned with Muḥammad's ascent than with the potential ascent of everyone engaged in philosophical theorizing. In this regard, Avicenna's *Ḥayy ibn Yaqẓān* presents one of the few non-prophetic versions of heavenly ascent in Islamic traditions.[22] Yet, as before, we witness a fundamental tension between normative Islamic accounts that recognize the religious perfection of Muḥammad and the Neoplatonic tradition that recognizes the intellectual perfection of the philosopher. What Avicenna seeks to accomplish in *Ḥayy ibn Yaqẓān,* then, is the invocation of the symbols associated with the *miʿrāj,* although now stripped of many of their particularities, to legitimate further philosophical speculation.

As in his *Miʿrājnāma,* Avicenna's *Ḥayy ibn Yaqẓān* recounts the soul's journey through a structured and hierarchical cosmos with the help of a celestial guide now called Ḥayy ibn Yaqẓān. In light of the Persian-language text, we can read Ḥayy, like Gabriel, as a personification of the Active Intellect. In addition, *Ḥayy ibn Yaqẓān,* unlike the *Miʿrājnāma,* leaves the person who undergoes the journey unnamed, most likely because this person symbolizes every person engaged in the philosophical journey. At the beginning of the narrative, the unnamed protagonist encounters Ḥayy for the first time, who describes himself in the following terms:

> My name is Ḥayy; my lineage, ibn Yaqẓān; as for my country, it is *al-bayt al-muqaddas* [The Sanctified House, often a reference to Jerusalem]. My profession is to be forever journeying, to travel about the universe so that I may know all of its conditions. My face is turned toward my father, who is Awake [*Yaqẓān*]. From him I have learned all sciences [*ʿulūm*]. He has shown me the road [*ṭarīq*] leading to the ends of the universe; because my journey embraces all of it, I transcend [the universe's] regions [*aqālīm*].[23]

Here, we again see how for Avicenna notions of ascent are symbolic of the philosophical quest. He asserts this, as the above passage well shows, by allegorizing philosophy as a road (*ṭarīq*) to the outermost reaches of the universe. He also subtly connects the innocuous notion of constant journeying around the universe with the more technical concept of Peripateticism, thereby grafting further the familiar concept of ascent with the less familiar one of Aristotelian science.

As the unnamed protagonist and Ḥayy ibn Yaqẓān begin their ascent, they encounter a number of individuals whom Ḥayy describes as pernicious to the journey that will follow. These "individuals" are actually allegorical personifications of the various faculties (e.g., the irascible faculty, the imaginative faculty) that get in the way of philosophical speculation. As the two proceed on their journey, they reach a threshold at which the unnamed protagonist must undergo a ritual initiation that will enable him to progress to the next level.[24] This occurs as Ḥayy and the initiate approach "a flowing spring near the tranquil spring of life" [*ᶜayn kharāra fī jiwār ᶜayn al-ḥayawān al-rākida*]. At this point,

> he [i.e., the initiate] cleanses himself [*tatahhara*] in [this spring] and drinks from its sweet waters, then a vigor is created in his limbs. This increases his power to cross vast deserts, and he does not sink in the surrounding waters [*al-baḥr al-muḥīt*]. He is able to climb Mount Qāf, and the wicked angels [*al-zabāniyya*] cannot fling him down into hell [*al-hāwiyya*].[25]

After the initiate immerses himself in the spring, drinking its healing waters, he is ritually purified and able to continue on his journey. The successful initiation, as Ḥayy tells him, enables him to cross vast deserts, walk on water, and ascend sacred mountains. The spring, Avicenna subsequently informs his readers, represents the threshold or barrier (*barzakh*) through which the protagonist must pass in order to attain the level of two vertical regions that comprise the upper universe.[26]

Following these ordeals, the unnamed protagonist enters into these two regions. The first is referred to as the West, and is composed of two types of matter: that which is allegorized corporeally as "all kinds of plants and animals,"[27] and that which is allegorized incorporeally as "a desert plain inhabited by strangers who come from distant places."[28] Following an understanding of these two levels of materiality, which is essentially tantamount to Aristotelian physics, Ḥayy ibn Yaqẓān introduces the initiate into each of the eight celestial spheres, which occupy the rest of the Western part of the universe on a vertical hierarchy, and which correspond to Aristotelian metaphysics. Each one of the spheres is associated with a particular planet, following the standard medieval cosmological system.[29] Textually, Avicenna's descriptions of these levels invoke the descriptive accounts that we have encountered above in the *Miᶜrājnāma*.[30]

After the above descriptions, Ḥayy ibn Yaqẓān turns toward the so-called Eastern part of the cosmos,[31] the region associated with form. Following an appropriate understanding of the Eastern and Western hemispheres of the universe, which, read in light of his more discursive treatises, is the same as understanding the relationship between form and matter (i.e., Aristotelian physics and metaphysics), Ḥayy leads the initiate toward the region that occupies the space above both East and West. Numerous ghosts and demons people the road and try to prevent the initiate from succeeding on his journey. This is the most difficult part of the journey, and not everyone who sets out on its path will complete it:

> He who succeeds in leaving this region enters the regions of the angels, among which the one that marches with the earth is a region in which the terrestrial regions dwell. These angels form two groups. One occupies the right side: they are the angels who know and order. Opposite them, a group occupies the left side: they are angels who obey and act [. . .].[32]

These angelic realms, based on his more discursive philosophical treatises, refer to the intellectual faculties that exist, *in potentia,* within each individual.[33] Read in this manner, we know that these two sets of angels refer to the theoretical intellect and practical intellect respectively. The first type of intellect, that which "knows and orders,"[34] is able to discriminate between true and false and is ultimately responsible for contemplating theoretical matters, such as God and the other celestial intellects. The other intellect, that which "obeys and acts," is responsible for the acquisition of good behavior and thus is responsible for the ethical behavior of the individual. Again, Avicenna takes the celestial topographies familiar from the narratives associated with the *miʿrāj* and re-signifies them so that they now refer to the Aristotelian distinction between two types of intellects, the theoretical and the practical, that exist within every person. The *miʿrāj* now becomes the journey that every philosopher, but interestingly not necessarily every Muslim, undertakes.

At the end of *Ḥayy ibn Yaqẓān,* as the unnamed protagonist reaches the end of his ascension, he encounters the king (*malik*):

> Among them all, the king is the most withdrawn into solitude. Whoever connects Him with an origin errs; whoever claims to pay him praise that is proportionate to him is an idle babbler. For the king escapes the power of the clever to bestow qualifications, just as here too all comparisons fail of their end. Let none, then, be so bold as to compare him to anything whatsoever. . . . His beauty is the veil of his beauty, his manifestation the cause of his occultation, and his epiphany is the cause of his hiddenness. . . . Whoever perceives a trace of his beauty fixes his contemplation upon it forever; never again, even for the twinkling of an eye, does he let himself be distracted from it.[35]

If we compare this description with Avicenna's comments to the *telos* of Muḥammad's *miʿrāj,* we know that "the king" refers not to a human being, but the Necessary Existent, i.e., that whose existence is necessary for the sustenance of the universe and all that it encompasses. The Necessary Existent, in typical Neoplatonic fashion, is neither created nor bound within any temporal or spatial framework; on the contrary, it exists so far beyond this world that one cannot even speak positively, let alone knowingly, about it. In fact, the only way that one can speak about it, as Avicenna himself does here, is through paradox or apophasis. Although the end of the journey culminates in vision, it is not a literal vision, as some versions of the *miʿrāj* narrative imply, but an intellectual one that takes places through reason as opposed to the ocular faculty.

The *Miʿrājnāma* and *Ḥayy ibn Yaqẓān* present two overlapping philosophical readings and interpretations of the *miʿrāj*. In so doing, they embed the theoretical teachings associated with Avicenna's more discursive philosophical work within the familiar terms and categories supplied by narratives of Muḥammad's ascent. Since both accounts stress ascent, gnosis, and vision, it became fairly easy to read each account in the light of the other. Yet, when understood on their own terms, the philosophical concept of ascent is predicated on a set of assumptions that are much different from those of the traditional Muslim narrative. It is precisely this tension that Avicenna sought to overcome in cross-pollinating the narratives, thereby attempting to legitimate his philosophical program by downplaying its novelty, and thus possible danger, to the majority of Muslims not necessarily interested in philosophy.

Abraham ibn Ezra's *Ḥay ben Meqitz*

In one of the few works of medieval Hebrew poetics, *Kitāb al-muḥāḍara wa'l-mudhākara* ("The Book of Conversation and Discussion"),[36] Moshe ibn Ezra (1055–1138)—no immediate relation to Abraham ibn Ezra—writes:

> If you should employ a motif that existed prior to you, behave prudently in the matter; either add to it or take away from it. An appropriate addition should not corrupt the motif and an appropriate omission should not put it to shame. . . . Concerning the argument of the plagiarists, al-Jāḥiẓ, a leader of the *mutakallimūn*, said: "I do not know of a poet who has invented an appropriate allegory or a remarkable motif or an original saying without another poet coming after him and claiming it for himself."[37]

This quotation gets to the heart of the manifold ambiguities and tensions endemic to Andalusi Jewish culture.[38] On the one hand it is certain that Moshe ibn Ezra, like his colleagues, was attracted to the pleasing language, verse, and prosody of Arab poetry, not to mention other literary and philosophical genres.[39] Yet, on the other hand, his attraction is filtered through the need to defend the Hebrew language and Judaism by arguing that literary creativity is not something that is solely the defining characteristic of Arabs. Out of this motivation, Moshe ibn Ezra wanted to demonstrate that Hebrew was not only the equal of Arabic, but actually superior to it. It is for this reason that the Hebrew poets returned time and again to the biblical narrative, to show that their craft was not one of innovation, but that of continuing an ancient and venerable literary tradition.[40]

Keeping in mind both the *miʿrāj* as providing a language of philosophical legitimation and the comments of Moshe ibn Ezra, I would now like to turn attention to *Ḥay ben Meqitz.* Abraham ibn Ezra was an important figure in poetry, philosophy, and biblical exegesis; he also translated many Arabic texts into Hebrew, thus functioning as an important conduit between the two traditions, in addition to being a major player in the development of medieval Hebrew science.[41] His *Ḥay ben Meqitz* is a text that works on multiple levels. On one level it is a pastiche of biblical phrases that enabled twelfth-century Jews to embrace and legitimate the intellectual and aesthetic ideals of Neoplatonism, in much the same manner that Avicenna's work did earlier. On another level *Ḥay ben Meqitz* is a rich philosophical-mystical narrative that culminates in the protagonist's ascent to and ultimate vision of the divine presence.

Despite a number of important philosophical differences between the two works, ibn Ezra, on a literary level, essentially adopts and adapts Avicenna's narrative to the concerns of a Jewish audience.[42] Although he borrows the basic plot, structure, and characters from Avicenna's text, he does so in such a manner that his new creation derives its vocabulary, terms of reference, and, ultimately, its potency from the biblical narrative. By doing this, ibn Ezra attempted to show to his Jewish audience, on a religious level, that his own version was better than Avicenna's; and, on a philosophical level, that latent in the biblical narrative resides the truths of philosophy. Explicit in his "judaization" of this work, then, is the notion that Jews no longer needed to read the original Arabic version of the narrative.[43]

In taking over Avicenna's basic plot and narrative structure, ibn Ezra was forced to engage with the theme of the *miʿrāj.* Indeed, he had to do so if he wanted to demonstrate that the themes of philosophical ascent and vision were not external impositions, whether from Neoplatonism or from Islamic literary traditions dealing with the *miʿrāj.* In what follows, I shall argue that ibn Ezra engages the *miʿrāj* in at least three ways: in dealing directly with the notion of ascent; in addressing the concept of initiation and how this enables the protagonist to move on to higher and higher celestial levels; and in his concern with providing rich descriptions of cosmic topography.

Ascent

Ibn Ezra, like Avicenna before him, is interested in grounding the concept of philosophical awakening in the familiar categories provided by his religious tradition. In addition, however, he also seeks to show how the motif of ascent is something that is not solely Islamic and, as Avicenna had implied, grounded within the semantic field of Muḥammad's *miʿrāj.* In this regard, ibn Ezra incorporates the motifs and images that are associated with earlier Jewish mystical sources and, much like Avicenna before him, manipulates them in the light of the categories provided by Neoplatonism. Ibn Ezra does this by re-signifying some of the generic features associated with the *mi*ʿ*rāj* narrative, at least broadly defined, in light of the vocabulary and categories associated with the biblical narrative.

For example, ibn Ezra writes of the unnamed protagonist's first encounter with Ḥay:

> An old man was walking in the field
> Praising God, giving thanks.
>
> His appearance was like that of kings
> An aura surrounding him, shining like the angels.
>
> Seasons had not changed him
> Years seemed not to overtake him. . . .[44]

Ibn Ezra's description of an individual meeting a celestial guide would certainly not have been foreign to a Jewish audience. It is, for instance, a very common motif within the early Jewish mystical sources. In the first century *Apocalypse of Abraham* we encounter the following:

> The angel he sent to me in the likeness of a man came, and he took me by my right hand and stood me on my feet. And he said to me, "Stand up, Abraham, friend of God who has loved you, let human trembling not enfold you! For lo! I am sent to you to strengthen you and to bless you in the name of God."[45]

Significantly, though, in much of the Apocalyptic and Hekhalot literature, the named protagonist, upon seeing the celestial guide, falls down in fear and awe.[46] The fact that ibn Ezra's unnamed protagonist does not fall down at this point may be owing to the natural component of the philosophical enterprise as opposed to the selective or supernatural one of mysticism. Whereas ibn Ezra's protagonist is unnamed, those of the Apocalyptic and Hekhalot tradition are usually named (e.g., Abraham, Enoch, Rabbi Ishmael). Ibn Ezra's protagonist is, like Avicenna's, a philosophical Everyman. In like manner, although ibn Ezra's guide, Ḥay ben Meqitz, is described in terms that compare him to an angel, he is actually a philosopher. (Or, if we follow Avicenna, he is personification of the Active Intellect.) In invoking the imagery and vocabulary from the earlier Jewish mystical traditions,[47] ibn Ezra not only makes Ḥay familiar, he also signals to his audience that some form of special knowledge or gnosis is to be imparted to the protagonist, as was the case in the earlier Hekhalot literature.

Initiation

In the following passage the main character, Ḥay ben Meqitz, takes the unnamed protagonist to a stream, in which he will undergo initiation. This spring, read philosophically, marks the border between the world of form and matter on the one hand, and that of the supra-lunar world on the other. Yet, when read from the perspective of the early Jewish mystical tradition, it is the immersion in water than enables the protagonist to ascend to higher levels and receive gnosis.[48] Keeping in mind both the basic cosmology and ritual structure provided in Avicenna's *Ḥayy ibn Yaqẓān,* the unnamed protagonist says:

> We approached the spring
> And stood beside it.
>
> He undressed me, my clothes he cast aside
> He led me naked toward it.
>
> He said, "Drink the water from its source
> The fluids flowing from its well!
>
> In it your fractures will be healed
> Your limbs will be dressed.
>
> You will have wings
> To fly in the heavens."
>
> I drank from the water of life
> The water that gives life to souls.
>
> My pains and my afflictions left me
> My loyal yet bad ailments.
>
> They became like a balsam
> To heal my fractures and soothe my limbs.
>
> I drank enough
> My sickness was cured.
>
> He reached out his hand and grabbed me
> He lifted me from the depth of the spring.[49]

In this passage, the water associated with the spring serves to purify the unnamed protagonist. Before he immerses himself in this water, however, his earthly clothes are removed.[50]

This act invokes an important trope that is also popular within early Jewish mystical sources. In 2Enoch, for example, we find:

> The Lord said to Michael, "Take Enoch, and extract [him] from the earthly clothing. And anoint him with delightful oil; and put him into the clothes of glory." And Michael extracted me from my clothes. He anointed me with the delightful oil; and the appearance of that oil is greater than the greatest light [. . .].[51]

The earthly clothes symbolize the corporeality of the individual; by discarding them, he divests himself of the hindrance of the body. Although this notion of purification by immersion in water is a universal symbol, it is a motif that recurs frequently throughout this genre of Jewish literature. The celestial sojourner often undergoes some form of contact with water (or, alternatively, fire) as a means of continuing his journey upward.[52] In 1Enoch, for example, we find:

> And they lifted me up into one place where there were [the ones] like the flaming fire. And when they [so] desire, they appear like men. And they took me into a place of whirlwind in the mountain; the top of its summit was reaching into heaven. And I saw chambers of light . . . and they lifted me up unto the waters of life, unto the occidental fire which receives every setting of the sun. And I came to the river of fire which flows like water and empties itself into the great sea in the direction of the West. . . . And I saw the mouths of all the rivers of the earth and the mouth of the seas.[53]

Although phenomenologically the narrative accounts that we encounter in *Ḥayy ibn Yaqẓān* and *Ḥay ben Meqitz* are virtually identical, ibn Ezra's text attempts to demonstrate that Jewish sources also deal directly and dramatically with notions of ascent.

Like Avicenna before him, ibn Ezra is interested in legitimating the potentially dangerous teachings of philosophy by grounding them within the familiar categories of his own religious and literary tradition. However, he also has to show his Jewish audience that the twin themes of ascent and vision, although central to Neoplatonism, do not resonate solely within the Islamic ascent narrative associated with the *miʿrāj. Ḥay ben Meqitz,* in other words, enables ibn Ezra to demonstrate that the symbols and images that Avicenna clearly associates with *miʿrāj* also have lengthy histories in Jewish texts, ones that moreover predate not only their Islamic counterparts, but even Muḥammad himself.

Ibn Ezra also implies that the ritualistic purification that makes ascent possible is not something that exists solely within the purview of Islamic sources. Whereas Avicenna had tried to show his audience that philosophical ascent was qualitatively similar to the *miʿrāj,* ibn Ezra here goes a step further: not only is the concept of philosophical ascent religious and something that religious texts endorse, it is a phenomenon that is as Jewish as it is Islamic, if not more so. This permits him to show his audience, who undoubtedly would have been familiar with Islamic claims to monotheistic legitimation through the *miʿrāj* narrative, that the themes of ascent, vision, and gnosis existed in Jewish sources, ones that predated the advent of Islam.

For example, when the unnamed protagonist and Ḥay ben Meqitz journey through the celestial world, stopping at the various planets in order to understand their personified inhabitants, they eventually arrive at the divine presence, another theme familiar from Jewish mystical sources.[54] Ibn Ezra's narrative describes this encounter in the following way:

> I was afraid, and said,
>   "How awesome is this place that I see."
>
> He replied: "From your feet
>   Remove your sandals.

From the matter of your corpse
  Lift your soul.

Forsake your thoughts,
  Relax your eyelids!

See by the eyes of your interior
  The pupils of your heart."[55]

In this passage, ibn Ezra uses a number of biblical prooftexts, images, and significations. The phrase "How awesome is this place" comes right out of Genesis 28:16; the original context is Jacob's dream at Bethel, where he sees the angels of God ascending and descending on a stairway. In like manner, the image of removing one's sandals immediately invokes for the reader Exodus 3:5, where Moses encounters the divine presence in the burning bush.[56] Once again we see here how ibn Ezra attempts to ground the ritual activity that Avicenna employed in his *Ḥayy ibn Yaqẓān* within the familiar language and categories of the biblical narrative. And again this has the effect of not only "judaizing" the generic theme of philosophical ascent, but also of showing that this theme was biblical.

Cosmology

Like Avicenna, ibn Ezra is also interested in providing rich cosmological descriptions. In his description of Jupiter and its heavenly sphere, for example, we read that:

In the sixth kingdom are righteous men
  Adhering to purity.

Their paths clear,
  Their deeds just.

They wash their hands of bribery.
  Looking upon evil their eyes are shut.

They practice righteousness,
  Despising profit.

They dwell in tents.
  They are teachers and judges,

Magistrates and officials,
  Judges and companions.

Prophets.
  Princes.

Priests.
  Academy Heads.[57]

In this quotation, ibn Ezra describes Jupiter as a kingdom with the stars as its inhabitants.[58] The planets, to whom God has delegated the governance of the sub-lunar world, exert certain influences on the earth. In speaking of Jupiter and its inhabitants, ibn Ezra uses a phrase from Habakkuk, whose original context describes God's justice: "Looking upon evil, your eyes are shut" (1:13). Ibn Ezra also makes this explicit when he uses the phrase "magistrates and officials." This phrase, as used in Deuteronomy 16:18,[59] refers to those individuals who are responsible for enforcing the divine legislation in Israel. Similarly, in the last sentence of this segment, ibn Ezra employs another text, this time from Psalm 45:7, to describes the righteousness of God's rule of the universe. In like manner "they dwell in tents" echoes Genesis 25:27.[60] That context describes the difference between Jacob and Esau. Esau, associated with the chaos and unruliness of the desert, is juxtaposed against Jacob, a "city dweller." The latter is a symbol of peace and calmness—the virtues of a judge—which are, not coincidentally, the same virtues used to describe the inhabitants of Jupiter.

As this passage, in addition to the ones described above, shows, ibn Ezra wrote his *Ḥay ben Meqitz* to demonstrate to his readers that all of the themes encountered in the phenomenon of philosophical ascent, themes that Avicenna had framed in terms of the *miʿrāj* tradition, are biblical and thus Jewish. Ibn Ezra is able to engage the motif of the *miʿrāj* in such a manner that the manifold themes associated with it became attached to the larger issue of Jewish cultural "nationalism."[61] That is, ibn Ezra is not so much interested in claiming that the *miʿrāj* is actually a Jewish symbol, but that, in writing his Jewish version of Avicenna's text, there exists an indigenous history of this trope in Judaism.

This study has examined how two particular Islamicate philosophers, one Muslim and one Jewish, dealt with the theme of the *miʿrāj*. This approach permitted us to look closely at a particular historical example of the ways in which this theme was absorbed, and ultimately contested, by a set of texts that were, on many levels, in conversation with one another. Such an approach avoids the positing of general themes associated with more generic concepts of ascent that can be found in each tradition, in addition to avoiding the positing of non-historical comparisons between Arabic and Hebrew texts written centuries apart from one another.[62]

This particular study revolves around the theoretical issue of the *miʿrāj* as providing a conceptual language of legitimation that works on a number of levels. On one level it enabled Avicenna, as a representative of the Islamic philosophical tradition, to legitimate the foreignness and thus the potential danger inherent in non-Muslim intellectual traditions. His *Miʿrājnāma* achieves this goal explicitly by providing a line-by-line commentary to the standard *miʿrāj* narrative, whereas his *Ḥay ibn Yaqẓān* achieves this same goal less explicitly by employing the same stations, initiations, and cosmic topography, but with the important caveat that it nowhere mentions Muḥammad. If the former text enables Avicenna to "islamicize" philosophy, the latter does this as well; moreover, it seeks to show how

Muḥammad's experiences of ascent, vision, and gnosis are not *sui generis,* but something to which every philosopher could aspire. This method enables Avicenna to legitimate not only foreign ideas, but also foreign practices.

Ibn Ezra's *Ḥay ben Meqitz* is one of the few Hebrew texts in which we can clearly witness a Jewish thinker engaging the *miʿrāj.* Although other Jewish thinkers certainly employ themes of ascent and vision, their accounts are of a more generic variety, and it is accordingly difficult to ascertain clearly whether or not they explicitly had this theme in mind when they composed their various works. However, because we know that ibn Ezra wrote his text with the primary intention of competing with Avicenna's, we are afforded a fairly clear insight into how he deals with the *miʿrāj.* He deals with it, as I argued above, by showing that the themes associated with this tradition were not Islamic, as Avicenna had implied, but firmly grounded in traditional Jewish texts. This approach enables ibn Ezra to legitimate both the intellectual project of philosophy, and the cultural project of dealing with Islamic ideas and modes of expression.

Notes

I would like to acknowledge Ross Brann, Frederick Colby, Christiane Gruber, Lisa A. Hughes, and Michael Sells for their suggestions and comments on this chapter, only some of which I was able to incorporate here. Any mistakes that remain are my own.

1. Regarding Muslim attitudes toward philosophy, see Fazlur Rahman, *Prophecy in Islam: Philosophy and Orthodoxy* (Chicago: University of Chicago Press, 1958). On the theme of Muslim attitudes toward *bidʿa* (innovation) more generally, see Michael Cook, *Commanding Right and Forbidding Wrong in Islamic Thought* (Cambridge: Cambridge University Press, 2000), 427–504.

2. Here I follow the lead of Steven M. Wasserstrom, who writes that "the ways in which one religion made the image of the other into an image of themselves, which image was then used to redefine and continuously legitimate themselves, constituted an interreligious imaginary that is perceptible to us today only from certain hermeneutical angles." See his *Between Muslim and Jew: The Problem of Symbiosis Under Early Islam* (Princeton: Princeton University Press, 1995), 206.

3. Interestingly, nowhere does Avicenna employ this term in his Ḥayy ibn Yaqẓān; yet, as I shall argue below, this work is quite clearly a philosophical treatment of the *miʿrāj.*

4. The name Ḥay ben Meqitz is the literal Hebrew translation of Ḥayy ibn Yaqẓān, both of which can be translated into English as "Living, Son of Awake."

5. In this regard, see my "A Case of 12th-Century Plagiarism? Abraham ibn Ezra's Ḥay ben Meqitz and Avicenna's Ḥayy ibn Yaqẓān," *Journal of Jewish Studies* 55/2 (2004), 306–331.

6. The term Neoplatonism is a fairly problematic one. Because it was coined in the nineteenth century, none of the thinkers we today think of as Neoplatonic (e.g., Plotinus, Iamblichus, Proclus) would have considered themselves to be part of a Neoplatonic school or to have engaged in a phenomenon know as Neoplatonic philosophy. Instead, they would have considered themselves to be explicating the work of Plato through, inter alia, the corpus of Aristotle. In this regard, see the insightful comments in Maria Luisa Gatti, "Plotinus: The Platonic Tradition and the Foundation of Neoplatonism," in *The Cambridge Companion to Plotinus,* ed. Lloyd P. Gerson (Cambridge: Cambridge University Press, 1992), esp. 22–27.

7. A critical edition of this work is *Miʿrājnāma* (The Book of Ascension), with a revised text by Shamsuddīn Ibrāhīm Abarqūhī, ed. N. Māyel Heravī (Mashhad: The Islamic Research Foundation, Āstān-i Quds-i Radavī, 1986). An English translation and analysis may be found in Peter Heath, *Allegory and Philosophy in Avicenna (Ibn Sīnā), with a Translation of the Book of the Prophet Muhammad's Ascent to Heaven* (Philadelphia: University of Pennsylvania Press, 1992), 111–143.

Although there have been some issues raised concerning the authenticity of this work's attribution to Avicenna, I concur with Heath, who argues that the burden of proof falls on those who do not want to attribute this text to Avicenna given that its doctrines are so closely in accord with his (*Allegory and Philosophy in Avicenna,* 110). Moreover, even if someone should unequivocally prove that Avicenna did not compose this text (which I think is unlikely), the fact still remains that the *Miʿrājnāma* grounds Avicennian philosophical terminology and concepts within the familiar categories of Islam.

8. In commenting on the *miʿrāj,* it is uncertain from what sources Avicenna draws his "base narrative." He does not, for example, use the collections of sound Sunni hadith reports in either Bukhārī or Muslim. Frederick Colby contends that it most likely derives from the versions often ascribed to Ibn ʿAbbās. See his *Narrating Muḥammad's Night Journey* (Albany: State University of New York Press, 2008), ch. 9.

9. Heath, *Allegory and Philosophy in Avicenna,* 124.

10. See the discussion in Herbert A. Davidson, *Alfarabi, Avicenna, and Averroes on Intellect: Their Cosmologies, Theories of the Active Intellect, and Theories of Human Intellect* (New York: Oxford University Press, 1992), 124–126.

11. Heath, *Allegory and Philosophy in Avicenna,* 125.

12. See Fazlur Rahman, *Avicenna's Psychology: An English Translation of* Kitāb al-Najāt, *Book II, Chapter VI With Historico-Philosophical Notes and Textual Improvements On the Cairo Edition* (Oxford: Oxford University Press, 1952), 24–69; for requisite secondary literature see, in particular, Fazlur Rahman, *Prophecy in Islam,*14–20; Davidson, *Alfarabi, Avicenna, and Averroes on Intellect,* 74–83.

13. See his autobiography, however, where he does say that when he had trouble finding a middle term, he would engage in prayer in addition to other things (e.g., drinking wine). See William E. Gohlman, *The Life of Ibn Sīnā: A Critical Edition and Annotated Translation* (Albany: State University of New York Press, 1974), 28–33.

14. In particular, see Michael E. Marmura, *Incoherence of the Philosophers: A Parallel English-Arabic Text Translated* (Provo, Utah: Brigham Young University Press, 1997), e.g., 1–4.

15. As I have argued elsewhere, however, even Ghazālī was not averse to such methods. See my "Imagining the Divine: Ghazālī's Defense of Dreams and Dreaming," *Journal of the American Academy of Religion* 70.1 (2002), esp. 45–48.

16. Interestingly, though, Avicenna does not spend much time in his commentary on the ritualistic initiation in the spring waters, something that he spends considerable time on in *Ḥayy ibn Yaqẓān,* as does ibn Ezra in his *Ḥay ben Meqitz.* The theme of waters, and their ritual properties, nevertheless, play a significant role in the more standard *miʿrāj* narratives (e.g., the opening of Muḥammad's chest and the washing of it with the waters of Zamzam). Mention could also be made of a much more rare reference (appearing in the Abū Hurayra narrative in Ṭabarī's *Tafsīr* and later narratives that appropriate it) of a ritual bathing in a river or sea in the seventh heaven or beyond.

17. Heath, *Allegory and Philosophy in Avicenna,* 129–130.

18. Ibid., 137.

19. For example, see the discussion in his *al-Shifāʾ, al-Ilāhiyyāt.* An English translation of the appropriate parts may be found in Arthur Hyman, "The Healing, Metaphysics," in *Philosophy in the Middle Ages,* 2nd ed., ed. Arthur Hyman and James J. Walsh (Indianapolis: Hackett, 1973), 244–247.

20. The tension here, of course, is palpable, since according to Muslim legend Muḥammad was *ummī,* or "illiterate."

21. This, incidentally, is a case that Averroes (1126–1198) would subsequently make in his *Faṣl al-maql*. Whereas Avicenna tries to justify the study of philosophy mythopoeically, however, Averroes does so legally.

22. An interesting parallel here is the autobiographical *miʿrāj* account attributed to the ninth-century Sufi Abū Yazīd al-Bisṭāmī. Bisṭāmī recounts how on the various cosmological levels he meets and confronts various angelic, as opposed to prophetic, guardians. Unlike Avicenna's *Ḥayy ibn Yaqẓān*, however, he retains the same terminology employed in Muḥammad's *miʿrāj*. Despite this, both texts nonetheless show how the trope of the *miʿrāj* could be transformed, recast, and adapted to various particular circumstances or worldviews. A translation of pertinent sections from this may be found in *Early Islamic Mysticism: Sufi, Qur'ān, Miʿrāj, Poetic and Theological Writings*, ed. and trans. Michael Sells (New York: Paulist Press, 1996), 242–250.

23. Avicenna, "Ḥayy ibn Yaqẓān," in *Ḥayy ibn Yaqẓān li ibn Sīnā wa ibn Tufayl wa al-Suhrawardī*, ed. Ahmad Amīn (Cairo: Dār al-maʿārif, 1959), 40. An English translation may be found in Henry Corbin, *Avicenna and the Visionary Recital*, trans. Willard Trask (Princeton, N.J.: Bollingen, 1960), 138.

24. I discuss the ritual component of this narrative in greater detail in my *The Texture of the Divine: Imagination in Medieval Islamic and Jewish Thought* (Bloomington: Indiana University Press, 2004), 125–128.

25. Avicenna, *Ḥayy ibn Yaqẓān*, 43 (Corbin, *Avicenna and the Visionary Recital*, 141–142).

26. Avicenna, ibid., 43 (Corbin, ibid., 142).

27. Avicenna, ibid., 44 (Corbin, ibid., 143).

28. Avicenna, ibid. (Corbin, ibid.).

29. See, for example, Davidson, *Alfarabi, Avicenna, and Averroes on Intellect*, 74–83; Seyyed Hossein Nasr, *An Introduction to Islamic Cosmological Doctrines: Conceptions of Nature and Methods Used for Its Study by the Ikhwān al-Ṣafā', Al-Bīrūnī, and Ibn Sīnā*, rev. ed. (Albany: State University of New York Press, 1993), 202–214.

30. Especially Heath, *Allegory and Philosophy in Avicenna*, 130–132. Unlike the cosmological system presupposed by *Ḥayy ibnYaqẓān*, however, the *Miʿrājnāma* adds a ninth sphere above the sphere of the Zodiac, the all-encompassing Empyrean.

31. Much has been made of Avicenna's "Oriental Wisdom" (*al-ḥikma al-mashriqiyya*), a debate which I have no intention of addressing here. For Corbin, this refers to some vague type of immediate and experiential system of gnosis that is juxtaposed against Avicenna's more philosophical works. For a survey of the major players and themes involved in this debate, see my *The Texture of the Divine*, 30–35.

32. Avicenna, *Ḥayy ibn Yaqẓān*, 48 (Corbin, *Avicenna and the Visionary Recital*, 148).

33. For a good discussion of the way in which "angels" were interpreted in the medieval Islamicate philosophical tradition, see Maimonides, *Guide of the Perplexed*, trans. Shlomo Pines (Chicago: University of Chicago Press, 1963), vol. 2, 6–7 (pp. 261–266).

34. See *Avicenna's Psychology*, 32–35.

35. Avicenna, *Ḥayy ibn Yaqẓān*, 49 (Corbin, *Avicenna and the Visionary Recital*, 149–150).

36. Moshe ibn Ezra, *Kitāb al-muḥāḍara wa'l-mudhākara (Sefer ha-ʿiyyunim ve ha-diyyunim)*, ed. and trans. into Hebrew A. S. Halkin (Jerusalem: Mekize Niramim, 1975). For requisite secondary literature, see Joseph Dana, *Poetics of Medieval Hebrew Literature according to Moshe ibn Ezra* [Hebrew] (Jerusalem: Dvir, 1982); Raymond P. Scheindlin, "Rabbi Moshe Ibn Ezra on the Legitimacy of Poetry," *Medievalia et Humanistica* 7 (1976), 101–116; Ross Brann, *The Compunctious Poet: Cultural Ambiguity and Hebrew Poetry in Muslim Spain* (Baltimore: Johns Hopkins University Press, 1991), 71–83.

37. Moshe ibn Ezra, *Kitāb al-muḥāḍara*, 174.

38. On the general religious and political contexts of al-Andalus in the eleventh and twelfth centuries, see David Wasserstein, *The Rise and Fall of the Party-Kings: Politics and Society in Islamic Spain, 1002–1086* (Princeton: Princeton University Press, 1985), esp. 190–223; idem, *The Caliphate in the West: An Islamic Political Institution in the Iberian Peninsula* (Oxford: Clarendon, 1993). More specifically to my concerns here, see Brann, *Power in the Portrayal:*

Representations of Jews and Muslims in Eleventh- and Twelfth-Century Islamic Spain (Princeton: Princeton University Press, 2002), 1–21.

39. On this attraction more generally, see my *The Art of Dialogue in Jewish Philosophy* (Bloomington: Indiana University Press, 2007), ch. 1.

40. Dan Pagis, *Hebrew Poetry of the Middle Ages and the Renaissance* (Berkeley: University of California Press, 1991), 5–23.

41. See Raphael Levy, *The Astrological Works of Abraham ibn Ezra: A Literary and Linguistic Study with Special Reference to the Old French Translation of the Hagin* (Baltimore, Md.: Johns Hopkins University Press, 1927); more recently see Shlomo Sela, *Abraham ibn Ezra and the Rise of Medieval Hebrew Science* (Leiden: E. J. Brill, 2003), esp. 75–78, 105–106.

42. On the philosophical differences between ibn Ezra and Avicenna, see my "The Three Worlds of ibn Ezra's Ḥay ben Meqitz," *Journal of Jewish Thought and Philosophy* 11.1 (2002), 1–24. Ibn Ezra composed his *Ḥay ben Meqitz* in response to a request from Shmuel ben Yaʿaqub ibn Jamʿa, a wealthy North African halakhist and poet. In this regard, see the comments in *Dīwān des Abraham Ibn Ezra mit seiner Allegorie Ḥai ben Mekiz,* ed. Jacob Egers (Berlin, 1886), 139–140. Here I follow the lead of Kaufmann, who surmised that ibn Ezra was responding to a poetic challenge by ibn Jamʿa. See David Kaufmann, *Studies in the Hebrew Literature of the Middle Ages* [Hebrew] (Jerusalem: Mossad ha-Rav Kook, 1962); see also Israel Levin, *Abraham ibn Ezra: His Life and Poetry* [Hebrew] (Tel Aviv: Ha-kibbutz ha-meuchad, 1969), 15.
Moreover, there exists in ibn Ezra's *Dīwān* an Arabic heading appended to *Ḥay ben Meqitz* stating that it was ibn Ezra's intention to follow "in the footsteps of Avicenna's Risāla *Ḥayy ibn Yaqẓān.*" See *Dīwān des Abraham Ibn Ezra mit seiner Allegorie Ḥai ben Mekiz,* 139; Levin, *Abraham ibn Ezra: His Life and Poetry,* 179.

43. On the role of this trope in medieval Jewish philosophy, see the important study of Steven Harvey, "Falaquera's Alfarabi: An Example of the Judaization of the Islamic Falāsifa," *Trumah* 12 (2002), 97–112.

44. Abraham ibn Ezra, *Iggeret Ḥay ben Meqitz,* ed. Israel Levin (Tel Aviv: Tel Aviv University Press, 1983), 50. This English translation comes from my critical translation of the entire work, in Hughes, *The Texture of the Divine,* 189–207.

45. *The Apocalypse of Abraham* 10:4–6. For this text I have consulted the English translation by R. Rubinkiewicz and H. G. Hunt in *The Old Testament Pseudepigrapha, vol. 1: Apocalyptic Literature and Testaments,* ed. James H. Charlesworth (New York: Doubleday, 1983), 693–694.

46. E.g., 1Enoch 14:24–25; 3Enoch 1:7. For these texts, I have consulted *The Old Testament Pseudepigrapha, vol. 1: Apocalyptic Literature and Testaments.*

47. For this notion of revelation in early Jewish mystical traditions, see Ithamar Gruenwald, *Apocalyptic and Merkavah Mysticism* (Leiden: E. J. Brill, 1980), 15–20.

48. For greater detail on the ritualistic component of *Ḥay ben Meqitz,* see my *Texture of the Divine,* 119–125.

49. Ibn Ezra, *Iggeret Ḥay ben Meqitz,* 60 (Hughes, *Texture of the Divine,* 195).

50. In a few of the Ibn ʿAbbās versions of the *miʿrāj,* although it seems not the one that Avicenna was using, there are references to Muḥammad being told to cast off his earthly attire and/or to don clothes of light. I would like to thank Rick Colby for drawing this point to my attention.

51. 2Enoch 22:8–9; see 3Enoch 12:1–5 (for bibliographic details, refer to n. 46 above).

52. On imagery associated with water and anointing in the Jewish mystical tradition, see Moshe Idel, *Studies in Ecstatic Kabbalah* (Albany: State University of New York Press, 1988), ch. 1; idem, *The Mystical Experience in Abraham Abulafia,* trans. Jonathan Chipman (Albany: State University of New York Press, 1988), 74–80.

53. 1Enoch 17:1–8; see 2Enoch 56:2; 3Enoch 42:1 (for bibliographic details, refer to n. 46 above).

54. In this regard, see Elliot R. Wolfson, *Through a Speculum That Shines: Vision and Imagination in Medieval Jewish Mysticism* (Princeton: Princeton University Press, 1994), esp. 41–51.

On the way that such elements were recycled in al-Andalus among Jewish rationalists, see *idem*, "Merkavah Traditions in Philosophical Garb: Judah Halevi Reconsidered," *Proceedings of the American Academy of Jewish Research* 57 (1991): 179–242.

55. Ibn Ezra, *Iggeret Ḥay ben Meqitz*, 83 (Hughes, *Texture of the Divine*, 205–206).

56. In some of the later Ibn ʿAbbās texts, such as those versions ascribed to Bakrī, God explicitly tells Muḥammad not to remove his sandals (see Colby, *Narrating Muḥammad's Night Journey*, ch. 8).

57. Ibn Ezra, *Iggeret Ḥay ben Meqitz*, 78 (Hughes, *Texture of the Divine*, 203).

58. On the role, function, and problematics associated with ibn Ezra's use of astrology, see the important essay of Langermann, "Some Astrological Themes," 28–85. Also, see Dov Schwartz, *Astrology and Magic in Medieval Jewish Thought* [Hebrew] (Ramat Gan: Bar Ilan University Press, 1999), 62–91.

59. See Levin's comments in ibn Ezra, *Iggeret Ḥay ben Meqitz*, 78.

60. Ibid.

61. According to Ross Brann, "Hebrew poetry was conceived as a linguistic and literary means of promoting Jewish cultural nationalism in al-Andalus. Its prosody and style imitated Arabic poetics and poetry, but its chosen language of expression was emphatically biblical Hebrew. To put this another way, the stimulus for the poets' linguistic ideology and literary practice came from the dynamic Arabo-Islamic host culture, yet their conscious objective was nationalistic." See his *The Compunctious Poet*, 24. On this theme, also see Raymond Scheindlin, "Merchants and Intellectuals, Rabbis and Poets: Judeo-Arabic Culture in the Golden Age of Islam," in *Cultures of the Jews: A New History*, ed. David Biale (New York: Schocken, 2002), 313–386.

62. As, for example, David J. Halperin does in his "Hekhalot and Miraj: Observations on the Heavenly Journey in Judaism and Islam," in *Death, Ecstasy, and Other Worldly Journeys*, eds. John J. Collins and Michael Fishbane (Albany: State University of New York Press, 1995), 265–284.

9

Pious Journey, Sacred Desire: Observations on the *Miʿrāj* in Early Anatolian Turkish Verse Narratives

SELİM S. KURU

The idea for this chapter originated from Victoria Holbrook's detailed reading of the late eighteenth-century Turkish lyric romance, *Ḥüsn ü ʿAşḳ* (Beauty and Love), by the esteemed Ottoman poet and Mevlevī sheikh, Ġālib. In her *Unreadable Shores of Love,* Holbrook skillfully analyzes and discusses this text, which was written in 1783 and is accepted today, in a somewhat ahistorical fashion, as the peak of Ottoman romance literature. In the introduction to the *Ḥüsn ü ʿAşḳ*, Ġālib, following the traditional form of lyric romances, includes a description of the Prophet Muḥammad's ascension immediately after the preliminary *naʿat,* or eulogy of the Prophet. Holbrook discusses Ġālib's "*miʿrāj* paradigm" by establishing a relationship between the author's description of the *miʿrāj* and his portrayal of the allegorical love between the story's two protagonists, *Ḥüsn* and *ʿAşḳ*, that is, Beauty and Love.[1] According to Holbrook, the Prophet Muḥammad's conversation with God described in the *miʿrāj* section is analogous to the dialogues between Beauty and Love. Holbrook draws parallels between the archangel Gabriel, the Prophet Muḥammad, and God, and Speech (*Sühan,* another character of Ġālib's romance), Love, and Beauty, respectively. She then concludes that "Galib's prefatory *miʿrāj* chapter is an interpretive paradigm for his tale."[2] This statement, however revealing, requires substantiation, since the *miʿrāj* had been treated in verse in Anatolian Turkish long before *Ḥüsn ü ʿAşḳ*, and using the *miʿrāj* as an interpretive paradigm may not be an invention of Ġālib.

Beginning early in Anatolian Turkish literary traditions, that is, in the fourteenth and fifteenth centuries, descriptions of the *miʿrāj* were included in the introductory sections of lyric romances.[3] In verse narratives, the invocation section about the testimony to God's oneness (*tevḥīd*) and prayers (*münācaʿāt*) directly precedes the *naʿat.* Some works in *meṣnevī* form, in particular the lyric romances, are organized so that the *naʿat* section is then followed by a chapter on the *miʿrāj.* The prefatory chapters of *Ḥüsn ü ʿAşḳ* show that although Ġālib was following a well established pattern, he was most likely developing the *miʿrāj* section in an unprecedented manner. As a result, Holbrook's argument that the *miʿrāj* provides a concise framework for understanding the spiritual content of Ġālib's tale offers a useful model, one that can be applied to the study of the development and function of verse narratives of *miʿrāj* chapters included in other Anatolian Turkish lyric romances.

Although the present study started with the question of the function of *miʿrāj* narratives in lyric romances, it inevitably has had to take into consideration ascension chapters present in earlier didactic verse narratives. These chapters consist either of accounts drawn from the biography of the Prophet Muḥammad or of didactic writings on Islamic creed. Whereas the Prophet Muḥammad's journey was employed to express piety in religio-didactic works, in lyric romances the *miʿrāj* was employed to express the most sacred form of desire, namely the Prophet's desire to see God.

To date, free-standing *miʿrāj* narratives in verse have been studied in an ahistorical fashion, and versified *miʿrāj* narratives that were included in larger compositions have been neglected by contemporary scholarship.[4] The aim of this study is to map the beginnings of the versification of the *miʿrāj* in early Anatolian Turkish traditions. Furthermore, it aims to offer a brief look at the story in the earliest lyric romances in Anatolian Turkish, which in turn reveals how the *miʿrāj* functions differently in various genres. This chapter seeks to meet these aims by first examining relevant excerpts from four key texts, and then presenting a detailed reading of the first *miʿrāj* section to appear in an extant lyric romance composed in Anatolian Turkish, the *Süheyl ü Nevbahār,* written in 1350.[5] A short comparison of this text to its corresponding section in *Ḥüsn ü ʿAşḳ* will then be offered.

It is a problematic task to compare individual texts as a means to analyze and interpret the themes that they share. Indeed, this process tends to erase idiosyncrasies and flatten the wrinkles created by individual authors' styles and/or the authorial voices they employ. Despite such shortcomings, the goal in this limited survey is to attempt to understand the different forms and functions of the *miʿrāj* story through an examination of verse narratives in different genres that were produced until the mid-fifteenth century.

The *Miʿrāj* in the Name of Piety

Studies of Anatolian Turkish literature consider the first instance of a *miʿrāj* narrative in verse to be contained in the *Ġarībnāme* (The Book of the Forlorn), composed by ʿĀşıḳ Paşa (d. 1333) in 1330. It was an original composition and a very popular guidebook of Islamic doctrine.[6] Separate chapters devoted exclusively to the *miʿrāj* then appear in Aḥmedī's (d. 1412) *İskendernāme* (Book of Alexander), Süleymān Çelebi's (d. 1422) influential *Vesīletü'n-necāt* (Path to Salvation), and finally the *Muḥammediyye* (Book of Muḥammad) written by Yazıcıoğlu Meḥemmed (d. 1451).[7] Written in Anatolia during the fourteenth and fifteenth centuries, these four texts exist in numerous illustrated and unillustrated manuscript copies, some of which were later employed as primers for the religious education of youth in the Ottoman Empire.

The *miʿrāj* tale has a remarkably adaptable character, and the distinct approaches to this tale are shaped by the different genres in which they appear. The earliest examples of *miʿrāj* narratives reveal two distinct approaches to storytelling. On the one hand, the story functions as a didactic narrative, stressing the importance of communal prayers (*ṣalāt*) assigned to the followers of the Prophet Muḥammad during his ascension. On the other hand, the story appears in the form of a descriptive narrative and is thus essentially expository in nature. As will be argued, both of these approaches are different from the allegorical function of the *miʿrāj* in lyric romances, even though they all are composed in the *mes̱nevī* form. All four of the early Anatolian Turkish texts that are surveyed briefly in what follows present the Prophet as the intercessor of mankind. This emphasis is not found in the earliest *miʿrāj* chapters found in lyric romances, and it thus illustrates how authors such as ʿĀşıḳ Paşa adapted the *miʿrāj* narrative to suit their particular aims.

In his monumental *Ġarībnāme* of ca. 1330, ʿĀşıḳ Paşa includes a preface in Persian and a long panegyric introduction.[8] This text is divided into ten chapters (*bāb*), each of which is subsequently divided into ten discourses (*faṣl*). Altogether, they form a collection of moral precepts and exhortations illustrated by quotations from the Qur'an and hadiths as well as relevant anecdotes. As soon as it was published, *Ġarībnāme* established itself as one of the most popular propaedeutic books in Anatolian Turkish.

The Prophet Muḥammad's *isrā'* is discussed twice in the *Ġarībnāme:* first in the second section of the eighth chapter and again in the seventh section of the ninth chapter. The first section provides the author with a pretext to describe the octagonal structure of the Dome of the Rock on the Temple Mount in Jerusalem. This detailed description appears to be the first of its kind to appear in Anatolian Turkish, and it points to the encyclopedic nature of the *Ġarībnāme*. Except for a description of the Prophet's footprint on the Rock, whence he departed to rise through the celestial spheres, all other details of his *miʿrāj* are absent in this one-hundred-couplet section.[9]

In contrast, the second instance of the *miʿrāj* in the *Ġarībnāme* provides a heaven-by-heaven description of the Prophet Muḥammad's ascension toward God. In each celestial heaven, Muḥammad witnesses angels in various postures of prayer. For example, in the third sphere the Prophet sees angels in prostration (*secde*). The eighth and ninth heavens are described as the states of "bewilderment and intoxication" (*hayrān ü mest*) and "obliteration and annihilation" (*maḥv ü fenā*), respectively. The designation of the eighth and ninth spheres for bewilderment and annihilation of the self extols the virtue of the mystic path of love and establishes prayer as a gateway to unity with God. It thus brings together mystic ideals and religious duties. ʿĀşıḳ Paşa's account of the *miʿrāj* does not mention the previous prophets Muḥammad meets in each heaven, nor does it include the names of the fixed stars, details almost always present in *miʿrāj* chapters inserted into lyric romances. Instead, the version of the *miʿrāj* given in the *Ġarībnāme* serves to explain the responsibilities of Muslims, specifically their performance of daily prayers, and also to depict the Prophet Muḥammad as the intercessor of mankind. This overlap of the function of the *miʿrāj*, both as an account of a miraculous journey that leads to oneness with God and as a disquisition on the significance of Muslim prayer, affords it religio-didactic and miraculous overtones.

ʿĀşıḳ Paşa's focus on the journey to Jerusalem and prayers in his *Ġarībnāme* are much more developed than the minor or even absent references to such themes in lyric romances, which typically allude to the journey to Jerusalem in only one or two couplets that conclude the *naʿat* chapter, thereby serving as a means to establish a transition from the *naʿat* chapter to the *miʿrāj* chapter, itself the main thrust of the ascension tale.[10] This distinction is related to the variable function of the ascension tale in different literary genres, as well as a reflection of the individual interests of each author. In the *Ġarībnāme,* then, the *miʿrāj* presents ʿĀşıḳ Paşa with the opportunity to introduce his readers to a description of the Dome of the Rock, and more importantly to formulate prayer as the basis of the Sufi path of knowledge—a path that leads to the purification of the self through bewilderment, and consequently the annihilation of the self in order to become one with God.

A similar utilization of the *miʿrāj* appears in the *Vesīletü'n-necāt* by Süleymān Çelebi, an extremely popular account of the Prophet Muḥammad's life written seventy years later in 1409 and commonly known as the *Mevlid-i Şerīf* (The Noble Birth). It was composed in response to the controversial statements of a preacher in Bursa, who had claimed that Muḥammad was not necessarily superior to Jesus.[11] Following the chapter that enumerates the miracles of the Prophet, the sixty-one-couplet *miʿrāj* chapter begins with the *isrā'* episode. Gabriel approaches the Prophet in Mecca and brings Burāḳ from heaven (10:14–15).[12] Mounting Burāḳ, the Prophet reaches Jerusalem to lead the souls of previous prophets in prayer (10:14–15). When a staircase of light (*nûrdan örülmiş nerdibân*) appears, Muḥammad climbs to the heavens, and as in ʿĀşıḳ Paşa's account, he witnesses there the angels in different postures of prayer (10:26, 34–39).

Süleymān Çelebi, like his predecessor ʿĀşıḳ Paşa, concentrates on the prayers and their significance in his narrative, omitting details about the heavenly spheres and their associated prophets and planets. Although his account does not refer to the mystical path of love as ʿĀşıḳ Paşa's does, it nevertheless includes a verse at the end of each chapter that stresses the importance of man's love of God:

Ger dilersiz bulasız oddan necât
Aşḳ ile derd ile eydün es-selât[13]

If you wish to save yourself from the fire
Pray in love and in suffering (9:51 and 10:61)

This repeated refrain emphasizes, in an extended manner, that every Muslim should pray in love and suffering in order to avoid hellfire. The special place of the

Prophet Muḥammad in the eyes of God is clear in the following verse in Süleymān Çelebi's *miʿrāj* chapter:

Bu kerâmetler ki Hak virdi sana
Virmedi hiç kimseye önden sonra

These abilities that God gave to you
He has not given to anyone before or after you (10:33)

The *Vesīletü'n-necāt* fails to describe many miraculous details of the *miʿrāj* story and concentrates instead on the necessity (and recompense) of prayer. In this function, it may be said to be influenced by ʿĀşıḳ Paşa's *Ġarībnāme.* However, by correlating prayer and the Prophet's miraculous ascent, Süleymān Çelebi suggests that prayer offers a vehicle for spiritual unity between God and His subjects. In these two popular early depictions of the *miʿrāj,* the story's major constituent details, such as cosmological and eschatological motifs, are lacking. Most probably, this lack was a result of the religious tendencies and intellectual interests of their authors, as well as the models of religio-didactic narratives that they tried to emulate.

Unlike the *Ġarībnāme* and the *Vesīletü'n-necāt,* both of which relate the *miʿrāj* in terms of those select parts that discuss prayer, the first to offer a rather straightforward telling of the ascension story in a versified historical account appears in Aḥmedī's *İskendernāme* of 1390 (and again later in Yazıcıoğlu Meḥemmed's *Muḥammediyye* of 1449). Aḥmedī presents a "universal history" by interpolating sections of an original story into his account of Alexander's adventures.[14] This insertion includes a *miʿrāj* chapter (Plate 15) as a part of the universal history told by Ḫıżır in response to Alexander's request to learn about the rulers of the world who would follow him.[15] Aḥmedī thus identifies the ascension as a central part of Muḥammad's life story, and this *miʿrāj* section in the *İskendernāme* provides one of the first fully detailed renderings of the ascension tale in Anatolian Turkish.

In Aḥmedī's account, the prophets whom Muḥammad meets on his way to the highest sphere are not identified. However, the fixed star of each sphere is mentioned in the subtitles to each section, and its contribution to the Prophet's maturity is identified in three to six verses. Verses describing the fourth heaven, for example, read as follows:

Resīden-i resūlu'l-lāh be-āsmān-ı çehārom ve dīden-i u Āftāb-rā

Gördi dördincide bir ulu melek
Rūşen anuñ nūrile yidi felek
ʿĀlem-i ecsāmı pür nūr eylemiş
Yir yüzini cümle maʿmūr eylemiş
Merḥabā diyüben aña söyledi
Müşkili kim vardı āsān eyledi
Baḫt ü devlet virdi feth ü ẓafer
ʿizzet ü te'yīd daḫı kerr ü fer[16]

The Arrival of the Messenger of God at the Fourth Heaven and his Meeting the Sun

He saw a huge angel in the fourth [heaven]
With his light the seven spheres shined
He cast the whole universe into light
He adorned the earth altogether
He called on him saying, "Welcome"
Whatever difficulty he had that angel resolved
He bestowed upon him good fortune and luck
Glory, corroboration, and power as well. (6406–6409)

Aḥmedī describes the eighth heaven, where Muḥammad reaches an incomprehensible place in which the human mind can neither conceive of time nor space (6424–6428). Then, in a valley called the Valley of Bewilderment (*Vādī-yi Ḥayret*), Muḥammad hears God's voice demanding praise of Himself. Muḥammad proves incapable of praising such a Superior Being:

Çün s̱enādan ᶜacz gösterdi ol resūl
Ol s̱enānuñ yirine oldı ḳabūl

Since the Prophet was not able to praise,
This helplessness is accepted as praise.[17] (6435)

God accepts Muḥammad's inability to laud Him as the highest form of devotion. Following a lengthy digression on true belief that cannot be expressed by false praises and insincere tears (6436–6468), Aḥmedī continues his narrative by relating Muḥammad's encounter with God. After opening thousands of veils, God asks Muḥammad what he wishes. Muḥammad answers that he only desires communion with Him, and then asks God to bless his followers. Aḥmedī concludes his *miᶜrāj* section by stating that Muslim prayer, holy war, and almsgiving were decreed as religious duties for Muslims at the time of this divine encounter (6478). This extremely popular version of the Alexander romance by a poet who had also composed a lyric romance[18] was the first in a series of *miᶜrāj* verse narratives that incorporated further details into the fabric of the story in Anatolian Turkish. Thus, along with the existing Persian models, Aḥmedī's popular version, which stands between didactic and lyric versions of the story, might have become a major source of inspiration for *miᶜrāj* chapters included in subsequent lyric romances.

One text that appears to draw upon Aḥmedī's *İskendernāme*, and the final text to be discussed in this brief survey of early Anatolian Turkish ascension accounts, appears in the *Muḥammediyye*, a biography-cum-Islamic guidebook, composed in 1449 by the famous author Yazıcıoğlu Meḥemmed. The *Muḥammediyye* was one of the most popular books in the Ottoman Empire until the Republican era, and it has remained revered until today.[19] It includes a brief history of Islam up to the Battle of Kerbela' (680 C.E.), and it furthermore describes both the mysteries of the universe and the miracles of the Sufis. Last, but certainly not least, it relates in detail the central events in the life of the Prophet and, at a total of two hundred eighty-six couplets, it includes the longest *miʿrāj* narrative of all early ascension texts composed in Anatolian Turkish (Plate 16).

Yazıcıoğlu's account of the *miʿrāj* appears somewhat like a liturgical text, with chapters in varying meter and rhyme that are linked with repetitions of the following verse throughout:

Ona evvel sıfâtiyle tecellî eyledi Allâh
Pes ondan sonra zâtiyle tecellî eyledi Allâh[20]

First with His attributes God manifested Himself to him
And then with His essence God manifested Himself to him

The *Muḥammediyye* is narrated mostly in the first person singular by the Prophet Muḥammad himself, with digressions that record the conflicting interpretations of certain events in his life. For example, different arguments surrounding the question of the Prophet's ascension as being a bodily or a spiritual experience are recorded by Yazıcıoğlu, in a manner not dissimilar from the Arab and Persian exegetes who preceded him:

Acem fazılları gerçi gönül göziyle gördü dir
Arab kamilleri haktır tutun bu sözi ta'lila

Although Persian scholars claimed he saw Him with the eye of his heart
Arab scholars are right, trust my word through reason (2261)

In this section, Yazıcıoğlu refers to the various accounts reported by Ibn ʿAbbās, ʿĀ'işe, and other eyewitnesses, ultimately taking the side of those who believe that the *miʿrāj* was a corporeal experience and thus unique to the Prophet. In this way, the *Muḥammediyye* transcends its potential role as simply another versified eulogy of the Prophet, and functions as a religious treatise informing its readers of interpretations surrounding the *miʿrāj*. As in the early Arab accounts, Yazıcıoğlu introduces the prophets whom Muḥammad meets in each sky, yet does not refer to the planets. His formulation of the *miʿrāj* is an ecstatic but informative versification, but it does not reach the lyric capacity of Aḥmedī's version. His work was most probably enjoyed as an informative religious hymn, which, unlike the other three accounts, concerns itself with a more learned telling of the *miʿrāj* that includes conflicting reports on the event.

Although these four popular texts describe the *miʿrāj* as a miraculous journey in the form of a testimony to God's selection of Muḥammad as His messenger, they nevertheless present two differing interpretations of, and functions for, the ascension story. In one instance, the *miʿrāj* acts as the key miracle of the Prophet Muḥammad through which God's assignment of ritual prayer to the Muslim community holds pride of place. Thus, the Prophet's ascension functions as a promotion of communal prayer and as a miraculous gateway for unification with God, as seen in the *Ġarībnāme* and the *Mevlid*. In other instances, the *miʿrāj* also is presented with select details—not necessarily with a focus on any particular theme such as prayer—and with attention to its essentially miraculous nature. While the former two texts presented more didactic versions of *miʿrāj*, the latter two might have been influenced more closely by the lyric versions available in Persian models, especially the various *miʿrāj* chapters included in Niẓāmī's *Khamsa* (Quintet).[21]

Three of these early texts, namely the *Muḥammediyye*, the *Vesīletü'n-necāt*, and to some degree the *Ġarībnāme*, target a less educated audience through their use of a colloquial language and simplified literary style. In the *İskendernāme*, on the other hand, the style of the narrative is modeled after Persian romances, suggesting an elite audience. Nevertheless, these four didactic texts of differing genres and emphases employ the story of the *miʿrāj* to legitimize Muḥammad's superior status, including his miraculous encounter with God as the symbol of his utmost rank. All these texts, with their extended narration of Muḥammad's *miʿrāj* in verse form, present the Prophet primarily as an intercessor of mankind, rather than as a Beloved or Lover of God.

The *Miʿrāj* in the Name of Love

The first *miʿrāj* chapter in a lyric romance appears in *Süheyl ü Nevbahār*, composed in 751/1350 (twenty years after ʿĀşıḳ Paşa's *Ġarībnāme* and forty years before Aḥmedī's *İskendernāme*) by Mesʿūd b. Aḥmed. It is generally accepted as the first profane lyric romance in Anatolian Turkish.[22] In this text, which was translated from a no longer extant Persian romance, the tale of the Prophet's ascension is presented within the *naʿat* chapter, rather than forming its own separate chapter, as would become common in later romances.

The first line of the eulogy describes the Prophet as "the mystery behind *levlāk*." This description makes a reference to the famous tradition that determines Muḥammad as the reason behind God's creation.[23] After a description of the Prophet as more handsome than even Joseph, the epitome of beauty in Turco-Persian literature (couplets 105–106),[24] Muḥammad's splitting of the moon in two is described as one of his miracles (108–109). This short introduction continues with his being chosen among all creation as the Messenger of God (110–119). These couplets chronicle the miracles of the Prophet that lead to the ultimate miracle that is the *miʿrāj*. In the process, Mesʿūd's *Süheyl ü Nevbahār* abides by a similar pattern displayed in didactic verse narratives, that is, the emphasis on enumerating Muḥammad's prophetic miracles.

At the end of this section of the *naʿat*, Mesʿūd relates that, after Muḥammad began to spread God's message, he wished to see God face to face:

Bir ol ḳaldıyidi ki Ḥaḳ ḥażretin
Göze göz göre isteye devletin

Only seeing Him eye to eye was left
And asking for his share of blessings. (120)

Here, the *miʿrāj* is presented as a symbol of the Prophet's unmatched propinquity to God. This point is further intensified in the following couplet, which compares him to Moses. Moses had asked God to see Him, but he was answered with the divine reply: "You cannot see Me" (*len-terānī*):[25]

Ki Mūsā kelīmu'llāh öküş zamān
Dürişdi vü işitdi kim len-terān

Remember how Moses, the Interlocutor,
Strived so long and heard, "You cannot see Me!" (121)

Unlike the Prophet Muḥammad, Moses was not able to bear seeing God. Appearing after references to the Prophet Muḥammad's miracles, the transitional verses (120–121) cited above serve as opening lines for the twenty-four-couplet account of the *miʿrāj.*

In Mesʿūd's account of the *miʿrāj,* Gabriel presents an analog to Moses in that he similarly is powerless to accompany Muḥammad in the final stages of the journey into the divine presence (125–126). At the Lote Tree of the Limit (*sidretü'l-müntehā*), Gabriel tells Muḥammad that he can go no further. This of course underscores the fact that was transmitted though the overt reference to Moses, namely that Muḥammad is the only chosen one. Neither Moses nor the highest of the angels were thus comparable to the Prophet Muḥammad in his closeness to God.

The next part of Mesʿūd's narrative starts by expressing the impossibility of describing Muḥammad's encounter with God:

Gönüldi ol aradka ḳodı anı
Neler gördügin dimege dil ḳanı

He left him behind and moved forward
There is no tongue to tell what he [Muḥammad] saw. (132)

The Prophet Muḥammad's uniqueness in his relationship to God is thus reinforced. Soon after, in three couplets, the author relates how Muḥammad passed through many curtains and opened many locked doors (133), and that many angels were so delighted by his sight that they prayed for him (134–136). Muḥammad then reaches the uppermost heaven (137–138), at which point Mesʿūd advises his audience to read the qur'anic verse 53:9, which relates that the Prophet was "two bows' length or even nearer" to God. The section then concludes with verses describing the impossibility of comprehending Muḥammad's union with God:

Yaḳıncaḳ nice bulduğın Ḥaḳı
Gerek bilesin ḳāb ḳavseyni okı

Niçe sır kelecisi söylendi bol
Arada anı Ḥaḳ bilür daḫı ol
Kişi fikri aña nasıl irişür
Ne var ᶜaḳl eger ḳavzanur dürişür

If you want to know how close he was to God,
Go read the *ḳāb ḳawsayn*[26]
Many words of mystery were uttered;
Yet, only God knows how it happened
The human mind cannot comprehend it,
However much it tries to imagine. (139–141)

The *miᶜrāj* section ends with three lines (142–144) in which Muḥammad is mentioned as the "*Tangrı'nuñ sevgülü dostı,*" that is, the Beloved Friend of God. These verses close the section with a reference to the saying that God created the universe for Muḥammad, "*levlāk,*" which was cited at the beginning:

Ki levlāk anuñ şānına indidi
Le-ᶜamrük başı üzre tāc indidi
Ger ol olmayadı bu gök ü bu yir
Yaradılmayadı Çalap böyle dir

Levlāk has been revealed in his name
Le-ᶜamrük[27] has crowned his head
If it were not for him, this earth
And this sky, says God, would not have been created. (143–144)

In this short eulogy, Mesᶜūd presents the *miᶜrāj* as a proof of the Prophet's closeness to God. Not even Moses or the archangel Gabriel could reach the level of proximity to God that Muḥammad achieved. Although his work proceeds with a story of worldly love between Süheyl and Nevbahār, Mesᶜūd does not necessarily employ the ascension chapter as an allegorical paradigm for his subsequent tale. However, unlike the stress on the Prophet's position as the intercessor of mankind in the didactic and historical accounts of *miᶜrāj,* here Mesᶜūd's stress on the uniqueness of the Prophet and his desire to see God symbolically allude to the position of a lover who is seeking his beloved.

Centuries later, after countless *miᶜrāj* chapters in many lyric romances, the convention that presented Muḥammad as the lover and the beloved of God comes to take a more refined form. Finally, Ġālib's lyric romance, *Hüsn ü Aşḳ* (Beauty and Love) includes a short invocation in eighteen couplets, as well as a forty-two-couplet eulogy titled "In Praise of the Leader of Creation" (*der naᶜt-ı seyyid-i kâinat*).[28] This eulogy lists praises for the Prophet (19–25) and compares him to a series of seven preceding prophets (Adam, Noah, Moses, Abraham, Enoch, Joseph, and Jesus). The subsection continues with a description of the uniqueness of the Messenger of God as a reflection of the unity of God. Praise for Muḥammad concludes with a reference to his night journey, followed by lines expressing how words are insufficient to describe the Prophet himself, since the Qur'an praises him in a perfect manner:

Söz olsa da menba-i kerâmet
Ḳuran'a nazire olmaz elbet
Ḳuran o resulü kıldı tavsif
Ahlak-ı azimin etti tarif

Even though words can create miracles
They can't match the Qur'an
The Qur'an praises the Prophet,
It explains his magnificent conduct. (40–41)

These laudatory verses are followed by another section bearing the title "The Story of the *Miʿrāj*" (*der menkabet-i miʿrāj*), which marks the launch of a ninety-four couplet verse narrative more elaborate than the one contained in *Süheyl ü Nevbahār.* Yet when we compare the thematic clusters of these ninety-four verses with the twenty-four verses in the latter, it is apparent that a similar line of development and reference is pursued in both:

44–64: The description of the night of the *miʿrāj*
65–77: The ascent of Muḥammad, Gabriel, and Burāḳ
78–81: The impossibility of telling the *miʿrāj*
82–106: Muḥammad's travel through the fixed stars
107–122: Muḥammad's travel through the sphere of the zodiac
123–130: Muḥammad reaches God's throne
131: Gabriel is not able to proceed forward
132–136: Ġālib expresses his inability to describe what happened and asks for God's intercession

Ġālib's account of the Prophet's ascension differs in one major way from Mesʿūd's narrative. The *miʿrāj* chapter in *Hüsn ü Aşḳ* contains detailed descriptions of the spheres of the fixed stars and the sphere of the zodiac. Apart from such descriptions, these two chapters are very similar to each other, even though Mesʿūd's tale is briefer in length and sparser in detail. While Mesʿūd compares Muḥammad solely to Moses and Joseph, Ġālib justifies the Prophet's superiority by comparing him to seven other prophets. Likewise, Ġālib does not stress the intermediary role of Gabriel except in two couplets that are parallel to Mesʿūd's own couplets mentioning Gabriel. Even though Ġālib refers to a few prophetic miracles that Mesʿūd omits, these are alluded to rather than elaborated upon by Ġālib.

In addition, there are formal differences in the attempts of both authors to render the *miʿrāj* as a vehicle for expressing praise of the Prophet. Ġālib treats this topic in a peripheral fashion, in which a description of the ascension forms a separate section from the one devoted to words of praise. He strives to create playful metaphors abounding with allegorical ambiguities and potential symbolic meanings. Moreover, he defies conventional modes of expression with his unusual parallels. For example, he implies that Muḥammad is the moon that reflects the light of the sun (God's light); the splitting of the moon mirrors the splitting of the Prophet's chest for the purpose of purification.

Earlier accounts in didactic verse narratives focus on Muḥammad's ascension as proof of his being the chosen intercessor between God and man. These works deliver traditional details and at times discuss debates around the *miʿrāj* as an event. Lyric romances, on the other hand, use the *miʿrāj* as an opportunity to underscore Muḥammad's desire to see God, as well as his unique status superior to that of other prophets. His miraculous ascent enables various authors to demonstrate their mastery of a highly refined vocabulary that they draw upon in order to evoke exuberant imagery, especially that pertaining to Islamic cosmology. Celestial spheres, names of planets, and creation stories are evoked in these lyric romances in an increasingly symbolic, and at times enigmatic, fashion.

The earliest verse narratives of the *miʿrāj* focus on the importance and miraculous nature of Muslim prayer, rather than on the aspect of love. These early religio-didactic verse narratives present distinct evaluations of issues raised by religious treatises in different languages, and they may also reflect hymns chanted during rituals. They depict the journey of the Prophet Muḥammad as blazing an exemplary path that can be emulated by the pious through prayer and faith-driven maturation. The journey of the perfect human being is explained as a journey to piety, and was interpreted as reflecting the Prophet's desire to deliver his people to their ultimate salvation.

On the other hand, the earliest verse account in Mesʿūd's romance, *Süheyl ü Nevbahār,* does not even mention the theme of prayer, instead focusing on the miracles of Muḥammad and his unification with God. Muḥammad's desire to see God and God's acceptance of his request comprise the core themes of *miʿrāj* sections in both of the lyric romances evaluated in this study. It is clear that the *miʿrāj* functioned differently in various contexts, according to the constraints of the particular genre to which it belonged. Unlike the versifiers of religious creed or biographers of the Prophet, the authors of lyric romances did not see it as their responsibility to narrate the tale of Muḥammad's *miʿrāj* in detail. Instead, for these particular writers, the *miʿrāj* served as a thematic template useful for displaying their mastery in creating vivid allusions and cosmic analogies.

It must be noted that the first *miʿrāj* story included in a lyric romance in Anatolian Turkish was translated into that language from Persian. Even though the original source of *Süheyl ü Nevbahār* is no longer extant, it can be assumed that Mesʿūd adapted the images and content of the tale from the Persian romance that he translated. The tale would continue to develop in the centuries that followed through the pens of authors writing in Turkish, while drawing on *miʿrāj* narratives composed in Turkish, Arabic, and Persian.

In Turkish lyric romances, the *miʿrāj* chapter comes to be divorced from the *naʿat* chapter eulogizing the Prophet Muḥammad as the most perfect creation, turning instead to focus on the subjects of the uniqueness of the Prophet in God's eyes and Muḥammad's desire for communion with Him. Both of the latter themes continue to serve as part of the authorial act of praising the Messenger of God in no uncertain terms. From the uniqueness of the Prophet by the reciprocation of his desire to see God in *Süheyl ü Nevbahār* to his maturation as he gathers the virtues of the planets he passes in *Ḥüsn ü Aşḳ*, the *miʿrāj* chapters in lyric romances tell the story of a sacred desire that is fulfilled through the prophetic ascent. Unlike the pious journey in religious verse narratives that present the believers with a template to follow in order to become good Muslims, the driving force in the lyric romances is the sacred desire to be one with the Creator. That desire foreshadows the ordeals that the heroes of the profane romances would face, namely Süheyl's journey to reach Nevbahār and Ḥüsn's adventures to be finally united with Aşḳ.

Notes

I am thankful to Christiane Gruber and Frederick Colby for their helpful feedback and criticism.

1. Holbrook, *The Unreadable Shores of Love,* 146–149.

2. Ibid., 148.

3. Free-standing verse descriptions of the *miʿrāj* appear later, after the chapters in larger texts and lyric romances (see Akar, *Türk Edebiyatında Manzum Mi'râc-nâmeler;* and Mustafa Uzun, "Mi'râciyye," 136–137).

4. William Hanaway, in a short essay, investigated Persian narratives in both prose and verse, where the *miʿrāj* story appears in different forms and functions. For a brief exploration of the *miʿrāj* as included in Persian lyric romances, see his "Some Accounts of the *Mi'râj* of the Prophet in Persian Literature," 556–559. Hanaway explains the function of the *miʿrāj* in Persian lyric romances around the pattern of a hero's journey who matures in search of love. Even though Hanaway's article does not include reference to Holbrook's work, it arrives at similar conclusions about the relation of the *miʿrāj* chapter in the lyric romance. Unlike Hanaway's more general approach, the present study focuses on the verse narratives of the *miʿrāj* produced specifically in Anatolian Turkish during the fourteenth and fifteenth centuries.

5. Mesʿūd b. Aḥmed, *Süheyl ü Nev-bahār.*

6. This work is available in a decent edition with a facsimile of one of the manuscripts, Āşıḳ Paşa-yı Veli, *Garib-nâme.* For a brief introduction to the author and his *Ġarībnāme,* see Fahir İz, "ʿĀşıḳ Paşa, ʿAlā' al-Dīn ʿAlī," 688, 699.

7. I used the edition of *Ġarībnāme* found in Yavuz, "Anadolu'da başlayan Türk edebiyatında görülen ilk Miraçnâmeler ve Âşık Paşa ve Miraçnâmesi." This work includes a prose summary and transcription of the *miʿrāj* sections in the *Ġaribnāme.* For the other three works, I used the following editions: Aḥmedī, *İskender-nāme;* Süleyman Çelebi, *Vesîletü'n-necât;* and Yazıcıoğlu Mehmet, *Muḥammediyye.*

8. Yavuz, "Anadolu'da başlayan Türk edebiyatında görülen ilk Miraçnâmeler ve Âşık Paşa ve Miraçnâmesi," 247.

9. Ibid., 257–260.

10. The omission of a detailed recounting of the *isrā'* in lyric romances is due to the fact that it is not related to the divine communion and the expression of love between the Prophet Muḥammad and God. The *isrā'* story is related to the identification of Jerusalem as a sacred site for Muslims, and also, since the Prophet Muḥammad leads all the previous prophets in prayer at the end of this journey, to the superiority of Muḥammad over all other prophets of God.

11. For an excellent analysis of this incident and on different recensions of the *Mevlid,* see Dedes, "Süleyman Çelebi's Mevlid: Text / Performance and Muslim-Christian Dialogue," 326–330.

12. The numbers in parentheses refer to the chapter and verse numbers assigned by Ateş (see Süleyman Çelebi, *Vesîletü'n-necât: Mevlid*).

13. In quotations from edited volumes, I have followed the editors' transcription system. Whenever I transcribed a text, I employed the transcription system that is commonly used in transcribing Ottoman Turkish.

14. For a description of the *İskendernāme* and this chapter, see Sawyer, "Revising Alexander: Structure and Evolution: Ahmedî's Ottoman Iskendernâme (c. 1400)," 225–243, for the "universal history"; and 229–230 for "mevlid" chapters.

15. The *miʿrāj* chapter is apparently added in a later recension in 809/1407, and it is claimed that Aḥmedī's insertion of a *miʿrāj* narrative in his *İskendernāme* was related to the same event that inspired Süleymān Çelebi's composition of the *Mevlid.* See Sawyer, "Revising Alexander," 229–230.

16. The verse numbers follow Ünver's facsimile edition of the *İskendernāme.* The translation and transcription are mine.

17. This is a reference to a widely circulated hadith. For further references, see al-Sulamī, *The Subtleties of the Ascension,* 243, note 104.

18. Aḥmedī's *Cemşīd ü Ḫurşīd,* an adaptation of a lyric romance of the same name by Salmān-i Sāvajī (778/1376), was composed before the *miʿrāj* in the *İskendernāme.* It does not include a separate *miʿrāj* chapter, but several allusions are made to the story in a twelve-couplet lyric digression in a different meter and rhyme scheme at the end of the *naʿat* chapter. See Ahmedî, *Cemşîd ü Ḫurşîd,* 64–65.

19. In his edition of the work, Çelebioğlu provides information on fifty-eight manuscript copies and thirteen print editions, which were published in the nineteenth century, along with several other manuscript copies in Anatolian and European libraries; see Yazıcıoğlu, *Muḥammediyye,* 53–67. Also see Plate 16 for a sample illustrated printed edition.

20. This verse is repeated throughout the *miʿrāj* section as lines 2089, 2111, 2131, 2176, 2197, 2219, 2239, 2260, 2281, 2302, and 2323 in the Çelebioğlu edition.

21. This argument needs further research to compare Niẓāmī's *miʿrāj* chapters with those in Anatolian Turkish. For an anthology of *miʿrāj* chapters included in Persian lyric romances, see Ranjbar, *Chand Miʿrājnāma.*

22. For a general evaluation of the early lyric romances in Anatolian Turkish, see Dilçin's introduction to his edition of *Süheyl ü Nev-bahar* (Mesʿūd b. Aḥmed, *Süheyl ü Nev-bahār,* 1–8). For information on Mesʿūd's life story, see ibid., 9–25.

23. For a brief notice on the use of the hadith ḳudsī, or saying uttered by God Himself and known as *levlāk* in Turkish, see Schimmel, *As Through a Veil,* 178. Here, Schimmel translates this tradition as follows: "If you had not been I would not have created the spheres." The *naʿat* chapters in the lyric romances consistently start with a reference to *levlāk.*

24. The couplet numbers follow the Dilçin edition.

25. Qur'an 7:143.

26. "Two bows' length," ibid., 53:9.

27. Ibid., 15:72, "*la-ʿamruka*" ("By your life"). In this verse of the Qur'an, God cites Muḥammad as the reason for all creation.

28. The couplet numbers follow Holbrook's edition of *Hüsn ü ʿAşḳ.*

10

Skepticism and Forgiveness: The *Mi*ʿ*rāc* in Veysī's *Dürretü t-tāc*

GOTTFRIED HAGEN

The Prophet Muḥammad's ascension to heaven stands out among the legends from his life for its particular symbolic meaning. It occurs in the course of his prophetic career without any direct connection to other events of his life; no events or developments around him lead up to it, or prompt it.[1] Whereas the majority of his famous miracles, like the splitting of the moon, serve as proofs of his prophethood (*şevāhid-i nübüvvet*),[2] the *mi*ʿ*rāc* and the closely related opening of his breast serve to demonstrate the Prophet's initiation into prophethood and his ascending proximity to God. In a semiotic analysis, these latter two miracles might be categorized as "vertical miracles," bearing a message first of all for the Prophet himself, and indicating his progress in the vertical dimension, from the worldly to the divine realm. They are distinct from "horizontal miracles," whose primary audience consists in the environment of the Prophet, conveying his special status.[3] The very notion of prophetic miracle in Islamic thought fits squarely into the latter category, as encapsulated in the term *mu*ʿ*ciza,* which combines the meanings of being impossible, inimitable, and incapacitating (i.e., the opponents). As a result of this distinction, the *mi*ʿ*rāc,* although categorized as a miracle in many Muslim accounts, may be missing in collections of "proofs of prophethood," such as the work of ʿAbdurraḥmān Cāmī (d. 1492).[4] On the other hand, it is never missing from narratives of the life of the Prophet, that is, works belonging to the biographical (*sīra*) genre.

The Ottoman author Üveys b. Meḥmed, better known under his pen-name Veysī, not only considered the *mi*ʿ*rāc* a central miracle in the career of the Prophet, but in fact attributed to it a special significance that merits detailed consideration in its historical and intellectual context. Born in 1561–1562, Veysī was trained in the *medreses* of Istanbul and went on to pursue a somewhat bumpy but overall unremarkable career in the Ottoman judiciary, serving as a judge or financial inspector in Egypt, Anatolia, and the Balkans. Veysī ended up being judge of Üsküb (today Skopje in Macedonia) a total of seven times, where he died in 1628.[5] He wrote both poetry and prose, but it is on the latter that his fame rests. Out of his numerous works two have become particularly famous, even popular. The first is his *Ḫābnāme* (Book of Dreams), a reflection on history and political advice in the form of a dream conversation between Sulṭān Aḥmed I and the paragon of successful rule, Alexander the Great. The other is his account of the life of the Prophet Muḥammad, titled *Dürretü t-tāc fī sīret ṣāḥibi l-miʿrāc* (The Pearl of the Crown: The Vita of The One Who Ascended).

The *Dürretü t-tāc* is considered a culmination of Ottoman artistic prose. The Ottoman polymath Kātib Çelebi (d. 1657), two generations younger and not necessarily a kindred spirit, expressed his appreciation of Veysī's vita in his bibliographic dictionary. Here, he describes it as "an abridgment in Turkish in which [Veysī] used every kind of ornamental style most proficiently."[6] Numerous manuscripts of Veysī's work exist, along with two printed editions produced during the nineteenth century, thus attesting to its relative popularity in Ottoman realms.[7] As the work remained unfinished after Veysī's death, numerous authors have tried their hand at completing it, but none of them has been considered entirely successful. Until Tanzimat literature in the nineteenth century began to reject the elitist sophistication of classical Ottoman poetry, Veysī's work remained a model for Ottoman *sīra* writing.

Veysī considered the *miʿrāc* a prominent enough occurrence in the Prophet's life to make it part of the title of his book and to use it as the emblematic event in Muḥammad's distinguished career. In the present study, I use Veysī's section on the *miʿrāc* from *Dürretü t-tāc* to demonstrate how an Ottoman author positioned himself vis-à-vis the *sīra* tradition,[8] as well as how he expanded the tradition by producing his own version, a rendering that reflected the religious concerns and intellectual currents of his time. Furthermore, the way in which style and content are inextricably intertwined in Veysī's work also draws attention to the literary quality of *sīra* writing in general, which in turn helps to elucidate questions of audience and Sitz im Leben of *sīra* literature.

Sīra Works in Ottoman Turkish: Translation and Originality

Veysī was the first Ottoman author to produce a narrative of the Prophet's life that is fully his own rather than a Turkish translation of a biography written in another Islamic language, especially in Arabic or Persian. Ottoman *sīra* (in Turkish, *siyer*) literature comprises a rather heterogeneous genre, itself subsumed under the broader corpus of works dedicated to narrating events in the life of the Prophet Muḥammad. Prior to the nineteenth century, this literature includes a vast number of poetic works—including poems on the birth of the Prophet (*mevlid*)[9] and full-fledged verse narratives, such as one by an otherwise unknown fifteenth-century author named Meḥmed[10]—whereas the number of works in prose is limited. Only prose texts will be discussed in this chapter. In order to assess Veysī's contribution to this genre, it will be necessary first to offer a brief survey of its history.

Beginning in the late fourteenth century, translations initially dominated the genre. Muṣṭafā Ḍarīr's voluminous work was written for the Mamluk sultan Barqūq (r. 1382–1399) and is called a translation in the title, i.e., *Tercüme-i Ḍarīr ve taqdimetü l-Ẓahīr.* Although it is based on the popular stories circulating especially in Egypt under the name of Abū'l-Ḥasan al-Bakrī (fl. thirteenth century?), blended with long borrowings from Ibn Hishām (d. 833 or 828),[11] it is still a highly original work, which was chosen for lavish illumination in Istanbul at the end of the sixteenth century (Plates 17 and 18). The voice of the author-translator is particularly perceptible in the numerous verse passages with which the six-volume opus is interspersed, and which comment on the narrative. The style, which is much indebted to popular Turkish heroic narratives, gives this text a flavor distinct from its Arabic models.[12] On the other hand, the translation of the Arabic-language study of the life of the Prophet titled *al-Mawāhib al-laduniyya,* written by the Egyptian Sufi scholar al-Qasṭallānī (d. 1517) and rendered into Turkish by the scholar and poet Bāqī (d. 1600) on the order of the Ottoman grand vizier Ṣoqollu Meḥmed Paşa (d. 1579), is a very faithful, almost literal, translation in which the voice of the translator is not present at all.[13]

Similarly, there exists great variation among the Turkish translations of Persian texts, which were more numerous than those from Arabic. While some translations are awaiting closer investigation to determine their degree of dependency (as the Persian *Siyar-i Kāzarūnī,* itself a translation from Arabic), translations of Cāmī's *Ṣavāhid-i nubuvvat* and of Molla Muʿīn-i Miskīn's (d. 1501–2) *Maʿāric-i nubuvvat* produced between the late fifteenth and the early seventeenth century range from creative rewriting to a more or less complete and faithful rendering of the original Persian into Ottoman Turkish.[14] The stylistic register of these translations also varies between rather straightforward, even clumsy, Turkish and a highly elaborate, multilingual, and ornate prose.

None of these works became part of a sustained tradition of teaching and transmitting the *sīra* in Turkish. Most translator-authors were well-known scholars, often with a strong Sufi connection, and the works they produced in Turkish certainly reflect their linguistic and scholarly skills. Yet subsequent generations of Ottoman writers—attempting to create their own *sīra* narratives—all went back to the biographical tradition in Arabic and Persian instead of using texts available in Turkish. This suggests that the place of Turkish *sīra* literature in the Ottoman-Islamic scholarly and literary canon was distinct from that of the originals, with which the translations continued to coexist.[15] In addition, it can be argued that the originals continued to command a higher degree of authority, and that the process of translating itself had a particular value as the performance of a religious act.[16]

In the early Islamic era, the *sīra* tradition included a number of reports strikingly at odds with the mainstream, in terms of content, or in terms of theological ideas, or both. Thus, it had been said that Muḥammad sacrificed an animal at one of the sacred stones of Mecca, or that in despair over the lapse of revelation, he attempted to commit suicide.[17] The progressing consolidation of the Prophet's image over time eliminated or marginalized such accounts, with the result that by the Ottoman period the tradition was largely homogeneous, and free of contradictions and theologically problematic stories. Thus, after the fourteenth-century Turkish *sīra* by Muṣṭafā Ḍarīr with all its legendary and non-canonical material had been relegated to private circles and to the harem, variation in terms of content occurs in Ottoman *sīra*s only within the rather strict limits of Sunni orthodoxy.

These Ottoman *sīra* texts provide the backdrop against which we have to consider Veysī's work as an expression not only of an individual genius but also of a specific milieu.[18] In this study, I compare Veysī's work to previous texts for methodological reasons. Ultimately, *sīra* writing is both a science and a literary activity or, especially in the Ottoman case outside of the *medrese*, a science and an art form. In a hermeneutical approach to Veysī's text, ideally we would pursue what Gadamer has called the "fusion of horizons."[19] Unfortunately, the current state of research on Ottoman literature and thought is still far from a reconstruction of this horizon. What modern scholars often perceive as the frustratingly hermetic character of this literature ultimately is nothing but a very tightly knit web of meanings, which appears so impenetrable to us today because all those who held a share in it were initiated through many years of practice and daily interaction. To add to these difficulties, Ottoman interpretive guidance was hardly ever written down and has not come down to us. Progress has been made in penetrating the semantic web of historical, political, and poetic discourse, whereas the same endeavor in terms of religious, spiritual, and theological texts has hardly begun—a daunting task given the vast canonical heritage accessible to the Ottomans, to which Kātib Çelebi's monumental bibliographical encyclopedia bears witness.[20] This heritage is mirrored in the stupendous erudition of Ottoman scholars and the ease of their movement through texts and meanings. Therefore, comparing the work to its predecessors, in order to understand the decisions authors had to make while producing their texts out of a preexisting stream of traditions, helps to assess the work at least within the limits of *sīra* discourse, and may be seen as a step toward a fuller hermeneutic approach.

Between Narrative, Exegesis, and Homily

The tradition of the *miʿrāc* in *sīra* literature regularly consists of two distinct levels: one narrative, and one exegetical. The narrative level is concerned with the surface details of the story itself, while the exegetical level is largely concerned with problems of contradictory traditions (e.g., regarding the place where the *miʿrāc* began or whether it involved the body or spirit), and with theological issues arising from the account (such as the nature of the Prophet's vision of God). Both are ultimately concerned with the understanding and reconstruction of the events. In addition, there can be a third, homiletic level, which builds upon the previous two levels and which, being primarily interpretive, is often closely related to the exegetical level. This homiletic level deals with the moral teachings and spiritual gains that can be derived from the event of *miʿrāc.* Ottoman authors of *sīra* works selected or combined these two or sometimes three levels in accordance with their expected audience and with their own particular interests.

For example, Muṣṭafā Ḍarīr, who was more of a storyteller than a scholar and narrated the Prophet's biography to a courtly audience of non-specialists, disregarded the exegetical level almost entirely and also showed very little interest in the *sīra*'s homiletic potential, that is, its use as a medium for moralizing discourse or doctrinal instruction.[21] Instead, he produced a linear tale of great detail, to a large extent narrated through the Prophet's own voice. Ḍarīr's biography includes a whole series of moral and cosmological legends that had been grafted onto the original plot without so much as acknowledging that there are divergent traditions and interpretations of events in the Prophet's ascension. The only concession to possible theological disputes in Ḍarīr's narrative-heavy version of the *miʿrāc* is that he records the Prophet declaring that God did not permit him to divulge the nature of his vision of God.[22]

Among *sīra* texts popular among the Ottomans, the other extreme is represented by Qāḍī ʿIyāḍ (d. 1149)—whose text was subject to illustration at this time (Plate 19)—and al-Qasṭallānī, who do not offer an uninterrupted chronological narration, but rather focus entirely on the problems of hadith criticism and theology, that is, on exegesis. Although in doing so they partly follow the chronology of the *miʿrāc* tale, a narrative does not emerge as a coherent whole. These works therefore only make sense to those familiar with the ascension story beforehand, and provide good examples of works that stress the exegetical dimension over and above the narrative dimension of the *sīra.*[23]

The homiletic concern is particularly visible in the work of Muʿīn-i Miskīn, whose text was widely read in its original form and in several translations. In his *Maʿāric-i nubuvvat,* the author presents a very detailed chronological narrative of the Prophet's ascension in which the tale is frequently suspended by means of exegetical digressions discussing divergent traditions. Even more frequently inserted, however, are sections that expose the moral or spiritual implications of the events just narrated. These latter digressions, usually titled *laṭīfa* (pleasant story), typically consist of short narratives or verses driving home the author's edifying message.[24] Muʿīn-i Miskīn's approach thus demonstrates how the homiletic level can be intertwined with the exegetical, while the narrative level is reduced to little more than an organizing principle. The homiletic emphasis corresponds with Muʿīn's interest in preaching, as opposed to Ḍarīr's narrative or Qāḍī ʿIyāḍ's teaching.

In composing his *miʿrāc* text, Veysī strikes more of a compromise between the three levels than any of his predecessors. His *miʿrāc* chapter, like his entire work, is very brief. In the printed edition in quarto (as compared to the folio-sized editions of al-Qasṭallānī and Muʿīn-i Miskīn), it occupies no more than a dozen pages. Kātib Çelebi indeed characterized Veysī's work as an abridgment (*muḫtaṣar*), which may mean that in the perception of contemporary readers it was considered as a category different from full *miʿrāc* accounts, such as those composed by Muʿīn-i Miskīn. At the very least, Kātib Çelebi's description demonstrates that he considered Veysī's account a condensed one. In his brief account of the ascension, Veysī first addresses the most pressing text-critical and exegetical questions, although, at the same time, he tries to avoid a debate, lest "theological dispute (*mübāḥeṣe-i kelāmīye*)" confound the "evidence-radiating events of the [life of the] Prophet."[25] That theology is not his main concern is also indicated by the fact that—as has been noted—he goes against the grain of the tradition in calling the *miʿrāc* a miracle. After this section, he launches into a very compressed chronological narration of the *miʿrāc*. We will see how Veysī shifts attention to certain aspects of the tale while giving no more than a nod to others or disregarding some altogether. At the very end of his narrative, however, he switches modes again and attaches a concluding anecdote that advances a homiletic interpretation of the entire *miʿrāc*.

Selectivity

The brevity of the entire chapter required Veysī to condense his account to a considerable degree—so much so, in fact, that several topics and motifs are barely skirted. The tightly knit web of narratives, symbols, and meanings that make the entire *miʿrāc* tradition so appealing as a vehicle to convey religious messages can be broken down into several complexes:

- The construction of the Prophet of Islam through his relation to earlier prophets, to the angels, and to the spirits, and ultimately through his encounter with God;
- The delineation of the Muslim community through certain practices—the five daily prayers, the prohibition of wine—as preordained distinctions, and the affirmation of the *miʿrāc* by members of the Muslim community as a mark of the Prophet's distinction;
- The endorsement of communal values and rules through the description of specific punishments to come;[26]
- The presentation of a complex cosmology, including God's throne (*ʿarş*) and footstool (*kursī*), the spheres of the planets, the seven heavens, paradise and hell, the Lote Tree of the Limit (*sidre-i müntehā*), the Basin in paradise (*kevṣer*), and the rivers of paradise (to these Ḍarīr adds several more elements, such as the Sea of Life, the Sea of the Flood, and the Sea of Sustenance).[27]

Veysī in turn is highly selective in the way he takes up these themes and motifs. The Prophet's inspection of paradise and of hell, the latter employed by previous scholars to dramatically illustrate the punishment of certain sins they deemed significant in their community, is glossed over in one sentence. The testing of the cups, an episode recorded in many variant narratives in order to emphasize the distinction of the Muslim community, is given only slightly more attention.[28] What constitutes probably one of the main interests for Muʿīn-i Miskīn—that is, the Prophet's visits to the seven heavens—is little more than a list of prophets' names in Veysī's account, and all the other things shown to the Prophet are summarized as follows: "In every sphere, he witnessed marvelous wonders beyond the comprehension of numbers."[29] Furthermore, Veysī leaves out some episodes that are relatively standard features in other *miʿrāc* accounts. For example, the vehement disbelief expressed by the pagan Meccans upon Muḥammad's return has traditionally stood as a symbol of the distinction between believers, represented by Abū Bakr (named with the honorific epithet al-Ṣiddīq at this time), and the unbelievers under their leader Abū Cahl.[30] This entire episode also is passed over in silence by Veysī. All these omissions suggest that, for Veysī, the imparting of moral advice, typically explored in homiletic interpretations of the heavenly spheres and the Prophet's confrontation with the Meccans, was not of prime interest.

Other omissions in the narrative can be explained by the context in which Veysī composed his work. For instance, Veysī did not see a need to elaborate on Muḥammad's encounter with the earlier prophets, which would firmly place him within the sequence of revelations that punctuate salvation history. Elsewhere in his work it becomes clear that for him the Prophet is so far above every other prophet, utterly unique, that such legitimating narratives are obsolete. Equally, Veysī is not concerned at all to connect Muḥammad to a genealogy of prophets, as his predecessors regularly did; his book begins only with Muḥammad's vita, not with earlier history leading up to the Prophet's life. In this respect, Veysī is in perfect accordance with a broader movement in Ottoman society, which resulted in a specifically Ottoman form of piety centered around the Prophet. The public and private veneration of the Prophet promoted by the Ottoman dynasty after the late sixteenth century, such as the cult of the Prophet's relics and the celebration of his birthday (*mevlid*), form the most conspicuous indicators of this process.[31]

Most surprisingly at first glance, the Prophet's encounter with God and the related debates over his vision of the Lord do not play any significant role in Veysī's account. Veysī relates that Muḥammad, while roaming through the heavenly realms, was beatified (*müstesʿid*) by reaching the foot of the throne of the Merciful, but then restricts himself to saying that he "attained infinite divine favors beyond what can be encompassed by words of speech."[32] The beatific vision has attracted much theological attention; moreover, the Sufi tradition in particular emphasized it as the ultimate—if unattainable—model of a human encounter with the divine. That Veysī did not further elaborate on it may be understood by taking seriously his assertion that it was "beyond what can be encompassed by words of speech." On the other hand, it is also plausible that he was reluctant to engage a theologically volatile topic.[33]

One important aspect of Veysī's selective approach to *miʿrāc* material is that for the most part he is concerned only with those episodes that are generally accepted and not contested by the standard authorities such as Qāḍī ʿIyāḍ or al-Qasṭallānī. Such episodes are regularly introduced by the author with phrases such as "This claim has also reached the rank of certainty,"[34] or "This tradition, too, has been written down in the records of acceptance."[35] These rhetorical strategies indicate that Veysī's concern lies with an innovative interpretation of received tradition, and this would certainly be more convincing if based on well-accepted narratives than drawn upon rare and potentially unsound traditions.

The Physical Aspects of the *Miʿrāc*

Two major themes emerge as central in Veysī's treatment of the *miʿrāc:* one is the physical character of the ascension, and together with this the physical reality of the transcendental world to which the Prophet traveled. This is largely an exegetical problem, whereas the second major theme is located on the homiletic level, to be discussed in the following section.

Whether the Prophet made the ascension awake or asleep, in body or only in spirit, or in the course of a vision, is the most important theological concern in the context of the *miʿrāc* tradition. As previously stated, the Ottoman *sīra* tradition is largely unvaried, which for the *miʿrāc* means that all authors agreed that the *miʿrāc* was experienced bodily, that the *isrā'* and *miʿrāc* occurred together in one night, that there was no opening of the breast during the *miʿrāc,*[36] that the visionary account of Qur'an 53:1–18 does in fact refer to the *miʿrāc,* and so forth.[37] Veysī is no exception, so that the long argumentative passage constituting about the first half of his *miʿrāc* chapter seems to be merely repeating the usual scriptural authorities. To my knowledge, all Ottoman *sīra* texts, as well as the major Ottoman commentary on the Qur'an, Ebū l-Suʿūd Efendi's (d. 1574) *Irşād al-ʿaql al-salīm,* agree on the physical character of the Prophet's *miʿrāc.*[38] The only widely read authoritative text that supported the notion of a *miʿrāc* in spirit was al-Zamaḫşarī's (d. 1144) commentary on the Qur'an titled *al-Kashshāf.*[39] Veysī thus follows the mainstream thought regarding the Prophet's *miʿrāc* in dealing with this particular theological issue.

Veysī appears to be weary of these types of theological disputes, which he does not want to interfere with the thrust of his *sīra.* As he declares: "In this short treatise, the black-tailed horse, the reed pen, is not allowed so much liberty of running to and fro that it should mix theological arguments with the evidence-radiating events of the [life of the] Prophet."[40] Nevertheless, he addresses the main points, adducing fairly standard arguments to show that Muḥammad went on the *miʿrāc* in spirit and body jointly while awake. This position leaves open the possibility that this physical ascension that the Prophet experienced while awake was preceded by another visionary *miʿrāc* that he experienced while asleep, because God had chosen to introduce the Prophet to the realities of heaven step by step, just as nightly visions had preceded the revelation of the Qur'an.[41]

The unique aspect of Veysī's argument lies elsewhere, especially in the way he takes on rationalist skeptics who deny the possibility of a bodily ascension to heaven. In the opening phrase of his ascension chapter, he rails against such "imitators of the philosophers, who have surrendered to the bridle of philosophy," according to whom "the virtue of mankind is limited to explaining the drawings in the *Almagest* with the key of Euclid the Wise." In "their permanent recourse to the mathematical laws of the Brahmins,"[42] they used to object that it is unacceptable to imagine that the substance of the celestial spheres should open and close [to let the Prophet and his company pass through], perforce making the *miʿrāc* a physical impossibility. Some of these "mathematicians"—who are "fettered by the deficient rules of Aristotle"[43]—also cited the qur'anic phrase "I am only a mortal like you" to demonstrate the physical impossibility of the Prophet's heavenly ascension.[44]

Objections based on the laws of physics were not a new phenomenon in *miʿrāc* discourse. In a famous passage, Faḫr al-dīn al-Rāzī (d.606/1209) had argued in his commentary on the Qur'an that the fast movement necessary to pass through space the way the Prophet must have done is in fact physically possible.[45] Veysī's reference not only to the "rules of reason" (*rüsūm-ı ʿaqlīye*) but also to the central works of Greek scientific lore as cultivated in the Islamic world suggests an intellectual context to this passage beyond the regular theological disputes. Rather, the author's tone suggests that he was addressing an ongoing debate that was raging in his own time.

Since the last decades of the sixteenth century, there seems to have been an increasing bifurcation between the religious sciences and more secular approaches to understanding the universe. Whereas some geographers invoked religious justification for their descriptions of the world, which were certainly often satisfying a "this-worldly" curiosity, we also observe a continuing and probably growing emphasis on Islamic cosmology based on hadith.[46] In 1577, for example, Sulṭān Murād III (r. 1574–1595) ordered a new observatory built on the hills between Galata and Tophane, but in 1580 another political faction managed to convince the sultan to have it torn down. This affair, a *cause célèbre* among historians of science, should not be reduced to an example of scientific progress thwarted by religious narrow-mindedness; rather, it indicates how religious arguments could be mustered against efforts to study the universe through measurement and observation.[47]

A few decades after Veysī, the polymath Kātib Çelebi deplored how philosophy and science, once highly regarded in Islam, were increasingly neglected since the days of Sulṭān Süleymān (r. 1520–1566) and how such neglect had lead to ignorance and misjudgments. He also drew on al-Ġazālī (d. 1111) to argue that disputing scientific truths on religious grounds was doing a disservice to religion.[48] There is good reason to assume that Kātib Çelebi was not alone with this belief, and that he represented a broader tendency in Ottoman society that favored a scientific worldview that was critical of phenomena considered legendary or mythical. Moreover, a few outspoken atheists are attested both before and after Veysī's time. One of them, Lārī Meḥmed Efendi (d. 1665), used to greet his friends with the exclamation "*yoq*," i.e., "there is no [god]."[49] Such atheists are documented because they were so outspoken that the authorities intervened and ultimately ordered them to be executed. Again, it is likely that they were only the tip of an iceberg of skepticism in Ottoman society.[50] All these examples suggest that the doubts cast on the *miʿrāc* on grounds of physics for Veysī were not merely a theoretical, but a very real, highly debated, and quite timely issue. The suggestion would also imply that this criticism emerged in close proximity to the circles frequented by Veysī, since the Ottoman intellectual elite did not distinguish in principle between religious or legal scholars on the one hand and scientists on the other; rather, these types of intellectuals were all closely interconnected.

But does Veysī simply reject scientific or philosophical arguments as invalid in principle? The phrase "the deficient rules of Aristotle" seems to suggest this, but other expressions indicate that his concern was more that these "rules" claimed to explain everything, while in his opinion they applied only to the external world. Thus he accuses these critics of being concerned with rules (or laws) and seeing only the outward (*ẓāhir*) side of things: *ol maqūle ẓāhir-bīnān-ı qawāʿid-pīşe.*[51] In contrast, Veysī seems to have been keen on demonstrating the physical reality of the other world. While he does not spend much time, as has been mentioned, on the cosmological aspects as such, he does describe the Prophet's mount, Burāq, and the Lote Tree of the Limit (*sidretü l-müntehā,* Qur'an 53:14) in great detail. In the case of Burāq, also praised in a long poem in Persian, the point is made through the juxtaposition of the physical description of this fantastic beast with its epithet "measuring the no-place" (*lā-mekān-peymā*).[52] The Lote Tree bears fruits like large buckets (*sebū-yi hucur*) and leaves like the ears of elephants; it is also surrounded by innumerable angels, and its shadow takes seventy years to traverse.[53] These kinds of physical details in an otherwise strongly abridged narrative seem to support his argument that the *miʿrāc* should be accepted wholesale as a physical reality, against scientific and philosophical objections.

Intercession and Forgiveness

The second major theme that seems to distinguish Veysī's account of the *miʿrāc* from that of his predecessors is the infinite and unmotivated divine grace and forgiveness (*maḥḍ-ı merḥamet-i bī-ʿillet-i aḥadīyet,* KV 115) revealed to the Prophet during his encounter with God. The topic is raised in a slightly different way than in the standard accounts of the imposition of the ritual prayers, in which Muḥammad, upon the advice of Moses, negotiates the reduction of obligatory daily prayers from fifty to five (Plate 18). Vuckovic interprets this story primarily as symbolizing Muslim superiority over the community of Moses, because Moses keeps encouraging Muḥammad to ask for an even lower number based on his own experience of the weakness of his followers.[54] Veysī, on the other hand, seems more interested in the expression of divine mercy as the heavy prayer obligations are diminished in number. He makes this clear by prefacing this section with the revelation of the final verse of the second *sūra* from the Qur'an, a rather unusual element in this context:

> God charges no soul save to its capacity; take us not to task if we forget, or make mistake. Our Lord, charge us not with a load such as Thou didst lay upon those before us. Our Lord, do Thou not burden us beyond what we have the strength to bear. And pardon us, and forgive us, and have mercy on us; Thou art our Protector. And help us against the people of the unbelievers.[55]

By citing these verses in connection to the reduction in the number of prayers the Muslim community is commanded to observe, Veysī suggests that God offers such a reduction as a mercy granted, made so as not to saddle the community with too heavy a burden.

Beyond his attribution of mercy to the reduction of prayers, Veysī makes an even more explicit and more unique interpretation of the *miʿrāc* as a manifestation of divine grace following the conclusion of the narrative, that is, after the Prophet's return to Mecca. Here, Veysī declares his intention to "impress the musk-seal [of a good conclusion] upon this fortunate session of the joy-radiating *miʿrāc,* with an inspiring whiff from the amber-wafting bouquet of divine favor."[56] This phrase constitutes the introduction to the narrative's terminal section, which I previously described as homiletic. With the background of God granting the Prophet's every request in the course of his *miʿrāc,* this section describes yet another request made at the same time: Muḥammad asks that on the Day of Judgment his community's books of deeds be given to him so that he can erase every sin recorded in them. This takes the quintessential role of the Prophet as intercessor (*ṣāfiʿ*, *ṣafīʿ*) for his community to the extreme.

Contrary to the classical traditions on the topic, intercession here is unconditional, since there is no mention of penitence, and all-encompassing, as no exceptions are made known. Its efficacy is guaranteed, as implied by the metaphor of the total erasing of sins from the books of deeds.[57] However, Veysī's version of this categorical promise of salvation goes even further: God responds that he does not even want Muḥammad to have to see the registers of his community's sins. His being the "veiler" (*sattār*) requires him to conceal their shame even from Muḥammad, and His being the "forgiver" (*ġaffār*) compels him not to send those who take refuge with Him to the place of execution (hell).[58] In other words, Veysī's account promises all Muslims redemption as a special favor being granted to Muḥammad on the night of the ascension.

This ultimate hyperbole of intercession is granted not in response to the plea of the Prophet as intercessor but as a tribute to him and his virtues. In this sense, Veysī has turned the *miʿrāc* into a complement of the *mevlid,* the celebration of the Prophet's birth. This *mevlid* account was encapsulated for Ottomans in a poem composed by Süleymān Çelebi in 1409, which subsequently became the centerpiece of all *mevlid* celebrations. Titled "Means of Salvation" (*Vesīletü l-necāt*), this poem extolled the birth of the Prophet as the single event that ensured salvation for the community of believers, privileging the veneration of the persona of the Prophet over revelation, law, and daily practice. As an expression of popular piety, and a response to it, the *mevlid* had offered consolation for the masses without the rigorous requirements of legal and ritual obligations.[59] In a new form of religiosity that emerged in the Ottoman elite after the late sixteenth century, an ostentatious cult of the prophet in public ceremonies or in the veneration of his relics played an important role. Beginning in 1589, one aspect of this cultural mode included the celebration of the *mevlid* in public by the Ottoman sultan, in the main mosque of Istanbul, along with recitations of Süleymān Çelebi's poem and sermons by the main preachers of the capital.[60] It is not only the poetic expressions in Veysī's work, which will be discussed below, that reflect this new mode of religiosity. Pious literature of the period seems to be imbued by the idea that human sins are so great that only divine grace, not individual betterment, can provide salvation. As we have seen, Veysī's interpretation of the *miʿrāc* builds on the tension between the inherent sinfulness of man and the gratuity of intercession. Thus, Veysī's reinterpretation of the *miʿrāc* as another manifestation of the promise of salvation can be seen once again to fit into the larger context of Ottoman religious praxis and thought.

Veysī's frequent praise for the night, i.e., the night of the *miʿrāc,* also takes on an additional meaning in this context, as it may indicate an attempt to legitimize the inclusion of the night of the ascension (*miʿrāc gecesi*) among the officially recognized and celebrated *kandil* nights, the non-canonical holidays specific to Turkish (or more precisely Ottoman) Islam. By the middle of the sixteenth century, there were only three recognized *kandil* nights, but the nights commemorating the *mevlid* and *miʿrāc* came to be added over time, most likely in the late sixteenth or seventeenth century.[61] Veysī's work may thus have helped the celebration of the night of the *miʿrāc* to gain more official acceptance in Ottoman Muslim practice.

Style and Meaning

Veysī's fame rests largely on his prose style, as indicated already by Kātib Çelebi and confirmed by other contemporary sources.[62] Ottoman ornate prose, developed in the imperial chancery and among the court chroniclers, used a wide variety of devices for rhetorical effect, such as paronomasia, parallelisms, and rhyme, employing Arabic and Persian vocabulary alongside Turkish. Thus, a rhyming phrase, such as the description of the appearance of the ladder to heaven as "*felek-i dünyāya merfūᶜ bir nerdbān-ı nūr-efşān ve miᶜrāc-ı raṣīnü l-erkān nümāyān oldı*" (KV 112), is frequent. The expressions *Burāq-ı berrāq* ("radiant Burāq") and the "bridle of philosophy" (*ḥakeme-i ḥikmet*) make use of words derived from homonymous roots in Arabic.[63] Other examples have been cited previously in this study.

Ornate prose (*inşā'*) significantly broadened an author's range of register, because he could employ such rhetorical *tours de force* in combination with other modes of expression. Veysī uses rather straightforward prose (albeit rarely), experiments with different degrees of ornamentation, and inserts short or long sections of poetry, mostly in Persian but also in Arabic and Turkish. Obviously, these devices can be used independently from the semantic level of the text, and can serve to amplify even the most mundane passage without adding anything in terms of content and meaning.[64]

The second store of rhetorical devices Veysī uses is the metaphor-rich language of Ottoman poetry.[65] By his time, the so-called Indian Style (*sabq-ı hindī*) had also begun to strike root in Turkish prose, allowing, among other things, for the intersection or combination of different metaphors in the same context, adding more complexity, more playfulness, but also more density to the texts.[66] That the Prophet had his every request granted from God is expressed with the metaphor of the royal falcon: every falcon (wish) that emerged and rose from the privacy of the tent of prophethood preyed on the pheasant of acceptance in the apogee of the sky (desire of proximity to God).[67] The Prophet's departure from Mecca combines the image of the night as a black veil for a woman with that of a king's procession: "Cibrā'īl and Mikā'īl were clinging to his throne-traversing stirrups from the right and left like power and glory, while the chaste "Mother of Cities" [Mecca] shrouded in black was raising her hand in praise and applause."[68] Mecca is a female figure that is suggestive of humbleness and honor. There is also here the unspoken idea that these processions used to be occasions at which time subjects could submit petitions to kings, possibly to seek out their mercy and forgiveness.

It is my contention that Veysī's reputation as a master of ornate prose rests on his ability not only to cloak his text in such ornamentation but also to use such stylistic devices, especially metaphors and images, to convey additional meanings or to guide an interpretation beyond the immediate semantics of the narrative. In Ottoman poetic language, symbols are multilayered: not only can they signify a variety of things, but they in turn can transform into other symbols. What Walter Andrews and Mehmet Kalpaklı state about Ottoman poetry is true for Veysī's prose as well: "One of the things that Ottoman poets could do because they worked with limited, stable, conventional components was to take wild flights of rhetorical fancy and revel in subtle allusions and barely perceptible connections."[69] In the limited scope of this study, a complete analysis of Veysī's rhetorical devices is not possible. However, I touch upon these devices here in order to highlight the poetic quality of his text and what this quality entails for contemporary and modern audiences.

In Veysī's account of the *miᶜrāc,* sometimes a single word can add an entire layer of meaning. For instance, having arrived in Jerusalem, Muḥammad ties the bridle of Burāq to the *ḥalqe-i iᶜtiṣām* that had been used by previous prophets to attach their own steeds. At the literal level, this means a ring to firmly hold onto,[70] but *iᶜtiṣām* also means "staying away from sinful behavior," and is etymologically related to *ᶜiṣma,* the doctrine of the Prophet's immunity against sin and error, which is here subtly extended to the preceding prophets.[71] When Muḥammad informs us that he saw the prophet Idrīs "presiding in the *medrese* of the fourth heaven,"[72] the *medrese* is not simply a synonym for the space of the fourth heaven, but indicates Idrīs's special place among the prophets as the inventor of writing and teaching. Examples of this kind can be multiplied with ease.[73]

Thus, the skilled use of symbolic imagery and multiple semantic levels helps Veysī to create a web of meanings in which every moment of the *sīra* is connected to every other, while at the same time allowing for the maximum condensing of the narrative itself, because many aspects can be expressed by way of a metaphorical code alone. To cut through this web to the "real" or "original" or "basic" meaning would simply be to deprive the text of its richness. To extract from it the main plot of the narrative, to paraphrase as I have done occasionally, impoverishes it; stripping it of the rhetoric destroys not only the sound, but also the meaning itself. It was not the plot of the ascension per se, which was widely known at this time, that truly delighted his literate audience. Rather, it was wandering through this web of meanings and disentangling the multiple allusions and cross-references that constituted the essential aesthetic appeal of Veysī's work.

Let us at this point return to the interpretation advanced in the homiletic conclusion of the *miᶜrāc* chapter. I argue that, to the informed reader, the final reference to the unconditional and unlimited grace of God as the essential outcome of the entire *miᶜrāc* does not come as a surprise to the literate audience because Veysī had used all kinds of stylistic and rhetorical devices to prepare them for it by dropping hints and clues along the way. References to the miserable and grief-stricken state of the community (e.g., KV 116: *ümmet-i ḫaste-ḥāl-i ġam-ḫwārī*) appear in several instances in the text; the dialogue between Moses and Muḥammad over the negotiation of the number of prayers sets the stage for the presentation of the community as too weak to bear the strict requirements (*riyāḍīyāt*) of Islam. At the same time, the Prophet returns to earth after the *miᶜrāc* as a "sign of [God's] grace" (*āyet-i raḥmet*). Again, this metaphor is coupled with an entirely different one: "The bird of paradise appears in the greenery of the world of mankind, the pheasant of *ᶜillīyīn* arrives in the area of the traps of mankind" (*dām-gāh-i beşerīyet,* KV 117). Such metaphors express how the Prophet appears, as a sign of grace, in the most unworthy context, "decorating the world with grace" (*cihānī şüd ez raḥmet āreste,* KV 117).

The Prophet's description of the Day of Judgment makes for another evocative contrast, as Veysī here employs many different images of bookkeeping, accounting, and dealing with money for the process of recording and calculating human guilt.

Thus, the inspection of the records becomes associated with a materialistic human activity known to be fraught with inaccuracy and injustice, and is even more powerfully contrasted to the divine grace that renders this entire process obsolete in granting wholesale forgiveness to the community of Muḥammad.[74] With these types of rhetorical clues strewn throughout the text, Veysī's literate audience becomes well prepared for this expression of God's mercy with which his *miʿrāc* account concludes.

The two main themes elaborated on in this chapter, the skepticism of those who insist on the laws of physics and the promise of infinite forgiveness, are never explicitly linked by Veysī. Certain connections, however, can be inferred. One is that the promise of forgiveness and salvation extends to every Muslim, and thus presumably also to the skeptics who raise objections against the physical reality of the *miʿrāc;* it is worth noting that their attitude is not condemned as sinful or heretic, but rather as intellectually insufficient. The other, more powerful aspect is that by insisting on the physical reality of the heavens and the bodily character of the Prophet's ascension, Veysī also—again, implicitly—attributes the highest degree of reality to the promise of salvation, which is embodied in the persona of the Prophet.

The level of sophistication in Veysī's writing in terms of his linguistic range and the scope of his stylistic register suggests an erudite, even elite, audience. This impression is supported by a number of references to scholarly authorities in the text. In the section on the *miʿrāc,* these include a number of widely read texts, such as Qāḍī ʿIyāḍ's *al-Şifā'* or al-Suhaylī's (d. 1185) *Rawḍ al-unuf,* but also some less popular works, such as al-Zarkaşī's *Kitāb iʿlām al-sācid bi-aḥkām al-masācid* or the unidentified work *Zayn al-qıṣaṣ.*[75] Despite its literary style, Veysī's text often abandons the narrative in favor of scholarly arguments about hadith criticism, scriptural proof, and philosophical implications, quoting evidence in the original Arabic. Ultimately, the two levels of narrative and exegesis are held together by the homily, moving swiftly between the two in extracting from the entire event the deeper message, which hinges on intercession and salvation. That Veysī called the chapter a *meclis,* or "session," suggests that the work was intended to be read in a learned circle of scholars, Sufis, and other learned connoisseurs. However, while the text may speak to a small initiated circle, the promise of salvation through the person of the Prophet Muḥammad as a truth above rationalistic criticism extends beyond this select audience and encompasses all Muslims. The chapter on the Prophet's *miʿrāc* in Veysī's work makes this point most forcefully, thus justifying the author's decision to name the entire work after it: *The Pearl of the Crown: the Vita of The One Who Ascended.*

Notes

Many thanks are due to Christiane Gruber and Frederick Colby for their thoughtful comments on several stages of this chapter. Needless to say, all remaining shortcomings are my own.

1. It is explained in some accounts as divine consolation of the Prophet in the "Year of Sadness," marked by the death of Abū Ṭālib and Ḫadīca (thanks to Frederick Colby for pointing this out). This connection, however, is obviously secondary, since many different dates are reported for the *miʿrāc*. So this explanation just underscores the awareness of the lack of an obvious link.

2. Throughout this chapter, I am using a modified Turkish system of transliteration, intended to not confuse the non-specialist, and to render satisfactory precision for the specialist. My translations of Veysī's prose are necessarily inadequate, oscillating between the vague but idiomatic, and the literal but awkward, depending on the point to be made.

3. This distinction is taken from Derouet, *Les possibilités d'interprétation sémiologique des textes hagiographiques,* and seems to me to be valid for the life of the Prophet as well. On the opening of the breast, see Rubin, *The Eye of the Beholder,* which also contains a discussion of the earlier literature.

4. On this work see Storey and Bregel, *Persidskaia Literatura,* 560–565; and Hagen, "Translations and Translators."

5. *Encyclopaedia of Islam,* new ed. (E.I.²), s.v. "Weysī"; for the most comprehensive Ottoman source see ʿAṭāʾī, *Ẕeyl-i şaqāʾiq* 1:713–716.

6. He writes, *"Aḥsana fī inşāʾihī kulla l-iḥsān."* See Kātib Çelebi, *Kaşf al-ẓunūn,* 738 f.

7. For this study, I have used the text in the second edition, *Külliyāt-ı Veysī,* Istanbul 1286, henceforth cited as *KV.*

8. By *sīra* tradition I mean the entire stream of hadith relating to the Prophet's life, as gathered in a wide variety of works. See Schöller, *Exegetisches Denken und Prophetenbiographie;* and Kister "The Sīrah Literature."

9. On *mevlid,* see Pekolcay, *Süleyman Çelebi: Mevlid (Vesîletü'n-necât);* Süleyman Çelebi, *The Mevlidi Sherif;* and most recently Dedes, "Süleyman Çelebi's Mevlid."

10. Berlin, Staatsbibliothek, Ms. or. fol. 3333 (Sohrweide, *Türkische Handschriften,* 236ff., Nr. 277).

11. It may be observed here that Ibn Hishām/Ibn Isḥāq and Abū l-Ḥasan al-Bakrī are much closer to one another than one would suspect from their respective places in scholarship. On this issue, see Sellheim, "Prophet, Chalif und Geschichte: Die Muhammad-Biographie des Ibn Isḥāq"; Shoshan, *Popular Culture in Medieval Cairo.* For the spurious character of attributions to al-Bakrī, see Rudi Paret, *Die legendäre Maghāzī-Literatur.*

12. Hagen, "Some Considerations about the *Tergüme-i Darir ve taqdimetü z-zahir.*"

13. E.I.², s.v. "al-Ḳasṭallānī" and "Bāqī." I am grateful to İsmail Eriş, Ph.D. candidate at the University of Michigan, for comparing the translation and the original for me during a summer research project.

14. Hagen, "Translations and Translators." On Muʿīn-i Miskīn and the Turkish translation by Altıparmaq Meḥmed Efendi, see the chapter by Özgen Felek in the present volume. On the *Siyar-i Kāzarūnī,* see Storey and Bregel, *Persidskaia Literatura,* 548–550.

15. This distinction also allows me, for the purpose of this chapter, to ignore the works written in Turkish in the same period in the Ottoman domain, but also written in Arabic, most prominently al-Diyārbakrī's (d. after 990/1582) *al-Taʾrīḫ al-ḫamīs fī sīrat anfas al-nafīs* and al-Ḥalabī's (d. 1044/1635) *al-Sīra al-Ḥalabīya* (Brockelmann, *Geschichte der Arabischen Litteratur,* 2:207, 381). These remained distinct, and there seems to be no exchange between them and the texts written in Turkish.

16. See Hagen, "Translations and Translators."

17. Rubin, *The Eye of the Beholder,* 78 and 113, respectively.

18. In Ottoman studies, the historical and sociological background of the field has led to a strong emphasis on the study of literary texts as products of their authors' social and political background, whereas the concept of an author as a unique individual is mostly forgotten.

19. Hans-Georg Gadamer, *Wahrheit und Methode. Grundzüge einer philosophischen Hermeneutik,* 286–290.

20. For exemplary studies of Ottoman intellectuals see Fleischer, *Bureaucrat and Intellec-*

tual; Schmidt, *Pure Water for Thirsty Muslims;* and Dankoff, *Evliya Çelebi: an Ottoman Mentality.* For a plea for Ottoman poetry, see Andrews, *Poetry's Voice, Society's Song.* On Kātib Çelebi's *Kaşf al-ẓunūn* as a canon of Ottoman knowledge, see Birnbaum, "The Questing Mind of Katib Chelebi, 1609–1657." Several young scholars have started to bring religious discourses back into focus, notably Derin Terzioğlu, Nabil al-Tikriti, Tijana Krstic, and John Curry.

21. His poetic digressions, mentioned before, may be the only exception.

22. Mustafa Darîr, *Siyer-i Nebî,* tr. Gürtunca, vol. 2, 166–224; on the vision of God, see ibid., 204.

23. Bāqī, *Maᶜālimü l-yaqīn,* 400–430; Qāḍī ᶜIyāḍ, *Şifā',* vol. 1, 343 ff.

24. Altıparmaq, *Delā'il-i nübuvvet-i Muḥammedī,* 297–376.

25. *KV,* 107. Al-Qasṭallānī as well as Qāḍī ᶜIyāḍ, on the other hand, had their entire works arranged systematically.

26. The first three of these have been studied in detail by Vuckovic, *Heavenly Journeys,* on the basis of early Muslim traditions.

27. Darîr, *Siyer-i Nebi,* vol. 2, 176–184.

28. *KV,* 113 f.

29. *KV,* 112: "*her felekde bīrūn-i ḥīṭa-ı şümār nice ᶜacā'ib-i ġarībe şühūd eyledi.*"

30. Vuckovic, *Heavenly Journeys,* 75–95.

31. On the relics of the Prophet in the Ottoman palace, see Öz, *Hırka-i Saadet dairesi ve Emanat-ı Mukaddese;* and Necipoğlu, *Architecture, Ceremonial, and Power,* 150–152. The institution of the *mevlid* is described by Dedes, *Süleyman Çelebi's Mevlid.*

32. *KV,* 115: "*iḥāṭa-ı niṭāq-ı nuṭqdan bīrūn elṭāf-ı mā-lā-nihāye-i ilāhīye fāyiz* [*sic*] *oldılar.*"

33. For the *miᶜrāc* in Sufi thought, see Böwering "From the Word of God to the Vision of God." I thank Frederick Colby for further comments on this question.

34. *KV,* 113: "*bu müddeᶜā daḫı rütbe-i s̱übūta vāṣıldur ki . . .*"

35. *KV,* 114: "*bu menqūl daḫı nüvişte-i sicill-i qabūl olmışdur ki . . .*"

36. This point had been made in an authoritative way by Qāḍī ᶜIyāḍ.

37. On the main theological questions, see Andrae, *Die person Muhammeds in lehre und glauben seiner gemeinde,* 71–73; and van Ess, "Le Miᶜrāğ et la vision de Dieu dans les premières spéculations théologiques en Islam."

38. Ebū s-Suᶜūd, *Tafsīr Abī l-suᶜūd: Irşād al-ᶜaql al-salīm,* vol. 3, 319 ff.

39. See Schimmel, *Mystical Dimensions of Islam,* 162. Schimmel attributes this position to the Muᶜtazilite character of al-Zamaḫşarī's work, an interpretation which, however, has been disputed (Lane, *A traditional Mu'tazilite Qur'an Commentary*).

40. *KV,* 107: "*Bu muḫtaṣar risālede kümeyt-i siyah-zānū-yı qaleme ol qadar ruḫṣat-ı tekāpū verilmez ki veqā'iᶜ-i sāṭiᶜü l-burhān-ı nebevīyeye ḫalṭ-ı mübāḥes̱e-i kelāmīye eyleye.*"

41. *KV,* 108, quoting Suhaylī's *Rawḍ al-unuf,* but the same argument is also found in Ebū l-Suᶜūd's *Tafsīr Abī l-suᶜūd.*

42. *KV,* 107: "*maġlūb-ı ḥakeme-i ḥikmet olan ṭarḥ-endāzān-ı uṣūl-ı felāsife ki hemīşe yanlarında fażīlet-i insānīye iqlīd-i iqlīdūs el-ḥakeme ile fetḥ-i eşkāl-ı Macestī etmege maqṣūrdur. O maqūle ẓāhir-bīnān-ı qavāᶜid-pīşe dā'imā maᶜāqid-i riyāḍīyāt-ı berhemenīye qānūnına ircāᶜ olmaġın . . .*"

43. *KV,* 107: "*qavāᶜid-i muḫtalle-i Aristū pā-bestesi olan ᶜulūm-ı riyāḍīye eṣḥābı.*"

44. Qur'an 18: 110 and 41: 6 (Arberry's translation).

45. See the paraphrase by Vuckovic, *Heavenly Journeys,* 80–81.

46. The famous *History of the West Indies* (*Tārīḫ-i Hind-i Ġarbī*) or the work of Sipāhīzāde most likely belong to the first category, and so also, to a degree, does the work of Meḥmed ᶜĀşıq (see Goodrich, *The Ottoman Turks and the New World;* Hagen, "Kâtib Çelebi and Sipahizade"; and Hagen, "Some Considerations on the Study of Ottoman Geographical Writings"). On Islamic cosmology by Ottoman scholars, see the introduction to Heinen, *Islamic Cosmology.*

47. Sayılı, *The Observatory in Islam,* 289–305, is still the authoritative account of the affair.

48. Katib Çelebi, *Cihānnümā*, 17–19.

49. Wurm, *Der osmanische Historiker Ḥüseyn b. Ǧa'fer, gen. Hezarfenn*, 68; see also Ocak, *Osmanlı toplumunda zındıklar ve mülhidler*, 243–248.

50. For the intellectual climate of the period see Gottfried Hagen, "Afterword: Ottoman Understandings of the World in the Seventeenth Century," 207–248.

51. *KV*, 107.

52. *KV*, 111. "*Lā-mekān*" also implies infinity, and as such the infinite speed of Burāq; elsewhere it is used as an epithet of God (Steingass, *A Persian-English Dictionary;* Zenker, *Türkisch-Arabisch-Persisches Handwörterbuch*, s.v. "mekān").

53. *KV*, 113.

54. Vuckovic, *Heavenly Journeys*, 64–73.

55. Qur'an 2:287.

56. *KV*, 116: "*Bu meclis-i ḥālet-baḫş-i miʿrāc-i bāhirü l-ibtihācı şemāme-i ʿanber-şemīm-i lüṭf-i ilāhīden bir nafḥa-ı rūḥ-efzā ile miskīyü l-ḥitām edüb.*"

57. On the concept and development of intercession, see E.I.[2], s.v. "Shafāʿa"; a more detailed discussion appears in Andrae, *Die person Muhammeds*, 229–245. A granting of intercession during the *miʿrāc* is mentioned by Andrae on p. 240, but the passage cited does not go as far as Veysī.

58. *KV*, 117.

59. Süleymān Çelebi's poem has been reconstructed from widely varying manuscripts by Ahmet Ateş, *Süleyman Çelebi: Vesîletü'n-necât*, and (in a different way) Neclâ Pekolcay, *Süleyman Çelebi: Mevlid (Vesîletü'n-necât)*. For an English translation, see *The Mevlidi Sherif*, trans. F. Lyman MacCallum. The history of Mevlid celebrations has been studied in detail by Kaptein, *Muḥammad's Birthday Festival*. For the Ottoman manifestation, see also Dedes, "Süleyman Çelebi's Mevlid."

60. *İslam Ansiklopedisi*, s.v. "Mevlid." The locale must initially have been Ayasofya, then the mosque of Sultan Ahmed (r. 1603–1617). In later times, *mevlids* in other mosques are mentioned as well.

61. Ebū l-Suʿūd Efendi's (d. 982/1574) fetvās mention only the Leyletü l-Reġā'ib, Berāt, and Qadr as the *kandil* nights (Düzdağ, *Şeyhülislâm Ebussu'ûd Efendi'nin fetvalarına göre Kanunî devrinde Osmanlı hayatı*, # 201). Today five "sacred nights" are regularly celebrated in Turkey. In addition to those mentioned, they are the night of Muhammed's birth (*Mevlid*) and the night of Muḥammad's ascension (*Miʿrāc*). Today "Regaip gecesi" is sometimes understood as referring to Muḥammed's conception (Özdemir and Frank, *Visible Islam in Modern Turkey*, 55 and Appendix F).

62. See, e.g., ʿAṭā'ī, *Zeyl-i şaqā'iq*, vol. 1, 714.

63. The latter example also employs a clever play with the notion of riding, which pervades the entire *miʿrāc* legend.

64. See Hagen, "Translations and Translators," for examples.

65. The most useful introduction in English is still Andrews, *An Introduction to Ottoman Poetry*.

66. See Lamers, "On Evliya's Style," for a brief discussion of the Indian Style in English; more recently, see Aynur, Çakır, and Koncu, eds., *Sözde ve anlamda farklılaşma: Sebk-i Hindî*. On *sebq-i Hindī* in Ottoman poetry, see Walter Feldman, "Imitatio in Ottoman Poetry: Three Ghazals of the Mid-Seventeenth Century," *Turkish Studies Association Bulletin* 21/2 (1997): 41–58.

67. *KV*, 116 f.: "*ve her şāhbāz-ı murād ki köşe-i surādiq-i risāletden ser-āġāz pervāz qıldı evc-i hevā-yı qurbda şayd-ı teẕerv-i qabūl etdi.*" The royal falcon was an image frequently employed in mystical poetry (see Renard, *All the King's Falcons*).

68. *KV*, 111: "*Cibrā'īl ve Mikā'īl devlet ve ʿizzet gibi yemīn ve yesārında mülāzım-ı rikāb-ı kürsī-peymāları olduqda muḥaddere-i siyahpūş-ı Ümmü l-qurā dest ber-āvarde-i medḥ u s̱enā olub.*"

69. Andrews, Black, and Kalpaklı, *Ottoman Lyric Poetry*, 14.

70. Steingass, *Persian-English Dictionary,* s.v. "*iʿtiṣām.*"

71. On the concept of *ʿiṣma,* see Andrae, *Die person Muhammeds;* Rubin, *The Eye of the Beholder;* E.I.², s.v. "*ʿiṣma.*" In many traditions, *ʿiṣma* is exclusively attributed to Muḥammad.

72. *KV,* 113: "*Idrīs ʿaleyhī s-selāmi ṣadr-ārā-yi medrese-i çehārom gördüm.*"

73. I suspect that the particularly elaborate forms used where Veysī cites a hadith from ʿĀ'işa is caused by the fact that, in due respect, Veysī rejects the hadith (*KV,* 109).

74. For the Ottoman manifestation of the notion that injustice is inherent in any form of worldly power, see Hagen, "World Order and Legitimacy."

75. Qāḍī ʿIyāḍ al-Yaḥṣubī's *Kitāb al-şifā' fī taʿrīf ḥuqūq al-Muṣṭafā* was one of the most influential works on all aspects of the life and deeds of the Prophet. Widely read among Ottoman scholars, it was also translated into Turkish in the nineteenth century (see Andrae, *Die person Muhammeds,* passim; E.I.², s.v. "ʿIyāḍ"). Al-Suhaylī's (d. 581/1285) *Rawḍ al-unuf* is a commentary on Ibn Hişām (Brockelmann, *Geschichte der arabischen Litteratur,* vol.1, 526). On al-Zarkaşī (d. 794/1392), see ibid., vol. 2, 92, and supplement, vol. 2, 108.

11

Mystical Love, Prophetic Compassion, and Ethics: An Ascension Narrative in the Medieval Bengali *Nabīvaṃśa* of Saiyad Sultān

AYESHA IRANI

The first biography of the Prophet Muḥammad to be composed in Bengali, Saiyad Sultān's *Nabīvaṃśa*, "The Prophet's Lineage," is an epic work from around the turn of the seventeenth century.[1] The author was a noted Sufi *pīr* who lived on the northeastern frontier of Islamic expansion in Bengal.[2] Practicing and writing in a sociocultural milieu in which membership in one religious group did not necessarily preclude affiliation with another, Saiyad Sultān (Sayyid Sulṭān in Arabic) was keenly involved with the reification of an Islamic identity for his community. Cognizant of the popularity of local models of epic and mythological story-telling, the author employed two distinct, yet comparable, genres—the local purāṇic model and the Islamic universal history model—to establish the superiority of the Prophet of Islam. In doing so, he straddles multiple worlds: while staking claim to the literary and cultural heritage of Arabo-Persian Islamic civilization, he simultaneously draws on the language and imagery of Bengal's rich literary and religious traditions. His version of the Prophet Muḥammad's *miʿrāj*, the focus of this chapter, is an episode in the larger project of writing an Islamic *purāṇa*—the *Nabīvaṃśa*—that he hoped would rival and ultimately replace existing Hindu epic and purāṇic literature.

Sultān was probably born into the ruling Sayyad family of Taraf *parganā* (administrative division) in Sylhet, a family of scholars and administrators, who were, at least in Sultān's time, closely associated with the courts of Arakan and Chittagong. Sultān's tomb in Sultānśi, Habigañj, to this day draws devotees.[3] While espousing distinctly Sufi beliefs, the author's esoteric practice as presented in his *Jñāna Pradīpa* (Lamp of Gnosis) employed local Nātha Yogic techniques to master the subtle body, a common feature of contemporary Sufi praxis in Bengal.[4] At a time when writing about Islam in Bengali was widely perceived by the Islamic elite to be a corruption of their faith, Saiyad Sultān went against convention, as did a few other Muslim Bengali writers of the period, thereby breaking new literary ground.[5]

In his account of the ascension, Sultān elevates the Prophet Muḥammad above all other sacred figures by presenting him as God's very own beloved. Depicted as the perfect *faqīr,* he is cultural role model for Sufi and layperson alike, one whose powers as intercessor make him the pragmatic choice for members of his own and other faiths. The Prophet's compassionate figure, much like that of the *guru* in Bengali culture, bridges the formidable nature of God's abstraction. Particularly when read in the context of his other works, Sultān's *miᶜrāj* serves three interlinked purposes, each one enriching the other: first, to supply an effective narrative platform by which to further enhance the sacredness of the Prophet; second, to provide an ethical template for individual and communal Islamic practice, serving to construct a community identity aligned around the axis of *pīr,* Prophet, and God; and third, to invite others to the faith by presenting the Prophet as intercessor, an attractive figure of compassion and power. While the *Nabīvaṃśa* comprises numerous narrative sections each of which serves one or more of the above ideological purposes, the ascension story is perhaps the only discrete narrative unit that simultaneously serves all three.

The Prophet's *miᶜrāj* had emerged out of the biographical-historical mode by the fourth/tenth century as an independent narrative genre: the *kitāb al-miᶜrāj* in Arabic, and the Persian and Turkish *miᶜrājnāma.*[6] The Books of Ascension in Persian and Chaghatay Turkish of the eleventh and twelfth centuries CE were notable for their deployment of pre-Islamic Zoroastrian and Buddhist motifs, thus creating "powerful, and recognizable, narratives that could be used for entertainment, education, and conversion" as Islam became rooted in Iran and Central Asia.[7] Later, from the twelfth to the sixteenth century, the *miᶜrājnāma* became distilled into the Prophetic encomium (*miᶜrāj naᶜt*) of Persian classical poetry.[8] A simultaneous trend to insert the *miᶜrāj* into the biographical cycle of the Prophet Muḥammad (*sīra*) included in universal histories of rulers is evident in Arabic and Persian literature of the fourteenth and fifteenth centuries, as well as in the west under the Ottomans in the late sixteenth century.[9] Roughly contemporaneous to the Ottoman trend, but on the new Islamic frontier in the east, Saiyad Sultān inserts the *miᶜrāj* narrative in his universal history of the Prophet.[10] By this time enriched by Islamic scholars, historians, Sufis, and mystical and popular poets alike, this palimpsestic narrative serves as a platform, time-honored and tested for persuasiveness by several centuries of Islamic literature, from which to establish the supremacy of the Prophet of Islam and spread the faith. Furthermore, as I will demonstrate at various points in this chapter, Sultān draws on the concepts, language, and imagery of Nātha Yoga and Gauṛīya Vaiṣṇavism in his transcreation of the *miᶜrāj,* thus producing a uniquely Bengali narrative to honor the sacred figure of the Prophet.

Saiyad Sultān and His Works

In an important essay building on the studies of several earlier authors, Mazharul Islam puts forward a strong argument linking the birthplace of Saiyad Sultān to

Laśkarpur, "a seat of learned scholars and administrators during the mediaeval age of Bengal."[11] Laśkarpur was the capital of Taraf, a vast territory of several *parganās*. Taraf's first Muslim ruler, Sayyad Nāṣir al-Dīn, was Saiyad Sultān's forefather, five generations removed.[12] Said to have migrated from the Middle East in the Mughal period, he helped the local population to clear jungle land and taught them how to cultivate it. He also introduced them to Islam.[13] The Sayyads were a family of scholars; legend has it that Sayyad Ibrāhīm, Nāṣir al-Dīn's great-grandson, was given the title *Mālik al-ʿUlamā'* ("Lord of the Learned") by the then Emperor of Delhi. The family was well connected to the courts of Arakan, Chittagong, and perhaps even Gauṛ. The Sayyads were held in such wide esteem that legend links the family in marriage to Sultān Jalāl al-Dīn Fatḥ Shāh of the Ilyās Shāhī dynasty, who ruled Bengal from 1481 to 1487, and to ʿAlā al-Dīn Ḥussain Shāh as well, who ruled between 1493 to 1519. Saiyad Sultān and his brother, Saiyad Musā, were intimately associated with the court of Arakan; according to Mazharul Islam, Ālāol, the famous poet at the Arakanese court, rendered Niẓāmī's *Haft Paykar* (Seven Beauties) into Bengali under Saiyad Musā's patronage. Sultān's disciple, Mohāmmad Khān, who wrote *Maktul Hosen* (Ḥusayn the Martyr), was a descendant of Rāstī Khān, the ruler of Chittagong, whose family administered the region until 1665.[14] The Sylhet of Sultān's time has been characterized by Richard Eaton as "Bengal's 'Wild East'"; despite being annexed by the Mughals in 1612 the Mughal presence does not seem to have made much impact.[15] In such a political climate, powerful families such as the Sayyads must have held sway over large parts of the region.[16] Today Laśkarpur exists as a village in the Habigañj district of Greater Sylhet. So does Sultānśi, the nearby village named after Sultān where he later settled (he lived there until his death, at a considerably old age, probably in the early 1650s).[17]

Saiyad Sultān composed numerous *padāvalīs*, lyrical songs that draw on Vaiṣṇava, Nātha, and Sufi themes; and a short piece titled *Jaykum Rājāra Laṛāi* (King Jaykum's Battle), in which Muḥammad and ʿAlī vanquish the infidel ruler Jaykum and bring Islam to his peoples.[18] In addition, he penned two Sufi practice manuals: *Jñāna Pradīpa* (Lamp of Gnosis) and a short piece, *Jñāna Cautiśā* (The Thirty-four [Verses] on Gnosis).[19] These stand testimony to his connection, as a Sufi of Bengal, to the practices of Nātha Yoga. Paying homage throughout the text to his *guru*, Shāh Hosen, in *Jñāna Pradīpa* Sultān depicts the Sufi path as based firmly on the principal tenets of Islam, while having among its goals the attainment of bodily immortality.[20] Sultān prescribes Sufi visualization techniques, integrated with the Nātha Yogic practices of breath control and *haṭha yoga*, a local body of praxis oriented toward attainment of immortality.

Nabīvaṃśa (The Prophet's Lineage),[21] Sultān's magnum opus composed in the traditional *payār* and *tripadi* meters,[22] is the first biography of the Prophet Muḥammad written in Bengali.[23] Conceived at once as a universal history and as a *purāṇa*—genres flexible and capacious enough to incorporate cosmogony and cosmology, mythology and hagiography, genealogy, ascetic and devotional praxis, and ethics—it begins with creation and culminates in the life of the Prophet of Islam. The author depicts cosmogony; the formation of the primordial pair, Mārij and Mārija,[24] from whom were born the gods and the demons; the eventual destruction of both parties by sin; and the futile creation of the four Vedas in order to reform humankind. According to Sultān, these divinely revealed Hindu texts acknowledge the future manifestation of the Prophet of Islam. Then follows the descent of various prophets identifiable as specific Hindu deities, such as Śiva, and various *avatāras* of Viṣṇu, including Rāma, all of whom were unsuccessful in eradicating evil from the earth. This leads to the eventual creation of Adam, and after him a line of prophets including Seth, Enoch, Noah, Abraham, Moses, David, Solomon, Zachariah, and Jesus, whose stories are told in some detail, culminating with the Prophet of Islam. A prophet born of the line of Kābila (i.e. Cain), Hari (i.e. Kr̥ṣṇa) is the only Hindu god who punctuates the line of Hebrew prophets after Adam. The narrative unit on Hari exemplifies Sultān's effort to minimize local competition to the Prophet of Islam: the inclusion of this "unsuccessful" prophet—one of the most popular deities of medieval Bengal—in Muḥammad's lineage subsumes and marginalizes a native rival.

The section of the *Nabīvaṃśa* on the Prophet's life, *Rasul Carita* (The Messenger's Deeds), is divided into three parts. Part one begins with a recapitulation of cosmogony elaborating on the bare principles delineated in the beginning of the *Nabīvaṃśa.* Then follows a description of Muḥammad's birth and his early life as a Prophet. Part two, *Śab-i Merāj* (The Night of the Ascension), begins with the ascension narrative (which alone constitutes approximately 854 verses), and continues beyond it to present, among other things, the migration to Medina, various battles of the Prophet, and his triumphant return to Mecca.[25] Part three, *Ophāt-i Rasul* (The Messenger's Death), concerns his last days and death, ending with a brief description of the conquests of the first three caliphs.[26]

We now turn to Sultān's expressed reasons for composing this sacred biography, which clearly has a pedagogical and proselytizing function. The author addresses "the Musalmāns of Vaṅgadeśa" with the following words:

> If there is in the land a learned man (*ālim*) who does not teach others, he will surely go to hell. Seizing the learned man if they sinned, men would beat him with a stick in the presence of God. You have all gathered in my presence; this is why I expound the teachings of the scriptures (*śāstra*). God will say, "You were a learned man! You did not prohibit human beings from committing sin" . . . When God asks you for an account of the good and the bad you've done, then you'll say to God, "I found a master (*guru*) but he did not teach me [how to discriminate between good and evil]." More than you, God will flog me: in my mind I constantly bear this fear. Thus, I thought to speak of the significance of the Prophet, hearing which humankind will not be drunk with sin. Brooding on this fear I composed the *Nabīvaṃśa,* listening to which sinful people will not be destroyed by sin.[27]

He is sensitive about being criticized by "hypocrites" for "hindu-izing" the teachings of the holy Book of Islam—an anxiety that reflects the wider perception of Islam becoming "impure" in local contexts.[28] He defends himself by highlighting the importance of translating the Book's message into the local language,[29] for the benefit of people who are born as Bengalis in Vaṅga "due to the fault of their [past] actions (*karmadoṣa*)."[30] Since they do not know Arabic they "do not understand a word of their own religion (*dīna*)"; "they ever read the stories of Rāma and Kṛṣṇa," and continue to possess "animal nature," ever submerged in sin.[31] Sultān's public posture for preaching thus casts his audience in a negative light; by instilling fear into the minds of his listeners he hopes to draw them into his sermon.

Furthermore, what emerges here is a picture of Sultān's active engagement as a *pīr* and author with the issue of Islamic identity and its construction in the Bengali sociocultural milieu. He desires to strengthen his community's understanding of Islam and invite others to the faith in a complex religious world, wherein those with Islamic affiliations, and certainly those who identified themselves as "Musalmān," were presumably still a minority group, one that had no linguistic access to the qur'anic word.[32] He was thus concerned with two issues: first, to construct a sacred biography of the Prophet that would compete with popular Hindu narrative texts such as the *Rāmāyaṇa*, the *Mahābhārata*, and the *Bhāgavata Purāṇa*;[33] and second, to establish a moral code for Islamic practice. In this regard his self-assigned task was a bit like that of the Islamic scholars writing between the first and third Islamic centuries (seventh to ninth centuries CE), who had to wrestle with communal definition and identity construction among a minority Muslim population surrounded in the Arabian peninsula by Jews and Christians, and outside of it in the Middle East by Christians and Zoroastrians.[34]

There are other reasons, however, for composing his sacred biography that remain unexpressed, chief among these being the construction of charismatic authority. It is evident that Sultān, himself a Sufi master, invested considerable authority in the role of the *guru/pīr*. (It is noteworthy that Sultān prefers to use the Indic term *guru* when referring to the Sufi preceptor.)[35] Attached to the master Śāh Hosen, Sultān repeatedly glorifies his virtues in *Jñāna Pradīpa*.[36] In the *Nabīvaṃśa*, the author explains the distinguishing characteristics of the true *guru*, and while paying obeisance to his own master, he emphasizes the importance of such an act should a *guru* desire similar devotion from his own disciples.[37] Sultān tells a story in which the baby Muḥammad is exchanged with another child in order to save him from being killed by the evil ruler Abū Jahl, known in the Islamic tradition as the Prophet's lifelong foe. Echoing the tale of Kṛṣṇa's birth, this narrative represents the complex interplay of appropriation and competition characteristic of the *Nabīvaṃśa*. The author explains that he read this story in a book, and insists that if people hear these words from the *guru's* mouth, they become more credible.[38] We are confronted here with the author's consciousness of the authority traditionally invested in the *guru*, and the special impact he expects his narrative to have on his audience.[39]

The intermittent insertion of the authorial voice within the narrative on the Prophet's life, whether through colophons or direct didacticism, constantly reminds us of the symbiotic relationship of power between Sultān as *pīr* and the figure of the Prophet. As much as Sultān, in his capacity as *pīr,* plays a crucial role in legitimizing the figure of the Prophet in Bengal, Sultān's own status as *pīr* derives greater spiritual legitimacy through the manner in which he constructs the Prophet of Islam. A section in the *miʿrāj* sheds light on Sultān's understanding of his role as one who provides moral and spiritual guidance to his followers. When Muḥammad meets God, we are told that the latter imparts to the Prophet knowledge of 90,000 matters (*kathā*): 30,000 of these were knowledge of the scriptures (*śāstra*); 30,000 were knowledge of Brahman, and the remaining third were secret expressions the author does not consider appropriate to reveal.[40] The God-Muḥammad master-disciple relationship presented here establishes the model for the *murshīd-murīd* (or, in Sultān's language, *guru-śiṣya*) relationship, institutionalizing and sanctifying the charismatic authority of the *guru.*

In *Jñāna Pradīpa* the author traces the Sufi spiritual lineage back to ʿAlī's apprenticeship to the Prophet, a lineage that can be traced back even further, as the *miʿrāj* passage discussed above suggests, to the Prophet's own supreme discipleship to God.[41] Moreover, while a primary concern of the *Nabīvaṃśa* is the genealogy of the Prophet Muḥammad, who is placed in a long line of Hindu gods, prophets, and cultural heroes, Sultān is also keen to affix his own spiritual lineage to that of the Prophet's; the Prophet of Islam brings God's latest revelation, while Sultān presents himself as its interpreter to the people of Vaṅga, who hitherto "knew nothing of all such matters."[42] Given his anxiety over detractors who deride him for corrupting the Islamic faith by writing about it in Bengali, this preoccupation with genealogies can perhaps be seen as a discursive move to allay such criticism by presenting the "purity" of his spiritual ancestry, credentials fortified by the title of "Saiyad" and his powerful sociopolitical standing.

In sum, Saiyad Sultān, as a *pīr* and writer of sacred biography, is concerned with creating a competitive narrative, an Islamic *purāṇa* on the Prophet Muḥammad, to draw the attention of local Bengalis from the myths of Rāma and Kṛṣṇa to the figure of the Prophet. Conscious of his power as *guru* to enhance the Prophet's status in his community, he simultaneously consolidates his own credentials as spiritual master by linking his Sufi genealogy directly to God, through the figure of the Prophet. And finally, in his endeavor to create a community identity, aligned around the spiritual axis of *pīr,* Prophet, and God, he is concerned with establishing a moral code for Islamic practice.

Saiyad Sultān's *Miʿrāj:* A Spectrum of Narrative Motifs

In her study on the *miʿrāj* myth, as shaped between the eighth and fourteenth centuries by the medieval scholarly elite, Brooke Olson Vuckovic provides a useful taxonomy of narrative motifs. Although introducing new elements, Sultān employs in his myth-making many of the standard medieval motifs identified by Vuckovic. These include, first, "readying events," such as, in this case, receiving instruction from the angel Gabriel, washing in the waters of Zamzam, the trial of the people (similar to Vuckovic's "trial of the voices") and the trial of drinks, and visiting sacred sites such as Jerusalem and Mt. Sinai; second, ascending into the heavens on the mythical beast, Burāq; third, the Prophet's meetings with "heavenly beings," such as, in this case, Satan (Iblīs) and the King of Hell; fourth, his meeting with the prophets, including Moses; fifth, reward and punishment in the afterlife; and finally, the reaction of the Prophet's community to his ascension.[43] Three themes not apparently typical in medieval scholarly sources add distinction to Sultān's work: first, meeting with the archangels; second, descent through the planetary spheres; and third, mystical love. In this third and most elaborately developed theme, discussed in the next section, Sultān introduces Nātha Yogic and Gauṛīya Vaiṣṇava concepts and imagery, which contribute to the uniquely Bengali flavor of his *miʿrāj*. But before we examine these themes, a brief outline of Sultān's *miʿrāj* is first provided.

Sultān's account of the mysterious night of the Prophet's ascension, the twenty-seventh night of the Rajab moon,[44] begins with God's command to his angels to bring his "friend, the Prophet Muḥammad" to him, so that they could sit as two friends on one throne and commune with each other.[45] Gabriel (Jibrā'īl), accompanied by Azrael (ʿAzrā'īl), Michael (Mikā'īl), and Isrāfīl, each with a band of 70,000 angels, is dispatched on this mission. At the Prophet's doorstep, Gabriel allays Muḥammad's fears of a nocturnal attack by Arabs—the multitudes of angels gathered around his dwelling were confused for the enemy—and advises him to mount Burāq and journey through the seven heavens to have a glimpse of God, thereby honoring God's wish. In order to further reassure Muḥammad, Gabriel, as eternal messenger of God's word to the prophets, presents an account of his spiritual credentials.[46]

Exhilarated, the Prophet flies on Burāq escorted by the angels to the *masjid* of Mecca. There, having washed at the Zamzam well, he enters the mosque and prays together with all the angels. Muḥammad ignores calls to tarry awhile. Traveling onward, the Prophet discovers two large bejewelled vessels (*kūpa*), one of honey and one of wine. He selects the vat of honey, and is informed by Gabriel that his choice has saved his community from destruction. Visiting Mount Sinai soon after, the Prophet once again prays in unison with all the angels.[47]

Next, the Prophet meets with Iblīs; in hell he sees the sufferings of Jews and Christians, and of women who have sinned.[48] After a brief meeting with the angel Ismāʿīl, he travels to the *bāyatul mokāddes* (*bayt al-muqaddas,* or Jerusalem); when he prays on the Holy Rock, his feet leave their sacred impression on it.[49] After a short interview with the personified form of the Holy Rock, the Prophet rides a second Burāq to ascend into the seven heavens. In the first five heavens the Prophet meets with Adam; a gigantic white rooster and its master, the angel Samā'īl/Ismāʿīl; Moses; Jesus; briefly, Aaron and Joseph; and ʿAzrā'īl, respectively. The sixth heaven is in fact hell, ruled by the King of Hell—a character distinct from Iblīs—who hesitantly shows him his land.[50] In the seventh heaven the Prophet meets with Abraham in his *masjid,* where Abraham as *khalīl* ("friend [of God]") leads the angels in prayer.[51] He also meets with the archangel Michael and the martyrs of paradise, who enjoy the delicious fruit of the jujube (*badarī*) tree, whose branches reach the throne of God.[52] At this tree ʿAzrā'īl appears once more, and then the Prophet encounters Isrāfīl; he sees the Pen and the Preserved Tablet, and also the angels who guard God's throne.[53] Beyond the seven heavens, Muḥammad visits paradise; finally left alone by Gabriel at the Lote Tree of the Limit (*sidrat al-muntahā*), Muḥammad traverses 70,000 veils of dense darkness to reach God's throne, on a horse named Rafraf.[54]

God and his beloved companion eventually meet, an encounter Sultān describes in rich detail.[55] Before he leaves, God asks Muḥammad to convey to his community that they should pray sixty times a day, fast for six months during the year, and perform ablutions seven times after enjoying conjugal relations.[56] Hearing this, Moses sends Muḥammad back repeatedly until God reduces the number of daily prayers to five, fasting to one month of the year, and performing ablutions to once after sexual intercourse.[57] The Prophet then begins his descent through the spheres, with the planets of each sphere prostrating before him. When he returns to his still-warm bed, his wives, ʿĀ'isha and Khadīja, are sleeping. Later he informs each of them about his journey, and then, at the time of collective morning prayers, speaks of it to his community.[58]

The Prophet as God's Beloved

Pursuing Vuckovic's path of dissecting narrative technique to reveal ideological motive, I now turn to the narrative devices that Sultān employs to exalt the Prophet over other prophets, and his community over those of other prophets. Since Vuckovic carefully deals with the manner in which the more typical *miʿrāj* motifs are used in "constructing the Prophet of God,"[59] I turn to Sultān's more unusual motifs, foremost of which is the theme of mystical love.[60] Sultān sets the tone for his *miʿrāj* with God's command to his angels to cast a veil of deep and contented slumber over the world. Humans resting in their beds and the dead in their graves should not be disturbed. The fires of hell must be doused, and sweet fragrances spewed along the pathways. The houris of paradise are to adorn themselves while the skies are to be lit with row upon row of lamps.[61] The scene is thus set at none other than God's command: the night is specially prepared for Muḥammad's secret ascent, ensconced in darkness, into the intimacy of God's presence. The Prophet thus seems to be transported through the heavens on the wings of God's desire to be together with his long-lost friend; God urges Gabriel to set forth, with these words:

O every moment I contemplate my love for him
the Prophet Muḥammad, my companion.
Thus from the mortal world shall I bring him here;
in person shall I give him audience.
We will sit as two friends on one throne;
we will converse with each other, he and I.
Go, all angels, and bring him;
explain to him my message.
Today is the twenty-seventh night of the Rajab moon—
tell him to come swiftly on this night.
Go together with all the angels; fetch him.
With him shall I be seated, this very night.[62]

The one who is "beyond need" has need for his beloved companion, a theme celebrated in Sufi poetry across the Islamic world.[63] Separated from his supreme friend at the beginning of creation, God pines to be united with him once more.[64] Here God is presented as the needy Sufi lover, who desires to enter into deep communion, *ṣuḥba,* with the beloved. Traditional roles are reversed, hierarchies broken down: Beloved (*maᶜshūq*) becomes lover (*ᶜāshiq*), and lover beloved—a transformation that immediately signals the central role of God's love in bringing about Muḥammad's ascent.[65]

Despite being accorded the welcome due a long-awaited beloved, Muḥammad approaches haltingly into God's presence, accepting his cordial invitation to sit beside him on his throne with trepidation and bewilderment. God then reminds him:

I created you from a part (*aṃśa*) of myself.
You and I were one, always:
for how many days you have been separated from me![66]

Sultān's idea that God is one, as well as his understanding that God and Muḥammad are essentially one but separated (as elaborated below), bear examination in the light of Tony Stewart's remarks on the connections between Islamic cosmogony and Gauṛīya Vaiṣṇava thought.[67] Like Ālī Rajā, an eighteenth-century Bengali Sufi, Sultān's cosmogonic ideas are compatible with the Gauṛīya Vaiṣṇava philosophy of *acintya bhedābheda,* defined by Stewart as "a simultaneous distinction and non-distinction between the ultimate and the created world that is cognitively unresolvable."[68] Furthermore, as Stewart points out concerning Ālī Rajā, Sultān too "asserts . . . the unity of the creator before creation, while noting the ineffable connection between this unity and the dualism necessary for all existent things to interact with the divine, the dualism necessary for a relationship of love to exist."[69]

Sultān makes Muḥammad the object of God's desire, with the creation itself taking place due to God's love for his beloved. God reprimands the King of Hell, who initially turns down the Prophet's request to view his realm, and informs the king that no person in the three worlds could equal Muḥammad, his "pure friend," for the love of whom he created the three worlds.[70] Again, when Muḥammad bids God farewell before his return to earth, Muḥammad is reminded:

> Other than you, I have no companion.
> My mind submerged in the juice of love (*pirīti rasa*) for you,
> I created these three worlds.
> I created the heavens and the earth because of you.
> Without you, all this would not have been created.[71]

These words echo the sentiment encapsulated in the divine saying, *lawlāka mā khalaqtu'l-aflāka,* "But for thee, I would not have created the heavens," favored in Sufi circles, while simultaneously drawing on the Gauṛīya Vaiṣṇava language of *prema rasa,* the sentiment or mood of love.[72] The impact of this Sufi motif, coupled with that of God's pining for their time of prior oneness, is greatly magnified when read in the context of Sultān's cosmogonic thought. He states that creation—the supreme soul (*paramāttamā*), the individual soul (*jīvāttamā*), the Throne, the Pen, the Tablet, the great mystic formulae (*mahāmantra*), and so on—emerged from the sweat produced when God's entranced gaze fell on his beloved companion, Nūr Muḥammad, himself (personified as this entity is in the text) an emanation from God.[73] The Muḥammad of Sultān's *miᶜrāj,* thus, is not merely the last prophet, but the first as well, the preexistent entity, Nūr Muḥammad, the Muḥammadan Light, whose essence passes from Adam through the line of prophets, as spermatic substance, down to the historical Muḥammad.[74] It is in this context that we can understand Sultān's designation for the Prophet, *ādi-antera rasula,* "the first and the last messenger"—a paradox that has been discussed in Islamic literature.[75] In his own elaboration on this theme, Sultān draws on the Vaiṣṇava theory of *aṃśa avatāra*s ("partial incarnations").[76] In its notion of partaking in the very substance of God, this parallels the concept of the Nūr Muḥammad as laid out in early hadith literature.[77]

To continue with God's entreaty to Muḥammad to sit beside him on his throne:

> You have been separated from me for an eternity.
> Come and look at me with the visible eye.
> With the hidden eye while meditating in *dhyāna* do you see me.
> Come and see your friend with the visible eye.[78]

Here, the author depicts the Prophet as a *yogī* who has a vision of God through the Nātha Yogic process of *dhyāna,* a form of meditation requiring sustained contemplation of the deity. The "secret" or "hidden" eye is suggestive of the yogic *ājñā cakra,* or "third" eye, one of the subtle centers for mental concentration in *dhyāna.* Furthermore, Sultān reifies the Sufi belief that the Prophet's ascension took place in body, rather than merely in spirit, and that his vision of God took place in a state of sober awareness rather than in a condition of mystical annihilation:[79] God asks Muḥammad to look upon him with his "manifest" or "visible" eyes, to perceive him externally, as opposed to the inner vision he has of him.[80] God then beseeches his beloved:

Come, come, Muḥammad, sit with me;
become a sea of grace on the waves of love.
. . . .
You are my beloved friend, of one body.
Sit close to me; let there be no distance.
One to the other, eye to eye, let us gaze.
One to the other, let us commune, forgetting ourselves.
Saying this, he drew the messenger close to himself—
as though the moon's radiance was in the sun's lap.
Two mirrors remained face to face,[81]
light merged into light, belying form.
When those two lights became united,
the two lights merged in one body.
When the two brows arch and knit together,
like two snakes intertwined,
lover (*bhāvaka*) and beloved (*bhāvinī*) become one in ecstasy—[82]
between two bows a single string.[83]

Sultān skillfully weaves esoteric and exoteric imagery in depicting Muḥammad's meeting with God as a reenactment of their time of primordial togetherness, an affirmation of the Prophetic saying, "I have a time with God."[84] Sufis, including Sultān, interpreted the qur'anic expression "two bows' length" (*qāb qawsayn*) to mean two drawn bows, their strings touching to make a circle signifying union.[85]

Some of Sultān's other images quoted here go farther, and might suggest that Muḥammad's communion with God in the *miʿrāj* involves ontological union. The image of the two facing mirrors is a particularly fertile one. God and Muḥammad see each other in these mirrors, eye to eye and face to face, their reflected forms reproducing themselves without beginning or end—a play on the idea that all created things emanate from God's love for Muḥammad, all forms here shown to be created in their conjoined image. Muḥammad himself, moreover, is presented as being created in God's own image, as an *aṃśa* would be. Additionally, by using the Vaiṣṇava literary terms *bhāvaka* (lover) and *bhāvinī* (beloved), Sultān frames Muḥammad's meeting with God in terms of the passionate Rādhā-Kṛṣṇa encounter. In this context, the trope of the multiplying mirror-images draws upon the idea that the love of Rādhā and Kṛṣṇa is like a hall of mirrors: Kṛṣṇa's love is reflected back to him by Rādhā, who ever magnifies it—and so their love grows in an endless spiral.[86] Thus, in his construction of the Prophet as God's beloved, Sultān employs Sufi imagery and ideas while embracing the language and concepts of Nātha Yoga and Vaiṣṇavism. Sultān's Prophet is made that much more glorious for being enriched and legitimized by religious and cultural images rooted in Bengal.

The Prophet's special status as God's friend leads him to be exalted by the heavenly beings and prophets he meets on his celestial journey. Typically, the Prophet has an encounter with the master(s) of each heaven and one or both of two narrative possibilities unfold. First, the Prophet is accorded a privileged position by his counterpart, for one or more reasons: doctrinal (as in the case of Jesus), on account of his status as God's friend, his intercessory powers (Adam, or the guards of hell), or the superior nature of his community (Moses, Jesus, and the archangel Michael).[87] Second, in encounters such as those with the archangels ʿAzrā'īl and Isrāfīl, and the King of Hell, the Prophet is empowered with special knowledge of God's eschatological plan. The deployment of these two narrative patterns establishes the Prophet's superior knowledge and spiritual mastery over all other prophets. A third narrative technique Sultān adopts lies in his depiction of the Prophet's ascent from one heaven to the other: the Prophet departs for the next heaven usually having led, as their *imām,* all the angels in prayer, a trope that literally and figuratively brings the Prophet to the fore.[88]

Not only do the prophets and other heavenly beings exalt Muḥammad's position, but Sultān puts into God's mouth praise of his holy stature, elevating him over all other prophets. While approaching the throne, the Prophet wishes to remove his sandals; God objects, but Muḥammad defends his position, citing the example of Moses, who was instructed to remove his sandals when he ascended Mt. Sinai. God refutes him, explaining that the purpose of this injunction was to have the holy dust of Mt. Sinai wash away Moses's sins; in the case of Muḥammad, his beloved companion "whose body is without sin," God's throne would gain stability from the holy dust of his sandals.[89]

While Sultān invokes the authority of the prophets, and even God, to exalt Muḥammad's position, he also employs the testimony of non-Islamic scriptures. Before Muḥammad leaves God's proximity in order to begin his descent through the seven spheres, God promises to broadcast his name in the four Vedas and the fourteen Hindu scriptures (*śāstra*), in the Torah, the Gospels *(injīl),* the Book of Psalms (*zabūr*) and the Furqān (Qur'an).[90] This serves a triple function: one, the anachrony of God's promise to Muḥammad immediately casts the Prophet's paradigmatic moment with God as an event outside of historical time, a pre-eternity when God and his beloved were one; two, it places Muḥammad's own revealed scripture, the Qur'an, on a continuum of revealed scriptures one more ancient than the other, giving the last Prophet and his Book the weight and wisdom of immemorial time; and three, it places the Bengali Hindus, who also rely on revealed scripture, within the Islamic category of "people of the Book."

Another unusual theme Sultān employs to exalt the Prophet's holy stature is that of his descent through the spheres. On his return journey Muḥammad meets with the personified forms of the presiding planets of each sphere, who prostrate themselves before him.[91] This narrative element, much like the trial of drinks used in certain instances in medieval literature, serves as confirmation of his divine stature, one that has been consecrated by his ascension into the presence of God.[92]

To conclude, Sultān employs a spectrum of narrative themes, both old and new, in the construction of the Prophet as God's beloved. While fleshing out these themes, he draws on diverse esoteric and devotional systems—Sufism, Nātha Yoga, and Gauṛīya Vaiṣṇavism—each one complementing the other to enhance the Prophet's holy stature. By invoking the authority of the prophets, God, and scripture, the author legitimizes the Prophet's status, and accords him preeminence over all other religious leaders.

The Prophet as Perfect *Faqīr:* Formulating Islamic Ethics

While Sultān's *miᶜrāj* indeed includes Sufi and other devotional elements, it does not seem conceived as a mystical text per se: given Sultān's interest in esoteric disciplines, as revealed by his *Jñāna Pradīpa,* it is striking that his narrative is not composed, for instance, as a mystical progression through the various stations and/or planetary spheres.[93] Rather it has been shaped primarily as a didactic treatise that sets the codes of Islamic practice. The treatment of the Prophet's experiences in the hereafter appears predicated entirely upon the author's preacherly engagement with his disciples in the here and now.

Much like medieval *miᶜrāj* accounts, Sultān's descriptions of the afterworld and his reinforcement of the qur'anic promise of paradise and the threat of hell remind the believer of the consequences of moral choice and the accountability of action within the overarching scheme of God's justice, while providing a coherent link to the teachings of the Qur'an.[94] So as not to repeat the descriptions found in the Qur'an, medieval accounts eschew descriptions of paradise per se, and focus rather on its inhabitants.[95] In contrast, Sultān's *miᶜrāj*—perhaps precisely because the Qur'an was inaccessible to the local Bengali—provides detailed descriptions of paradise (*bhihist/svarga*) and hell (*naraka*), along with an account of those who are punished.[96] Other than the martyrs, those who are rewarded with paradise are not specifically listed and become the default category—members of the Prophet's community who do not commit the sins punishable by hell, and instead enjoy the sensual delights of paradise.

As we encounter elsewhere in his *miᶜrāj,* Sultān, in his depictions of heaven and hell, was creatively adapting, much like other Bengali poets of his time, the whole spectrum of Arabo-Persian Islamic civilization to the Bengali cultural world.[97] The author uses powerful visual imagery in portraying the glories and beauty of paradise, in which exquisitely adorned houris, depicted according to the conventions of classical Indian poetry, entreat God to bestow on them husbands from among the Prophet's community, reminding him that they have been practicing austerities and mantra recitation (*tapa japa*) to be so blessed.[98] These images are sharply contrasted with the revolting nature of hell, whose swampy areas infested with mosquitoes, worms, scorpions, pythons, snakes, and fearsome aquatic denizens conjure up the fetid ponds and mangroves of Bengal.[99] Through this juxtaposition the author confronts his audience with the pragmatic importance of making the right choices.

Though Sultān does not provide in his *mi^crāj* a categorization of the virtuous who inhabit paradise nor names exemplary Muslims who live there, he does supply an ideal model for emulation in the form of the Prophet himself—the "beautiful model," *uswa ḥasana,* of the Qur'an.[100] In his conversation with the Prophet upon his ascent, God presses Muḥammad a second time to ask for a boon.[101] This time Muḥammad makes several entreaties to him:

> Let my body always burn with hunger and thirst. Do not grant me a stomach-full of food; grant me the daily means to eat for the day.... The moment men ask [something] of me, I ask that I can give [it] away immediately. Order that my hands be great givers; let them promptly donate whatever someone asks. Command also that my body ever remain in your service . . . and that I may be known in the three worlds as the *faqīr* who continually takes the Lord's name (*nāma dhari phakir*).[102]

In effect, the Prophet asks to be made the quintessential Sufi—a desire that, according to this account, greatly pleases God.[103] Much as the culmination of Sultān's teachings in his Sufi practice manual *Jñāna Pradīpa* is the presentation of a process of visualizing the Unblemished Lord, Prabhu Nirañjana, in the heart-lotus, it seems clear that the high point of Sultān's ethical teachings in his *mi^crāj* lies here.[104] In his presentation of the "life as model" ideal for emulation, in his representation of the Prophet as cultural role model—an ascetic, munificent, *dhikr-* (recollection-) absorbed *faqīr*—Sultān is sketching a Sufi self-portrait for his Bengali audience. In doing so, he simultaneously makes the Prophet a familiar, approachable figure, and casts the *pīr* in the Prophet's likeness.

As do medieval accounts, Sultān lists specific categories of sinners punishable in hell, providing an exhaustive, if mostly normative,[105] categorization of sin that includes lack of belief in the basic tenets of Islamic piety; non-abidance by the pillars of Islam; financial sins; sins against what is lawfully appropriate in terms of diet or sexual relations; sins associated with ritual purity; and a wide variety of social sins including those that relate to a lack of respect for the authority of parents, *guru, faqīrs* and dervishes, and learned men—*^cālims* and *mawlānās*. Proper behavior between the genders is laid down in some detail, while Sultān speaks out against violating lawful sexual relationships.[106] The author thus compiles a minimal obligatory code of conduct for the Muslim, following which the upright believer would be assured a place in paradise. In Sultān's worldview, however, the disbeliever, no matter how virtuous, finds no place in paradise; instead the other "people of the Book"—Christians and Jews—associated as they are with the basic "evil" of giving false testimony, are automatically dispatched to hell.[107] Going against the grain of medieval *mi^crāj* descriptions, which confirm the qur'anic view in depicting the virtuous members of various communities gathered around their respective prophets in paradise, Sultān here presents a bleaker future for the Christian and the Jew.[108]

What, then, does Sultān have to say about the Hindu disbeliever?[109] As we have seen, the author places Hindu gods and scripture in his universal history at the service of an Islamic teleology, tacitly acknowledging Hindus as being "people of the Book." Throughout the *Nabīvaṃśa,* however, the author emphasizes the evils of idol worship. In doing so, he adopts the standard discursive strategy that Muslim writers use to speak of non-Muslims, associating them all with the age of ignorance. In accounts of pre-Islamic prophets, the author weaves elaborate tales of the destruction of idols and idolaters, suggesting that his audience included new converts for whom he feared wavering and backsliding into their previously idolatrous ways.[110]

The account of the prophet Hari/Kr̥ṣṇa particularly stands out. In Sultān's retelling of key episodes of Kr̥ṣṇa's life, probably familiar to him from the tenth book of the *Bhāgavata Purāṇa* in which he is famously celebrated, the author depicts Kr̥ṣṇa's sport with the married women of Vraja as being a depravity, the result of Iblīs's machinations. When a heavenly voice finally awakens Kr̥ṣṇa to his deluded nature and his deplorable failure as a prophet, he decides to abandon these women and his previous ways forever. Arjuna comes upon him full of remorse and lends an ear to his confessions of sin. Together they journey, on their very own ascension, through celestial worlds on the back of Garuṛa, the mythical prince of birds, the traditional mount of Viṣṇu (whose *avatāra* Kr̥ṣṇa is). Arriving, eventually, at a paradisiacal city, Kr̥ṣṇa is attracted to the beautiful and virtuous resident women whose amorous favors he desires. Instead these women, who invite comparison with the Islamic houris, pelt him with bricks and abuse, not allowing him to enter their city. While censuring the doctrine of *avatāravāda* (divine manifestation), they reprimand him for his wretched life on earth and for stealing other men's wives, and they make clear that they are only to be enjoyed by men who do not commit adultery. To redeem himself, Kr̥ṣṇa has to return to earth to disabuse his devotees of their belief in him as Supreme Being and to prohibit them from worshipping idols dedicated to him and his beloved, Rādhā.[111]

Sultān's polemical presentation of Kr̥ṣṇa's exploits—the manner in which he seeks to humiliate this popular deity at every narrative turn, and in particular, setting up Kr̥ṣṇa's failed ascension as a foil to the Prophet Muḥammad's vastly successful one—suggests that the Vaiṣṇavas, especially the Gauṛīyas, would surely be denied a place in Sultān's paradise.

In the author's understanding, a large part of *kufr* (unbelief) is idolatory: a *kāfir* is one of animal nature, who does not worship the Unblemished Lord, who, not knowing the essence of the Islamic faith, commits all sorts of irreligious acts, and ever worships idols.[112] In the *miʿrāj,* Sultān relates a striking anecdote about the mythical beast Burāq. Waiting outside the Prophet's abode in order to bear him through the heavens, Burāq flees when he smells the Prophet's hands. Muḥammad's hands are apparently tainted as a consequence of slapping the idol in Mecca across the head, in a fit of moral outrage—though the author is quick to clarify that Burāq fled only as a reminder to human beings of the evils of idol-worship, for no stench could truly cling to the Prophet's hands.[113] Thus while there is no direct mention of the fate of the idolater in Sultān's descriptions of hell, by introducing wisdom through the guise of the mythical beast Burāq in the first section of the *miʿrāj,* he provides unambiguous warning to such disbelievers at the very outset.

In the colophon that closes the opening section of the *miʿrāj,* in which the foregoing incident of Burāq is related, Sultān issues a stern warning to idolaters, perhaps softened by the alternative he provides:

> Those who worship idols in the hope of gaining paradise,
> will be utterly destroyed having fallen into hell.
> Listen, O men, says Saiyad Sultān:
> remain in refuge at the Prophet's feet.[114]

Here, the author offers the hitherto idol-worshipping neophyte with an attractive exchange: the Prophet's feet for an idol of stone. The Prophet's anthropomorphism, much like the figure of the tantric *guru,* becomes a conduit for negotiating the formidable nature of God's abstraction.[115]

The Prophet as Intercessor: Invitation to the Faith

This brings us to another related issue: while Sultān is concerned with strengthening the Islamic community by establishing a moral code of conduct for individual practice and communal interaction, he is also interested to invite others to the faith. Given the array of religious options available within the Bengali sociocultural milieu of the late sixteenth century, how does Sultān manage to project Islam as the most expedient and desirable? The answer lies partly in an examination of the techniques Sultān uses to accord preeminence to the Prophet in his biography—an issue that has been explored earlier. What follows is a discussion of images, in the *miʿrāj,* of the Prophet as intercessor for his community, images that seem to be closely related to Sultān's desire to spread the Islamic faith.

In his discussion of the literature of Satya Pīr, Tony Stewart emphasizes that the importance of this religious and cultural, albeit mythical, figure lies in his dealing with "pragmatic concerns of survival—not overt ideology, theology or ritual"; devotees simply "accept that he has the power to make their lives better."[116] While Satya Pīr is worshipped for his power to make life on earth "better," Sultān presents the Prophet as one who has the power to make the afterlife experience of his disciples better. In the colophon above, the Prophet is depicted as the pragmatic choice for the Hindu idolater concerned with enjoying the pleasures of paradise, since the Prophet alone can win the most sinful of sinners a place in paradise—once such a sinner has sought shelter at his feet.

In keeping with legends of the Prophet in popular piety across the Islamic world, Sultān portrays Muḥammad as one who truly cares for his flock, a negotiator and intercessor for his community even at great personal cost.[117] His Muḥammad is one who ensures the maximum leniency permissible to the worst of his followers, and for the best among them he brokers privileges often rivaling his own. The Prophet thus makes sure he inspects the seventh hell, reserved for sinners of his community, in order to gain intimate knowledge of the sufferings some of his people might face. Guided through this formidable hell by its king, the Prophet fears for the members of his community and entreats God to save them from hell. God tests him by asking him to choose between saving his parents or his community from hell. The Prophet elects the latter: a predictable but nonetheless endearing choice.[118] Again, before mounting Burāq the Prophet takes assurance from Gabriel that good people from within his community would eventually also be able to ride this fantastic beast—that is, journey to the heavens.[119]

When Muḥammad comes into the presence of God, the Lord offers him anything he desires in the universe, including his throne and footstool, and even paradise. The Prophet instead begs that his community be forgiven its sins. At first God forgives a third of the Prophet's community. But the Prophet continues to plead with him until he forgives another third. Not entirely satisfied, the Prophet continues to press God, who finally grants that all those who recite the *kalima* will be completely forgiven of sin.[120] Furthermore, when God tells him to stay on with him if he wishes, the Prophet expresses his sense of obligation to return to earth for the sake of his community.[121] He worries that his people might go astray, like those of Enoch and Jesus, who left their followers in order to live in paradise.[122] Here Sultān not only portrays the Prophet as God's friend, superior to all other prophets, but also presents him as the unfailing friend of his people, making him thus an attractive figure for love and veneration. Even more than through the rewards of paradise, Sultān intends to win people to this new religion of Bengal through the figure of the Prophet of Islam, in whom the qualities of *jamāl* are justly matched by *jalāl:* he whose compassion, self-sacrifice, and attentiveness to his people rival his glory, majesty, and most importantly, influence with God.

Saiyad Sultān's ascension narrative on the Prophet Muḥammad is a significant chapter in his larger project, the *Nabīvaṃśa*—a literary attempt to gain wider acceptance for the Prophet Muḥammad and his religion in the Bengali sociocultural world. "To be widely accepted," as Richard Eaton points out, a deity "had to be perceived not only as powerful and efficacious, but as genuinely local."[123] Sultān knew well that the success of his mission lay in how effectively he could make the Prophet a truly Bengali figure. In reformulating the Arabic *mi*^{c}*rāj* genre for a Bengali audience, he translates Perso-Arabic Islamic literary and aesthetic sensibilities into a Bengali cultural and literary aesthetic. Introducing the "alien" figure of the Prophet, he presents new Islamic teachings in terms of the familiar, the authentically local. Thus, in his various depictions of the Prophet—as God's beloved, as ideal Bengali *faqīr,* as *guru*-like guardian and intercessor for his disciples—and in his eidetic images of otherworldly regions, the author invokes Bengal's literary, religious, and cultural vocabulary. While the author uses many motifs of the medieval *miʿrāj* in his ascension narrative, and effectively employs the language and imagery of Sufism, his construction of the Prophet as God's beloved simultaneously draws on the ascetic and devotional systems of Bengal—Nātha Yoga and Gauṛīya Vaiṣṇavism. It is through the leitmotiv of mystical love that Sultān accomplishes his foremost task: the consolidation of the Prophet's supremacy over all other religious figures.

By reading Sultān's *miʿrāj* in the context of the *Nabīvaṃśa* and his other works, and through an analysis of its narrative motifs and techniques, we see how the biographer and his subject are entwined in a relationship of mutual legitimation: while the Prophet of Islam, as the subject of sacred biography, derives credibility from the charismatic authority that Saiyad Sultān wields as *pīr* over his community, Sultān's own office is sanctified by the manner in which he constructs the Prophet of Islam. All the models of the Prophet that Sultān presents—God's beloved, the *faqīr*, and the intercessor—coalesce in the image of the Prophet as paradigmatic Sufi *pīr*, who embodies all three roles. Having affirmed a spiritual axis of *pīr*, Prophet, and God around which to orient his community, Sultān provides, through his *miʿrāj* tale, an ethical framework to strengthen community identity and differentiate believers from disbelievers. While a minimal obligatory code of conduct is laid down for the ordinary Muslim, the Prophet as ideal *faqīr* is held up as the perfect cultural model for emulation. In his attempt to invite others to the faith, Sultān uses imagery of the Prophet as intercessor for his community: likened to the figure of the *guru* in Bengali culture, Sultān's Prophet is an exemplary guide and guardian of his disciples. In his charismatic persona reside the twin qualities of grace and power that then make him the most pragmatic choice for the people of Bengal.

Notes

I am grateful to those who generously offered their comments and suggestions on this chapter: Aditya Behl, Frederick Colby, Thibaut d'Hubert, Shaman Hatley, Kathleen Kesson, Rachel McDermott, and Tony Stewart. For her editorial comments and considerable support in developing this chapter, I extend special thanks to Christiane Gruber.

1. For the purpose of this study I rely on Ahmad Sharif's critical edition of Saiyad Sultān's *Nabīvaṃśa: Saiyad Sultān viracita Nabīvaṃśa*, ed. Ahmad Sharif, 2 vols. (Dhaka: Bangla Academy, 1978; henceforth in citations I refer to this work as the *NV*). Vol. 2 also contains Sharif's critical editions of Sultān's other works mentioned in the course of this chapter: *Jaykum Rājāra Laṛāi, Jñāna Pradīpa, Jñāna Cautiśā,* and his *padāvalī*s. For a discussion of the date of composition of the *NV*, see n. 23 of this chapter.

2. Concerning the emergence of Bengal's Muslim population between the late sixteenth and the mid-eighteenth centuries, refer to part II in Richard M. Eaton, *The Rise of Islam and the Bengal Frontier, 1204–1760* (Berkeley: University of California Press, 1993).

3. Mazharul Islam, "Saiyad Sul'tān: His Birthplace and Time," in *Essays on Middle Ben-*

gali Literature, ed. Rahul Peter Das (Calcutta: Firma KLM Private Limited, 1999), 141, 143, 150–151.

4. For further details about the yogic practices of Bengali Sufis refer to Shaman Hatley, "Mapping the Esoteric Body in the Islamic Yoga of Bengal," *History of Religions,* 46 (2007), 351–368. Hatley shows how Bengali Sufis adopted tantric practices for mastery of the subtle body, reconfigured within an Islamic doctrinal framework.

5. See Asim Roy, *The Islamic Syncretistic Tradition in Bengal* (Princeton, N.J.: Princeton University Press, 1983), 58, 67–69. See also Asim Roy, "The Interface of Middle Bengali Muslim Literature and the Process of Islamisation in Bengal," in *Essays on Middle Bengali Literature,* ed. Rahul Peter Das (Calcutta: Firma KLM, 1999), 183.

6. Christiane Gruber, "The Prophet Muḥammad's Ascension (*Miʿrāj*) in Islamic Art and Literature, 1300–1600" (Ph.D. diss., University of Pennsylvania, 2005), 17.

7. Ibid., 46.

8. Ibid., 240. Classical Persian literary works usually open with a *ḥamd,* a lyrical invocation praising God, followed by the *naʿt,* in praise of the Prophet Muḥammad.

9. Rashīd al-Dīn's *Jāmiʿ al-Tawārīkh* (Compendium of Chronicles) in Arabic, Mīrkhwānd's *Rawḍat al-Ṣafā'* (Garden of Purity) in Persian, and Sayyid Luqmān's *Zubdat al-Tawārīkh* (Cream of Histories) from Ottoman Turkey are examples of such universal histories. Ibid., 37, 321–322.

10. I use the term "universal history" to describe the *NV,* since the Prophet Muḥammad is its apogee. However, the work could be considered a purāṇic extension of the Islamic *qiṣaṣ al-anbiyā'* (tales of the prophets) genre, a genre that constitutes an important part of universal histories, the difference being that Sultān does not present any sources or chains of transmission for his tales. While many medieval authors eschew the *sīra* in their *qiṣaṣ,* authors such as al-Rabghūzī incorporate it, including as well the ascension narrative. See Al-Rabghūzī, *The Stories of the Prophets:* Qiṣaṣ al-Anbiyā'. *An Eastern Turkish Version,* vol. 1, ed. H. E. Boeschoten, M. Vandamme, and S. Tezcan, vol. 2 trans. H. E. Boeschoten, J. O'Kane, and M. Vandamme (Leiden: E. J. Brill, 1995).

11. Islam, "Saiyad Sul'tān: His Birthplace and Time," 132. Islam refutes the view first put forward by Muhammad Enamul Haq, and later endorsed by scholars such as Ali Ahmad and Ahmad Sharif, that Sultān was born in Parāgalpur, Chittagong. Ibid., 131–132, 134.

12. Ibid., 140. For the Saiyad family tree, refer to 142.

13. Concerning Nāṣir al-Dīn, see Eaton, *The Rise of Islam and the Bengal Frontier,* 208.

14. Islam, "Saiyad Sul'tān: His Birthplace and Time," 140–143.

15. Eaton, *The Rise of Islam and the Bengal Frontier,* 259.

16. For details on the religious gentry of Sylhet, see ibid., 258–267.

17. Islam, "Saiyad Sul'tān: His Birthplace and Time," 145, 150–151. Mazharul Islam presents various possible calculations for the date of composition of the *NV* (see n. 23 below); however, the exact dates of Sultān's birth and death remain unknown. The date of completion of Mohāmmad Khān's *Maktul Hosen* is 1645 CE; while this date delimits Sultān's death date (ibid., 143, 152–155), the attempt to establish the date of the composition of the *NV* should take into account the textual evidence that attests to the author's knowledge of Gauṛīya Vaiṣṇava praxis.

18. Ahmad Sharif assigns this piece to a popular genre in Islamic Bengali literature, which he designates as *kāphir vijaya kāvya,* literary works on the theme of trouncing the infidel. Sharif, introduction to *NV* 2:xix.

19. In addition to these four works and the *NV,* there is some debate on whether the *Iblisnāmā* (The Chronicle of Iblīs) could also be ascribed to Sultān. See Muhammad Enamul Haq, *Muslim Bāṇglā Sāhitya,* in *Muhammad Enāmul Hak Racanāvalī,* vol. 1, ed. Monsur Musa (Dhaka: Bangla Academy, 1991), 298, 304–305; and Ahmad Sharif, appendix 'Kha' in *NV* 2:696–697.

20. *Jñāna Pradīpa* in *NV* 2:577, 597. It is not entirely clear whether Sultān advocates ontological union. Traditionists may argue that the desire for immortality (and ontological union, *ittiḥād*) would be heretical, as it constituted *shirk,* but it was indeed the common esoteric goal

of many Bengali Sufi *tarīqas*. See Hatley, "Mapping the Esoteric Body in the Islamic Yoga of Bengal," 358.

21. Since number is ambiguous in such a construction, an alternative translation, such as that suggested by Asim Roy, might be "The Line of the Prophets." Roy, *The Islamic Syncretistic Tradition in Bengal,* 12. However, I prefer "The Prophet's Lineage," since it is clear that the author intends the Prophet of Islam to be the teleological and theological fulfillment of the line of the prophets. Titles of other works, such as Sekh Cānda's *Rasul Vijaya* (The Messenger's Victory), the section of the *NV* titled *Rasul Carita* (The Messenger's Deeds), and particularly the *Harivaṃśa* (Hari's Lineage)—on which Sultān's title could have been modeled—make a case for accepting the singular number in such a construction. Concerning the *Nabīvaṃśa* being modeled on the *Harivaṃśa,* see Sukumar Sen, *History of Bengali Literature* (New Delhi: Sahitya Akademi, 1979), 143.

22. *Payār* is a couplet, while *tripadi* is a six-line stanza in the rhyme-scheme *aabccb.*

23. Scholars are divided in their opinions on the exact date of composition of the *NV.* Their arguments are based largely on a passage in Sultān's introduction to the *NV*—lines that Sharif quotes in his introduction to the text but which, for some reason, as detailed in n. 33 below, he does not include in the critical edition. Mazharul Islam summarizes these opinions and then presents other possibilities. The proposed dates for Saiyad Sultān's inauguration of his epic work range from 1584–1586 to 1630. Islam, "Saiyad Sul'tān: His Birthplace and Time," 152–515. See also n. 17 of this chapter.

24. Sharif's edition reads "Mārica" and "Pārijāta," which I propose are corrupt readings of the Islamic terms for the primordial *jann,* Mārij (probably rendered by Sultān into Bengali as "Mārija") and his mate, Mārija (probably "Mārijā" in Bengali). *NV* 1:7. From Mārij and Mārija, according to popular Islamic *qiṣaṣ al-anbiyā',* tales of the prophets, were born two clans of *jinn,* whom Sultān styles the *sura,* gods, and the *asura,* demons. Muḥammad ibn 'Abd Allāh al-Kisā'i, *Tales of the Prophets (Qiṣaṣ al-anbiyā'),* trans. Wheeler M. Thackston Jr. (Chicago: Great Books of the Islamic World, Inc., 1997), 19. Sultān follows the Islamic tradition by reiterating their creation from a smokeless fire. He also states that the Hindus call this pair Īśvara (i.e., Śiva) and Pārvatī. *NV* 1:8.

25. The question arises as to whether the *NV* is in fact a single text, for no single manuscript that I have seen transmits the entirety of what Sharif publishes as the *NV.* As I have personally assessed a representative selection of the manuscripts in the Dhaka University archives, some of which Sharif uses in his edition, it is clear that Sharif's categorization of the manuscripts under the titles *Nabīvaṃśa* and *Rasul Carita* is based on the scribal tradition. The *Nabīvaṃśa* manuscripts (corresponding to Sharif's vol. 1) begin with the story of creation and present the tales of the prophets up to Jesus, while the *Rasul Carita* manuscripts (corresponding to Sharif's second volume) contain the biography of the Prophet Muḥammad from birth to death, and usually include the ascension narrative. Independent manuscripts of certain sections of *Rasul Carita*—*Śab-i Merāj* and *Ophāt-i Rasul*—also exist. See appendix 'Kha,' *NV* 2:690–699. The subsection titles in the critical edition are entirely Sharif's; the manuscripts I studied very rarely contain such demarcations, but instead mark changes in meter and *rāga* (which Sharif also indicates). Nonetheless, the editor was probably right in considering all these manuscripts to transmit sections of a single text, the *Nabīvaṃśa,* since remarks throughout the text identify it as such. In this chapter, when I speak of Sultān's *mi'rāj* I refer to the section which specifically deals with the Prophet's ascent (the first 814 verses). Though I take into account the reactions of the Prophet's community to his ascent—a 40-verse section that immediately follows the sectional colophon of the *Śab-i Merāj*—I do not consider the other narratives about the Prophet's mid-life to be a part of the ascension narrative, even though they fall under the editorial subtitle *Śab-i Merāj.*

26. Passages in Mohāmmad Khān's *Maktul Hosen* inform us that as soon as Sultān completed the section on the Prophet's death in the *NV,* he instructed his disciple, Khān, to complete his work. Khān wrote concerning the story of Karbalā and the eschaton in eleven cantos, thus taking upon himself to complete, so he tells us, his master's unfinished work. For details

on Khān's work, see Islam, "Saiyad Sul'tān: His Birthplace and Time," 143. See also Munshi Abdul Karim and Ahmad Sharif, *A Descriptive Catalogue of Bengali Manuscripts in Munshi Abdul Karim's Collection* (Dacca: Asiatic Society of Pakistan, 1960), 344–367; and M. E. Haq, *Muslim Bāṅglā Sāhitya*, 296, 297, 302–304. To my mind, however, Sultān's *Nabīvaṃśa* is a complete work for two reasons. First, the title itself is certainly appropriate to the author's chosen subject, a universal history of the Prophet Muḥammad. Second, in his conclusion to the *NV*, Sultān appears to allude to future projects, specifically mentioning the possibility of composing "another book" (*bhinna eka pustaka*) when the opportunity arises. *NV* 2:547. While this suggests that he considered the *NV* to be complete, it does not eschew the possibility that Sultān later asked his disciple, Khān, to carry forward his literary legacy by taking up the projects he himself was unable to work on.

27. *deśeta ālima thāki yadi nā jānāe / se ālima narake yāiba sarvathāe // nara sabe pāpa kaile ālimaka dhari / āllāra sākṣāte māribenta daṇḍa vāri // tomharā sabera mele mora utapana / tekāraṇe kahi āmhi śāstrera vacana // āllāe buliba torā ālima āchilā / manuṣye karite pāpa niṣedha nā kailā // . . . ilāhie tomhāre yekhane jijñāsiba / bhāla manda ye karicha hisāba laïba // seikṣaṇe kahibā tumhi āllāra gocare / guru bheṭilāma guru nā jānāila more // tomhāra adhika more tāṛiba āllāe / ehi bhae bhāvi āmhi maneta sadāe // e buliyā bhāvilāma nabīra mahattva / śuni nara sabe yena pāpe nahe matta // ehi bhae bhāviyā racila nabīvaṃśa / śuni pāpī gaṇe yena pāpe nahe dhvaṃśa // NV* 2:476–477.

28. See *munāphike bole āmhi kitābetu kāṛi / kitābera kathā dilūṁ hinduyānī kari //* Ibid., 477.

29. *ālime kitāba paṛi vākhāne ye kāle / hinduyāni kari yadi nā vākhāni bole // vaṅgadeśī sakalare kirūpe bujhāiba / vākhānī ārabī bhāṣe bujhāite nāriba //* Ibid., 480. Elsewhere he states that he has written the "hindi *Nabī Vaṃśa*"—"hindi" here apparently signifying a language of Hind (i.e., Hindustān). Ibid., 1:696.

30. Ibid., 2:479.

31. Ibid.

32. Girish Chandra Sen wrote the first Bengali translation and commentary on the Qur'an, the first volume of which appeared in 1881. Sufia M. Uddin, *Constructing Bangladesh: Religion, Ethnicity, and Language in an Islamic Nation* (Chapel Hill: University of North Carolina Press, 2006), 87.

33. M. E. Haq and Ahmad Sharif refer to a passage in which Sultān states that he draws inspiration from the first Bengali *Mahābhārata*, composed by Kavīndra Parameśvara Dās under the patronage of Parāgal Khān, the governor of Caṭṭagrām (Chittagong) appointed by ʿAlā al-Dīn Ḥussain Shāh, ruler of Bengal between 1493 and 1519. See Kalpana Bhowmik, introduction to *Kavīndra Mahābhārata: Lipitāttvika-Bhāṣātāttvika Samīkṣā o Saṃskṛta Mahābhāratera Saṅge Tulanā*, 2 vols. (Dhaka: Bangla Academy, 1999), 1:12. For dates of Ḥussain Shāh's rule, see Richard Eaton, *The Rise of Islam and the Bengal Frontier 1204–1760*, 325. Haq states that the passage in question is found in the preface to the *Śab-i Merāja. Muslim Vāṅglā Sāhitya*, 294–295. Strangely enough, this passage is nowhere to be found in the published edition of the *NV*, even though Sharif too quotes it in his introductions to both volumes, without indicating its location in the text. Introductions to *NV* 1:9 and 2:7. See also n. 23 of this chapter.

34. See Brooke Olson Vuckovic, *Heavenly Journeys, Earthly Concerns: The Legacy of the Miʿraj in the Formation of Islam* (New York: Routledge, 2005), 42.

35. Concerning such usage in rural Bengal, see Ralph W. Nicholas, "Vaiṣṇavism and Islam in Rural Bengal," in *Bengal Regional Identity*, ed. David Kopf (East Lansing: Michigan State University, 1969), 41. For the use of this term in Islamic Bengali literature, see Roy, "The Interface of Middle Bengali Muslim Literature and the Process of Islamisation in Bengal," 188.

36. Little is known about Sultān's master. Mazharul Islam and others identify Shāh Hosen with a mystical poet and *pīr* by the name of Shāh Hosen Ālam, who was born in Viśvanāth, not far from Laśkarpur; in the early seventeenth century, he wrote *Bhedasāra* (The Essence of Distinctions), mystic verses that, according to Mazharul Islam, resemble the esoteric themes and

language of Sultān's *padāvalis* and *Jñāna Pradīpa*. Islam, "Saiyad Sul'tān: His Birthplace and Time," 147–148.

37. *NV* 1:287–289.

38. Ibid. 2:52. It is impossible to determine from the language of the text whether the book in question is "the Book," or merely "a book."

39. Textual evidence about the place of the *guru/pīr* in the social organization of rural Bengal seems to be corroborated by anthropological evidence. See Nicholas, "Vaiṣṇavism and Islam in Rural Bengal," 40–45.

40. *NV* 2:270. See also 283. For the idea of God granting secret knowledge to Muḥammad as depicted in Sufi sayings on the Prophet's ascent, see Abū ʿAbd al-Raḥmān Sulamī, *The Subtleties of the Ascension,* trans. Frederick Colby, 64–65, 82–83. Concerning God's revelation of "three times thirty thousand mysteries" to Muḥammad, as presented in ʿAṭṭār's depiction of the Prophet's ascent in the *Ilāhīnāma,* see Annemarie Schimmel, *And Muhammad is His Messenger: The Veneration of the Prophet in Islamic Piety* (Chapel Hill: University of North Carolina Press, 1985), 168.

41. Reminiscent of Bengali verses on the greatness of the *guru* as conduit to liberation, ʿAlī is represented, in the *Jñāna Pradīpa,* as beseeching the Prophet to lead him across the sea of existence (*bhava sāgara*), and teach him the secrets of incinerating his internal enemies (*ripus*), such that his body need never be cremated. The climactic moment is reached when, on ʿAlī's entreaty, the Prophet gives him a glimpse of the Unblemished Lord (Prabhu Nirañjana)—a moment of truth that echoes Kṛṣṇa's revelation of the cosmic form to Arjuna: ʿAlī is shown a form of light, shining like "crores and crores of suns." As the Prophet is to the Sufi master, ʿAlī is to the disciple: the perfect giver and the perfect recipient of grace, respectively. *Jñāna Pradīpa* in *NV* 2:601–602.

42. *vaṅgeta e saba kathā keha nā jānila / nabī vaṃśa pāñcālīta sakala kahila //.* Ibid., 481.

43. Vuckovic, *Heavenly Journeys*: "readying events," 17–35; ascension on Burāq, 44–47; meetings with heavenly beings, 34–39; meeting with prophets, 51–72; the afterlife, 97; the community's reaction, 75.

44. *NV* 2:200. Ibn Saʿd relates that Muḥammad's ascent took place "on the night of Saturday, 27 Ramaḍān, eighteen months before the Hijra." Quoted in Trude Ehlert, "Muḥammad," in *Encyclopedia of Islam,* new ed., 7:366. See also Schimmel, *And Muhammad is His Messenger,* 161.

45. *NV* 2:200.

46. Ibid., 201–203.

47. Ibid., 206–212.

48. Ibid., 213–217.

49. Ibid., 217–218. Concerning the angel Ismāʿīl in medieval *miʿrāj* accounts, see Vuckovic, *Heavenly Journeys,* 46–47. For the footprints on the Holy Rock, see ibid., 219; also Christiane Gruber, "Prophet's Footprint," in *Encyclopedia of Sacred Sites and Religious Icons,* ed. Dennis Spillman and Cynthia Clark Northrup, 3 vols. (New York: Facts on File, forthcoming).

50. "King of Hell," *Naraka Nṛpati,* appears to refer to Mālik, whom Vuckovic describes as "the guardian of hell, the word meaning both lord and possessor." Mālik is also "the character . . . who shows Muḥammad hell." Vuckovic, *Heavenly Journeys,* 36–37.

51. *NV* 2:243. There seems to be a conflation here between the *masjid*—for which Sultān again uses the term *bāyatul mukāddes* (*bayt al-muqaddas*)—and *bayt al-maʿmūr,* the heavenly prototype of the *masjid al-ḥarām,* the Holy Mosque of Mecca. Ibn Isḥāq describes Abraham "as a man sitting on a throne at the gate of the immortal mansion (*bayt al-maʿmūr*)." *Sīrat Rasūl Allāh,* trans. Alfred Guillaume (Oxford: Oxford University Press, 1955), 183.

52. *NV* 2:244–247.

53. Ibid., 248–249.

54. For the reference to 70,000 veils, see ibid., 264. See Annemarie Schimmel, *The Mystery of Numbers* (New York: Oxford University Press, 1993), 133; and Sulamī, *The Subtleties of the Ascension: Early Mystical Sayings on Muḥammad's Heavenly Journey,* trans. Frederick Colby

(Louisville: Fons Vitae, 2006), 66–68. On Rafraf: Ahmad Sharif reads "Pharad," but the manuscripts also attest "Pharphar" and "Raphar." *NV* 2:263 (n. 2). I conjecture that Sultān wrote "Raphraph," conflating the horse with the flying cushion, *rafraf,* which, in some *miʿrāj* accounts, is exchanged for Burāq at the Lote Tree of the Limit. See Schimmel, *And Muhammad is His Messenger,* 171. See also Gruber, "The Prophet Muḥammad's Ascension (*Miʿrāj*)," 60.

55. A brief outline of the meeting between God and Muḥammad is as follows: first, the incident of the removal of sandals before God's throne; second, God's invitation to Muḥammad to sit beside him on the throne and Muḥammad's final acceptance, which includes a depiction of mystical love; third, bargaining between Muḥammad and God as a consequence of Muḥammad's entreaty to God to forgive his community of its sins; fourth, God's initiating the Prophet into 90,000 mysteries; fifth, Muḥammad's declining of God's invitation to remain with him, and instead returning to earth for the sake of his community; sixth, Muḥammad's entreaties to God to be made the model *faqīr;* seventh; God's praise of Muḥammad, stating that he would spread the Prophet's glory in various scriptures; finally, a description of God's throne studded with the planets and constellations, studying which empowered Muḥammad with knowledge of prognostication. *NV* 2:263–274.

56. Ibid., 275. Medieval accounts of the *miʿrāj* give the original number of daily prayers prescribed by God as fifty. No mention is made in these accounts of God fixing the requirement for fasting or ritual ablutions. Vuckovic, *Heavenly Journeys,* 65–72.

57. *NV* 2:276–278.

58. Ibid., 279–284.

59. Quoted from the title of chapter 1 in Vuckovic, *Heavenly Journeys.*

60. While esoteric themes have been employed by prominent Sufis, such as Abū Yazīd al-Bisṭāmī, Ibn al-ʿArabī, and Muḥammad Ghawth Gwāliorī, in elaborations of their own personal ascension narratives, the theme of mystical love is not typical in medieval accounts of the Prophet's *miʿrāj.* See Gruber, "The Prophet Muḥammad's Ascension (*Miʿrāj*)," 42–44. Also see Scott Kugle, "Heaven's Witness: The Uses and Abuses of Muḥammad Ghawth's Mystical Ascension," *Journal of Islamic Studies* 14:1 (2003), 16.

61. *NV* 2:199–200.

62. *tabe prabhu nirañjana saṃsārera sāra / jibarila sambodhiyā lāgilā kahibāra // ohi ye mohora sakhā muhammada nabī / anukṣaṇa tāhāne sneha āmhi bhābi // se tāhāne martya honte ānimu ethāta / dibāma darśana āmhi tāhāna sakṣāta // dui mitra eka siṃhāsaneta basimu / anye anye tāñi muñi ālāpa karimu // āna giyā yatheka phiristā gaṇe yāi / mohora samvāda tāne kahia bujhāi // rajaba cāndera āji sātāiśa rāti / ei rātri āsite bulibā śīghra gati // phiristā sakale mili āna giyā tāne / āji rātri ekatre basimu tāna sane //.* Ibid., 200.

63. See, in the case of Rumi, for instance, William L. Chittick, *The Sufi Path of Love: The Spiritual Teachings of Rumi* (Albany: State University of New York, 1983), 197.

64. Sultān's cosmogonic ideas are discussed below.

65. Qur'an 17:1 depicts God as being the one who caused Muḥammad's night journey. Furthermore, the idea that Muḥammad is "sent for" occurs in Qurtubī's thirteenth-century work, *Aḥkām al-Qur'ān.* Vuckovic, *Heavenly Journeys,* 47. See also the fourteenth-century Turkish mystic Yūnus Emre's poem, in which God sent Gabriel to bring Muḥammad to him. Schimmel, *As Through a Veil: Mystical Poetry in Islam* (Oxford: Oneworld Publications, 1982, 2001), 183. For the idea of God becoming the lover of the Muḥammadan Light, see Schimmel's translation of an excerpt from Meḥmed Bey Khāqānī's Turkish *Ḥilya-i sharīf:*

> God (*ḥaqq*) loved this light and said: "My beloved friend (*ḥabībī*)!"
> And became enamored (*ʿāshiq*) of this light . . .

Schimmel, *And Muhammad is His Messenger,* 127.

66. *āpanā aṃśatu āmhi sṛjichi tomhāre // tumhi āmhi ekatre āchila anudina / āmhā honte katha dina haiyācha bhina // NV* 2:266.

67. See ibid., 1:1 and 2:3.

68. Tony Stewart, "In Search of Equivalence: Conceiving Muslim-Hindu Encounter through Translation Theory," *History of Religions* 40, no. 3 (2001), 284.

69. Ibid.

70. *ehi muhammada nabī śuddha sakhā mora / tribhubane eka nāhi tāna samasara // tāna preme sr̥jiyāchi e tina bhuvana / dekhāo tāhāne niyā naraka ekhana // NV* 2:233.

71. *tumhi chāṛi mohora dosara nāhi āra // tomhāra pirīti rase maji mora mana / sr̥jana karila āmhi e tina bhuvana // sr̥jiluma ākāśa kṣiti tomhāra kāraṇa / tumhi vine e sakala nā haita sr̥jana //* Ibid., 274.

72. See Annemarie Schimmel, *Mystical Dimensions of Islam* (Chapel Hill: The University of North Carolina Press, 1975), 215. See also Chittick, *The Sufi Path of Love,* 197–198.

73. See *NV* 1:4–6 and 2:3–9. According to Schimmel the idea of creation from sweat can be traced back to Ibn ʿArabī and his contemporary Najm Dāya Rāzī, and even further back in time to Thaʿlabī. Schimmel, *And Muhammad Is His Messenger,* 127. In many details (not all of which are provided here), Sultān's account of creation is similar to Imām ʿAbd al-Raḥīm b. Aḥmad al-Qāḍī's *Daqā'iq al-akhbār fī dhikr al-janna wa'l-nār.* Cf. ʿĀ'isha ʿAbd al-Raḥmān, *Islamic Book of the Dead: A Collection of Hadiths on the Fire & the Garden* (Wood Dalling and San Francisco: Diwan Press, 1977), 20–22.

74. Sultān supplies a detailed account of how the Lord, while creating Adam, deposited a part of himself (*nija aṁśa*)—light from his companion Nūr Muḥammad—into him, as a result of which Adam's forehead shone. This light passed down from Adam to his son Seth, from whom it passed through a long line of descendants, individually listed by Sultān, to ʿAbdullāh, who transmitted it to his son Muḥammad. In ʿAbdullāh's case, the Lord told Gabriel to take a flower from the Rabbānur tree and caress ʿAbdullāh's body with it. Seeing this, the Nūr Muḥammad entered his body, as a result of which it became radiant, and fragrant like musk. *NV* 2:9–15. Sultān thus draws on Islamic ideas of prophetic light and its primordiality. See Uri Rubin, "Pre-existence and Light: Aspects of the Concept of Nūr Muḥammad," *Israel Oriental Studies* 5 (1975): 62–119. Sultān also follows the hagiographical tradition in depicting the male progenitors of prophets as possessing a prophetic blaze on their foreheads, which then transfers to their female partners when the new prophet of the age is conceived. See, for instance, in the case of ʿAbdullāh, Muḥammad's father, *NV* 2:16–27; and in the case of Abraham, *NV* 1:444. See *Sīrat Rasūl Allāh,* trans. Alfred Guillaume (Oxford, New York: Oxford University Press, 1955), 68–69.

75. These words, credited to Muḥammad—"The first thing God created was my spirit," and "I was a prophet while Adam was still between water and clay"—have been much discussed by Islamic scholars. Schimmel, *Mystical Dimensions of Islam,* 215. Also, see Rubin, "Pre-existence and Light," 68–70.

76. See *NV* 1:2. While Sultān was probably familiar with this theory from Vaiṣṇava purāṇic literature, such as the *Bhāgavata Purāṇa* and the *Viṣṇu Purāṇa,* he was also aware, as alluded to in n. 17 above, of Gauṛīya Vaiṣṇava conceptions of *avatāras.* Concerning the latter, see Edward Dimock and Tony Stewart, introduction to *Caitanya Caritāmr̥ta of Kr̥ṣṇadāsa Kavirāja,* trans. Edward Dimock Jr., ed. Tony Stewart (Cambridge, Mass.: Harvard University Press, 1999), especially 142–143.

77. See Uri Rubin, "Nūr Muḥammadī," in *Encyclopedia of Islam,* 2nd ed., 8:125.

78. *cirakāla viccheda haiche mora sane / dekha āsi tumhi mora vekata nayāne // gopta āṁkhi dhyāneta dheyāi pāicha dekhā / vyakta āṁkhi dekha āsi āpanāra sakhā //. NV* 2:266.

79. See Schimmel, *And Muhammad Is His Messenger,* 162–163.

80. On his return to earth, when asked about his vision of God first by his wife ʿĀ'isha, then Khadijā, and finally by his community, the Prophet emphasizes each time that he had seen him with the inner as well as the outer eye. *NV* 2:281–284.

81. The translation and interpretation of this complex passage owe much to suggestions by Tony Stewart. In fact, I directly quote his translation of the two lines: "When the two brows . . . intertwined, . . ." Personal correspondence, 16 January 2008.

82. *Bhāvaka* and *bhāvinī* are common terms in Vaiṣṇava literature. *Bhāvaka* can mean all

of the following: thinker, creator, meditator, and connoisseur (*rasika, rasajña*). Haricharan Bandyopadhyay, *Baṅgīya Śabdakoṣa* (New Delhi: Sahitya Academy, 1996), 1671. *Bhāvinī*, its paired term in the feminine gender, used here to describe Muḥammad, is often used to describe Rādhā, the lover of Kṛṣṇa. Sailendra Biswas, *Samsad Bengali-English Dictionary* (Kolkata: Sahitya Samsad, 1994), 710.

83. *āisa āisa muhammada baisa mora sange / kṛpāra sāgara hauka premera tarange // . . . tumhi mora prema-sakhā eka kalevara / mohora nikaṭe baisa nā haïa antara // anye anye nayāne nayāne dekhā kari / anye anye kathā kahi āpanā pāsari // e buliyā rasulaka nilā nija pāśa / rabira koleta yena candrera prakāśa // duikhāna darpaṇa rahila mukhā mukhi / joteta milila jota ākāra upekṣi // yadi se haila dui jota ekattara / dui jota mili haila eka kalevara // dui bhuru madhye yena lalāṭa udae / eka kuṇḍalita dui dhānukī baisae // bhāvaka bhāvinī bhāve haila eka khaṇḍa / dui dhanu madhyeta rahila guṇa daṇḍa // NV* 2:266–267.

84. Schimmel, *Mystical Dimensions of Islam*, 220–221.

85. Quoted from Abdullah Yusuf Ali's annotation on Sūra 53:9. *The Qur'an: Text, Translation and Commentary*, ed., trans. Abdullah Yusuf Ali, 4th U.S. ed. (Elmhurst: Tahrike Tarsile Qur'an, 2002), 1444 (n. 5089).

86. I am grateful to Tony Stewart for his suggestions on the interpretation of this passage, and for directing my attention to the "hall of mirrors" image in Gauṛīya Vaiṣṇava theology. Personal correspondence, 16 January 2008. See *Caitanya Caritāmṛta of Kṛṣṇadāsa Kavirāja*, trans. Dimock, ed. Stewart, 199–200, and Dimock and Stewart's introduction to the same text, 101–102.

87. For Jesus, see *NV* 2:228. For Adam, see *tomhāra pirīti ati āllāra sahita / nirbodha pāpera bhāra khaṇḍāo turita //*, ibid., 223. For the guards of hell, see *tumhi se āllāra sakhā apāpa śarīra / karibā uddhāra tumhi yatha nārakīra // āmhi pāpī saba prati kara avadhāna / khaṇḍāo āmhāra pāpa māgi prabhu sthāna // naraka yantraṇā honte rakṣā pāibāra / ghucāo āmhāra duḥkha prasāde tomhāra //*, ibid., 233. For Moses, see *āmhā honte lākha guṇa mahimā tomhāra / tumhita parama priya rasula āllāra //*, ibid., 225. For Jesus, cf. *mohora ummata honte tomhāra ummata / rākhiyāche bahula mahimā yatha sat //*, ibid., 228. For Michael, see *rasule bulilā tabe ki kāje tomhārā sabe ethā rahi thāka anukṣaṇa / bulilā tomhāra lāgi prabhu pade vara māgi ethā rahi tomhāra kāraṇa // tomhāra ummata sabe daruda kahila yabe laïla tomhāra yadi nāma / ehi samudrera jala hae ati sunirmala taraṅga uṭhae aviśrāma //*, ibid., 245.

88. Ibid., 224, 226, etc.

89. Ibid., 264–265. See also 205. Concerning traditions that describe the role that Muḥammad's name plays in stabilizing God's throne, see Rubin, "Pre-existence and Light," 106.

90. *NV* 2:272–73. See also ibid., 1:24–25, and the introduction to Sultān and the *NV* in this chapter.

91. Many Prophetic encomia (*naᶜt*) of Persian classical poetry that appropriate, in their praise of him, the theme of the Prophet's ascension describe the Prophet's meeting with the presiding planet of each sphere, endowing, as he ascends, each of these planets with one of his special qualities. Gruber, "The Prophet Muḥammad's Ascension (*Miᶜrāj*)," 242–243, 280–281, 316. Sultān presents a variation on this trope in his description of the Prophet's descent.

92. Vuckovic, *Heavenly Journeys*, 27–29.

93. See the account of al-Bisṭāmī's personal ascension, Michael Sells, ed., trans., *Early Islamic Mysticism: Sufi, Qur'ān, Miᶜrāj, Poetic and Theological Writings* (Mahwah, N.J.: Paulist Press, 1996), 244–250.

94. Vuckovic, *Heavenly Journeys*, 120.

95. Ibid., 98.

96. The King of Hell, whom he meets in the sixth heaven, introduces the Prophet to the seven hells, set up as a sliding scale starting with the worst, which has 70,000 types of torments (*duḥkha*), to the seventh, which has 10,000; the latter is specially designed for Muḥammad's followers, who are described as weaker in physique than the robust heroes of yore. *NV* 2:235.

97. See Eaton, *The Rise of Islam and the Bengal Frontier*, 276–277.

98. *NV* 2:260.

99. Ibid., 236.

100. In the *mi^crāj,* Sultān grants a place of honor to four exemplary women: the Pharaoh's wife (whom he names Āsmā), Mary, Khadīja, and Fātima. These chaste women, *satī nārī,* have each been reserved a bejeweled pavilion in the third heaven. Ibid., 226. See Vuckovic, *Heavenly Journeys,* 106–112. For the "beautiful model": Qur'an 33:21, quoted in Schimmel, *As Through a Veil,* 172.

101. The first time Muḥammad asks the Lord to forgive his community for their sins. See below. For the "ask and be given" trope in Sufi sayings on Muḥammad's conversation with God during his ascent, see Sulamī, *The Subtleties of the Ascension,* trans. Colby, 132–133.

102. *rasule bulilā ehi māgie tomhāe / kṣudhāe tṛṣṇāe aṅga dahuka sadāe // khāite udara bhari nā dio āmhāre / dinera sambala dibā dine khāibāre // . . . nara sabe yekhane māge mora ṭhām̐i / ei māgi sabhānere dibāre jhāṭāi // ājñā kara ati dātā haüka mora kara / ye yei māgae tāre dibāre satvara // āra ājñā kara more śarīra sadāe / tomhāra sevāta rahi thāüka sarvathāe // . . . āra ājñā kara more e tina bhuvane / nāma dhari phakira ḍāuka sarvajane //* *NV* 2:272.

103. Several hadith reveal the Prophet as one who insisted on poverty so as to be closer to God. See Schimmel, *And Muhammad Is His Messenger,* 48.

104. *Jñāna Pradīpa,* in *NV* 2:645–646. In Sultān's writings Prabhu Nirañjana is an epithet for Allāh.

105. By normative, I refer to the categorizations of sin found in medieval *mi^crāj* accounts. See Vuckovic, *Heavenly Journeys,* 112–120.

106. *NV* 2:237–239. Vuckovic's perceptive remark on the sexual sins laid out in medieval accounts applies here as well: "The women are punished for what they do to the men of their family, not for what they do against God's decrees." Vuckovic, *Heavenly Journeys,* 120.

107. *NV* 2:216–217.

108.See Vuckovic, *Heavenly Journeys,* 99. See also Uri Rubin, "Prophets and Prophethood," in *Encyclopaedia of the Qur'ān,* vol. 4, ed. Jane Dammen McAuliffe, 289–307.

109. Sultān does not use the term "Hindu" in this particular section—though he does elsewhere in the *NV*—yet it is clear from the context that the "idolaters" and "*kāfirs*" he speaks of are members of local Bengali religious sects.

110. See, for instance, Seth (*NV* 1:180), Noah (ibid., 317), and Abraham (ibid., 347–353). Sultān narrates how people in Abraham's time bought idols and named them Brahma or Viṣṇu, and sacrificed goats before them—a comment on the religious practices of the author's own time. Ibid., 380.

111. *NV* 1:477–499. For a fuller description of the account of Hari/Kr̥ṣṇa in the *NV,* see Roy's account in *The Islamic Syncretistic Tradition in Bengal,* 96–98.

112. *tr̥tīe kāphira nāme paśura carita / nirañjana nā bhāviyā sebe mūrti nita // . . . kāphire nā jāne emā isalāmera marma / mūrti sebi kare nitya nānāna adharma //.* Ibid., 2:47.

113. Ibid., 207–208. Similar incidents concerning Burāq occur in other *mi^crāj* narratives; see *The Subtleties of the Ascension,* trans. Colby, 136.

114. *mūrti pūji se sakale svarge yāite āśa / narake paṛiyā haiba samūle vināśa // kahe saiyada sulatāne śuna naragaṇa / rasulera padayuge rahuka śaraṇa //* *NV* 2:208. Also, see the colophons on 212 and 221.

115. Placed in the context of Sultān's praise for his own *guru,* this serves to reinforce the axial alignment of *guru* and Prophet. Additionally, regarding the similarity in roles played by Muslim and Vaiṣṇava masters in the Bengali sociocultural world, see Nicholas, "Vaiṣṇavism and Islam in Rural Bengal," 40–41.

116. Tony Stewart, "Alternate Structures of Authority: Satya Pīr on the Frontiers of Bengal," in *Beyond Hindu and Muslim: Multiple Identity in Narratives from Village India,* ed. Peter Gottschalk (Oxford: Oxford University Press, 2004), 23.

117. See Annemarie Schimmel, *Deciphering the Signs of God: A Phenomenological Approach to Islam* (Albany: State University of New York, 1994), 202. See also the representation of the Prophet as intercessor in the *mi^crāj* motifs of classical Persian poetry, such as in ^cAṭṭār's

Ilāhīnāma. Schimmel, *And Muhammad Is His Messenger,* 166–168. For Sufi sayings on the Prophet's ascent with special reference to his role as intercessor, see Sulamī, *The Subtleties of the Ascension,* trans. Colby, 123–124, 132–133.

118. *janaka jananī kibā ummata tomhāra / kāhāre naraka honte karibā uddhāra // . . . rasule bolae āmhi māgie tomhāe / uddhārite ummata māgie sarvathāe // NV* 2:242. Concerning a similar trope in *miʿrāj* literature, see Gruber, "The Prophet Muḥammad's Ascension (*Miʿrāj*)," 50–51.

119. *NV* 2:206. Before he allows the Prophet to mount him, Burāq makes him promise to allow his community to eventually ride the beast into the heavens. Ibid.

120. Ibid., 269–270.

121. See Schimmel, *And Muhammad Is His Messenger,* 164.

122. *NV* 2:269–271.

123. Eaton, *The Rise of Islam and the Bengal Frontier,* 303.

12

Persian Illustrated Lithographed Books on the *Miʿrāj*: Improving Children's Shiʿi Beliefs in the Qajar Period

ALI BOOZARI

Religious painting is one of the most important genres in Persian pictorial traditions, and it is especially present in illustrated manuscripts and lithographed books. Although painting was practiced in Arab lands during the early years of Islam, figural imagery and especially religious sentiment as expressed in pictorial form flourished in Persian lands especially from the Safavid period onward. By the Qajar period (1785–1925), pious stories and religious painting became very popular, as evidenced by the many materials that have survived.[1]

Religious themes begin to appear in Islamic painting in the thirteenth century. The rise of the genre appears connected with the Mongols' conversion to Islam and the particular cultural environment of Iran during the medieval period.[2] At this time, a number of illustrated manuscripts depicting events in the life of the Prophet Muḥammad were produced with an eye toward presenting and teaching Islamic history to a recently converted Mongol elite. Illustrated works produced during the middle to late Ilkhanid period (ca. 1300–1350) included Rashīd al-Dīn's *Jāmiʿ al-Tavārīkh* (Compendium of Chronicles),[3] al-Bīrūnī's *al-Āthār al-Bāqiyya ʿan al-Qurūn al-Khāliyya* (Chronology of Ancient Nations),[4] and the anonymous *Miʿrājnāma* (Book of Ascension).[5] Among the many bio-historical themes that were represented, the Prophet Muḥammad's ascension (*miʿrāj*) held a prominent place. At this time, it is quite possible that the story of the prophetic ascent, along with its depiction, was used in procedures of religious indoctrination and missionary activities.

The ascension continued to be of prime interest to writers and painters during the Timurid and Safavid periods (ca. 1400–1700) as well. During the Timurid period, an autonomous *Miʿrājnāma* illustrated with over sixty paintings is believed to have been produced for Shāhrukh (r. 1401–1447) in Herat in 840/1436–1437 (Plates 4, 5, 6, 10, and 11). The manuscript stands out for having been written in Chaghatay Turkish using the Uighur script, as well as for a pictorial program that shows a clear indebtedness to the Sino-Buddhist scriptural arts of Central Asia.

This manuscript appears to have been used to legitimize Timurid Muslim rule at the height of Ming-Timurid cultural exchange and political competition in Asia.[6]

During the Timurid and especially the Safavid periods, the *miʿrāj* became aligned with Sufi thought and, as indicative of a potential spiritual journey of inspiration, was adopted for illustration at the beginning of illustrated texts, especially encomia to the Prophet included in such texts as ʿAṭṭār's *Mihr u Mushtarī* (Plate 20), Ibn Ḥusām's *Khavarānnāma* (The Book of Eastern Exploits) (Plate 21), and Niẓāmī's *Khamsa* (Quintet) (Plate 25).[7] The Shiʿi Safavid rulers also added a distinct sectarian overlay to the ascension story, using it as a means to legitimize Imām ʿAlī's vicegerency (*vilāyat*). For these reasons, Safavid paintings of the *miʿrāj* oftentimes depict ʿAlī, in the Prophet's encounter with him, as an angelic lion (Plates 27–28). In turn, such images provide pictorial support of the Shiʿi Safavid politico-religious system over the course of the sixteenth and seventeenth centuries.[8]

Illustrated manuscripts produced in Iran from the Ilkhanid to the Safavid period were available to an elite audience and overwhelmingly remained in the private domain. Even during the Qajar period, a number of manuscripts continued to be produced for private clients, and such manuscripts included illustrated *Miʿrājnāmas* with texts of unmistakable Shiʿi character (Plate 22). However, with the advent of the printing press in Iran during the nineteenth century, printed books started to replace the manuscript tradition. Books were produced in large quantities and thus were available to a much broader readership than ever before. Poetic compendia, heroic legends, and religious themes appealed to a learned elite, while books of simpler language and incorporating folkloric content were directed toward a lay public. Illustrated books with popular myths and tales may have been aimed at an illiterate audience in particular, because their illustrations helped to convey the story when the text may have lacked a capable readership.

Religious subjects thrived within the sphere of lithographic printing from the mid-nineteenth century onward. Texts such as the *ʿAqā'id al-Shīʿa* (Shiʿi Beliefs) were published numerous times. These texts recounted the life stories of the Prophet Muḥammad, Imām ʿAlī, Imām Ḥusayn, and members of the Prophet's household (*ahl al-bayt*), stressing in particular their exploits and courage. In these books, Muḥammad's *miʿrāj* comprises a frequently recurring theme, both as a subject unto itself (i.e., as an independent *Miʿrājnāma*) and as a theme inserted into heroic tales otherwise unrelated to the ascension. Illustrations are plentiful as well, and many continue the Safavid trope of representing Imām ʿAlī as a main protagonist, as a leonine angel and for the first time in human form, in the Prophet's ascension. These details reveal the continued effect and development of Shiʿi cultural and religious beliefs in the pictorial arts during the Qajar period.

Along with their didactic and religious applications, books treating the Prophet's ascension or containing segments dealing with the *miʿrāj* also recounted a number of entertaining stories of adventure that are particular to Persian traditions. Through both text and image, these kinds of illustrated printed books were helpful in inculcating a young audience into Islamic and Iranian literary traditions. As will be demonstrated, many of these illustrated books essentially function as graphic novels aimed toward a juvenile readership. As a consequence, illustrated books containing ascension stories should be understood as falling under the rubric of children's literature (*bachcha-khānī*). Propaedeutic and entertaining, Qajar lithographed books and their images were used to teach children of elementary school age Shiʿi tenets through the oftentimes conflated use of heroic legends and the Prophet's *miʿrāj*. For these reasons, such materials provide a fascinating lens through which to view the development of the ascension story in the modern period, along with its connection to a number of Persian tales and its potential use in teaching religious principles to young children.

A Brief Overview of Printing in Iran

Before discussing the lithographed books, a brief examination of the history of the printing press in Iran helps to frame the materials within their technological contexts. Lithographic printing was a widely used method of printing in Iran for over a century, from ca. 1843 until 1925.[9] Printing from movable type also was used at this time. Its official beginning was a direct result of the efforts of ʿAbbās Mīrzā Nā'ib al-Ṣalṭana, the son of Fatḥ ʿAlī Shāh Qājār (r. 1797–1834).[10] After Iran signed the Gulistan Agreement with Russia in 1812, ʿAbbās Mīrzā wanted to acquire printing presses from Russia. He sent a man by the name of Zayn al-ʿĀbidīn Tabrīzī to St. Petersburg to learn how to run a printing press and how to make inks.

Zayn al-ʿĀbidīn returned to Iran four years later in 1817 with a printing press. Upon his arrival, he established the Tabriz printing house (*chāpkhāna*).[11] After some time, the printer moved to Tehran at the behest of Fatḥ ʿAlī Shāh and set up the Tehran printing house. This establishment belonged to one of the most important politicians of the time, Manūchihr Khān-i Gurjī Muʿtamid al-Dawla.[12] In addition to the Tehran printing house, he also owned another in Isfahan.

In these early years when printing from movable type was popular in Iran, about fifty-four books were published in Tehran, Tabriz, and Isfahan. All were unillustrated except for a copy of the *Mukhtārnāma* (Book of Mukhtār), which contained eight illustrations.[13] It is quite possible that the production process for these early printed books restricted the number of images, as these were manually created as woodcuts inserted into a book produced by movable type. They were therefore inconvenient, expensive, and time-consuming.

The first lithographic printing house was established in Tabriz in 1832–1833, twenty-two years before printing from movable type was abolished. At this time, ʿAbbās Mīrzā sent Muḥammad Ṣāliḥ b. Ḥājj Bāqirkhān-i Shīrāzī to London and ordered that he bring back a lithographic printing press to Tabriz. He succeeded in doing so and established the Tabriz printing house in 1832. Shortly thereafter, other printing houses were opened in a number of other cities, including Tehran.[14]

Although printing from movable type and lithographic printing were used concurrently, lithography became a favored technique and the only method of printing by about 1854. There may have been two reasons for its popularity: Iranians preferred the appearance of hand-executed Persian calligraphy over the rather awkward characters of movable type, and printing from movable type was difficult and unwieldy. Furthermore, one of the advantages of lithographic printing was that both the text and its accompanying illustrations could be printed by one and the same method, yielding a simpler, one-step process guided by an overarching aesthetic template. Perhaps most importantly, these printed books resembled manuscripts in their conceptualization and layout, and thus formed a comfortable transition from the manuscript to the printed book. They were essentially "printed manuscripts"[15] that continued a long-lasting tradition of illustrated texts in Persian lands at the same time as they became more publicly available thanks to the tools of modern reprographic technology.

Lithographed Books on the *Miʿrāj*

Miʿrāj images appear in various printed versions of the Book of Ascension, as well as in the tale of Żarīr-i Khuzāʾī (a man who sought revenge for Imām Ḥusayn's death) and the *Ḥamla-i Ḥaydarī* (Ḥaydar's Battle, a poetical account of the life of Imām ʿAlī). Much like the tale of Żarīr-i Khuzāʾī and the *Ḥamla-i Ḥaydarī,* illustrated *Miʿrājnāmas* carried unmistakable Shiʿi messages and themes. In fact, these kinds of books dislodged the more "ecumenical" works that typically included ascension encomia and images. For example, unlike the manuscript tradition, there exist no printed illustrated books of Ibn Ḥusām's *Khavarānnāma* and Niẓāmī's *Khamsa,* quite possibly because these two texts were not overtly Shiʿi in character and because their literary style was too arduous for a non-elite and young audience.

The first printed *Miʿrājnāma* was composed in verse form by Shujāʿī Mashhadī. Very little is known about the author of this particular Qajar-period Book of Ascension. Indeed, it appears to be his only known work, and it is itself of rather questionable literary value because of many problems in its rhyme, rhythm, and figures of speech. Similarly, Shujāʿī Mashhadī includes idiosyncratic interpretations of the Prophet's ascension, claiming for instance that the Prophet Muḥammad embarked on his ascension from the house of Umm Salama in Mecca. *Miʿrāj* narratives usually present Muḥammad's ascent as occurring from the house of Umm Hāniʾ or the Zamzam well.

Perhaps more interestingly, Shujāʿī Mashhadī's narrative includes Imām ʿAlī as present during various moments in the Prophet's ascension, thus giving it a clear Shiʿi tinge. Imām ʿAlī is present in Mecca when Gabriel arrives with Burāq; he appears again beyond the seventh heaven to offer Muḥammad celestial food (Figure

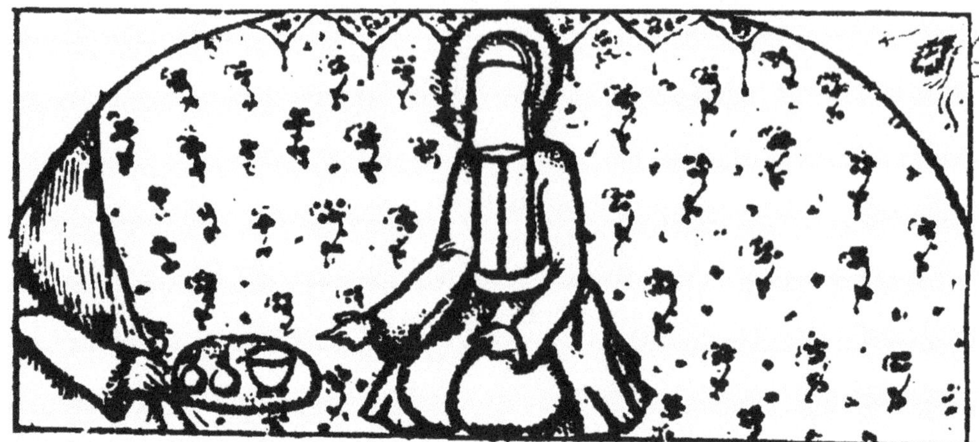

FIGURE 12.1. Imām ʿAlī shares food with the Prophet from behind a veil, Shujāʿī Mashhadī, *Miʿrājnāma*, 1271/1854.

12.1); and he is present once more upon the Prophet's return to Mecca, at which time he tells Muḥammad that he was protecting him during his ascension and, as proof of his presence along the way, ʿAlī shows him an apple from paradise tucked underneath his sleeve. Imām ʿAlī therefore assumes a role arguably more critical than the ascending protagonist, since it is he who shares food with Muḥammad and it is he who provides final proof of his protection and, as a result, the Prophet's own otherwordly successes.

The conclusion of Shujāʿī Mashhadī's *Miʿrājnāma* is also of particular interest, because it extends the questioning of Abū Jahl and the Quraysh tribesmen to include the doubting of Zaʿfar. Like Abū Jahl, the author informs us, Zaʿfar doubted the Prophet's ascension and, as a result of his disbelief, was turned into a woman. Once a woman, Zaʿfar is noticed by a man who later marries him (Figure 12.2); Zaʿfar gives birth to five boys and after nine years transforms back into a man. The moral of the tale is quite clear: the doubting Zaʿfar is punished for his disbelief by being transformed into a woman, a trope that one finds in folk tales from various traditions.[16] In all printed copies of Shujāʿī Mashhadī's *Miʿrājnāma,* the doubting of Zaʿfar is then followed by various tales (*dāstāns*) of heroic exploits, such as those of the prophet Khiżr and Imām ʿAlī, which were particularly popular in Persian lands.

Shujāʿī Mashhadī's illustrated *Miʿrājnāma* was a very popular tale of the Prophet's ascension. It was published as a lithographed book a total of seven times between 1851 and 1889.[17] Furthermore, the end of his text, which includes the tale of Zaʿfar's doubting, was published as an individual book intended, we are told, for children.[18] Based on this data, we can hypothesize that Shujāʿī Mashhadī's *Miʿrājnāma* was a popular tale put to pictures with a target audience of schoolchildren. Through its simple rhetoric and its blending of Shiʿi motifs and Persian tales, the work became a "bestseller" as an educational tool to teach both Islamic (Shiʿi) creedal systems and Persian literature.

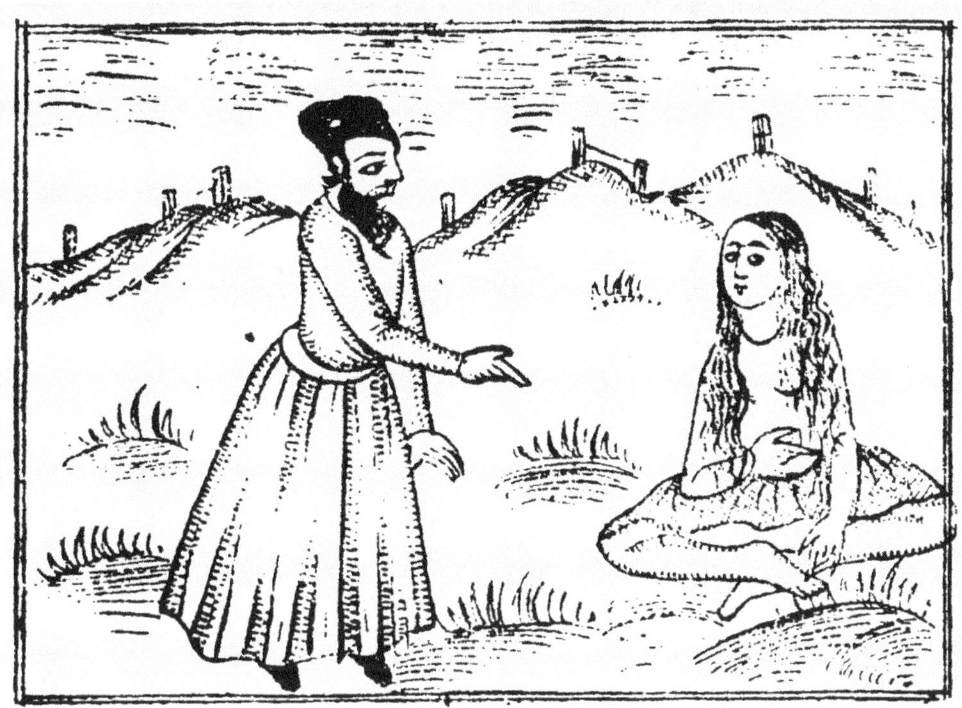

FIGURE 12.2. Zaʿfar is transformed into a woman and is observed by his/her future husband, Shujāʿī Mashhadī, *Miʿrājnāma,* 1291/1874.

There also exists a *Miʿrājnāma* in prose composed by an anonymous author, whose details recall the Book of Ascension of Shujāʿī Mashhadī. Its language is more fluent and lucid, and its structure and narrative details are more "normative." After the conclusion of the ascension narrative proper, further Persian *dāstāns* appear, along with a discourse on bodily health and a treatise on Shiʿi beliefs (*ʿAqā'id al-Shīʿa*). Publication details reveal that these texts were intended to be published in one single volume from the beginning.[19] As a result, we see a clear blending of the ascension, bio-religious stories, epic tales, and even the rules of hygiene necessary for a child's "core curriculum."

This anonymous Book of Ascension stands out for two reasons: because it exists in only one edition dated 1846, and because it is considered the earliest illustrated lithographed copy of a *Miʿrājnāma*. In addition, it contains twenty-nine finely executed illustrations depicting various moments in the Prophet's ascension. These include, for example, Muḥammad's encounter with Imām ʿAlī in human form (Figure 12.3). This is the first instance in which ʿAlī is rendered as a haloed and unveiled male rather than a leonine angel, hence displacing the metaphorical language of Safavid paintings and replacing it with a more literal emphasis on the figural embodiment of Shiʿi Islam.

Another Book of Ascension titled *Baḥr-i Tavīl-i Miʿrājnāma* was composed by Ḥamīd al-Dīn Maḥmūd Jawharī, a poet of the Qajar period. This book comprises a

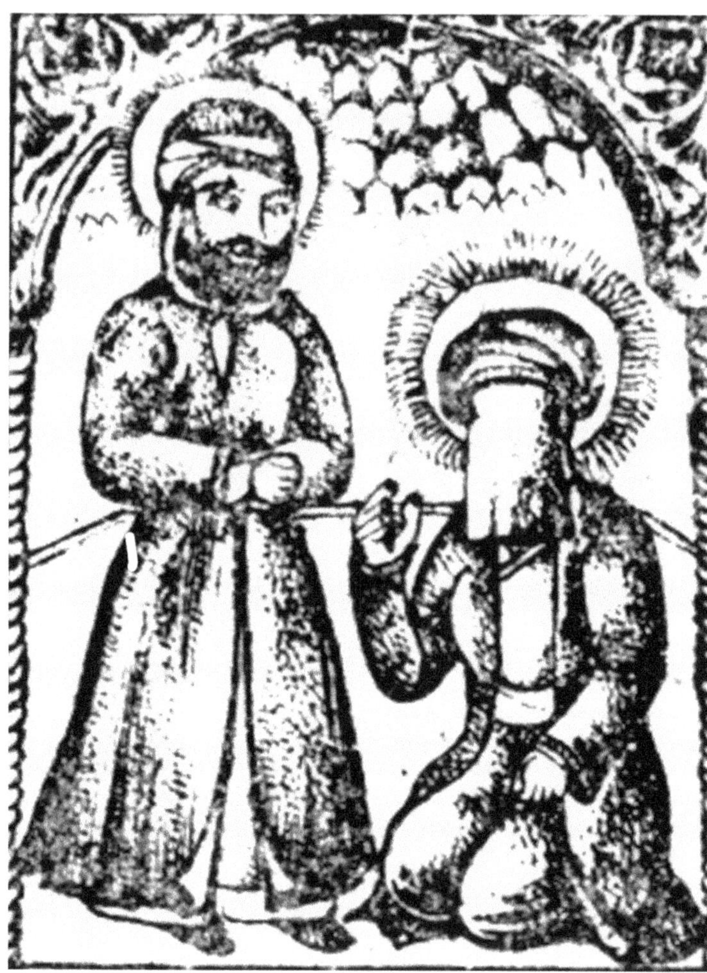

FIGURE 12.3. Imām ʿAlī, represented as a standing man with unveiled face, next to the seated Prophet Muḥammad with a veiled face, anonymous, *Miʿrājnāma*, 1263/1846.

chapter praising God and the Prophet Muḥammad, followed by an account of the *miʿrāj.* Jawharī's treatment of the ascension is very brief: he describes only Gabriel's arrival in Mecca, the Prophet's riding on Burāq, his passing through the skies and stars, and his meeting with an angelic lion (Imām ʿAlī). Its brevity makes it markedly different from the two previously mentioned *Miʿrājnāmas*.[20]

Besides these three *Miʿrājnāmas*, other lithographed books include texts and illustrations describing the Prophet's ascension. One of them is the *Ḥamla-i Ḥaydarī* (Ḥaydar's Battle) composed by Mulā Būman ʿAlī, known by the nickname *(laqab)* of Rājī Kirmānī. This popular work, published in no less than seven editions, provides an account of early Islamic history and also describes the Prophet's ascension in detail on two occasions: first, upon Muḥammad's return to Mecca it discusses the ascension as a vehicle for the praise of Imām ʿAlī, and second, when the author wishes to provide an explanation of the Ṭūbā tree in paradise. The work's high literary value is matched by its lavishly detailed illustrations, which include, for example, a depiction of groups of angels welcoming the Prophet into the skies (Figure 12.4).[21]

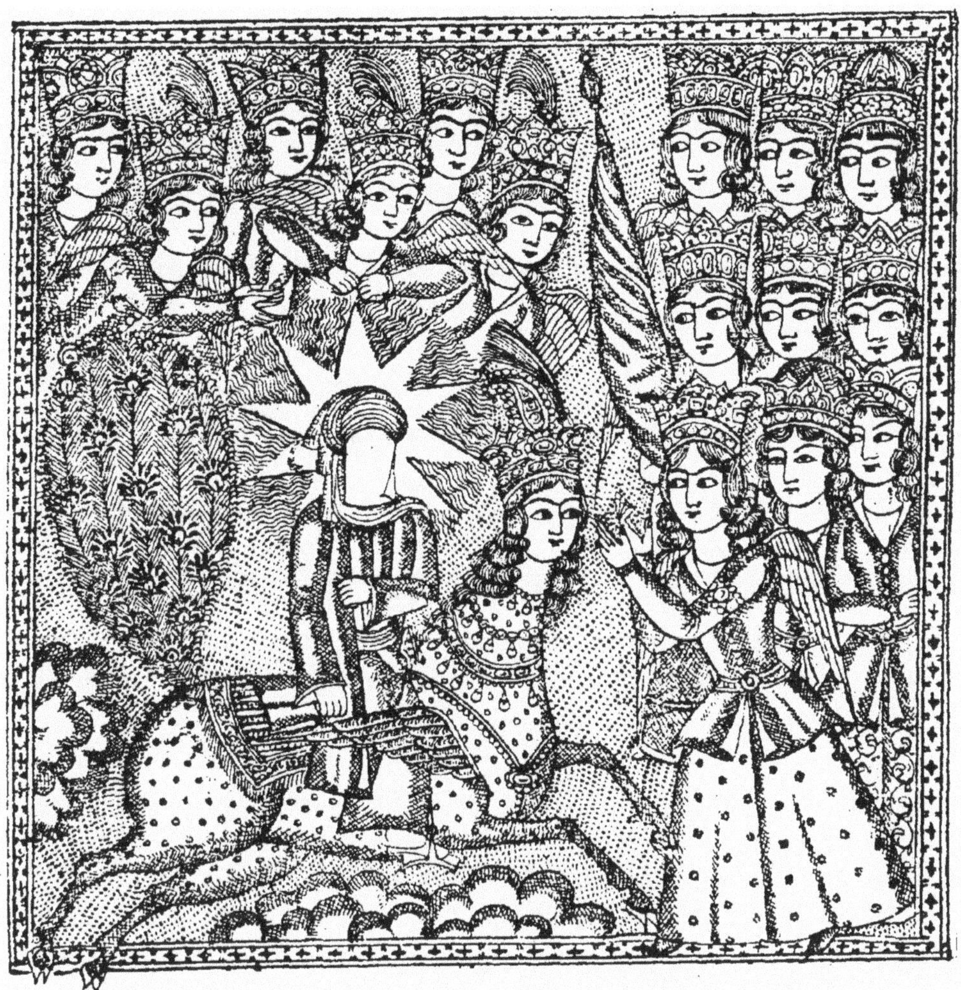

FIGURE 12.4. The Prophet Muḥammad, riding Burāq, is welcomed by angels into the heavens, Mulā Būman ᶜAlī, *Ḥamla-i Ḥaydarī,* illustrated by ᶜAlī-Qulī Khū'ī, 1264/1847.

The printed text of *Żarīr-i Khuzā'ī,* which recounts its protagonist's quest to avenge the murder of Imām Ḥusayn and his companions, exists in three different illustrated editions. Only one of them, dated 1848, however, includes a depiction of the *miᶜrāj* (Figure 12.5).[22] This illustration stands out for two complementary reasons: on the one hand, the ascension appears as a decoration above the opening of the text rather than being included within the text proper, while, on the other, it transforms a typically ornamental headpiece (*sarloh*) into a figurative representation, itself a very rare, if not unique, motif. It is quite possible that this *miᶜrāj sarloh* was not original to the lithographed text, but rather was commissioned specifically for the 1848 edition at the request of the patron or interest of the illustrator, who may have felt that—in order to stay in line with the manuscript tradition of including an ascension painting in the preliminary textual encomium to God and the Prophet Muḥammad—this

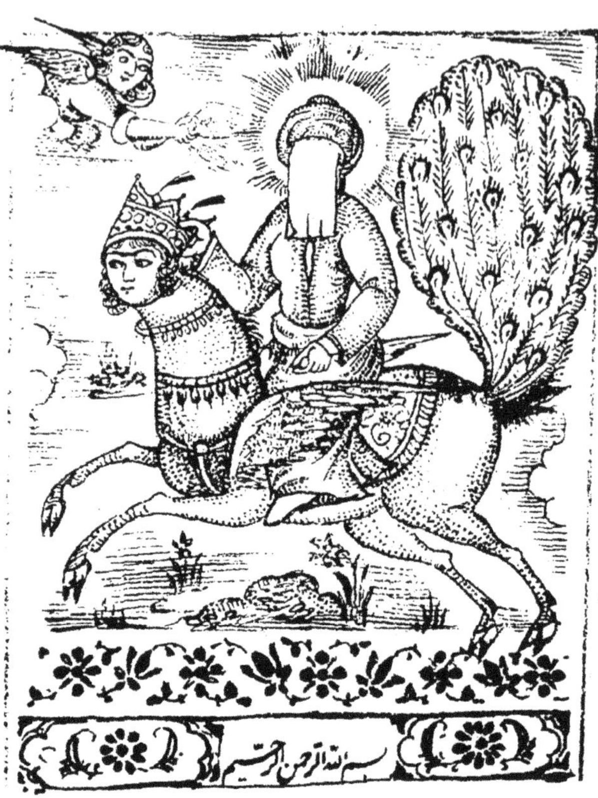

FIGURE 12.5. *Mi^c^rāj sarloh, Żarīr-i Khuzā'ī,* 1265/1848.

particular edition of the tale of *Żarīr-i Khuzā'ī* would not have been "complete" without its own version of a pictorial tribute to Muḥammad's *mi^c^rāj.*

The last text of interest is Maktabī Shīrāzī's *Laylā va Majnūn,* a popular Qajar text largely inspired by Niẓāmī's tale of the two ill-fated lovers in his *Khamsa.* Although there exist seven illustrated lithographed editions of Maktabī Shīrāzī's text, only one published in 1853 contains an illustration of the ascension depicting the veiled Prophet on Burāq encountering two angels in the sky.[23] A rather standard Qajar depiction of the ascension, it resembles other *mi^c^rāj* paintings included in illustrated manuscripts of Maktabī Shīrāzī's *Laylā va Majnūn,* which were produced during the first half of the nineteenth century.[24] The coexistence of manuscripts and lithographed books meant that certain pictorial motifs, such as those present in ascension compositions, could be borrowed and adopted rather freely based on a patron's wish and/or inherited artistic tradition.

Iconographic Motifs and Themes

Excluding illustrations belonging to some of the *dāstāns* added after the conclusion of certain ascension narratives, there exist a total of 119 *mi^c^rāj* depictions in illustrated lithographed books produced during the Qajar period. These represent

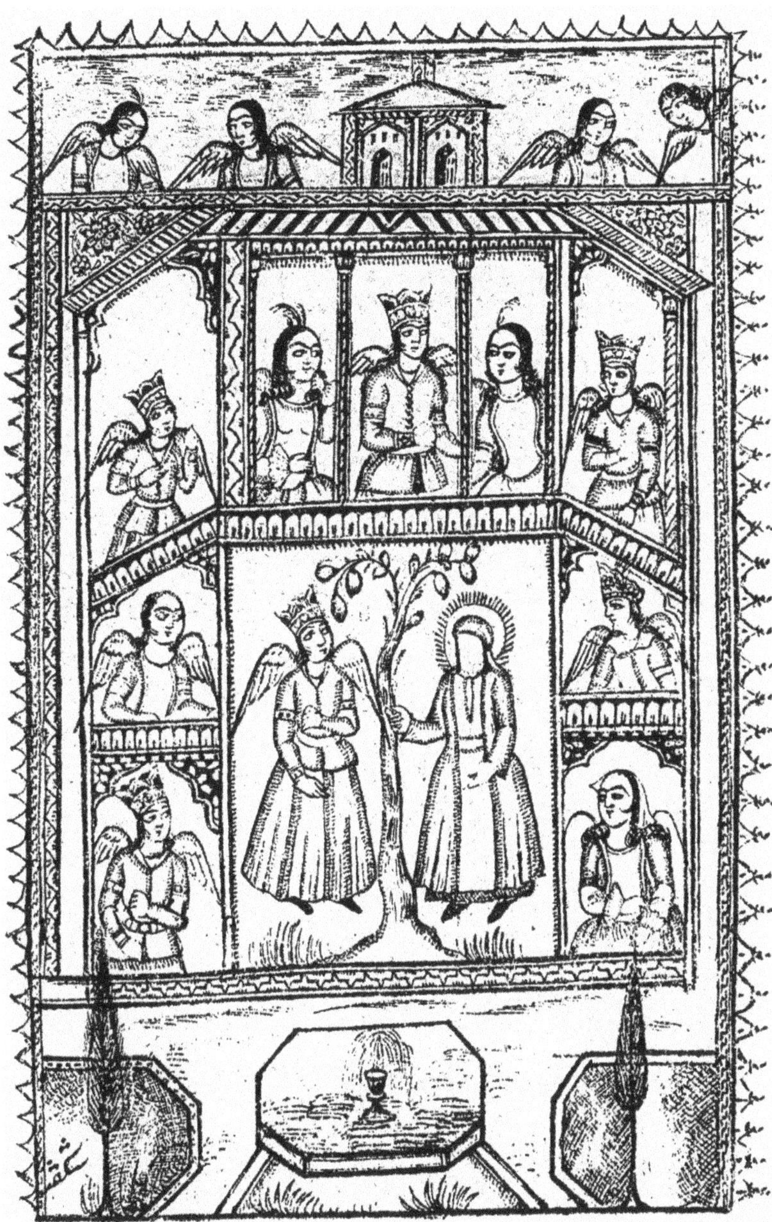

FIGURE 12.6. The Prophet Muḥammad stands next to the angel Gabriel and observes paradise and the Kawthar pool from a pavilion, anonymous, *Miʿrājnāma*, 1272/1855.

a number of episodes or key moments in the ascension, such as Muḥammad's encounter with Gabriel and Burāq, his visit of the heavens and angels, and his witnessing of heaven and hell.

The illustrations typically appear between poetical verses and sections of text so that the great majority of them—excluding the *miʿrāj sarloh*—are contained within a square or rectangular frame. Only in the *Miʿrājnāma* of 1854 do some illustrations appear in the form of a parallelogram or polygon in the margins. Some other illustrations also appear unframed, as in the *Miʿrājnāma* of 1846. To render space and the illusion of depth, illustrators use objects or motifs indicative

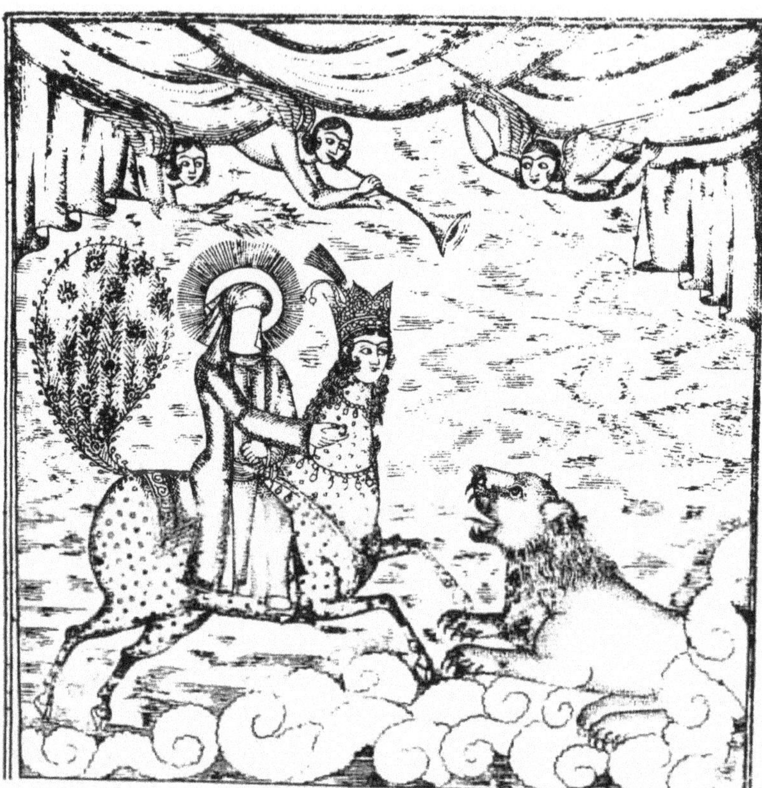

FIGURE 12.7. The Prophet Muḥammad, riding Burāq, encounters Imām ʿAlī in the shape of an angelic lion, Mulā Būman ʿAlī, *Ḥamla-yi Ḥaydarī*, illustrated by ʿAlī-Qulī Khū'ī, 1267/1850.

of location. For example, heavenly regions are keyed by the inclusion of clouds or the sun (as in the *Miʿrājnāma* of 1855). Some include trees as markers of a garden space, while others use columns, curtains, and other architectural details to denote an interior space or a pavilion (Figure 12.6). So although the compositions remain rather flat and stiff, a limited range of pictorial devices effectively suggest either an earthly or heavenly location, or an external or internal space.

Figural imagery includes depictions of the Prophet Muḥammad, as well as other prophets, Imām ʿAlī, Burāq, and angels. The Prophet appears consistently in illustrative cycles since he is the story's main protagonist. Without exception, he is represented wearing a turban and a facial veil, with a glowing halo encircling his head. The facial veil begins to be adopted as a marker of prophetic portraiture in Persian painting from the early sixteenth century onward for reasons that are complex; they are linked not just to a prohibition of representing the Prophet's facial features but to other religious and political factors particular to the early Safavid period.[25] With its gradual establishment as a "codified" marker of the Prophet Muḥammad and his sacredness over the course of several centuries, the facial veil had become standard in prophetic iconography by the Qajar period.

Like Muḥammad, other prophets and saints are depicted with aureoles and covered faces. Only in one book, the *Miʿrājnāma* of 1846, however, are all saints (except for the Prophet Muḥammad) depicted with facial features. Imām ʿAlī is shown as a

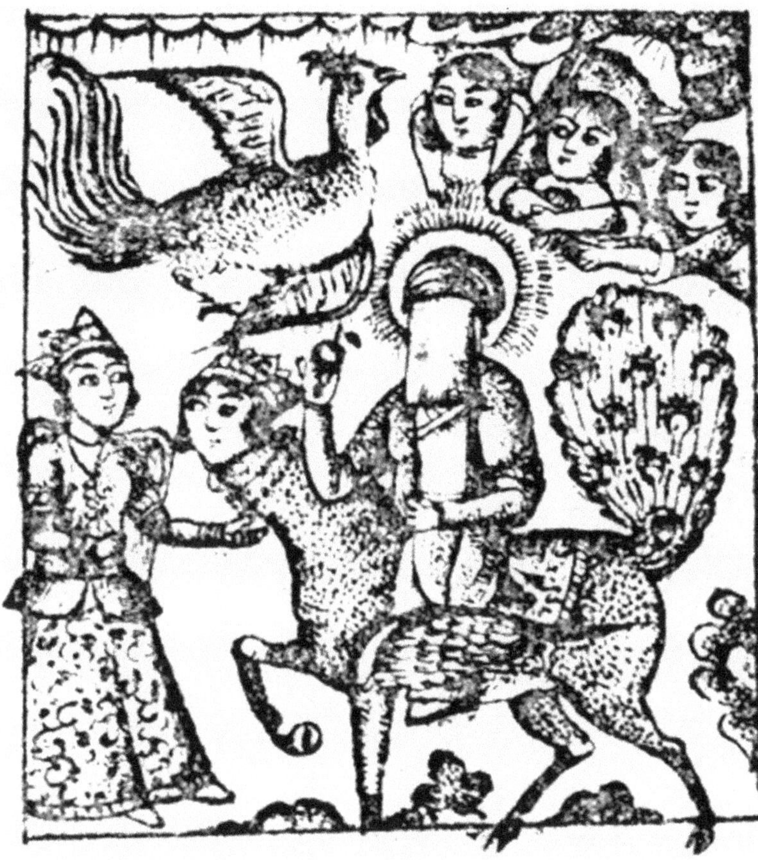

FIGURE 12.8. The Prophet Muḥammad, riding Burāq, observes the rooster angel, anonymous, *Miʿrājnāma,* 1263/1846.

human figure wearing a turban rather than a crown (Figure 12.3). In other cases, ʿAlī appears in the angelic shape of a lion (Figure 12.7), a motif that is carried over into Qajar lithographed books from Safavid ascension paintings. What is also new at this time is ʿAlī's presence in many episodes in the Prophet's ascension, and not just beyond the seventh heaven. He appears in Mecca at the beginning of the *miʿrāj;* he shares food with Muḥammad from behind a veil in the heavenly realms (Figure 12.1); and he confirms his companionship with the Prophet upon his return to Mecca. As Shujāʿī Mashhadī records in his *Miʿrājnāma,* Muḥammad is offered rice pudding and two apples in paradise, but he refuses to eat his meal without his faithful companion:

> *Ka tanhā nakhūrdam man hargiz ṭaʿām / magar bā rafīqam ʿAlī wa'l-salām*
>
> I have never eaten food by myself / only with my friend ʿAlī, peace be upon him

These many elements place Imām ʿAlī on par with the Prophet Muḥammad or even highlight ʿAlī's superiority to Muḥammad through his ability to accompany and protect the Messenger of Islam during his *miʿrāj.* Without a doubt, such elements would have catered to a Shiʿi audience disposed to welcome a sectarian reading (and visualizing) of the ascension tale.

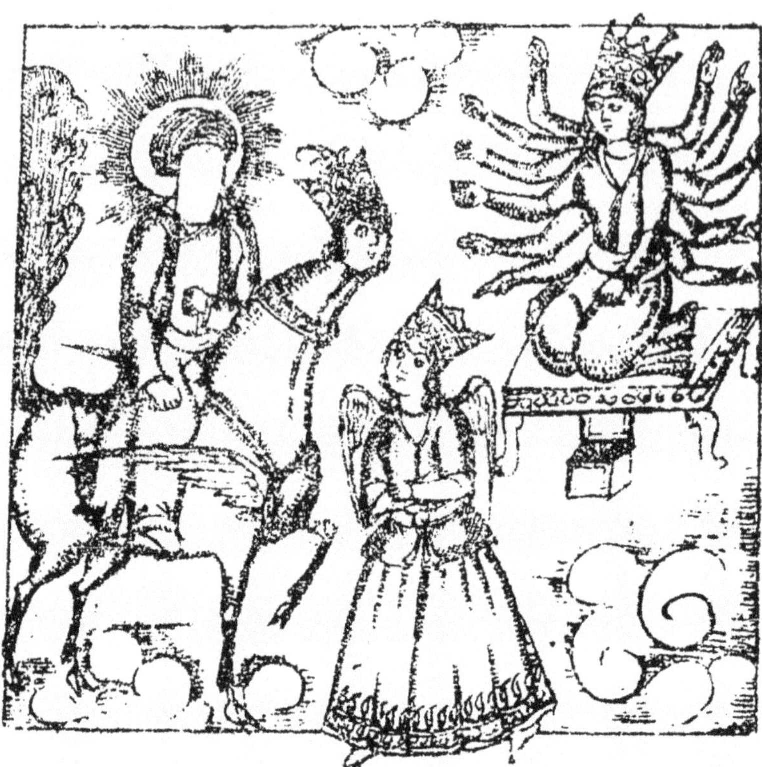

FIGURE 12.9. The Prophet Muḥammad, riding Burāq, sees the polylimbed angel Shāghāvā'īl, Shujāʿī Mashhadī, *Miʿrājnāma*, 1268/1851.

The angels in Qajar lithographed books also extend painterly traditions and alter inherited motifs to a certain extent. For example, Burāq is almost always represented as a flying steed with a female human head wearing a crown and a tail in the shape of a peacock's tail. Although Burāq's gender is never completely fixed prior to the Qajar period, it seems that at this time it is interpreted as a female creature. Similarly, the peacock's tail appears, albeit unsystematically, in earlier illustrations—here too, it is not until the Qajar period that Burāq's form is more fully crystallized.[26]

Angels in the skies wear long- and short-sleeved tunics and long skirts that are usually decorated with patterns or stippling, typical of Qajar costumes that are frequently depicted in large-scale oil paintings as well.[27] The angels are often represented wearing crowns and with wings stretched out. In other instances, they wear plumes or have hairdos parted at the middle, and their facial features include the readily recognizable Qajar monobrow. And still in other cases, the angels look like *putti*, thus revealing the extent to which European motifs had infiltrated Iran by this time.

The Prophet encounters a number of other angels: these include the rooster angel (Figure 12.8), an angel that usually appears in the first heaven in ascension paintings and that symbolizes God's calling to prayer from the heavenly spheres to the earthly realms (see Plate 8). Another angel not encountered in Persian pictorial traditions and that only appears in Qajar lithographed books is the angel by the name of Shāghāvā'īl, who is depicted as a crowned angel with many arms, seated on a throne (Figure 12.9). Although the Timurid *Miʿrājnāma* of ca. 1436 includes several depictions of polycephalous angels whose iconography appears indebted to Central Asian Buddhist depictions of the god of compassion Avalokitesvara (also known as Guanyin), this Qajar depiction of Shāghāvā'īl may have been influenced by depictions of the Hindu goddess Durga, a supreme form of Devi, who can appear in physical form with up to eighteen arms.[28]

The *Miʿrāj* as a Shiʿi Moralizing Tale For Children

Mīrzā ʿAbd al-Vaḥḥāb, a poet of the Qajar period and a secretary to Fatḥ ʿAlī Shāh, wrote a compendium of poetry titled *Ganjīna* (Treasury) in 1864–1865. At the end of his work, he includes an index *(fihrist)* describing a large number of printed lithographic books produced during his time. These include prayer books, poems, stories, fairy tales, as well as books discussed in the present study, namely various *Miʿrājnāmas*, the tale of Żarīr-i Khuzā'ī, and Maktabī Shīrāzī's *Laylā va Majnūn*. Interestingly, he classifies all these works under the rubric of children's literature (*bachcha-khānī*).[29] This provides a contemporaneous attestation that such illustrated books were produced with a young audience or a lay and/or relatively uneducated public in mind.

The Prophet's ascension, which is filled with fabulous adventures and stories of the otherworld, was indeed well suited for children. Entertaining and awe-inspiring, it also included religious themes to teach youngsters the biography of the Prophet and the basic tenets of the Islamic, and more particularly the Shiʿi, faith. Moralizing and entertaining, *miʿrāj* stories at this time seem to fit into a particular branch of children's literature, that is, religious advice literature. Such works were used as didactic tools, and without a doubt lithographed books containing descriptions and illustrations of the Prophet Muḥammad and the tale of his heavenly ascension must have appealed to teachers and their students. The printed books' relative simplicity and affordability facilitated their availability and, by extension, their use in both the private and public domain.

Qajar illustrated lithographed books dealing with the *miʿrāj* expand upon more than six centuries of narrating and depicting the Prophet's ascension in Persian artistic traditions. New texts blending Shiʿi motifs and Persian *dāstān*s reveal the extent to which religious traditions in Iran during the Qajar period went hand in hand and were reinforced by Persian folk tales. Similarly, the illustrations experiment with new forms and motifs, and for the first time depict Imām ʿAlī as the physical stand-in of Shiʿi Islam. These new narrative elements and visual devices all contributed to the development of the *miʿrāj* narrative in Iran during the modern period, and reveal the degree to which the tale of the Prophet's ascension could be expanded and adapted depending on cultural and religious traditions particular to the day.

Notes

I wish to thank Ulrich Marzolph, Seyed Mohammad Reza Fazel Hashemi, Sam Zand, and Mahsa Sedigh for their help. I also am very grateful to Christiane Gruber for discussing various topics related to my research and for her kind assistance in expanding my chapter and rendering it into English. The illustrations included in this chapter belong to the collection of Ulrich Marzolph, Göttingen, Germany.

1. See Peter Chelkowski, "Narrative Painting and Painting Recitation in Qajar Iran," *Muqarnas* 6 (1989), 98–111; and idem, "Popular Arts: Patronage and Piety," in *Royal Persian Paintings: The Qajar Epoch, 1785–1925,* ed. Layla Diba and Maryam Ekhtiar (London: I. B. Tauris, 1998), 90–97.

2. On book arts during the Ilkhanid period, see Robert Hillenbrand, "The Arts of the Book in Ilkhanid Iran," in *The Legacy of Genghis Khan: Courtly Art and Culture in Western Asia, 1256–1353,* ed. Linda Komaroff and Stefano Carboni (New York and New Haven: Metropolitan Museum of Art with Yale University Press, 2002), 134–167.

3. See Sheila Blair, *A Compendium of Chronicles: Rashid al-Din's Illustrated History of the World, The Nasser D. Khalili Collection of Islamic Art,* vol. 27 (London: Nour Foundation in association with Azimuth Editions and Oxford University Press, 1995).

4. Robert Hillenbrand, "Images of Muhammad in al-Biruni's *Chronology of Ancient Nations,*" in *Persian Painting from the Mongols to the Qajars: Studies in Honour of Basil W. Robinson,* ed. idem (London and New York: I.B. Tauris, 2000), 129–146.

5. For a discussion of the Ilkhanid illustrated *Miʿrājnāma* of ca. 1317–1335, see Christiane Gruber's chapter in this volume. Also see her *The Ilkhanid Book of Ascension: A Persian-Sunni Devotional Tale* (London: I. B. Tauris, 2009).

6. See Christiane Gruber, *The Timurid Book of Ascension (Miʿrajnama): A Study of Text and Image in a Pan-Asian Context* (Valencia: Patrimonio Ediciones, 2008); and Marie-Rose Séguy, *The Miraculous Journey of Mahomet: Mirâj Nâmeh, Bibliothèque Nationale, Paris (Manuscrit Supplément Turc 190),* trans. Richard Pevear (New York: G. Braziller, 1977). The text is available in English translation in Wheeler Thackston, "The Paris *Miʿrajnama,*" *Journal of Turkish Studies* 18 (1994), 263–299.

7. For a discussion of Safavid ascension images, see Christiane Gruber, "The Prophet Muhammad's Ascension (*Miʿrāj*) in Islamic Art and Literature, 1300–1600," (Ph.D. diss., University of Pennsylvania, 2005), 240–303.

8. Christiane Gruber, "When *Nubuvvat* Encounters *Valāyat:* Safavid Paintings of the Prophet Muhammad's *Miʿrāj,* ca. 1500–1550," in *Shiʿite Art and Material Culture,* ed. Pedram Khosronejad (London: I. B. Tauris, 2010).

9. For a history of printing in Iran, see Farīd Qāsimī, *Sarguzasht-i Maṭbūʿāt-i Īrān: Rūzgār-i Muḥammad Shāh va Nāṣir al-Dīn Shāh,* 2 vols. (Tehran: Vizārat-i Farhang va Irshād-i Islāmī, 1380/2001); and Ḥusayn Gulpāyigānī, *Ta'rīkh-i Chāp va Chāpkhāna dar Īrān* (Tehran: Nashr-i Gulshān, 1378/1999). For illustrated lithographed books, see Ulrich Marzolph, *Narrative Illustration in Persian Lithographed Books* (Leiden: Brill, 2001).

10. For further information about ʿAbbās Mīrzā, see Karīm Sulaymānī, *Alqāb-i Rijāl-i Dura-i Qājār* (Tehran: Ney, 1379/1959), 192–193.

11. Saʿīd Nafīsī, "Ṣanʿat-i Chāp-i Muṣavvar dar Īrān," *Payām-i Nu* 5 (1352/1974), 23.

12. Muʿtamid al-Dawla was one of the slaves of Āghā Muḥammad Khān (r. 1794–1797). He was brought to Iran from Tiflis in 1209/1794. His position improved at the Qajar court, and he was appointed governor of Kermanshah, Luristan, and Isfahan in 1254/1838. See Sulaymānī, *Alqāb-i Rijāl-i Dura-i Qājār,* 160.

13. *Mukhtārnāma,* dated 1261/1845, 177 folios, paper size: 16 × 26.5 cm; dimensions of written surface: 13.5 × 23 cm, 28 lines text/page; printed from movable type; 8 illustrations produced by wood engraving; published by ʿAbd ʿAlī Karīm.

14. Shahlā Bābāzāda, *Ta'rīkh-i Chāp dar Īrān* (Tehran: Kitābkhāna-i Ṭahūrī, 1378/1988), 21.

15. Ulrich Marzolph, "Early Printing History in Iran (1817–ca. 1900). Part I: Printed Man-

uscript," in *Middle Eastern Languages and the Print Revolution: A Cross-Cultural Encounter*, ed. Eva Hanebutt-Benz, Dagmar Glass, and Geoffrey Roper (Westhofen: Wva-Verlag Skulima, 2002), 263–267.

16. For gender transformation as a form of punishment, see Michio Sato, *Enzyklopädie des Märchens* (Berlin and New York: Walter de Gruyter, 1987), vol. 5, 1138–1142 (entry titled "Geschlechtswechsel").

17. I-*Miʿrājnāma*, dated 1268/1851; 24 folios; dimensions of written surface: 11.5 × 18 cm including diagonal writing in the margins; inner frame: 8 ×12 cm, 2 columns and 15 lines of text/page; 17 illustrations.

II-*Miʿrājnāma*, dated 1271/1854; 22 folios; dimensions of written surface: 12 × 19 cm including diagonal writing in the margins; inner frame: 9 × 12 cm, 2 columns and 15 lines of text/page; 17 illustrations; published by Mullā Muḥammad ʿAlī.

III-*Miʿrājnāma*, dated 1272/1855; dimensions of written surface: 15 × 24 cm including diagonal writing in the margins; 2 columns of text/page; 17 illustrations.

IV-*Miʿrājnāma*, dated 1276/1859; dimensions of written surface: 12 × 20 cm including diagonal writing in the margins; inner frame: 8.5 × 13 cm; 2 columns and 18 lines of text/page; 8 illustrations.

V-*Miʿrājnāma*, dated 1291/1874; 19 folios, dimensions of written surface: 14.5 × 19.5 cm including diagonal writing in the margins; inner frame: 9 × 13 cm; 2 columns and 15 lines of text/page; 10 illustrations.

VI-*Miʿrājnāma*, dated 1305/1887; 20 folios; dimensions of written surface: 12 × 16.5 cm including diagonal writing in the margins; 2 columns and 19 lines of text/page; scribe: Muḥammad Mahdī Gulpāyigānī; 6 illustrations; published by Mashhadī ʿAlī Naqī; printed by Ustād Mīrzā Ḥabīb Allāh.

VII-*Miʿrājnāma*, dated 1307/1889; 32 pages; dimensions of written surface: 12 × 19 cm including diagonal writing in the margins; inner frame: 9 × 12 cm; 2 columns and 15 lines of text/page; scribe: Muḥammad Mahdī Gulpāyigānī; 9 illustrations.

18. The tale of Zaʿfar was titled *Sarguzasht-i Mard-i Shakāk*, undated, scribe: Muḥammad Ṣanaʿī; 4 illustrations by Muḥammad Ṣānaʿī; published by ʿAlī Shīrāzī. Also see Muḥammad Hādī Muḥammadī and Zuhra Qāʾinī, *Taʾrīkh-i Adabīyāt-i Kūdakān-i Īrān* (Tehran: Chīstā, 1379/200–2001), vol. 4, 703.

19. *Miʿrājnāma*, dated 1263/1846; 20 folios; paper size: 15 × 20.5 cm; dimensions of written surface: 9.5 × 18 cm; 29 lines of text/page; 29 illustrations; scribe: Muṣṭafā Qulī b. Muḥammad Hādī Ṣulṭān-i Kajūrī-yi Balada; published by Mullā ʿAbbās ʿAlī; printers: Mashhadī Ḥājjī Muḥammad Tabrīzī and Muḥammad ʿAlī Ṣaḥḥāf b. Mullā Āghā Kuchak-i Iṣfahānī al-Aṣl.

20. There exist two editions of the *Baḥr-i Tavīl-i Miʿrājnāma:*

I-*Baḥr-i Tavīl-i Miʿrājnāma*, dated 1299 /1881; 9 folios; scribe: Aḥmad Khānsārī; published by Ghulām Riżā Mashhadī; printed by Mashhadī and Muḥammad Taqī.

II-*Baḥr-i Tavīl-i Miʿrājnāma*, undated; 9 folios; dimensions: 17.5 × 11 cm; 3 illustrations; published by Faraj Allāh Khalaf-i Marḥūm-i Āghā Ḥusayn-i Khānsārī.

21. There exist seven editions of the *Ḥamla-yi Ḥaydarī:*

I-*Ḥamla-i Ḥaydarī*, undated; 208 folios; dimensions of written surface: 17 × 29 cm; 4 columns and 36 lines of text/page; scribe: Mīrzā Āghā Kamraʾī; 51 illustrations; published by Ḥājjī Muḥammad Nuṣayr; printed by Karbalāʾī Muḥammad Ḥusayn.

II-*Ḥamla-i Ḥaydarī*, dated 1264/1847; 46 folios; paper size: 21 × 34.5 cm; dimensions of written surface: 16 × 28.5 cm; 4 columns and 37 lines of text/page; scribe: ʿAlī Aṣghar; 51 illustrations attributed to ʿAlī Qulī Khūʾī.

III-*Ḥamla-i Ḥaydarī*, dated 1269/1852; 199 folios; dimensions of written surface: 16 × 28.5 cm; 4 columns and 37 lines of text/page; scribe: ʿAbd al-Ṣamad b. Mullā Muḥammad Riżā Khurāsānī; 39 illustrations by Mīrzā ʿAlī Qulī Khūʾī; printed by Khān Rustam ʿAlī.

IV-*Ḥamla-i Ḥaydarī*, dated 1270/1853; 415 pages; paper size: 21 × 36.5 cm; dimensions of written surface: 17 × 28.5 cm; 37 lines of text/page; scribe: Mīrzā Āghā Kamraʾī; 51 illustrations.

V-*Ḥamla-i Ḥaydarī*, dated 1277/1860; 208 folios; paper size: 21.5 × 34 cm; dimensions of written surface: 17 × 29.5 cm; 4 columns and 37 lines of text/page; scribe: Muḥammad Ṣādiq al-Ḥusaynī al-Gulpāyigānī; 51 illustrations; published by Āghā Karbalā'ī Ghulām Riżā.

VI-*Ḥamla-i Ḥaydarī,* dated 1283/1866; 208 folios; paper size: 20.5 × 34 cm; dimensions of written surface: 16.5 × 28 cm; 37 lines of text/page; scribe: Mīrzā Āghā Kamra'ī; 52 illustrations; published by Abū'l-Ḥasan b. Mullā Zayn al-ʿĀbidīn Khūshnavīs; printed by Karbalā'ī Muḥammad Qulī and Karbalā'ī Muḥammad Ḥusayn.

VII-*Ḥamla-i Ḥaydarī,* dated 1312/1894; 209 folios; paper size: 21 × 33 cm; dimensions of written surface: 16.5 × 29 cm; 37 lines of text/page; scribe: Muḥammad Ismāʿīl b. Mullā ʿAlī Akbar al-Shāhrūdī; 50 illustrations by ʿAlī Khān; printed by Mīrzā Ḥabīb Allāh Tafrishī.

22. *Żarīr-i Khuzāʾī,* dated 1265/1848; 28 folios; paper size: 16 × 22 cm; dimensions of written surface: 11.5 × 19 cm including diagonal writing in the margins; inner frame: 7.5 × 13.5 cm; 2 columns and 15 lines of text/page; scribe: Ghulām Ḥusayn b. ʿAlī Akbar; 15 illustrations.

23. *Laylā va Majnūn,* dated 1270/1853; 33 folios; paper size: 14.5 × 23cm; dimensions of written surface: 10.5 × 19.5 cm including diagonal writing in the margins; inner frame: 8 × 14 cm; 2 columns and 18 lines of text/page; 25 illustrations.

24. See the illustrated manuscript of Maktabī Shīrāzī's *Laylā va Majnūn* dated 1240/1824 and its ascension painting on folio 7v in Basil Robinson (ed.), *Islamic Painting and the Arts of the Book* (London: Faber and Faber Ltd, 1976), 216, and cat. no. III.407.

25. For a discussion of the Prophet's facial veil, see Gruber, "When *Nubuvvat* Encounters *Valāyat.*"

26. On the iconography of Burāq in Islamic painting, see Thomas Arnold, *Painting in Islam: A Study of the Place of Pictorial Art in Muslim Culture* (New York: Dover, 1965), 117–122.

27. See comparative Qajar costumes depicted in various Qajar paintings published in Diba and Ekhtiar, *Royal Persian Paintings.*

28. On the Timurid *Miʿrājnāma*'s depictions of polycephalous angels and their pictorial and symbolic links to Avalokitesvara/Guanyin, see Gruber, *The Timurid Book of Ascension,* 317–319.

29. Hādī and Qā'inī, *Ta'rīkh-i Adabīyāt-i Kūdakān-i Īrān,* vol. 3, 45–46. For further information about Mīrzā ʿAbd al-Vaḥḥāb, see Sulaymānī, *Alqāb-i Rijāl-i Dura-i Qājār,* 160.

PART 3

☾

The Miʿrāj *as Performance and Ritual*

13

Reading the *Mi*ʿ*rāj* Account as a Theatrical Performance: The Case of *Ma*ʿ*ārij al-Nubuwwa*

ÖZGEN FELEK

The story of the Prophet's *mi*ʿ*rāj* can be analyzed from multiple perspectives as a telling of one of the most spectacular miracles of the Prophet. The present study aims to interpret the tale through a specific lens, namely through the form and mechanisms provided by theatrical dramas. In this endeavor, I have chosen to examine the *mi*ʿ*rāj* section of *Ma*ʿ*ārij al-nubuwwa fī madārij al-futuwwa* (The Stages of Prophecy on the Paths to Magnanimity)[1] composed in Persian by Muʿīn al-Dīn Muḥammad Amīn b. Ḥājjī Muḥammad al-Farāhī al-Harawī, also known as Muʿīn al-Miskīn (d. 908/1501–1502).[2] By examining the text through the methodological tools provided by the fields of narratology and performance, it will become clear that thanks to its highly presentational style and its sequential structure, the ascension narrative gives concrete and vivid substance to the otherwise abstract teachings of Islam. Likewise, it makes the existence of the otherworld immediate and tangible by catering to the expectations of its audience. This study aims to demonstrate—as Jerome Bruner effectively notes in his article "The Narrative Construction of Reality"—"how narrative operates as an instrument of mind in the construction of reality."[3] By presenting the Prophet's *mi*ʿ*rāj* as the symbolic and performative enactment of the otherworld, this cross-disciplinary investigation aims to highlight the complex audience dynamics evinced by the telling of the *mi*ʿ*rāj* narrative as well.

*Ma*ʿ*ārij al-nubuwwa* consists of an introduction, four main chapters, and a conclusion. After a brief introduction that focuses on the characteristics of the Prophet, the first chapter discusses the Prophet's primordial light (*nūr Muḥammad*), which is believed to have been transmitted through the former prophets to the Prophet's mother, Āmina.[4] After recounting the events from the Prophet's birth to the first revelation in the second chapter, the author writes about the period between the Prophet's first revelation and the *hijra* in the third chapter, more than half of which also covers the ascension of the Prophet. In the last chapter, he discusses the period after the *hijra* to his death, while the conclusion is mainly dedicated to the Prophet's miracles.

The *miʿrāj* section in *Maʿārij al-nubuwwa,* appearing in the third chapter (the Prophet Muḥammad's prophetic career from its beginning through *hijra*), consists of about two hundred pages, and its extensive treatment of the subject allows us to analyze this section as a quasi-independent *Miʿrājnāma* (Book of Ascension). Furthermore, its descriptions of exotic landscapes and locales in the heavens, paradise, and hell, allow us to read it as a kind of otherworldly *siyāḥatnāma,* or travel account. It is also possible to interpret it as an *ʿajā'ibnāma,* or book of marvels, because of the unusual creatures and places that the Prophet witnesses during his ascension through the skies.[5] Although it is a literary account that is meant to be read, it could additionally be understood as a highly visual experience, splendidly constructed and embellished with colorful and rich images. The multi-genre approach taken by Muʿīn al-Miskīn to present the heavenly journey of the Prophet could be compared to today's multi-media theatrical productions.

Indeed, Muʿīn al-Miskīn represents the ascension of the Prophet through a quintessentially dramatic structure. Although it is impossible to argue that he intended to present the story as a play, the text contains many elements that can be usefully analyzed through concepts and theories derived from narratology and dramatology, such as set design, plot, characters, and dialogues. This particularly dynamic approach may have been selected purposefully by the author, a devoted preacher, in order to convey the Prophet's ascent to his audience members, most of whom would not have read his text but would have had it read to them, in an especially vivid fashion. This kind of religious storytelling provides a hybrid form that mixes drama and written narrative, justifying the "lens" suggested in the present study. Taking this hypothesis as a starting point, in the analysis that follows I will look at particular narrative aspects of *Maʿārij al-nubuwwa* and examine the dramatic structure of its story line, with the aim to answer the question of how Muʿīn al-Miskīn "create[s] an illusion, an effect, a semblance of mimesis"[6] through his work, and how the story of the *miʿrāj* helps him establish himself not only as a solid scholar, but also as a successful narrator.

There are many theoretical approaches to narrative, yet in analyzing the narrative aspects of the text, I will closely follow Mieke Bal's analytical approach used in her *Narratology: Introduction to the Theory of Narrative,*[7] a theory well suited to the study of narrative aspects of *Maʿārij al-nubuwwa.* In her study, Bal proposes a three-level division of narrative: the *fabula,* the *story,* and the *text.* Of these, the *fabula* is "a series of logically and chronologically related events caused or experienced by actors," which contains four main elements: events, actors, time, and location. The *story* refers to the several aspects that are the ways the text manipulates the presentation of those elements. The last division of narrative is the *text,* by which language signs are used to convey a story produced by an agent who relates the story. This last division is devoted to the narrator, non-narrative comments, description, and levels of narration. Bal's theoretical concept of narrative is particularly useful for the analysis of Muʿīn al-Miskīn's text, for it brings greater clarity to our understanding of the relationship between the well-known *miʿrāj* story and the way it is presented by this particular narrator, a preacher and scholar who seems to have been highly aware of the expectations and taste of his audience members, themselves especially receptive to textual and visual metaphor.

In addition to drawing upon Bal's narratological theories, I will also refer to studies dealing with drama and performance. Among these, our main guides will be *The Art of Drama*, by Fred B. Millett and Gerald Eades Bentley,[8] along with Edwin Wilson's *The Theatre Experience.*[9] In the last chapter of *The Art of Drama*, after briefly discussing substance and form, Millett examines dramatic work in terms of its plot, characterization, dialogue, and setting. Wilson's work deals with the roles and responsibilities of the audience, the performance, the director, the designers, and the playwright. He also clarifies the functions of other technical elements necessary in dramas. Elements from each of these theoretical works will help to explain key features in Muʿīn al-Miskīn's *Maʿārij al-nubuwwa.*

Maʿārij al-nubuwwa is not a work of drama, but rather a prose narrative, and the story of the ascension can be considered as an embedded narrative in the primary text, itself a *sīra* or biography of the Prophet Muḥammad. Each one of these two narratives, both the *sīra* and the *miʿrāj*, has a unique *fabula* with its own independent and theoretically separate thrust. Yet, in analyzing the *miʿrājnāma* chapter of *Maʿārij al-nubuwwa*, its *fabula* can be again divided in two main segments: the *isrāʾ*, which refers to the night journey of the Prophet from Mecca to Jerusalem, and the *miʿrāj*, his heavenly journey through the skies. In this study, I will focus on the *miʿrāj* chapter's *fabula*, which is presented as a piece of drama. However, since the *story* and the *text* are just as fundamental a part of a narrative as the *fabula*, it is also essential to also look at several aspects of the narrative—such as sequential ordering, rhythm, frequency, along with the transformation of actor(s) to character(s) and of a place to space—to analyze the *story.* I will introduce the *text*, dealing with its narrator(s), non-narrative comments, description, and levels of narration after providing some basic background on the author and the historical, literary, and artistic context in which he composed his text.

Muʿīn al-Miskīn and his *Maʿārij al-Nubuwwa*

Muʿīn al-Miskīn was a scholar of hadith and a preacher for about thirty-one years,[10] serving for some time as the leader (*imām*) at the major mosque of Herat, presently located in western Afghanistan.[11] In addition to his *Maʿārij al-nubuwwa*, Muʿīn al-Miskīn also wrote a number of other works, including the following: *Muʿjizāt-i Mūsawī*, also called *Taʾrīkh-i Mūsawī* or *Qiṣṣa-yi Mūsawī*, a detailed history of the Prophet Moses; *Aḥsan al-Qiṣaṣ*, the story of Joseph (Yūsuf) and Zulaykhā, the wife of ʿAzīz, the king known as Potiphar in the Hebrew Bible; and *Tafsīr-i Ḥadāʾiq al-Ḥaqāʾiq*, a commentary on Sūrat Yūsuf (Qurʾan 12).[12] Muʿīn al-Miskīn also composed a collection of poetry (*dīwān*), which unfortunately does not survive today.

Although he composed numerous works of both prose and poetry, Muʿīn al-Miskīn, as he unabashedly claimed, seems to have built his reputation as a famous preacher through his private *majlis*es in addition to his regular sermons at the mosque in Herat.[13] His reputation was cemented more as a preacher by biographers: for example, Mīr ʿAlī Shīr Nawāʾī, in his *Majālis al-nafāʾis,* praises Muʿīn al-Miskīn as a successful sermonizer. However, he calls our author and his followers "*dīwāne,*" ecstatic mystics, and asserts that they were always in a state of ecstasy.[14] According to Nawāʾī, "because [Muʿīn al-Miskīn] was a *dīwāne,* he used to talk in the way that pleased himself while preaching from the pulpit; but none blamed him for his speeches, for nobody could hold a *dīwāne* and *ʿāshiḳ* [the ecstatic mystic who is deeply in love with the Divine] responsible [for anything]."[15] Nawāʾī also cites Ḳadi Mawlānā Nizāmuddīn, Muʿīn al-Miskīn's brother, and his appreciation of Muʿīn al-Miskīn's talent as a preacher.[16] According to Nizāmuddīn, Muʿīn al-Miskīn was "a good young person, but he should not be at the pulpit, because his talent is being wasted."[17] Since the content of his message is rarely noted, we can assume that it was a special charisma that made him a renowned preacher rather than his ability as a scholar.

As Muʿīn al-Miskīn himself states in the introduction to his *Maʿārij al-nubuwwa*, in addition to delivering sermons at the mosque, he held fifty sequential private gatherings (*majlis*es) devoted to the life of the Prophet.[18] These gatherings were reportedly attended by both the learned elite and common people (*khāss u ʿawām*), some of whom had traveled from a distance to attend his preaching sessions. Muʿīn al-Miskīn reports that during these gatherings he read his text aloud, and that members of his audience would listen to him with great interest.[19] He also states that he included different stories (*ḥikāyāt*) and pleasant phrases (*laṭīf ibārāt*), derived from the Qur'an.[20] As can be seen from his work, he seems to have invested his interest and energy in the stories of both pre-Islamic and Islamic prophets, which were among the topics favored by preachers and storytellers (*quṣṣāṣ*).[21] Furthermore, his use of pragmatic signals such as "*Ay darwīsh*" (O Sufi), "*rajaʿnā ilā al-qiṣṣa*" (we have returned to the narrative), and "*al-rujūʿilā al-qiṣṣa*" (return to the narrative), as well as his very use of the term "*qiṣṣa*" (narrative) throughout both his *Maʿārij al-nubuwwa* and his *Tafsīr-i Ḥadāʾiq al-Ḥaqāʾiq* underlines his interest in stories and his particular affinity for storytelling.[22]

In *Maʿārij al-nubuwwa* as well as in his other works, Muʿīn al-Miskīn's stylish use of language and visual descriptions allow him to create a fluency of expression that would have appealed to a varied audience attracted in the first instance by his talent as a preacher. Indeed, although his *Maʿārij al-nubuwwa* is a scholarly work containing quotations from the Qur'an and hadith, it is primarily an entertaining narrative enriched with colorful imagery and melodic harmonies. In reading *Maʿārij al-nubuwwa,* realism and immediacy in the descriptions and dialogues immediately strike the reader. I believe that the roots of this kind of realism could have derived from the artistic and cultural milieu in which the text was created. The sophisticated and lively cultural scene in later Timurid Herat, and especially its court-generated visual culture, must have inspired Muʿīn al-Miskīn as well; he seems to have been engaged in a process of image-making much as artists were at the time. This trend toward evocations of immediacy and tactility can be seen in particular in the descriptive images of paradise and hell. However, he seems to have drawn upon his rhetorical talent to make his story more tangible by including any detail that might help his audience visualize the events narrated in the story.

During the time that Muʿīn al-Miskīn was working on his *Maʿārij al-nubuwwa* (1461–1486), Herat served as the Timurid capital and thus was an important center of art and culture. By the time of Sultan Ḥusayn Bayqara's reign (1470–1507), Herat had been already a cultural mecca in the area for some time.[23] In 1486, when Muʿīn al-Miskīn completed his *Maʿārij al-nubuwwa,* Sultan Bayqara's vizier and milk-brother ʿAlī Shīr Nawāʾī was the greatest Timurid patron of the arts. As a statesman and connoisseur, as well as a poet, musician, and author in his own right, Nawāʾī created a vibrant courtly milieu of painters, poets, musicians, and calligraphers.[24] During this time, artists not only maintained a meticulous attention to detail but showed interest in depicting vignettes of everyday life with a new sense of realism.[25] This cultural oasis created a vast literary and artistic output, to which Muʿīn al-Miskīn undoubtedly contributed.

One artist from this milieu whose work demonstrates such an approach to both detail and realism is Kamāl al-Dīn Bihzād (1455–1535/6), who is widely acknowledged to have been the greatest painter of the Persian tradition.[26] Bihzād and his contemporaries worked within received pictorial conventions, but they also explored novel techniques and subjects, a late Timurid pictorial fusion that Thomas Lentz has called "New Painting." Bihzād and other painters contributed to illustrated texts that are contemporary to Muʿīn al-Miskīn's narrative, and therefore a clear dialectical relationship existed between authors and artists in Timurid Herat involving a new attention to realism.

For example, in an illustrated folio from a manuscript copy of Niẓāmī's *Makhzan al-Asrār* (Treasury of Secrets), produced in 1494–1495, a painting attributed to Bihzād shows traces of the New Style (Figure 13.1 and Plate 23). Here, the Prophet is depicted ascending above Mecca and the Kaʿba, and the vivid colors and the liveliness of the bright stars serve to convey a sense of tactility and immediacy not encountered in earlier Timurid art.[27] Even though the size of Kaʿba and the shapes and colors of the clouds are not "realistic," the painter clearly distinguishes between this world and the otherworld throughout which the Prophet travels by drawing them by means of different pictorial conventions; the evocation of three-dimensionality in buildings and spaces in the lower world stands in sharp contrast to the flat colors and ornamental shapes of the clouds in the heavenly realm.

Another key example appears in a different illustrated folio, dated to the same era, by Bihzād's contemporary Shāh Muẓaffar (Figure 13.2 and Plate 24). Shāh Muẓaffar was praised most especially for his ability to paint dainty portraits and to

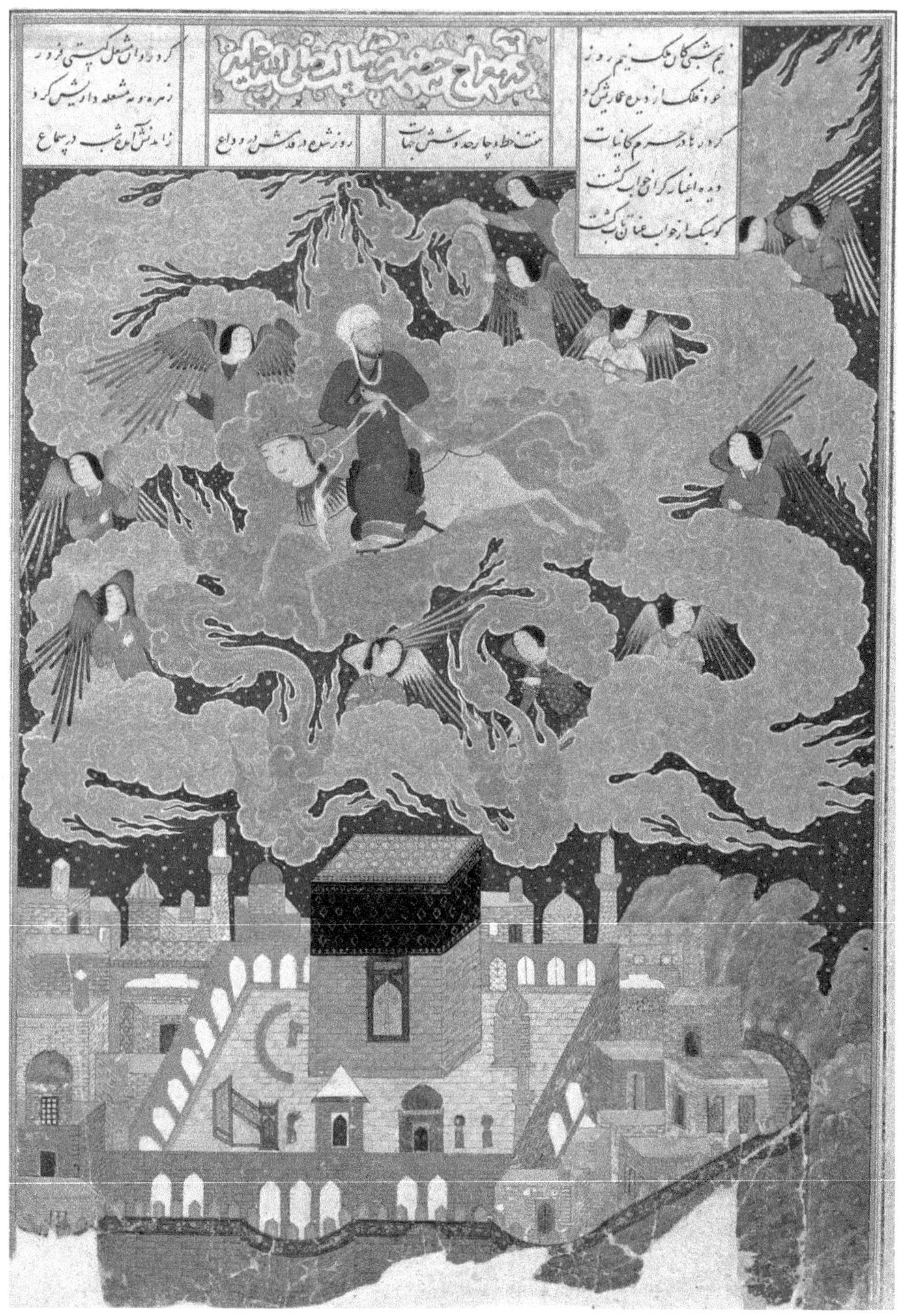

FIGURE 13.1. The Prophet ascends above Mecca and the Kaʿba, Niẓāmī, *Makhzan al-Asrār* (Treasury of Secrets), Herat, 1494–1495. London, British Library, Or. 6810, folio 5v. See color plate 23.

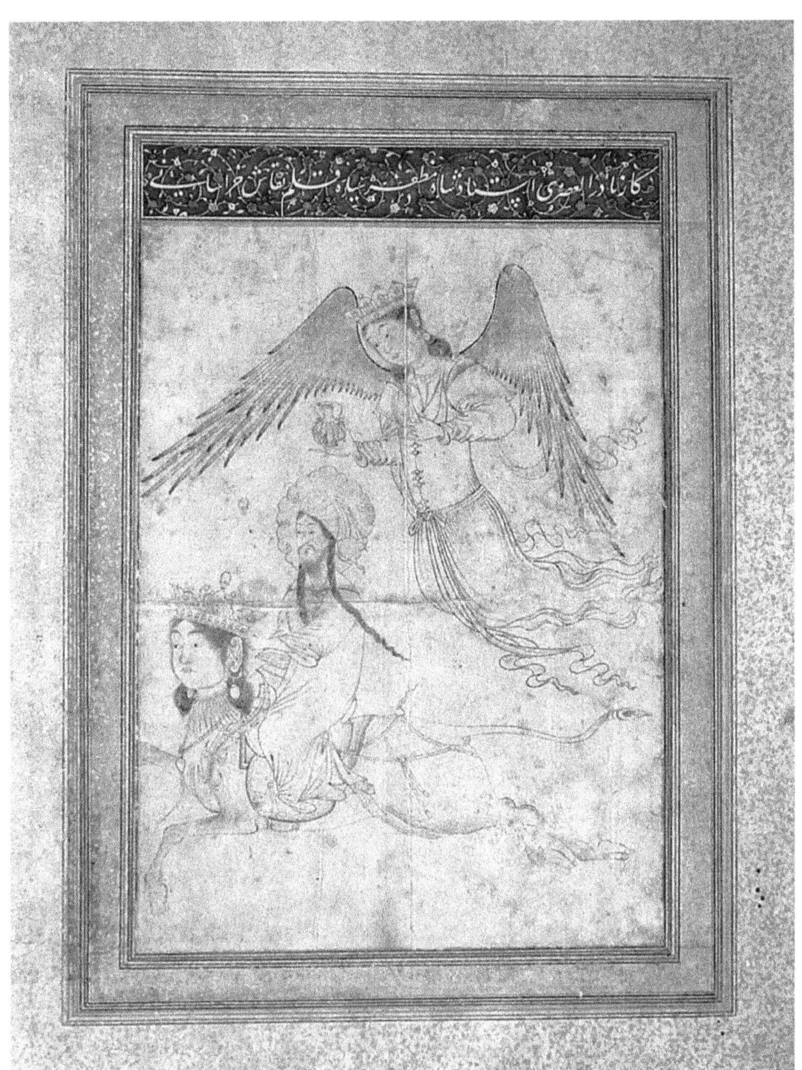

FIGURE 13.2. Shāh Muẓaffar (attr.), ink sketch of the Prophet ascending on Burāq, Herat, ca. 1475–1500. Istanbul, Topkapı Palace Library, H. 2154, folio 40v. See color plate 24 .

represent hair very precisely.[28] As clearly seen in this drawing of the Prophet in mid-air on the back of his human-headed, winged steed Burāq, and accompanied by the angel Gabriel, the closely scrutinized details of hair, beard, and eyebrows of the principal figures together with the delicate rendering of their clothing all suggest Shāh Muẓaffar's care and diligence in providing a believable image that, like Bihzād's work and subsequent ascension paintings (Plate 25), provides a sense of immediacy and realism.[29]

This tendency toward realism that seems to have been quite effective in the pictorial arts at the time is reflected in the narrative of Muʿīn al-Miskīn as well. His emphasis on depicting scenes and costumes, as well as on making dialogues as lively as possible, suggests his familiarity with and interest in the detail and realism that was effectively exploited by contemporary painters.

The *Story*

Having looked at the biography of Muʿīn al-Miskīn and the cultural and artistic environment in which he lived, preached, and produced his text, we now turn to a very brief and introductory analysis of the *story* and the *text* of his *Maʿārij al-nubuwwa* by following the analytical methods espoused by Mieke Bal, who defines a narrative level as distinct from text and *fabula*. According to Bal, "if one regards the *fabula* primarily as the product of imagination, the *story* could be regarded as the result of an *ordering*."[30] In dealing with the story aspects, she differentiates the features that distinguish the structured story from the *fabula*. These features, which she calls the *aspects*, are sequential ordering, rhythm, transformation of actor(s) to character(s), transformation of a place to the space, and focalization.

Bal's theory of narrative level can be examined in three parts: time-related aspects, which are sequential ordering and rhythm; space/place/setting-related aspects; and character and focalization. Of the time-related aspects, sequential ordering refers to the relationship between the sequence of the events in the story and their chronological order in the *fabula*. Following the way Bal describes the characteristics of story in her argument, one can see that in the narrative of *Maʿārij al-nubuwwa*, events are demonstrated in sequential ordering, all related in the past tense. Since there is no internal thought or emotion reflected to the audience, the narrator simply follows a sequential order in the past tense form.

As for rhythm, Bal argues that in narrative there are five distinguishable, different tempi, and "every narrative can be divided up into pieces which each correspond to one of these five tempi":[31] ellipsis, summary, scene, slow-down, and pause. Of them, in *Maʿārij al-nubuwwa*, the summary appears especially during travels over vast distances. For example, in a single instant, the Prophet travels vast distances from one level of heaven to another one, which normally would take someone five hundred years to travel. Even though a five-hundred-year distance is mentioned to only indicate the vastness of the heavenly realm, this still suggests the existence of such a vast distance between different levels. These distances endow the ascension narrative with a distinct tempo.

Pause also is often used in establishing rhythm in Muʿīn al-Miskīn's text. Pauses occur mostly between the different levels of the Prophet's journey. When he enters a new place, first the place is described in detail. This slows down the speed of the event and yet gives enough time for the actor (and the audience) to become acquainted with a place. The descriptions provided during these pauses will be discussed to a greater extent while analyzing the *fabula* under the subsection of *Setting*.

To Bal, another aspect of the story related to time is frequency of events, which refers to "a real *repetition* when an event occurs only once and is presented a number of times."[32] The rhythm of the narrative in *Maʿārij al-nubuwwa* is created through alternative presentations of events that the Prophet experienced during his heavenly journey. The same event is narrated repeatedly according to different hadith accounts from different hadith transmitters. Yet the repetition is not systematic, due to the numbers of hadith accounts relating different events. Some events are narrated only once or twice, whereas others are mentioned several times thanks to the existence of numerous accounts of the same event.

Bal also underlines the relations between place and space. Place is a physical shape of spatial dimensions, whereas the space is what is seen in relation to its perception. Thus, in determining the space, three senses in particular (sight, hearing, and touching) allow the actor to experience the place. In terms of its functions, place is either a place of action, or an object of presentation by becoming an acting place. That is, it is either a steady space in which events take place, or a dynamically functioning space that allows the actor to move.[33]

In *Maʿārij al-nubuwwa,* space appears to be both a dynamically functioning space and a steady space. It is not only a "place of action" in which events take place, but it is also thematized by becoming "an object of presentation itself," turning into an "acting place." Thus, space functions dynamically by allowing the Prophet to move when he has to travel through a vast array of different places. Between his departure and his return to Mecca, he moves from one space to another, and these spaces are sometimes arranged in opposites, such as sky vs. earth or paradise vs. hell. The relation between space and events is set in accordance with "fixed combinations"[34] presenting the characteristics of these spaces. For example, there are no scenes of people happy in hell, just as there are no scenes of grief in heaven. As it will be demonstrated in detail in analyzing the *fabula,* under the subsection of *Actors,* all the characters are properly situated in the literary space devoted to them.[35]

Bal also emphasizes that an actor with distinctive characteristics creates the effect of a character,[36] thereby transforming a mere actor into full character. The term actor refers to the abstract meaning of "the agent that acts," whereas the character is the actant with his/her own individuality.[37] In *Maʿārij al-nubuwwa,* characters are constructed either through direct definitions and/or adjectives that name their trait(s), or through indirect presentations that display the characters by using actions, speech, external appearances, and the environment in which they are situated.[38] The Prophet, the main actor, is determined on the basis of data provided in the previous chapters of *Maʿārij al-nubuwwa.* His traits are thus not given explicitly in the *miʿrāj* tale, mainly because his characteristics have already been established in the larger story, embedded within the *sīra.* Therefore, the audience is already familiar with his identity. Yet, Muḥammad's status as a prophet serves to continue to build his identity, and the narrator keeps constructing this characterization process by displaying, for example, the Prophet's meeting with God, his treatment and respect by angels, and the environment in which he appears.

Not only are the traits of the Prophet known; those of the archangels, previous prophets, and God are as well, based on the data presented in the *sīra.* In the same way, for example, God's being *God* is continuously expanded throughout the primary narration. The remaining characters, such as the thousands upon thousands of angels or the individuals encountered in hell or in paradise, could be labeled, in Bal's terms, as *referential* characters, who, because of their obvious slots in a frame of reference, act according to a given pattern.[39] The audience thus can easily predict their traits and behaviors. For example, we do not see any prophets or angels rebel against God or cause chaos.

The last aspect of the story is focalization, which is described by Bal as "the relationship between the vision, the agent that sees, and that which is seen."[40] She argues that the narration is determined by both the narrator and focalization, which she understands as "the relations between the elements presented and the vision through which they are presented."[41] In *Maʿārij al-nubuwwa,* both Muʿīn al-Miskīn and the Prophet serve as focalizors. Yet, Muʿīn al-Miskīn functions, borrowing Bal's term, as an "external focalizor" who is not a character but rather a conveyor of the events that happen to this "internal focalizor," the Prophet, who narrates his own visual experiences through numerous hadith accounts. This situation is best expressed through the author's statement: "I [Muʿīn al-Miskīn, the preacher] say that the Prophet says, 'I saw.'" This also gives the narrator the freedom to switch from an external focalizor to an internal one. Focalization thus alternates between these two predominant narrators: Muʿīn al-Miskīn and the Prophet. On the one hand, the Prophet, as the internal focalizor, seems to have the advantage over Muʿīn al-Miskīn, who watches the events through the eyes of the Prophet and consequently needs to refer to him for details. On the other, by locating himself at a point above the object(s) of his perception, Muʿīn al-Miskīn yields a panoramic view of all the events that happen during the journey of the Prophet, and he makes the Prophet his "focalized object." Thus, in the end, it is not the focalizor who changes, but the focalized.[42]

The *Text*

In addition to what one can learn about Muʿīn al-Miskīn's ascension narrative by examining its elements on the level of *story,* one can also learn a great deal by analyzing the narrative on the level of *text.* Since a narrative text is a text in which a narrative agent tells a story, then the narrative agent or narrator is, according to Bal, "the linguistic subject, a function, and not a person, which expresses itself in the language that constitutes the text."[43] One way that the narrator creates the *text* is through nonnarrative comments, which are the commentary of the external narrator that "may far exceed the function of *narrating.*"[44] In addition, Bal sees different types of descriptions as part of the *text,* since only motivation can make the contents of the narrative believable, and this motivation can be provided via speaking about (or describing) or looking at what the actor sees.[45] This motivates the actor(s) to act and move on. She also argues that levels of narration, which deal with the relationships between speakers in a narrative, cannot be separated from the *text.* In particular, relations between primary and embedded texts shape the *text* to a great extent.[46]

The complexity of the ascension text in *Maᶜārij al-nubuwwa* rests on its being narrated in a story with many narratives, most with more than one narrator. By allowing the Prophet to narrate his story in the first person, along with Gabriel, Muᶜīn al-Miskīn turns his narrative into a narrative within narrative(s).[47] Moreover, he enables the Prophet to repeat the episode by providing different hadith accounts on the same event. At times, he also allows God to intervene in the narrative by bringing in verses from the Qur'an. Muᶜīn al-Miskīn needs these other narrators' voices in order to establish himself as a reliable narrator[48] in the eyes of his audience;[49] in turn, this authorial blending also changes his text into a polyphonic narrative when it expands to include many other voices: of hadith transmitters, the choruses of angels and prophets who recite verses from the Qur'an and sing prayer invocations to God, and great poets such as Rūmī or ᶜAṭṭār who participate through their poetical verses. In the narration, the voice belongs to Muᶜīn al-Miskīn, the preacher. As the speaking agent, although he does not mention himself, it is he who narrates what the Prophet describes as the first-person narrator.

The narrator of the *miᶜrāj* story not only relates what his actor, the Prophet, has experienced, but also offers information and explanations, such as verses from the Qur'an and their explanations, outside of the *fabula*—these are what Bal would call "non-narrative comments." These statements function in different ways. Even though they cause a pause in the narrative and slow it down, they are necessary for the narrator to clarify what is happening in certain scenes, or to support his own reliability in the eyes of his audience. Besides, as discussed above, these pauses and slow-downs provide a rhythm to the narrative.

In examining *Maᶜārij al-nubuwwa,* one of the most striking aspects of the text rests on its levels of narration, due to the textual interference that shapes the text to a great degree. The primary text of the narrator, Muᶜīn al-Miskīn the preacher, and the embedded text of the main actor, the Prophet (embedded through hadith accounts transmitted through several hadith transmitters, each of whom also adds his own voice at certain points), are so closely related that these two texts at some points can hardly be distinguished from each other. Adding to the mix and complexity of authorial voices, embedded text creates a hierarchical structure among the narrators.

The *Fabula*

As mentioned above, the *fabula* is a series of logically and chronologically related events caused or experienced by actors. It contains four main elements—events, actors, time, and location—and, in turn, the story is determined by the way in which the *fabula* is presented.[50] Therefore, the presentation style of the *miᶜrāj* story's *fabula* is important. The wider story told in *Maᶜārij al-nubuwwa,* as the primary narrative, has its own *fabula* based on the accounts of the Prophet Muḥammad, a real-life person, and on his relations with real-life characters, such as his companions and opponents. Yet, the story of the *miʿrāj* is another narrative, embedded in the primary narrative, which has its own distinctive *fabula* that employs unusual characters, such as Burāq and angels as well as previous prophets who are not even alive any more, occurring in an unknown and unearthly sphere.

However, the *miʿrāj* narrative itself is divided into two parts: the *isrā'* and the *miʿrāj*. In the subsection "Dramatic Style in the *Miʿrāj*," I will analyze the *fabula*, following this division by mainly looking at how this *fabula* is presented by the narrator(s) as a dramatic performance. In this analysis, I will treat the frame *fabula* of this entire chapter as a series of events that occur "backstage" and the second *fabula* as a series of events that occur "on stage." In examining the second *fabula*, I will mainly examine the plot (events), actors (and dialogues), and setting (location).

Dramatic Style in the *Miʿrāj*: Setting as Backstage

In almost all *sīras* and *miʿrāj-nāmas*, the Prophet's ascension is narrated in a two-part fashion: first from Mecca to Jerusalem, and then from Jerusalem through the heavens toward God. My reading of the story follows this split structure by dividing the story into two parts: first the Earth, and second the Sky. The Earth provides the foundation before the play is enacted, whereas the Sky serves as a stage on which the main action of the play is performed.

The first five chapters of the *miʿrāj* section of *Maʿārij al-nubuwwa* serve as introductory chapters to the story. In a sense, the narrator informs his audience that he will tell them a true, but bizarre, story and attempts to clear doubts that his audience may have about both the authenticity of the story and the reliability of its narrator. After addressing the issues on the meaning behind and the reasons for the *miʿrāj* in the first chapter, Muʿīn al-Miskīn explains to his audience why this heavenly journey happened during the night, instead of daytime, in the following chapter. The third chapter offers ten proofs, discussed in detail, for the possibility of such travel. In the fourth chapter, the audience is given information about where and when this play on the *miʿrāj* is performed, and the Prophet is described as being prepared for the play by the archangel Gabriel. In the fifth chapter, both the audience and the protagonist, the Prophet, are introduced to the previous prophets and archangels Gabriel, Michael, and Isrāfīl, who will perform later on stage as well. In what follows, the preliminary preparations of the "play" depicted in the fourth and the fifth chapters of the text will be analyzed as the play's backstage.

Our story begins at the house of Umm Hāni', which one might interpret as the backstage where the angel Gabriel helps the protagonist to prepare for the upcoming play (Plate 17). First the Prophet performs his ablutions or bathes (*ghusl*) in pure water (*kawthar*).[51] Next, Gabriel clothes and adorns him. His vestments consist of vibrant colors—a cloak of light, a belt of ruby, a whip of emerald, and a pair of emerald clogs:

He was dressed in a cloak of light (*nūr*) and a turban of light was put on his blessed head [. . .], then Gabriel, peace be upon him, put a cloak on his blessed back and put green emerald clogs on his blessed feet and wrapped a belt of ruby around his blessed waist and gave him an emerald whip that was decorated with four hundred pearls. Each pearl shone like the star Venus.[52]

Burāq is also described in polychromic terms:

Its chest shines like ruby, its back is white like silver, its feet are of emerald, its tail is of red coral, and its neck is of ruby.[53]

While the main actor is being prepared for his celestial journey and is described as awash in color, the supporting characters and the technicians involved in the production prepare themselves in a different dimension (the Sky) as well. By putting Gabriel in charge, God, in a role similar to that of a stage director, manages the backstage and the technicians. First, silence and calm are obtained both backstage and on stage by this Director's divine command:

Bejewel [your] wings again with the gems of paradise and put on the belt of service and put the crown and mandate (*firmān*) on and tell Michael to stop the distribution of daily sustenance, and tell Isrāfīl to stop blowing his trumpet (*ṣūr*) for an hour, tell ʿAzrāʾīl to abstain from catching the souls, [. . .] admonish Mālik to close the doors of hell with the key of calm and quietness, [. . .] and the ocean and winds to be still and not to move, [. . .] let even the spheres delay turning and rest, tell the demons of hell not to move, [. . .] go to earth, and stop the torment of all the graves in the east and west.[54]

After these preliminary preparations, the lights on stage are turned on by God's proclamation, "Command the angels of light (*nūr*; divine illumination) to fill the skies with lights."[55] The supporting actors are ordered to get ready for the play by taking their places on stage and by holding the props they will need in their respective roles:

Have the *ḥūrīs* in paradise dress up and take plates in their hands to distribute gems, let them stand in rows in the palaces of paradise. [. . .] Call Adam, Noah, Abraham, Moses, and Jesus, blessing be upon all of them, and perfume their glorious souls.[56]

Finally, the heavenly stage itself is decorated:

Tell *Riḍwān* to decorate the eight heavens, [. . .] tell the servants of the throne to put the blessed clothes on the sky of satin and put the blessed crown on the throne.[57]

When all the preparations are complete, time is suspended and all movements are brought to a halt.[58] Once the whole universe is silently ready to watch the drama of the ascension unfold, the archangel Gabriel is sent to invite the Prophet to appear on stage.

On his way from Mecca to Jerusalem (Plate 10), an unidentified woman attempts to stop Muḥammad, but he does not pay attention to her, for he was already admonished by Gabriel to carry on.[59] In Jerusalem, he meets a number of secondary actors, the earlier prophets, Adam, Noah, Abraham, Moses, and Jesus. There, he serves as prayer leader, at which time all other prophets arrange themselves behind him (Plate 11). Then, he climbs the stairs, or in the author's words "*miʿrāj yaʿnī nardubān,*" and he arrives in the heavenly realm (see Plate 22).[60] In essence, the *curtain* has been raised, allowing the *play* proper to move full speed ahead in the domain of the Sky.

Before describing the *play* itself, a few words on its conclusion must be offered here. At the very end of this play, the Prophet returns to the dressing room, i.e., the Earth. When he returns to the backstage location, everything reverts back to normal: it is nighttime and dark, of course, as it should be. The colorful, lavishly textured, and imposing scenes disappear, and a great silence reigns over the night. Compared to the dazzling show presented in the skies, the Prophet's return is fairly plain—one might even say earthy:

> Then, parting from them, I went to Jerusalem. I saw Burāq tied at the ring of the mosque. I entered the *masjid* and performed a two-*rakʿat* prayer of *shukr* [being grateful for the blessings of God]. I thanked God for the miracles and blessings [that He gave me]. Then Gabriel showed me a vision of the prophets, peace be upon them. I saw my own face among them, and Abū Bakr was on my right and ʿUmar, may God be pleased with them, was on my left. Then I went out, and Gabriel, peace be upon him, told me to ride on Burāq, and I did. I found myself back in Mecca in the blink of an eye. My bed was still warm.[61]

The next day, when the Prophet relates his night journey, not surprisingly, his greatest companion Abū Bakr believes him without hesitation or doubt, whereas Abū Jahl, his lifetime opponent, ridicules him for his claim (Plate 9). He is even tested by the disbelievers of Mecca.[62] Life carries on in its own natural way, devoid of extraordinary visual and rhetorical flourishes.

It seems that whatever happens on the surface of the Earth should remain simple and different from the world of the heavens. The author's use of sensory details and descriptive language full of images and colors for the Sky contrasts with his rather unadorned language for the Earth. Thus, Muʿīn al-Miskīn clearly distinguishes this world from the other world in the skies, in a manner similar to the pictorial techniques used by artists, who adorn the heavenly realms in their paintings with swirling clouds of gold (Figure 13.1 and Plates 23 and 25).

Dramatic Style in the *Miʿrāj*: On Stage

Having discussed the pre-play (chapters 1–5) and post-play settings (chapters 23–24) that collectively serve as a backdrop for the play's main action, let us move on to the essential aspects of the drama (chapters 6–22) that forms the heart of the *miʿrāj* story. After briefly reviewing key concepts of drama theory and re-structuring the outlines of the plot, I will look at the set design, the characteristics of the protagonist and other actors, and the dialogues among these characters, in order to see how Muʿīn al-Miskīn dramatizes the story of *miʿrāj*, combining his knowledge and skills to produce especially appealing images in his narrative. In doing so, I will draw upon Fred Millett's analysis in *The Art of Drama* and Edwin Wilson's approach in *The Theatre Experience*, along with various theories drawn from other works in the field of dramatology.

Among the different types of dramatic structures, Wilson introduces three different forms of plot: the climactic plot, the episodic plot, and the combination of the two. The climactic and the episodic plots differ from each other in terms of their approaches to the fundamental elements of a play. The climactic plot begins quite late, almost toward the climax, itself the crisis of maximum emotion and tension,[63] whereas the episodic plot begins relatively early and moves through time frames. As opposed to the extended span of time, the numerous locations, and a large cast of characters in the episodic plot, the climactic plot usually occurs in a limited time period (a few days), with a limited cast. Yet, these two plots, as often seen in modern dramas, can be combined, sometimes by allowing one of them to dominate the other.[64]

Actors and characters are key elements of dramatic structure. Wilson offers four types of dramatic characters: extraordinary characters with historical importance such as kings and queens; prototypical characters who are exceptional in the way they embody the characteristics of an entire group;[65] stereotypical or stock characters, always the same and one-sided insofar as they symbolize some particular type of person or characteristic; and finally non-human elements, which are richly employed in the *miʿrāj* tale—for example Burāq, angels, scorpions, serpents, worms, and snakes of fire.[66]

Plot

The text consists of twenty-four main chapters (*faṣls*) numbered by the author, and each chapter includes several subdivisions (*laṭīfa* or *ḥikmat*). Although it is possible to examine all chapters, they best fit into three major acts, through which narrative tension escalates until the story's climax. Examining this play in three acts will help to show how tension is built up in the story and how it moves from beginning to end.

The Prophet's ascent through the skies forms Act I (chapters 6–12); his journey from the seventh sky up to his meeting with God and the archangels forms Act II (chapters 13–18); and his journey back through paradise and hell en route to earth forms Act III (chapters 19–22).

The tension that captures the audience's curiosity begins in Act I. Here, the Prophet encounters several unusual beings and witnesses strange phenomena. These many otherworldly elements create suspense for the reader-listener as he ponders where the hero will go and just what he will encounter next. At the end of Act I, the Prophet stands at the Lote Tree of the Limit (*sidrat al-muntahā*), a cosmic tree mentioned in the Qur'an (53:14). This cosmic tree is depicted as standing on the boundary of the existing universe and the divine realm that begins after the seventh heaven, where the Prophet is about to meet with God. After a significant amount of tension builds through the expectation of this upcoming divine encounter, the curtain drops on Act I.

Act II opens at the *sidrat al-muntahā*. Here, the Prophet waits to be presented to God, once again heightening the tale's dramatic suspense. First, the Prophet passes through thousands of curtains to reach God's throne. When he reaches it, he is placed on the throne; and once a drop (*qaṭra*) falls into his mouth, he is able to start speaking to God. The author's tale reaches a climax not only due to the auspicious nature of this encounter but also because the audience wonders whether the Prophet can actually see God face to face (Plate 14). This dramatic climax functions to present the narrative's central scene: the Prophet's meeting and conversation with God.

Act III, the last part of the narrative, prolongs the vector of the narrative with the Prophet's visits to paradise and hell. Coming after the play's climax, it functions as the denouement by presenting both the literal and symbolic action of falling. Act III keeps the tension high to some degree, though it is not as crisp as it was in the scene at the *sidrat al-muntahā*. At the very end of this act, however, the tension rises once again when the Prophet meets Moses, who declares that the number of daily prayers that God demands of the Prophet's community is excessive (Plate 18). Moses advises him to beseech God for a reduction in the number of prayers required each day. The Prophet begs God for leniency several times until the number of prayers is decreased from fifty to five. Watching the drama unfold, the audience waits to see how this process of negotiation between God and the Prophet will be resolved. By rejecting Moses's last recommendation to return to God, the Prophet ends this ongoing series of negotiations. This episode serves as an instructive story that functions as a moralizing anecdote with practical consequences: the five daily prayers that Muslims traditionally observe are explained and taught to the audience by the narrator, a devoted preacher, through the ascension tale.

Actors

Certainly, Muḥammad, as the tale's chief protagonist, is an extraordinary character due to his position as Prophet. Yet the story is populated by a variety of actors, such as God, who is in the play but never shown nor physically described to the audience; the previous prophets; the four archangels (Gabriel, Michael, Isrāfīl, and

ʿAzrāʾīl); the *ḥūrīs* of paradise; and thousands upon thousands of angels who can be labeled as stereotypical or stock characters.

God, who serves as the director and stage manager before the play, appears in the climax, but only through His voice, intensifying His mysteriousness. The audience is not given any description of Him, due to the common practice of avoiding endowing God with anthropomorphic features.

During his travel through the heavens the Prophet encounters the previous prophets, who are introduced to the audience right before the play, when the Prophet is about to enter on stage. These prophets are briefly introduced to the audience with their prophetic merits, rather than their physical descriptions, in a sense reminding the members of the audience what they already know about these characters. For example, Moses is remembered by the story of his parting of the sea, and Abraham is mentioned in connection with Nimrod and the fire.[67]

As opposed to other secondary characters, the angels are clearer to the audience because of the narrator's descriptions, although these descriptions are mostly limited to the numbers of their wings. As the chorus characters they serve as dramatic devices, originally a convention in drama, which are not involved directly but rather comment on angels or events.[68] By chanting in unison, they either salute the Prophet or recall God, adding the dimension of music as well as of dialogue. Additionally, we encounter different groups of individuals who appear to be pantomimic actors with no voices or identities. Not only the Prophet but also other characters to whom we are introduced during his journey are constructed by their physical surroundings, though they are not meticulously described: the denizens of hell are not good, whereas those in heaven are good. In fact, their external descriptions speak for them, despite the fact that in *Maʿārij al-nubuwwa* their traits are never explicated by the narrator. They function in the plot as prototypical characters. I would contend that these characters in paradise and hell are left underdeveloped in this fashion because this vagueness allows the audience members to project themselves (consciously or not) into these roles as the drama unfolds.

As one might expect of this famous preacher, Muʿīn al-Miskīn's target audience was largely his fellow Muslims. However, the inclusion of non-Muslims in the narrative suggests strongly that Muʿīn al-Miskīn's target demographic was not comprised exclusively of Muslims. Except for a few named individuals such as Nimrod, Pharaoh, and Qārūn, the other non-Muslim inhabitants of hell are briefly referred to only as polytheists, Christians, Jews, and pagans.[69] Along with this very brief statement about non-Muslims, the author adds that all sinners remain tortured in hell *ad eternum,* thus responding to questions about hell and its duration, which may have been posed by his audience members.[70] This avoids any possible allegation that hell is reserved for non-Muslims alone. Most of these prototypical characters in paradise and hell are not given actual names; rather, they are subsumed under a general title, such as "group of people" (*jamāʿatī*) with no mention of their religious background. For example, the characters we encounter in hell are liars, adulterers, murderers, wine drinkers, flatterers of tyrants, gossipers, perjurers, rebellious wives, rebellious children, and hypocrites (Plates 4 and 5). It seems that it is more important for the reader-listener to recognize the classes of sins[71] rather than to know who precisely engaged in such wayward behaviors. All members of the audience, regardless of religious background, can see themselves potentially engaged in or drawn to such sins and make connections between the dramatic situations they observe and their own deeds. Consequently, the audience is given a part to play as the unnamed denizens of hell, thereby becoming actors in the *miʿrāj* tale. By bringing several lessons worthy of telling and hearing, the stories of sinners heighten the sense of drama and the "tellability"[72] of the story. Furthermore, the technique of audience-mirroring provides the audience's interaction with and projection into the narrative through emotionally identifying with, and empathetically experiencing, the emotions of those situated in these particular scenes. As Pavis cogently notes: "No creator of theater would ever really risk writing a text or constructing a performance without taking the conditions of the public's receptivity into account."[73] Therefore, it is clear that Muʿīn al-Miskīn constructs his dramatic performance with his audience in mind, particularly when it comes to his depiction of the Prophet's visit to heaven and hell.

Setting

Most playwrights have in mind the setting form of their works before they set out to write them down.[74] Even though our author, Muʿīn al-Miskīn, does not call himself a "playwright," the aesthetic understanding of his time reveals itself in the setting of his *miʿrāj* tale as well. Much as Timurid painting makes use of lavish pigment to paint a scene, the author Muʿīn al-Miskīn uses his pen to illustrate every item on his meticulously managed stage. He turns his written text into an artwork, painting it with words with the fastidiousness of an artist, not overlooking any detail that might contribute to the visual impact of his narrative. He carefully depicts colors, textures, and materials. For example, buildings in paradise are multihued and are described by the author with the cutting precision of a gemologist:

> The door of paradise was of red gold, [. . .] its nails were of pearls, ruby, and emerald. It had four hundred nails and in the middle of them was a big ring of ruby. [. . .] I saw the walls. One brick was of gold, one of silver, one of ruby, one of green chrysolite, and one of pearl. [Paradise's] soil was of musk and amber, and its plants were of saffron and redbud. [. . .] Emerald, ruby, and pearl were used instead of pebbles. [. . .] I saw kiosks, some of which had ruby eaves, some had pearl eaves, some had gems, some had emerald eaves, some had golden eaves, and some had silver eaves, and the sides of the rivers and springs were gold, silver, pearl, and ruby, while the stones in the rivers were gems, pearls, and rubies.[75]

Once the Prophet enters each scene, the stage is appropriately illuminated by props, precious stones, and rays of light. The spheres of the heavens themselves are decked out in valuable materials. For example, in one case the author describes the whole stage itself as a shiny and luminous pearl:[76] "When I entered [the third heaven] I saw that it was created of a bright and shining white pearl, and its door was of white light and it had a lock of light on it."[77] Consequently, the text becomes so resplendent from beginning to end that it dazzles the audience. This very sentiment is even articulated by the Prophet himself, when he steps on stage in Act I, Scene II, in the second heaven: "It was extremely bright (*nūrānī*). It was so bright that it could not be looked at because the eyes would be dazzled."[78] This celestial resplendence comes together in the description of the sites in the vicinity of the *sidrat al-muntahā*. For example the *Bayt al-Maᶜmūr,* the celestial prototype of the Kaᶜba, is described as being made of ruby and provided with two emerald doors. Inside this sacred temple hang ten thousand red gold lamps filled with rubies and pearls, each one brighter than the sun. Next to the door, there is a pulpit of gold and a minaret of silver. Near the *Bayt al-Maᶜmūr,* there is also an ocean of light (*nūr*), in which angels wearing robes of light (*nūr*) are bathing or performing their ablutions.[79] The light emanates not only from the lamps in the *Bayt al-Maᶜmūr,* but also from its doors, the ocean, and the angelic actors, and altogether these bright locations and actors function as a kind of "spotlight" to illuminate the episode.[80]

Just as divine light functions to illuminate the scenes of heaven, so fire functions in the scenes of hell. Yet in contrast to the description of the heavens, the description of hell in *Maᶜārij al-nubuwwa* is brief. The dominant color in hell is a flaming red. Indeed, much as light and gems illuminate the heavens, hell is lit up by the fire emanating from fiery houses, valleys, mountains, rivers, oceans, and trees:

> [On the first level] I saw seventy thousand mountains of fire; on each mountain were seventy thousand rivers; in each valley were seventy thousand branches; in each branch were seventy thousand cities; in each city were seventy thousand palaces of fire; in each palace were seventy thousand houses; in each house was a chest and all chests were of fire; in each chest were many different torments. [. . .] I saw valleys where there were trees of fire with countless fruits of fire.[81]

These sharp and detailed descriptions of hell scenes appear in earlier ascension narratives and hadith reports as well.[82] Yet, compared to these earlier reports, Muᶜīn al-Miskīn describes hell in an especially detailed way so that the audience can immediately visualize it. These notations help the audience envisage much more precise images. Furthermore, the next most frequently used props in these scenes are the scorpions, serpents, worms, and snakes of fire. Yet these innumerable scorpions and snakes are covered beneath a cloth of fire. By covering them, the dread that might emerge from the scene is, to some extent, mitigated: "I saw a valley there which was covered with a cloth of fire. Gabriel, peace be upon him, told me to remove the cloth. When I removed it, I saw so many serpents and scorpions that only God most High knows their numbers."[83] In developing the setting, the generous use of gold (and silver) in painting palaces, doors, characters, and costumes with freshness and brightness reminds the audience of the illumination and palette of Timurid paintings. Furthermore, the meticulously described details, colors, and shapes, together with the inclusion of props, costumes, and lush sets allow the audience to envision the story as it is richly and vividly illustrated with words, thus activating the audience's imagination. This visual emphasis in the text bridges the gap between the *miʿrāj* account in the narrative of *Maʿārij al-nubuwwa* and its visual manifestation in *miʿrāj* paintings, thereby revealing how such methods of storytelling can effectively link text to image.

Dialogues

The ascension narrative in *Maʿārij al-nubuwwa* is a didactic piece full of "utilitarian" dialogues that present the *miʿrāj* as a workshop for the Prophet's instruction as well as for the believer's own edification. It is structured in such a manner as to inform the reader-listener about the otherworld. In addition to dialogues, Muʿīn al-Miskīn employs other narrative types: poetry, which Millett would call "non-utilitarian" but which attracts the audience's interest; verses from the Qur'an; and prayer invocations to God, often meaningfully uttered or sung by a chorus of angels or by the prophets, thereby providing musicality that is sustained throughout the narrative.[84]

The conversational structure of the text also maximizes audience participation. Although Muʿīn al-Miskīn occasionally addresses his audience members directly, he does not preach to them. Instead, he prefers to let the characters convey key messages through dialogue. For example, conversations typically occur between the following combinations of actors: a) Gabriel and the Prophet, b) Gabriel and an angel who is in charge of a particular location (the heavens, paradise, or hell), c) the Prophet and the other archangels (Michael, ʿAzrāʾīl, and Isrāfīl), d) the Prophet and previous prophets, e) God and the Prophet, and f) God and angels.

The characters often speak directly to each other in one-to-one dialogues, not in dynamic conversations, even when they convene as a group. Most of the characters the Prophet encounters are silent and nameless, and Gabriel tends to speak on their behalf. A prominent exception is found in the character of Moses, who has more than one opportunity to speak and voices a strong opinion. During the play, we first encounter him in Act I, Scene IV, when the Prophet ascends through the heavens, and again later in Act III, Scene IV, when the Prophet returns to earth. In their first meeting, Moses appears as a mentor, offering honor to the Prophet; during their second encounter, he acts as a persuasive facilitator in reducing the daily prayers from fifty to five. Moses's character is more developed than other secondary characters in the narrative, and he speaks for himself rather than needing Gabriel as his go-between.

The Prophet's unfamiliarity with the heavenly realms is made obvious through his questions to Gabriel about the places they visit and people they encounter during the journey. However, in Act II, when he meets with the four archangels Gabriel, Michael, ʿAzrāʾīl, and Isrāfīl, he becomes the knowledgeable one. The archangels ask him generally about salvation, and, after the Prophet responds to each question acting as a purveyor of eschatological knowledge, his answer is approved by God with the words "*ṣadaqta yā Muḥammad* (O Muḥammad, you said the truth)!"[85] Muḥammad's superiority to Gabriel is thereby established, even though he continues to need his angelic guide to proceed upward.

The most crucial dialogue that the audience has been promised is held between God and the Prophet in Act II. After having passed the *sidrat al-muntahā,* the Prophet comes before a curtain/veil with Isrāfīl, and after Isrāfīl's departure he is left all alone. The curtain/veil moves and an angel whose identity is not given takes him past seventy thousand curtains. In front of each curtain this unidentified angel is asked about his and his guest's identities. Eventually they pass through the last curtain and the angel places the Prophet on the throne. Although the text is full of images, colors, and props from the beginning, the scene in which God and the Prophet meet is a magnificent show using only one prop, the throne, which is made of white pearl with legs of red coral. All of a sudden, from behind the curtains, the Prophet hears a voice that calls out his name: "*yā Muḥammad* (O Muḥammad)!" He is so petrified by this voice that he almost falls off the throne. At this moment, a drop falls into his mouth; he opens his mouth and swallows it. He describes the drop saying that no one has ever tasted anything more delicious than it. Then, he becomes calm, relaxed, and able to speak, and his conversation with God commences.

The intense power of the conversation carries the entire scene and delivers its powerful message. Through hadith accounts, the audience is informed about the contents of the divine colloquy that comprises Muḥammad's being informed of his prophetic status, so that his assertions on the Earth are confirmed by God himself in the Sky. The dialogue is rather extensive: it includes the *attahiyyāt,* a prayer recited in the last sitting of every prayer,[86] as well as the last two verses of the *Sūrat al-Baqara* (Q 2: 285–286). Muʿīn al-Miskīn interrupts narrating this dialogue to provide exegesis of these two verses, even dedicating an entire chapter to them (chapter 17). In chapter 18, the dialogue between God and the Prophet, which is mainly based on what the members of audience would apparently need to know about their relationship with and responsibility to God, continues as based on the reports of several hadith transmitters. This long conversation consists of topics such as intercession and forgiveness of sins and offers answers to questions about what distinguishes the followers of the Prophet Muḥammad as superior to other communities of faith.

Even though *Maʿārij al-nubuwwa* is not just a purely educational exercise with little plot or tension, it nevertheless remains a didactic piece, intended to motivate the audience to action. For example, the angels who remain in the physical attitudes of prayer, *ṣalāt,* not only serve the author's aim of teaching the required parts of one *rakʿat,* but also indirectly provide an opportunity for the audience to get involved in the play by indicating to them that their daily prayers are part of the angelic action they are watching unfold. The famous Islamic teaching that "*ṣalāt* is the *miʿrāj* of every Muslim"[87] supports and legitimizes the spectator's involvement in the play. The teaching purpose of Muʿīn al-Miskīn is achieved through the conversational structure built into the text in order to make it more energetic and animated. Instead of preaching directly to his audience, he prefers to let his characters carry the message forward. The dialogues are written in a relatively simple language compared to the descriptions of the decorative elements. The common point of all the dialogues is that they serve a specifically didactic function. We could say that there is almost no word said without an educational purpose. Finally, the dialogues are primarily constructed in a question and answer format, a structure that is suggestive of the author's educational aims.

In Muʿīn al-Miskīn's *Maʿārij al-nubuwwa,* the Prophet's ascension is presented as a marvelous and dramatic show full of light, colors, poetry, and music provided through cantillated invocations. These many descriptive and decorative strategies coalesce to form a rich narrative that is designed to appeal to a varied audience. The fact that Muʿīn al-Miskīn was active in his position as a preacher in Herat for over thirty years certainly provides a strong indication that he was successful in his calling. In fact, he himself was, in his own way, always on stage in front of a large group of listeners.

Muʿīn al-Miskīn transforms the story of the Prophet's miraculous journey into a multi-media text that combines different stylistic ingredients, offering everything that an early-modern attendee would enjoy reading, listening to, and viewing.[88] For those who took pleasure hearing unusual and adventurous stories, the book offers a *siyāḥatnāma* or an *ʿajā'ibnāma.* For those with an interest in the visual arts, it serves as a carefully constructed tale filled with colorful details, reflected in contemporary Timurid paintings produced in Herat by master artists such as Bihzād and Shāh Muẓaffar. For those drawn to poetry, the text is appealing thanks to its recurring melodies and choral refrains as well as the poetical verses composed by Muʿīn al-Miskīn himself or quoted from great poets such as Rūmī or ʿAṭṭār. For scholars, who would be more interested in the ascension miracle per se and its pedagogical applications, the text closely chronicles the story in the light of the hadith. Muʿīn al-Miskīn was a hadith scholar, and his analysis of the verses along with the ascension story turn his text into a practice of narrative exegesis not only for scholars but also in a form comprehensible for a more general audience.

The text also can be seen to include all the essentials of a drama, such as actors, a producer, a director, a stage, decorative elements that set the stage, and an audience interested in watching such a play, if only in their mind's eye. This dramatic dimension to Muʿīn al-Miskīn's text allows us to examine his opus as if it were a play that could conceivably be enacted on stage, thanks to its highly presentational style and its sequential structure, as well as its use of actors performing directly in front of an audience. The narrative gives concrete and vivid substance to the abstract teachings of religion, especially with regards to the descriptions of the heavens, paradise, and hell. At the same time, just as all drama experiences are figurative representations of life, the Prophet's *miʿrāj* serves as the symbolic and performative enactment of the otherworld, thereby making its existence immediate and tangible to an audience receptive to textual and visual metaphor.

Notes

This chapter is based on a paper presented at the MESA conference (Boston, November 19, 2006). I would like to thank Walter G. Andrews, Gottfried Hagen, Christiane Gruber, and Frederick Colby for their insightful comments, and Behrad Aghaei and Kathryn Babayan for their help with particularly difficult passages in *Maʿārij al-nubuwwa*. Alexander Knysh's and Victoria Gardner's comments on an early draft of this paper were very helpful in its revision. I am also greatly indebted to Joshua Gass for references to and thoughtful comments on narratology. All mistakes and shortcomings are of course my own.

1. Muʿīn al-Dīn Muḥammad Amīn b. Ḥājjī Muḥammad al-Farāhī al-Harawī, *Maʿārij al-nubuwwa fī madārij al-futuwwa*, Istanbul, Süleymaniye Library, ms. Ayasofya 3442, dated 898/1492. The translation of the title belongs to Felix Tauer in Jan Rypka, *History of Iranian Literature* (Dordrecht: D. Reidel, 1968), 450.

2. See E. Berthels, "Muʿīn al-Miskīn," *Encyclopaedia of Islam*, new ed., vol. 7, 481. In examining *Maʿārij al-nubuwwa*, I also consulted the *Delā'il-i Nübüvvet-i Muḥammadī ve-Şemā'il-i Fütüvvet-i Aḥmedī* (The Evidences of the Prophethood of the Prophet and the Description of the Virtuous Character of Aḥmed), Istanbul: n.p., 1257/1841, an Ottoman Turkish translation of Muʿīn al-Miskīn's text produced around 1620 by Muḥammad b. Muḥammad, known as Altıparmak (d. 1033/1623–1624). Although the translation retains the organization of the original text, there are some parts missing in the translation, such as poetry. For a thorough comparison of the differences between the original text of Muʿīn al-Miskīn and the translation of Altıparmak, see Gottfried Hagen, "Translations and Translators in a Multilingual Society: A Case Study of Persian-Ottoman Translations, Late 15th to Early 17th Century," *Eurasian Studies* 2, no. (2003): 95–134.

3. Jerome Bruner, "The Narrative Construction of Reality," *Critical Inquiry* 18 (Autumn 1991): 1–21. I thank Joshua Gass for bringing this article to my attention.

4. Uri Rubin, "Pre-existence and Light: Aspects of the Concept of Nur Muhammad," *Israel Oriental Studies*, 5 (1975): 62–119.

5. In the beginning of some sections, the author himself even describes the content of the section as *ʿajā'ib* or *ʿajāyib u gharā'ib*.

6. Shlomith Rimmon-Kenan, *Narrative Fiction: Contemporary Poetics* (London: Methuen, 1983), 108.

7. Mieke Bal, *Narratology: Introduction to the Theory of Narrative* (Toronto: University of Toronto Press, 1985).

8. Fred B. Millett and Gerald Eades Bentley, *The Art of Drama* (New York: D. Appleton-Century, 1935).

9. Edwin Wilson, *The Theater Experience* (New York: McGraw-Hill, 1980).

10. Though he is said to have preached about thirty-one years, there is no indication of either the beginning or the end of this time period.

11. Little is known about Muʿīn al-Miskīn. His birth date is unknown and we have no information regarding his childhood. His father, Mawlānā Sharafuddīn Ḥājjī Muḥammad Farāhī, was a preacher also interested in poetry, who also used the *makhlaṣ* "Miskīn." His

brother Qaḍī Niẓāmuddīn Muḥammad was a prominent judge in Herat. It is said that he was buried in the shrine of Ḥāje ʿAbdullāh-i Anṣārī near the tomb of his brother. See Muʿīn al-Miskīn, *Maʿārij al-nubuwwa,* folio 4v; Jaʿfar Sajjādī, *Tafsīr-i Ḥadā'iq al-Ḥaqā'iq: Qismat-i Sūrah-i Yūsuf,* "The Biography of the Author" (Tihrān: Mu'asasah-i Intishārāt-i Amīr Kabīr, 1364), no page number; and ʿAlī Shīr Nawā'ī, *Majālis al-nafā'is, [The] "Galaxy of Poets" of Mīr ʿAlī Shīr Nawā'ī: Two 16th-Century Persian Translations* (Tehran: Bank Melli Press, 1945), 269.

12. His other two books are *Baḥr al-Durar,* a commentary on the Qur'an, and *Rawḍat al-Wāʿiẓīn,* a collection of sayings in the Forty Hadith genre (Jaʿfar Sajjādī, ed., *Tafsīr-i Ḥadā'iq al-Ḥaqā'iq,* "The Biography of the Author").

13. Ibid.

14. It is not clear in the text what Nawā'ī means by "his followers." It might refer to his disciples or simply to his audience. I have not come across any specific information on Muʿīn al-Miskīn's affiliation with a specific Sufi path, but he is reported to have been a *zāhid* (ascetic) and *ʿārif* (a gnostic Sufi), who withdrew himself from this world (Jaʿfar Sajjādī, *Tafsīr-i Ḥadā'iq al-Ḥaqā'iq,* "the Biography of the Author"). In addition, the language Nawā'ī uses in reference to Muʿīn al-Miskīn suggests that he might have been involved in a Sufi path, although he does not explicitly state it.

15. Nawā'ī, *Majālis al-nafā'is,* 269.

16. Niẓāmuddīn was Muʿīn al-Miskīn's brother.

17. Nawā'ī, *Majālis al-nafā'is,* 269.

18. Muʿīn al-Miskīn, *Maʿārij al-nubuwwa,* folio 5r.

19. Ibid., folio 5r.

20. Ibid., folios 5r–6v.

21. Jonathan P. Berkey, *Popular Preaching and Religious Authority in the Medieval Islamic Near East* (Seattle: University of Washington Press, 2001), 40.

22. Muʿīn-i Miskīn, *Maʿārij al-nubuwwa,* folio 4v; Nawā'ī, *Majālis al-nafā'is,* 269.

23. Eleanor Sims with Boris I. Marshak and Ernst J. Grube, *Peerless Images: Persian Painting and Its Sources* (New Haven: Yale University Press, 2002), 57–58.

24. Agah Sırrı Levend, *Ali Şir Nevai, Hayatı, Sanatı ve Kişiliği* (Ankara: Türk Tarih Kurumu Basımevi, 1965), 227–229; Sheila Blair and Jonathan Bloom, *Islamic Arts* (London: Phaidon Press, 1997), 50.

25. Marie Lukens-Swietochowski, "The School of Herat from 1450 to 1506," in *The Arts of the Book in Central Asia, 14th–16th Centuries,* ed. Basil Gray (Boulder, Colo.: Shambhala Publications, 1979), 179–211; Thomas Lentz, "Changing Worlds: Behzad and the New Painting," in *Persian Masters: Five Centuries of Painting,* ed. Sheila Canby (Bombay: J. J. Bhabha, 1990), 39–54.

26. Thomas Lentz and Glenn Lowry, *Timur and the Princely Vision: Persian Art and Culture in the Fifteenth Century* (Los Angeles: Los Angeles County Museum of Art, 1989), 285–292; R. W. Ferrier, *The Arts of Persia* (New Haven: Yale University Press, 1989); Basil Gray, *Persian Painting* (Geneva: Skira, 1961), 109–125; Mohammad Ali Karimzadeh Tabrizi, *Aḥvāl va āsār-i naqqāshān-i qadīm-i Īrān va barkhī az mashāhīr-i nigār gar-i Hind va ʿUsmānī* (London, 1985), 106–120; and Norah M. Titley, *Persian Miniature Painting and Its Influence on the Art of Turkey and India* (London: British Library, 1983), 72–74.

27. For a discussion of ascension paintings and manuscripts, see Christiane Gruber's studies, in particular her review article "*Meʿrāj* II. Illustrations," in *Encyclopedia Iranica,* ed. Ehsan Yarshater (New York: Columbia University, 2008), www.iranica.com.

28. Babur (Emperor of Hindustan). *The Bábar-Náma,* ed. Annette Beveridge (London: Printed for the trustees of the "E.J.W. Gibb Memorial" and published by Messrs. Luzac, 1971), 182a/181b; Babur, *Babur-nāme (Babur'un Hatıratı)* ed. Reşit Rahmeti Arat (Ankara: Kültür ve Turizm Bakanlığı Yayınları, 1985), 283; Lentz and Lowry, *Timur and the Princely Vision;* David Roxburgh, *Prefacing the Image: The Writing of Art History in Sixteenth-Century Iran* (Leiden: Brill, 2001) and his *The Persian Album* (New Haven: Yale University Press, 2005); and Ebādollah Bahārī, *Bihzād: Master of Persian Painting* (London: I. B. Tauris, 1996). However, since he died at the young age of twenty-four, there are few examples of his paintings. For further information, see Mohammad Ali Karimzadeh Tabrizi, *Aḥvāl va āsār-i naqqāshān-i qadīm-i Īrān,* 245.

29. I am grateful to Susan Babaie for her thoughtful comments in analyzing these two figures.

30. Bal, *Narratology: Introduction to the Theory of Narrative,* 49.

31. Ibid., 71.

32. Ibid., 78.

33. Ibid., 92–99.

34. Ibid., 97.

35. For a thorough discussion on literary space, see Chatman, *Story and Discourse: Narrative Structure in Fiction and Film* (Ithaca, N.Y., and London: Cornell University Press, 1978) 96–106, 138–145.

36. Bal, *Narratology: Introduction to the Theory of Narrative,* 79.

37. Bal, "Narration and Focalization," in *On Story-Telling Essays in Narratology,* ed. David Jobling (Sonoma: Polebridge Press, 1991), 86.

38. For characterization, see Rimmon-Kenan, *Narrative Fiction: Contemporary Poetics,* 66.

39. Bal, *Narratology: Introduction to the Theory of Narrative,* 83.

40. Ibid., 104.

41. Ibid., 100.

42. Ibid., 106–110; for "the focalized" also see her "Narration and Focalization," 75–108. This article is also available in *A Mieke Bal Reader* (Chicago: University of Chicago Press, 2006).

43. Bal, *Narratology: Introduction to the Theory of Narrative,* 119.

44. Ibid., 127.

45. Ibid., 130.

46. Ibid., 142.

47. Rimmon-Kenan, *Narrative Fiction,* 91.

48. Rimmon-Kenan describes the reliable narrator as "one whose rendering of the story and commentary on it the reader is supposed to take as an authoritative account of the fictional truth." See Rimmon-Kenan, *Narrative Fiction,* 100. The story of the *miʿrāj,* of course, is not a *fiction* created by Muʿīn al-Miskīn; but, as a narrator/preacher, he needs to establish himself as a reliable narrator. Regarding the reliability of the narrator, see also Gerald Prince, *The Form and Functioning of Narrative: Narratology* (Berlin: Mouton, 1982), 12.

49. The narrator's effort to establish himself as a reliable narrator is clearly seen even in the last chapter of the *miʿrāj* section of *Maʿārij al-nubuwwa,* when he presents the names of the thirty hadith transmitters who reported on the *miʿrāj* tale. See Muʿīn al-Miskīn, *Maʿārij al-nubuwwa,* folio 294r.

50. Bal, *Narratology: Introduction to the Theory of Narrative,* 93.

51. Muʿīn al-Miskīn, *Maʿārij al-nubuwwa,* folio 251v. Here, Muʿīn al-Miskīn provides different accounts on the nature of the cleansing. According to some accounts, he says, the Prophet performs ablutions, whereas in others, he bathes.

52. Ibid., folios 251v–252r.

53. Ibid., folio 252v.

54. Ibid.

55. Ibid.

56. Ibid.

57. Ibid.

58. Ibid., folio 251v.

59. Ibid., folio 254r.

60. Ibid., folio 256r.

61. Ibid., folio 292r.

62. Ibid., folio 293r.

63. Millett, *The Art of Drama,* 193.

64. Wilson, *The Theater Experience,* 253–267.

65. Ibid., 225.

66. Ibid., 221–237.

67. Muʿīn al-Miskīn, *Maʿārij al-nubuwwa,* folio 255r.

68. Wilson, *The Theater Experience,* 264–267; and R. Kerry White, "Chorus," in *An Annotated Dictionary of Technical, Historical, and Stylistic Terms Relating to Theatre and Drama* (Lewinston, Queenston, Lampeter: Edwin Mellen Press, 1995), 26–27.

69. Muʿīn al-Miskīn, *Maʿārij al-nubuwwa,* folio 287r.

70. Ibid., folio 252r.

71. In this regard, see Roberto Tottoli's contribution to this volume; also see Brooke Olson Vuckovic, *Heavenly Journeys, Earthly Concerns: The Legacy of the Mi'raj in the Formation of Islam* (New York: Routledge, 2005), 112–121.

72. See William Labov, "The Transformation of Experience in Narrative Syntax," in his *Language in the Inner City: Studies in the Black English Vernacular* (Philadelphia: University of Pennsylvania Press, 1972), 354–396; and Marie-Laure Ryan, "Virtuality and Tellability," in her *Possible Worlds, Artificial Intelligence, and Narrative Theory* (Bloomington: Indiana University Press, 1991), 148–174.

73. Patrice Pavis, "Production and Reception in the Theatre," in *New Directions in Theatre,* ed. Julian Hilton (New York: St. Martin's Press, 1993), 25.

74. Millett, *The Art of Drama,* 230.

75. Muʿīn al-Miskīn, *Maʿārij al-nubuwwa,* folios 282v–283r.

76. Material descriptions of each of the seven heavens, a common aspect of *miʿrāj* narratives, is not specific to the account of Muʿīn al-Miskīn. This description can be traced back to the ascension tales attributed to Ibn ʿAbbās. See Muḥyī al-Dīn al-Ṭuʿmī's *Taṭrīz al-Dībāj bi-Ḥaqā'iq al-Isrā' wa'l-Miʿrāj,* (Beirut: Dār wa-Maktabat al-Hilāl, 1994), 12–22.

77. Muʿīn al-Miskīn, *Maʿārij al-nubuwwa,* folio 259r.

78. Ibid., folio 258v.

79. Ibid., folio 261v.

80. For the further functions of light in drama, see Wilson, *The Theater Experience,* 179–193.

81. Muʿīn al-Miskīn, *Maʿārij al-nubuwwa,* folios 286v–287r.

82. al-Ṭuʿmī, *Taṭrīz al-Dībāj bi-Ḥaqā'iq al-Isrā' wa'l-Miʿrāj* , 17–18.

83. Muʿīn al-Miskīn, *Maʿārij al-nubuwwa,* 286v.

84. In its Ottoman Turkish translation by Altıparmak, although mostly loyal to the original text, all the poetic elements are lost. This could be explained by the difficulty of translating poetry, in particular classical Persian poetry. Moreover, it is also possible that the translator might have found poetry a frivolous element that diminishes the dignity of this specific miracle of the Prophet.

85. Muʿīn al-Miskīn, *Maʿārij al-nubuwwa,* folios 276r–276v.

86. Ibid., folios 270v–271r. For a brief discussion of the nature of the gift(s), see Abū ʿAbd al-Raḥmān Sulamī, *The Subtleties of the Ascension: Early Mystical Sayings on the Prophet's Heavenly Journey,* trans. Frederick Colby (Louisville: Fons Vitae, 2006), 44–45.

87. Annemarie Schimmel, *Mystical Dimensions of Islam* (Chapel Hill: University of North Carolina Press, 1975), 218–219.

88. Though Tauer points out "the greatest popularity" of the text in the past, I have been unable to determine whether the text still retains its popularity today. See Rypka, *History of Iranian Literature,* 450.

14

Reworking the Ascension in Ottoman Lands: An Eighteenth-Century *Miʿrājnāma* in Greek from Epirus

PHOKION P. KOTZAGEORGIS

Introduction

The legend of Muḥammad's nocturnal ascension to heaven is one of the most beloved tales in Islamic traditions. Its popularity owes much to the "imaginability" of the legend, and so it is not by chance that a number of lavishly produced Islamic manuscripts narrate and illustrate the legend. In this chapter, however, I move beyond a traditionally "Islamic" context and present a fascinating example of this Islamic legend originating in a Greek cultural milieu. My aim is to explore the various mechanisms of adaptation that this particular text features due to the environment in which it was produced. These mechanisms include the place of Jesus Christ in the legend, the date the ascension took place, and the oral character of the text, leading to some particularities in the development of the legend (ritual movements, audience, etc.).

The Ottoman Archive of the Prime Minister's Office (*Başbakanlık Osmanlı Arşivi*) in Istanbul preserves a manuscript under the title *Rumca bir shiir* (A Poem in Greek).[1] The manuscript actually consists of two separate manuscripts bound together into one volume. The first one is numbered in Latin numerals (folios I–XVI) and the second one in Arabic numerals (folios 1–94). The entire corpus is in a poor condition of preservation. Three poems constitute the main body of the whole manuscript, supplemented with some secondary texts (an oath, some commercial notes, and a practical medicine recipe).[2] Neither the place nor the date of the volume of these texts has been recorded. However, one does find some dates in the secondary texts, and one in the second poem can help us to date the manuscript. The date written at the end of the second poem is 1133/1720–1721. It seems very probable that the main body of the manuscript was compiled in that year or later, and the owner(s) of the manuscript subsequently added notes from a later period (end of the eighteenth to the beginning of the nineteenth century). By extension, the other texts included in the volume also appear to date from the eighteenth century or the first decade of the nineteenth century.

The place of compilation is completely unknown. The only element upon which to base a probable hypothesis is the language of the texts proper. Through a linguistic analysis of the texts and particularly several morphological types, in my previous work I have been able to conclude that the Greek dialect in which the book was written likely comes from Epirus and especially the Jannina region.[3] Therefore, the whole manuscript needs to be placed among the Greek *aljamiado* literature, i.e., literature written in the Arabic script but in Greek language.[4] Although Greek texts (in both prose or verse form) written in Arabic script date from the time of the famous Anatolian mystic Jalāl al-Dīn Rūmī (1207–1273), the main bulk of Greek *aljamiado* literature was developed around the middle of the seventeenth century. Its themes were mainly of a religious nature and its form was poetic.[5]

The element that makes this text a *unicum* is that it is written in Greek script. In the Ottoman Empire, the primary criterion for the selection of an alphabet in which to write was religion.[6] Thus, people who did not speak—or even know—the official language of their religion used to write their religious texts in the languages that they knew, though in the alphabet where the sacred texts of that religion were written. Thus, the Grecophone Catholics of Chios wrote using the Latin alphabet, but in the Greek language (*frangochiotika*); the Turcophone Orthodox Christians of Cappadocia wrote their Turkish texts using the Greek alphabet (*karamanlidika*); and the Grecophone Muslims of the Greek peninsula wrote in Greek language using the Arabic alphabet (*tourkogianniotika, tourkokretika*). Our case is much stranger, since it is a quite early example for that kind of literature and because it is largely concerned with religious themes.

The second and by far the longest of the three poems, dated 1133/1720, is a narrative recounting Muḥammad's ascension (*Miʿrājnāma*). It consists of 3,482 verses arranged in quatrains. The verse-type, which is a common element in the three poems, is that of the 15-syllable rhymed couplet.[7] To be more precise, the poem consists of approximately 860 rhymed couplets.[8] This verse-type is most widely used in Greek popular literature, although it remains unclear why the author "broke" the 15-syllable verse into two separate hemistiches and thus formed a quatrain. The compilation of such a poem in couplets is very common in Islamic literature as well, under the poetic type known as the *mathnawī*. External evidence offers no clues as to whether the author preferred drawing upon the Islamic or Greek poetic tradition. The fact that the cultural background of the author and/or audience was Greek draws me to argue for Greek influence, albeit the "breaking" of the 15-syllable verse was not very common in that tradition. That both of the above-mentioned verse-types had a memotechnic advantage, however, helps to explain the usage of such a form in texts addressed to people whose culture was primarily oral in character.

The Greek Text and its Related Narratives

The first problem that this peculiar *Miʿrājnāma* poses is the tradition by which it was influenced. The most widespread narrative tradition in the Islamic world with regard to the diffusion of the *miʿrāj* legend is that which came to us under the name of Ibn ʿAbbās.[9] The comparison between the Greek *Miʿrājnāma* and Ibn ʿAbbās' narrative shows that there are many elements in common.[10] In fact, the narrative's structure is similar in both texts, describing Muḥammad's ascension from Mecca to Jerusalem and thence through the heavens, his visit of the seven heavens, his arrival at God's throne, his tour of paradise and hell, and his final return to Mecca. Upon examination of the two texts, it is clear that the pseudo al-Bakrī version of the Ibn ʿAbbās narrative coincides even more closely with the Greek text.[11] This version thus provides another text that can shed light on the Greek *Miʿrājnāma* and the various ascension traditions in which it emerged.

Another noteworthy and well-known text on the *miʿrāj* produced in western Europe is the *Liber Scale Machometi* (The Book of Muḥammad's Ladder), translated from Castilian into Latin and Old French in the thirteenth and fourteenth centuries.[12] The Greek *Miʿrājnāma* has many elements in common with this text as well. The way the Latin text might have influenced the Greek version remains unknown. However, all of the above-mentioned ascension texts have a common narrative structure, suggesting that they may in fact have originated from a rather unified oral tradition.

Keeping in mind that the Ibn ʿAbbās tradition is attested to in Ottoman Turkish literature, one might wonder how this early Arabic tradition found its way into an Ottoman context. One text on the *miʿrāj* written in an Ottoman milieu (albeit in the Arabic language) is that of al-Iznīkī (d. 1434).[13] This text was written in the vicinity of Iznik (Nicaea), a city located in the western part of present-day Turkey, sometime near the end of the fourteenth or the beginning of the fifteenth century. The author was a learned theologian who relied heavily upon Arabic sources. The similarities between these many texts are not coincidental since the Ibn ʿAbbās tradition, as present in and elaborated upon in al-Iznīkī's text, must have facilitated its transmission to an Ottoman milieu.

A fifth ascension text that can be used for comparison with the Greek *Miʿrājnāma* comes from the Turco-Iranian cultural area, which also directly influenced the Ottoman cultural environment. This famous text was written in Chaghatay Turkish using Uighur script, and is believed to have been copied in Herat ca. 840/1436–1437.[14] Although this text does not contain many motifs that are directly parallel with the Greek *Miʿrājnāma,* it nevertheless bears some intriguing similarities with the Greek text, such as the ninety thousand words God gave to Muḥammad, some details concerning paradise (the Kawthar pool, the four corners, ʿUmar's pavilion), Mount Qāf, and the cities Jabalsa and Jabalqa.

From a similar cultural milieu comes another account of the legend. It is found in a manuscript dated 685/1286 and compiled in an Ilkhanid milieu, a text discussed at further length in Christiane Gruber's contribution to this volume.[15] This text helps us to investigate the possible influences of a purely Persian account on the Greek narrative.

In the Ottoman domain, the first ascension poem composed in Ottoman

Turkish verse is dated 808/1405–6 and comprises 497 couplets (*beyt*). It was discovered between folia of a manuscript containing Aḥmedī's *İskendernāme* (The Book of Alexander) and is preserved in the Süleymaniye Library in Istanbul.[16] From that time forward, the genre became well developed in Ottoman literature.[17] For the present study I have used the motifs elaborated by Dr. Metin Akar in his study of thirteen unpublished *Miʿrājnāma* texts in verse form composed in Ottoman Anatolia; these were penned between the fourteenth and nineteenth centuries, and thus give us a broad overview of the structures and contents of Ottoman ascension poems both before and during the time of the compilation of the Greek text under consideration.[18]

Comparison and Analysis of the Text's Motifs

In comparing the Greek *Miʿrājnāma* poem with the aforementioned texts, some interesting remarks may be made.[19] To begin with, the date that the ascent occurred in the Greek text diverges from the general pattern. While the Ibn ʿAbbās tradition specifies that the *miʿrāj* took place on 27 Rajab, and Ibn Saʿd states that it occurred on 17 Ramaḍān, the Anatolian Ottoman *Miʿrājnāmas* refer either to 17 or 27 of the months of Rabīʿ I, Rabīʿ II, or Rajab.[20] Unlike the rest of these works, the Greek *Miʿrājnāma* text under consideration here gives the date of the event as 27 Ramaḍān.[21] Rather than the result of a *lapsus memoriae,* this date corresponds with the only public feast that was performed by the Muslims of Jannina during the Ottoman period, at least before the end of the nineteenth century.[22] The local tradition said that the only case in which Greek was officially accepted as a common language by the Ottoman authorities was on 27 Ramaḍān. On that day the *shaykh* of the mosque located inside Jannina castle recited the *duʿā* in Greek in front of the mosque. Two other *khodjas* silently read verses of the Qur'an in Arabic. It is reported that this feast was performed on the occasion of the end of the pilgrimage (*ḥājj*). Therefore, on the question of the date of Muḥammad's *miʿrāj,* the differentiation of the Greek text from the general pattern seems to be due to local religious custom.

Special concern in the Greek text has been made for the religious duties that Muḥammad performed before accepting the angel Gabriel's call: Muḥammad said his last prayer of the day (*yatsi*) and Gabriel asked him to perform the ritual purification (*abdest*).[23] This motif is a reminiscence of one of the three component elements in the development of *miʿrāj* literature, namely that of the angels' opening of Muḥammad's chest and the cleansing of his heart.[24] However, most probably one finds in this motif the author's concern to preach to his audience indirectly about their religious duties through the story of Muḥammad's experiences that special night. So to speak, the duties Muḥammad performed during his ascension are the same ones that every believer has to attend to before proceeding with a sacred action. Through this clue, we see one subtle method the author uses to preach to his audience. In the section on the night journey to Jerusalem (*isrā'*), the Greek text does not contain any remarkable differences from those versions presented in our group of sample texts, including in the selection of the cups (Plate 26).[25] However, it does vary in subtle ways from other comparative narratives. In the Greek text, when Muḥammad is about to enter the first heaven, he sees a green sea suspended between the heavens and the earth. Its description in the Greek text may be connected with the Ilkhanid and Chaghatay *Miᶜrājnāma*s more than with the Arabic tradition.[26] Furthermore, among the angels Muḥammad encounters during his journey, only three are named: in the first heaven the *raitis* (from the Arabic *raᶜd,* "Thunder"), in the second the *kasimis* (from the Arabic *qāsim,* "Divider") and in the fourth the *kasouris* (perhaps from the Arabic *qāsir,* "Compeller," or *qaswar,* "Sturdy" and "Lion"). These names do not appear in any of the other sample texts.[27] The names of the first two angels come from the description of their function given in the text: the first arranges the thunder, and the second divides the bread among the people. The third name may be in fact an adjective of the angel and not a name; put otherwise, the author does not describe the angel's function. Since the three names exactly correspond with the meanings of the relevant Arabic verbs *raᶜada, qassama,* and *qasara,* I would conjecture that they were created by the author, and not necessarily drawn from any other tradition. In that case, the author might be said to have a good knowledge of the Arabic language and a talent in improvisation.

The archangel Michael is described in the Greek *Miᶜrājnāma* as present in the fifth heaven and as holding scales. This motif should be compared to that of the unnamed angel holding a balance in the sixth heaven according to al-Iznīkī's text.[28] Other similarities between these two texts in their descriptions of Muḥammad's ascension include the following: a) the snowy mountain of the Greek text and the sea of snow in al-Iznīkī's narrative (in the fourth heaven in both texts), and b) the Sea of Resurrection (*baḥr al-qiyāma,* in the first heaven in al-Iznīkī, but in the third heaven in the Greek *Miᶜrājnāma*).[29] It is noteworthy that in the texts of my sample from the classical Arabic tradition, the seas are typically placed before God's throne, while only in al-Iznīkī's and the Chaghatay texts is the sea motif present throughout the seven heavens.[30]

As for the order of the prophets in the various heavens,[31] in the Greek *Miᶜrājnāma* Moses inhabits the third heaven, while in all the texts of the sample he appears in the fourth heaven or above.[32] Interestingly, the opposite is observed for the position of Jesus Christ in the heavens: in the Greek text, Jesus is placed in the fourth heaven, which is the highest position given to him in any of the *Miᶜrājnāma*s. Furthermore, Jesus Christ's residence, according to the Greek text, is none other than the *Bayt al-Maᶜmūr,* the abode usually associated with the seventh heaven and considered as being the prototype of Kaᶜba in the heavens.[33] It is thus possible that the privileged treatment of Jesus Christ in the Greek text can be ascribed to the surrounding Christian culture, which predominated in the region in which this text was composed. The audience and/or the author of this text might be of Christian origin and thus familiar with Jesus Christ and the Christian faith in general. Although converts usually developed hostility toward their previous religion, this may not be the case for the Jannina region. The peaceful coexistence of Muslims, Jews, and Greeks notwithstanding, the adoption of Christian culture as it is reflected in the language meant that these people were not cut from their origins and, as a result, had preserved a respect for Jesus Christ.

In Muḥammad's intimate conversation with God, the usual motifs can be observed, with the addition of a noteworthy remark: the Greek *Miʿrājnāma* includes the motif that God gives to Muḥammad ninety thousand words containing the *sharīʿat, ṭarīqat,* and *ḥaqīqat.* This motif exists only in the Chaghatay text of the sample.[34] While in the Greek text the above terms are not mentioned, they are explained instead. Thus, Muḥammad was asked by God to tell the thirty thousand words (i.e., *ṭarīqat*) to everyone, another thirty thousand (i.e., *sharīʿat*) to the scholars, and the last thirty thousand (i.e., *ḥaqīqat*) to no one, but to keep these last words in his heart alone. By this motif, in my opinion, the prophetic charisma of Muḥammad is to be strengthened as compared with that of other prophets. The wisdom Muḥammad received from God is divided into three parts, which correspond with three categories of Muslims: the common believers, the learned men (*ʿulamā'*), and Muḥammad himself. Since these three categories all possess knowledge of the truth, then the person of Muḥammad is elevated to an extremely high rank, above the other prophets and their communities. By highlighting Muḥammad's position, the author thus tries to promote the Islamic faith to members of his audience and to protect them from following the "wrong" (possibly Christian) path.

The Greek text places Muḥammad's tour of hell after his tour of paradise, as do the Latin, al-Iznīkī, and Chaghatay texts. The other texts of my sample place hell in the fifth heaven.[35] The description is quite extensive; however, it is different from the relevant section in the Latin text and al-Iznīkī's version, both of which are much longer.[36] The major variance is related to the classes of sinners: the Greek text mentions fourteen cases of sinners' tortures, while al-Iznīkī's narrative mentions thirty-four, Ibn ʿAbbās twenty-four, and the Chaghatay text sixteen. The difference between the Greek text and the others is not the number of tortures and/or the proportion of the hell section in the whole text, but the detailed description of the tortures. It is clear that the author's intention is not to enumerate the tortures of hell but to arouse feelings by their extended description. Thus, the fear of the tortures of hell becomes a pedagogical vehicle for maintaining and strengthening of the audience's faith.

In the section describing Muḥammad's return to earth, two of the most interesting motifs appear in the Greek text: a) the city of Jabalqa, which Muḥammad visits after Mount Qāf and b) the motif of the ox and the fish, which support the earth. The first motif is found only in al-Iznīkī's, the Ilkhanid, and the Chaghatay texts, while the second is found and extensively elaborated upon in the Latin one.[37] The first motif, which is quite long in the Greek text (thirty-three couplets), is related with to the process of conversion.[38] This is very interesting for both author and audience of the Greek text. Since they probably were converts, by this motif the act of conversion to Islam is praised. Therefore, the audience is subtly paralleled with these imitable people of Jabalqa, and thus their conversion to Islam is justified. The fact that the people of Jabalqa converted to Islam were Jews does not make a substantial difference in the conversion process aimed toward Christians. The second motif, which is more briefly developed (five couplets), belongs to the mythical cosmology of Islam and is mentioned along with the Mount Qāf motif. By this motif, the author again catechizes to his audience, here giving a simpler doctrine rather than a more complex, theological one. This kind of motif fits well with the popular character of the Greek text, by its nature (and/or genre).

Although these sample texts do not offer us the possibility for an exhaustive analysis of the text's motifs, they nevertheless give a general overview of the development of the legend in the Greek text and the diffusion of the various traditions that influenced the Ottoman world. Naturally, the way to determine which tradition the Greek author relies upon the most would be to offer a detailed study of the text's central motifs. However, even the above-mentioned comparisons are sufficient to allow for some general conclusions. Although the Greek *Miʿrājnāma* as a whole follows the basic outlines of the Arabic textual tradition, it also shows some striking similarities with the al-Iznīkī and Chaghatay texts. This fact likely points to the diffusion of particular *miʿrāj* motifs in Ottoman lands and/or the use of some possible common sources among the latter texts. Conversely, it is noteworthy that the Greek text does not closely resemble many of the Ottoman Anatolian *miʿrāj* texts. Although this lack of resemblance is curious, it does imply that a variety of sources and/or traditions concerning the *miʿrāj* legend existed in the Ottoman world. Even though it is extremely difficult to find the sources of the Greek text, one may suggest that al-Iznīkī's text (or, perhaps more accurately, the wider tradition that this text represented) would be among the sources the Greek version would have drawn upon and adapted.

The Greek *Miʿrājnāma* does contain some peculiar elements concerning the development of the legend. The most distinctive motif, discussed earlier, is the position of Jesus Christ in the text. This fascinating feature may be explained by the possible Christian origin of the author and/or his Greek audience, together with the cultural environment of the area.[39] Even though this opinion cannot be satisfactorily proven, the prevalent Christian culture in the region likely played a decisive role for this choice. For instance, the preponderance of the Greek language is reflected in the bilingual (in Ottoman-Turkish and Greek) publication of the official newspaper of the province (*Vilâyet gazetesi*), first published in 1285/1868. Furthermore, in the famous Greek high school of Jannina, the Zossimaia Schole, Christians and Muslim Ottoman subjects were equally educated.[40] The second peculiar element in the Greek text analyzed above is the date given for the *miʿrāj* (27 Ramaḍān). Here, a local holiday appears to influence (and alter) the general pattern. Consequently, these two elements underscore the adaptation process this Islamic legend underwent in a Christian milieu, isolated from the main urban, Islamic centers of the Ottoman state. The Greek text shows how a particular ascension text could develop inside a long (and foreign) tradition, but alter it according to the particularities of the dominant, non-Islamic culture.

The Text's Linguistic Features

A distinguishing characteristic of the Greek *Miʿrājnāma* is that the tale is told in the third person singular, while the predominant manner in which the legend is narrated is through Muḥammad's first person narration.[41] In order to interpret this peculiarity of the text, we must examine the way this poem was compiled and the state of its performance as an oral composition.

The narrative of the Greek text is structured around a first-person singular narration (a narrator's report about what Muḥammad does and experiences), a third-person singular description (what Muḥammad says about his experience), and a second person plural exhortation (addressed to the audience). In many instances, other features are presented depending mainly on the use of direct or indirect comments by the author, which appear frequently in the text. In contrast with the Arabic texts, in which the first person almost invariably refers to Muḥammad as the narrator of his account, in the Greek text the first person narrator refers to the author, and the person who acts in the narrative (Muḥammad) remains in the third person singular. Hence, the crucial element in the linguistic development of the Greek version of the *miʿrāj* revolves around the function of the author.

The Greek *Miʿrājnāma* is actually a part of a wider poetic synthesis. The poem is the second of a series of three religious poems, which are placed one after the other in the manuscript. In the last verse of this synthesis appears the author's signature in prose form: "*I, Molla Murād b. ʿAlī sipahi [a cavalry soldier],*[42] *wrote all of it.*"[43] Based upon this reference, it is possible that this Murād b. ʿAlī is none other than the author of all three poems.

An even more striking detail is the way Murād b. ʿAlī moves from the first to the second poem. After reporting the basic religious duties of a Muslim, he starts the last page of the first poem with the phrase: "Listen to me, O righteous community, I am going to tell you the praises of virtuous Muḥammad."[44] The page ends with a two-verse title in prose form, stating: "*Here are reported the many honors and wonderful marks with which Muḥammad was born.*"[45] On the next page, the *miʿrāj* poem begins in earnest. However, the first three folios of the second poem actually offer an extended praise to Muḥammad, underscoring in particular his superiority over all other prophets.[46] The last quatrain of the Greek *Miʿrājnāma* contains the chronogram, i.e., the compilation year in verse form, giving the impression that the synthesis is finished. However, the third poem begins with the adverb "afterward,"[47] revealing that the author continues his narrative and thus that the third poem needs to be considered a part of the whole synthesis as well.

The use of first person in the Greek *Miʿrājnāma* is reserved for the author.[48] The selection of the third person for Muḥammad's role in the text, therefore, is due to the incorporation of the *Miʿrājnāma* into a wider body of texts as told by another narratorial voice. Hence, the problem of the way these three poems were composed is interrelated with the question of the third person narrative. Regarding the way the Greek *Miʿrājnāma* has come down to us, one might speculate that it reflects: a) a copy of a lost prototype, a suggestion that would not affect the development of the legend and bears only philological implications; b) a transcription of an identical text written in Arabic script (a typically *aljamiado* one), a suggestion that similarly has a mainly philological-linguistic character, and does not affect the development of the legend; c) a translation of an original text compiled in Ottoman Turkish or in Arabic, a suggestion that is not valid in my view since there is no reference to a translation process in the text; d) an original work composed by Murād b. ʿAlī; and/or e) a record of an oral recital.[49] This last suggestion does not exclude the penultimate one, since it focuses on the delivery of the text and not its content. As I will argue in what follows, the Greek *Miʿrājnāma* should be considered an original text used for oral recital, compiled based on a number of possible prototypes but nonetheless "original" in its form and its use for storytelling in a Greek milieu.

Several elements within the Greek *Miʿrājnāma* provide evidence for it being an original composition linked to oral delivery. First, one notices the existence of single verses that function as titles of the sections: "Here it is reported that in the [first, second, etc.] heaven."[50] Second, there are some verses in which words or letters were erased by the scribe.[51] Third, some tetrastichs are written in three verses, and in one case there is a six-verse couplet. In three cases the verse is accompanied by a comment, which has a prose form and doesn't keep the rhythm of the verse.[52] Fourth, there is inconsistency in describing the rivers of the paradise; it is initially written that they are four in number while few verses later they are mentioned as five.[53] Fifth, the author reports the first and third layers of hell under the same name (*Jahannam*).[54] In other cases, references to the sources the author used for this poem are provided. In some of them there is the implication that the author had read or consulted well-known versions of the legend.[55] In three cases the author makes direct references to standard texts or those transmitted by "learned" men.[56] Allusions to the Qur'an show that the author knew (and used) the sacred book of Islam as well.[57]

In numerous cases the author uses the imperative form (e.g., "Listen, I will tell you, ask a scholar [ʿālim]"). This feature implies that he addressed the work orally to a live audience. When, for instance, the author begins the *Miʿrājnāma*, he addresses his audience, saying, "[During] the time when the prestigious, the Prophet of all the world, God's beloved, was born, it is necessary for us, my brother, to be gathered, to kneel and to listen."[58] This tetrastich describes the way this poem may have been performed. Kneeling is a ritual movement, a movement of respect for the texts to be read (or recited). If we contextualize this tetrastich in the three texts of the Greek manuscript, we could suggest that it reflects the ritual aspect of a general performance.

Moreover, if we connect the kneeling pattern with other ritual events (such as prayer rituals in celebration of Muḥammad's birth), we can infer that the kneeling pattern does reflect the general ritual character of the three poems.

The way this text was compiled resembles very much how Muslim storytellers or *quṣṣāṣ* are said to have performed religious poems.[59] This includes delivering a tale in a poetic form, which is appropriate for a memotechnic organization and memorization of the material. The verse and the rhyme-type that the author selected for the text were the most familiar to its Greek audience, and probably the most convenient for educational purposes. The inconsistencies mentioned above are easily explained by the oral character of the text. The frequent presence of the second person singular in an imperative form testifies to the fact that the author had an audience in front of him, and that he tried to arouse their feelings. The high quantity of exhortational verses strengthen the evidence supporting this hypothesis.[60] Even the vividness of motifs in the hell section also serve this function, and provide further evidence in support of the theory that the text was composed with an oral delivery in mind.

The Text's Audience

The audience for the Greek *Miʿrājnāma* was most certainly Greek-speaking Muslims, in particular the so-called *Tourkogianniotes* (literally, the Turks of Jannina).[61] Although few examples have been discovered as yet, it seems that these people developed a religious literature mainly composed in verse form. This literary form constituted the mainstream of Greek *aljamiado* literature from the middle of the seventeenth century until the population exchange between Greece and Turkey in 1923. *Tourkogianniotes* were probably of Christian origin and were Islamized sometime during the seventeenth century. They did not speak any language other than Greek. Thus, even their frequency in attending mosque services did not provide them with the necessary knowledge about their faith. Given their low level of literacy, one important way that they could learn about their faith was to listen to religiously edifying texts such as the Greek *Miʿrājnāma.*

Only scattered pieces of information on the culture and everyday life of the Turks of Jannina have come to us. A Greek scholar from Jannina, Vassileios Pyrsinellas, in an article written in 1937,[62] offers some interesting remarks concerning their poems in Greek, basing his analysis mainly on personal experiences drawn from the contact with those people before their compulsory emigration from Greece in 1923.[63] The *Tourkogianniotes* called these poems *homologies* (confession poems). There were, according to Pyrsinellas, written texts using the Arabic alphabet but in the Greek language, composed in verse form and bearing religious content. They functioned as a kind of catechism for the local Muslim population, whose mother tongue was Greek. These poems belonged to the general poetic tradition of the region, since Greeks and Jews of Jannina were keen on composing poems or even single verses in rhymed form.[64] The poems were chanted in homes, as Pyrsinellas notes: "[they] were chanted in gatherings that took place in houses, mainly those of women, according to the manner in which the ritual prayers were performed in the mosques."[65] This image fits well the way in which the Greek *Miʿrājnāma* was composed. As it is stated in the previous section, the text was composed as part of a wider synthesis aiming to be recited during a religious feast. The poetic form of the text might be relevant with the chanting character of the texts mentioned by Pyrsinellas. The recitation in the houses can equally be connected both with the oral character of the text and with the Greek language, which was prohibited from being read in the mosques. Thus, the audience of the Greek *Miʿrājnāma* could be women and/or men engaged in home gatherings, through which they could learn more about their faith.

Furthermore, an intriguing connection can be made between the day this poem was recited and the only public prayer of the *Tourkogianniotes.* According to Pyrsinellas, as mentioned at the beginning of this chapter, the Greek language was used by these Greek-speaking Muslims in an official ceremony only during a prayer that took place at the mosque of Arslan Paşa (inside Jannina's castle) on 27 Ramaḍān, celebrating the end of the *ḥājj.* In this festival, the *shaykh* of the mosque read a *duʿā* and other *khodjas* recited phrases from the Qur'an.[66] Despite the fact that Pyrsinellas mentions only these texts to be read, there is a strong connection between the feast day and the day the author of the *Miʿrājnāma* starts his narrative.[67] So, this ceremony helps to explain why the *Miʿrājnāma* appears along with the other two poems that were recited on this particular feast day, and suggests strongly that this particular Book of Ascension was used in connection with a yearly festival in Jannina, recited either publicly and/or in private house gatherings.

The Greek *Miʿrājnāma* forms a product that is a mixture of a learned elite and a traditional society. The "learned" part derives from the identity of the persons who transmitted or compiled these texts. They were all members of the local religious establishment. Due to their identity, they had to rely on so-called "official" texts and/or traditions, showing regard to the religious topics with which they dealt in an authoritative fashion. It is not surprising to suppose that the author was a religious man, a *molla.* He probably was the only person who could understand a foreign (and Islamic) language—such as Arabic, Persian, or Turkish—and it was among his duties to catechize among members of his community. On the other side, the "traditional" part consists of the audience. It was not only their illiteracy but mainly their cultural isolation that separated them from access to the doctrines of Islam. This isolation was twofold: linguistic and geographic. The only thing that distinguished the former from the latter was faith. The Greek Muslims had to adhere to their faith to maintain their distinctive identity, and the most effective way for these illiterate people, who could not understand Arabic prayers in a mosque setting, was to adhere to their faith by listening to poems written in praise of the Prophet in their own vernacular.

The legend of the *miʿrāj* is, first and foremost, an image. As J. Bencheikh has accurately pointed out, "*Le mi'radj est un récit fait à des auditeurs présents. . . . Le text fait surgir une vision, il ne donne pas à penser, mais à voir. L'image est, ici, souveraine.*"[68] This statement convincingly justifies the selection of the legend by the *molla* of Jannina to incorporate it into his synthesis, along with the focal role this legend played for the Islamic faith in general. The elaboration of the legend in its Greek manifestation indeed presents vivid imagery and a rich collection of motifs, even though we cannot determine definitively which narrative the Greek author selected in order to create his own text.[69] The positive treatment of Jesus Christ may appear a minor characteristic of the Greek *Miʿrājnāma;* however, it is notable and unique, and thus must be understood in relation to the text's surrounding Christian environment. The high esteem for Jesus Christ can also be traced by the reference in the Greek text that the "Frequented House" (*bayt al-maʿmūr*), the prototype of the Kaʿba in the heavens, is Jesus Christ's residence. Conversely, the low position given to Moses in the heavens may be explained by a possible degradation of Jews in favor of Christians.

Although not sufficiently proved, the *Tourkogianniotes* would be converts of Christian origin. The presence of some specifically Persian and eastern motifs can be adequately explained by the general Ottoman environment. The third person narration, moreover, results from the way this poem was presented as an oral text for teaching basic Muslim themes to a largely illiterate Greek audience. The orality of the text highlights the way it was recited (or generally performed): the kneeling as a position to listen to this text suggests that the text was a part of a wider synthesis with a ritual character and was publicly read. The latter element corresponds well to the selection of the date the *miʿrāj* occurred (27 Ramaḍān), which coincides with the date of the only official public feast during which the Greek language was used by the Muslims of Jannina for religious purposes.

Therefore, the evidence from the Greek *Miʿrājnāma* suggests that the adaptation of a central Islamic legend into a marginal area in the Ottoman Islamic world does not necessarily produce any major structural changes in the narrative. Rather, it offers a good example of how local societies, particularly culturally and religiously marginalized ones, can adopt these legends and adapt them to their environments. Furthermore, this fundamental legend operated as a kind of catechism for maintaining and/or preaching the faith of Islam in a community surrounded by (and originating from) Christians. This particular community of believers did not speak the "three languages" (*elsine-i selase*) of Islam in Ottoman lands—namely Ottoman-Turkish, Arabic, and Persian—so they used Greek as their own "sacred" language.

Notes

I wish to thank Christiane Gruber and Frederick Colby for their valuable comments on an early version of this chapter. I also thank F. Colby for providing me a copy of his Ph.D. dissertation, "Constructing an Islamic Ascension Narrative," and Christiane Gruber for providing me a copy of the English translation of the Ilkhanid *Miʿrājnāma*.

1. *Başbakanlık Osmanlı Arşivi,* Collection Kāmil Kepeci, no. 859. Professor J. C. Alexander, Aristotle University of Thessaloniki, discovered this manuscript and kindly provided me with a copy for study as I wrote my master's thesis.

2. The whole manuscript has been edited by the present author. See my *To Islam sta Valkania: Ena hellenophono mousoulmaniko cheirographo apo ten Epiro tou 18ou aiona* [Islam in the Balkans: An 18th-Century Islamic Manuscript in Greek from Epirus] (Athens: Syllogos ton en Athinais Megalosholiton, 1997).

3. See the linguistic analysis of the three poems in ibid., 89–106.

4. For *aljamiado* literature in general see: s.v. "Aljamia," E. Lévi-Provençal, *Encyclopaedia of Islam,* new ed. (E.I.²). For Greek *aljamiado* literature, see Georgios Dedes, "Was there a Greek *Aljamiado* Literature?" in *The Balance of Truth: Essays in Honour of Professor Geoffrey Lewis,* ed. Ç. Balım Harding and C. Imber (Istanbul: Eren Kitabevi, 2000), 83–98.

5. For the dates (and genres) of the first examples of Greek *aljamiado* literature, see Kotzageorgis, *To Islam,* 68–72.

6. For an overview of the alphabets used in the Balkans during the Ottoman period, see Evangelos Zakhos-Papazahariou, "Babel balkanique: histoire politique des alphabets utilisés dans les Balkans," *Cahiers du monde russe et soviétique* 13/2 (1972): 145–179.

7. For this kind of verse in modern Greek poetry, see Linos Polites, "Neoteres apopseis gia te gennese kai te dome tou dekapentasyllabou" [Recent Views on the Origin and the Structure of the 15-syllable Verse], *Praktika Akademias Athenon* 56/2 (1981): 211–228.

8. Some of the verses consist of a tristich or a pentastich, and others are in the form of title-verse. The *Miʿrājnāma* extends from folios 1v to 88v. It was untitled but has a colophon. In sixteen folios there are isolated verses, which are in fact titles of the following "chapter."

9. For this tradition, see Jamel Eddine Bencheikh, *Le voyage nocturne de Mahomet,* Paris: Imprimerie Nationale, 1988, 235–237. See also the article in E.I.², s.v. "Miʿrādj" (J. E. Bencheikh); and the discussion of the history of this narrative by Frederick Colby in his "Constructing an Islamic Ascension Narrative," Ph.D. diss., Duke University, 2002; and idem, *Narrating Muḥammad's Night Journey* (Albany: State University of New York Press, 2008).

10. For the Ibn ʿAbbās narrative, I have relied upon the English translation in Nazeer El-ʿAẓma, *Al-Miʿrāj wa'l-ramz al-ṣūfī* [The *Miʿrāj* and Sufi Symbolism] (Beirut: Dar al-Bahith, 1982), 19–48, henceforth: Ibn ʿAbbās. See also Bencheikh, *Le voyage nocturne,* 13–179. For methodological reasons I refer to this version as the Ibn ʿAbbās narrative, although it is known that both the Ibn ʿAbbās and subsequent al-Bakrī traditions are richer and more complex in motifs. For the Greek text, see my *To Islam,* 126–220, henceforth: Greek *Miʿrājnāma.*

11. On Abū al-Ḥasan al-Bakrī see E.I.², s. v. "Al-Bakrī" (F. Rosenthal); Bencheikh, *Le voyage nocturne,* 238. Also see Colby, "Constructing an Islamic Ascension Narrative," appendix B.

12. I used a Greek translation made from the Latin original text in *I scala tou Moameth* [Muḥammad's Ladder], trans. Demetres Melas (Athens: Enalios, n.d.), henceforth: Latin.

13. I used the Turkish translation of this text in el-Musa b. Hacı Hüseyin İzniki, *Mi'rac,* trans. Hikmet Özdemir (Istanbul: Gonca Yayınevi, 1986), henceforth: Iznīkī. Colby, in his "Constructing an Islamic Ascension Narrative," discusses some of the commonalities between the Iznīkī text and the Ibn ʿAbbās ascension narrative.

14. I used the English translation in Wheeler Thackston, "The Paris *Mi'rājnāma,*" *Journal of Turkish Studies* 18 (1994), 263–299, henceforth: Chaghatay. For a recent edition and study of this text and its iconography, see Christiane Gruber, *The Timurid Book of Ascension (Miʿrajnama): A Study of Text and Image in a Pan-Asian Context* (Valencia: Patrimonio Ediciones, 2008). In this study, Gruber proves that the Chaghatay manuscript arrived in Istanbul by the early sixteenth century, so it may have influenced the Ottoman tradition on the legend.

15. See Christiane J. Gruber, *The Ilkhanid Book of Ascension: A Persian-Sunni Devotional Tale* (London: I. B. Tauris, 2009), henceforth: Ilkhanid.

16. Yaşar Akdoğan, "Mi'rac, Mi'rac-nâme ve Ahmedi'nin bilinmeyen Mi'râc-nâmesi," *Osmanlı Araştırmaları* 9 (1989): 263–310.

17. For a discussion of Ottoman lyric poems on the ascension, see Selim Kuru's chapter in this volume.

18. Metin Akar, *Türk Edebiyatında Manzum Mi'râc-Nâmeler,* Ankara: Kültür ve Turizm Bakanlığı Yayınları, 1987, henceforth: Ottoman Anatolia.

19. It is beyond the scope of this study to meticulously analyze all the motifs of the poem. I only extract those I think are remarkable and thus deserve special attention.

20. Ibn ʿAbbās, 19; "Miʿrādj," E.I.² 7:100 (B. Schrieke-[J. Horovitz]); and Ottoman Anatolia, 209.

21. Greek *Miʿrājnāma,* 129 (f. 4r, ln. 7).

22. Vassileios Pyrsinellas, "Hoi tourkogianniotikes *homologies*" [The confession poems of the Turkogianniotes], *Epirotika Chronika* 12 (1937), 164. I was not able to find further material on this feast. Pyrsinellas relied on what some old men had remembered and reported to him before they were exchanged according to the Greek-Turkish Treaty of Lausanne in 1923.

23. Greek *Miʿrājnāma,* 129 (f. 4r, ln. 13), 130 (f. 4v, ln. 19–20).

24. Bencheikh, *Le voyage nocturne,* 271.

25. On the road, Muḥammad hears three voices and sees a beautiful woman, as well as an ox coming out of a hole, a man felling trees and transferring the logs from one side to the other, and a bucket dropping into a well and coming up dry (Greek *Miʿrājnāma,* 136–137 [f. 10v]; cf. Iznīkī, 41). An interesting detail is the interpretation of the three voices: while one comes from the Christians and another from the fire-worshippers, for the last no mention of the Jews has been made. In the testing of the cups, Michael offers Muḥammad only two liquids: milk and wine (Greek *Miʿrājnāma,* 137 [f. 11r–11v, ln. 12]). See Ottoman Anatolia, 238–239, where the motif of the two cups goes back to the time of Anas b. Mālik. The motif of the cups is presented in other *miʿrāj* narratives as well, but in a different location. See for example the Latin version (Latin, 150–153 [ch. LII]), where the cups are offered to Muḥammad in paradise. For an elaborated version of the motifs of voices and other events on the road to Jerusalem, see Ilkhanid, ff. 11v–15v). In this text the testing of the cups is placed just before the ascension to the first heaven (ibid., f. 18r).

26. Greek *Miʿrājnāma,* 141 (f. 15r); Ilkhanid, f. 19v, where the sea is called *qāẓiyya* (fate); Chaghatay, 268, where the sea is called *Baḥr al-Kawthar,* without giving further details. In the Ibn ʿAbbās and al-Bakrī narratives, along with the Latin version, before the first heaven Muḥammad meets with the angel ʿAzrāʾīl. Furthermore, two Anatolian *Miʿrājnāmas* refer either to a river (from the fifteenth century) or a sea (from late eighteenth century) in the same position (Ottoman Anatolia, 278–279).

27. Greek *Miʿrājnāma,* 144–145 (f. 18r, ln. 9–18v, ln. 8), 146–147 (f. 20r, ln.1–20v, ln. 8), 150–151 (f. 23v ln. 5–18).

28. Greek *Miʿrājnāma,* 156 (f. 28v, ln. 8–20); and Iznīkī, 72–73.

29. Cf. Greek *Miʿrājnāma,* 149–150 (f. 22r, ln. 17–22v, ln. 16) and 154 (26v, ln. 13–20); and Iznīkī, 53 and 66.

30. See for example: Ibn ʿAbbās, 34–35; Latin, 85–86, where the water motif is analyzed. Also see Iznīkī, 53, 58, 66, 70, 73; Chaghatay, 268 (7v), 269 (11v), 271 (22v), 272 (30v); and Ilkhanid ff. 45r–46r. In the Ottoman Anatolian texts, the sea under God's throne is only mentioned in the oldest examples (Ottoman Anatolia, 283). Together with the motif of the seas throughout the heavens, the sea motif before God's throne is referred to in the Greek text as well (Greek *Miʿrājnāma,* 164 [f. 35v, ln. 18–36r, ln. 4]). In the "total and complete" narrative of al-Bakrī's tradition, one also finds the motif of the seas alongside the seven heavens. See Colby, *Narrating Muhammad's Night Journey,* Appendix B.

31. In the *Miʿrājnāmas* of the sample, there is no unanimity for the correspondence of a prophet with a heaven. Even in the first heaven, where it seems that the Arabic tradition places Adam, in the Latin version Jesus Christ and John the Baptist are to be found (Latin, 50–51 [ch. XII]). Curiously, Bencheikh argues that the relevant description follows the Ibn ʿAbbās narrative and not the Latin one, while he refers to Jesus and John as presented in the first heaven (Bencheikh, *Le voyage nocturne,* 39 and 188 n. 16).

32. Greek *Mi'rājnāma,* 148 (f. 21v, ln. 11). See Ibn 'Abbās, 33 (sixth heaven); Latin, 58–60 [ch. XVI] (fifth heaven); Iznīkī, 58–59 (fourth heaven); Chaghatay, 271 (sixth heaven); Ilkhanid, ff. 36v–38r (sixth heaven); and Ottoman Anatolia, 252–253 (sixth or seventh heaven). On the importance of Moses, see Bencheikh, *Le voyage nocturne,* 189, n. 28.

33. Greek *Mi'rājnāma,* 151 (f. 24r). See Ibn 'Abbās, 24 (second heaven); Latin, 50–51 [ch. XII] (first heaven); Iznīkī, 54 (second heaven without John); Ilkhanid, ff. 23v–24r (third heaven); and Ottoman Anatolia, 254 (second heaven). In the missing folios of the Chaghatay text, which correspond to the description of the fourth heaven, Jesus Christ may perhaps be placed in the fourth heaven as well.

34. Greek *Mi'rājnāma,* 206–207 (75r, ln. 5–20); and Chaghatay, 276 (40v). In the Greek text, the motif occurs when Muḥammad returns from his tour of paradise and hell, and just before he reaches earth. In the Chaghatay text only *ṭarīqat* and *ḥaqīqat* are included.

35. Cf. Ibn 'Abbās, 29–32; Latin, 155–171 (ch. LIV–LXI), 194–222 (ch. LXXI–LXXIX); Iznīkī, 126–146; Chaghatay, 280–283 (53a–67v); Ilkhanid, ff. 28r–34v; and Bencheikh, *Le voyage nocturne,* 187 n. 11, 196–197 n. 1, and 219 n. 15. The Anatolian texts place hell either in the first or in the fourth heaven, following the ḥadīths (Ottoman Anatolia, 284–285). On the tour of hell scenes, see Roberto Tottoli's contribution to this volume.

36. However, I roughly count that the proportion the Greek text presents for the hell section is higher than that of Iznīkī's and comparable only with the Latin one (20 percent versus a little bit more than 10 percent). Furthermore, we should keep in mind that the Greek text is a poem, in which the potential for extensive description is more limited than in a prose text.

37. Greek *Mi'rājnāma,* 207–211 (ff. 76r–80v); Latin, 172–174 (ch. LXII); Iznīkī, 155–156; Ilkhanid, ff. 57v–58r [only for the two cities]; and Chaghatay, 284 [67v]). However, the Latin text refers to these animals when it describes hell. The Greek text has by far the longest description of the city of Jabalqa, though it does not mention the city of Jabalsa, which is mentioned together with Jabalqa in the other three texts. An interesting detail is that apart from the description of Jabalqa, in the Greek text alone, a reference to the *jinns*' world is given in connection with Jabalqa (Greek, 212 [f. 80v]).

38. For the motif of Mount Qāf and the conversion of the righteous Jews, see the discussion by Maria Subtelny in this volume.

39. For the views concerning the origin of these populations, see my *To Islam,* 77–87.

40. Johann Strauss, "Das Vilayet Janina 1881–1912. Wirtschaft und Gesellschaft in einer 'geretteten Provinz'," in *Türkische Wirtschafts- und Sozialgeschichte von 1071 bis 1920,* ed. H. G. Majer and R. Motika (Wiesbaden; Harrassowitz, 1995), 306–307. For the well-documented prevalence of Greek culture in this region, see Grigorij Arsh, *He Albania kai he Epiros sta tele tou ih' kai stis arches tou ith' aiona: Ta dytikobalkanika pasalikia tes Othomanikes Autokratorias* [Albania and Epirus in the end of the eighteenth and the beginning of the nineteenth century: The Pashaliks of the Ottoman Empire in the Western Balkans], Gr. trans. Antonia Dialla (Athens: Gutenberg, 1994), 279–281.

41. See the interesting remarks on the use of the first person singular in the Latin version in Jean-Patrick Guillaume, "'Moi, Mahomet, Prophète et Messager de Dieu . . .': Traduction et adaptation dans le *Liber Scale Machometi,*" in *Le voyage initiatique en terre d'Islam,* Mohammad Ali Amir-Moezzi, ed. (Louvain: Peeters, 1991), 92–95.

42. A *sipahi* might have belonged to the local Muslim elite rather than being a simple soldier.

43. Greek *Mi'rājnāma,* 226 (f. 94r, ln. 22–23).

44. Ibid., 125 (f. XVIr, ln. 1–4).

45. Ibid., 126 (f. XVIr, ln. 17–18).

46. Ibid., 126–129 (ff. 1v–3v).

47. Ibid., 220 (f. 89v, ln. 1).

48. See for example note 42 above.

49. See an analysis of the problem in my *To Islam,* 29–34.

50. Greek *Mi'rājnāma,* 141 (f. 14v, ln. 17), 145 (f. 18v, ln. 13), 147 (f. 20v, ln. 9), 150 (f. 22v, ln.

17), 154 (f. 27r, ln. 5), 157 (f. 29v, ln. 9), 158 (f. 30v, ln. 5), 163 (f. 35v, ln. 5), 164 (f. 36r, ln. 5), 174 (f. 45r, ln. 5), 185 (f. 55v, ln. 13), 207 (f. 76r, ln. 1), 212 (f. 81r, ln. 5). In my view, the subject of the verb is the poem and not the author; therefore, the single verses function as an explanation of what follows.

51. For example: Greek *Miʿrājnāma,* 176 (f. 46v, ln. 18–19), 178 (f. 48v, ln. 12–13).

52. Ibid., 127 (f. 2r, ln. 5–7), 128 (f. 2v, ln. 21–23), 147 (f. 20r, ln. 21–23), 207 (f. 75v, ln. 13–18). The explanatory phrases are on pp. 152 (f. 24v, ln. 24: for the angel ʿAzrā'īl), 154 (f. 26v, ln. 20: for the mountain in the fourth heaven), and 156 (f. 28v, ln. 8: for the angel Michael).

53. Ibid., 177 (f. 48r, ln. 3 and ln. 18). However, these inconsistencies occur even in a more scholarly text such as Ilkhanid, f. 18r, which first refers to three cups and then describes four.

54. Greek *Miʿrājnāma,* 202 (f. 70v, ln. 2 and 6). For a similar inconsistency, see Ilkhanid, ff. 31v-32r, where two of the seven valleys of hell bear the same name, *Hāviya.*

55. This may be the conclusion drawn from the similarity, in terms of existing motifs, between the Greek *Miʿrājnāma* and Iznīkī's version of the *miʿrāj.*

56. Greek *Miʿrājnāma,* 164 (f. 36v, ln. 2: "the hukamā' tell us"), and 180 (f. 50v, ln. 5–6: "and the books testify and narrate to us"; 51r, ln. 10: "the ʿulamā' say").

57. Ibid., 172 (f. 43r, ln. 13), 177 (f. 48r, ln. 4), and 209 (f. 77v, ln. 15).

58. Ibid., 126–127 (f. 1v, ln. 1–8).

59. For the importance of the *quṣṣāṣ* in the development of the *miʿrāj* legend, see Bencheikh, *Le voyage nocturne,* 246–251.

60. Apart from the numerous verses scattered throughout the poem, on the last page, before the quatrain narrating the year of the compilation of the poem, there are two others urging the audience that one who does not believe to Muḥammad goes to hell (Greek *Miʿrājnāma,* 220 [f. 88v, ln. 1–8]).

61. For this group and the relevant bibliography, see my *To Islam,* 77–87.

62. Pyrsinellas, "Hoi tourkogianniotikes *homologies,*" 160–169. For the Greek text of such a poem, see also Demetrios Salamangkas, "Mia tourkogianniotike *homologia*" [A Tourkogianniot "confession poem"], *Epeirotike Zoe* 1/6 (1946): 14–15 and 24.

63. These people had been exchanged according to the Greek-Turkish Treaty of Peace of Lausanne in 1923 and were settled mainly in western Turkey along the Aegean coast. For the immigration of various ethnic groups in Turkey, see Peter A. Andrews, *Ethnic Groups in the Republic of Turkey* (Wiesbaden: Dr. Ludwig Reichert Verlag, 1989). For the population exchange between Turkey and Greece see Demetrios Pentzopoulos, *The Balkan Exchange of Minorities and its Impact on Greece* (The Hague: Mouton, 1962).

64. These small poems are known as *stichoplakia* ("short rhymed verses" or "singled couplets"). See Demetrios Salamangkas, "To gianniotiko stichoplaki ki oi paragontes tou" [The Jannina short-rhymed verse and its factors], *Epeirotike Hestia* 4 (1955), 807–814; and Aristoteles Brelles, *Epeirotika stichoplakia: Eisagoge-keimeno-lexilogio* [Short-rhymed verses from Epirus. Introduction, text, vocabulary], Ph.D. diss., University of Jannina, 1980.

65. Pyrsinellas, "Hoi tourkogianniotikes *homologies,*" 164.

66. Ibid.

67. See notes 21–22 above.

68. Bencheikh, *Le voyage nocturne,* 262.

69. For this purpose, a general study of the diffusion of the *miʿrāj* in Ottoman lands would be of great value. To my knowledge, such a study has not yet been undertaken. However, for a preliminary discussion of the subject, see the chapters by Gottfried Hagen and Selim Kuru in this volume.

15

Shāh Ismāʿīl Ṣafevī and the *Miʿrāj*: H̬aṭā'ī's Vision of a Sacred Assembly

AMELIA GALLAGHER

The poetry related to the *miʿrāj* complex that is attributed to Shāh Ismāʿīl Ṣafevī (d. 1524) collectively constitutes one of the most important statements of a unique Islamic mythology. Shāh Ismāʿīl's *mah̬laṣ* (pen-name) is H̬aṭā'ī, which has come to mean "The Fallible" or the "The One with Fault."[1] H̬aṭā'ī is also an identity eventually associated with a literary corpus that has expanded since the death of the historical poet-monarch, a corpus that reflects the religious imagination of the Alevi and other similar traditions considered heterodox.[2] Through Shāh Ismāʿīl's accounts of the *miʿrāj* we see how he continued to give shape to Anatolian heterodox religiosity posthumously. The poetic treatments of the *miʿrāj* attributed to Shāh Ismāʿīl further reveal how he endured as a voice of a poetic legacy spanning centuries, from the time of his successor, Shāh Tahmāsp (r. 1524–1576) until the present century.[3]

First, a few words regarding the religious culture in which this poetry flourished are necessary. This study limits itself to the Alevi tradition confined mainly to present-day Turkey. The Alevi form one of the sects whose adherents were known by traditional heresiographers as "exaggerators" (pl. *ghulāt*) due to the exalted status in which they held the Prophet Muḥammad's son-in-law and the first Shiʿi imām, ʿAlī ibn Abī Ṭālib (d. 661).[4] While the precise relations among ʿAlid sects remain problematic, the beliefs of various communities in Turkey presently categorized under the term Alevism (Turkish: *Alevilik*) that concern us here bear strong parallels with those of the Bektashi order, and are also related to the extinct Safavid order, as evidenced by their former appellation Qızılbāş.[5] Although the technical characterization of the Alevi as "twelver" Shiʿa is an accurate reflection of their *imāmī* piety, the designation is misleading in view of the distinct development of the *ithnā ʿasharī* tradition in Iran and elsewhere. The Alevi can be seen to represent an earlier form of Safavid religiosity, but, as we shall see, the Alevi also underwent their own crucial development since the time of their formation in the fifteenth century. Turkish remains their liturgical and literary language. Indeed, the poetry attributed to Shāh Ismāʿīl can be seen across the development of premodern Turkish and sometimes even is composed in a stylistic imitation of the original southern Turkish, or Azeri, dialect.

Accounts of the Prophet's night journey (*isrā'*) and ascent (*miʿrāj*) have served as powerful forums for the expression of distinctive sectarian postures, as seen in the various Imāmī, Ismaʿīlī, and Nuṣayrī *miʿrāj* elaborations recounted in both poetry and prose.[6] Shāh Ismāʿīl is thus one of the mystical-literary figures contributing to this tendency. Within the Alevi tradition, and Ḫaṭā'ī's contribution to its literary culture in particular, the imagery associated with this event has a distinct precedent: ʿAlī appears as a central figure of the *miʿrāj* and makes his presence known to the Prophet Muḥammad during its various stages, often appearing as a mysterious lion in possession of the Prophet's signet ring, an image indicating ʿAlī's place as the living culmination of the divine message and, as such, superior to the Prophet (Plates 27 and 28).[7] However, the poems recounting the *miʿrāj* attributed to Ḫaṭā'ī that are taken from the Qızılbāş tradition, which developed after Shāh Ismāʿīl's death, diverge considerably from *miʿrāj* accounts found in other Shiʿi and Ṣūfī contexts. Indeed, these poetic visions of the *miʿrāj* expand considerably on Shāh Ismāʿīl's own historical works. This particular vision of the *miʿrāj* likely emerged as Alevi ritual practice configured in the sixteenth and seventeenth centuries. It is a context in which poetic song is used to express sectarian myths, such as the primordial origin of ʿAlī as well as the origin of ritual itself. Myths such as these find continual poetic expression through the *miʿrāj*.

The Poetry of Shāh Ismāʿīl I

For over a century, Safavid historians have held a particular fascination with the literary output of Shāh Ismāʿīl (1487–1524) as the hereditary leader of the Safavid brotherhood and the founder of the Safavid dynasty.[8] Charged with the penetrating translations of Vladimir Minorsky,[9] who first exploited his Paris *dīvān*, historians have maintained Shāh Ismāʿīl's program of propaganda involved poetic incitement aimed at the Qızılbāş partisans of the Safavid family. This conditioning helped lead the Safavids to startling military victory over the Aqqūyūnlū dynastic warlords. The young Ismāʿīl provides an example of a successfully activated charisma, supported in turn by the poetic pronouncements of the adolescent demagogue himself:

> I am the bird of paradise,
> I am a commander over legions of soldiers,
> I am the comrade of the Sufis,
> Declare me the Shāh, *ġāzis*!
>
> From the eve come forth,
> Bring in the New Year, reach the Shāh,
> Prostrate yourselves, *ġāzis*,
> Declare me the Shāh, *ġāzis*!

I am Ḫaṭā'ī, on the red steed,
Like his words of sugar, I stand as sweet,
I am with Mürtażā ʿAlī,
Declare me the Shāh, *ġāzīs*![10]

In the above piece, (perhaps intended as a soldiers' march, for it is set to a simple meter), the legion of Sufi soldiers is led to their destiny: the new shah who demands and deserves prostration as much as the ephemeral Shah he represents. In this way Shāh Ismāʿīl's poetry has come to be the foremost source revealing the spectacular "heresy" of the Safavid *shaykhs*, which included the belief in their immortality as well as their divine identity. Clearly, the dominant religious themes running throughout Shāh Ismāʿīl's *dīvān* poetry distinguish it from the "orthodox" Imāmī Shiʿism that would indeed characterize the later Safavid ethos as it developed under the *ithnā ʿasharī* clerical elements allied with Shāh Ismāʿīl's successors. Instead, the verses of Shāh Ismāʿīl's *dīvān* poetry reveal a sacred incarnation identified with the living scion of the Safavid order and the first of their monarchs. This poetic voice sometimes presents Shāh Ismāʿīl as the Hidden *imām*, sometimes as an incarnation of ʿAlī, and, in one striking verse, as the eye of God.[11] By skillful use of meter, the new shah deliberately confounds his persona with those of a vast sacred past:

I am the immortal Ḫıżır, Jesus, Mary
And the Alexander of this age.

The point of my sword conquered the world,
I am ʿAlī Mürtażā's faithful servant.

My great *şeyḫ* is Ṣafī, my father is Ḥayder,
I am the true Caʿfer of the brave.

As Ḥüseyn, I curse Yezīd,
I am Ḫaṭā'ī, a slave of the Shāh.[12]

These sorts of poetic illustrations of metaphysical bravado that fuse the author with luminaries of scripture and legend are taken from Shāh Ismāʿīl's earliest formal collections of poetry (*dīvān*) and are thus considered authentic.[13] While references to the Prophet's *miʿrāj* within these original collections are encountered only sparingly, these references are also quite conventional relative to verses containing what remain audacious, though not unprecedented, statements of the author's divine status.[14] In fact, Shāh Ismāʿīl's *dīvān* poetry treats the *miʿrāj* only in a passing allusion. Found in the oldest *dīvān*s, the following curt reference to the *miʿrāj* reads:

It was Muḥammad who ascended the ladder from below,
It was ʿAlī who was the lion he saw at the sanctuary.[15]

This couplet (*beyt*) is taken from one of numerous poems of encomia to ʿAlī. The significance of ʿAlī, and the poet's estimation of his significance, provides the overriding theme throughout Shāh Ismāʿīl's authentic collections, even beyond the self-glorifying content, for which the *dīvān* is notorious. Although the allusion to the *miʿrāj* in this poem remains confined to a single couplet, it nevertheless serves as the basis for further developments of the *miʿrāj* mythology in the later Ḫaṭā'ī tradition—that is, the Turkic poetry bearing his name that carried on after his death. Employing the iconic representation of ʿAlī as an angelic lion, and as part of the dominant strategy of establishing ʿAlī's cosmic supremacy (even above that of the Prophet), the preceding couplet reveals a dispensation in which Muḥammad is ascending to heights that ʿAlī has already achieved.

The following verses are also taken from Shāh Ismāʿīl's older *dīvāns*. As in the verse above, the poet conspicuously links ʿAlī to the *miʿrāj*, by twice making reference to Burāq, the beast-vehicle of the Prophet's ascent, who here serves ʿAlī along with his traditional mount, Düldül:[16]

> His attributes are "*elif-lām*" and "*yā-sīn*,"[17]
> He has reached the place without place,
> His perch is the miraculous Burāḳ,
> He illuminates all that is obscured.
> It is ʿAlī, it is ʿAlī, it is ʿAlī, ʿAlī,
> ʿAlī, the glorious intercessor, the friend of God.
>
> He is always living, ever-lasting,
> He is who mounts Düldül and Burāḳ,
> Always in conformity [*ittfāḳı olan*] with the Divine Reality,
> The cup-bearer of the water of Kevser,[18]
> It is ʿAlī, it is ʿAlī, it is ʿAlī, ʿAlī,
> ʿAlī, the glorious intercessor, the friend of God.[19]

The work from which these verses are taken is singular in its classification as a *müseddes*—a six-line stanzaic form that is rare in Shāh Ismāʿīl's *dīvān* collections.[20] Throughout the piece, the rhythmic repetition of ʿAlī's name in the last distich of each sestet suggests a performance intention for the piece. That this *müseddes* is one of few poems from Shāh Ismāʿīl's *dīvān* included in a collection featuring the work of varied Alevi-Bektashi poets would further suggest its ritual application.[21] Shāh Ismāʿīl's association with ritual indeed has proved an intriguing question: some authors maintain that he is the "architect" of Alevi ritual as it has come down to us today.[22]

The significant historical accounts attesting to the association of Shāh Ismāʿīl with Qızılbāş ritual before modern times include the observation of the intrepid European traveler Michel Membré. As a Venetian agent intent on securing Safavid support against Ottoman interests, Membré stayed in Tabriz with high-ranking Qızılbāş officials in 1540–1541. Privy to the rituals performed by the Qızılbāş, and also a curious participant on at least one occasion, Membré leaves us an intriguing reference to the deceased shah during the ritual performance of his hosts:

> . . . then they begin to sing certain songs in praise of the Shah, composed by Shāh Ismāʿīl and the said Tahmāsp . . . that is Ḫaṭā'ī; and after that is done, there sits

> one with a tambour, and he begins to call very loudly the names of all who are there, one by one; and then each one whose name he calls says "*Shāh bāsh,*" that is "The Shah is head" . . .[23]

Membré's mention of the "songs" composed by Shāh Ismāʿīl are explicitly identified with the pen-name "Khaṭā'ī." Nearly a century later, during the year 1028/1619, an Ottoman source containing a summarized account of the "confessions" of heretics (*mülḥid*) also cites Shāh Ismāʿīl "Ḫaṭā'ī"'s association with the liturgy of the accursed. According to the official: "They have many prayers [*duʿā*] in praise of the wayward [*gümrāh*] shah—May God of the Most High destroy them!—During which they cite the words of Shāh Ismāʿīl, Ḫaṭā'ī, which they call *maʿnī*."[24] Amid the polemic, the document strongly points to the fact that the "words" of the despised shah still hold sacred value among those branded as renegades by the state.

The Ottoman document on heretical activity further reveals that the "words" of Shāh Ismāʿīl continued to serve as an integral element of heterodox ritual, similar to the rituals of the Safavid Qızılbāş Membré had described several decades before. In both sources these "words" and "songs" are mentioned in connection with praise (*sitāyiş*)of the shah.[25] The author of the Ottoman account locates the identity of the shah within the Safavid house, condemning him as heretical or astray (*gümrāh*). This position of the shah in the ritual might suggest that the Shāh Ismāʿīl continued to serve as an object of worship in the seventeenth century. But without specific reference to the "songs" in question, both the significance of Shāh Ismāʿīl within the ritual and the authenticity of the "songs" attributed to him would be impossible to ascertain. The credit given to Shāh Ismāʿīl in the construction of Qızılbāş-Alevi ritual may be premature at this point; however, the claim is certainly testimony to the perception of his towering influence among the Alevi in Turkey today.

Evidenced by numerous manuscripts of folk poetry containing attributions to Shāh Ismāʿīl located throughout Turkey, what can be assumed is that significant expansion of Shāh Ismāʿīl's existent poetic legacy occurred as the Qızılbāş developed into a permanent sectarian community in Ottoman territory. Ḫaṭā'ī's use of poetry to expound upon ritual procedure characterizes one prominent example taken from one of the earliest known collections of these pious inventions—a Qızılbāş "catechism" dated from the sixteenth century.[26] This expansion of the Ḫaṭā'ī tradition from the sixteenth to the twentieth century also includes several extended treatments of the *miʿrāj,* works that stand outside the official *dīvān* collections of Shāh Ismāʿīl's poetry.

Ḥaṭā'ī in the Turkish Alevi Tradition

Following Edward G. Browne, literary historians have tended to dismiss dubious attributions to Shāh Ismāʿīl's corpus as "pseudo-Ḫaṭā'ī."[27] Although these attributions are indeed questionable, they still deserve scholarly attention, for they become the vehicle by which Shāh Ismāʿīl's significance was transformed and preserved through a process of pseudonymity in the decades and centuries following his death. While certain verses and poems from later collections were changed in order to salvage orthodox respectability within Safavid Persia,[28] this larger transformation of Shāh Ismāʿīl's persona among the Qızılbāş went beyond a cosmetic alteration of his existent poetic works. Among Anatolian Qızılbāş communities, the new image of Shāh Ismāʿīl emerged primarily through the expansion of his corpus. In keeping with this transformation, the *miʿrāj* poetry grew to reflect the mythical imagination of Qızılbāş-Alevi development.

These later works present the Qızılbāş/Alevi understanding of the true prophetic mission of the *miʿrāj,* that is, the recognition of ʿAlī's supreme place within Muḥammad's ascension, and by extension, his cosmic status. As is the case of many ʿAlī-based traditions, the theological relevance of ʿAlī's position is best drawn through artistic developments; dogmatic expositions upon the subject are rare compared to the massive volume of poetic sources. In this way, the poetry related to the *miʿrāj* provides yet another narrative paradigm in which to express ʿAlī's association with the divine. This poetry further constitutes a source from which to gain insight into the development of the Qızılbāş as a sectarian religious community, a community declaring its own sacredness through clear poetic parallels. In Ḫaṭāʾī's *miʿrāj* poetry, ʿAlī's followers take their place beside him at the height of the ascent and thereby claim the exalted status of the group. Recalling the lone reference from Shāh Ismāʿīl's *dīvān* in which ʿAlī stands as a lion guarding the portal of a sanctuary during the Prophet's ascent, the numerous *miʿrāj* poems attributed to Shāh Ismāʿīl document a scenario in which the listener is led inside the sanctuary in order to witness the significance of the assembly gathered within.

According to the poetic typology of the Alevi-Bektashi, the term *miʿrāçlama* is applied to poetic narratives of the *miʿrāj.* Unlike classical forms of Islamicate poetry, Alevi-Bektashi poems (generally termed *nefes*) are categorized according to content, rather than formal structure. And like other categories of these works, such as the *düvāz imām* (elegy to the Twelve Imāms) or the *mersiye* (lament for the tragedy of Karbalāʾ), the *miʿrāçlama* also serves a ritual function. As Ahmet Yürür's study of the *miʿrāçlama* has shown, although the form is also attributed to other Alevi-Bektashi poets, versions of the *miʿrāçlama* attributed to Ḫaṭāʾī predominate in the ritual context.[29] The ascension of the Prophet Muḥammad inspires a complex of narratives contained in Alevi-Bektashi *miʿrāçlama* and elsewhere, unfolding as ʿAlī appears to the Prophet during his ascent.[30] Ḫaṭāʾī envisions ʿAlī in a variety of ways throughout these presentations of the *miʿrāj:* as the ubiquitous lion, as the stern bearer of the scales of judgment, or, as seen below, as a child perched on the shoulders of Selmān Fārsī, the legendary hero of the ʿAbbāsid revolution:

One day, Muḥammad sat at home,
Four angels brought him a proclamation.
Selmān carried a young child on his shoulder,
A strange and glorious word he has brought.

Muḥammad received the child's greeting,
Showing respect he stood up,
With much effort, he humbled himself in prayer,
The child passed to sit on the prayer rug.

Behold Muḥammad, that child is ʿAlī,
The master of men, *cinn*, and angels,
A blessing, the path of the saints,
Muḥammad brought to him a decree.

ʿAlī submitted his hand,
Muḥammed saw his ring and called him "friend,"
Gabriel wanted a sign from ʿAlī,
He brought him before the star of Venus.[31]

In the last stanza cited above we see the child ʿAlī revealing his possession of the Prophet's ring. Whether this ring is revealed to Muḥammad on the hand of the child ʿAlī or in the mouth of ʿAlī's lion incarnation, it is commonplace throughout Ḫaṭā'ī's presentations of the *miʿrāj* that recognition of the ring triggers an epiphany in the Prophet. Some authors insist that this revelation to the Prophet consists of his recognition of ʿAlī's divinity. The *miʿrāj* poetry attributed to Ḫaṭā'ī makes it clear that ʿAlī commands the events of the *miʿrāj*, and certainly a good deal more. While the appearance of the Prophet's ring on ʿAlī 's finger is a necessary scene in virtually all Alevi narratives of the *miʿrāj*, this particular presentation goes on to reveal a more unusual display of ʿAlī's power. Here he is associated with an ability to create an iconic entourage (made up of his daughter, sword, and beasts of burden) through his division of an apple brought from paradise:

They knew who that boy was,
All of the angels stood in his presence,
They put forth many injustices,
One of them brought an apple from paradise.

He expounded upon the apple they carried,
The Shāh took the apple and divided it into four pieces,
One of the pieces Muḥammad took for himself,
The angels took the other three pieces to the sanctuary.

God looked kindly upon this,
The Shāh was given the holy ones,
One became Düldül, one became Zülfıḳār,
They brought to him Fāṭima and Ḳanber.[32]

The preceding selections are taken from a *miʿrāçlama* attributed to Ḫaṭā'ī included in one of several dozen manuscripts featuring traditional Alevi-Bektashi poets housed at the Mevlana Museum in Konya.[33] What may be a disappointing feature about this work and others of these collections would be the lack of Shāh Ismāʿīl's historical voice as the "commander of legions," slashing heathens at their root.[34] While these brazen images remain important sources for Safavid history, this militant image of Shāh Ismāʿīl did not endure within the Anatolian Qızılbāş tradition. Instead, the descendants of a once fanatical military culture collectively created a more appropriate leader bearing the same pen-name. With his role as the divine warrior compromised, Shāh Ismāʿīl emerged from unfulfilled messianic promises with the vigor of a new vision entirely.

At the same time, a tenuous memory recalls the voice of the historical poet. Traces of the authentic voice are deliberately recalled in these later works of pseudo-Ḫaṭā'ī. Certainly, the *ghuluww* cosmology revolving around the figure of ʿAlī remains a central poetic theme. As the following couplet taken from one of Ḫaṭā'ī's *miʿrāçlama*s shows, the theomorphic tendencies the tradition grants ʿAlī are seen though his co-eternity with God:

> Before the ground, before the sky, before the throne,
> He who established the scale of reality is ʿAlī.[35]

This emphasis on the primordial status of ʿAlī—and ʿAlī exclusively—is representative of a crucial departure for the poetry associated with Shāh Ismāʿīl. To illustrate this, we return to the authentic *dīvān* poetry of this charismatic monarch. Here it is seen how the poet inserts himself into the primordial schema, while ʿAlī is not mentioned whatsoever:

> Before there was earth, before there was sky, since the beginning of time
> I was.
> For years I was a compass, encircling your incomparable gem.
>
> I rendered the gem like water, it permeated the world end to end,
> I veiled the sky, the earth, and the throne of God from the beloved.
>
> At one time, with Ḥüseyn, the *ḳadi*s flayed my skin,
> At one time I wore Manṣūr's clothes, I declared *enā'l-ḥaḳḳ* in the gallows.[36]
>
> I wore the garments of man, so that no one knew my secret,
> I was in that house of God since the beginning of time.
>
> I came revolving with 18,000 worlds,
> And I was a commander, a commander with God.
>
> From His world, I knew His secret and He knew mine,
> Under the sea I stoked the fires of hell.
>
> I am Ḫaṭā'ī, I know *ḥaḳḳ* as *ḥaḳḳ*,
> And I was present thus at the beginning of creation.[37]

In this example from Shāh Ismāʿīl's *dīvān* poetry, the voice is not merely of a commander, but a "Commander with God," coeval if not consubstantial. It is no wonder that before the contents of these collections were studied, historians took with a grain of salt the European reports of Safavid partisans throwing themselves into battle unarmed. Since the publication of the contents of Shāh Ismāʿīl's *dīvān,* these accounts are taken literally.[38]

Further Elaborations of the *Miʿrāj*

Irène Mélikoff rightly maintains that Alevi-Bektashi versions of the *miʿrāj* stand as the prototype for the central Alevi ritual, the *ayīn-i cemʿ* (ritual of assembly). These ritual elements reflect their mythical origins during an episode in which Muḥammad is led to the "Assembly of the Forty."[39] While it is difficult to point to a single culmination within a ritual as complex as the *ayīn-i cemʿ*, which constitutes several discrete episodes and can last several days, the frequent appearance of the Forty within Alevi liturgical poetry suggests a central symbolic understanding. For Ḫaṭā'ī, the "Forty" represent the beatific reward for entry into the sanctuary, and in most versions the Prophet stands astonished at the scene he witnesses inside.

Within the *miʿrāj* complex, most of the forty individuals present at this assembly remain unidentified, as various constellations of the Forty constitute a pervasive feature of Anatolian saintly devotion.[40] Some of the figures mentioned in these *mirʿāçlama* include the angel Gabriel, Fāṭima, and other members of the Prophet's family. Selmān Fārsī is also prominent in the assembly, as shown in the following verses attributed to Ḫaṭā'ī describing Muḥammad's struggle to understand this gathering of the Forty:

> They call you the Forty,
> Then why is one missing?
> Selmān has gone to beg for alms,
> He is the one missing from among us.
>
> Selman returned from begging for alms,
> Enunciating *hū* he entered the assembly,[41]
> With that, Muḥammad became intoxicated,
> His crown falling from his head.[42]

The ritual greeting " *hū*," the begging for alms, and the intoxication of ecstatic dancing serve to mark the preceding scene with traditional dervish precept. Within this familiar environment, the heavenly host can be seen as a parallel gathering repeated in earthly sanctuaries. The structure of the *miʿrāçlama* cited below also establishes the connection to the living participants of the ritual. This poem repeatedly returns to the supreme metaphysical significance of ʿAlī, which provides a dominant strategy for both the authentic and pseudo-Ḫaṭā'ī. Following established convention, ʿAlī first appears to Muḥammad as a lion, guarding the entrance of the sacred assembly, but his presence multiplies by the end of the piece: from a lion to the holder of divine mysteries, finally appearing as the miracle-working master of the ceremony. In this final incarnation, the author points beyond the figure of ʿAlī to the assembly over which he presides. The Forty are thereby revealed as the performers of an ecstatic *semāʿ* or ritual dance. With this privileged vision of the assembly, the ritual parallels are seen:

> Muḥammad, on the night of the *miʿrāc*, saw
> The lion at the door is ʿAlī.
>
> He took off his ring and gave it as a sign,
> The one he saw reciting the glories of God is ʿAlī.
>
> He spoke 90,000 words with *ḥaḳḳ*
> Who holds the 30,000 secrets is ʿAlī.
>
> At that moment, he took off from the face of the earth to heavens,
> He who brought "Raḥmān" is ʿAlī.[43]
>
> He saw upon the ground a dome was made,
> He who is the wondrous green dome is ʿAlī.
>
> Inside, he enunciates the secrets of Divine Truth,
> He who sets up the scales of the Last Judgment is ʿAlī.
>
> He walked ahead, he pushed at the door,
> He who asks, "Who are you?" is ʿAlī.
>
> He said I am he who is the servant worthy of the Women,[44]
> He who also opens the door is ʿAlī.
>
> When he saw the Forty, the mystery of God,
> Inside, the prince of the brave is ʿAlī.
>
> Upon entering, they spoke affectionately,
> He who turns the Forty into one is ʿAlī
>
> Aḥmed stayed within this enigma,
> He who brings the enigma to light is ʿAlī.
>
> He struck the lance to one; from the Forty flowed (blood),
> He who wields the lance is ʿAlī.
>
> He procured a single grape, flowing,
> He whose hand bears the ring is ʿAlī.
>
> Crushed into drink, they drank
> He who is intoxicated with love and admiration is ʿAlī.
>
> They played, the *semāʿ* began,
> The drunkard who intoxicates them is ʿAlī.

The nectar consumed, the veil was torn,
He who shows the ring as a sign is ᶜAlī.[45]

The final role accorded ᶜAlī in this piece is leader of the ecstatic dance or *semāᶜ*, employing the traditional symbolic associations of intoxication. Reflecting the cosmic structure of Ḫaṭā'ī's *miᶜrāj* account above, the *ayīn-i cemᶜ* emulates the events by actual ritual procedure: according to most accounts of the ritual, the performance of the *miᶜrāçlama* directly leads to the performance of the *semāᶜ*.[46] The following *semāᶜ*, attributed to Ḫaṭā'ī is an example of the most common version of the ritual, termed the "*semāᶜ* of the Forty." This particular example is a poetic form related to the *miᶜrāj*, but it assumes an understanding of the event and bypasses it entirely in order to directly focus on the significance of the sacred assembly:

I arrived at the stage of the Forty,
Come here brother, they said.
I greeted them with respect,
Come to the stage, they said.

The Forty stood in one place,
Sit, they said, they gave me a space.
They set a table before me,
Extend your hand to the sacred sustenance, they said.

The heart of the Forty is clear,
The mind of the one who comes is pure,
Free from the blood of the one who returns,
Say who you are, they said.

Enter the *semāᶜ*, dance together here,
May your heart always be a mirror.
Boiling in the cauldron forty years,
This flesh is still raw, they said.

What you have seen with your eye,
Do not express by words.
Then, together with us,
You will also be a guest, they said.

Do not fall into worldly torments,
Be a follower in the presence of God,
Into the water of Zemzem,
Dip your finger, they said.

I am Shāh Ḫaṭā'ī, what is your state?
Give thanks to God, raise your hand.
Cut your tongue away from slander,
Show justice to everyone, they said.[47]

In this "*semāᶜ* of the Forty," the author is truly anonymous, representing a humble servant admitted to the sacred gathering of the ritual performance. It is through such symbolism that the community participates in the events of the *miᶜrāj.* Whether struggling for political supremacy or surviving under secrecy, it is not uncommon among heterodox groups to articulate self-understandings of their transcendence beyond normal human categories by presenting a dichotomy in which they are triumphant. This distinction between the members of the group and their opponents and persecutors extends back to Shāh Ismāᶜīl's rise to power, and it provided a useful trope that penetrated his poetic works. Not surprisingly, this stark portrayal of binary opposites adopts a militant character in his historical works. Shāh Ismāᶜīl's partisans make up a characteristic amalgam of the mystical, militant, and martial. Described as his precious *ġāzī*s, "the people of divine truth," (*ehl-i ḥaḳḳ*), or "the people of purity" (*ṣafā ehli*), they make their frequent appearance in his *dīvān* pitted against the nefarious "outsiders":

> The angels have descended from the sky, announcing good news to the gnostics [*ehl-i ᶜarifāne*],
> The hour of death to the outsiders [*ḫavāric*] and disaster to the Yezīds have come.[48]
>
> If the world-conquering *ġāzī*s enter the field,
> The outsiders [*ḫavāric*] will be turned upside-down.[49]
>
> Not permitting outsiders [*ḫavāric*] to root in the world,
> I am Ḫaṭā'ī, as a testament I have now come.[50]

These examples are taken from separate works in Shāh Ismāᶜīl's genuine poetry in which this dichotomy constitutes a recurring theme. Here the Manichean Ḫaṭā'ī reveals himself as the leader of the righteous side of a vivid sectarian divide. But for pseudo-Ḫaṭā'ī, it is the ritual space, rather than the battlefield, that is the setting for his new chosen people. Here, in a *nefes* related to the *miᶜrāj,* the author makes explicit that the inspiration for the ritual gathering is the heavenly assembly of the Forty. The members of this elite assembly are no longer cast as warriors and their possessions are figurative: that is, gems of theological knowledge gained through direct encounter with the divine:

> I came upon a group of the saved,
> They had all joined hands,
> I said to them, where is your station?
> The station held the hand of Divine Truth.
>
> They held the rubies and pearls they carried,
> They priced them on a scale,
> They sowed affection in the garden of the lover,
> Learn the gardener's language.

They had taken their milk from the lake of omnipotence,
They had mixed their yeast from the Forty,
They fasted, the duties were fulfilled,
God did not oppress his creatures.

If you have knowledge, purify,
If you are a ratified lover, look to the letter,
Straighten out your obstinacy,
Understand the torrent of love.

He who drinks the nectar of love is needy.
He who serves the Forty is wanting,
I am Shāh Ḫaṭā'ī, consenting to servitude
You are as a sacred prison of the imams' slaves.[51]

In this piece taken from the varied and dispersed corpus of pseudo-Ḫaṭā'ī, a group comprised of the needy, the wanting, and the thirsty is immediately identified as a "group of the saved." For pseudo-Ḫaṭā'ī, knowledge, love, and fasting mark the new spiritual elite, creating a poetic landscape reflective of a people among whom the world-conquering *ġāzī*s, now long defeated, no longer have a place.

Historians locate the fall of Shāh Ismāʿīl's "messianic pretensions" to the battlefield of Chaldiran, where he suffered a moral and military defeat against the Ottoman Sultan Selim I in 1514. Literature produced in memory of Shāh Ismāʿīl's identity achieved transcendence over his personal divine associations, reeling from his humiliation in 1514 and further squandered until his premature death in 1524. Just as the *dīvān* poetry of Shāh Ismāʿīl shaped his image as a living authority, his authority as a voice of the subsequent tradition comes through his extra-*dīvān* attributions and generations of pious imitators.

The importance of these pseudonymous works is not how they betray the original poetic mission of Shāh Ismāʿīl, but how they deflect it to ʿAlī and the sacred assembly gathered in his name, reconstructed and strengthened during each ritual performance. Through these *miʿrāj* accounts, the true demise of Shāh Ismāʿīl's messianic pretensions lies within a literary ascent to a heavenly gathering rather than within any historical event. No longer the centre of the poem's strategy, Shāh Ismāʿīl has become merely one of the anonymous refugees, gathered for the ritual of assembly, as the following *miʿrāçlama* concludes:

I am Shāh Ḫaṭā'ī to those who know the assembly,
To those who look and find the jewel within themselves,
To those who are perfect before the master,
To those who reach the Divine Truth.[52]

Notes

1. Through his internal analysis of Shāh Ismāʿīl's Paris *dīvān,* Vladimir Minorsky notes that "Khaṭā'ī" likely derives from the medieval Persian placename for China, "Khaṭā(y)." Vladimir Minorsky, "The Poetry of Shāh Ismāʿīl I," *Bulletin of the School of Oriental and African Studies* 4 (1939–1942), 1028. İbrahim Arslanoğlu relates a tradition in which Shāh Ismāʿīl styled his pen name to mimic the name of ʿAlī Şīr Navā'ī (d. 1501), as he admired this Chaghatay poet. İbrahim Arslanoğlu, *Şah İsmail Hatayî: Divan, Dehnâme, Nasihatnâme ve Anadolu Hatayîleri* (Istanbul: Der Yayınevi, 1992), 14. Among the Alevi-Bektashi, however, the association of Shāh Ismāʿīl's *maḫlaṣ* with the concept of culpability is more pervasive, deriving from the term "*ḫaṭa*" (error, transgression).

2. Vladimir Minorsky first observed Shāh Ismāʿīl's place among the Ahl-i Ḥaḳḳ in Minorsky, "The Poetry of Shāh Ismāʿīl I," 1007. Irène Mélikoff relates the supreme position of Shāh Ismail's *dīvān* among the Ḳırklar, a small sectarian community related to the Ahl-i Ḥaḳḳ. See her "Le problème Bektaşi-Alévi: quelques dernières considérations," *Turcica* 31 (1999): 27. See also Martin van Bruinessen, "Shabak," in *Encyclopaedia of Islam*, new ed., vol. 9, 152–153. Frederick de Jong's observations of Bulgarian Alevi sects are also noteworthy regarding the centrality of Shāh Ismāʿīl within their religiosity. See "Problems Concerning the Origins of the Qızılbāş in Bulgaria: Remnants of the Ṣafaviyya?" in *Convegno sul tema: la Shī'a nell'impero Ottomano (Roma, 15 Aprile 1991)* (Roma: Accademia nazionale dei Lincei, 1993), 210.

3. Portions of this paper are taken from my dissertation, which explored the wider issue of Shāh Ismāʿīl's literary legacy. However, there I did not address at length the poetry related to the *miʿrāj* that is attributed to him. See Amelia Gallagher, "The Fallible Master of Perfection: Shah Ismail in the Alevi-Bektashi Tradition" (Ph.D. diss., McGill University, 2004).

4. Jean During suggests the term "hyper-Shiʿa" to designate sects centered on the theological primacy of the first Shiʿi *imām,* ʿAlī. See Jean During, "A Critical Survey on Ahl-e Haqq Studies in Europe and Iran," in *Alevi Identity: Cultural, Religious and Social Perspectives: Papers Read at a Conference Held at the Swedish Research Institute in Istanbul, November 25–27, 1996,* ed. Tord Olsson, Elisabeth Özdalga, and Catharina Raudvere (Istanbul: Swedish Research Institute, 1998), 105. While the beliefs in ʿAlī's divinity are central to the "extremist" sects, other fundamental mythical understandings also characterize these *ghuluww* worldviews. See Kathryn Babayan, *Mystics, Monarchs, and Messiahs: Cultural Landscapes of Early Modern Iran* (Cambridge: Harvard University Press, 2002).

5. Literally meaning "red head," the designation Qızılbāş (Ottoman: Ḳızılbāş) was originally a derisive term applied to those tribes under the command of Shāh Ismāʿīl's father Ḥaydar (d. 893/ 1488), because of their red head-dress. This term remained in usage beyond the affiliation of these populations with the Safavid order as they developed into a permanent sectarian community in Ottoman-Turkish society during the sixteenth and seventeenth centuries. By the time of Frederick Hasluck's research, the term Alevi (*ʿalawī,* pertaining to ʿAlī) had replaced the term Qızılbāş, at least in scholarly circles. Frederick William Hasluck, *Christianity and Islam Under the Sultans,* ed. Margaret M. Hasluck (Oxford: Clarendon Press, 1929), vol. 1, 140.

6. On Shiʿi sectarian presentations of the event, see the following articles from Mohammad Ali Amir-Moezzi, ed., *Le Voyage initiatique en terre d'Islam* (Louvain: Peeters, 1996): Mohammad Ali Amir-Moezzi, "L'Imām dans le ciel: Ascension et initiation (aspects de l'imāmologie duodécimaine III)," 99–116; reprinted in idem, *La religion discrète: croyances et pratiques spirituelles dans l'islam shiʿite* (Paris: Librarie Philosophique J. Vrin, 2006); M. M. Bar-Asher and A. Kofsky, "L'ascension céleste du gnostique Nuṣayrite et le voyage nocturne du prophète Muḥammad," 133–148; Yves Marquet, "L'ascension spirituelle chez quelques auteurs ismailiens," in *Le Voyage initiatique,* ed. Amir-Moezzi, 117–132. See also Frederick Colby's chapter in the present volume, "Early Imami Shiʿi Narratives."

7. For early accounts of ʿAlī's presence during the *miʿrāj,* see Amir-Moezzi, "L'imām dans le ciel: Ascension et initiation (aspects de l'imāmologie duodécimaine III)"; idem, "L'imām dans le ciel," in *La religion discrète;* Colby, "Early Imami Shiʿi Narratives." On the visual ren-

dering of this image during Shāh Ismāʿīl's reign, see Christiane Gruber, "When *Nubuvvat* Encounters *Valāyat:* Safavid Paintings of the Prophet's *Miʿrāj,* ca. 1500–1550," in *Shi'ite Art and Material Culture,* ed. Pedram Khosronejad (London: I. B. Taurus, 2009).

8. Once in power, the Qızılbāş became increasingly a liability to the emerging Safavid religious and political establishment, and as a result, Qızılbāş beliefs were increasingly suppressed. See Kathryn Babayan, "The Safavid Synthesis: From Qızılbāş Islam to Imamite Shiʿism," *Iranian Studies* 27 (1994): 135–161. As witnessed by thriving Alevi communities in Turkey today, the efforts to eradicate Qızılbāş elements from Safavid Persia were considerably more effective than in Ottoman territory, where the Qızılbāş survived in secrecy.

9. Vladimir Minorsky, "The Poetry of Shāh Ismāʿīl I," 1007–1053.

10. From the Paris *dīvān* reproduced in Tourkhan Gandjeï, ed., *Il Canzoniere di Šāh Ismāʿīl Ḫaṭā'ī* (Napoli: Istituto Universitario Orientale, 1959), no. 20.

11. "I am God's eye, I am God's eye, I am God's eye!/ O wayward blind soul, come and behold the Divine Truth." Gandjeï, ed., *Il Canzoniere di Šāh Ismāʿīl Ḫaṭā'ī,* no. 207.

12. Gandjeï, ed., *Il Canzoniere di Šāh Ismāʿil Ḫaṭā'ī,* no. 16.

13. Long thought to be the oldest and therefore the most authentic of Shāh Ismāʿīl's poetic collections, the Paris *dīvān* should be evaluated in conjunction with at least two other collections contending for this status. According to Wheeler Thackston, an incomplete and damaged manuscript housed in the Sackler Gallery in Washington D.C. was likely transcribed during Shāh Ismāʿīl's lifetime. See Wheeler Thackston, "The *Diwan* of Khata'i: Pictures for the Poetry of Shah Isma'il I," *Asian Art* 1 (1989), 61. This manuscript, however, is unavailable for consultation at present; a copy of its contents provided by Wheeler Thackston was used here (hereafter cited as *Dīvān of Shāh Ismāʿīl Ḫaṭā'ī,* MS, Sackler Gallery, s86.0060, transcription by Wheeler Thackston). A manuscript in Tashkent also antedates that of Paris. Its contents are transcribed in Azizaga Memedov, ed., *Shah Ismaiyl Khatai: Asarlari,* 2 vols., (Baku: Elm Nashriiiaty, 1966–1973). See Azizaga Memedov, "Le plus ancien manuscrit du *dīvān* de Shah Ismail Khatayi," *Turcica* 6 (1972): 8–23.

14. As I have discussed previously, Shāh Ismāʿīl's self-glorifying poetry should also be viewed as part of the established the mystical-literary convention of "ecstatic utterances" (*shaṭḥiyyāt*). In both his *dīvān* and in subsequent attributions, Shāh Ismāʿīl pays notable homage to the best known virtuoso of the audacious phrase-makers, Manṣūr ("I am the Divine Truth") al-Ḥallāj (executed in 309/922). Gallagher, "The Fallible Master of Perfection," ch. 4. On the early development of this literary-mystical phenomenon, see Carl Ernst, *Words of Ecstasy in Sufism* (Albany: State University of New York Press, 1985).

15. Gandjeï, ed., *Il Canzoniere di Šāh Ismāʿīl Ḫaṭā'ī,* no. 17.

16. The name of the Prophet's mule bequeathed to ʿAlī as a gift. According to tradition, ʿAlī rode Düldül during the battles of the Camel and Ṣiffīn.

17. These letters provide reference to the hidden significance of the free-standing letters in the Qur'an, the dominant cabbalist influence at this time being the Ḥurūfī tradition.

18. From *sūra* 108, titled al-Kawthar ("abundance"); identified as a basin or river in paradise.

19. Stanzas 9 and 14 in Gandjeï, ed., *Il Canzoniere di Šāh Ismāʿīl Ḫaṭā'ī,* no. 15; Memedov, ed., *Shah Ismaiyl Khatai: Asarlari* 1: no. 5; *Dīvān of Shāh Ismāʿīl Ḫaṭā'ī* (Wheeler Thackston), no. 152.

20. The Paris *dīvān,* beyond the dominant *ḳaṣīde-ġazel* stanzaic forms, includes one *murabbaʿ*, one *müseddes* and three *mesnevī*s in addition to a single poem in the syllabic meter of the Turkish folk style. The Tashkent *dīvān* also includes a selection of *rubāʿī* which the Paris *dīvān* omits.

21. *Macmūʿa* no. 181 MS, Mevlânâ Müzesi, folios 148r–v.

22. See Ahmet Yaşar Ocak, "Un aperçu général sur l'hétérodoxie musulmane en Turquie: Réflexions sur les origines et les caractéristiques du Kızılbachisme (Alévisme) dans la perspective de l'histoire," in *Syncretistic Religious Communities in the Near East: Collected Papers of the International Symposium "Alevism in Turkey and Comparable Syncretistic Religious Com-*

munities in the Near East in the Past and Present," Berlin, 14–17 April 1995, ed. Krisztina Kehl-Bodrogi, Barbara Kellner-Heinkele, and Anke Otter-Beaujean (Leiden: Brill, 1997), 201.

23. Andrew H. Morton, ed. and trans., *Mission to the Lord Sophy of Persia (1539–1542)* (London: School of Oriental and African Studies, 1993), 42. For a detailed analysis of the ritual of Membré's account see Andrew Morton, "The *chūb-i tarīq* and Qızılbāş Ritual in Safavid Persia," in *Études Safavides,* ed. Jean Calmard (Paris: Institut français de recherche en Iran, 1993), 225–245.

24. M. A. Danon, "Un interrogatoire d'hérétiques musulmans (1619)," *Journal Asiatique* 17 (1921), 293. According to Minorsky, this reference to *maʿnī* could be taken in the sense of *maʿnā* (lit., meaning or spiritual reality), that is, a "(saying full of) meaning," indicating a further derivative of *maʿnā,* the independent quatrain common in Turkish folk poetry, the *maʿnī.* In this case, the use of *manī* would be similar to Membré's use of the term "songs" (*canzone*). In fact, the *maʿnī* stanzaic form is common in Alevi-Bektashi poetry, a small corpus of which is also attributed to Ḫaṭā'i. For selections of *manī* attributed to Shāh Ismāʿīl see Gölpınarlı, Abdülbâki, ed., *Alevî-Bektaşî Nefesleri* (Istanbul: Remzi Kitabevi, 1963); Özmen, İsmail, ed., *Alevi-Bektaşi Şiirleri Antolojisi* (Ankara: Saypa Yayınları, 1995), vol. 2, 215–216.

25. Danon, "Un interrogatoire d'hérétiques musulmans (1619)," 293.

26. *Menāḳıb ül-Asrār Behcet ül-Aḥrar,* no. 1172, MS, Mevlânâ Müzesi. Translated as "Narrative of the Mysteries of the Joy of the Liberated"; for further discussion on the category of the manuscript see Abdülbâki Gölpınarlı, *Mevlânâ Müzesi Yazmalar Kataloğu* (Ankara: Türk Tarih Kurumu Basımevi, 1972), 3: 431. According to Gölpınarlı, although the manuscript dates from the reign of Shāh ʿAbbās (r. 995–1038/ 1587–1629), he attributes the work to one Bısāṭī from the reign of Shāh Ṭahmāsp (930–984/ 1524–1576), based on a parallel manuscript in his private collection. Works classified under this genre, although attributed to the first Safavid *shaykh,* Ṣafī al-Dīn (650–735/ 1252–1334), likely date back to the period of active Safavid military activity in Anatolia under the leadership of Shāh Ismāʿīl's grandfather Junayd (d. 864/ 1460) and father Ḥaydar (d. 893/ 1488). For a discussion of the genre of these manuals, referred to as *buyruḳ* ("order") see Gallagher, "The Fallible Master of Perfection," ch. 5.

27. See Tourkhan Gandjeï, "Pseudo-Khaṭā'ī," in *Iran and Islam in Memory of the Late Vladimir Minorsky,* ed. C. E. Bosworth (Edinburgh: Edinburgh University, 1971), 263–266.

28. Minorsky, "The Poetry of Shāh Ismāʿīl I," 1026.

29. Ahmet Yürür, "Miʿraçlama in the Liturgy of the Alevi of Turkey: A Structural and Gnostic Analysis" (Ph.D. diss., University of Maryland, 1989), 14–15.

30. A prose version of the *miʿrāj* is narrated in Sefer Aytekin, ed. *Buyruk* (Ankara: Emek Basım Yayınevi, 1958), 7. For other summaries of the Alevi-Bektashi *miʿrāj,* see Frederick de Jong, "The Iconography of Bektashism: A Survey of the Themes and Symbolism in Clerical Costume, Liturgical Objects and Pictorial Art," *Manuscripts of the Middle East* 4 (1989), 8; Irène Mélikoff, "Le problème Bektaşi-Alévi," 7–34; and John Kingsley Birge, *The Bektashi Order of Dervishes* (Hartford: Hartford Seminary, 1937), 137–138.

31. *Macmūʿa* no. 181, MS, Mevlânâ Müzesi, folios 32–33.

32. Ibid.

33. For poems attributed to Shāh Ismāʿīl in the collection, see Abdülbâki Gölpınarlı, *Mevlânâ Müzesi Yazmalar Kataloğu* .

34. Because of the varied nature of the manuscripts containing attributions to Shāh Ismāʿīl, the extent of this corpus can only be estimated at this point. Important collections of Alevi-Bektashi poetry are located in Konya, Istanbul, Sivas and the village of Hacıbektaş. Moreover, many manuscripts remain in private collections for liturgical use.

35. *Macmūʿa* no. 82, MS, Mevlânâ Müzesi, folios 120r–v.

36. A reference (one of several found throughout Shāh Ismāʿīl's *dīvān*s) to the well known ecstatic utterance "I am the Divine Truth," mentioned above in note 14, ascribed to Manṣūr al-Ḥallāj (executed in 309/922).

37. Memedov, ed., *Shah Ismaiyl Khatai: Asarlari,* vol. 1, 372–373.

38. As encouraged by Vladimir Minorsky, see Minorsky, "Persia: Religion and History," in *Iranica: Twenty Articles* (Tehran: University of Tehran, 1964), 252.

39. Irène Mélikoff, "La cérémonie du *ayn-i djem* (Anatolie centrale)," in *Bektachiyya: Études sur l'ordre mystique des Bektachis et les groups relevant de Hadji Bektach,* ed. Alexandre Popovic and Gilles Veinstein (Istanbul: Isis, 1995), 65. For a further discussion of Alevi ritual, see Vernon Schubel's chapter in the present volume.

40. See Hasluck, *Christianity and Islam Under the Sultans,* vol. 2, 391–402 on the significance of the Forty in Christian and Islamic piety.

41. Literally, "He." In this context, the Arabic third-person singular pronoun refers to God. The articulation of *hū* is employed as a salutation and a close to prayers and other liturgical segments.

42. Mehmet Yaman, *Alevilikte Cem: İnanç, İbadet, Erkân* (Istanbul: Ufuk Reklamcılık ve Matbaacılık, 1998), 64.

43. The fifty-fifth *sūra* of the Qur'an, "al-Raḥmān" describes the topography of paradise. In addition, "al-Raḥmān" is one of the beautiful names of God, and one of two that appears at the beginning of nearly every chapter of the Qur'an.

44. Reference to the fourth qur'anic *sūra* "al-Nisā'."

45. *Macmūʿa* no. 82, MS, Mevlânâ Müzesi, folios 120r–v.

46. See for example, Mehmet Yaman, *Alevilikte Cem: İnanç, İbadet, Erkân.*

47. *Macmūʿa* no. 82, MS, Mevlânâ Müzesi, folios 120r.

48. Gandjeï, ed., *Il Canzoniere di Šāh Ismāʿīl Ḫaṭā'ī,* no. 252.

49. *Beyt* 8 in Memedov, ed., *Shah Ismaiyl Khatai: Asarlari,* vol. 1, 129–131; and Gandjeï, ed., *Il Canzoniere di Šāh Ismāʿīl Ḫaṭā'ī,* no. 7.

50. Gandjeï, ed., *Il Canzoniere di Šāh Ismāʿīl Ḫaṭā'ī,* no. 171.

51. *Macmūʿa* no. *82,* MS, Mevlânâ Müzesi, folios 109r.

52. Ibid., no. 181, folios 32–33.

16

When the Prophet Went on the *Miraç* He Saw a Lion on the Road: The *Miraç* in the Alevi-Bektaşi Tradition

VERNON SCHUBEL

Know for a certainty that ʿAli is the calculation of the proof,
ʿAli is the manifestation of the *tevhit*[1] of the Qur'an,
On the evening when Muḥammad went on the *miraç*
ʿAli was the lion he saw at the door.

He took his ring off of his finger and gave it as a sign,
He saw Reality and ʿAli was its Glory.
He spoke 90,000 words with God (*Hak*),
30,000 were secret, secret with ʿAli.

When there was no earth or sky or throne,
ʿAli established the scales of Truth (*Hakikat*).
ʿAli is the refuge of the wretched Hatayi,
He is the cure for incurable pain.[2]

The above poem above is from the *Miracname* of Shah Ismaʿil Hatayi (d. 1524), the founder of the Safavid dynasty (1501–1722), as it is recorded by the Turkish musicians Ali Rıza and Hüseyin Albayrak on a remarkable compact disc (CD) entitled *Shah Hatayi Deyişleri* (*Devotional Songs of Shah Hatayi*). Assisted by the legendary guitarist and *bağlama* virtuoso Erkan Oğur, *Shah Hatayi Deyişleri* was a top selling folk music CD in Turkey in 2006.[3] Ali Rıza and Hüseyin Albayrak are only two of dozens of popular recording artists producing music from the Alevi-Bektaşi tradition. In fact, Alevi music has long been the central tradition in the thriving *türkü* or folk music scene in Turkey. Moreover, one of the critically important themes in Alevi-Bektaşi music is the *miraç*.

The importance of the *miraç* in Alevi-Bektaşi music is not surprising. Of all the Islamic communities there is probably none for whom the *miraç* narrative figures more prominently than for the Alevi-Bektaşi community of Anatolia. The story of the *miraç* in many ways provides the cosmogonic narrative of the creation of the Alevi community, as it describes the creation of the central ritual of the Alevis known as the *ayin-i cem*.[4]

Although the *ayin-i cem* varies in form and content from region to region, and even village to village, its basic structure remains remarkably consistent. Members of the Alevi community gather together before their *dede*, their *pir*, who is a descendant of ʿAli and Muḥammad. They greet the *pir* and each other and reconcile disputes they might have with any other members of the community. Gathered together, they show the *pir* respect and honor while listening to songs honoring ʿAli, Muḥammad, the Twelve Imams and the *pir*s of their tradition. The *cem* can last for hours. Sometimes people break for conversation. Sometimes the participants share food. Sometimes they discuss religious issues. Often the *cem* culminates in *semah*, in which men and women dance together in a circular movement to songs accompanied by the long-necked lute known as the *bağlama*, showing their devotion to God and Muḥammad in a manner reminiscent of the dance of the Forty (*kırklar*) described in the Alevi *miraç* story.

Not only is the story of the *miraç* the first and longest narrative in *Buyruk*, one of the most important religious texts associated with the Alevi tradition, but the *miraç* makes itself present in other ways as well. Important rituals in the Alevi community, such as the *ikrar* ceremony and the *görge cem*, are themselves ritual reenactments of the *miraç*, and they conclude with the participants greeting each other with the phrase "*miracın kutlu olsun*" (may your *miraç* be blessed).[5]

Shah Ismaʿil's poetry describing the *miraç* is held in high esteem by Alevis.[6] It is performed in the context of the *cem* and has been republished numerous times in both scholarly and popular formats. The 1995 edition of Sefer Aytekin's transliteration of Hacı Bektaş's biography, the *Vilayetname*, which has a picture of Hacı Bektaş on the front cover, also has a medieval miniature of a scene from the *miraç* (with the Prophet's face uncovered) on the back. A similar picture is found on the back of the 2000 republication of Aytekin's transliteration of *Buyruk*. Understanding the *miraç* narrative of the Alevis is crucial to understanding their religious worldview, as the *miraç* narrative is a kind of code laying out in broad strokes the most essential aspects of Alevi thought and practice.[7]

The story of the *miraç* provides the opening narrative in *Buyruk*, one the most important of all Alevi texts. *Buyruk* purports to be a compilation of the esoteric teachings of the sixth imam, Cafer-i Sadık, to his community. Originally composed in Turkish, rather than being a translation from a Persian or Arabic source, its precise historical origins are in dispute, although the prolific twentieth-century Turkish scholar of religion and autodidact Gölpınarlı makes a strong case that it was likely compiled during the reign of Shah Ismaʿil's son Shah Tahmasb (d. 1576).[8]

Buyruk is a living document. There is no single definitive version agreed upon by all Alevis. Numerous versions of the text exist in manuscript form. It is readily available in a variety of inexpensive published versions. Although these versions differ both in length and content, they generally contain a similar collection of narratives, descriptions of ritual, poetry, and explanations of theology.

The central theological claims of *Buyruk* are esoteric (*batıni*) in nature. It argues that there are four doors into Islam: *şeriat, tarikat, marifet*, and *hakikat*. The *şeriat* (Islamic law) is the lowest level of spiritual practice, the beginning of a journey whose goal is mystical union with the Divine. As with many other *batıni* perspectives, *Buyruk* emphasizes the necessity of allegiance to ʿAli, the Shiʿi imams, and their legitimate spiritual successors. From the standpoint of *Buyruk*, ʿAli is the gateway to the esoteric truths of Islam. While the worldview of *Buyruk* is in crucial ways very different from more exoteric understandings of Islam, it nevertheless clearly represents an Islamic perspective rooted in Muslim symbols and concepts.

The following version of the *miraç* narrative is taken from a translation of *Buyruk* into modern Turkish published in 2006 by the Alevi scholar Fuad Bozkurt.[9] He has based his translation on several versions, including the manuscript versions transliterated and published by Sefer Aytekin in the 1950s.[10] My choice of a contemporary Turkish rendering of the text for this volume is in part meant to reflect the dynamic nature and contemporary relevance of this narrative.

The *Cem* of the Forty

One day while Hz.[11] Muḥammad was going on the *miraç*, suddenly a lion (*aslan*) appeared on the road. The lion suddenly began to roar. Muḥammad wondered what to do, when all of a sudden a voice called out, "O Muḥammad, put your ring in the lion's mouth." (Plates 27 and 28).

Muḥammad did as he was told and put his ring in the lion's mouth. As soon as the lion took this sign, he became calm. Muḥammad continued on his way. He arrived at the highest level of the heavens. And there he met with his Friend (*Dost*). He spoke ninety thousand words with him: thirty thousand of these were about the *şeriat* (Islamic law) and were sent down to the believers. The remaining sixty thousand stayed secret with ʿAli.[12]

In paradise (*cennet*), food came to Muḥammad composed of honey, milk, and apples. These foods were especially chosen. For human beings milk and honey each have a hundred benefits. As soon as apple is added to them, a thousand benefits are found in these three foods. The honeycomb represents the essence of the human being; the breast, from which milk comes, is the womb of the mother; and the peel of the apple is a person's skin. God has bestowed affection on milk, love on honey, and friendship on the apple, and He sent all three of these as the food of paradise to humans.

While Muḥammad was returning from the *miraç* he saw a dome in the city. This dome attracted his attention. He walked up to it and came to its door. The people inside were conversing with each other. They were engaged in conversation (*sohbet*). Hz. Muḥammad knocked on the door in order to go inside. A voice came from within:

"Who are you, and why have you come?" it asked.

The Prophet replied, "I am the *peygamber* (Prophet). Open up and let me in. Let me see the beautiful faces of the *erenler*."[13]

From inside they said, "A *peygamber* will not fit among us. Go and perform your prophethood (*peygamberlik*) for your community (*ümmet*)."

At that the Prophet went away from the door. Suddenly a voice came from God (*Tanrı*). It commanded, "O Muḥammad, go back to that door."

According to this command of God, Muḥammad once again went to the door and knocked.

"Who is it?" they asked again from inside.

He replied, "I am the *peygamber.* Open up and let me come in. Let me see your blessed faces."

They said, "There is no room among us for a *peygamber.* Besides, we have no need of a *peygamber.*"

The Envoy (*Elçi*) of God, on hearing these words, again turned away. Before he had gone very far, a voice came from God commanding, "O Muḥammad, go back. Where are you going? Go and open that door."

The Messenger of God again went to the door. He knocked on the door with its knocker. From inside a voice came asking, "Who are you?"

He replied, "I am the son of a poor man who came from nothing. I have come to see you. Is there permission for me to enter?" He didn't tell them that he was the same person returning again.

At that moment the door opened. Those inside said, "Hello, welcome, good fortune to you. Let your coming be blessed." And they called him inside.

In that gathering (*meclis*) the Forty were seated and speaking among themselves. The Prophet said, "The holy door, the door of blessings, has opened."

Saying, "In the name of God, the compassionate, the merciful" (*bismillah-ar-rahman-ar-rahim*), and placing his right foot in first, he stepped inside the door. Inside thirty-nine believing souls were seated. Muḥammad saw when he looked that twenty-two of them were men and seventeen were women. A voice came from the hidden realm saying, "Muḥammad the Prophet has come."

The believers stood up in order to let Muḥammad come in. They all showed him a place for him to sit. Hz. ʿAli was also there. Hz. Muḥammad sat next to Hz. ʿAli, but he did not recognize that he was Hz. ʿAli. Some questions came to Hz. Muḥammad's mind: "Who are they? Are they all on the same level?" He thought to himself, "Who are the greatest among them and who are the least?" He recognized that these questions were not necessary, but he could not help but ask.

"Who are you? What do they call you?" he asked.

Those inside replied, "We are the Forty."

Hz. Muḥammad said, "Well, I cannot understand who among you is greater and who is lesser."

The Forty replied, "Our greatest is great. Our least is also great. The Forty of us are one and each one of us is the Forty."

Hz. Muḥammad asked, "One of you is missing. What happened to that one?"

The Forty said, "That one of us is Selman. He left for the provinces. He went to Iran. But why do you ask? Selman is also here. We consider him to be among us."

Hz. Muḥammad wanted the Forty to demonstrate this, so Hz. ʿAli extended his blessed hand. One of the forty, saying "By your leave," struck ʿAli's arm with a knife. Blood began to flow from Hz. ʿAli's arm. At the same time, blood flowed from the wrists of all the forty. At that same moment, a drop of blood came in through the window and fell amid them. This blood was blood from the arm of Selman, who was out in the provinces. Later one of the Forty bandaged Hz. ʿAli's arm. The blood of all the other Forty stopped flowing.

At that time they saw Selman Farsi coming from Iran. Selman brought one single grape. The Forty took this grape and placed it in front of Hz. Muḥammad.

They said, "O servant of the poor, perform a service and divide this grape among us."

Hz. Muḥammad looked at the situation and thought, "There are forty people and there is only one grape. How can I divide this grape among them?"

At that moment God commanded (the angel) Cebrail[14] saying, "My dear one (Muḥammad) is in difficulty. Go quickly, take a platter of light from heaven and deliver it to him. Let him crush the grape inside the platter and make *şerbet* and give it to the Forty to drink."

Cebrail took a platter made of light (*nur*) and came in front of the Messenger of God. Bringing greetings from God, he placed the platter in front of Muḥammad. He said, "O Muḥammad, turn it into *şerbet*."

Meanwhile the Forty were watching to see what Muḥammad would do with the grape. Suddenly they saw the platter of light appear in front of Hz. Muḥammad. The platter shone like the sun. Muḥammad placed a drop of water in the platter. Then with his finger he crushed the single grape inside the platter of light and made *şerbet*. He placed the platter in front of the Forty.

The Forty drank from the *şerbet*. All of them became as drunk as they were on the Day of Alast when they were first created.[15] They all stood up where they were seated. Saying at once "Ya Allah!" they joined hands with one another. Naked (*üryan büryan*), they entered into *semah* (mystical dance) with each other. Muḥammad also entered into *semah* with them. The Forty's *semah* continued, bathed in a holy light. While doing *semah*, Hz. Muḥammad's blessed turban (*imame*) fell from his head. His turban divided into forty pieces. Each one of the Forty took one piece. They made a robe of each piece and put it on.

Hz. Muḥammad asked them, "Who are the *pirs* and the leaders (*rehberler*)?"

The Forty said, "Our *Pir* is *Shah-i Merdan* (the King of the Heroes) ʿAli, without doubt and without debate, and our guide is Cebrail, peace be upon them (*alleyhissalem*)."

At that moment Hz. Muḥammad realized that Hz. ʿAli was there. Hz. ʿAli walked straight towards Hz. Muḥammad. When Hz. Muḥammad saw Hz. ʿAli coming, he bowed down with respect and affection, and invited Hz. ʿAli to sit next to him. The Forty also joined Muḥammad in bowing in respect in front of Hz. ʿAli, opening the way and showing him a place. At that time Hz. Muḥammad saw his ring upon the finger of Hz. ʿAli.[16]

Analysis of the Narrative

By any standard this is indeed a remarkable story. While from the standpoint of exoteric Islam—especially non-mystical forms of Sunni Islam—it may at first glance appear to be heretical and syncretistic, it is remarkable how deeply Islamic it is in its symbolism and underlying worldview. It maintains clear resonances with the larger Shiʿi and Sufi traditions. Rather than understanding this work as a piece of Turkic folklore, it needs to be seen as an example of a particular kind of *daʿwa,* calling people to affirm their obedience and loyalty to Muḥammad and his family (*ehl-i beyt*).[17]

The narrative begins with the Prophet encountering a lion while on his *miraç.* This symbolism draws heavily on elements of Shiʿi imagery, which are also shared with much of the Sufi tradition. A lion is, of course, a standard symbol for ʿAli, who is commonly known by the name Ḥaydar, the Arabic word for lion. ʿAli is also known by the title "the Lion (*Aslan*) of God."

It is interesting that Muḥammad does not initially recognize the lion as ʿAli. Despite Muḥammad's extraordinary status as the Prophet of God, there are things that he does not immediately know. The Prophet's growing knowledge of hidden things is a crucial and recurring theme in the narrative. And yet throughout the narrative there are many things that the Prophet knows as the result of spiritual guidance from the hidden realm (*gaip*). Muḥammad is clearly in contact with the divine spiritual realm. In moments of crisis he is given explicit guidance either by God or the angel Cebrail. And throughout the story, the Prophet obeys these commands.

In the first instance of these commands, the Prophet is told by a voice to place his ring, which is the sign of the seal of his prophecy, into the mouth of the lion. The Prophet thus foreshadows in the spiritual realm the events of Gadiri Humm, the well where the Prophet declared ʿAli his *mawla* with the famous statement, "I am his *mawla* and he is mine."[18] The terma *mawla* connotes multiple meanings including friend, servant, and master. For the Shiʿa, this is the moment when Muḥammad publicly announces that ʿAli is the Imam and his successor. For the Alevis, the events at Gadiri Humm irreparably divide the Muslim community (*ümmet*) between those who accepted Muḥammad's recognition of ʿAli and became his true followers and those who rejected ʿAli and thus follow the path of apostasy (*murtad*). The passing of the ring affirms that the Prophet's authority is passed on to ʿAli and that those who follow Muḥammad are obligated to follow ʿAli as well.

Having passed his ring of authority to ʿAli, the Prophet continues on to the Divine Throne, where he encounters God, identified here as the Friend (*Dost*). The text affirms the Prophet's role as the giver of exoteric teachings, noting that he speaks ninety thousand words with his Friend, thirty thousand of which concern *şeriat* and are shared with his community, while the remaining sixty thousand stay a secret between him and ʿAli.[19] Thus, Muḥammad is confirmed as the master of the *şeriat* and the exoteric knowledge of Islam, while ʿAli is confirmed as the keeper of the esoteric teachings of Islam. But it should be noted that Muḥammad is also privy to these secrets, so neither he nor ʿAli is said to possess knowledge not available to the other. This scene asserts the intimacy between Muḥammad, ʿAli, and God, and thus the necessity of belief in and devotion to all three.

Before the Prophet descends from his journey, mention is made of the food of paradise (apples, honey, and milk) that are brought to the Prophet. These foods resonate with the ancient Jewish notions of the Promised Land, that is, a land of milk and honey. Interestingly, these are all foods which are produced naturally, without the need of human intervention or the slaughtering of living things. It should be noted that before the actual ritual of the *cem* begins, participants bring food, oftentimes fruit, to be blessed by the spiritual leader or *dede*, and later to be distributed to those in attendance as *lokma*.

As the Prophet descends to earth, he comes across a domed building where the Forty are holding their sacred gathering or *meclis*. The Forty whom Muḥammad encounters there are engaged in *sohbet*. The term *sohbet* (related to the Arabic word *ṣaḥābah*, or companions) literally means "conversation" in Turkish, but it also carries the notion of a gathering of Sufis in the Turkish mystical lexicon. Muḥammad clearly identifies the *meclis* as a gathering of the *erenler*, "those who have attained." The Prophet recognizes the *erenler* as "holy," and he desires to enter the domed building in order to see their beauty.

Although he wishes to enter their gathering, he is initially refused entrance, a common theme in Sufi literature. In a manner reminiscent of many classical Sufi tales, Muḥammad comes to the door three times.[20] Twice he is declined entrance and walks away. Both times he is sent back to the door by the angel Cebrail. Each time he is rejected because he attempts to enter in his role as Prophet (*peygamber*). He finally gains entrance only when he identifies himself not as the *peygamber*, but simply as a *fakir*, "a poor man who came from nothing." Again, the necessity of exhibiting true humility is a common theme in the Sufi tradition. This is often expressed through voluntary poverty, which interestingly is seen as having its origins in the poverty of the Prophet.

Entering on his right foot and reciting the *bismallah* and thus following the proper etiquette (*edep*) for entering a mosque or a tomb, Muḥammad is greeted warmly. Despite the fact that he was denied entrance when he identified himself as the Prophet, at the moment he enters, a voice from the hidden realm (*gaip*) in fact announces him as the *peygamber*. Muḥammad then enters to see a mixed gathering of men and women, mirroring the Alevi *ayin-i cem* ritual itself, which, unlike exoteric communal prayers (*ṣalāt*), takes place in a mixed gender environment where men and women freely interact, especially during the *semah*.

There are only thirty-nine people present. The one who is missing turns out to be Selman-i Farsi, an important companion of the Prophet (especially in Shiʿi narrative), beloved for his devotion to the *ehl-i beyt.* The presence of Selman both roots the *erenler* as actual and specific people from the Prophet's historical time, and also identifies the Forty as a group that includes at least one non-Arab. The membership in the Forty is therefore not limited by either gender or ethnicity. Symbolically, the *cem* could thus be considered an expression of universal humanity, a crucial concept in Alevi thought.

Within this self-professed egalitarian environment of the *cem,* the Prophet is initially concerned with issues of hierarchy, an issue that falls within the realm of exoteric or *zahiri* matters. Although he intuitively recognizes that this concern is inappropriate in this esoteric or *batıni* context, he nevertheless asks out of curiosity, "Who is the greater? Who is the lesser?" They reply that they are all equal, insisting that matters of hierarchy play no role in the *cem.*

Muḥammad's role as *peygamber* initially keeps him out of the *cem* precisely because the *cem* is a place of equality and not a place of hierarchy. The Forty are all equals. They are a community of equals who share all things in common. There is no lesser or greater among them. Their equality is manifested in their shared poverty; they are all *fakirs.* Their poverty is apparent in the fact that Selman returns from his journey to the provinces with only one grape. Part of the purpose of the text is clearly to both contrast and connect the exoteric role of Muḥammad—the *peygamber* and lawgiver who creates a social structure with its necessary boundaries and hierarchies—and the *batıni* role of ʿAli and the *erenler,* who manifest the anti-hierarchical aspects of equality, shared suffering, and communal poverty.

While I hesitate to bring an "*etic*" model to an analysis of this text, Victor Turner's notion of liminality, and its corollary sense of *communitas,* provide an effective interpretive tool for illuminating this narrative. For Turner, all societies maintain both modes of structure and modes of idyllic anti-structure that he calls *communitas.* The realm of structure is, of course, to be found in a model of society based in legal and hierarchical relationships. *Communitas* provides a model of society rooted in unmediated relationships between persons in a homogeneous and unstructured manner.[21]

In his book *The Ritual Process,* Turner lists a number of characteristics of "the liminal," almost all of which coincide with characteristics of the *cem* of the Forty. These include: equality, anonymity, absence of property, absence of status, nakedness, the minimization of sex distinctions, absence of rank, humility, and sacredness.[22] In terms of Turner's *schema,* Muḥammad could be portrayed as a man of structure, providing the necessary elements of hierarchy, rank, and status one needs to build and maintain a community.[23] Conversely, the *erenler* could be said to represent *communitas.* Muḥammad's role as lawgiver is necessary to provide a structure for the *ümmet.* But the *cem* of the *erenler* is, on the other hand, a liminal place of *communitas,* offering an environment of "lowliness and sacredness, of homogeneity and comradeship."[24] The *cem* attempts to transcend the relative egalitarianism that is found in the *şeriat* and approach the mystical equality of the Day of Alast.

Within the liminal context of the *cem,* which takes place in a realm between worlds, the *erenler* are all one, rejecting hierarchy and marks of status. Men and women mix freely. It is indeed a place of humility and sacredness. There is a sense of anonymity about the *cem,* so much so that the Prophet does not even recognize his beloved son-in-law ʿAli as he is seated among the *erenler.* They are all perceived as equal, and on a certain level they have all become one.

The *communitas* of the forty is dramatically demonstrated by the fact that even though they are not all of the *ehl-i beyt,* in a very real sense they all share the same blood. Thus, when ʿAli is cut and bleeds they all bleed. Even Selman bleeds, despite his absence from the *meclis,* and his blood flows into the room to join the blood of the others. Similarly, when ʿAli is bandaged, all their blood stops flowing. On one level they are all ʿAli. Clearly this narrative implies a shared suffering with ʿAli and the *ehl-i beyt,* which is a crucial defining characteristic of the Alevi community, as it is for the exoteric Twelver Shiʿi community. For both of these communities, this shared suffering represents a sign of their individual and collective love for ʿAli.[25]

Muḥammad is given a challenge by the Forty in his role as the "servant of the poor." He is asked to divide the one grape brought by Selman among all of the Forty. Seeing the challenge, God sends Cebrail to help "His beloved." He tells Cebrail to take a platter of light to Muḥammad and to instruct him to crush the grape into *şerbet.*[26] Muḥammad follows those instructions, making the *şerbet* that they all drink and become drunk as they were on the Day of Alast. They all rise naked (*üryan*) and join in *semah,* and Muḥammad joins in as well. The nakedness of the Forty in the narrative is symbolic of rebirth and purity, and is emblematic of the *communitas* of the *erenler.* The Forty become naked as they were on the day of the primordial covenant mentioned in the Qur'an, when all of humanity was asked by God, "Am I not your Lord?" and they responded in the affimative. The *cem* should thus be understood as a symbolic recreation of that Day of Alast.[27]

Perhaps even more importantly, the *cem* narrative ends with the Forty wrapped in robes made from fragments of the Prophet's blessed turban or *imame.* During the *semah* the Prophet's *imame* fell from his head, and is divided into forty pieces, each of the *erenler* taking a piece as his or her robe. By donning these robes, the *erenler* are all cloaked in Muḥammad's clothing. Symbolically the *batıni* community of the *erenler* is now forever bound to the larger exoteric community of Muḥammad.

At one point Muḥammad asks one last question about authority, not who is greater or lesser but instead a more esoteric question: "Who is your *pir* and who is your guide?" They reply: "Our *pir* is Shah-i Merdan ʿAli and our guide is Cebrail." It is only at this point that Muḥammad finally recognizes that the entire time he was seated next to ʿAli and discovers that his ring—the sign of his authority which he gave to the lion on his *miraç*—is on the finger of ʿAli, the Lion of God. Through his participation in the *semah* just as the *erenler* have wrapped themselves in his mantle, Muḥammad affirms the role of ʿAli as *pir*, i.e., the mystical leader of the community.

On one level this is a story about the succession to the Prophet's authority. However, it is expressed not in terms of the exoteric issue of caliphate, which is actually a secondary issue from the *batıni* perspective, but rather the spiritual succession to the Prophet. The question is one of *imamet,* not one of the caliphate. For the Alevis, as for the Shi'a, the great tragedy of early Islam was not simply that the community rejected ʿAli as its political leader.

Much more importantly, the majority of the companions had failed to recognize ʿAli's spiritual rank as the imam. ʿAli's status as the imam is inherent; it is his very nature. Unlike the caliphate, which is a political office chosen by the community, ʿAli cannot be denied the *imamet*, because he is the imam and has been since the beginning of time. When the Prophet dies, his specific prophetic message (*risalet*) ends. But as in exoteric Shiʿism, the leadership of the Prophet, his personal *imamet,* continues through the person of ʿAli and the other imams of the Twelver lineage.

Beyond this, for the Alevis this is also a narrative about the relationship between the exoteric and esoteric paths in Islam. The majority of the companions of the Prophet not only rejected ʿAli as caliph and imam, they also rejected him in his role as *Shah-i Evliya* (King of the "Saints"), thus fundamentally turning away from the presence of Divine light (*nur*) in the world. This rejection is especially crucial for the Alevis, because for them the spiritual authority (*vilayet*) of ʿAli continues beyond the Twelve Imams and is maintained in the *vilayet* of the *erenler.* This is, in fact, the fundamental proposition of *Alevilik* that distinguishes it from Twelver Shiʿism.

The idea of a continuing line of authority through the "saints" is particularly crucial in the absence of the Twelfth Imam. For the Alevis, Bektaşis, and Safaviyyah—along with other similar movements that Hodgson brilliantly identifies as *tarikat* Shiʿism[28]—the *vilayet* of the Imam continues in the *pirs* of their lineages. For the Alevis it incorporates Shah Ismaʿil, Hacı Bektaş, and the lineage of their own religious figures called *dedes*.

The Alevi community regularly affirms the esoteric connection between Muḥammad, ʿAli, and the *erenler* through participation in the *ayin-i cem*, which takes place in the presence of a *dede* and culminates in the *semah* ceremony, performed to the singing of mystical poetry accompanied by the *bağlama.* The ritual recreation of the *cem* of the Forty, which in some communities takes place as often as weekly during most of the year, clearly reflects the importance of this *miraç* narrative in the Alevi community.[29] It is interesting to note that the popularity of the music of the *cem,* which extends far beyond the confines of the Alevi community, has maintained the esoteric motifs of the Alevi worldview as a deeply rooted component of Turkish Islamic culture.

The narrative of the *miraç* in *Buyruk* upholds a vision of the essential symbiosis, common spiritual purpose, and unity of ʿAli, Muḥammad, and God. Muḥammad is the *peygamber* establishing the *şeriat,* the first door of the spiritual path, and providing the exoteric boundaries of Islam. ʿAli is the gateway to the esoteric realm, the *pir* of the *erenler,*[30] and the *Shah-i Evliya.* ʿAli and Muḥammad are intimate with God and each other.

The *miraç* provides the occasion for the integration of the exoteric and esoteric elements of Islam. It presents ʿAli in the role of Muḥammad's spiritual inheritor, establishing the necessity of obedience to him as well as the authority of the *erenler* and their spiritual identity with ʿAli. Furthermore, the basic structure of *cem* and its *semah* are also grounded in the *illo tempore* of the *miraç,* to be established on earth in the form of the *ayin-i cem.* Thus the *miraç* provides the cosmogonic creation myth of the Alevi community, rooting it in the secret (*sır*) of the Divine unity of God, Muḥammad, and ʿAli.

These basic themes of the *miraç* narrative are confirmed and expanded in the narrative that immediately follows it in *Buyruk.* In the subsequent tale, the Prophet returns to his home after the *miraç* and his companions come to see him, asking him to reveal the secret (*sır*) that he learned at the throne of God. He asks them to go and bring ʿAli. He then commands each believer to take another believer as a brother, thus establishing the Alevi tradition of *musahıplık,* in which Alevis similarly form brotherly relationships with other members of the community.

Then he draws ʿAli to his breast. They put on the same shirt so that their two heads appear to be connected to one body. He then recites these words: "His flesh is my flesh, His body is my body, his spirit is my spirit, his life is my life."[31] Some of his companions who witness this occurrence are troubled by these words. They become jealous of ʿAli, thinking to themselves, "Look, first he gives him his daughter and now he says 'he is my brother.'" According to one version of *Buyruk,* at that moment "their faith was broken and they became unbelievers. They became apostates and enemies of the family of ʿAli."[32] This call for the true faithful to recognize the necessity of devotion to both ʿAli and Muḥammad set into motion a definitive split within the community, dividing it from that point on between those who accepted the authority of ʿAli and those who rejected him out of jealousy, turning instead to the path of apostasy (*murtad*).

The rejection of ʿAli is not merely political. According to Alevi thought, it is the rejection of the esoteric path of Islam, and thus, from the standpoint of *Buyruk,* tantamount to the rejection of Islam itself. As one version puts it:

> From Adam until the coming of the seal of the Prophets, the rules of conduct (*erkan*) of the path (*yol*) were nonexistent. Then Muḥammad and ʿAli Murtaza came as blessing to everyone and made the religion (*din*) apparent. They established the rules of conduct. The *şeriat* is *zahir* (exoteric). The *tarikat* and *hakikat* are secret. The *şeriat* is Muḥammad's. The *tarikat* and *hakikat* are a matter for ʿAli.[33]

The teaching of *Buyruk* is that Islam requires following a true *pir,* one who knows and understands not only *şeriat* but also the mysteries of *tarikat, marifet,* and *hakikat*. And those *pirs* are to be found only among the true followers of both Muḥammad and ʿAli. To reject one is to reject the other, and the true path is the path of both ʿAli and Muḥammad. For the Alevis, this lesson forms the core message of the Prophet Muḥammad's *miraç*.

Notes

1. *Tevhit* refers to the concept of unity, particularly the unity of God, which in the Alevi tradition contains a strong notion of mystical union. Most of the technical Islamic terms in this chapter are rendered in modern Turkish; thus, for example, I am using *tevhit* rather than *tawḥīd* to refer to the concept of the unity of God, *hakikat* rather than *haqīqat* for ultimate reality, and *şeriat* rather than *sharīʿah* for Islamic law. The sources I used for this chapter were largely contemporary Alevi sources written in modern Turkish. As this is a living tradition that conducts its rituals in Turkish, I decided to use the terms that are actually used by the community rather than replace them with transliterated Arabic words from which they were derived. For some words, I did use the Arabic transliteration, including the now common and standard English spellings of Shiʿa and Shiʿi, and Imam ʿAli (as opposed to the commonplace Turkish name Ali). I have also maintained the standard English spelling of "Shah" as a title as in Shah Hatayi and Shah-i Merdan. Similarly I use "Imam" rather than "İmam." For Muḥammad, I am following the convention observed in this volume as a whole.

2. Ali Rıza and Hüseyin Albayrak, *Shah Hatayi Deyişleri*, Kalan Music, 2006.

3. It is, in fact, the second CD of music by Ali Rıza and Hüseyin Albayrak. Their first, *Batini Nefes*, was also very well received. It was often heard playing from the shops in the town of Hacıbektaş, which I visited in 2004.

4. The *ayin-i cem* is a common term for the gathering of Alevis for ritual practices. The term "*cem*" means a gathering or congregation and is commonly used to refer to any ritual and devotional gathering of Alevis. I will use the term *cem* in this way throughout the chapter.

5. Esat Korkmaz, *Alevilik Bektaşi Terimleri Sözlüğü* (Istanbul: Anahtar Kıtaplar Yayınevi, 2005), 486.

6. For a discussion of poetry attributed to Shah Ismaʿil, see the chapter by Amelia Gallagher in the present volume.

7. For more thorough discussions of Alevi ritual and world view, see Tord Olsson, Elizabeth Özdalga, Catherine Raudevere, eds. *Alevi Identity* (Istanbul: Swedish Research Institute in Istanbul, 1998).

8. Abdülbâki Gölpınarlı, *Tarih Boyunca İslam Mezhepleri ve Şiilik* (Istanbul: Der Yayınları, 2003), 178–179.

9. Fuat Bozkurt, *Buyruk; Imam Cafer-i Sadık Buyruğu* (Istanbul: Kapı Yayınları, 2006).

10. Sefer Aytekin, *Buyruk*, (Ankara: Ayıldız Yayınları, 2000).

11. Hz. is the common abbreviation for the honorific title *Hazreti* in a genitive construct that is often affixed before a holy person's name; for example Hazreti ʿAli, Hazreti Muḥammad, and Hazreti Pir, as well as a common way of referring to Hacı Bektaş Veli.

12. Most versions of *Buyruk* identify the larger portion of the conversation as secret. Interestingly, this is not the case in the poem quoted at the beginning of this chapter, where it is the thirty thousand words that are secret and the sixty thousand that refer to law.

13. The term *erenler* literally means "those who have attained"; it is the most common word in the Turkish Alevi tradition for identifying Sufi "saints" or *evliyalar*—literally, "the friends." I hesitate to use the word "saint," as it is a Christian term. The closest word in Arabic for a Sufi "saint" is *walī*, meaning "friend" or, more specifically, a friend of God. The plural is *awliyā'*, hence *evliya* in Turkish.

14. This is the angel known in English as Gabriel.

15. This allusion to Q 7:172 refers to the day when all of humanity was brought forth from the loins of humanity and asked by God, "Am I not your Lord?" (*alastu bi-rabbikum*). This is a crucial concept, especially in the mystical traditions of Islam, as it demonstrates the equality of all souls before God and the innate tendency of all of humanity to submit to God. As shall become clear, the *cem* is in many ways a recreation of the Day of Alast.

16. Bozkurt, *Buyruk*, 13–18.

17. There is in my mind no reason to draw a clear distinction between vernacular expressions of Islam, often referred to a "popular Islam," and "Islamic orthodoxy," which is often identified with Islamic *şeriat*. Such a dichotomy, I believe, provides a distorted view of Islam, identifying obedience to the *şeriat* not as a manifestation of Islamic piety but instead as Islamic piety itself. This view is particularly problematic when dealing with communities like the Alevis, who have developed their own vernacular forms of devotion (*'ibadat*) that differ dramatically from *şeriat* practice. If Islam is *şeriat*, then the Alevis are clearly not Muslims. But the majority of Alevis, in fact, consider themselves to be Muslim. They sing a version of the first *shahadah* (*Hakk La illaha ilallah*) in the *cem*. And they claim to be the true followers of the esoteric teachings of Muḥammad and ʿAli. As devotees of God, Muḥammad, and ʿAli, I believe they have to be seen as Muslims. For the Alevis true Islam is rooted in *ahlak* (good morals) rather than *şeriat*, and they frequently quote ḥadīths from the Prophet affirming their position. Thus they reject the *şeriat* while affirming Islam. I believe it is crucial that we approach the study of the Alevis recognizing and accepting their connection to the larger *ümmet* of Islam, rather than seeing them as simply a form of pre-Islamic practice draped in Muslim clothing. To do otherwise is to do a disservice to their tradition.

18. The incident at Gadiri Humm is considered crucial both by Shʿi Muslims, who see this event as confirming ʿAli's status as the Imam, and by many Sufi groups that frequently call ʿAli "Mawla ʿAli." For a full account see Shaykh al-Mufid, *Kitab al-Irshad: The Book of Guidance into the Lives of the Twelve Imams*, trans. I. K. A. Howard (Qum, Iran: Ansariyan, n.d.), 123–126.

19. Bozkurt notes that this could be read as identifying God and ʿAli, but it should be noted that nowhere in the text is such an explicit identification made. While such identification may be implied, the text always remains ambiguous. There is, however, a similar identification implied between ʿAli and Muḥammad, which is in fact stated much more clearly later in *Buyruk*.

20. This is of course most famously found in the story associated with Rumi about the man who approaches the door of his beloved and twice answers the question "Who is there?" by saying "I." On the third time he answers "Thou," and the door opens. One runs into this theme in a variety of contexts. As in Zen stories, refusing entrance is a way of testing the sincerity of disciples. The Alevi *pir* and poet Pir Sultan Abdal initially rejected his disciple Hızr Paşa warning him that he would eventually betray him to the Sultan. Ultimately he did. I once met a Sufi *murid* in Pakistan who described how he was rejected by a particular *pir* several times until asked to undergo a trial of faith by jumping into a flooded canal. He did so, and emerged perfectly dry. The *pir* then told him that he was destined to be the follower of another *pir* and told him where to meet him.

21. Victor Turner, *The Ritual Process* (Ithaca, N.Y.: Cornell University Press, 1977), 132.

22. Ibid., 106.

23. Of course, there are elements of egalitarianism even in the exoteric message of the Prophet, which calls for the spiritual equality of all believers. However, that egalitarianism is but a reflection of the absolute *communitas* of the Day of Alast and the Day of Resurrection (*qiyamet*), which are so clearly referenced in this and other mystical narratives.

24. Turner, *The Ritual Process*, 96.

25. In my opinion, the term "Alevi" should not be misunderstood to imply a community of those who worship ʿAli—as its detractors assert—but rather a community of those who are united in their love and devotion for ʿAli.

26. Interestingly, when Cebrail arrives only the Prophet can see the angel; the rest only see the platter of light shining like the sun. This follows the general Islamic understanding that only prophets can recognize the presence of angels.

27. I hesitate to translate this line about the Forty becoming drunk and naked, as for centuries the detractors of the Alevi community have accused the Alevis of drinking wine in the *cem* and (more perversely) wrongly interpreted the fraternizing of men and women in the *cem* as evidence of sexual licentiousness. First, while wine is ritually consumed in small quantities in some *cem evis*, they are in the minority. Most Alevis do not consume alcohol in the *cem*. Most importantly, the ritual of the *ayin-i cem* that culminates in *semah* is not performed naked. In fact, in my experience the earthly *cem* is in no way a sexually charged arena. From the Alevi perspective, men and women can freely associate precisely because they are a spiritual community.

28. Marshall Hodgson, *The Venture of Islam* (Chicago: University of Chicago Press, 1977), 2: 493.

29. The *ayin-i cem* is performed in many Alevi communities every Thursday night. As there is no centralized version of Alevi Islam, the actual details of the ritual vary from village to village. In many villages it is not performed in the spring and summer, because agricultural work is seen itself as a form of devotion. In urban environments, the content of the *cem* takes on elements of the villages from which the *dede* or the congregants have migrated. The culmination of the *cem* in *semah,* in which both men and women participate, has clear resonance with the *miraç* narrative.

30. This of course affirms the famous hadith in which Muḥammad refers to himself as the city of knowledge and names ʿAli as its gate.

31. Aytekin, *Buyruk*, 122.

32. Ibid.

33. Ibid. Interestingly, in this early version of *Buyruk*, only three of the classical four gates are mentioned; *marifet* (gnosis) is not listed.

Bibliography

This bibliography contains a list of the published books and articles that appear in the notes sections of all the chapters in this volume. With few exceptions, it does not contain entries for unpublished works that are mentioned in the notes, such as unpublished original manuscripts, nor does it contain entries for encyclopedia articles. Those readers who are interested in the details of such works are directed to consult the notes sections of individual chapters.

ʿAbd al-Muṭṭalib, Rifʿat Fawzī. *Aḥādīth al-isrā' wa al-mi'rāj: Dirāsa tawthīqiyya.* Cairo: Maktabat al-Khānjī, 1400/1980.

ʿAbd al-Raḥmān, ʿĀ'isha. *Islamic Book of the Dead: A Collection of Hadiths on the Fire & the Garden.* Wood Dalling and San Francisco: Diwan Press, 1977.

ʿAbd al-Razzāq b. Ḥammām al-Himyarī. *Tafsīr al-Qur'ān.* 3 vols. in 4. Riyadh: Maktabat al-Rushd, 1989.

Abdul Karim, Munshi, and Ahmad Sharif. *A Descriptive Catalogue of Bengali Manuscripts in Munshi Abdul Karim's Collection.* Dacca: Asiatic Society of Pakistan, 1960.

Abel, Armand. "L'apocalypse de Balūqīya." In *Eschatologie et cosmologie,* ed. Armand et al. Brussels: Éditions de l'Institut de Sociologie, Université Libre de Bruxelles, 1969.

Abū Dāwūd, Sulaymān b. al-Ashʿath al-Sijistānī. *Sunan.* 5 vols. Cairo: Dār al-ḥadīth, 1999.

Abū Yaʿlā. *Musnad.* 16 vols. Beirut: Dār al-Ma'mūn li-'l-turāth, 1984–1992.

Adang, Camilla. *Muslim Writers on Judaism and the Hebrew Bible: From Ibn Rabban to Ibn Hazm.* Leiden: E. J. Brill, 1996.

Aḥmedī. *Cemşîd ü Ḫurşîd.* Ed. Mehmet Akalın. Ankara: Atatürk Üniversitesi Yayınları, 1975.

———. *İskender-nāme: İnceleme, Tıpkıbasım.* Ed. İsmail Ünver. Ankara: Türk Dil Kurumu Yayınları, 1983.

al-ʿAjlūnī, Ismāʿīl b. Muḥammad al-Jarrāḥī. *Kashf al-Khafā' wa-muzīl al-ilbās ʿammā ishtahara min al-aḥādīth ʿalā alsinat al-nās.* 2 vols. Aleppo: Maktabat al-Turāth al-Islāmī, 1973.

Akar, Metin, *Türk Edebiyatında Manzum Mi'râc-Nâmeler.* Ankara: Kültür ve Turizm Bakanlığı Yayınları, 1987.

Akdoğan, Yaşar. "Mi'rac, Mi'rac-nâme ve Ahmedi'nin bilinmeyen Mi'râc-nâmesi." *Osmanlı Araştırmaları* 9 (1989): 263–310.

Alexander, P., trans. "3 (Hebrew Apocalypse of) Enoch (Fifth–Sixth Century A. D.): A New Translation and Introduction." In *The Old Testament Pseudepigrapha,* vol. 1, *Apocalyptic Literature and Testaments,* ed. James H. Charlesworth. New York: Doubleday, 1983.

Alexandrin, Elizabeth. "The 'Sphere of *Walāyah*': Ismāʿīlī *Ta'wīl* in Practice according to al-Mu'ayyad (d. ca. 1078 C.E.)." Ph.D. diss., McGill University, 2006.

Ali, Abdullah Yusuf, ed. and trans. *The Qur'an: Text, Translation and Commentary.* 4th U.S. ed. Elmhurst: Tahrike Tarsile Qur'an, 2002.

Ali, Ahmed. *Al-Qur'ān,* 5th ed. Princeton, N.J.: Princeton University Press, 1994.

Altıparmak Meḥmed. *Delā'il-i nübuvvet-i Muḥammedī ve şemā'il-i fütuvvet-i Aḥmedī* [translation of Muʿīn-i Miskīn, Maʿāriğ-i nubuwwa]. Istanbul, 1257/1841.

Amir-Moezzi, Mohammad Ali. *The Divine Guide in Early Shiʿism: The Sources of Esotericism in Islam.* Trans. David Streight. Albany: State University of New York Press, 1994.

———. *Le Guide divin dans le shi'isme originel.* Lagrasse: Verdier, 1992.

———. "L'Imām dans le ciel: Ascension et initiation (aspects de l'imāmologie duodécimaine)." In *Le Voyage initiatique en terre d'Islam*, ed. Amir-Moezzi. Louvain: Peeters, 1996.

———. *La religion discrète: croyances et pratiques spirituelles dans l'islam shiʿite.* Paris: Librarie Philosophique J. Vrin, 2006.

Amir-Moezzi, Mohammad Ali, ed. *Le Voyage initiatique en terre d'Islam: ascensions célestes et itinéraires spirituels.* Louvain: Peeters, 1996.

Amitai, Reuven. "The Conversion of Tegüder Ilkhan to Islam." *Jerusalem Studies in Arabic and Islam* 25 (2001): 15–43.

Andrae, Tor. *Die person Muhammeds in Lehre und Glauben seiner Gemeinde.* Stockholm: Kungl. boktryckeriet. P. A. Norstedt & Söner, 1918.

Andrews, Peter A. *Ethnic Groups in the Republic of Turkey.* Wiesbaden: Dr. Ludwig Reichert Verlag, 1989.

Andrews, Walter G. *An Introduction to Ottoman Poetry.* Minneapolis: Bibliotheca Islamica, 1976.

———. *Poetry's Voice, Society's Song: Ottoman Lyric Poetry.* Seattle: University of Washington Press, 1985.

Andrews, Walter G., Najaat Black, and Mehmet Kalpaklı. *Ottoman Lyric Poetry: An Anthology.* Seattle: University of Washington Press, 2006.

The Apocalypse of Abraham. Trans. R. Rubinkiewicz and H. G. Hunt. In *The Old Testament Pseudepigrapha.* Vol. 1, *Apocalyptic Literature and Testaments,* ed. James H. Charlesworth. New York: Doubleday, 1983.

Arberry, A. J. "The Divine Colloquy in Islam." *The Bulletin of the John Rylands Library* (1956–1957): 18–44.

———, trans. *Muslim Saints and Mystics: Episodes from the Tadhkirat al-Auliya' ("Memorial of the Saints") by Farid al-Din Attar.* London: Routledge and Kegan Paul, 1966; repr. ed., 1979.

Arnold, Thomas. *Painting in Islam: A Study of the Place of Pictorial Art in Muslim Culture.* New York: Dover, 1965.

Arsh Grigori. *He Albania Kai he Epiros sta tele tou ih' Kai stis arches tou ith' aiona: Ta dytikobalkanika pasalikia tes Othimanikes Autokratorias.* [Albania and Epirius in the End of the Eighteeenth and the Begining of the Nineteenth Century: The Pashaliks of the Ottoman Empire in the Western Balkans]. Trans (into Greek) Antonia Dialla. Athens: Gutenberg, 1994.

Arslanoğlu, İbrahim. *Şah İsmail Hatayî: Divan, Dehnâme, Nasihatnâme ve Anadolu Hatayîleri.* Istanbul: Der Yayınevi, 1992.

Āşıḳ Paşa-yı Veli. *Garib-nâme: Tıpkıbasım, Karşılaştırmalı Metin ve Aktarma.* Ed. Kemal Yavuz. 4 vols. Istanbul: Türk Dil Kurumu, 2000.

Asín Palacios, Miguel. *La escatología musulmana en la Divina Comedia.* Madrid: Real Academia Española, 1919.

ʿAṭāī [Nev'îzade], *Ẕeyl-i şaqā'iq [ḥadā'iqu l-ḥaqā'iq fī tekmileti şaqā'iq].* Istanbul: Maṭbaʿa-i ʿĀmire, 1268/1851–1852.

Ateş, Ahmet, ed. *Süleyman Çelebi: Vesîletü'n-necât.* Ankara: Türk Tarih Kurumu, 1954.

ʿAṭṭār, Farīd al-Dīn Nīshāpūrī. *Tadhkirat al-awliyā'.* Ed. Muḥammad Istiʿlāmī. Repr. ed. Tehran: Kitābkhāna-i Millī-i Īrān, 1382/2003–2004.

Avicenna (Ibn Sīnā). "Ḥayy ibn Yaqẓān." In *Ḥayy ibn Yaqẓān li ibn Sīnā wa ibn Tufayl wa al-Suhrawardī,* ed. Aḥmad Amīn. Cairo: Dār al-maʿārif, 1959.

———. *Miʿrājnāma* (The Book of Ascension), with a revised text by Shamsuddīn Ibrāhīm Abarqūhī. Ed. N. Māyel Heravī. Mashhad: The Islamic Research Foundation, Āstān-i Quds-i Rezavī, 1986.

———. *al-Shifā', al-Ilāhiyyāt* [selections:] "The Healing, Metaphysics." In *Philosophy in the Middle Ages,* 2nd ed. Ed. Arthur Hyman and James J. Walsh. Indianapolis: Hackett, 1973.

Aynur, Hatice, Müjgân Çakır, and Hanife Koncu, eds. *Sözde ve anlamda farklılaşma: Sebk-i Hindî; 29 Nisan 2005: Bildiriler.* Istanbul: Turkuaz, 2005.

Aytekin, Sefer, ed. *Buyruk*. Ankara: Emek Basım Yayınevi, 1958; Ankara: Ayıldız Yayınları, 2000.

El-ʿAẓma, Nazeer. *Al-Miʿrāj wa-i-razm al-ṣūfī*. Beirut: Dār al-Bāḥith, 1982.

Babayan, Kathryn. *Mystics, Monarchs, and Messiahs: Cultural Landscapes of Early Modern Iran*. Cambridge, Mass.: Harvard University Press, 2002.

———. "The Safavid Synthesis: From Qizilbash Islam to Imamite Shiʿism." *Iranian Studies* 27 (1994): 135–161.

Bābāzāda, Shahlā. *Ta'rīkh-i Chāp dar Īrān*. Tehran: Kitābkhāna-i Ṭahūrī, 1378/1988.

Bābur (Emperor of Hindustan). *The Bábar-Náma*. Ed. Annette Beveridge. London: Printed for the trustees of the "E.J.W. Gibb Memorial" and published by Messrs. Luzac, 1971.

———. *Babur-nāme (Babur'un Hatıratı)*. Ed. Reşit Rahmeti Arat. Ankara: Kültür ve Turizm Bakanlığı Yayınları, 1985.

Bacher, Wilhelm. *Ein hebräisch-persisches Wörterbuch aus dem vierzehnten Jahrhundert*. Strassburg: Karl Trübner, 1900.

———. "Ein hebräisch-persisches Wörterbuch aus dem 15. Jahrhundert." *Zeitschrift für die alttestamentliche Wissenschaft* 16 (1896): 201–247.

al-Baghawī, Abū Muḥammad al-Ḥusayn b. Masʿūd. *Maṣābīḥ al-sunna*. Ed. Yūsuf ʿAbd al-Raḥmān al-Marʿashlī, Muḥammad Salīm Ibrāhīm Samāra, and Jamāl Ḥamdī al-Dhahabī. 4 vols. Beirut: Dār al-Ma ʿrifa, 1407/1987.

Bahārī, Ebādollah. *Bihzād: Master of Persian Painting*. London: I. B. Tauris, 1996.

Bal, Mieke. *A Mieke Bal Reader*. Chicago: University of Chicago Press, 2006.

———. "Narration and Focalization." In *On Story-Telling Essays in Narratology*, ed. David Jobling. Sonoma, Calif.: Polebridge Press, 1991.

———. *Narratology: Introduction to the Theory of Narrative*. Trans. Christine van Boheemen. Toronto: University of Toronto Press, 1985.

Baldick, Julian. *Imaginary Muslims: The Uwaysi Sufis of Central Asia*. New York: New York University Press, 1993.

Bandyopadhyay, Haricharan. *Baṅgīya Śabdakoṣa*. New Delhi: Sahitya Academy, 1996.

Bāqī, *Maʿālimü l-yaqīn fi sīrat seyyidi l-mürselīn* [also known as *Mevahib-i ledüniye tercümesi*]. Istanbul: Maṭbaʿa-i ʿĀmire, 1261/1845.

Bar-Asher, M. M. and A. Kofsky. "L'ascension céleste du gnostique Nuṣayrite et le voyage nocturne du prophète Muḥammad." In *Le Voyage initiatique en terre d'Islam*, ed. Amir-Moezzi.

Bartholomae, Christian. *Altiranisches Wörterbuch*. Strassburg: K. J. Trübner, 1904; repr. ed., Berlin: Walter de Gruyter, 1979.

al-Bayhaqī, Abū Bakr Aḥmad b. Ḥusayn. *Dalā'il al-nubuwwa wa maʿrifat aḥwāl ṣāḥib al-sharīʿa*. Ed. ʿAbd al-Muʿṭī Amīn Qalʿajī. 7 vols. Beirut: Dār al-kutub al-ʿilmiyya, 1985.

Bazin, Louis, et al. *Philologiae Turcicae Fundamenta*. Wiesbaden: Franz Steiner, 1964.

Bekkum, Wout Jac. van, ed. and trans. *A Hebrew Alexander Romance According to MS Héb. 671.5 Paris, Bibliothèque Nationale*. Groningen: Styx, 1994.

———. *A Hebrew Alexander Romance According to MS London, Jews' College, no. 145*. Louvain: Peeters and Departement Oriëntalistiek, 1992.

Bencheikh, Jamel Eddine. *Le voyage nocturne de Mahomet*. Paris: Imprimerie Nationale, 1988.

Berkey, Jonathan P. *Popular Preaching and Religious Authority in the Medieval Islamic Near East*. Seattle: University of Washington Press, 2001.

Besson, Gisèle, and Michèle Brossard-Dandré, eds. and trans. *Le livre de l'échelle de Mahomet (Liber Scale Machometi): Édition nouvelle*. Paris: Le Livre de Poche, 1991.

Birge, John Kingsley. *The Bektashi Order of Dervishes*. Hartford: Hartford Seminary, 1937.

Birnbaum, Eleazar. "The Questing Mind: Katib Chelebi, 1609-1657: A Chapter in Ottoman Intellectual History." In *Corolla Torontonensis: Festschrift for Ronald Morton Smith*, ed. E. Robbins, Stella Sandahl. Toronto: TSAR, 1994.

Biswas, Sailendra. *Samsad Bengali-English Dictionary*. Kolkata: Sahitya Samsad, 1994.

Blair, Sheila. "The Coinage of the Later Ilkhanids: A Typological Analysis." *Journal of the Economic and Social History of the Orient* 26 (1983): 285–317.

———. *A Compendium of Chronicles: Rashid al-Din's Illustrated History of the World, The Nasser D. Khalili Collection of Islamic Art,* vol. 27., ed. Julian Raby. London: Nour Foundation in association with Azimuth Editions and Oxford University Press, 1995.

———. "The Development of the Illustrated Book in Iran." *Muqarnas* 10 (1993): 266–74.

———. "The Mongol Capital of Sulṭāniyya, 'The Imperial.'" *Iran* 24 (1986): 139–152.

———. "The Religious Art of the Ilkhanids." In *The Legacy of Genghis Khan: Courtly Art and Culture in Western Asia,* ed. Linda Komaroff and Stefano Carboni. New York: Metropolitan Museum of Art, 2003.

Blair, Sheila, and Jonathan Bloom. *Islamic Arts.* London: Phaidon Press, 1997.

Blochet, Edgar. *Catalogue des manuscrits turcs.* 2 vols. Paris: Bibliothèque nationale de France, 1932–1933.

———. "Études sur l'histoire religieuse de l'Iran, II: L'ascension au ciel du prophète Mohammed." *Revue de l'histoire des religions* 40 (1899): 1–25, 203–236.

Bodrogligeti, András J. E. "Yasavī Ideology in Muḥammad Shaybānī Khān's Vision of an Uzbek Islamic Empire." *Journal of Turkish Studies* 18 (1994): 41–57.

Böwering, Gerhard. "From the Word of God to the Vision of God: Muḥammad's Heavenly Journey in Classical Ṣūfī Qur'ān Commentary." In *Le Voyage initiatique en terre d'Islam,* ed. Amir-Moezzi.

———. *The Mystical Vision of Existence in Classical Islam.* Berlin and New York: de Gruyter, 1980.

Bozkurt, Fuat. *Buyruk: Imam Cafer-i Sadık Buyruğu.* Istanbul: Kapı Yayınları, 2006.

Brann, Ross. *The Compunctious Poet: Cultural Ambiguity and Hebrew Poetry in Muslim Spain.* Baltimore: Johns Hopkins University Press, 1991.

———. *Power in the Portrayal: Representations of Jews and Muslims in Eleventh- and Twelfth-Century Islamic Spain.* Princeton, N.J.: Princeton University Press, 2002.

Brelles, Aristoteles. "Epeirotika stichoplakia: Eisagoge-keimeno-lexilogio [Short rhymed verses from Jannina. Introduction, text, vocabulary]." Ph.D. diss., University of Jannina, 1980.

Brockelmann, Carl. 1949. *Geschichte der Arabischen Literatur.* 2 vols. and 2 supplements. Leiden: E. J. Brill, 1949.

Bruner, Jerome. "The Narrative Construction of Reality." *Critical Inquiry* 18 (Autumn 1991): 1–21.

Buber, Martin. *Tales of the Hasidim,* trans. Olga Marx, 2 books in 1. New York: Schocken Books, 1947; repr. ed., 1991.

al-Bukhārī, Muḥammad b. Ismāʿīl. *Kitāb Rafʿ al-Yadayn fī'l-Ṣalāh.* Ed. Badīʿ al-Dīn al-Rāshidī. Beirut: Dār Ibn Ḥazm, 1417/1996.

———. *Ṣaḥīḥ.* Beirut: Dār al-kutub al-ʿilmiyya, n.d.

———. *Ṣaḥīḥ Bukhārī.* Ed. Muḥammad Nizār Tamīm and Haytham Nizār Tamīm. Beirut: Sharikhat Dār al-Arqām b. Abī Arqām, n.d.

Bulliet, Richard. "Conversion to Islam and the Emergence of a Muslim Society in Iran." In *Conversion to Islam,*ed. Nehemia Levtzion. New York: Holmes and Meier, 1979.

———. *Conversion to Islam in the Medieval Period: An Essay in Quantitative History.* Cambridge, Mass.: Harvard University Press, 1979.

Busse, Heribert. "Jerusalem in the Story of Muḥammad's Night Journey and Ascension." *Jerusalem Studies in Arabic and Islam* 14 (1991): 1–40.

Caferoğlu, Ahmet. "La littérature turque de l'époque des Karakhanides." In *Philologiae Turcicae Fundamenta,* ed. Louis Bazin et al., vol. 2. Wiesbaden: Franz Steiner, 1964

Caitanya Caritāmṛta of Kṛṣṇadāsa Kavirāja. Trans. Edward C. Dimock, Jr., ed. Tony K. Stewart. Cambridge, Mass.: Harvard University Press, 1999.

Calmard, Jean. "Le chiisme imamite sous les Ilkhans." In *L'Iran face à la domination mongole,* ed. Denise Aigle. Tehran: Institut Français de Recherche en Iran, 1997.

———. "Les rituels shiites et le pouvoir: L'imposition du shiisme safavide; eulogies et malédic-

tions canoniques." In *Études Safavides*, ed. Jean Calmard. Tehran: Institut Français de Recherche en Iran, 1993.
———. *Études Safavides*. Paris: Institut Français de Recherche en Iran, 1993.
Çelebi, Süleyman. *The Mevlidi Sherif.* Trans. F. Lyman MacCallum. London: J. Murray, 1943 (repr. edn. 1957).
———. *Vesîletü'n-Necât: Mevlid.* Ed. Ahmet Ateş. Ankara: Türk Tarih Kurumu, 1954.
Cerulli, Enrico. *Il "Libro della scala" e la questione delle fonti arabospagnole della Divina commedia.* Vatican: Biblioteca Apostolica Vaticana, 1949.
Charlesworth, James H., ed. *The Old Testament Pseudepigrapha.* Vol. 1, *Apocalyptic Literature and Testaments.* New York: Doubleday, 1983.
Chatman, Seymour. *Story and Discourse: Narrative Structure in Fiction and Film.* Ithaca, N.Y.: Cornell University Press, 1978.
Chelkowski, Peter. "Narrative Painting and Painting Recitation in Qajar Iran." *Muqarnas* 6 (1989): 98–111.
———. "Popular Arts: Patronage and Piety." In *Royal Persian Paintings: The Qajar Epoch, 1785–1925,* ed. Layla Diba and Maryam Ekhtiar. London: I. B. Tauris, 1998.
Chittick, William L. *The Sufi Path of Love: The Spiritual Teachings of Rumi.* Albany: State University of New York, 1983.
Choksy, Jamsheed K. *Conflict and Cooperation: Zoroastrian Subalterns and Muslim Elites in Medieval Iranian Society.* New York: Columbia University Press, 1977.
Cisneros, Fernando. *El Libro del viaje nocturno y la ascensión del Profeta.* México: El Colegio de México, 1998.
Colby, Frederick. "Constructing an Islamic Ascension Narrative: The Interplay of Official and Popular Culture in Pseudo-Ibn ʿAbbās." Ph.D. diss., Duke University, 2002.
———. *Narrating Muḥammad's Night Journey: Tracing the Development of the Ibn ʿAbbās Ascension Discourse.* Albany: State University of New York Press, 2008.
Collins, John J. *The Apocalyptic Imagination: An Introduction to the Jewish Matrix of Christianity.* New York: Crossroad, 1989.
———. "Towards the Morphology of the Genre." In "Apocalypse: The Morphology of a Genre," ed. John J. Collins, special issue, *Semeia* 14 (1979): 5–9.
Collins, Roger. *Early Medieval Spain: Unity in Diversity, 400–1000.* New York: St. Martin's Press, 1983.
Conklin Akbari, Suzanne. "The Rhetoric of Antichrist in Western Lives of Muhammad." *Islam and Christian-Muslim Relations* 8/3 (1997): 281–293.
Cook, Michael. *Commanding Right and Forbidding Wrong in Islamic Thought.* Cambridge: Cambridge University Press, 2000.
Coope, Jessica. *The Martyrs of Córdoba: Community and Family Conflict in an Age of Mass Conversion.* Lincoln: University of Nebraska Press, 1995.
Corbin, Henri. *Avicenna and the Visionary Recital.* Trans. Willard Trask. Princeton, N.J.: Bollingen, 1960.
———. *Face de Dieu, face de l'homme.* Paris: Flammarion, 1983.
———. "L'Histoire secrète des prophètes, d'après le *Kitab Asas al-Ta'wil* de Qazi No'man." In *Itinéraire d'un enseignement,* ed. Christian Jambet. Tehran and Paris: Bibliothèque Iranienne, 1993.
Dalley, Stephanie. "Gilgamesh in the Arabian Nights." *Journal of the Royal Asiatic Society,* ser. 3, vol. 1, no. 1 (1991): 1–17.
———. "The Tale of Bulūqiyā and the *Alexander Romance* in Jewish and Sufi Mystical Circles." In *Tracing the Threads: Studies in the Vitality of Jewish Pseudepigrapha,* ed. John C. Reeves. Altanta: Scholars Press, 1994.
Dana, Joseph. *Poetics of Medieval Hebrew Literature According to Moshe ibn Ezra* [Hebrew]. Jerusalem: Dvir, 1982.
Dankoff, Robert. *Evliya Çelebi: An Ottoman Mentality.* Leiden: E. J. Brill, 2004.
Danon, M. A. "Un interrogatoire d'hérétiques musulmans (1619)." *Journal Asiatique* 17 (1921): 280–293.

Darîr, Mustafa. *Siyer-i Nebî.* Trans. [into Turkish] M. Faruk Gürtunca. Istanbul: Dogus Kültür Hizmetleri, 1995.

Davidson, Gustav. *A Dictionary of Angels, Including the Fallen Angels.* New York: Free Press, 1967.

Davidson, Herbert A. *Alfarabi, Avicenna, and Averroes on Intellect: Their Cosmologies, Theories of the Active Intellect, and Theories of Human Intellect.* New York: Oxford University Press, 1992.

De Epalza, Mikel. "Mozarabs: An Emblematic Christian Minority in Islamic al-Andalus." In *The Legacy of Muslim Spain*, ed. Salma Khadra Jayyusi. Leiden: E. J. Brill, 1992.

———. "Mozarabs: An Emblematic Christian Minority in Islamic Al-Andalus." In *The Legacy of Muslim Spain*, ed. Salma Khadra Jayyusi. Leiden: E. J. Brill, 1992.

Dedes, Georgios. "Was there a Greek *Aljamiado* Literature?" In *The Balance of Truth: Essays in Honour of Professor Geoffrey Lewis*, ed. Ç. Balim Harding and C. Imber. Istanbul: Eren Kitabevi, 2000.

Dedes, Yorgo. "Süleyman Çelebi's Mevlid: Text / Performance and Muslim-Christian Dialogue." In *Şinasi Tekin'in Anısına: Uygurlardan Osmanlıya*, ed. G. Kut and F. Büyükkarcı. Istanbul: Simurg Yayınevi, 2005.

D'Emilio, James. "The Royal Convent of Las Huelgas: Dynastic Politics, Religious Reform and Artistic Change in Medieval Castile." In *Studies in Cistercian Art and Architecture*, ed. Meredith Parsons Lillich, vol. 6. Kalamazoo, Mich.: Cistercian Publications, 2005.

Deny, J. "Un *soyurgal* du Timouride Šāhruḫ en écriture ouigoure." *Journal asiatique* 245, no. 3 (1957): 253–266.

Derouet, Jean Louis. "Les possibilités d'interprétation sémiologique des textes hagiographiques." *Revue d'Histoire de l'Église de France* 62 (1976): 153–162.

DeWeese, Devin. *Islamization and Native Religion in the Golden Horde: Baba Tükles and Conversion to Islam in Historical and Epic Tradition.* University Park: Pennsylvania State University Press, 1994.

———. "The *Mashā'ikh-i Turk* and the *Khojagān:* Rethinking the Links between the Yasavī and Naqshbandī Sufi Traditions." *Journal of Islamic Studies* 7/2 (1996): 180–207.

———. "Sayyid ʿAlī Hamadānī and Kubrawī Hagiographical Traditions." In *The Legacy of Mediaeval Persian Sufism*, ed. Leonard Lewisohn. London: Khaniqahi Nimatullahi Publications, 1992.

———. "Yasavian Legends on the Islamization of Turkistan." In *Aspects of Altaic Civilization, III: Proceedings of the Thirtieth Meeting of the Permanent International Altaistic Conference, Indiana University, Bloomington, Indiana, June 19–25, 1987*, ed. Denis Sinor. Bloomington: Research Institute for Inner Asian Studies, Indiana University, 1990.

Diba, Layla, and Maryam Ekhtiar, eds. *Royal Persian Paintings: The Qajar Epoch, 1785–1925.* London: I. B. Tauris, 1998.

Diyārbakrī. *al-Ta'rīkh al-khamīs fī sīrat anfas al-nafīs.* 2 vols. in 1. Beirut: Mu'assasat Sha'ban, 1970–1979.

Dodds, Jerrilynn. *Architecture and Ideology in Early Medieval Spain.* University Park: Pennsylvania State University Press, 1989.

———. "The Great Mosque of Córdoba." In *Al-Andalus: the Art of Islamic Spain*, ed. Dodds. New York: Abrams, 1992.

———. "Islam, Christianity, and the Problem of Christian Art." In *The Art of Medieval Spain, 500–1200 A.D.* New York: Abrams, 1993.

Doerfer, Gerhard. *Türkische und mongolische Elemente im Neupersischen: Unter besonderer Berücksichtigung älterer neupersischer Geschichtsquellen, vor allem der Mongolen- und Timuridenzeit.* 4 vols. Wiesbaden: Franz Steiner, 1963–1975.

Dozy, Reinhart. *Dictionnaire détaillé des noms des vêtements chez les arabes.* Amsterdam: J. Müller, 1845.

Dughlat, Mirza Haydar. *Tarikh-i Rashidi: A History of the Khans of Moghulistan.* Ed. and trans. W. M. Thackston. 2 vols. Cambridge, Mass.: Dept. of Near Eastern Languages and Civilizations, Harvard University, 1996.

During, Jean. "A Critical Survey on Ahl-e Haqq Studies in Europe and Iran." In *Alevi Identity,* ed. Tord Olsson, Elisabeth Özdalga, and Catharina Raudvere. Richmond: Curzon, 1998.

Dutton, Yasin. "*ʿAmal v. Ḥadīth* in Islamic Law: the Case of *Sadl al-Yadayn* (Holding One's Hands by One's Sides) When Doing the Prayer." *Islamic Law and Society* 3/1 (February 1996): 13–40.

Düzdağ, M. Ertuğrul. *Şeyhülislâm Ebussu'ûd Efendi'nin fetvalarına göre Kanunî devrinde Osmanlı hayatı: fetâvâ-yı Ebussu'ûd Efendi.* Çemberlitaş, Istanbul: Şûle Yayınları, 1998.

Eaton, Richard. *The Rise of Islam and the Bengal Frontier, 1204–1760.* Berkeley: University of California Press, 1993.

Ebū s-Suʿūd. *Tafsīr Abī l-suʿūd: Irşād al-ʿaql al-salīm ilā mazāyā al-kitāb al-karīm.* [Beirut]: Dār al-Fikr, n.d.

Echevarría, Ana. "Eschatology or Biography? Alfonso X, Muhammad's Ladder and a Jewish Go-Between." In *Under the Influence: Questioning the Comparative in Medieval Castile,* ed. Cynthia Robinson and Leyla Rouhi. Leiden: E. J. Brill, 2005.

Eckmann, János. "Das Chwarezmtürkische." In *Philologiae Turcicae Fundamenta,* ed. Louis Bazin et al., vol. 1. Wiesbaden: Franz Steiner, 1959.

———. "Die Kiptschakische Literatur." In *Philologiae Turcicae Fundamenta,* ed. Louis Bazin et al., vol. 2. Wiesbaden: Franz Steiner, 1964.

———. "Das Tschaghataische." In *Philologiae Turcicae Fundamenta,* ed. Louis Bazin et al., vol. 1. Wiesbaden: Franz Steiner, 1959.

———. "Nehcü'l-Feradis'in bilinmiyen bir yazması." In János Eckmann, *Harezm, Kipçak ve Çağatay Türkçesi üzerine araştırmalar,* ed. Osman Fikri Sertkaya. Ankara: Türk Dil Kurumu, 1996.

———. "Zur Charakteristik der islamischen mittelasiatisch-türkischen Literatursprache." In *Studia Altaica (Festschrift für Nikolaus Poppe zum 60. Geburtstag am 8. August 1957).* Wiesbaden: O. Harrassowitz, 1957.

Eckmann, János, ed. *Nehcü'l-feradis.* 3 vols. Ankara: Türk Tarih Kurumu Basımevi, 1956–1998.

Ehrman, Bart D. *The New Testament: A Historical Introduction to the Early Christian Writings.* 3rd ed. New York: Oxford University Press, 2004.

Encyclopaedia of Islam, new ed. (E.I.²). Ed. H. A. R. Gibb et al. 12 vols. Leiden: E. J. Brill, 1960–2005.

Encyclopaedia of the Qur'ān. Ed. Jane Dammen McAuliffe. Leiden: Brill, 2001–2006.

Encyclopedia Iranica (E. Ir.). Ed. Ehsan Yar-Shater. 12 vols. New York: Columbia University, 1996–.

Encyclopedia of Islam and the Muslim World. Ed. Richard C. Martin. New York: Macmillan, 2004.

Encyclopedia of Religion. Ed. Mircea Eliade et al. 16 vols. New York: Macmillan, 1987.

Enzyklopädie des Märchens. Ed. Kurt Ranke et al. Berlin and New York: Walter de Gruyter, 1987.

Eraslan, Kemal, ed. *Ahmed-i Yesevî, Dîvân-i Hikmet'ten Seçmeler.* Ankara: Başbakanlık Basımevi, 1983; Ankara: Özkan Matbaası, 1991.

———. "Alî Şîr Nevâyî, Nesâyimü 'l-Mahabbe min Şemâyimi 'l-Fütüvve." Ph.D. diss. (Doktora Tezi), Istanbul Edebiyat Fakültesi Basımevi, 1979.

———. "Hakîm Ata ve Mi'râc-Nâmesi," *Atatürk Üniversitesi Edebiyat Fakültesi Araştırma Dergisi* 10 (1979): 243–304.

Ernst, Carl. *Following Muḥammad.* Chapel Hill: University of North Carolina Press, 2003.

———. *Words of Ecstasy in Sufism.* Albany: State University of New York Press, 1985.

Esin, Emil. "The Bakhshi in the 14th to 16th Centuries: The Masters of the Pre-Muslim Tradition of the Arts of the Book in Central Asia." In *The Arts of the Book in Central Asia, 14th–16th Centuries,* ed. Basil Gray. London: Serindia; Paris: UNESCO, 1979.

Ess, Josef van. "Le *miʿrāǧ* et la vision de Dieu dans les premières spéculations théologiques en Islam." In *Le voyage initiatique en terre d'Islam,* ed. Amir-Moezzi.

———. *Theologie und Gesellschaft im 2. und 3. Jahrhundert Hidschra: Eine Geschichte des religiösen Denkens im frühen Islam.* 6 vols. Berlin: Walter de Gruyter, 1991–1997.

Ettinghausen, Richard. "Persian Ascension Miniatures of the Fourteenth Century." In *Convegno di Scienze Morali Storiche e Filologiche, Symposium on Orient and Occident during the Middle Ages, May 27–June 1, 1956.* Rome: Accademia nazionale dei Lincei, 1957 (republished in Ettinghausen, *Islamic Art and Archaeology: Collected Papers,* ed. Miriam Rosen-Ayalon [Berlin: G. Mann Verlag, 1984]).

Feki, Habib *Les Idées religieuses et philosophiques de l'ismaelisme fatimide.* Tunis: Université de Tunis, 1978.

Feldman, Walter. "Imitatio in Ottoman Poetry: Three Ghazals of the Mid-Seventeenth Century." *Turkish Studies Association Bulletin* 21/2 (1997): 41–58.

Fernández Arenas, José. *Mozarabic Architecture.* Greenwich, Conn.: New York Graphic Society, 1972.

Ferrier, R. W. *The Arts of Persia.* New Haven, Conn.: Yale University Press, 1989.

Fischel, Walter J. "Isfahān: The Story of a Jewish Community in Persia." In *The Joshua Starr Memorial Volume: Studies in History and Philology.* New York: Conference on Jewish Relations, 1953.

———. "The Jews of Central Asia (Khorasan) in Medieval Hebrew and Islamic Literature." *Historia Judaica* 7, no. 1 (1945): 35–43.

Fleischer, Cornell H. *Bureaucrat and Intellectual in the Ottoman Empire: The Historian Mustafa Ali (1541–1600).* Princeton, N.J.: Princeton University Press, 1986.

Flórez, Enrique. *Sancti Beati, Presbyteri Hispani Liebanensis, in Apocalypsin, ac Plurimas Ultriusque Foederis Paginas Commentaria, ex Veteribus, Nonnullisque Desideratis Patribus, Mille Retro Annis Collecta, Nunc Primum Editia.* Madrid: Matriti, Catholicae Majestatis Typographum, 1770.

de Fouchécour, Charles-Henri. *Moralia: Les notions morales dans la littérature persane du 3e/9e au 7e/13e siècle.* Paris: Éditions Recherche sur les Civilisations, 1986.

Frembgen, Jürgen. *Derwische: Gelebter Sufismus; Wandernde Mystiker und Asketen im islamischen Orient.* Cologne: DuMont Buchverlag, 1993.

Friedmann, Yohanan. *Tolerance and Coercion in Islam: Interfaith Relations in the Muslim Tradition.* Cambridge: Cambridge University Press, 2003.

Gadamer, Hans-Georg. *Wahrheit und Methode: Grundzüge einer philosophischen Hermeneutik.* Tübingen: Mohr, 1960.

Gallagher, Amelia. "The Fallible Master of Perfection: Shah Ismail in the Alevi-Bektashi Tradition" Ph.D. diss., McGill University, 2004.

Gandjeï, Tourkhan, ed. *Il Canzoniere di Šāh Ismāʿīl Ḫaṭā'ī.* Napoli: Istituto Universitario Orientale, 1959.

———. "Note on the Colophon of the *Laṭāfat-nāma* in Uighur Characters from the Kabul Museum." *Annali dell'Istituto Universitario Orientale di Napoli,* n.s., 14 (1964): 161–165.

———. "Pseudo-Khaṭā'ī." In *Iran and Islam in Memory of the Late Vladimir Minorsky,* ed. C. E. Bosworth. Edinburgh: Edinburgh University, 1971.

García-Tejedor, Carlos Miranda. "Stylistic Analysis of the Gerona Beatus." In *Codex of Gerona: Commentarius in Apocalypsin,* vol. 2 [Commentary volume accompanying facsimile edition], ed. Mónica Miró. Barcelona: M. Moleiro, 2004.

Garrett Fisher, Carol. "A Reconstruction of the Pictorial Cycle of the *Siyar-i Nabi* of Murad III," *Ars Orientalis* 14 (1984), 75–94.

———. "The Pictorial Cycle of the *Siyer-i Nebi*: A Late Sixteenth-Century Manuscript of the Life of Muhammad." Ph.D. diss., Michigan State University, 1981.

Gatti, Maria Luisa. "Plotinus: The Platonic Tradition and the Foundation of Neoplatonism." In *The Cambridge Companion to Plotinus,* ed. Lloyd P. Gerson. Cambridge: Cambridge University Press, 1992.

Genequand, Charles. "Alexandre et les sages de l'Inde." *Arabic and Middle Eastern Literatures* 4, no. 2 (2001): 137–144.

al-Ghayṭī, Najm al-Dīn Muḥammad b. Aḥmad. *Qiṣṣat al-miʿrāj al-kubrā.* Cairo: Muṣṭafā al-Bābī al-Ḥalabī, 1949.
al-Ghazālī, Abū Ḥāmid. *Incoherence of the Philosophers: A Parallel English-Arabic Text.* Trans. Michael E. Marmura. Provo, Utah: Brigham Young Univeristy Press, 1997.
Gieschen, Charles A. "Baptismal Praxis in the Book of Revelation." In *Paradise Now: Essays on Early Jewish and Christian Mysticism,* ed. April D. DeConick. SBL Symposium Series 11, Atlanta: Society of Biblical Literature, 2006.
Gil, Juan, ed. *Corpus scriptorum muzarabicorum.* 2 vols. Madrid: Instituto Antonio de Nebrija, 1973.
Gil, Moshe. *Jews in Islamic Countries in the Middle Ages.* Trans. David Strassler. Leiden: E. J. Brill, 2004.
Gilliot, Claude. "Abraham eût-il un regard peccamineux?" In *Autour du regard.* Mélanges Gimaret, ed. Eric Chaumont with the collaboration of Denis Aigle, Mohammad Ali Amir-Moezzi, and Pierre Lory. Louvain: Peeters, 2003.
Gimaret, Daniel. "Au coeur du *Miʿrāǧ,* un hadith interpolé." In *Le voyage initiatique en terre d'Islam,* ed. Amir-Moezzi.
Ginzberg, Louis, comp. *Legends of the Jews.* Trans. Henrietta Szold and Paul Radin. 2nd ed. 2 vols. Philadelphia: The Jewish Publication Society, 2003.
Godard, André. "The Mausoleum of Öljeitü at Sultaniya." In *A Survey of Persian Art,* ed. Arthur Upham Pope and Phyllis Ackerman. Tehran: Soroush Press, 1977.
Gohlman, William E. *The Life of Ibn Sīnā: A Critical Edition and Annotated Translation.* Albany: State University of New York Press, 1974.
Gölpınarlı, Abdülbâki, ed. *Alevî-Bektaşî Nefesleri.* Istanbul: Remzi Kitabevi, 1963.
———. *Mevlânâ Müzesi Yazmalar Kataloğu.* Ankara: Türk Tarih Kurumu Basımevi, 1972.
———. *Tarih Boyunca İslam Mezhepleri ve Şiilik.* Istanbul: Der Yayınları, 2003.
Goodrich, Thomas D. *The Ottoman Turks and the New World: A Study of Tarih-i Hind-i Garbi and Sixteenth-Century Ottoman Americana.* Wiesbaden: O. Harrassowitz, 1990.
Grabar, Oleg. *Mostly Miniatures: An Introduction to Persian Painting.* Princeton, N.J.: Princeton University Press, 2000.
Grabar, Oleg, and Sheila Blair. *Epic Images and Contemporary History: The Illustrations of the Great Mongol Shahnama.* Chicago: University of Chicago Press, 1980.
Graham, William A. *Divine Word and Prophetic Word in Early Islam: A Reconsideration of the Sources, with Special Reference to the Divine Saying or* Ḥadîth Qudsî. The Hague: Mouton, 1977.
Gray, Basil. *Persian Painting.* Treasures of Asia Series. New York: Skira, 1961.
Grube, Ernst. *Persian Painting in the Fourteenth Century: A Research Report. Supplement n. 17 to the Annali of the Naples Oriental Institute* 38/4. Naples: Istituto Orientale di Napoli, 1978.
Gruber, Christiane. *The Ilkhanid Book of Ascension: A Persian-Sunni Devotional Tale.* London: I. B. Tauris, 2009.
———. "The Prophet Muḥammad's Ascension (*Miʿrāj*) in Islamic Art and Literature, ca. 1300–1600." Ph.D. diss., University of Pennsylvania, 2005.
———. *The Timurid Book of Ascension (Miʿrajnama): A Study of Text and Image in a Pan-Asian Context.* Valencia, Spain: Patrimonio Ediciones, 2008.
———. "When *Nubuvvat* Encounters *Valāyat:* Safavid Paintings of the Prophet Muhammad's *Miʿrāj,* ca. 1500–1550." In *Shiʿite Art and Material Culture,* ed. Pedram Khosronejad. London: I. B. Tauris, 2010).
Gruenwald, Ithamar. *Apocalyptic and Merkavah Mysticism.* Leiden: E. J. Brill, 1980.
Gryson, Roger, ed. *Apocalypsis Johannis. Vetus Latina. Die Reste der altlateinischen Bibel. Nach Petrus Sabatier neu gesammelt und herausgegeben von der Erzabtei Beuron unter der Leitung* 26/2. Freiburg: Herder, 2000.
Guillaume, Alfred, trans. *The Life of Muhammad: A Translation of Isḥāq's* Sīrat Rasūl Allāh. London: Oxford University Press, 1955.

Guillaume, Jean-Patrick. "'Moi, Mahomet, Prophète et Messager de Dieu . . .': Traduction et adaptation dans le *Liber Scale Machometi*." In *Le voyage initiatique en terre d'Islam*, ed. Amir-Moezzi.
Gulpāyigānī, Ḥusayn. *Ta'rīkh-i Chāp va Chāpkhāna dar Īrān*. Tehran: Nashr-i Gulshān, 1378/1999.
Hādī Muḥammadī, Muḥammad, and Zuhra Qā'inī. *Ta'rīkh-i Adabīyāt-i Kūdakān-i Īrān*. Tehran: Chīstā, 1379/2000–2001.
Hagen, Gottfried. "Afterword: Ottoman Understandings of the World in the Seventeenth Century." In *An Ottoman Mentality: Evliya Çelebi*, ed. Robert Dankoff. Leiden: E. J. Brill, 2004.
———. "Kâtib Çelebi and Sipahizade." In *Essays in honour of Ekmeleddin İhsanoğlu*, ed. Mustafa Kaçar and Zeynep Durukal. Istanbul: IRCICA, 2006.
———. "Some Considerations about the *Tergüme-i Darir ve taqdimetü z-zahir*, based on Manuscripts in German Libraries." *Journal of Turkish Studies / Türklük Bilgisi Araştırmaları* 26 (Barbara Flemming Armağanı, ed. Jan Schmidt), no. 1 (2002): 323–337.
———. "Some Considerations on the Study of Ottoman Geographical Writings." *Archivum Ottomanicum* 18 (2000): 183–193.
———. "Translations and Translators in a Multilingual Society: A Case Study of Persian-Ottoman Translations, Late 15th to Early 17th Century." *Eurasian Studies* 2, no. 1 (2003): 95–134.
———. "World Order and Legitimacy." In *Legitimizing the Order: Ottoman Rhetoric of State Power*, ed. Maurus Reinkowski and Hakan Karateke. Leiden: E. J. Brill, 2005.
Ḥājib, Yūsuf Khāṣṣ. *Kutadgu bilig*. Vol. 1, *Viyana nüshası*. Facsimile ed. Istanbul: Alâeddin Kıral, 1942.
———. *Wisdom of Royal Glory (Kutadgu Bilig): A Turko-Islamic Mirror for Princes*. Trans. Robert Dankoff. Chicago: University of Chicago Press, 1983.
al-Ḥākim, Muḥammad b. ʿAbdallāh b. Muḥammad Abū ʿAbdallāh b. al-Bayyiʿ al-Naysābūrī. *al-Mustadrak ʿalā Ṣaḥīḥayn fī 'l-ḥadīth*. 4 vols. Hyderabad: Dā'irat al-Maʿārif al-Niẓāmiyya, 1917–1924.
al-Ḥalabī, ʿAlī b. Ibrāhīm. *al-Sīra al-Ḥalabīya*. Damascus: Dār al-Maʿrifa, 1989.
Halm, Heinz. *The Empire of the Mahdi*. Leiden: E. J. Brill, 1996.
———. "The Ismāʿīlī Oath of Allegiance (*ʿahd*) and the Sessions of Wisdom (*majālis al-ḥikma*) in Fāṭimid Times." In *Medieval Ismāʿīlī History and Thought*, ed. Farhad Daftary. Cambridge: Cambridge University Press, 1996.
Halperin, David J. "*Hehalot* and *Miraj*: Observations on the Heavenly Journey in Judaism and Islam." In *Death, Ecstasy, and Other Worldly Journeys*, ed. John J. Collins and Michael Fishbane. Albany: State University of New York Press, 1995.
al-Ḥamawī, Yāqūt. *Muʿjam al-buldān*. 7 vols. Beirut: Dār Ṣādir, 1955–1957; repr. ed., 1995.
Hames, Harvey J. *The Art of Conversion: Christianity and Kabbalah in the Thirteenth Century*. Leiden: E. J. Brill, 2000.
Hanaway, William. "Some Accounts of the *Mi'râj* of the Prophet in Persian Literature." In *Cultural Horizons: A Festschrift in Honor of Talat S. Halman*, ed. Jayne L. Warner. Syracuse, N.Y.: Syracuse University Press, 2001.
Haq, Muhammad Enamul. *Muslim Bāṇglā Sāhitya*. In *Muhammad Enāmul Hak Racanāvalī*. Vol. 1. Ed. Monsur Musa. Dhaka: Bangla Academy, 1991.
Harder, Hans. "Bangladesch." In *Der Islam in der Gegegenwart*. 5th ed. Ed. Werner Ende and Udo Steinbach, 363–371. Munich: C. H. Beck, 2005.
Hartmann, Richard . "Die Himmelsreise Muhammeds und ihre Bedeutung in der Religion des Islam." In "Über die Vorstellungen von der Himmelsreise der Seele," special issue, *Vorträge der Bibliothek Warburg* 8 (1928–1929): 42–65.
Harvey, Steven. "Falaquera's Alfarabi: An Example of the Judaization of the Islamic Falāsifa." *Trumah* 12 (2002): 97–112.
Hasluck, Frederick William. *Christianity and Islam Under the Sultans*, ed. Margaret M. Hasluck. Oxford: Clarendon, 1929.

Hatley, Shaman. "Mapping the Esoteric Body in the Islamic Yoga of Bengal." *History of Religions* 46 (2007): 351–368.

Heath, Peter. *Allegory and Philosophy in Avicenna (Ibn Sīnā), with a Translation of the Book of the Prophet Muhammad's Ascent to Heaven.* Philadelphia: University of Pennsylvania Press, 1992.

Heinen, Anton M. *Islamic Cosmology: A Study of as-Suyūṭī's al-Hay'a as-sanīya fī l-hay'a as-sunnīya.* Beirut: Franz Steiner, Wiesbaden, 1982.

Heullant-Donat, I., and M.-A. Polo de Beaulieu. "Histoire d'une traduction: le livre de l'échelle de Mahomet." In *Le Livre de l'Échelle de Mahomet (Liber Scale Machometi)*, ed. and trans. Besson and Brossard-Dandré.

Hillenbrand, Robert. "The Arts of the Book in Ilkhanid Iran." In *The Legacy of Genghis Khan: Courtly Art and Culture in Western Asia, 1256–1353*, ed. Linda Komaroff and Stefano Carboni. New York: Metropolitan Museum of Art, 2002.

———. "Images of Muḥammad in al-Biruni's *Chronology of Ancient Nations.*" In *Persian Painting from the Mongols to the Qajars: Studies in Honour of Basil W. Robinson*, ed. Robert Hillenbrand. London: I. B. Tauris, 2000.

Hodgson, Marshall. *The Venture of Islam.* 3 vols. Chicago: University of Chicago Press, 1974.

Holbrook, Victoria. *The Unreadable Shores of Love: Turkish Modernity and Mystic Romance.* Austin: Texas University Press 1994.

Hood, William. "Saint Dominic's Manners of Praying: Gestures in Fra Angelico's Cell Frescoes at San Marco." *The Art Bulletin* 68/2 (June 1986): 195–206.

Horovitz, Josef. "Bulūqjā." *Zeitschrift der Deutschen Morgenländischen Gesellschaft* 55 (1901): 519–525.

Howorth, Henry. *History of the Mongols from the 9th to the 19th Century.* London: Longmans, Green, 1888.

Hūd b. Muḥakkam Hawārī. *Tafsīr kitāb Allāh al-ʿazīz.* 4 vols. Beirut: Dār al-Gharb al-Islāmī, 1990.

Hughes, Aaron. *The Art of Dialogue in Jewish Philosophy.* Bloomington: Indiana University Press, 2007.

———. "A Case of 12th-Century Plagiarism? Abraham ibn Ezra's Ḥay ben Meqitz and Avicenna's Ḥayy ibn Yaqẓān." *Journal of Jewish Studies* 55/2 (2004): 306–31.

———. "Imagining the Divine: Ghazālī on Imagination, Dreams, and Dreaming." *Journal of the American Academy of Religion* 70.1 (2002): 33–53.

———. *The Texture of the Divine: Imagination in Medieval Islamic and Jewish Thought.* Bloomington: Indiana University Press, 2004.

———. "The Three Worlds of ibn Ezra's Ḥay ben Meqitz." *Journal of Jewish Thought and Philosophy* 11/1 (2002): 1–24.

Humphreys, R. Stephen. *Islamic History: A Framework for Inquiry.* Rev. ed. Princeton, N.J.: Princeton University Press, 1991.

Hyatte, Reginald, trans. *The Prophet of Islam in Old French: "The Romance of Muhammad" (1258) and "The Book of Muhammad's Ladder" (1264).* Leiden: E. J. Brill, 1997.

I scala tou Moameth [Muhammad's Ladder]. Trans. Demetres Melas. Athens: Enalios, n.d.

Ibn ʿAbbās, ʿAbd Allāh. *Hādhā miʿrāj al-nabī (ṣ) ta'līf al-Imām Ibn ʿAbbās.* Damascus: Maktabat Muḥammad al-Ḥalabī, 1948.

———. *al-Isrā' wa-'l-Miʿrāj.* Damascus: Maktabat al-Mahāynī, n.d.

———. "al-Isrā' wa'l-Miʿrāj." In *Taṭrīz al-Dībāj bi-Ḥaqā'iq al-Isrā' wa'l-Miʿrāj*, ed. Muḥyī al-Dīn al-Ṭuʿmī. Beirut: Dār wa Maktabat al-Hilāl, 1994.

———. *al-Isrā' wa-l-miʿrāj li-l-imām Ibn ʿAbbās.* Cairo: Maktabat al-Qāhira, n.d.

Ibn Abī Shayba, *Muṣannaf.* Beirut: Dār al-kutub al-ʿilmiyya, 1995.

Ibn ʿArabshāh. *ʿAjā'ib al-maqdūr fī nawā'ib Taymūr.* Ed. Aḥmad Fā'iz al-Ḥimṣī. Beirut: Mu'assasat al-Risāla, 1407/1986.

Ibn Bābawayh, *ʿUyūn akhbār al-Riḍā.* 2 vols. Beirut: Mu'assasat al-aʿlamī li-'l-maṭbūʿāt, 2005.

Ibn Diḥya al-Kalbī. *al-Ibtihāj fī aḥādīth al-miʿrāj.* Cairo: Maktabat al-Khānjī, 1996.

Ibn Ezra, Abraham. *Dīwān des Abraham Ibn Ezra mit seiner Allegorie Ḥai ben Mekiz.* Ed. Jacob Egers. Berlin: n.p., 1886.

———. *Iggeret Ḥay ben Meqitz.* Ed. Israel Levin. Tel Aviv University Press, Tel Aviv, 1983.

Ibn Ezra, Moshe. *Kitāb al-muḥāḍara wa'l-mudhākara (Sefer ha-ʿiyyunim ve ha-diyyunim).* Ed. and trans. into Hebrew by A. S. Halkin. Jerusalem: Mekize Niramim, 1975.

Ibn Ḥajar ʿAsqalānī, Aḥmad b. ʿAlī, and Jalāl al-Dīn Suyūṭī. *al-Isrā' wa-l-miʿrāj.* Cairo: Dār al-Ḥadīth, 1989.

Ibn Ḥanbal, Aḥmad. *Musnad.* Beirut: Dār al-Fikr, 1991.

Ibn Hishām, ʿAbd al-Mālik. *The Life of Muhammad: a Translation of Ibn Isḥāq's* Sirat rasul Allah. Intro., trans., and notes A. Guillaume. London: Oxford University Press, 1955.

———. *al-Sīra al-nabawiyya.* Beirut: Dār al-Fikr, 1992.

———. *al-Sīra al-nabawiyya.* Ed. Muṣṭafā al-Saqqā, Ibrāhīm al-Abyārī, and ʿAbd al-Ḥafīẓ Shalabī. 4 vols. Repr. ed. Beirut: Dār Iḥyā' al-Turāth al-ʿArabī, n.d.

———. *Sīrat Rasūl Allāh.* Ed. Ferdinand Wüstenfeld. 2 vols. in 3. Göttingen: n.p, 1856.

Ibn Isḥāq, Muḥammad. *The Life of Muhammad: A Translation of Isḥāq's* Sīrat Rasūl Allāh. Trans. Alfred Guillaume. Lahore: Pakistan Branch, Oxford University Press, 1955.

Ibn Māja, Muḥammad b. Yazīd. *Sunan.* Cairo: Muṣṭafā al-Bābī al-Ḥalabī, n.d.

Ibn Saʿd, Muḥammad. *al-Ṭabaqāt al-kubrā.* 9 vols. Beirut: Dār al-Ṣādir, 1957–68.

Idel, Moshe. *The Mystical Experience in Abraham Abulafia.* Trans. Jonathan Chipman. Albany: State University of New York Press, 1988.

———. *Studies in Ecstatic Kabbalah.* Albany: State University of New York Press, 1988.

İpşiroğlu, Mazhar. *Painting and Culture of the Mongols.* Trans. E. D. Phillips. New York: Abrams, 1996.

İpşiroğlu, Mazhar and Sebahattin Eyüboğlu. *Fatih Alumuna Bir Bakış, Sur l'Album du Conquérant.* Istanbul: Maarif Basımevi, 1955.

İslâm Ansiklopedisi (İ.A.). Istanbul: Türkiye Diyanet Vakfı, 1988–.

Islam, Mazharul. "Saiyad Sul'tān: His Birthplace and Time." In *Essays on Middle Bengali Literature,* ed. Rahul Peter Das. Calcutta: Firma KLM Private Limited, 1999.

el-İznikî, Mûsâ b. Hacı Hüseyin. *Miʿrac.* Trans. Hikmet Özdemir. Istanbul: Gonca, 1986.

Jahn, Karl. "The Still Missing Works of Rashid al-Din." *Central Asiatic Journal* 9 (1964): 113–122.

James, David. *The Master Scribes: Qur'ans of the 10th to 14th Centuries AD, The Nasser D. Khalili Collection of Islamic Art.* Vol. 2. Ed. Julian Raby. New York: Nour Foundation, in association with Azimuth Editions and Oxford University Press, 1992.

Jeffery, Arthur. *A Reader on Islam.* The Hague: Mouton, 1962.

Jong, Frederick de. "The Iconography of Bektashism: A Survey of the Themes and Symbolism in Clerical Costume, Liturgical Objects and Pictorial Art." *Manuscripts of the Middle East* 4 (1989): 7–29.

———. "Problems Concerning the Origins of the Qızılbāş, in Bulgaria: Remnants of the Ṣafaviyya?" In *Convegno sul tema: la Shī'a nell'impero Ottomano (Roma, 15 Aprile 1991),* Rome: Accademia nazionale dei Lincei, 1993.

Kappler, Claude et al., eds. *Apocalypses et voyages dans l'au-delà.* Paris: CERF, 1987.

Kaptein, N. J. G. *Muḥammad's Birthday Festival: Early History in the Central Muslim Lands and Development in the Muslim West until the 10th/16th Century.* Leiden: E. J. Brill, 1993.

Karimzadeh Tabrizi, Mohammad Ali. *Aḥvāl va āsār-i naqqāshān-i qadīm-i Īrān va barkhī az mashāhīr-i nigār gar-i Hind va ʿUsmānī.* London: Karimzadeh Tabrizi, 1985.

———. *The Lives & Arts of Old Painters of Iran and a Selection of Masters from the Ottoman & Indian Regions.* London: Interlink Longraph, 1985.

Kassis, Hanna E. *A Concordance of the Qur'an.* Berkeley and Los Angeles: University of California Press, 1983.

Katib Çelebi, Ismail. *Cihānnümā.* Istanbul: Müteferrika, 1732.

———. *Kitāb kashf al-ẓunūn ʿan asmā' al-kutub wa'l-funūn.* 6 vols. Istanbul, 1941–1955.

Kaufmann, David. *Studies in the Hebrew Literature of the Middle Ages* [Hebrew]. Jerusalem: Mossad ha-Rav Kook, 1962.

Kauz, Ralph. *Politik und Handel zwischen Ming und Timuriden: China, Iran und Zentralasien im Spätmittelalter.* Wiesbaden: Reichert, 2005.

Kavīndra Mahābhārata: Lipitāttvika-Bhāṣātāttvika Samīkṣā o Saṃskṛta Mahābhāratera Saṅge Tulanā. 2 vols. Ed. and intro. Kalpana Bhowmik. Dhaka: Bangla Academy, 1999.

Khosronejad, Pedram, ed. *Shiᶜite Art and Material Culture.* London: I. B. Tauris, 2010.

Khwāndamīr, Ghiyāth al-Dīn b. Humām al-Dīn al-Ḥusaynī. *Tārīkh-i Ḥabīb al-siyar fī akhbār afrād-i bashar.* Ed. Jalāl al-Dīn Humā'ī. 4 vols. Tehran: Khayyām, 1333/1954–1955; repr. ed., 1362/1984.

al-Kirmānī, Ḥamīd al-Dīn. *Kitāb al-Riyāḍ.* Ed. ᶜĀrif Tāmir. Beirut: Dār al-Thaqāfa, 1960.

al-Kisā', Muḥammad ibn ᶜAbd Allāh. Tales of the Prophets (Qiṣaṣ al-anbiyā'). Trans. Wheeler M. Thackston, Jr. Chicago: Great Books of the Islamic World, 1997.

Kister, M. J. "The sīrah Literature." In *Arabic Literature to the End of the Umayyad Period,* ed. A. F .L. Beeston et al. Cambridge: Cambridge University Press, 1983.

Klein, Peter. *Der ältere Beatus-Kodex Vitr. 14–1 der Biblioteca Nacional zu Madrid: Studien zur Beatus-Illustration und der Spanischen Buchmalerei des 10. Jahrhunderts* (Studien zur Kunstgeschichte, 8). Hildesheim and New York: Olms, 1976.

———. "Beatus v. Liébana." *Lexikon des Mittelalters,* I, col. 1746–1747. Munich: Artemis Verlag, 1980.

———. "Eschatological Expectations and the Revised Beatus." In *Church, State, Vellum and Stone: Essays on Medieval Spain in Honor of John Williams,* ed. Therese Martin and Julie A. Harris. [Medieval and early Modern Iberian World v. 26]. Leiden: E. J. Brill, 2005.

———. "The Illumination of the Las Huelgas Beatus Codex." In *Estudio del Manuscrito del Beato de las Huelgas M. 429,* vol. 2 [Commentary volume accompanying facsimile edition titled *Beato del Monasterio de Santa Maria la Real de Huelgas de Burgos*], ed. William Voelkle, Peter Klein et al. Valencia: Scriptorium, 2004.

———. "La tradición pictória de los Beatos." In *Actas del Simposio para el studio de los códices del "Comentario al Apocalipsis" de Beato de Liébana,* vol. 2. Madrid: Joyas Bibliográficas, 1980.

Klemm, Verena. *Die Mission des fāṭimidischen Agenten al-Mu'ayyad fī d-Dīn in Sīrāz.* Frankfurt: P. Lang, 1989.

Köprülü, Mehmed Fuad. *Early Mystics in Turkish Literature.* Trans., ed., and intro. Gary Leiser and Robert Dankoff; foreword, Devin DeWeese. London: Routledge, 2006.

Korkmaz, Esat. *Alevilik Bektaşi Terimleri Sözlüğü.* Istanbul: Anahtar Kıtaplar Yayınevi, 2005.

Kotzageorgis, Phokion. *To Islam sta Valkania: Ena hellenophono mousoulmaniko cheirographo apo ten Epiro tou 18ou aiona [Islam in the Balkans. An 18th-Century Islamic Manuscript in Greek from Epirus].* Athens: Syllogos ton en Athinais Megalosholiton, 1997.

Kūfī, Furāt b. Furāt. *Tafsīr Furāt al-Kūfī.* Ed. Muḥammad al-Kāẓim. Tehran: Mu'assasat al-Ṭabᶜ wa'l-Nashr, 1990.

Kugle, Scott. "Heaven's Witness: The Uses and Abuses of Muḥammad Ghawth's Mystical Ascension." *Journal of Islamic Studies* 14:1 (2003): 1–36.

Labov, William. "The Transformation of Experience in Narrative Syntax." In *Language in the Inner City: Studies in the Black English Vernacular.* Philadelphia: University of Pennsylvania Press, 1972.

Lamers, Hanneke. "On Evliya's Style." In *Evliya Çelebi in Diyarbekir: the Relevant Section of the Seyahatname edited with translation, commentary and introduction,* ed. Martin van Bruinessen and Hendrik Boeschoten. Leiden: E. J. Brill, 1988.

Landolt, Hermann. "Ghazālī and '*Religionswissenschaft*': Some Notes on the *Mishkāt al-Anwār* for Professor Charles J. Adams." *Asiatische Studien (Etudes asiatiques)* 45/1(1991): 1–72.

Lane, Andrew J. *A Traditional Mu'tazilite Qur'an Commentary: The Kashshaf of Jar Allah al-Zamakhshari.* Leiden: E. J. Brill, 2006.

Laut, Jens Peter. *Uigurische Sünden, Silk Road Studies V. De Dunhuang à Istanbul. (Hommage à James Russell Hamilton, présenté par Louis Bazin et Peter Zieme).* Turnhout: Brepols, 2001.

———. "Vielfalt türkischer Religionen." *Spirita* 10/1 (1996): 24–36.
Lentz, Thomas W. "Changing Worlds: Behzad and the New Painting." In *Persian Masters: Five Centuries of Painting*, ed. Sheila Canby. Bombay: J. J. Bhabha, 1990.
———, and Glenn D. Lowry, *Timur and the Princely Vision: Persian Art and Culture in the Fifteenth Century.* Los Angeles: Los Angeles County Museum of Art; Washington, DC: Arthur M. Sackler Gallery, Smithsonian Institution, and Smithsonian Institution Press, 1989.
Levend, Agah Sırrı. *Ali Şir Nevai, Hayatı, Sanatı ve Kişiliği.* Ankara: Türk Tarih Kurumu Basımevi, 1965.
Levin, Israel. *Abraham ibn Ezra: His Life and Poetry* [Hebrew]. Tel Aviv: Ha-kibbutz hameuchad, 1969.
Levy, Raphael. *The Astrological Works of Abraham ibn Ezra: A Literary and Linguistic Study with Special Reference to the Old French Translation of the Hagin.* Baltimore: Johns Hopkins University Press, 1927.
Lewis, Suzanne. *Reading Images: Narrative Discourse and Reception in the Thirteenth-Century Apocalpyse.* Cambridge: Cambridge University Press, 1995.
Liber Scale Machometi (Le Livre de l'Échelle de Mahomet). Trans. Gisèle Besson and Michèle Brossard-Dandré. Paris: Librairie Générale Française, 1991.
López Gómez, Margarita. "The Mozarabs: Worthy Bearers of Islamic Culture." In *The Legacy of Muslim Spain*, ed. Salma Khadra Jayyusi. Leiden: E. J. Brill, 1992.
Lukens-Swietochowski, Marie. "The School of Herat from 1450 to 1506." In *The Arts of the Book in Central Asia, 14th–16th Centuries*, ed. Basil Gray. Boulder, Colo.: Shambala Publications, 1979.
Maimonides. *Guide of the Perplexed.* Trans. Shlomo Pines. Chicago: University of Chicago Press, 1963.
Majlisī, Muḥammad Bāqir. *Biḥār al-anwār al-jāmiʿa li'l-durār akhbār al-ā'imma al-athār.* 2nd. ed. 111 vols. Beirut: Mu'assasat al-wafā', 1983.
———. *Biḥār al-anwār.* 110 vols. Tehran and Qum: Ḥaydarī, 1956–1972.
Mansuroğlu, Mecdut. "Das Karakhanidische." In *Philologiae Turcicae Fundamenta,* vol. 1, ed. Louis Bazin et al. Wiesbaden: Franz Steiner, 1964.
Marquet, Yves. "L'ascension spirituelle chez quelques auteurs ismailiens." In *Le voyage initiatique en terre d'Islam,* ed. Amir-Moezzi.
Marzolph, Ulrich. "Early Printing History in Iran (1817–ca. 1900). Part I: Printed Manuscript." In *Middle Eastern Languages and the Print Revolution: A Cross-Cultural Encounter,* ed. Eva Hanebutt-Benz, Dagmar Glass, and Geoffrey Roper. Westhofen: Wva-Verlag Skulima, 2002.
———. *Narrative Illustration in Persian Lithographed Books.* Leiden: E. J. Brill, 2001.
Massignon, Louis. "Le 'Jour du covenant' (*Yawm al-Mīthāq*)." *Oriens* 16 (1962): 86–92.
McGinn, Bernard. "Introduction: John's Apocalypse and the Apocalyptic Mentality." In *The Apocalypse in the Middle Ages,* ed. Richard K. Emmerson and Bernard McGinn. Ithaca, N.Y.: Cornell University Press, 1992.
McKendrick, Melveena. *A Concise History of Spain.* London: Cassell, 1972.
Mélikoff, Irène. "La cérémonie du *ayn-i djem* (Anatolie centrale)." In *Bektachiyya: Études sur l'ordre mystique des Bektachis et les groups relevant de Hadji Bektach,* ed. Alexandre Popovic and Gilles Veinstein. Istanbul: Isis, 1995.
———. "Le problème Bektaşi-Alévi: Quelques dernières considérations," *Turcica* 31 (1999): 7–34.
Melville, Charles. "Abū Saʿīd and the Revolt of the Amirs in 1319." In *L'Iran face à la domination mongole,* ed. Denise Aigle. Tehran: Institut Français de Recherche en Iran, 1997.
———. *The Fall of Amir Chupan and the Decline of the Ilkhanate, 1327–37.* Bloomington: Indiana University Press, 1999.
Memedov, Azizaga. "Le plus ancien manuscrit du *dīvān* de Shah Ismail Khatayi." *Turcica* 6 (1972): 8–23.
———, ed. *Shah Ismaiyl Khatai: Asarlari,* 2 vols. Baku: Elm Nashriiiaty, 1966–1973.

Menéndez Pidal, Gonzalo. "Mozárabes y asturianos en la cultura de la Alta Edad Media en relación especial con la historia de los conocimientos geográficos." *Boletín de la Real Academia de la Historia* 134 (1954): 137–291.

Mentré, Mireille. *Illuminated Manuscripts of Medieval Spain.* London: Thames and Hudson, 1996.

Merrick, James. *The Life and Religion of Muḥammad.* Boston: Phillips, Sampson, 1850.

Mesᶜūd bin Aḥmed. *Süheyl ü Nev-bahār: inceleme, metin, sözlük.* Ed. Cem Dilçin. Ankara: Atatürk Kültür Merkezi, 1991.

Mezoughi, Noureddine. "Le fragment de Beatus illustré conserve a Silos." *Cahiers de Saint Michel de Cuxá* 13 (1982): 125–151.

Millett, Fred B., and Gerald Eades Bentley. *The Art of Drama.* New York, London: D. Appleton-Century, 1935.

Millie, Julian. "The Narrative Potential of Mi'râj: Two Contexts for Its Interpretation." In *Epic Adventures: Heroic Narrative in the Oral Performance Traditions of Four Continents,* ed. Jan Jansen and Henk M. J. Maier. Münster: LIT Verlag, 2004.

Milstein, Rachel et al. *Stories of the Prophets: Illustrated Manuscripts of Qiṣaṣ al-Anbiyā.* Costa Mesa, Calif.: Mazda Publishers, 1999.

Minorsky, Vladimir. "Persia: Religion and History." In *Iranica: Twenty Articles.* Tehran: University of Tehran, 1964.

———. "The Poetry of Shāh Ismāᶜīl I." *Bulletin of the School of Oriental and African Studies* 4 (1939–1942): 1006a–1053a.

Morris, James W. "Situating Islamic 'Mysticism': Between Written Traditions and Popular Spirituality." In *Mystics of the Book: Themes, Topics, and Typologies,* ed. Richard Herrera. New York/Berlin: P. Lang, 1993.

Morton, Andrew H. "The *chūb-i tarīq* and Qizilbash Ritual in Safavid Persia," In *Études Safavides,* ed. Jean Calmard. Paris: Institut Français de Recherche en Iran, 1993.

Morton, Andrew H., ed. and trans. *Mission to the Lord Sophy of Persia (1539–1542).* London: School of Oriental and African Studies, 1993.

al-Mu'ayyad fī al-Dīn al-Shīrāzī. *Majālis al-Mu'ayyadiyyah.* Ed. Muṣṭafā Ghālib. Beirut: Dār al-Andalus, 1976–1984.

———. *Majālis al-Mu'ayyadiyyah.* Ed. Ḥātim Ḥamīd al-Dīn. Oxford: Z. H. Nooruddin/Leaders Press Private Limited, 1395–1407/1975–1986.

Muḥammad b. Muḥammad (Altıparmak). *Delā'il-i Nübüvvet-i Muḥammedī ve-Şemā'il-i Fütüvvet-i Aḥmedī.* Istanbul, 1257/1841.

Muhsin Khan, Muḥammad. *Ṣaḥīḥ al-Bukhārī: The Translation of the Meanings of Ṣaḥīḥ al-Bukhārī, Arabic–English,* vol. 6. New Delhi: Kitab Bhavan, 1984.

Muᶜizz al-ansāb (Proslavliaiushchee genealogii). Facsimile. Ed. and trans. Sh. Kh. Vokhidov. Alma Ata: Daik, 2006.

Müller, Hans. "Die Islamisierung des subsaharischen Afrika." In *Der Islam in der Gegenwart.* 5th ed. Ed. Werner Ende and Udo Steinbach. Munich: C. H. Beck, 2005.

Muñoz Sendino, José, ed. and trans. *La Escala de Mahoma: Traducción del Árabe al Castellano, Latín y Francés, Ordenada par Alfonso X el Sabio.* Madrid: Ministerio de Asuntos Esteriores, Dirección General de Relaciones Culturales, 1949.

Muqātil b. Sulaymān. *Tafsīr Muqātil.* 5 vols. Cairo: al-Ḥay'a al-miṣriyya, 1979–1989.

Muslim b. Ḥajjāj al-Qushayrī al-Naysābūrī. *Ṣaḥīḥ Muslim.* 5 vols. Beirut: Dār al-Kutub al-ᶜIlmiyya, 1990.

Nafīsī, Saᶜīd. "Ṣanᶜat-i Chāp-i Muṣavvar dar Īrān." *Payām-i Nu* 5 (1352/1974): 22–35.

al-Nasā'ī, Abū ᶜAbd al-Raḥmān Aḥmad b. Shuᶜayb. *Kitāb al-sunan al-kubrā.* 12 vols. Beirut: Risālah Publishers, 2001.

Nasr, Seyyed Hossein. *An Introduction to Islamic Cosmological Doctrines: Conceptions of Nature and Methods Used for Its Study by the Ikhwān al-Ṣafā', Al-Bīrūnī, and Ibn Sīnā.* Rev. ed. Albany: State University of New York Press, 1993.

———. *Islamic Art and Spirituality.* Albany: State University of New York Press, 1987.

Nawā'ī, ʿAlī Shīr. *Majālisu'n-Nafā'is, "[The] Galaxy of Poets" of Mīr ʿAlī Şīr Nawā'ī: Two 16th-Century Persian Translations.* Tehran: Bank Melli Press, 1945.

Necipoğlu, Gülru. *Architecture, Ceremonial, and Power: The Topkapi Palace in the Fifteenth and Sixteenth Centuries.* New York: Architectural History Foundation; Cambridge: MIT Press, 1991.

Neuss, Wilhelm. *Die Apokalypse des hl. Johannes in der altspanischen und altchristlichen Bibel-Illustration* (Spanische Forschungen der Görresgesellschaft, Reihe II, 2 and 3), Münster in Westfalen: Aschendorff, 1931.

———. "Probleme der christlichen Kunst in maurischen Spanien des 10. Jahrhunderts." In *Neue Beträge zur Kunstgeschichte des 1. Jahrtausends: Frühmittelalterliche Kunst,* Ed. A. Alföndi. Vol. 1.; 2nd ed.. Baden-Baden: Verlag für Kunst und Wissenschaft, 1954.

Nicholas, Ralph W. "Vaiṣṇavism and Islam in Rural Bengal." In *Bengal Regional Identity,* ed. David Kopf. East Lansing: Michigan State University, 1969.

Nomoto, Shin. "Early Ismāʿīlī Thought on Prophecy according to the *Kitāb al-Iṣlāḥ* by Abū Ḥātim al-Rāzī (d. ca. 322/ 934–5)." Ph.D. diss., McGill University, 2000.

Ocak, Ahmet Yaşar. "Un aperçu général sur l'hétérodoxie musulmane en Turquie: Réflexions sur les origines et les caractéristiques du Kızılbachisme (Alévisme) dans la perspective de l'histoire." In *Syncretistic Religious Communities in the Near East: Collected Papers of the International Symposium "Alevism in Turkey and Comparable Syncretistic Religious Communities in the Near East in the Past and Present," Berlin, 14–17 April 1995,* ed. Krisztina Kehl-Bodrogi, Barbara Kellner-Heinkele and Anke Otter-Beaujean. Leiden: E. J. Brill, 1997.

———. *Osmanlı toplumunda zındıklar ve mülhidler: 15.-17. yüzyıllar.* Beşiktaş, Istanbul: Türkiye Ekonomik ve Toplumsal Tarih Vakfı Yayınları, 1998.

O'Callaghan, J. F. "The Integration of Christian Spain into Europe: the Role of Alfonso VI of León-Castile." In *Santiago, Saint-Denis and Saint Peter: The Reception of the Roman Liturgy in León-Castile in 1080,* ed. Bernard F. Reilly. New York: Fordham University Press, 1985.

———. *The Learned King: the Reign of Alfonso X of Castile.* Philadelphia: University of Pennsylvania Press, 1993.

———. *Reconquest and Crusade in Medieval Spain.* Philadelphia: University of Pennsylvania Press, 2003.

Olsson, Tord, Elizabeth Özdalga, and Catherine Raudevere, eds. *Alevi Identity: Cultural, Religious and Social Perspectives; Papers Read at a Conference Held at the Swedish Research Institute in Istanbul, November 25–27, 1996.* Istanbul: Swedish Research Institute in Istanbul, 1998.

O'Shaughnessy, Thomas. "The Seven Names for Hell in the Qur'an." *Bulletin of the School of Oriental and African Studies* 24/3 (1961): 444–469.

Öz, Tahsin. *Hırka-i Saadet Dairesi ve Emanat-ı Mukaddese.* Istanbul: İsmail Akgün Matb., 1953.

Özdemir, Adil, and Kenneth Frank. *Visible Islam in Modern Turkey.* Foreword, Annemarie Schimmel. Houndmills, Basingstoke, Hampshire: Macmillan, 2000.

Özmen, İsmail, ed. *Alevi-Bektaşi Şiirleri Antolojisi.* Ankara: Saypa Yayınları, 1995.

Pagis, Dan. *Hebrew Poetry of the Middle Ages and the Renaissance.* Berkeley: University of California Press, 1991.

Paret, Rudi. *Die legendäre Maghāzī-Literatur: Arabische Dichtungen über die muslimischen Kriegszüge zu Mohammeds Zeit.* Tübingen: J. C. B. Mohr, 1930.

Pavet de Courteille, Abel. *Mirâdj-Nâmeh, Récit de l'Ascension de Mahomet au Ciel Composé A.H. 840/1436–1437: Texte turk-oriental, publié pour la première fois d'après le manuscript ouïgour de la Bibliothèque Nationale et traduit en français.* Paris, 1882. Repr. ed. Amsterdam: Philo Press, 1985.

Pavis, Patrice. "Production and Reception in the Theatre." Trans. Susan Melrose. In *New Directions in Theatre,* ed. Julian Hilton. New York: St. Martin's Press, 1993.

Pekolcay, Necla, ed. *Süleyman Çelebi: Mevlid (Vesîletü'n-necât).* Istanbul: Dergâh, 1980.

Pentzopoulos, Demetrios. *The Balkan Exchange of Minorities and its Impact on Greece.* The Hague: Mouton, 1962.
Pereira, A. S. Rodrigues, "Two Syriac Verse Homilies on Joseph." *Ex Oriente Lux* 31 (1989–1990): 95–120.
Pfeiffer, Judith. "Conversion Versions: Sultan Öljeytü's Conversion to Shiʿism (709/1309) in Muslim Narrative Sources." *Mongolian Studies* 22 (1999): 35–67.
Piemontese, Angelo M. "Le voyage de Mahomet au Paradis et en Enfer: Une version persane du *miʿrâj.*" In *Apocalypses et voyages dans l'au-delà*, ed. Claude Kappler et al. Paris: CERF, 1987.
Polites, Linos. "Neoteres apopseis gia te gennese kai te dome tou dekapentasyllabou" [Recent Views on the Origin and the Structure of the 15-Syllable Verse]. *Praktika Akademias Athenon* 56/2 (1981): 211–228.
Prince, Gerald. *The Form and Functioning of Narrative: Narratology.* Berlin: Mouton, 1982.
Pyrsinellas, Vassileios. "Hoi tourkogianniotikes homologies" [The confession poems of the Turkogianniotes]. *Epirotika Chronika* 12 (1937): 160–169.
Qāḍī ʿIyāḍ b. Mūsā al-Yaḥṣubī. *al-Shifā bi-taʿrīf ḥuqūq al-Muṣṭafā.* Amman: Dār al-faiḥā', 1986.
Qāḍī al-Nuʿmān. *Asās al-Ta'wīl.* Ed. ʿĀrif Ṭāmir. Beirut: Dār al-Thaqāfa, 1966.
Qāsimī, Farīd. *Sarguzasht-i Maṭbūʿāt-i Īrān: Rūzgār-i Muḥammad Shāh va Nāṣir al-Dīn Shāh.* 2 vols. Tehran: Vizārat-i Farhang va Irshād-i Islāmī, 1380/2001.
al-Qazwīnī, Zakariyyā b. Muḥammad b. Maḥmūd. *Āthār al-bilād wa akhbār al-ʿibād.* Beirut: Dār Ṣādir, 1380/1960.
al-Qummī, ʿAlī b. Ibrāhīm. *Kitāb tafsīr ʿAlī b. Ibrāhīm.* Tabriz lithograph, 1895.
———. *Tafsīr al-Qummī.* 2 vols. Beirut: Dār al-surūr, 1991.
al-Qushayrī, *Kitāb al-Miʿrāj.* Ed. ʿAlī Ḥasan ʿAbd al-Qādir. Cairo: Dār al-Kutub al-Ḥadīth, 1384/1964.
al-Rabghūzī [Nosiruddin Burhonuddin]. *The Stories of the Prophets:* Qiṣaṣ al-Anbiyā'. *An Eastern Turkish Version.* Ed. H. E. Boeschoten, M. Vandamme, and S. Tezcan. Trans. H. E. Boeschoten, J. O'Kane, and M. Vandamme. 2 vols. Leiden: E. J. Brill, 1995.
Rahman, Fazlur. *Avicenna's Psychology: An English Translation of* Kitāb al-Najāt, *Book II, Chapter VI With Historico-Philosophical Notes and Textual Improvements On the Cairo Edition.* Oxford: Oxford University Press, 1952.
———. *Prophecy in Islam: Philosophy and Orthodoxy.* Chicago: University of Chicago Press, 1958.
Raizman, David. "A Rediscovered Illuminated Manuscript of St. Ildefonsus' *De Virginitate Beatae Mariae* in the Biblioteca Nacional in Madrid." *Gesta* 26/1 (1987): 37–46.
———. "The Church of Santa Cruz and the Beginnings of Mudejar Architecture in Toledo." *Gesta* 38/2 (1999): 128–141.
———. "The Later Beatus (M. 429) in the Morgan Library: Description, Function, Style, and Provenance." In *Estudio del Manuscrito del Beato de las Huelgas M. 429,* vol. 2 [Commentary volume accompanying facsimile edition titled *Beato del Monasterio de Santa Maria la Real de Huelgas de Burgos*], William M. Voelkle, Peter K. Klein, David Raizman, Alberto del Campo Hernández, Joaquín González Echegaray, and Les G. Freeman. Valencia: Scriptorium, 2004.
———. "Prayer, Patronage, and Piety at Las Huelgas: New Observations on the Later Morgan Beatus (M. 429)." In *Church, State, Vellum and Stone: Essays on Medieval Spain in Honor of John Williams,* ed. Therese Martin and Julie A. Harris. Leiden: E. J. Brill, 2005.
Ranjbar, Ahmad. *Chand Miʿrājnāma.* Tehran: Mu'assasah-i Intishārāt-i Amīr Kabīr, 1396/1990.
Rāzī, Abū al-Futūḥ. *Rawḍ al-jinān wa rawḥ al-janān fī tafsīr al-Qur'ān.* Ed. Muḥammad Jaʿfar Yāḥaqqī and Muḥammad Mahdī Nāṣiḥ. 20 vols. Repr. ed. Mashhad: Intishārāt-i Āstān-i Quds-i Riḍavī, 1378/1999.

Reilly, Bernard F. *The Kingdom of León Castilla under King Alfonso VI, 1065–1109.* Princeton, N.J.: Princeton University Press, 1988.
Renard, John. *All the King's Falcons: Rumi on Prophets and Revelation.* Albany: State University of New York Press, 1994.
———, ed. *Windows on the House of Islam.* Berkeley: University of California Press, 1998.
Renaud, Étienne. "Le Récit du *mi*ʿ*rāj*: une version arabe de l'ascension du Prophète, dans le *Tafsīr* de Tabarī." In *Apocalypses et voyages dans l'au-delà,* ed. Claude Kappler. Paris: CERF, 1987.
Richard, Francis. *Catalogue des manuscrits persans.* Vol. 1, *Ancien fonds.* Paris: Bibliothèque nationale de France, 1989.
———. *Splendeurs persanes: Manuscrits du XIIe au XVIIe siècle.* Paris: Bibliothèque nationale de France, 1997.
Rimmon-Kenan, Shlomith. *Narrative Fiction: Contemporary Poetics.* London; New York: Methuen, 1983.
Ritter, Helmut. "Philologika XIV. Farīduddīn ʿAṭṭār. II." *Oriens* 11 (1958): 1–76.
Rıza, Ali, and Hüseyin Albayrak. *Shah Hatayi Deyişleri.* CD Recording. Kalan Music, 2006.
Robinson, Basil, ed. *Islamic Painting and the Arts of the Book.* London: Faber and Faber Ltd, 1976.
Rogers, Michael. "The Genesis of Safawid Religious Painting." *Vth International Congress of Iranian Art and Archaeology, Tehran-Isfahan-Shiraz, 11th-18th April 1968.* Vol. 2 of 2. Tehran: Ministry of Culture and Arts, 1968.
Rothschild, Jean-Pierre. "Alexandre hébreu, ou Micromégas." *Mélanges de l'École Française de Rome* 112, no. 1 (2000): 27–42.
Roxburgh, David. J. *The Persian Album, 1400–1600: From dispersal to collection.* New Haven, Conn.: Yale University Press, 2005.
———. *Prefacing the Image: The Writing of Art History in Sixteenth-Century Iran.* Leiden: E. J. Brill, 2001.
Roy, Asim. "The Interface of Middle Bengali Muslim Literature and the Process of Islamisation in Bengal." In *Essays on Middle Bengali Literature*, ed. Rahul Peter Das. Calcutta: Firma KLM, 1999.
———. *The Islamic Syncretistic Tradition in Bengal.* Princeton, N.J.: Princeton University Press, 1983.
Rubin, Uri. *The Eye of the Beholder: The Life of Muḥammad as Viewed by the Early Muslims: a Textual Analysis.* Princeton, N.J.: Darwin Press, 1995.
———. "Pre-Existence and Light: Aspects of the Concept of Nur Muhammad." *Israel Oriental Studies* 5 (1975): 62–119.
Rūmī, Jalāl al-Dīn. *Kitāb-i Mathnawī-i ma*ʿ*nawī.* Ed. and trans. Reynold A. Nicholson. 6 bks. in 8 vols. London: Luzac, 1925–1940; repr. ed., vols. 1–6, 1985.
Ryan, Marie-Laure. "Virtuality and Tellability." In *Possible Worlds, Artificial Intelligence, and Narrative Theory.* Bloomington: Indiana University Press, 1991.
Rypka, Jan. *History of Iranian Literature.* Written in collaboration with Otakar Klima et al. Ed. Karl Jahn. Dordrecht: D. Reidel, 1968.
Ṣaffar Qummī, Muḥammad b. Ḥasan. *Baṣā'ir al-darajāt fi faḍā'il Āl Muḥammad.* Ed. Mīrzā Muḥsin Kuchabāghī Tabrīzī. Qum: Maktabat Āyat Allāh al-ʿUẓmā Marʿashī Najafī, 1982.
Saiyad Sultān. *Nabīvaṃśa: Saiyad Sultān viracita Nabīvaṃśa.* Ed. Ahmad Sharif. 2 vols. Dhaka: Bangla Academy, 1978.
Sajjādī, Jaʿfar, ed. *Tafsīr-i Ḥadā'iq al-Ḥaqā'iq: Qismat-i Sūrah-i Yūsuf,* "The Biography of the Author." Tihrān: Mu'asasah-i Intishārāt-i Amīr Kabīr, 1364/1944.
Salamangkas, Demetrios. "Mia tourkogianniotike *homologia*" [A Tourkogianniot 'confession poem']. *Epeirotike Zoe* 1/6 (1946): 14–15 and 24.
———. "To gianniotiko stichoplaki ki oi paragontes tou" [The 'short rhymed verse' and its factors]. *Epeirotike Hestia* 4 (1955): 807–814.
al-Samarrai, Qassim. *The Theme of Ascension in Mystical Writings: A Study of the Theme in Is-*

lamic and non-Islamic Mystical Writings. Baghdad: National Printing and Publishing, 1968.

Sanders, Henry, ed. *Beati in Apocalipsin libri duodecim.* Rome: American Academy, 1930.

Sawyer, Caroline G. "Revising Alexander: Structure and Evolution: Ahmedî's Ottoman Iskendernâme (c. 1400)." *Edebiyât* 13:2 (2003): 225–243.

Sayılı, Aydın. *The Observatory in Islam and Its Place in the General History of the Observatory.* Ankara: Türk Tarih Kurumu Basımevi, 1960.

Schäfer, Peter. *The Hidden and Manifest God.* Trans. Alan Pomerance. Albany: State University of New York Press, 1992.

Scharlipp, Wolfgang Ekkehard. *Die alttürkische Literatur: Einführung in das vorislamische Schrifttum.* Engelschoff: Verlag auf dem Ruffel, 2005.

Scheindlin, Raymond P. "Merchants and Intellectuals, Rabbis and Poets: Judeo-Arabic Culture in the Golden Age of Islam." In *Cultures of the Jews: A New History,* ed. David Biale. New York: Schocken, 2002.

———. "Rabbi Moshe Ibn Ezra on the Legitimacy of Poetry." *Medievalia et Humanistica* 7 (1976): 101–116.

Scherberger, Max, ed. and trans. *Das Miʿrāǧnāme: Die Himmel- und Höllenfahrt des Propheten Muḥammad in der osttürkischen Überlieferung, Arbeitsmaterialien zum Orient* 14. Würzburg: Ergon Verlag, 2003.

Schimanowski, Gottfried. "Connecting Heaven and Earth: The Function of Hymns in Revelation 4–5." In *Heavenly Realms and Earthly Realities in Late Antique Religions,* ed. Ra'anan Boustan and Annette Yoshiko Reed. Cambridge: Cambridge University Press, 2004.

Schimmel, Annemarie. *And Muhammad Is His Messenger: The Veneration of the Prophet in Islamic Piety.* Chapel Hill: University of North Carolina Press, 1985.

———. *As Through a Veil: Mystical Poetry in Islam.* Oxford: Oneworld Publications, 2001.

———. *Deciphering the Signs of God: A Phenomenological Approach to Islam.* Albany: State University of New York, 1994.

———. *The Mystery of Numbers.* New York: Oxford University Press, 1993.

———. *Mystical Dimensions of Islam.* Chapel Hill: University of North Carolina Press, 1975.

———. *Mystische Dimensionen des Islam: Die Geschichte des Sufismus.* Frankfurt a. M. / Leipzig: Insel Verlag, 1995.

———. *Und Muhammad ist Sein Prophet. Die Verehrung des Propheten in der islamischen Frömmigkeit.* 3rd ed. Munich: Eugen Diederichs Verlag, 1995.

Schmidt, Jan. *Pure Water for Thirsty Muslims: A study of Muṣṭafā ʿĀlī of Gallipoli's Künhü l-aḫbār.* Leiden: Het Oosters Instituut, 1991.

Schöller, Marco. *Exegetisches Denken und Prophetenbiographie: eine quellenkritische Analyse der Sīra-Überlieferung zu Muḥammads Konflikt mit den Juden.* Wiesbaden: O. Harrassowitz, 1998.

Schwartz, Dov. *Astrology and Magic in Medieval Jewish Thought* [Hebrew]. Ramat Gan: Bar Ilan University Press, 1999.

Séguy, Marie-Rose, *The Miraculous Journey of Mahomet: Mirâj Nâmeh, Bibliothèque Nationale, Paris (Manuscrit Supplément Turc 190).* Trans. Richard Pevear. New York: G. Braziller, 1977.

Sela, Shlomo. *Abraham ibn Ezra and the Rise of Medieval Hebrew Science.* Leiden: E. J. Brill, 2003.

Sellheim, Rudolf. "Prophet, Chalif und Geschichte: Die Muhammad-Biographie des Ibn Isḥāq." *Oriens* 18–19 (1965): 33–91.

Sells, Michael. Ed. and trans. *Early Islamic Mysticism: Sufi, Qur'ān, Miʿrāj, Poetic and Theological Writings.* Mahwah, N.J.: Paulist Press, 1996.

Sen, Sukumar. *History of Bengali Literature.* New Delhi: Sahitya Akademi, 1979.

Shāmī, Muḥammad b. Yūsuf. *Khulāṣat al-faḍl al-fā'iq fī miʿrāj khayr al-khalā'iq.* Cairo: Dār Ibn Ḥazm, 2003.

Shaykh al-Mufid. *Kitab al-Irshad: The Book of Guidance into the Lives of the Twelve Imams.* Trans. I. K. A. Howard. Qum, Iran: Ansariyan, n.d.

Shorter Encyclopaedia of Islam. Ed. H. A. R. Gibb and J. H. Kramers. Leiden: E. J. Brill, 1961.

Shoshan, Boaz. *Popular Culture in Medieval Cairo.* Cambridge: Cambridge University Press, 1993.

Shterenshis, Michael. *Tamerlane and the Jews.* London: RoutledgeCurzon, 2002.

Sijistānī, Abū Yaʿqūb. *Kashf al-Maḥjūb.* Ed. Henri Corbin. Tehran/Paris: Institut Franco-Iranien, 1949.

———. *Kashf al-Maḥjūb.* Trans. Hermann Landolt. In *An Anthology of Philosophy in Persia,* ed. Seyyed Hossein Nasr and Mehdi Aminrazavi. Oxford: Oxford University Press, 2001.

———. *Kitāb al-Yanābīʿ.* In *Trilogie ismaélienne,* ed. Henri Corbin. Tehran: Département d'Iranologie de l'Institut francoiranien, 1961.

———. *Kitāb al-Yanābīʿ* [*Wellsprings of Wisdom*]. Trans. Paul Walker. Salt Lake City: University of Utah Press, 1994.

Sims, Eleanor, with Boris I. Marshak and Ernst J. Grube. *Peerless Images: Persian Painting and Its Sources.* New Haven, Conn.: Yale University Press, 2002.

Smith, Jane Idleman, and Yvonne Yazbeck Haddad. *The Islamic Understanding of Death and Resurrection.* Albany: State University of New York Press, 1981.

Smith, R. Payne. *Thesaurus Syriacus.* 2 vols. Oxford: Clarendon, 1879–1901; repr. ed., Hildesheim: Georg Olms, 1981.

Sohrweide, Hanna. *Türkische Handschriften. 5. Beschrieben von Hanna Sohrweide.* Vol. 13, 5, *Verzeichnis der orientalischen Handschriften in Deutschland.* Wiesbaden: Franz Steiner Verlag, 1981.

Soucek, Priscilla. "The Life of the Prophet: Illustrated Versions." In *Content and Context of Visual Arts in the Islamic World: Papers from a Colloquium in Memory of Richard Ettinghausen, Institute of Fine Arts, New York University, 2–4 April 1980,* ed. Priscilla Soucek. University Park: Pennsylvania State University Press, 1988.

Sourdel, Dominique. *L'Imāmisme vu par le cheikh al-Mufīd.* Paris: Guethner, 1974.

Soulen, Richard N. and R. Kendall Soulen, *Handbook of Biblical Criticism.* 3rd rev. ed. Louisville, Ky.: Westminster John Knox Press, 2001.

Southgate, Minoo S., trans.. *Iskandarnamah: A Persian Medieval Alexander-Romance.* New York: Columbia University Press, 1978.

Spuler, Bertold. *History of the Mongols Based on Eastern and Western Accounts of the Thirteenth and Fourteenth Centuries.* Berkeley and Los Angeles: University of California Press, 1972.

Stchoukine, Ivan. "Les images de Sultân Hosayn dans un manuscrit de son *Dîvân* de 897/1492." *Syria* 53 (1976): 141–148.

Steingass, Francis Joseph. *A Comprehensive Persian-English Dictionary, including the Arabic words and phrases to be met with in Persian Literature.* London: K. Paul, Trench, Trubner, [1930].

Stewart, Tony K. "Alternate Structures of Authority: Satya Pīr on the Frontiers of Bengal." In *Beyond Hindu and Muslim: Multiple Identity in Narratives from Village India,* ed. Peter Gottschalk. Oxford: Oxford University Press, 2004.

———. "In Search of Equivalence: Conceiving Muslim-Hindu Encounter through Translation Theory." *History of Religions* 40, no. 3 (2001): 260–287.

Stoneman, Richard, trans. *The Greek Alexander Romance.* London: Penguin Books, 1991.

Storey, C. A., and Yuri. E. Bregel. *Persidskaia Literatura: bio-bibliograficheskii obzor.* Moscow: [Nauka], Glav. ped. Vostochnoi literatury, 1972.

Strauss, Johann. "Das Vilayet Janina 1881–1912. Wirtschaft und Gesellschaft in einer 'geretteten Provinz.'" In *Türkische Wirtschafts- und Sozialgeschichte von 1071 bis 1920,* ed. H. G. Majer and R. Motika. Wiesbaden: O. Harrassowitz, 1995.

Subtelny, Maria E. "ʿAlī Shīr Navāʾī: *Bakhshī* and *Beg.*" In "Eucharisterion: Essays Presented to Omeljan Pritsak on His Sixtieth Birthday by His Colleagues and Students," ed. Ihor

Ševčenko and Frank E. Sysyn, special issue, *Harvard Ukrainian Studies* 3–4 (1979–1980): 797–807.

———. "The Sunni Revival under Shāh-Rukh and Its Promoters: A Study of the Connection between Ideology and Higher Learning in Timurid Iran." In *Proceedings of the 27th Meeting of Haneda Memorial Hall: Symposium on Central Asia and Iran, August 30, 1993*. Kyoto: Haneda Memorial Hall, Institute of Inner Asian Studies, Kyoto University, 1994.

———. *Timurids in Transition: Turko-Persian Politics and Acculturation in Medieval Iran*. Leiden: E. J. Brill, 2007.

———. "Zoroastrian Elements in the Islamic Ascension Narrative." In *Proceedings of the 6th European Conference in Iranian Studies*, in press.

Subtelney, Maria E., and Anas B. Khalidov. "The Curriculum of Islamic Higher Learning in Timurid Iran in the Light of the Sunni Revival under Shāh-Rukh." *Journal of the American Oriental Society* 115, no. 2 (1995): 210–236.

Suhaylī, ʿAbd al-Raḥmān b. ʿAbd Allāh. *Rawḍ al-unuf fī sharḥ al-sīrat al-nabawiyya li-Ibn Hishām*. 7 vols. Cairo: Dār al-Kutub al-Ḥadītha, 1967–1970.

Sulamī, Abū ʿAbd al-Raḥmān. *The Subtleties of the Ascension: Early Mystical Sayings on Muḥammad's Heavenly Journey*. Trans. Frederick Colby. Louisville, Ky.: Fons Vitae, 2006.

Sulaymānī, Karīm. *Alqāb-i Rijāl-i Dura-i Qājār*. Tehran: Ney, 1379/1959.

al-Suyūṭī, Jalāl al-Dīn. *al-Āya al-kubrā fī sharḥ qiṣṣat al-isrā'*. Ed. Muḥyī al-Dīn Mistū. 2nd ed. Damascus: Dār Ibn Kathīr, 1987.

———. *al-Durr al-manthūr fī 'l-tafsīr al-ma'thūr*. 8 vols. Beirut: Dār al-Fikr, 1983.

———. *La'āli' al-maṣnūʿa fī aḥādīth al-mawḍūʿa*. Ed. Abū ʿAbd al-Raḥmān Ṣalāḥ b. Muḥammad b. ʿUwayḍa. 2 vols. Beirut: Dār al-Kutub al-ʿIlmiyya, 1996.

———. *Masālik al-ḥunafā' fī wāliday al-muṣṭafā*. Cairo: Dār al-Amīn, 1993.

al-Ṭabarī, Muḥammad b. Jarīr. *The History of al-Ṭabarī (Ta'rīkh al-rusul wa'l-mulūk)*. Vol. 1, *General Introduction* and *From the Creation to the Flood*. Trans. Franz Rosenthal. Albany: State University of New York Press, 1989.

———. *Jāmiʿ al-bayān ʿan ta'wīl āy al-Qur'ān*. 30 vols. in 12. Cairo: Muṣṭafā al-Bābī al-Ḥalabī, 1968.

———. *Tafsīr al-Ṭabarī*. 13 vols. Beirut: Dār al-Kutub al-ʿIlmiyya, 1992.

Tamani, Giuliano. "La tradizione ebraica del *Romanzo di Alessandro*." In *La diffusione dell'eredità classica nell'età tardoantica e medievale: Forme e modi di trasmissione*, ed. Alfredo Valvo. Alessandria: Edizioni dell'Orso, 1997.

Tanındı, Zeren. *Siyer-i Nebî: İslam Tasvir Sanatında Hz. Muhammedin Hayatı*. Istanbul: Hürriyet Vakfı Yayınları, 1984.

Tanındı, Zeren, and Filiz Çağman. *The Topkapı Saray Museum: The Albums and Illustrated Manuscripts*. Trans. J. M. Rogers. Boston: Little, Brown, 1986.

Tauer, Felix. "History and Biography," in *History of Iranian Literature*. Written in collaboration with Otakar Klima et al. Ed. Karl Jahn. 438–459. Dordrecht: D. Reidel, 1968.

Thackston, Wheeler. *Album Prefaces and Other Documents on the History of Calligraphers and Painters, Studies and Sources in Islamic Art and Architecture: Supplements to Muqarnas*, vol. 10. Leiden: E. J. Brill, 2001.

———. "The *Diwan* of Khata'i: Pictures for the Poetry of Shah Isma'il I." *Asian Art* 1 (1989): 37–63.

———. "The Paris *Miʿrājnāma*." In "Annemarie Schimmel Festschrift: Essays Presented to Annemarie Schimmel on the Occasion of Her Retirement from Harvard University by Her Colleagues, Students and Friends," ed. Maria Eva Subtelny, special issue, *Journal of Turkish Studies* 18 (1994): 263–299.

al-Thaʿlabī, Abū Isḥāq Aḥmad b. Muḥammad. *ʿArā'is al-majālis fī qiṣaṣ al-anbiyā' or "Lives of the Prophets" as Recounted by Abū Isḥāq Aḥmad ibn Muḥammad ibn Ibrāhīm al-Thaʿlabī*. Trans. William M. Brinner. Leiden: E. J. Brill, 2002.

———. *al-Kashf wa al-bayān, al-maʿrūf Tafsīr al-Thaʿlabī*. Ed. Abū Muḥammad b. ʿĀshūr. 10 vols. Beirut: Dār Iḥyā' al-Turāth al-ʿArabī, 1422/2002.

Titley, Norah M. *Persian Miniature Painting and Its Influence on the Art of Turkey and India.* London: British Library, 1983.

Tolan, John V. *Saracens: Islam in the Medieval European Imagination.* New York: Columbia University Press, 2002.

Tottoli, Roberto. "The Story of Jesus and the Skull in Arabic Literature: the Emergence and Growth of a Religious Tradition." *Jerusalem Studies in Arabic and Islam* 28 (2003): 225–259.

———. "Two *Kitāb al-miʿrāj* in the Manuscripts Collection of the Paul Kahle Library of the University of Turin." *Loquentes Linguis: Studi linguistici e orientali in onore di Fabrizio A. Pennacchietti.* Ed. Pier Giorgio Borbone et al. Wiesbaden: O. Harrassowitz Verlag, 2006.

Tugwell, Simon. "The Nine Ways of Prayer of St. Dominic." In *Early Dominicans: Selected Writings,* ed. Tugwell. New York: Paulist Press, 1982.

al-Ṭuʿmī, Muḥyī al-Dīn. *Taṭrīz al-Dībāj bi-Ḥaqā'iq al-Isrā' wa'l-Miʿrāj.* Beirut: Dār wa Maktabat al-Hilāl, 1994.

Turner, Victor. *The Ritual Process.* Ithaca, N.Y.: Cornell University Press, 1977.

Uddin, Sufia M. *Constructing Bangladesh: Religion, Ethnicity, and Language in an Islamic Nation.* Chapel Hill: University of North Carolina Press, 2006.

al-Ujhūrī, Nūr al-Dīn. *al-Nūr al-wahhāj fī al-kalām ʿalā al-isrā' wa-l-miʿrāj.* Beirut: Dār al-Kutub al-ʿIlmiyya, 2003.

Veysī, Üveys b. Meḥmed. *Külliyāt-ı Veysī.* Istanbul: n. p., 1286/1869.

Vives, José, ed. *Concilios visigóticos e hispano-romanos.* Barcelona: Consejo Superior de Investigaciones Científicas, Instituto Enrique Flórez, 1963.

Vuckovic, Brooke Olson. *Heavenly Journeys, Earthly Concerns: The Legacy of the Miʿraj in the Formation of Islam.* New York: Routledge, 2005.

Walker, Rose. *Views of Transition: Liturgy and Illumination in Medieval Spain.* London: British Library Press, 1998.

Wasserstein, David. *The Caliphate in the West: An Islamic Political Institution in the Iberian Peninsula.* Oxford: Clarendon, 1993.

———. *The Rise and Fall of the Party-Kings: Politics and Society in Islamic Spain, 1002–1086.* Princeton, N.J.: Princeton University Press, 1985.

Wasserstrom, Steven M. *Between Muslim and Jew: The Problem of Symbiosis Under Early Islam.* Princeton, N.J.: Princeton University Press, 1995.

———. "Jewish Pseudepigrapha and *Qiṣaṣ al-Anbiyā'.*" In *Judaism and Islam: Boundaries, Communication and Interaction: Essays in Honor of William M. Brinner,* ed. Benjamin H. Hary, John L. Hayes, and Fred Astren. Leiden: E. J. Brill, 2000.

Werkmeister, Otto. "The First Romanesque Beatus Manuscripts and the Liturgy of Death." In *Actas del Simposio para el Estudio de los Codices del 'Comentario al Apocalipsis' de Beato de Liébana,'* vol. 1. Madrid: Joyas Bibliográficas, 1980.

———. "Art of the Frontier: Mozarabic Monasticism." In *The Art of Medieval Spain.* New York: Metropolitan Museum of Art, distrib. H. N. Abrams, 1993.

———. "The Islamic Rider in the Beatus of Girona." *Gesta* 36/2 (1997): 101–108.

Werner, Edeltraud, ed. *Liber Scale Machometi: die Lateinische Fassung des Kitab al-Mi'radj.* Düsseldorf: Droste, 1986.

Wheeler, Brannon M. *Moses in the Quran and Islamic Exegesis.* London: RoutledgeCurzon, 2002.

———. "The Prophet Muḥammad Dhu al-Qarnayn: His Journey to the Cities at the Ends of the Earth." In "The Acts of Alexander the Great: The Unique Monument of Medieval Toreutics Found in the Village Muzhi of Yamal-Nenetz Autonomic District. Proceedings of the Colloquium Held by the Saint-Petersburg Society for Byzantine and Slavic Studies, September 10–12th, 1998" (Russian title page: "Deianiia tsaria Aleksandra"), ed. C. C. Akentiev and B. I. Marshak, special issue, *Byzantinorossica/Vizantinorossika* 2 (2003): 179–219.

Wilber, Donald. *Architecture of Islamic Iran: The Il Khānid Period.* Princeton, N.J.: Princeton University Press, 1995.

Williams, John. *Early Spanish Manuscript Illumination.* New York: George Braziller, 1977.

———. "Purpose and Imagery in the Apocalypse Commentary of Beatus of Liébana." In *The Apocalypse in the Middle Ages,* ed. Richard K. Emmerson and Bernard McGinn. Ithaca, N.Y.: Cornell University Press, 1992.

———. *The Illustrated Beatus: A Corpus of Illustrations of the Commentary on the Apocalypse.* London: Harvey Miller, 1994.

Wilson, Edwin. *The Theater Experience.* New York: McGraw-Hill, 1980.

Wolf, Kenneth Baxter. *Christian Martyrs in Muslim Spain.* Cambridge: Cambridge University Press, 1988.

———. "The Earliest Latin Lives of Muhammad." In *Conversion and Continuity: Indigenous Christian Communities in Islamic Lands, Eighth to Eighteenth Centuries,* ed. Michael Gervers and Ramzi Jibran Bikhazi. Toronto: Pontifical Institute of Mediaeval Studies, 1990.

———. "The Earliest Spanish-Christian Views of Islam." *Church History* 55, no. 3 (Sept. 1986): 281–293.

———. "Muhammad as Antichrist in Ninth-Century Córdoba." In *Christians, Muslims, and Jews in Medieval and Early Modern Spain,* ed. Mark D. Meyerson and Edward D. English. South Bend, Ind.: Notre Dame Press, 1999.

Wolfson, Elliot R. "Merkavah Traditions in Philosophical Garb: Judah Halevi Reconsidered." *Proceedings of the American Academy of Jewish Research* 57 (1991): 179–242.

———. *Through a Speculum That Shines: Vision and Imagination in Medieval Jewish Mysticism.* Princeton, N.J.: Princeton University Press, 1994.

Wunderli, Peter. *Études sur "Le livre de l'eschiele Mahomet." Prolégomènes à une nouvelle édition de la version française d'une traduction alphonsine.* Winterthur: P. G. Keller, 1965.

Wurm, Heidrun. *Der osmanische Historiker Ḥüseyn b. Ǧa'fer, gen. Hezarfenn, und die Istanbuler Gesellschaft des 17. Jahrhunderts.* Vol. 13, *Islamkundliche Untersuchungen.* Freiburg i.Br.: K. Schwarz, 1971.

Yāḥaqqī, Muḥammad Jaʿfar. *Farhang-i asāṭīr wa dāstānwārahā dar adabiyāt-i fārsī.* Tehran: Farhang Mu'āṣir, 1386/2007.

Yaḥyā Ibn Sallām. *Tafsīr min sūrat al-Naḥl ilā sūrat al-ṣaffāt.* 2 vols. Beirut: Dār al-Kutub al-ʿIlmiyya, 2004.

Yaman, Mehmet. *Alevilikte Cem: İnanç, İbadet, Erkân.* Istanbul: Ufuk Reklamcılık ve Matbaacılık, 1998.

Yürür, Ahmet. "Miʿraçlama in the Liturgy of the Alevi of Turkey: A Structural and Gnostic Analysis." Ph.D. dissertation, University of Maryland, 1989.

Yarbro Collins, Adela. *The Apocalypse* [New Testament Message: A Biblical-Theological Commentary, vol. 2]. Collegeville, Minn.: Liturgical Press, 1979.

Yavuz, Kemal. "Anadolu'da başlayan Türk edebiyatında görülen ilk Miraçnâmeler ve Âşık Paşa ve Miraçnâmesi." *İlmi Araştırmalar* 8 (1999): 247–266.

Yazıcıoğlu, Mehmet. *Muḥammediye.* Ed. Âmil Çelebioğlu. Istanbul: Milli Eğitim Bakanlığı Yayınları, 1996.

Zakhos-Papazahariou, Evangelos. "Babel balkanique: Histoire politique des alphabets utilisés dans les Balkans." *Cahiers du monde russe et soviétique* 13/2 (1972): 145–179.

Zenker, Julius Theodor. *Türkisch-Arabisch-Persisches Handwörterbuch.* Hildesheim: G. Olms, 1967.

Contributors

Elizabeth R. Alexandrin is Assistant Professor of Islamic Studies in the Department of Religion at the University of Manitoba. Her recent scholarly contributions grapple with a wide range of issues in medieval Islamic philosophy and mysticism, such as "Râzî and His Mediaeval Opponents: Discussions concerning *Tanâsukh* and the Afterlife," published in *Cahiers de Studia Iranica.*

Mohammad Ali Amir-Moezzi is Professor of Islamic Theology at l'École Pratique des Hautes Études (Sorbonne, Paris). He is author of *The Divine Guide in Early Shiᶜism,* translated from the French original of 1992, and *Revelation and Falsification* (with Etan Kohlberg). He is the author of several other books and more than sixty articles, and also served as editor of *Le voyage initiatique en terre d'Islam: ascensions célestes et itinéraires spirituels.*

Ali Boozari is an independent researcher and practicing artist in Iran. He is the author of articles included in the *Encyclopedia of Art* and the *Encyclopedia of Iran.* He served as research assistant for Ulrich Marzolph's *Narrative Illustration in Persian Lithographed Books.*

Heather M. Coffey is a Ph.D. candidate in the Department of Art History at Indiana University Bloomington. Her research centers upon the art and architecture of twelfth- and thirteenth-century Italy. The arts of the Islamic world remain a favorite secondary research area.

Frederick Colby is Associate Professor of Religious Studies at the University of Oregon. His is editor and translator of a work by Abu ʿAbd al-Rahman Sulami entitled *The Subtleties of the Ascension: Early Mystical Sayings on Muhammad's Heavenly Journey.* His second book is *Narrating Muhammad's Night Journey: Tracing the Development of the Ibn ᶜAbbas Ascension Discourse.*

Özgen Felek is a Ph.D. candidate in Near Eastern Studies at the University of Michigan. Her scholarly interests include classical Ottoman literature and the dramatization of poetry. She is editor with Walter G. Andrews of *Victoria R. Holbrook'a*

Armağan, and is author of "Mehmet Emirî Efendi and His Poetry," published in the *Journal of Social Science, Firat University.*

Amelia Gallagher is Assistant Professor of Religious Studies at Niagara University. Her research interests include the various Alevi groups of Turkey, including the Nusayri Alevis of the Hatay. She is currently preparing her dissertation for publication in a volume that analyzes the religious poetry of Shah Ismaʿil I (d. 1524).

Christiane Gruber is Assistant Professor of Islamic Art at Indiana University Bloomington. She has written a number of articles on Islamic painting and the Prophet's ascension. Her books include *The Timurid Book of Ascension (Mi'rajnama): A Study of Text and Image in a Pan-Asian Context* and *The Ilkhanid Book of Ascension: A Persian-Sunni Devotional Tale.*

Gottfried Hagen is Associate Professor of Turkish Studies at the University of Michigan. His research focuses on Ottoman ideas, literature, and religion, with a particular interest in views of the cosmos, earth, and history. He is the author of numerous publications on Ottoman geographical and historiographical texts, and is now working on a book-length study of Ottoman Turkish *sira* literature entitled "The Myth of the Prophet Muhammad and Ottoman Muslim Religiosity."

Aaron W. Hughes is Associate Professor of History and the Gordon and Gretchen Gross Professor in the Institute of Jewish Thought and Heritage at the University of Buffalo, SUNY. In addition to numerous articles and book chapters, he is author of *The Texture of the Divine: Imagination in Medieval Islamic and Jewish Thought* (Indiana University Press, 2004), *Situating Islam: The Past and Future of an Academic Discipline* (Equinox, 2007), and *The Art of Dialogue in Jewish Philosophy* (Indiana University Press, 2008).

Ayesha Irani is a Ph.D. candidate in South Asia Studies at the University of Pennsylvania. The subject of her dissertation is the medieval Bangali *Nabīvaṃśa* of Saiyad Sultān. Her research interests include Islam in pre-modern Bengal, South Asian Sufi and *bhakti* literatures, as well as classical Persian poetry.

Phokion P. Kotzageorgis is Lecturer in Early Modern Greek History at Aristotle University of Thessaloniki. He studies the history of the Greek Peninsula in the Ottoman period. His works (in Greek) include *Islam in the Balkans: An 18th-Century Islamic Text from Epirus Written in Greek Script* and *The Athonite Monastery of Saint Paul during the Ottoman Period.*

Selim S. Kuru is Associate Professor of Turkish Studies in the Department of Near Eastern Languages and Civilizations, University of Washington, Seattle. His current research focuses on Ottoman Turkish text and gender studies. His articles include "Naming the Beloved in Ottoman Turkish Gazel: The Case of Ishak Çelebi (d. 1537–8)," published in *Ghazal as World Literature II: From a Literary Genre to a Great Tradition.*

Max Scherberger is a Ph.D. candidate in the Orientalisches Seminar at Albert-Ludwigs-University in Freiburg, Germany. His dissertation focuses on language reform in the Turkish Republic. He is author of *Das Miʿragname: Die Himmel- und Höllenfahrt des Propheten Muhammad in der osttürkischen Überlieferung* as well as the recent article "Weitere osmanische Paraphrasierungen der Pariser Handschrift des *Miʿragname,*" published in *Materialia Turcica.*

Vernon Schubel is N. E. H. Distinguished Teaching Professor of Religious Studies at Kenyon College. His research has focused on issues of Shiʿi and Sufi ritual in South Asia and Central Asia, as well as Alevi-Bektaşi traditions in Anatolia. He is the author of numerous articles and the book *Religious Performance in Contemporary Islam: Shiʿi Devotional Rituals in South Asia.*

Maria E. Subtelny is Professor of Persian and Islamic Studies in the Department of Near and Middle Eastern Civilizations at the University of Toronto. Her research focuses on the history and culture of medieval Iran, including classical Persian literature and Perso-Islamic mysticism. Her recent and forthcoming books include *Le monde est un jardin: Aspects de l'histoire culturelle de l'Iran médiéval* and *Timurids in Transition: Turko-Persian Politics and Acculturation in Medieval Iran.*

Roberto Tottoli is Associate Professor of Islamic Studies and Muslim Literature in the Department of Asian Studies at the University of Naples "L'Orientale." He has published extensively both in Italian and in English on early Muslim literature and in particular on the biblical tradition in Islam. His publications include *Biblical Prophets in the Qur'an and in Muslim Literature* and *The Stories of the Prophets by Ibn Mutarrif al-Tarafi.*

Index

Page numbers in italics indicate photographs and illustrations.

www.ingramcontent.com/pod-product-compliance
Lightning Source LLC
LaVergne TN
LVHW070403060826
844660LV00009B/287

9780253353610